SUBJECT & STRATEGY
A Writer's Reader

Eleventh Edition

SUBJECT & STRATEGY
A Writer's Reader

Paul Eschholz
Alfred Rosa
University of Vermont

BEDFORD/ST. MARTIN'S
Boston ■ *New York*

For Bedford/St. Martin's

Developmental Editor: Nathan Odell
Production Editor: Jessica Skrocki
Production Supervisor: Jennifer Peterson
Senior Marketing Manager: Karita dos Santos
Art Director: Lucky Krikorian
Text Design: Linda M. Robertson
Copy Editor: Virginia Rubens
Photo Research: Sue McDermott Barlow
Cover Design: Trudi Gershenov
Composition: TexTech International
Printing and Binding: R. R. Donnelley & Sons Company

President: Joan E. Feinberg
Editorial Director: Denise B. Wydra
Editor in Chief: Karen S. Henry
Director of Development: Erica T. Appel
Director of Marketing: Karen Melton Soeltz
Director of Editing, Design, and Production: Marcia Cohen
Managing Editor: Shuli Traub

Library of Congress Control Number: 2007934705

Copyright © 2008 by Bedford / St. Martin's

Manufactured in the United States of America.

2 1 0
f e

For information, write: Bedford/St. Martin's, 75 Arlington Street, Boston, MA 02116   (617-399-4000)

ISBN-10: 0-312-46290-5
ISBN-13: 978-0-312-46290-1

Acknowledgments

Preface

Subject & Strategy is a reader for college writers. The selections in this text will entertain, inform, and contribute to students' self-awareness and understanding of the world around them. But above all, the sixty-two reading selections by professional writers, the twelve student essays, and the numerous visual texts in this edition were chosen to help students become better observers and better writers, and especially to help them grasp and master nine widely used and versatile writing strategies.

Subject & Strategy, as its title suggests, places equal emphasis on the content and form of an essay — that is, on what an essay has to say and on the techniques used to say it. All readers pay attention to content, to the substance of what writers are saying. Far fewer readers, however, notice the strategies that writers use to organize their writing and to make it understandable and effective. Because these strategies — most of which students intuitively use already — are such an essential element of the writer's craft, students need first to become aware of them and then to practice using them to write well-crafted essays. The most important purpose of *Subject & Strategy* is to help students understand how a given strategy, alone or in combination, can be used most effectively to communicate a subject to an audience.

FAVORITE FEATURES OF *SUBJECT & STRATEGY*

We continue to include the key features — developed and refined over ten previous editions — that have made *Subject & Strategy* a classic.

Timely, Teachable, and Diverse Readings

Seventy-four readings—including twelve student essays and sixty-two professional essays by some of the best classic and contemporary writers—offer a broad spectrum of subjects, styles, and cultural points of view. These engaging selections, by well-known writers including Thomas L. Friedman, Deborah Tannen, Alice Walker, Edward Abbey, Malcolm X, Annie Dillard, Mark Twain, Martin Luther King Jr., Nikki Giovanni, George Orwell, and Jonathan Rauch, demonstrate for students the versatility and strengths of the different rhetorical strategies.

Thorough Coverage of the Reading and Writing Process

In Chapter 1, "The Reading Process," students are introduced to the five steps of the reading process and an illustration of that process in "The Reading Process in Action: Thomas L. Friedman's 'My Favorite Teacher.'" In Chapter 2, "The Writing Process," students will learn about the five steps in the writing process and how it applies to their own writing. In addition, we provide a case study of a student paper in progress, which neatly illustrates the writing process and shows students what can be accomplished with careful, thoughtful revision. In Chapter 3, "Five Writers on Writing," Russell Baker, Anne Lamott, Linda Flower, William Zinsser, and Donald Murray offer students inspiration, insight, and advice to validate their experiences in the writing classroom and enrich their own writing processes.

Detailed Introductions to Each Rhetorical Strategy

The introduction to each rhetorical chapter opens with a definition of the rhetorical strategy under discussion and then examines examples of that strategy put into practice. After discussing the various purposes for which writers use each strategy, we offer advice on how to use the strategy in the various college disciplines students are likely to encounter beyond their writing course. Next, a complete, annotated student essay gives students a model for that strategy. Finally, we give sound, practical advice on how to write an essay using that strategy, including guidelines on selecting topics, developing thesis statements, considering audiences, gathering evidence, choosing organizational patterns, and using other rhetorical strategies in support of the dominant strategy.

Annotated Student Essays

An annotated student essay appears in each chapter introduction, offering students realistic examples of how they can successfully incorporate rhetorical strategies into their own writing. Discussion questions follow each student essay, encouraging students to analyze and evaluate the overall effectiveness of the rhetorical strategies employed in the example.

Extensive Rhetorical Apparatus

The abundant study materials accompanying each essay teach students how to use each strategy to make their own writing more effective by linking their reading to their writing.

- *Preparing to Read* prompts ask students to write about their own experiences with the issues discussed in the selection. *Thinking Critically about the Text* post-reading prompts ask students to analyze, elaborate on, or take issue with a key aspect of the selection. From time to time, discussion questions and writing assignments ask students to return to these writings and reflect on their early thinking before moving ahead with more formal writing tasks.
- *Questions on Subject* focus students' attention on the content of each selection as well as on the author's purpose. These questions help students check their comprehension of the selection, and they provide a basis for classroom discussion.
- *Questions on Strategy* direct students to the various rhetorical strategies and writing techniques the writer has used. These questions encourage students to put themselves in the writer's place and to consider how they might employ the strategies in their own writing. In addition, questions in this section ask students to identify and analyze places where the author has used one or more rhetorical strategies to enhance or develop the essay's dominant strategy.
- *Questions on Diction and Vocabulary* emphasize the importance of diction, word choice, and verbal context.
- *Classroom Activities* that follow each essay suggest that students work individually, in small groups, or as a class on short exercises— usually ten to fifteen minutes in length—that further enhance both their understanding and their application of each strategy.
- *Writing Suggestions* follow each professional essay. These typically focus on the particular rhetorical strategy under discussion and/or explore the topic of the essay or a related topic.

End-of-Chapter Writing Suggestions

As in previous editions, there are a number of writing suggestions at the end of Chapters 4 through 13. These writing suggestions provide additional topics suitable to the strategy covered in each chapter.

In preparing the suggestions, we made an effort to tie them to particular selections or pairs of selections in the chapter. Instructors can use these writing suggestions as complements to or substitutes for the more focused writing topics that accompany individual selections.

Advice for Writing Researched Essays

Chapter 15, "Writing a Researched Essay," includes guidelines for conducting print and online research; evaluating the reliability and timeliness of print and online sources; taking notes and integrating quotations into an essay; and avoiding plagiarism. In addition, the chapter features model MLA citations for the most widely used sources, including electronic databases, and a sample documented student essay.

Thematic Table of Contents

Immediately after the main table of contents, a second table of contents classifies the reading selections into general thematic categories. This thematic table of contents is designed to make it easier for instructors to identify groups of essays that have common subject matter, thus providing further opportunities for discussion and writing based on the content of individual selections and on various rhetorical approaches to common themes.

Glossary of Rhetorical Terms

The glossary at the end of *Subject & Strategy* provides concise definitions of terms useful in working with the rhetorical strategies presented in the text. Wherever we thought that information in the glossary might assist students in answering a study question in the text, we placed a cross-reference to the appropriate glossary entry next to the question.

NEW TO THIS EDITION OF *SUBJECT & STRATEGY*

Substantially updated for its eleventh edition, *Subject & Strategy* combines the currency of a brand-new text with the effectiveness of a thoroughly class-tested one as it continues to address the needs of a wide range of students and instructors. Guided by comments and advice from instructors and students across the country who have used the previous editions, we have made some dramatic changes designed primarily to expand and strengthen the writing instruction offered in the text.

Engaging New Readings, Compelling Perspectives

Twenty-three readings—nearly forty percent of this edition's selections—are new, including new argument pairs and high-interest, teachable pieces by such well-known writers as:

- Andrew Sullivan, who explores how iPods have changed the way people interact with the world
- Pico Iyer, who compares and contrasts two very interesting kinds of people
- Maya Angelou, who describes a person who was instrumental in teaching her to love language
- Russell Baker, who narrates how he discovered his abilities as a writer and the power of his words
- Pat Mora, who describes her aunt with wonderful detail and touching devotion
- Mitch Albom, who uses illustrative stories of five people to find out what they would do if they had one more day with a loved one

New Chapter on Editing for Grammar, Punctuation, and Sentence Style

Chapter 14, "Editing for Grammar, Punctuation, and Sentence Style," provides students with advice for finding, correcting, and avoiding errors in their writing. This chapter includes such topics as comma splices, fragments, comma faults, subject/verb agreement problems, pronoun reference problems, and sentence variety.

New Emphasis on the Elements of Writing

The eleventh edition emphasizes the idea that the basic elements of all good writing—thesis, organization, unity, effective sentences, diction—are also the foundation of strong academic writing. Chapter 1 now demonstrates how active reading can reveal the elements at work in professional essays, while Chapter 2 adds new coverage of how to use the elements as focal points for the revision process. The student essay in each strategy chapter includes annotations that call attention to the basic elements of the essay, modeling both the active reading skills from Chapter 1 and the revision techniques from Chapter 2.

New "Across the Disciplines" Boxes

To show students how rhetorical strategies are used outside the composition classroom, we include "Across the Disciplines" boxes in the strategy chapter introductions. Each box demonstrates how a strategy works for subjects in the humanities, the social sciences, or the natural and applied sciences.

New "Classroom Activities"

These in-class group activities following each reading encourage students to collaborate and explore the practical and academic uses of the various rhetorical strategies.

New Author Headshots

To reinforce the concepts of audience and authorship, author photographs accompany almost all professional essays. These photographs remind students that every essay has been written by a person, and encourage them to think of themselves as writers who have individual voices and interesting things to communicate to an audience.

ACKNOWLEDGMENTS

We are gratified by the reception and use of the ten previous editions of *Subject & Strategy*. Composition teachers in hundreds of community colleges, liberal arts colleges, and universities have used the book. Many teachers responded to our detailed review questionnaire, thus helping tremendously in conceptualizing the improvements to this edition. We thank Sarita Batongmalaque, Pierce College; James Boswell, Harrisburg Area Community College; Arnold J. Bradford, Northern Virginia Community College–Loudoun; Deb Dusek, North Dakota State College of Science; Dan Erlacher, North Idaho College; Jeannette L. Gregory, Cloud County Community College; Roderick Hofer, Indian River Community College; Lori Huth, Houghton College; Susan Keith, Massasoit Community College; Isera Kelley Tyson, Manatee Community College; Lisa A. Kirby, North Carolina Wesleyan College; Monique Kluczykowski, Gainesville State College; Elaine Kromhout, Indian River Community College; John Larkin, Castleton State College; Anna Maheshwari, Schoolcraft College; Peter J. Pellegrin, Cloud County Community College; Regina St. John, Ball State University; Patricia Jo Teel, Victor Valley College; David Waskin, Washtenaw Community College; Linda S. Weeks, Dyersburg State Community College; Judith C. White, Cleary University; and Nancy Zenger-Beneda, Cloud County Community College.

At Bedford/St. Martin's, we thank our longtime friend and editor, Nancy Perry, and our talented and enthusiastic developmental editors,

Gregory S. Johnson and Nathan Odell, for their commitment to *Subject & Strategy*. Together we have charted some new territories for this enduring text, and the process has been truly exciting. Thanks go also to the rest of the Bedford/St. Martin's team: Joan Feinberg, Denise Wydra, Erica Appel, Karen Melton Soeltz, Rachel Falk, Marcia Cohen, Jessica Skrocki, Donna Dennison, Lucy Krikorian, and Sandy Schechter. Special thanks go to Sarah Federman for preparing the *Instructor's Manual*. We are also happy to recognize those students whose work appears in *Subject & Strategy* for their willingness to contribute their time and effort in writing and rewriting their essays: Barbara Bowman, Gerald Cleary, Kevin Cunningham, Keith Eldred, Mark Jackson, Tara E. Ketch, Laura LaPierre, Shoshanna Lew, Howard Solomon Jr., Carrie White, and James Blake Wilson. We are grateful to our own writing students at the University of Vermont for their enthusiasm for writing and for their invaluable responses to materials included in this book. And we also thank our families for sharing in our commitment to quality teaching and textbook writing.

Finally, we thank each other. Beginning in 1971 we have collaborated on many textbooks on language and writing, all of which have gone into multiple editions. With this eleventh edition of *Subject & Strategy*, we enter the thirty-seventh year of working together. Ours must be one of the longest-running and most mutually satisfying writing partnerships in college textbook publishing. The journey has been invigorating and challenging as we have come to understand the complexities and joys of good writing and have sought new ways to help students become better writers.

Paul Eschholz
Alfred Rosa

Contents

3 Five Writers on Writing   39

"And he started to read. My words! He was reading *my words* out loud to the entire class. What's more, the entire class was listening."

"All writers write them. This is how they end up with good second drafts and terrific third drafts."

6 Illustration   150

What Is Illustration?   150

Using Illustration as a Writing Strategy   152
> ▸ *Using Illustration across the Disciplines*   152

Sample Student Essay Using Illustration as a Writing Strategy   154
> Carrie White, "Family Portraits"   154
> ▸ *Analyzing Carrie White's Essay of Illustration: Questions for Discussion*   156

Suggestions for Using Illustration as a Writing Strategy   157
> Planning Your Essay of Illustration   157
> Organizing Your Essay of Illustration   160
> Revising and Editing Your Essay of Illustration   160
> ▸ *Questions for Revising and Editing: Illustration*   161

Natalie Goldberg, *Be Specific*   162
> "Don't say 'fruit.' Tell what kind of fruit—'It is a pomegranate.' Give things the dignity of their names."

Mitch Albom, *If You Had One Day with Someone Who's Gone*   166
> "Have you ever lost someone you love and wanted one more conversation, one more day to make up for the time when you thought they would be here forever?"

Deborah Tannen, *How to Give Orders Like a Man*   171
> "I challenge the assumption that talking in an indirect way necessarily reveals powerlessness, lack of self-confidence or anything else about the character of the speaker. Indirectness is a fundamental element in human communication."

Isaac Asimov, *Those Crazy Ideas*   181
> "How does one go about creating or inventing or dreaming up or stumbling over a new and revolutionary scientific principle?"

Alice Walker, *In Search of Our Mothers' Gardens*   193
> "How was the creativity of the black woman kept alive, year after year and century after century, when for most of the years black people have been in America, it was a punishable crime for a black person to read or write?"

Writing Suggestions for Illustration   205

7 Process Analysis   207

What Is Process Analysis?   207

Using Process Analysis as a Writing Strategy   208
> Directional Process Analysis   208
> Informational Process Analysis   209
> Evaluative Process Analysis   210
> ▸ *Using Process Analysis across the Disciplines*   210

"We hold these truths to be self-evident, that all men are created equal, that they are endowed by their Creator with certain unalienable rights, that among these are Life, Liberty, and the Pursuit of Happiness."

"A lot of small words, more than you might think, can meet your needs with a strength, grace, and charm that large words do not have."

"I have a dream that my four little children will one day live in a nation where they will not be judged by the color of their skin but by the content of their character."

"Many superpatriots say they love America because of its freedom. Supposedly, we can say what we like. Here again, the claim should be greeted skeptically or at least carefully qualified. We are not as free as we think."

"We offspring are recognizing the right that was stripped from us at birth—the right to know who both our parents are. And we're ready to reclaim it."

". . . recent studies have found professional women are more likely to get divorced, more likely to cheat, less likely to have children, and, if they do have kids, they are more likely to be unhappy about it."

". . . rather than rush to blame the woman, let's not overlook the other key variable: What is the guy doing?"

Thematic Contents

The Minority Experience

The Natural World

Science, Technology, and the Internet

A Sense of Place

A Sense of Self

Women and Men

SUBJECT & STRATEGY
A Writer's Reader

Introduction for Students

Subject & Strategy is a reader for writers. The selections in this book will entertain you, inform you, and even contribute to your self-awareness and understanding of the world around you. In addition, they will help you grasp and master nine versatile and widely used writing strategies—narration, description, illustration, process analysis, comparison and contrast, division and classification, definition, cause and effect analysis, and argumentation—as well as show you how to combine these strategies. *Subject & Strategy* devotes one chapter to each of these strategies. In each chapter, an introduction defines the strategy, illustrates it with examples, presents an annotated student essay using the strategy, and offers suggestions for using the strategy in your own writing. Each chapter then offers selections from professional writers, chosen because they serve as excellent models of the strategy in question.

Subject & Strategy places equal emphasis on the content and form of a selection—that is, on what an essay has to say and on the strategy used to say it. All readers pay attention to content, to the substance of what an author is saying. Far fewer, however, notice the strategies authors use to organize their writing, to make it clear, logical, and effective. Yet using these strategies is an essential element of the writer's craft, one that writers must master to write well. Because these strategies are such a vital component of the writer's craft, you will need first to become more aware of them in your reading and then to master your use of them to become a better writer.

As the readings in this text demonstrate, content and form are unified in all good writing. Indeed, the two actually help determine one another. A writer who wants to relate the details of an event, to "tell

1

what happened," for example, will naturally choose narration; at the same time, the requirements of the narrative form will influence the content of the written story. On the other hand, if the writer wants to examine *why* something happened, storytelling alone will not do the job. It will be necessary to use the strategy of cause and effect analysis, and this strategy will determine the ultimate content. As you write, you will often tentatively plan your strategy before you start, consciously deciding which strategy or which combination of strategies best fits what you have to say and what you want to accomplish with your writing. Sooner or later, you will have to look back at what you have written, making sure that your choice of strategy serves the purpose of your writing and that it expresses your content accurately and effectively.

One good way for you to become a stronger writer is to become a stronger, more active reader. By becoming more familiar with different types of writing, you will sharpen your critical thinking skills and learn how good writers make decisions in their writing. After reading an article or essay, most people feel more confident talking about the content of the piece than about the style. Content is more tangible than style, which always seems so elusive. In large part, this discrepancy results from our schooling. Most of us have been taught to read for ideas. Not many of us, however, have been trained to read with a writer's eye, to ask why we like one piece of writing and not another. Likewise, most of us do not ask ourselves why one piece of writing is more believable or convincing than another. When you learn to read with a writer's eye, you begin to answer these important questions, and in the process you come to appreciate the craftsmanship involved in writing—how a writer selects descriptive details, uses an unobtrusive organizational strategy, opts for fresh and lively language, chooses representative and persuasive examples, and emphasizes important points with sentence variety.

We have designed this text to help you improve your reading and writing skills. The two processes go hand in hand and should be studied that way because writing, after all, is the making of reading. The more sensitive you become to the content and style decisions made by the writers in this text, the more skilled you will be at making similar decisions in your own writing.

CHAPTER 1

The Reading Process

Active, analytical reading requires, first of all, that you commit time and effort. Second, try to take a positive interest in what you are reading, even if the subject matter is not immediately appealing. Remember, you are not reading for content alone but also to understand a writer's craft—to see firsthand how writers use strategies that fit their subject and purpose.

To help you get the most out of your reading, this chapter provides guidelines for the five steps of the reading process.

STEP 1: PREPARE YOURSELF TO READ THE SELECTION

Instead of diving right into any given selection in *Subject & Strategy*, there are things you can do beforehand to get the most out of what you will be reading. It's helpful, for example, to get a context for what you'll be reading. What's the essay about? What do you know about the writer's background and reputation? Where was the essay first published? Who was the intended audience? And, finally, how much do you already know about the subject of the selection?

We encourage you to consider carefully the materials that precede each selection in this book: the *title, headnote,* and *Preparing to Read* prompt. From the *title* you often discover the writer's position on an issue or attitude toward the topic. The title can also give clues about the intended audience and the writer's purpose in writing the piece. In addition to the writer's photograph, the *headnote* contains three essential elements:

1. The *biographical note* provides information about the writer's life and work, as well as his or her reputation and authority to write on the chosen subject.

2. The *publication information* tells you when the essay was published, where it appeared, and what other works the writer has published. This information can also give you insight about the intended audience.

3. The *content and rhetorical highlights* preview the topic and outline key aspects of how the selection was written.

Finally, the *Preparing to Read* prompt encourages you to collect and record your thoughts and opinions about the topic before you begin reading.

STEP 2: READ THE SELECTION

Always read the selection at least twice, no matter how long it is. The first reading lets you get acquainted with the essay and form general impressions of it. You will want to get an overall sense of what the writer is saying, keeping in mind the essay's title and what you know about the writer. The essay will present information, ideas, and arguments — some you may expect, some you may not. As you read, you may find yourself modifying your sense of the writer's message and purpose. Circle words you do not recognize so that you can look them up in a dictionary. Put a question mark alongside any passages that are not immediately clear. However, you will probably want to delay most of your annotating until a second reading so that your first reading can be fast, enabling you to concentrate on the larger issues of message and purpose.

STEP 3: REREAD THE SELECTION

Your second reading should be quite different from your first. You will know what the essay is about, where it is going, and how it gets there; now you can relate the individual parts of the essay more accurately to the whole. Use your second reading to test your first impressions, developing and deepening your sense of how (and how well) the essay is written. Because you now have a general understanding of the essay, you can pay special attention to the author's purpose and means of achieving it. You can look for features of organization and style and adapt them to your own work.

STEP 4: ANNOTATE THE SELECTION

When you annotate a selection you should do more than simply underline what you think are important points. It is easy to underline so much that the notations become almost meaningless because you forget why you underlined passages in the first place. Instead, as you read, write down your thoughts in the margins or on a separate piece of paper. Mark the selection's main point when you find it stated directly. Look for the strategy or strategies the author uses to explore and support that point, and jot the information down. If you disagree with a statement or conclusion, object in the margin: "No!" If you feel skeptical, indicate that response: "Why?" or "Explain." If you are impressed by an argument or turn of phrase, compliment the writer: "Good point!" Place vertical lines or a star in the margin to indicate important points.

What to Annotate in a Text

Here are some examples of what you may want to mark in a selection as you read:

- Memorable statements of important points
- Key terms or concepts
- Central issues or themes
- Examples that support a main point
- Unfamiliar words
- Questions you have about a point or passage
- Your responses to a specific point or passage

Jot down whatever marginal notes come naturally to you. Most readers combine brief written responses with underlining, circling, highlighting, stars, or question marks.

Remember that there are no hard-and-fast rules for annotating elements. Choose a method of annotation that will make sense to you when you go back to recollect your thoughts and responses to the essay. Don't let annotating become burdensome. A word or phrase is usually as good as a sentence. One helpful way to focus your annotations is to ask yourself questions such as those on page 6 while reading the selection a second time.

STEP 5: ANALYZE AND EVALUATE THE SELECTION

As you continue to study the selection, analyze it for a deeper understanding and appreciation of the author's craft and try to evaluate its overall effectiveness as a piece of writing. Our students have found it helpful to ask some basic questions about an essay's content and form as they analyze and evaluate it. Here are some questions you may find helpful as you start the process of analyzing and evaluating a selection:

1. What does the writer want to say? What is the writer's main point or thesis?
2. Why does the writer want to make this point? What is the writer's purpose?
3. What strategy or strategies does the writer use? Where are the strategies used?
4. How does the writer's strategy suit his or her subject and purpose?
5. What, if anything, is noteworthy about the writer's use of this strategy?
6. How effective is the essay? Does the writer make his or her points clear?

Each essay in *Subject & Strategy* is followed by study questions similar to these but specific to the essay. The subject questions help you analyze the content of an essay, while the strategy questions analyze the writer's use of the rhetorical strategies. In addition, there are questions about the writer's diction and vocabulary. As you read the essay a second time, look for details related to these questions, and then answer the questions as fully as you can.

THE READING PROCESS IN ACTION: THOMAS L. FRIEDMAN'S "MY FAVORITE TEACHER"

To illustrate the five-step reading process that we have just explored, we have fully annotated an essay by Thomas L. Friedman, including the headnote material and the Preparing to Read prompt. In addition, we have provided answers to the basic questions for analyzing and evaluating an essay. Before you read Friedman's essay, think about the title, the biographical and rhetorical information in the headnote, and the Preparing to Read prompt. Make some notes of your expectations about the essay and write out a response to the prompt. Next, use the five-step process outlined in this chapter as you read this essay. You may find it helpful to cover up our annotations until after you have had an opportunity to read and react to the essay yourself. As you read the essay for the first time, try not to stop; take it all in as if in one breath. The second time through, pause to annotate the text. Next, using the following six questions, analyze and evaluate the essay. Finally, compare your annotations and answers to ours.

1. What does Friedman want to say? What is his main point or thesis?
2. Why does he want to make this point? What is his purpose?
3. What strategy or strategies does Friedman use?
4. How does Friedman's strategy or strategies suit his subject and purpose?
5. What is noteworthy about Friedman's use of this strategy?
6. How effective is Friedman's essay? Why?

Clear indication of topic in the title

My Favorite Teacher
Thomas L. Friedman

Acclaimed journalist

Book titles demonstrate expertise in journalism, especially reporting on Middle East affairs.

Rhetorical highlight: collective impact of descriptive details

New York Times *foreign affairs columnist Thomas L. Friedman was born in Minneapolis, Minnesota, in 1953. He graduated from Brandeis University in 1975 and received a Marshall Scholarship to pursue modern Middle East studies at St. Anthony's College, Oxford University, where he earned a master's degree. He has worked for the* New York Times *since 1981—first in Lebanon, then in Israel, and since 1989 in Washington, D.C. He was awarded the Pulitzer Prize in 1983 and 1988 for his reporting and again in 2002 for his commentary. Friedman's 1989 best-seller,* From Beirut to Jerusalem, *received the National Book Award for nonfiction. His most recent books are* The Lexus and the Olive Tree: Understanding Globalization *(2000),* Longitudes and Attitudes: Exploring the World after September 11 *(2002), and* The World is Flat: A Brief History of the Twenty-First Century *(2005).*

In the following essay, which first appeared in the New York Times *on January 9, 2001, Friedman pays tribute to his tenth-grade journalism teacher. As you read Friedman's profile of Hattie M. Steinberg, note the descriptive detail he selects to create the dominant impression of "a woman of clarity in an age of uncertainty."*

PREPARING TO READ

Prompt asks you to reflect on who your favorite teacher was and explain why.

If you had to name your three favorite teachers of all time, who would they be? Why do you consider each one a favorite? Which one, if any, are you likely to remember twenty-five years from now? Why?

Last Sunday's *New York Times Magazine* published its annual review of people who died last year who left a particular mark on the world. I am sure all readers have their own such list. I certainly do. Indeed, someone who made the most important difference in my life died last year—my high school journalism teacher, Hattie M. Steinberg. 1

I grew up in a small suburb of Minneapolis, and Hattie was the legendary journalism teacher at St. Louis Park High School, Room 313. I took her intro to journalism course in 10th grade, back in 1969, and have never needed, or taken, another course in journalism since. She was that good. 2

Hattie was a woman who believed that the secret for success in life was getting the fundamentals right. And boy, she pounded the fundamentals of journalism into her students—not simply how to write a lead or accurately transcribe a quote, but, more important, how to comport yourself in a professional way and to always do quality work. To this day, when I forget to wear a tie on assignment, I think of Hattie scolding me. I once interviewed an ad exec for our high school paper who used a four-letter word. We debated whether to run it. Hattie ruled yes. That ad man almost lost his job when it appeared. She wanted to teach us about consequences. 3

Hattie was the toughest teacher I ever had. After you took her journalism course in 10th grade, you tried out for the paper, *The Echo*, which she supervised. Competition was fierce. In 11th grade, I didn't quite come up to her writing standards, so she made me business manager, selling ads to the local pizza parlors. That year, though, she let me write one story. It was about an Israeli general who had been a hero in the Six-Day War, who was giving a lecture at the University of Minnesota. I covered his lecture and interviewed him briefly. His name was Ariel Sharon. First story I ever got published. 4

Those of us on the paper, and the yearbook that she also supervised, lived in Hattie's classroom. We hung out there before and after school. Now, you have to understand, Hattie was a single woman, nearing 60 at the time, and this was the 1960's. She was the polar opposite of "cool," but we hung around her classroom like it was a malt shop and she was Wolfman Jack. None of us could have articulated it then, but it was 5

*Dramatic conclud-
ing sentence*

because we enjoyed being harangued by her, disci-
plined by her and taught by her. She was a woman of
clarity in an age of uncertainty.

*Narration helps
develop profile of
Hattie as a teacher
who treated stu-
dents as family.*

We remained friends for 30 years, and she followed, 6
bragged about and critiqued every twist in my career.
After she died, her friends sent me a pile of my stories
that she had saved over the years. Indeed, her students
were her family—only closer. Judy Harrington, one of
Hattie's former students, remarked about other friends
who were on Hattie's newspapers and yearbooks: "We
all graduated 41 years ago; and yet nearly each day in
our lives something comes up—some mental image,
some admonition that makes us think of Hattie."

*Quotation shows
Hattie's forceful
personality.*

Judy also told the story of one of Hattie's last birth- 7
day parties, when one man said he had to leave early to
take his daughter somewhere. "Sit down," said Hattie.
"You're not leaving yet. She can just be a little late."

*Short, dramatic
paragraph*

That was my teacher! I sit up straight just thinkin' 8
about her.

*Fundamental of
reading The
Times—repeats
"Room 313"*

Among the fundamentals Hattie introduced me to 9
was *The New York Times*. Every morning it was delivered to Room 313. I had never seen it before then. Real
journalists, she taught us, start their day by reading
The Times and columnists like Anthony Lewis and
James Reston.

*Explains "dot-
com" collapse*

I have been thinking about Hattie a lot this year, 10
not just because she died on July 31, but because the
lessons she imparted seem so relevant now. We've just
gone through this huge dot-com-Internet-globalization
bubble—during which a lot of smart people got
carried away and forgot the fundamentals of how
you build a profitable company, a lasting portfolio, a
nation state or a thriving student. It turns out that
the real secret of success in the information age is what
it always was: fundamentals—reading, writing and
arithmetic, church, synagogue and mosque, the rule of
law and good governance.

*Friedman believes
in fundamentals,
too.*

*Emphasizes funda-
mentals*

The Internet can make you smarter, but it can't 11
make you smart. It can extend your reach, but it will
never tell you what to say at a P.T.A. meeting. These
fundamentals cannot be downloaded. You can only
upload them, the old-fashioned way, one by one, in
places like Room 313 at St. Louis Park High. I only
regret that I didn't write this column when the woman
who taught me all that was still alive.

*Repeats "Room
313"*

*Ends with "only
regret"*

Once you have read and reread Friedman's essay, write your own answers to the six basic questions listed earlier. Then compare your answers with those that follow.

1. *What does Friedman want to say?*

Friedman wants to tell his readers about his high school journalism teacher, Hattie M. Steinberg, because she was "someone who made the most important difference in my life" (paragraph 1). His main point seems to be that "Hattie was a woman who believed that the secret for success in life was getting the fundamentals right" (3). Friedman learned this from Hattie and applied it to his own life. He firmly believes that "the real secret of success in the information age is what it always was: fundamentals" (10).

2. *Why does he want to make this point?*

Friedman's purpose is to memorialize Hattie Steinberg, his former journalism teacher, and to explain the importance of the fundamentals that she taught him more than thirty years ago. He wants his readers to appreciate the examples of fundamentals offered by his journalism teacher and to realize that there are no shortcuts or quick fixes on the road to success. Without the fundamentals, success often eludes people.

3. *What strategy or strategies does Friedman use?*

Overall, Friedman uses the strategy of illustration. Hattie M. Steinberg is a detailed example of a person on Friedman's list of important people who died last year. Friedman fleshes out his profile of Steinberg with specific examples of the fundamentals she instilled in her students (paragraphs 3 and 9). Friedman uses description as well to develop his profile of Steinberg. We learn that she was Friedman's "toughest teacher" (4), that she was "a single woman, nearing 60 at the time," that she was "the polar opposite of 'cool,'" and that she was "a woman of clarity in an age of uncertainty" (5). Finally, Friedman's brief narratives about his interview of an advertising executive, his interview of Ariel Sharon, hanging out in Steinberg's classroom, and one of the teacher's last birthday parties give readers insight into her personality by showing us what she was like instead of simply telling us.

4. *How does Friedman's strategy or strategies suit his subject and purpose?*

Friedman selects exemplification as a strategy because his purpose is to show why Hattie M. Steinberg deserves a place on his list of people who died last year who left a particular mark on the world. She was the person who had the greatest impact on his life. Friedman knew that he was not telling Steinberg's story, a narration, so much as he was showing what a great teacher she was. Using examples of how Hattie affected his life and molded his journalistic skills allows Friedman to introduce his teacher as well as to demonstrate her importance.

5. *What is noteworthy about Friedman's use of the strategy?*

In developing his portrait of Hattie M. Steinberg, Friedman relies on the fundamentals of good journalism. He selects brief examples that give us insight into Steinberg's character and personality. When taken collectively, these examples create a poignant picture of this unforgettable teacher. One would have to think that Steinberg herself would have been proud to see how her former student demonstrates his journalistic skills in paying tribute to the woman who taught him his craft so long ago.

6. *How effective is the essay? Why?*

Friedman's essay is effective because it serves his purpose extremely well. He helps his readers visualize Hattie M. Steinberg and understand the gifts that she gave to each of her journalism students. In his concluding two paragraphs, Friedman shows us that Steinberg's message is as relevant today as it was more than thirty years ago in St. Louis Park High School, Room 313.

THE READING-WRITING CONNECTION

Reading and writing are two sides of the same coin. Many people view writing as the making of reading, but the connection does not end there. Active reading is one of the best ways to learn to write and to improve writing skills. By reading we can see how others have communicated their experiences, ideas, thoughts, and feelings in their writing. We can study how they have effectively used the various elements of the essay — thesis, organization, beginnings and endings, paragraphs, transitions, effective sentences, word choice, tone, and figurative language — to say what they wanted to say. By studying the style, technique, and rhetorical strategies of other writers we learn how we might effectively do the same. The more we read and write, the more we begin to read as writers and, in turn, to write knowing what readers expect.

Reading as a Writer

What does it mean to read as a writer? Most of us have not been taught to read with a writer's eye, to ask why we like one piece of writing and not another. Likewise, most of us do not ask ourselves why one piece of writing is more believable or convincing than another. When you learn to read with a writer's eye, you begin to answer these important questions and, in the process, come to appreciate what is involved in selecting a subject. Also, you begin to understand the craftsmanship involved in writing—how a writer selects descriptive details, uses an unobtrusive organizational pattern, opts for fresh and lively language, chooses representative and persuasive examples, and emphasizes important points with sentence variety.

At one level, reading stimulates your imagination by providing you with subjects. After reading Malcolm X's "Coming to an Awareness of Language," David P. Bardeen's "Not Close Enough for Comfort," or Mary Winstead's "Up in Smoke," you might decide to write about a "turning point" in your life. Or, by reading Pat Mora's "Remembering Lobo," Edward Abbey's "Aravaipa Canyon," or Robert Ramírez's "The Barrio," you would see how each writer creates a dominant impression of an important person or place in his or her life, and you could write about a person or place of similar personal significance.

On a second level, reading provides you with information, ideas, and perspectives for developing your own essay. For example, after reading Rosalind Wiseman's "The Queen Bee and Her Court," you might want to elaborate on what she has written, agreeing with her examples or generating better ones; qualify her argument or take issue with it; or use a variation of her classification scheme to discuss male relationships (i.e., "The King and His Court"). Similarly, if you wanted to write an essay in which you take a stand on an issue, you would find the paired essays on contentious subjects in the Argumentation chapter an invaluable resource.

On a third level, reading can increase your awareness of how others' writing affects you, making you more sensitive to how your writing will affect readers. For example, if you have been impressed by an author who uses convincing evidence to support her claims, you might be more likely to back up your own claims carefully. If you have been impressed by an apt turn of phrase or a memorable choice of words, you may be more inclined to take care with your diction. More to the point, however, the active, analytical reading that you will be encouraged to do in *Subject & Strategy* will help you recognize and analyze the essay's essential elements. When you see, for example, how Deborah Tannen uses a strong thesis statement about the value of directness and indirectness in human communication to control the parts of her essay, you can better appreciate the importance of having a clear thesis statement in your writing. When you see the way Diane Ackerman uses transitions to link key phrases and important ideas so that readers can recognize how the parts of her essay are meant to flow together, you have a better idea of how to achieve such coherence in your writing. And when you see how Suzanne Britt uses a point-by-point organizational pattern to show the differences between neat and sloppy people, you see a powerful way in which you can organize an essay using the strategy of comparison and contrast.

Finally, another important reason to master the skill of reading like a writer is that, for everything you write, you will be your own first reader. How well you scrutinize your own drafts will affect how well you revise them, and revising well is crucial to writing well. So reading others' writing with a critical eye is useful and important practice; the more you read, the more practice you will have in sharpening your skills.

Remember, writing is the making of reading. The more sensitive you become to the content and style decisions made by the writers in *Subject & Strategy*, the more skilled you will become at making similar decisions in your writing.

CHAPTER 2

The Writing Process

Writers cannot rely on inspiration alone to produce an effective piece of writing. Good writers follow a writing process: They understand their assignment, gather ideas, draft, revise, and edit and proofread. It is worth remembering, however, that the writing process is rarely as simple and straightforward as this. Often the process is recursive, moving back and forth among the five stages. Moreover, writing is personal—no two people go about it exactly the same way. Still, it is possible to describe the steps in the writing process and thereby have a reassuring and reliable method for undertaking a writing task.

STEP 1: UNDERSTAND YOUR ASSIGNMENT

A great deal of the writing you do in college will be in response to very specific assignments. Your American history professor, for example, may ask you write a paper in which you explain the causes of the Spanish-American War; your environmental studies professor may ask you to report both the pro and con arguments for regulating industrial carbon emissions; or your English professor may ask you to compare and contrast the text and film versions of H. G. Wells's *The War of the Worlds*. It is important, therefore, that you understand exactly what your instructor is asking you to do. The best way to understand assignments such as these (or exam questions, for that matter) is to identify *subject* words (words that indicate the content of the assignment) and *direction* words (words that indicate your purpose or the writing strategy you should use). In the first example given above, the subject words are *Spanish-American War* and the direction word is *explain*. In the second example, the subject words are *industrial carbon emissions* and the direction word is *report*. Finally, the subject words in the third example are *text and film versions of H. G. Wells's* The War of the Worlds, while the direction words are *compare and contrast*.

Most direction words are familiar to us, but we are not always sure how they differ from one another or exactly what they are asking us to do. The following list of direction words, along with explanations of what they call for, will help you analyze paper and exam assignments.

Analyze: take apart and examine closely

Argue: make a case for a particular position

Categorize: place into meaningful groups

Compare: look for differences; stress similarities

Contrast: look for similarities; stress differences

Critique: point out positive and negative features

Define: provide the meaning for a term or concept

Evaluate: judge according to some standard

Explain: make plain or comprehensible

Illustrate: show through examples

Interpret: explain the meaning of something

List: catalog or list steps in a process

Outline: provide abbreviated structure for key elements

Prove: demonstrate truth through logic, fact, or example

Review: summarize key points

Synthesize: bring together or make connections among elements

Trace: delineate a sequence of events

Finding a Subject Area and Focusing on a Topic

Although you will usually be given specific assignments in your writing course, you may sometimes be given the freedom to choose your subject matter and topic. In either case, when selecting your specific topic you should determine whether you know something about it and whether it interests you.

When your instructor leaves you free to choose your own topic, begin by determining a broad subject that you like to think about and might enjoy writing about—a general subject like the Internet, popular culture, or foreign travel. Something you've recently read—one of the essays in *Subject & Strategy*, for example—may help bring particular subjects to mind. You might consider a subject related to your career ambitions—perhaps business, journalism, teaching, law, medicine, architecture, or computer programming. Another option is to list some subjects you enjoy discussing with friends: food, sports, television programs, or politics. Select several likely subjects, and let your mind explore their potential for interesting topics. Your goal is to arrive at an appropriately narrowed topic.

Suppose, for example, you select as possible subject areas "farming" and "advertising." You could develop each according to the following chart.

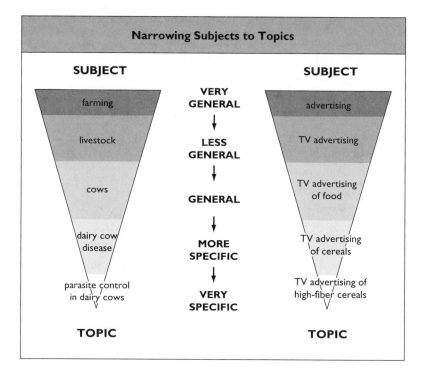

Narrowing Subjects to Topics

SUBJECT		SUBJECT
farming	VERY GENERAL	advertising
livestock	LESS GENERAL	TV advertising
cows	GENERAL	TV advertising of food
dairy cow disease	MORE SPECIFIC	TV advertising of cereals
parasite control in dairy cows	VERY SPECIFIC	TV advertising of high-fiber cereals
TOPIC		TOPIC

Determine Your Purpose.   All effective writing is written with a purpose. Good writing seeks to accomplish any one of three purposes:

- To express thoughts and feelings about life experiences
- To inform readers by explaining something about the world around them
- To persuade readers to adopt some belief or take some action

In *expressive writing*, or writing from experience, you put your thoughts and feelings before all other concerns. When Annie Dillard reacts to being caught throwing a snowball at a car (Chapter 4), when

Malcolm X shows his frustration at not having appropriate language to express himself (Chapter 4), and when Edward Abbey describes a hike in Aravaipa Canyon with two friends (Chapter 5), each one is writing from experience. In each case, the writer has clarified an important life experience and has conveyed what he or she learned from it.

Informative writing focuses on telling the reader something about the outside world. In informative writing, you report, explain, analyze, define, classify, compare, describe a process, or examine causes and effects. When Kennedy P. Maize explains what happens when the residents of Kern County declare war on the mouse population (Chapter 11) and when Deborah Tannen discusses examples of orders given and received in the workplace (Chapter 6), each one is writing to inform.

Argumentative writing seeks to influence readers' thinking and attitudes toward a subject and, in some cases, to move them to a particular course of action. Such persuasive writing uses logical reasoning, authoritative evidence, and testimony and sometimes includes emotionally charged language and examples. Richard Lederer uses numerous examples to show us the power of short words (Chapter 12), and Thomas Jefferson uses evidence to argue that the fledgling American colonies are within their rights to break away from Britain (Chapter 12).

Know Your Audience.   The best writers always keep their audience in mind. Once they have decided on a topic and a purpose, writers present their material in a way that empathizes with their readers, addresses their difficulties and concerns, and appeals to their rational and emotional faculties. Based on knowledge of their audience, writers make conscious decisions on content, sentence structure, and word choice.

An audience might be an individual (your instructor), a group (the students in your class), a specialized group (art history majors), or a general readership (readers of your student newspaper). To help identify your audience, ask yourself the following questions:

Questions about Audience

- Who are my readers?
- Are they a specialized or a general group?
- What do I know about my audience's age, gender, education, religious affiliation, economic status, and political views?
- What does my audience know about my subject? Are they experts or novices?
- What does my audience need to know that I can tell them?

(continued on next page)

(continued from previous page)

- Will my audience be interested, open-minded, resistant, or hostile to what I have to say?
- Do I need to explain any specialized language so that my audience can understand my subject? Is there any language that I should avoid?
- What do I want my audience to do as a result of reading my essay?

STEP 2: GATHER IDEAS AND FORMULATE A THESIS

Ideas and information lie at the heart of good prose. Ideas grow out of information (facts and details); information supports ideas. Gather as many ideas as possible and as much information as you can about your topic in order to inform and stimulate your readers intellectually. If you try to write before doing such work, you run the risk of producing a shallow, boring draft.

Brainstorming

A good way to generate ideas and information about your topic is to *brainstorm*. Simply list everything you know about your topic, freely associating one idea with another. At this point, order is not important. Try to capture everything that comes to mind because you never know what might prove valuable later. Write quickly, but if you get stalled, reread what you have written; doing so will jog your mind in new directions. Keep your list handy so that you can add to it over the course of several days. Here, for example, is a student's brainstorming list on why Martin Luther King Jr.'s "I Have a Dream" speech (page 486) is enduring:

WHY "I HAVE A DREAM" IS MEMORABLE

- Civil rights demonstration in Washington, D.C.
- Delivered on the steps of Lincoln Memorial
- Repetition of "I have a dream"
- Allusions to the Bible, spirituals
- "Bad check" metaphor

- Other memorable figures of speech
- Crowd of more than 200,000 people
- Echoes other great American writings — Declaration of Independence and Gettysburg Address
- Refers to various parts of the country
- Embraces all races and religions
- Sermon format
- Displays energy and passion

Clustering

Clustering allows you to generate material and to sort it into meaningful groupings. Put your topic, or a key word or phrase about your topic, in the center of a sheet of paper and draw a circle around it. Draw four or five (or more) lines radiating out from this circle, and jot down main ideas about your topic; draw circles around them as well. Repeat the process by drawing lines from the secondary circles and adding examples, details, and any questions you have. You may find yourself pursuing one line of thought through many connected circles before beginning a new cluster. Do whatever works for you. Here, for example, is a student's cluster on television news programs:

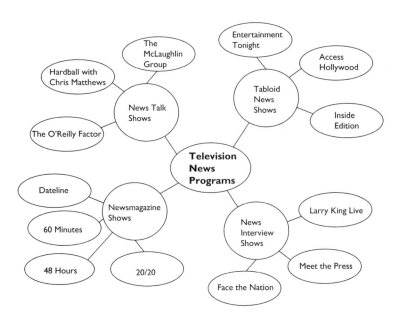

Researching

You may want to supplement what you know about your topic with research. This does not necessarily mean formal library work. Firsthand observations and interviews with people knowledgeable about your topic are also forms of research and are usually more up to date than library research. Whatever your form of research, take careful notes, so you can accurately paraphrase an author or quote an interviewee.

Rehearsing Ideas

Try rehearsing what you are going to write by running ideas or phrasings, even sentences, through your mind until they are fairly well crafted before you transfer them to paper. The image of the writer, pencil in hand, staring off into space, perhaps best captures the essence of this technique. Rehearsing may suit your personality and the way you think. Moreover, because it is a thoughtful practice, rehearsing may help you generate ideas. Sometimes rehearsing may even be done orally. Try taking ten or fifteen minutes to talk your way through your paper with a roommate, friend, or family member.

Formulating a Thesis

The thesis of an essay is its main idea, the major point the writer is trying to make. Because all the content in an essay must in some way be logically connected to the thesis statement, it has a lot of power in controlling the content and direction of your essay. The thesis is often expressed in one or two sentences called a thesis statement. Here's an example of a thesis statement about television news programs:

> The so-called serious news programs are becoming too like tabloid news shows in both their content and their presentation.

A thesis should be

- The most important point you make about your topic
- More general than the ideas and facts used to support it
- Focused enough to be covered in the space allotted for the essay

A thesis statement should not be a question but an assertion. If you find yourself writing a question for a thesis statement, answer the question first—this answer will be your thesis statement.

An effective strategy for developing a thesis statement is to begin by writing, "What I want to say is that . . ."

What I want to say is that unless language barriers between patients and health care providers are bridged, many patients' lives in our most culturally diverse cities will be endangered.

Later you can delete the formulaic opening, and you will be left with a thesis statement.

Unless language barriers between patients and health care providers are bridged, many patients' lives in our most culturally diverse cities will be endangered.

To determine whether your thesis is too general or too specific, think hard about how easy it will be to present data—that is, facts, statistics, names, examples or illustrations, and opinions of authorities—to support it. If you stray too far in either direction, your task will become much more difficult. A thesis statement that is too general will leave you overwhelmed by the number of issues you must address. For example, the statement "Malls have ruined the fabric of American life" would lead to the question "How?" To answer it, you would probably have to include information about traffic patterns, urban decay, environmental damage, economic studies, and so on. You would obviously have to take shortcuts, and your paper would be ineffective. On the other hand, too specific a thesis statement will leave you with too little information to present. "The Big City Mall should not have been built because it reduced retail sales at existing Big City stores by 21.4 percent" does not leave you with any opportunity to develop an argument.

Will Your Thesis Hold Water?

Once you have a possible thesis statement in mind for an essay, ask yourself the following questions:

- Does my thesis statement take a clear position on an issue? If so, what is that position?
- Is my thesis too general?
- Is my thesis too specific?
- Is my thesis the most important point I make about my topic?

The thesis statement is usually set forth near the beginning of the essay, although writers sometimes first offer a few sentences that establish a context for the piece. One common practice is to position the thesis statement as the final sentence of the first paragraph.

STEP 3: ORGANIZE AND WRITE YOUR FIRST DRAFT

There is nothing mysterious or difficult about the nine rhetorical strategies discussed in this book. You're probably familiar with some of them already. When you want to tell a story, for example, you naturally use the strategy of narration. When you want to make a choice, you naturally compare and contrast the things you must choose between. When you want to explain how to make a pizza, you fall automatically into the strategy of process analysis. These and other strategies are ways we think about the world and our experiences in it. What might make these strategies seem unfamiliar, especially in writing, is that most people use them more or less intuitively, with little awareness of their use. Sophisticated thinking and writing do not come from simply using these structures—everyone does that—but from using them consciously and purposefully.

Writing strategies, however, are not like blueprints or plaster molds that determine in advance exactly how the final product will be shaped. Good essays usually employ components of more than one strategy, and the options for how to use them effectively are numerous. Rather, these strategies are flexible and versatile, with only a few fundamental rules or directions to define their shape—like the rules for basketball, chess, or other strategic games. Such directions leave plenty of room for all the imagination and variety you can put into your writing and for all the things you may want to write about. In addition, because these strategies are fundamental ways of thinking, they will help you in all stages of the writing process—from prewriting and writing a first draft through revising and editing your piece.

Writing Strategies	
Narration	Telling a story or giving an account of an event
Description	Presenting a picture with words
Illustration	Using examples to illustrate a point or idea
Process Analysis	Explaining how something is done or happens
Comparison and Contrast	Demonstrating likenesses and differences
Division and Classification	Dividing a subject into its parts and placing them in appropriate categories

(continued on next page)

(continued from previous page)

Definition	Explaining what something is
Cause and Effect Analysis	Explaining the causes of an event or the effects of an action
Argumentation	Using reason and logic to persuade someone to your way of thinking

Determining a Strategy for Developing Your Essay

If you have been given a writing assignment, your instructor wants to make sure you carry out the writing task with certain goals in mind. The language used in the writing assignment is, therefore, very important. If a description is called for, or you need to examine causes and effects, or, as is often the case, you are asked to argue for a position on an important issue, the language of the assignment will include key direction words and phrases that will indicate the strategy or strategies you should use in developing your essay.

The first column in the following chart lists some key direction words and phrases you may encounter in your writing assignments. The second column lists the strategy that is most likely called for by the use of those words and, therefore, the strategy you should pursue in developing your essay.

Key Direction Words and Phrases	Suggested Writing Strategy
Give an account of; tell the story of; relate the events of	*Narration*
Describe; present a picture; discuss the details of	*Description*
Show; demonstrate; enumerate; discuss; give examples of	*Illustration*
Explain how something is done; explain how something works; explain what happens; analyze the steps	*Process Analysis*
Compare; contrast; explain differences; explain similarities; evaluate	*Comparison and Contrast*
Divide and classify; explain what the components are; analyze the parts of	*Division and Classification*

Explain; define a person, place, or thing; give the meaning of	*Definition*
Explain causes; explain effects; give the reasons for; what are the consequences of	*Cause and Effect Analysis*
Argue for or against; make a case for or against; state your views on; persuade; convince; justify	*Argumentation*

Choosing Strategies across the Disciplines.   Often in academic writing your instructor may not give you a specific assignment; instead, he or she may ask you to treat one of the topics in the course according to your own interests, asking only that you write a paper of a specific length. In such cases you are left to determine for yourself what strategy or strategies might best accomplish your purpose. If you are uncertain as to what strategy or strategies you should use in developing your essay, you might try the following four-step method:

1. State the main idea of your essay in a single phrase or sentence.
2. Restate the main idea as a question — in effect, the question your essay will answer.
3. Look closely at both the main idea and the question for key words or concepts that go with a particular strategy, just as you would when working with an assignment that specifies a topic.
4. Consider other strategies that would support your primary strategy.

AMERICAN LITERATURE

MAIN IDEA: John Updike relies on religion as a major theme in his fiction.

QUESTION: In what instances does John Updike use religion as a major theme?

STRATEGY: Illustration. The phrase *in what instances* signals that it is necessary to show examples of where Updike uses the theme of religion to further his narrative purposes.

SUPPORTING STRATEGIES: Definition. What is meant by religion needs to be clear.

BIOLOGY

MAIN IDEA: Mitosis is the process by which cells divide.

QUESTION: How does the process of mitosis work?

STRATEGY: Process Analysis. The words *how*, *process*, and *work* signal a process analysis essay.

SUPPORTING STRATEGIES: Illustration. A good process analysis includes examples of each step in the process.

POLITICAL SCIENCE

MAIN IDEA: The threat of terrorism has changed the way people think about air travel.

QUESTION: What effects does terrorism have on air travel?

STRATEGY: Cause and Effect Analysis. The phrase *what effects* asks for a listing of the effects.

SUPPORTING STRATEGIES: Illustration. The best presentation of effects is through vivid examples.

These are just a few examples of how to decide on a writing strategy and supporting strategies that are suitable for your topic. In every case, your reading can guide you in recognizing the best plan to follow. In Chapter 13, you will learn more about combining strategies.

Writing Your First Draft

First drafts are exploratory and sometimes unpredictable. While writing your first draft, you may find yourself getting away from your original plan. What started as a definition essay may develop into a process analysis or an effort at argumentation. For example, a definition of "school spirit" could turn into a process analysis of how a pep rally is organized or an argument about why school spirit is important (or detrimental). A definition of "manners" could become an instructive process analysis on how to be a good host, or it could turn into an argument that respect is based on the ways people treat one another. A definition of "democracy" could evolve into a process analysis of how democracy works in the United States or into an argument for democratic forms of government. If your draft is leaning toward another strategy, don't force yourself to revert to your original plan. Allow your inspiration to take you where it will. When you finish your draft, you can see whether the new strategy works better than the old one or whether it would be best to go back to your initial strategy. Use your first draft to explore your ideas; you will always have a chance to revise later.

It may also happen that while writing your first draft, you run into a difficulty that prevents you from moving forward. For example, suppose you want to tell about something that happened to you, but you aren't certain whether you should be using the pronoun *I* so often. If you turn to the essays in Chapter 4 to see how authors of narrative essays handle this problem, you will find that it isn't necessarily a problem at all. For an account of a personal experience, it's perfectly acceptable to write *I* as often as you need to. Or suppose that after writing several pages describing someone you think is quite a character, you find that your draft seems flat and doesn't express how lively and funny the person really is. If you read the introduction to Chapter 5, you will learn that descriptions need lots of factual, concrete detail, and the chapter selections give further proof of this. You suddenly realize that just such detail is what's missing from your draft. Reading, then, is helpful because it enables you to see how other writers have successfully dealt with problems similar to yours.

If you do run into difficulties writing your first draft, don't worry or get upset. Even experienced writers run into problems at the beginning. Just try to keep going and take pressure off yourself. Think about your topic, and consider your details and what you want to say. You might even want to go back and look over the information you've gathered.

Checklist for Your First Draft

- Triple-space your draft so that you can make changes more easily.
- Make revisions on a hard copy of your paper.
- Read your paper aloud, listening for parts that do not make sense.
- Have a fellow student read your essay and critique it.

STEP 4: REVISE YOUR ESSAY

Once you have completed your first draft, have set it aside awhile, and have had at least one peer critiquing session, you are ready to revise your essay. Revision is a vital part of the writing process. It is not to be confused with editing or "cleaning up" a draft but should be regarded as a set of activities wherein a rough draft may be transformed from a more or less acceptable piece of writing into a polished essay that powerfully expresses your ideas. In fact, many writers believe that all writing is essentially rewriting. When you revise, you give yourself a chance to re-see how well you have captured your subject, to see what has worked and what still needs to be done. Perhaps you need to reorganize your paragraphs or the sentences within some paragraphs, generate more information because you have too few examples, revise your thesis statement so that it better fits your argument, or find better transitions to bind your sentences and thoughts together. Rather than an arduous task, many writers find revision a very satisfying process because they are able to bring their work into sharper focus and give themselves a better chance of connecting with their audience. In another sense, revision is a payoff for all the hard work that went into the prewriting activities of brainstorming, gathering information, researching, trying out strategies, and drafting. The following sections offer proven techniques for initiating and carring out one or more revisions of your developing essays.

Taking Advantage of Peer Critiques

When you critique work with other students—yours or theirs—it is important to maximize the effectiveness and efficiency of the exercise. The tips outlined in the following box will help you get the most out of peer critiques.

A Brief Guide to Peer Critiquing

When critiquing someone else's work:

- Read the essay carefully. Read it to yourself first and, if possible, have the writer read it to you at the beginning of the session. Some flaws become obvious when read aloud.
- Ask the writer to state his or her purpose for writing and to identify the thesis statement within the paper itself.
- Be positive, but be honest. Never denigrate the paper's content or the writer's effort, but do your best to identify how the writer can improve the paper through revision.
- Try to address the most important issues first. Think about the thesis and the organization of the paper before moving on to more specific topics like word choice.
- Do not be dismissive, and do not dictate changes. Ask questions that encourage the writer to reconsider parts of the paper that you find confusing or ineffective.

When someone critiques your work:

- Give your reviewer a copy of your essay before your meeting.
- Listen carefully to your reviewer, and try not to discuss or argue each issue. Record comments, and evaluate them later.
- Do not get defensive or explain what you wanted to say if the reviewer misunderstands what you meant. Try to understand the reviewer's point of view, and learn what you need to revise to clear up the misunderstanding.

(continued on next page)

(continued from previous page)

- Consider every suggestion, but only use the ones that make sense to you in your revision.
- Be sure to thank your reviewer for his or her effort on your behalf.

Revising the Large Elements of Your Essay

During the revision stage of the writing process, you will focus on the large issues of thesis, purpose, content, organization, and paragraph structure to make sure that your writing says what you want it to say. But first, it is crucial that you set your draft aside and give yourself a rest. Then you can come back to it with some freshness and objectivity. When you do, resist the temptation to plunge immediately into a second draft. Scattered changes will not necessarily improve the piece. Try to look at your writing as a whole and tackle your writing problems systematically.

One way to begin the revision process is to make an informal outline of your first draft—not as you planned it, but as it actually came out. What does your outline tell you about the strategy you used? Does this strategy suit your purpose? Perhaps you meant to compare your two grandmothers, but you have not clearly shown their similarities and differences. Consequently, your draft is not one unified comparison and contrast essay but two descriptive essays spliced together. Or perhaps your outline will show you that you set out to write about two religions, but you never had a definite purpose in mind. Outlining your first draft helps you see that, despite some differences, both religions are very much alike in all the ways that matter. This gives you both a point to make and a strategy for making it: comparison and contrast.

Even if you are satisfied with the overall strategy of your draft, an outline can still help you make improvements. Perhaps your directions for preparing a pizza leave out an important step in the process—adding oregano to the tomato sauce, for example. Or perhaps your classification essay on types of college students is confusing because you create overlapping categories: computer science majors, athletes, and foreign students (a computer science major could, of course, be an athlete, a foreign student, or both). You may uncover a flaw in your organization, such as a lack of logic in an argument or a faulty parallelism in a comparison and contrast. Now is the time to discover these problems and to fix them.

Another method you can use in revising is to start with large-scale issues, such as your overall structure, and then concentrate on finer and finer points. As you examine your essay, ask yourself questions about what you have written. The following list of questions addresses the large elements of your essay: thesis, purpose, organization, paragraphs, and evidence.

Questions for Revising the Large Elements of Your Essay

- Have I focused my topic?
- Does my thesis statement clearly identify my topic and make an assertion about it?
- Is the writing strategy I have chosen the best one for my purpose?
- Are my paragraphs adequately developed, and does each support my thesis?
- Have I accomplished my purpose?
- Is my beginning effective in capturing my reader's interest and introducing my topic?
- Is my conclusion effective? Does it grow naturally from what I've said in the rest of my essay?

Revising the Smaller Elements of Your Essay

Once you have addressed the major problems in your essay by writing a second draft, you should turn your attention to the finer elements of sentence structure, word choice, and usage. The following questions focus on these concerns.

Questions for Revising Sentences

- Do my sentences convey my thoughts clearly, and do they emphasize the most important parts of my thinking?
- Are all my sentences complete sentences?
- Are my sentences stylistically varied? Do I alter their pattern and rhythm for emphasis? Do I use some short sentences for dramatic effect?
- Are all my sentences written in the active voice?
- Do I use strong action verbs and concrete nouns?
- Is my diction fresh and forceful, or is my writing verbose?
- Have I committed any errors in usage?

Finally, if you find yourself dissatisfied with specific elements of your draft, look at several essays in *Subject & Strategy* to see how other writers have dealt with similar situations. For example, if you don't like the way the essay starts, find some beginnings you think are particularly effective. If your paragraphs don't seem to flow into one another, examine how various writers use transitions. If an example seems unconvincing, examine the way other writers include details, anecdotes, facts, and statistics to strengthen their illustrations. Remember that the readings in this text are a resource for you as you write, as are the strategy chapter introductions, which outline the basic features of each strategy. In addition, the six readings in Chapter 3, "Five Writers on Writing," will provide you with inspiration and advice to help you through the writing process.

Notes on Beginnings and Endings

Beginnings and endings are very important to the effectiveness of an essay, but they can be daunting to write. Inexperienced writers often feel they must write their essays sequentially when, in fact, it is usually better to write both the beginning and the ending after you have completed most or all of the rest of your essay. Once you see how your essay develops, you will know better how to catch your reader's attention and introduce the rest of the essay. As you work through the revision process, ask yourself:

- Does my introduction grab the reader's attention?
- Is my introduction confusing in any way? How well does it relate to the rest of the essay?
- If I state my thesis in the introduction, how effectively is it presented?
- Does my essay come to a logical conclusion or does it seem to just stop?
- How well does the conclusion relate to the rest of the essay? Am I careful not to introduce new topics or issues that I did not address in the essay?
- Does my conclusion help to underscore or illuminate important aspects of the body of the essay or is it redundant, a mechanical rehashing of what I wrote earlier?

STEP 5: EDIT AND PROOFREAD YOUR ESSAY

Now that you have made your essay "right," it is time to think about making it "correct." During the *editing* stage of the writing process, you check your writing for errors in grammar, punctuation, capitalization, spelling, and manuscript format. Both your dictionary and your grammar handbook will help you in answering specific editing questions about your essay. You may also refer to Chapter 14 for additional advice on editing your essay.

Having revised and edited your essay, you are ready to print your final copy. Always proofread your work before turning it in. Even though you may have used your computer's spell-checker, you might find that you have typed *worm* instead of *word* or *form* instead of *from*.

Questions to Ask during Editing and Proofreading

- Do my verbs agree in number with their antecedents?
- Do my pronouns have clear antecedents—that is, do they clearly refer to specific earlier nouns?
- Do I have any sentence fragments, comma splices, or run-on sentences?
- Have I made any unnecessary shifts in person, tense, or number?
- Have I used commas properly in all instances?
- Have I checked for misspellings, mistakes in capitalization, and typos?
- Have I inadvertently confused words like *their*, *they're*, and *there* or *it's* and *its*?
- Have I followed the prescribed guidelines for formatting my manuscript?

A STUDENT ESSAY IN PROGRESS

When he was a first-year student at the University of Vermont, Keith Eldred enrolled in Written Expression, an introductory writing course.

Step 1: Keith's Assignment

Somewhere near the middle of the semester, Keith's assignment was to read Chapter 10 in *Subject & Strategy* and to write a three-to-five-page essay of definition.

Step 2: Keith's Ideas

Keith had already been introduced to the Hindu concept of the mantra, and he decided that he would like to explore this concept and to narrow his focus to the topic of mantras as they operate in the secular world.

Having made this decision, he began to brainstorm some notes to help him get started. These notes provided him with several examples of what he intended to call "secular mantras"; a dictionary definition of the word *mantra*; and the idea that a good starting point for his rough draft might be the story of "The Little Engine That Could." Here are the notes he jotted down.

> Mantra: "a mystical formula of invocation or incantation" (Webster's)
> Counting to ten when angry
> "Little Engine That Could" (possible beginning)
> "Let's Go Bulls" → action because crowd wants players to say it to themselves
> Swearing (not always a mantra)
> Tennis star—"Get serious!"
> "Come on, come on" (at traffic light)
> "Geronimo" "Ouch!"
> Hindu mythology

Step 3: Keith's First Draft

After mulling over his list, Keith began to organize his ideas with the following scratch outline:

1. Begin with story of "Little Engine That Could"
2. Talk about the magic of secular mantras
3. Dictionary definition and Hindu connections
4. Examples of individuals using mantras
5. Crowd chants as mantras—Bulls
6. Conclusion—talk about how you can't get through the day without using mantras

Based on this outline as well as what he learned in reading about definition as a writing strategy—formal definition, how to put a term in a class and differentiate it from other terms in its class, synonymous definition, as well as the need for examples—Keith came up with the following first draft of his essay.

Secular Mantras: Magic Words
Keith Eldred

Do you remember "The Little Engine That Could"? If you recall, it's the story about the tiny locomotive that hauled the train over the mountain when the big, rugged locomotives wouldn't. Do you remember how the Little Engine strained and heaved and chugged "I think I can—I think I can—I think I can" until she reached the top of the mountain? That's a perfect example of a secular mantra in action.

A secular mantra (pronounced man-truh) is any word or group of words that helps a person use his or her energy. The key word here is "helps" — repeating a secular mantra doesn't *create* energy; it just makes it easier to channel a given amount. The Little Engine, for instance, obviously had the strength to pull the train up the mountain; apparently, she could have done it without saying a word. But we all know she wouldn't have been able to, any more than any one of us would be able to sky-dive the first time without yelling "Geronimo" or not exclaim "Ouch" if we touched a hot stove. Some words and phrases simply have a certain magic that makes a job easier or that makes us feel better when we repeat them. These are secular mantras.

It is because of their magical quality that these expressions are called "secular mantras" in the first place. A mantra (Sanskrit for "sacred counsel") is "a mystical formula of invocation or incantation" used in Hinduism (*Webster's*). According to Hindu mythology, Manu, lawgiver and progenitor of humankind, created the first language by teaching people the thought-forms of objects and substances. "VAM," for example, is the thought-form of what we call "water." Mantras, groups of these ancient words, can summon any object or deity if they are miraculously revealed to a seer and properly repeated silently or vocally. Hindus use divine mantras to communicate with gods, acquire superhuman powers, cure diseases, and for many other purposes. Hence, everyday words that people concentrate on to help themselves accomplish tasks or cope with stress act as secular mantras.

All sorts of people use all sorts of secular mantras for all sorts of reasons. A father counts to 10 before saying anything when his son brings the car home dented. A tennis player faults and chides himself, "Get serious!" A frustrated mother pacing with her wailing baby mutters, "You'll have your own kids someday." A college student writhing before an exam instructs himself not to panic. A freshly spanked child glares at his mother's back and repeatedly promises never to speak to her again. Secular mantras are everywhere.

Usually, we use secular mantras to make ourselves walk faster or keep silent or do some other act. But we can also use them to influence the actions of other persons. Say, for instance, the Chicago Bulls are behind in the final minutes of a game. Ten thousand fans who want them to win scream, "Let's go, Bulls!" The Bulls are roused and win by 20 points. Chalk up the victory to the fans' secular mantra, which transferred their energy to the players on the court.

If you're not convinced of the power of secular mantras, try to complete a day without using any. Don't mutter anything to force yourself out of bed. Don't utter a sound when the water in the shower is cold. Don't grumble when the traffic lights are long. Don't speak to the computer when it's slow to boot up. And don't be surprised if you have an unusually long, painful, frustrating day.

Step 4: Keith's Revised Essay

Keith read his paper aloud in class, and other students had an opportunity to ask him questions about secular mantras. As a result of this experience, Keith had a good idea of what he needed to do in subsequent drafts, and he made the following notes so that he wouldn't forget what he needed to do.

- Do a better job of defining secular mantra — expand it and be more specific — maybe tell what secular mantras are *not*
- Get more examples, especially from everyday experiences and TV
- Don't eliminate background information about mantras
- Class thought Bulls examples didn't work — keep or delete?
- Keep "The Little Engine That Could" example at beginning of paper
- Get new conclusion — present conclusion doesn't follow from paper

In subsequent drafts, Keith worked on each of the areas he had listed. While revising, he found it helpful to reread portions of the selections in the definition chapter. His reading led him to new insights about how to strengthen his essay. As he revised further, he found that he needed to make yet other unanticipated changes.

Keith revised his definition of mantra and secular mantra to include the following meanings for the related terms.

Historical definition of mantra revised

"Mantra" means "sacred counsel" in Sanskrit. The term refers to a "mystical formula of invocation or incantation" used in Hinduism (*Webster's*). According to Hindu mythology, the god Manu created the first language by teaching humans the thought-form of every object and substance. "VAM," for example, was what he told them to call the stuff we call "water." But people altered or forgot most of Manu's thought-forms. Followers of Hinduism believe mantras, groups of these ancient words revealed anew by gods to seers, can summon specific objects or deities if they are properly repeated, silently or vocally. Hindus repeat mantras to gain superhuman powers, cure diseases, and for many other purposes. Sideshow fakirs chant "AUM" ("I agree" or "I accept") to become immune to pain when lying on beds of nails.

Definition of secular mantra expanded

Our "mantras" are "secular" because, unlike Hindus, we do not attribute them to gods. Instead, we borrow them from tradition or invent them to fit a situation, as the Little Engine did. They work not by divine power but because they help us, in a way, to govern transmissions along our central nervous systems.

Explanation of how secular mantras work added

Secular mantras give our brains a sort of dual signal-boosting and signal-damping capacity. The act of repeating them pushes messages, or impulses, with extra force along our nerves or interferes with incoming messages we would rather ignore. We can then perform actions more easily or cope with stress that might keep us from functioning the way we want to. We may even accomplish both tasks at once. A sky-diver might yell "Geronimo," for example, both to amplify the signals telling his legs to jump and to drown out the ones warning him he's dizzy or scared.

He also rewrote the conclusion, adding yet more examples of secular mantras, this time drawn largely from television advertising. Finally, he made his conclusion more of a natural outgrowth of his thesis and purpose and thus a more fitting conclusion for his essay.

Sentence of examples moved from paragraph 4

You probably have favorite secular mantras already. Think about it. How many of us haven't uttered the following at least once: "Just do it"; "I'm lovin' it"; "Got milk?"; "Can you hear me now?"; or "Have it your way"? How about the phrases you mumble to yourself from your warm bed on chilly mornings? And those words you chant to ease your impatience when the traffic lights are endless? And the reminders you mutter so that you'll

Final sentence, which links to thesis and purpose, added

remember to buy bread at the store? And you must see how much less painful and frustrating your life is because of those magic words and phrases.

Step 5: Keith's Edited Essay

After expanding his definitions and strengthening his conclusion, as well as making other necessary revisions, Keith was now ready to edit his essay and to correct those smaller but equally important errors in word choice, spelling, punctuation, and mechanics. He had put aside these errors to make sure his essay had the appropriate content. Now he needed to make sure it was grammatically correct. For example, here is how he edited the first paragraph of his essay:

~~Do you~~ Remember "The Little Engine That Could"? ~~If you recall, it's~~ That's the story about the tiny locomotive that hauled the train over the mountain when the big, rugged locomotives wouldn't. ~~Do you~~ Remember how the Little Engine strained and heaved and chugged,"I think I can — I think I can — I think I can" until she reached the top of the mountain? That's a perfect example of a secular mantra in action.

By the deadline, Keith had written his essay, revised and edited it, printed it, proofread it one last time, and turned it in. Here is the final draft of his essay:

Secular Mantras
Keith Eldred

Remember "The Little Engine That Could"? That's the story about the tiny locomotive that hauled the train over the mountain when the big, rugged loco-motives wouldn't. Remember how the Little Engine strained and heaved and chugged, "I think I can — I think I can — I think I can" until she reached the top of the mountain? That's a perfect example of a secular mantra in action. 1

You probably have used a secular mantra — pronounce it "mantruh" — already today. It's any word or group of words that helps you use your energy when you consciously repeat it to yourself. You must understand two things about secular mantras to be able to recognize one. 2

First of all, a secular mantra is not simply any word or phrase you say to yourself. It must help you use your energy. Thus, "I wish I were home" is not a secular mantra if you just think the words. But the sentence is a secular mantra if, walking home on a cold day, you repeat it each time you take a step, willing your feet to move in a fast rhythm. By the same token, every swear word you mutter to bear down on a job is a secular mantra, while every one you unthink-ingly repeat is simple profanity. 3

Secondly, secular mantras only help you use your energy. They don't create energy. The Little Engine, for instance, obviously had enough power to pull the train up the mountainside — she could have done it without a peep. But we all know that puffing "I think I can" somehow made her job easier, just like, say, chanting "left-right-left" makes it easier for us to march in step. Any such word or phrase that magically seems to help you perform an action when you purposefully utter it is a secular mantra. 4

In fact, it is to highlight this apparent magic that I dubbed these expressions with so odd a title as "secular mantras." 5

"Mantra" means "sacred counsel" in Sanskrit. The term refers to a "mystical formula of invocation or incantation" used in Hinduism (*Webster's*). According to Hindu mythology, the god Manu created the first language by teaching humans the thought-form of every object and substance. "VAM," for example, was what he told them to call the stuff we call "water." But people altered or forgot most 6 of Manu's thought-forms. Followers of Hinduism believe mantras, groups of these ancient words revealed anew by gods to seers, can summon specific objects or deities if they are properly repeated, silently or vocally. Hindus repeat mantras to gain superhuman powers, cure diseases, and for many other purposes. Sideshow fakirs chant "AUM" ("I agree" or "I accept") to become immune to pain when lying on beds of nails.

Our "mantras" are "secular" because, unlike Hindus, we do not attribute them to gods. Instead, we borrow them from tradition or invent them to fit a situation, as the Little Engine did. They work not by divine power but because they help us, in a way, to govern transmissions along our central nervous systems.   7

Secular mantras give our brains a sort of dual signal-boosting and signal-damping capacity. The act of repeating them pushes messages, or impulses, with extra force along our nerves or interferes with incoming messages we would rather ignore. We can then perform actions more easily or cope with stress that might keep us from functioning the way we want to. We may even accomplish both tasks at once. A sky-diver might yell "Geronimo," for example, both to amplify the signals telling his legs to jump and to drown out the ones warning him he's dizzy or scared.   8

Any one of us can use any words in this way to help himself or herself do any task. A father might count to ten to keep from bellowing when junior brings the car home dented. A tennis player who faults may chide himself "Get serious!" as he swings, to concentrate harder on directing the ball. A sleepy mother pacing with her wailing baby can make her chore less painful by muttering, "You'll have kids someday." Chanting "Grease cartridge" always cools my temper because doing that once kept me from exploding at my father when we were working on a cantankerous Buick.   9

You probably have favorite secular mantras already. Think about it. How many of us haven't uttered the following at least once: "Just do it"; "I'm lovin' it"; "Got milk?"; "Can you hear me now?"; or "Have it your way"? How about the phrases you mumble to yourself from your warm bed on chilly mornings? And those words you chant to ease your impatience when the traffic lights are endless? And the reminders you mutter so that you'll remember to buy bread at the store? You know what I'm talking about. And you must see how much less painful and frustrating your life is because of those magic words and phrases.   10

"Secular Mantras" is a fine essay of definition. Keith provides a clear explanation of the concept, offers numerous examples to illustrate it, and suggests how mantras work and how we use them. More importantly, Keith's notes, rough draft, samples of revised and edited paragraphs, and final draft demonstrate how writing is accomplished. By reading analytically — both his own writing and that of experienced writers — Keith discovered and understood the requirements of the strategy of definition. An honest and thorough appraisal of his rough draft led to thoughtful revisions, resulting in a stronger and more effective piece of writing. Finally, note how Keith's essay combines the strategies of illustration and definition to become more interesting and convincing.

CHAPTER 3

Five Writers
on Writing

Like any other craft, writing involves learning basic skills as well as more sophisticated techniques that can be refined and then passed between practitioners. Some of the most important lessons a student writer encounters may come from the experiences of other writers: suggestions, advice, cautions, corrections, encouragement. This chapter contains essays in which writers discuss their habits, difficulties, and judgments while they express both the joy of writing and the hard work it can entail. These writers deal with the full range of the writing process—from freeing the imagination in journal entries to correcting punctuation errors for the final draft—and the advice they offer is pertinent and sound. The skills and techniques presented here can help you exert more control over your writing and, in the process, become more confident of how best to achieve your goals.

Discovering the Power of My Words

Russell Baker

 *Russell Baker has had a long and distinguished career as a newspaper reporter and columnist. He was born in Morrisonville, Virginia, in 1925 and enlisted in the navy in 1943 after graduating from Johns Hopkins University. In 1947, he secured his first newspaper job, as a reporter for the* Baltimore Sun, *then moved to the* New York Times *in 1954, where he wrote the "Observer" column from 1962 to 1998. Baker's columns have been collected in numerous books over the years. In 1979, he was awarded the Pulitzer Prize, journalism's highest award, as well as the George Polk Award for Commentary. Baker's memoir,* Growing Up *(1983), also received a Pulitzer. His autobiographical follow-up,* The Good Times, *was published in 1989. His other works include* Russell Baker's Book of American Humor *(1993);* Inventing the Truth: The Art and Craft of Memoir, *with William Zinsser and Jill Ker Conway (revised 1998); and* Looking Back *(2002), a collection of Baker's essays for the* New York Review of Books. *From 1993 to 2004 he hosted the distinguished PBS series* Exxon Mobil Masterpiece Theatre.*

The following selection is from Growing Up. *As you read Baker's account of how he discovered his abilities as a writer, particularly the power of his own words, note the joy he felt hearing his own words read aloud.*

PREPARING TO READ

What has been your experience with writing teachers in school? Have any of them helped you become a better writer? What kind of writer do you consider yourself now—excellent, above average, good, below average? Why?

The notion of becoming a writer had flickered off and on in my head . . . but it wasn't until my third year in high school that the possibility took hold. Until then I'd been bored by everything associated with English courses. I found English grammar dull and baffling. I hated the assignments to turn out "compositions," and went at them like heavy labor, turning out laden, lackluster paragraphs that were agonies for teachers to read and for me to write. The classics thrust on me to read seemed as deadening as chloroform. 1

When our class was assigned to Mr. Fleagle for third-year English I anticipated another grim year in that dreariest of subjects. Mr. Fleagle was notorious among City students for dullness and inability to inspire. He was said to be stuffy, dull, and hopelessly out of date. To me he looked to be sixty or seventy and prim to a fault. He wore primly severe eyeglasses, his wavy hair was primly cut and primly combed. He wore prim vested suits with neckties blocked primly against the collar 2 buttons of his primly starched white shirts. He had a primly pointed jaw, a primly straight nose, and a prim manner of speaking that was so correct, so gentlemanly, that he seemed a comic antique.

I anticipated a listless, unfruitful year with Mr. Fleagle and for a long time was not disappointed. We read *Macbeth*. Mr. Fleagle loved *Macbeth* and wanted us to love it too, but he lacked the gift of infecting others with his own passion. He tried to convey the murderous ferocity of Lady Macbeth one day by reading aloud the passage that concludes

> . . . I have given suck, and know
> How tender 'tis to love the babe that milks me.
> I would, while it was smiling in my face,
> Have plucked my nipple from his boneless gums . . .

The idea of prim Mr. Fleagle plucking his nipple from boneless gums was too much for the class. We burst into gasps of irrepressible snickering. Mr. Fleagle stopped.

"There is nothing funny, boys, about giving suck to a babe. It is the—the very essence of motherhood, don't you see."

He constantly sprinkled his sentences with "don't you see." It wasn't a question but an exclamation of mild surprise at our ignorance. "Your pronoun needs an antecedent, don't you see," he would say, very primly. "The purpose of the Porter's scene, boys, is to provide comic relief from the horror, don't you see."

Late in the year we tackled the informal essay. "The essay, don't you see, is the . . ." My mind went numb. Of all forms of writing, none seemed so boring as the essay. Naturally we would have to write informal essays. Mr. Fleagle distributed a homework sheet offering us a choice of topics. None was quite so simpleminded as "What I Did on My Summer Vacation," but most seemed to be almost as dull. I took the list home and dawdled until the night before the essay was due. Sprawled on the sofa, I finally faced up to the grim task, took the list out of my notebook, and scanned it. The topic on which my eye stopped was "The Art of Eating Spaghetti."

This title produced an extraordinary sequence of mental images. Surging up from the depths of memory came a vivid recollection of a night in Belleville when all of us were seated around the supper table— Uncle Allen, my mother, Uncle Charlie, Doris, Uncle Hal—and Aunt Pat served spaghetti for supper. Spaghetti was an exotic treat in those days. Neither Doris nor I had ever eaten spaghetti, and none of the adults had enough experience to be good at it. All the good humor of Uncle Allen's house reawoke in my mind as I recalled the laughing arguments we had that night about the socially respectable method for moving spaghetti from plate to mouth.

Suddenly I wanted to write about that, about the warmth and good   8
feeling of it, but I wanted to put it down simply for my own joy, not for
Mr. Fleagle. It was a moment I wanted to recapture and hold for myself.
I wanted to relive the pleasure of an evening at New Street. To write it as
I wanted, however, would violate all the rules of formal composition I'd
learned in school, and Mr. Fleagle would surely give it a failing grade.
Never mind. I would write something else for Mr. Fleagle after I had
written this thing for myself.

When I finished it the night was half gone and there was no time   9
left to compose a proper, respectable essay for Mr. Fleagle. There was no
choice next morning but to turn in my private reminiscence of
Belleville. Two days passed before Mr. Fleagle returned the graded
papers, and he returned everyone's but mine. I was bracing myself for a
command to report to Mr. Fleagle immediately after school for discipline when I saw him lift my paper from his desk and rap for the class's
attention.

"Now, boys," he said, "I want to read you an essay. This is titled   10
'The Art of Eating Spaghetti.'"

And he started to read. My words! He was reading *my words* out   11
loud to the entire class. What's more, the entire class was listening. Listening attentively. Then somebody laughed, then the entire class was
laughing, and not in contempt and ridicule, but with open-hearted
enjoyment. Even Mr. Fleagle stopped two or three times to repress a
small prim smile.

I did my best to avoid showing pleasure, but what I was feeling was   12
pure ecstasy at this startling demonstration that my words had the
power to make people laugh. In the eleventh grade, at the eleventh
hour as it were, I had discovered a calling. It was the happiest moment
of my entire school career. When Mr. Fleagle finished he put the final
seal on my happiness by saying, "Now that, boys, is an essay, don't you
see. It's—don't you see—it's of the very essence of the essay, don't you
see. Congratulations, Mr. Baker."

For the first time, light shone on a possibility. It wasn't a very heart-   13
ening possibility, to be sure. Writing couldn't lead to a job after high
school, and it was hardly honest work, but Mr. Fleagle had opened a
door for me. After that I ranked Mr. Fleagle among the finest teachers in
the school.

THINKING CRITICALLY ABOUT THE TEXT

In his opening paragraph Baker states, "I hated the assignments to turn out
'compositions,' and went at them like heavy labor, turning out laden, lackluster paragraphs that were agonies for teachers to read and for me to write."
Have you ever had any assignments like these? How are such assignments different from Mr. Fleagle's assignment to write an informal essay about "The
Art of Eating Spaghetti"?

DISCUSSING THE CRAFT OF WRITING

1. How does Baker describe his teacher, Mr. Fleagle, in the second paragraph? What dominant impression does Baker create of this man? (Glossary: *Dominant Impression*)

2. Mr. Fleagle's homework assignment offered Baker and his classmates "a choice of topics." Is it important to have a "choice" of what you write about? Explain.

3. Once Baker's eye hits the topic of "The Art of Eating Spaghetti" on Mr. Fleagle's list, what happens? What triggers Baker's urge to write about the night his Aunt Pat served spaghetti for supper?

4. Why is Baker reluctant to submit his finished essay?

5. In paragraph 11 Baker states, "And he started to read. My words! He was reading *my words* out loud to the entire class. What's more, the entire class was listening. Listening attentively." Why do you suppose this episode was so memorable to Baker? What surprised him most about it?

6. What insights into the nature of writing does Baker's narrative offer? Explain.

Shitty First Drafts

Anne Lamott

Born in San Francisco in 1954, Anne Lamott graduated from Goucher College in Baltimore and is the author of six novels, including Rose *(1983),* All the New People *(1989),* Crooked Little Heart *(1997), and* Blue Shoes *(2002). She has also been a food reviewer for* California *magazine, a book reviewer for* Mademoiselle, *and a columnist for Salon.com. Her nonfiction books include* Operating Instructions: A Journal of My Son's First Year *(1993), in which she describes life as a single parent;* Traveling Mercies: Some Thoughts on Faith *(1999), in which she charts her journey toward faith in God;* Plan B: Further Thoughts on Faith *(2005); and* Grace (Eventually): Thoughts on Faith *(2007). Lamott has taught at the University of California–Davis, as well as at writing conferences around the country.*

In the following selection, taken from Lamott's popular book about writing, Bird by Bird: Some Instructions on Writing and Life *(1994), she argues for the need to let go and write those "shitty first drafts" that lead to clarity and sometimes brilliance in subsequent drafts.*

PREPARING TO READ

Many professional writers view first drafts as something they have to do before they can begin the real work of writing—revision. How do you view the writing of your first drafts? What patterns, if any, do you see in your writing behavior when working on them? Is the work liberating or restricting? Pleasant or unpleasant?

N ow, practically even better news than that of short assignments is the idea of shitty first drafts. All good writers write them. This is how they end up with good second drafts and terrific third drafts. People tend to look at successful writers, writers who are getting their books published and maybe even doing well financially, and think that they sit down at their desks every morning feeling like a million dollars, feeling great about who they are and how much talent they have and what a great story they have to tell; that they take in a few deep breaths, push back their sleeves, roll their necks a few times to get all the cricks out, and dive in, typing fully formed passages as fast as a court reporter. But this is just the fantasy of the uninitiated. I know some very great writers, writers you love who write beautifully and have made a great deal of money, and not *one* of them sits down routinely feeling wildly enthusiastic and confident. Not one of them writes elegant first drafts. All right, one of them does, but we do not like her very much. We do not think that she has a rich inner life or that

1

God likes her or can even stand her. (Although when I mentioned this to my priest friend Tom, he said you can safely assume you've created God in your own image when it turns out that God hates all the same people you do.)

Very few writers really know what they are doing until they've done it. Nor do they go about their business feeling dewy and thrilled. They do not type a few stiff warm-up sentences and then find themselves bounding along like huskies across the snow. One writer I know tells me that he sits down every morning and says to himself nicely, "It's not like you don't have a choice, because you do—you can either type or kill yourself." We all often feel like we are pulling teeth, even those writers whose prose ends up being the most natural and fluid. The right words and sentences just do not come pouring out like ticker tape most of the time. Now, Muriel Spark is said to have felt that she was taking dictation from God every morning—sitting there, one supposes, plugged into a Dictaphone, typing away, humming. But this is a very hostile and aggressive position. One might hope for bad things to rain down on a person like this.

For me and most of the other writers I know, writing is not rapturous. In fact, the only way I can get anything written at all is to write really, really shitty first drafts.

The first draft is the child's draft, where you let it all pour out and then let it romp all over the place, knowing that no one is going to see it and that you can shape it later. You just let this childlike part of you channel whatever voices and visions come through and onto the page. If one of the characters wants to say, "Well, so what, Mr. Poopy Pants?," you let her. No one is going to see it. If the kid wants to get into really sentimental, weepy, emotional territory, you let him. Just get it all down on paper, because there may be something great in those six crazy pages that you would never have gotten to by more rational, grown-up means. There may be something in the very last line of the very last paragraph on page six that you just love, that is so beautiful or wild that you now know what you're supposed to be writing about, more or less, or in what direction you might go—but there was no way to get to this without first getting through the first five and a half pages.

I used to write food reviews for *California* magazine before it folded. (My writing food reviews had nothing to do with the magazine folding, although every single review did cause a couple of canceled subscriptions. Some readers took umbrage at my comparing mounds of vegetable puree with various ex-presidents' brains.) These reviews always took two days to write. First I'd go to a restaurant several times with a few opinionated, articulate friends in tow. I'd sit there writing down everything anyone said that was at all interesting or funny. Then on the following Monday I'd sit down at my desk with my notes, and try to write the review. Even after I'd been doing this for years, panic would set in. I'd try to write a lead, but instead I'd write a couple of dreadful sentences, xx them out, try again, xx everything out, and then feel despair and worry settle on my chest like an x-ray apron. It's over, I'd think, calmly. I'm not going to be able to get the magic to work this time. I'm ruined. I'm through. I'm toast. Maybe, I'd think, I can get my old job back as a clerk-typist. But probably not. I'd get up and study my teeth in the mirror for a while. Then I'd stop, remember to breathe, make a few phone calls, hit the kitchen and chow down. Eventually I'd go back and sit down at my desk, and sigh for the next ten minutes. Finally I would pick up my one-inch picture frame, stare into it as if for the answer, and every time the answer would come: all I had to do was to write a really shitty first draft of, say, the opening paragraph. And no one was going to see it.

So I'd start writing without reining myself in. It was almost just typing, just making my fingers move. And the writing would be *terrible*. I'd write a lead paragraph that was a whole page, even though the entire review could only be three pages long, and then I'd start writing up descriptions of the food, one dish at a time, bird by bird, and the critics would be sitting on my shoulders, commenting like cartoon characters. They'd be pretending to snore, or rolling their eyes at my overwrought descriptions, no matter how hard I tried to tone those descriptions down, no matter how conscious I was of what a friend said to me gently in my early days of restaurant reviewing. "Annie," she said, "it is just a piece of *chicken*. It is just a bit of *cake*." 6

But because by then I had been writing for so long, I would eventually let myself trust the process—sort of, more or less. I'd write a first draft that was maybe twice as long as it should be, with a self-indulgent and boring beginning, stupefying descriptions of the meal, lots of quotes from my black-humored friends that made them sound more like the Manson girls than food lovers, and no ending to speak of. The whole thing would be so long and incoherent and hideous that for the rest of the day I'd obsess about getting creamed by a car before I could write a decent second draft. I'd worry that people would read what I'd written and believe that the accident had really been a suicide, that I had panicked because my talent was waning and my mind was shot. 7

The next day, though, I'd sit down, go through it all with a colored pen, take out everything I possibly could, find a new lead somewhere on the second page, figure out a kicky place to end it, and then write a second draft. It always turned out fine, sometimes even funny and weird and helpful. I'd go over it one more time and mail it in. 8

Then, a month later, when it was time for another review, the whole process would start again, complete with the fears that people would find my first draft before I could rewrite it. 9

Almost all good writing begins with terrible first efforts. You need to start somewhere. Start by getting something—anything—down on 10 paper. A friend of mine says that the first draft is the down draft—you just get it down. The second draft is the up draft—you fix it up. You try to say what you have to say more accurately. And the third draft is the dental draft, where you check every tooth, to see if it's loose or cramped or decayed, or even, God help us, healthy.

What I've learned to do when I sit down to work on a shitty first draft is to quiet the voices in my head. First there's the vinegar-lipped Reader Lady, who says primly, "Well, *that's* not very interesting, is it?" And there's the emaciated German male who writes these Orwellian memos detailing your thought crimes. And there are your parents, agonizing over your lack of loyalty and discretion; and there's William Burroughs, dozing off or shooting up because he finds you as bold and articulate as a houseplant; and so on. And there are also the dogs: let's not forget the dogs, the dogs in their pen who will surely hurtle and snarl their way out if you ever *stop* writing, because writing is, for some of us, the latch that keeps the door of the pen closed, keeps those crazy ravenous dogs contained.

Quieting these voices is at least half the battle I fight daily. But this is better than it used to be. It used to be 87 percent. Left to its own devices, my mind spends much of its time having conversations with people who aren't there. I walk along defending myself to people, or exchanging repartee with them, or rationalizing my behavior, or seducing them with gossip, or pretending I'm on their TV talk show or whatever. I speed or run an aging yellow light or don't come to a full stop, and one nanosecond later am explaining to imaginary cops exactly why I had to do what I did, or insisting that I did not in fact do it.

I happened to mention this to a hypnotist I saw many years ago, and he looked at me very nicely. At first I thought he was feeling around on the floor for the silent alarm button, but then he gave me the following exercise, which I still use to this day.

Close your eyes and get quiet for a minute, until the chatter starts up. Then isolate one of the voices and imagine the person speaking as a mouse. Pick it up by the tail and drop it into a mason jar. Then isolate another voice, pick it up by the tail, drop it in the jar. And so on. Drop in any high-maintenance parental units, drop in any contractors, lawyers, colleagues, children, anyone who is whining in your head. Then put the lid on, and watch all these mouse people clawing at the glass, jabbering away, trying to make you feel like shit because you won't do what they want—won't give them more money, won't be more successful, won't see them more often. Then imagine that there is a volume-control button on the bottle. Turn it all the way up for a minute, and listen to the stream of angry, neglected, guilt-mongering voices. Then turn it all the way down and watch the frantic mice lunge at the glass, trying to get to you. Leave it down, and get back to your shitty first draft.

11

12

13

14

A writer friend of mine suggests opening the jar and shooting them all in the head. But I think he's a little angry, and I'm sure nothing like this would ever occur to you. 15

THINKING CRITICALLY ABOUT THE TEXT

What do you think of Lamott's use of the word *shitty* in her title and in the essay itself? Is it in keeping with her tone? (Glossary: *Tone*) Are you offended by the word? Explain. What would be lost or gained if she used a different word?

DISCUSSING THE CRAFT OF WRITING

1. Lamott says that the perception most people have of how writers work is different from the reality. She refers to this in paragraph 1 as the "fantasy of the uninitiated." What does she mean?

2. In paragraph 7 Lamott refers to a time when, through experience, she "eventually let [herself] trust the process—sort of, more or less." She is referring to the writing process, of course, but why "more or less"? Do you think her wariness is personal, or is she speaking for all writers? Explain.

3. From what Lamott has to say, is writing a first draft more about content or psychology? Do you agree when it comes to your own first drafts? Explain.

4. What is Lamott's thesis? (Glossary: *Thesis*)

5. Lamott adds humor to her argument for "shitty first drafts." Give some examples. Does her humor add or detract from the points she makes? Explain.

6. In paragraph 5, Lamott narrates her experiences in writing a food review, during which she refers to an almost ritualistic set of behaviors. What is her purpose in telling her readers this story about her difficulties? (Glossary: *Purpose*) Is this information helpful for us? Explain.

Writing for an Audience

Linda Flower

Linda Flower is a professor of English at Carnegie Mellon University, where she directed the Business Communication program for a number of years and is currently the director of the Center for the Study of Writing and Literacy. She has been a leading researcher on the composing process, and the results of her investigations shaped and informed her influential writing text Problem-Solving Strategies for Writing in College and Community *(1997). She has also written* The Construction of Negotiated Meaning: A Social Cognitive Theory of Writing *(1994).*

In this selection, which is taken from Problem-Solving Strategies, *Flower's focus is on audience—the people for whom we write. She believes that writers must establish a "common ground" between themselves and their readers that lessens their differences in knowledge, attitudes, and needs. Although we can never be certain who might read what we write, it is nevertheless important for us to have a target audience in mind. Many of the decisions that we make as writers are influenced by that real or imagined reader.*

PREPARING TO READ

Imagine for a moment that you just received a speeding ticket for going sixty-five miles per hour in a thirty-mile-per-hour zone. How would you describe the episode to your best friend? To your parents? To the judge in court? Sketch out the three versions. What differences, if any, do you find in the three versions? Explain.

The goal of the writer is to create a momentary common ground between the reader and the writer. You want the reader to share your knowledge and your attitude toward that knowledge. Even if the reader eventually disagrees, you want him or her to be able for the moment to *see things as you see them.* A good piece of writing closes the gap between you and the reader. 1

Analyze Your Audience

The first step in closing that gap is to gauge the distance between the two of you. Imagine, for example, that you are a student writing your parents, who have always lived in New York City, about a wilderness survival expedition you want to go on over spring break. Sometimes obvious differences such as age or background will be important, but the critical differences for writers usually fall into three areas: the reader's *knowledge* about the topic; his or her *attitude* toward it; and his 2 or her personal or professional *needs*. Because these differences often exist, good writers do more than simply express their meaning; they pinpoint the critical differences between themselves and their reader and design their writing to reduce those differences. Let us look at these areas in more detail.

Knowledge. This is usually the easiest difference to handle. What does your reader need to know? What are the main ideas you hope to teach? Does your reader have enough background knowledge to really understand you? If not, what would he or she have to learn? 3

Attitudes. When we say a person has knowledge, we usually refer to his conscious awareness of explicit facts and clearly defined concepts. This kind of knowledge can be easily written down or told to someone else. However, much of what we "know" is not held in this formal, explicit way. Instead it is held as an attitude or image — as a loose cluster of associations. For instance, my image of lakes includes associations many people would have, including fishing, water skiing, stalled outboards, and lots of kids catching night crawlers with flashlights. However, the most salient or powerful parts of my image, which strongly color my whole attitude toward lakes, are thoughts of cloudy skies, long rainy days, and feeling generally cold and damp. By contrast, one of my best friends has a very different cluster of associations: to him a lake means sun, swimming, sailing, and happily sitting on the end of a dock. Needless to say, our differing images cause us to react quite differently to a proposal that we visit a lake. Likewise, one reason people often find it difficult to discuss religion and politics is that terms such as "capitalism" conjure up radically different images. 4

As you can see, a reader's image of a subject is often the source of attitudes and feelings that are unexpected and, at times, impervious to mere facts. A simple statement that seems quite persuasive to you, such as "Lake Wampago would be a great place to locate the new music camp," could have little impact on your reader if he or she simply doesn't visualize a lake as a "great place." In fact, many people accept uncritically any statement that fits in with their own attitudes — and reject, just as uncritically, anything that does not. 5

Whether your purpose is to persuade or simply to present your perspective, it helps to know the image and attitudes that your reader already holds. The more these differ from your own, the more you will have to do to make him or her *see* what you mean. 6

Needs. When writers discover a large gap between their own knowledge and attitudes and those of the reader, they usually try to change the reader in some way. Needs, however, are different. When you 7 analyze a reader's needs, it is so that you, the writer, can adapt to him. If you ask a friend majoring in biology how to keep your fish tank from clouding, you don't want to hear a textbook recitation on the life processes of algae. You expect a friend to adapt his or knowledge and tell you exactly how to solve your problem.

The ability to adapt your knowledge to the needs of the reader is often crucial to your success as a writer. This is especially true in writing done on a job. For example, as producer of a public affairs program for a television station, 80 percent of your time may be taken up planning the details of new shows, contacting guests, and scheduling the taping sessions. But when you write a program proposal to the station director, your job is to show how the program will fit into the cost guidelines, the FCC requirements for relevance, and the overall programming plan for the station. When you write that report, your role in the organization changes from producer to proposal writer. Why? Because your reader needs that information in order to make a decision. He may be *interested* in your scheduling problems and the specific content of the shows, but he *reads* your report because of his own needs as station director of the organization. He has to act. 8

In college, where the reader is also a teacher, the reader's needs are a little less concrete but just as important. Most papers are assigned as a way to teach something. So the real purpose of a paper may be for you to make connections between two historical periods, to discover for yourself the principle behind a laboratory experiment, or to develop and support your own interpretation of a novel. A good college paper doesn't just rehash the facts; it demonstrates what your reader, as a teacher, needs to know—that you are learning the thinking skills his or her course is trying to teach. 9

Effective writers are not simply expressing what they know, like a student madly filling up an examination bluebook. Instead they are *using* their knowledge: reorganizing, maybe even rethinking their ideas to meet the demands of an assignment or the needs of their reader. 10

THINKING CRITICALLY ABOUT THE TEXT

What does Flower believe constitutes a "good college paper" (paragraph 9)? Do you agree? Why or why not?

DISCUSSING THE CRAFT OF WRITING

1. How, according to Flower, does a competent writer achieve the goal of closing the gap between himself or herself and the reader? How does a writer determine what a reader's "personal or professional needs" (paragraph 2) are?

2. What, for Flower, is the difference between knowledge and attitude? Why is it important for writers to understand this difference?

3. In paragraph 4, Flower discusses the fact that many words have both positive and negative associations. How do you think words come to have associations? (Glossary: *Connotation/Denotation*) Consider, for example, such words as *home, anger, royalty, welfare, politician,* and *strawberry shortcake.*

4. Flower wrote this selection for college students. How well did she assess your needs as a member of this audience? Does Flower's use of language and examples show a sensitivity to her audience? Provide specific examples to support your view.

5. When using technical language in a paper on a subject you are familiar with, why is it important for you to know your audience? Explain. How could your classmates, friends, or parents help you?

Simplicity

William Zinsser

Born in New York City in 1922, William Zinsser was edu-cated at Princeton University. After serving in the army in World War II, he worked at the New York Herald Tribune *as an editor, writer, and critic. During the 1970s he taught a popular course in nonfiction at Yale University, and from 1979 to 1987 he was general editor of the Book-of-the-Month Club. Zinsser has written more than a dozen books, including* The City Dwellers *(1962),* Pop Goes America *(1966),* Spring Training *(1989), and three widely used books on writing:* On Writing Well, 30th Anniversary Edition: The Classic Guide to Writing Nonfiction *(2006);* Writing with a Word Processor *(1983); and* Writing to Learn *(1988). Currently, he teaches journalism at Colum-bia University, and his freelance writing regularly appears in leading magazines.*

The following selection is taken from On Writing Well. *This book grew out of Zinsser's many years of experience as a professional writer and teacher. In this essay, Zinsser exposes what he believes is the writer's number one problem — "clutter." He sees Americans "strangling in unnecessary words, circular constructions, pompous frills, and meaningless jargon." His solution is simple: Writers must know what they want to say and must be thinking clearly as they start to compose. Then self-discipline and hard work are necessary to achieve clear, simple prose. No matter what your experience as a writer has been, you will find Zinsser's observations sound and his advice practical.*

PREPARING TO READ

Some people view writing as "thinking on paper." They believe that by seeing something written on a page they are better able to "see what they think." Write about the relationship, for you, between writing and thinking. Are you one of those people who like to "see" ideas on paper while trying to work things out? Or do you like to think through ideas before writing about them?

C lutter is the disease of American writing. We are a society stran-gling in unnecessary words, circular constructions, pompous frills, and meaningless jargon. 1

Who can understand the viscous language of everyday American commerce: the memo, the corporation report, the business letter, the notice from the bank explaining its latest "simplified" statement? What member of an insurance or medical plan can decipher the brochure explaining his costs and benefits? What father or mother can put together a child's toy from the instructions on the box? Our national ten-dency is to inflate and thereby sound important. The airline pilot who announces that he is presently anticipating experiencing considerable 2 precipitation wouldn't think of saying it may rain. The sentence is too simple—there must be something wrong with it.

But the secret of good writing is to strip every sentence to its cleanest components. Every word that serves no function, every long word that could be a short word, every adverb that carries the same meaning that's already in the verb, every passive construction that leaves the reader unsure of who is doing what—these are the thousand and one adulterants that weaken the strength of a sentence. And they usually occur in proportion to education and rank.

During the 1960s the president of my university wrote a letter to mollify the alumni after a spell of campus unrest. "You are probably aware," he began, "that we have been experiencing very considerable potentially explosive expressions of dissatisfaction on issues only partially related." He meant the students had been hassling them about different things. I was far more upset by the president's English than by the students' potentially explosive expressions of dissatisfaction. I would have preferred the presidential approach taken by Franklin D. Roosevelt when he tried to convert into English his own government's memos, such as this blackout order of 1942:

> Such preparations shall be made as will completely obscure all Federal buildings and non-Federal buildings occupied by the Federal government during an air raid for any period of time from visibility by reason of internal or external illumination.

"Tell them," Roosevelt said, "that in buildings where they have to keep the work going to put something across the windows."

Simplify, simplify. Thoreau said it, as we are so often reminded, and no American writer more consistently practiced what he preached. Open *Walden* to any page and you will find a man saying in a plain and orderly way what is on his mind:

> I went to the woods because I wished to live deliberately, to front only the essential facts of life, and see if I could not learn what it had to teach, and not, when I came to die, discover that I had not lived.

How can the rest of us achieve such enviable freedom from clutter? The answer is to clear our heads of clutter. Clear thinking becomes clear writing; one can't exist without the other. It's impossible for a muddy thinker to write good English. You may get away with it for a paragraph or two, but soon the reader will be lost, and there's no sin so grave, for the reader will not easily be lured back.

Who is this elusive creature, the reader? The reader is someone with an attention span of about 30 seconds—a person assailed by other forces competing for attention. At one time these forces weren't so numerous: newspapers, radio, spouse, home, children. Today they also include a "home entertainment center" (TV, VCR, tapes, CDs), pets, a fitness program, a yard and all the gadgets that have been bought to keep it spruce, and that most potent of competitors, sleep. The person snoozing in a chair with a magazine or a book is a person who was being given too much unnecessary trouble by the writer.

It won't do to say that the reader is too dumb or too lazy to keep pace with the train of thought. If the reader is lost, it's usually because the writer hasn't been careful enough. The carelessness can take any number of forms. Perhaps a sentence is so excessively cluttered that the reader, hacking through the verbiage, simply doesn't know what it means. Perhaps a sentence has been so shoddily constructed that the reader could read it in several ways. Perhaps the writer has switched pronouns in mid-sentence, or has switched tenses, so the reader loses track of who is talking or when the action took place. Perhaps Sentence B is not a logical sequel to Sentence A—the writer, in whose head the connection is clear, hasn't bothered to provide the missing link. Perhaps the writer has used an important word incorrectly by not taking the trouble to look it up. The writer may think "sanguine" and "sanguinary" mean the same thing, but the difference is a bloody big one. The reader can only infer (speaking of big differences) what the writer is trying to imply.

9

Faced with such obstacles, readers are at first tenacious. They blame themselves—they obviously missed something, and they go back over the mystifying sentence, or over the whole paragraph, piecing it out like an ancient rune, making guesses and moving on. But they won't do this for long. The writer is making them work too hard, and they will look for one who is better at the craft.

10

Writers must therefore constantly ask: What am I trying to say? Surprisingly often they don't know. Then they must look at what they have written and ask: Have I said it? Is it clear to someone encountering the subject for the first time? If it's not, some fuzz has worked its way into the machinery. The clear writer is someone clearheaded enough to see this stuff for what it is: fuzz.

11

I don't mean that some people are born clearheaded and are therefore natural writers, whereas others are naturally fuzzy and will never write well. Thinking clearly is a conscious act that writers must force upon themselves, as if they were working on any other project that requires logic: adding up a laundry list or doing an algebra problem. Good writing doesn't come naturally, though most people obviously think it does. Professional writers are constantly being bearded by strangers who say they'd like to "try a little writing sometime"—meaning when they retire from their real profession, which is difficult,

12

like insurance or real estate. Or they say, "I could write a book about that." I doubt it.

Writing is hard work. A clear sentence is no accident. Very few sen- 13 tences come out right the first time, or even the third time. Remember this in moments of despair. If you find that writing is hard, it's because it *is* hard. It's one of the hardest things people do.

THINKING CRITICALLY ABOUT THE TEXT

What assumptions does Zinsser make about readers? According to Zinsser, what responsibilities do writers have to readers? How do these responsibilities manifest themselves in Zinsser's writing?

DISCUSSING THE CRAFT OF WRITING

1. What exactly is clutter? When do words qualify as clutter, and when do they not?
2. In paragraph 2, Zinsser states that "Our national tendency is to inflate and thereby sound important." What do you think he means by *inflate*? Provide several examples to illustrate how people use language to inflate.
3. One would hope that education would help in the battle against clutter, but, as Zinsser notes, wordiness "usually occur[s] in proportion to education and rank" (paragraph 3). Do your own experiences or observations support Zinsser's claim? Explain.
4. Zinsser believes that writers need to ask themselves two questions— "What am I trying to say?" and "Have I said it?"—constantly as they write. How would these questions help you eliminate clutter from your own writing? Give some examples from one of your essays.
5. In order "to strip every sentence to its cleanest components," we need to be sensitive to the words we use and know how they function within our sentences. For each of the "adulterants that weaken the strength of a sentence," which Zinsser identifies in paragraph 3, provide an example from your own writing.
6. Zinsser knows that sentence variety is an important feature of good writing. Locate several examples of the short sentences (seven or fewer words) he uses in this essay, and explain how each relates in length, meaning, and impact to the sentences around it.

The Maker's Eye: Revising Your Own Manuscripts

Donald M. Murray

 *Donald M. Murray (1924–2006) was born in Boston, Massa-
chusetts. He taught writing for many years at the University
of New Hampshire, his alma mater. He served as an editor at
Time magazine, and he won the Pulitzer Prize in 1954 for
editorials that appeared in the Boston Globe. Murray's published works include novels, short stories, poetry, and source-
books for teachers of writing, like* A Writer Teaches Writing
(revised 2003), The Craft of Revision *(5th ed., 2003), and*
Learning by Teaching *(1982), in which he explores aspects
of the writing process.* Write to Learn *(6th ed., 1998), a text-
book for college composition courses, is based on Murray's belief that writers learn to
write by writing—by taking a piece of writing through the whole process, from
invention to revision. In 2001 he published* My Twice-Lived Life: A Memoir. *Until
his death in December 2006, he wrote the weekly column "Now and Then" for the*
Boston Globe.*

In the following essay, first published in the Writer *in October 1973 and later
revised, Murray discusses the importance of revision to the work of the writer. Most
professional writers live by the maxim that "writing is rewriting." And to rewrite or
revise effectively, we need to become better readers of our own work, open to discovering new meanings and sensitive to our use of language. Murray draws on the experiences of many writers to make a compelling argument for careful revising and
editing.*

PREPARING TO READ

Thinking back on your education to date, what did you think you had to do
when teachers told you to revise a piece of your writing? How did the request
to revise make you feel? Write about your earliest memories of revising some
of your writing. What kinds of changes do you remember making?

When students complete a first draft, they consider the job of   1
writing done—and their teachers too often agree. When professional writers complete a first draft, they usually feel that they are at
the start of the writing process. When a draft is completed, the job of
writing can begin.

That difference in attitude is the difference between amateur and   2
professional, inexperience and experience, journeyman and craftsman.
Peter F. Drucker, the prolific business writer, calls his first draft "the zero
draft"—after that he can start counting. Most writers share the feeling
that the first draft, and all of those which follow, are opportunities to
discover what they have to say and how best they can say it.

To produce a progression of drafts, each of which says more and
says it more clearly, the writer has to develop a special kind of reading
skill. In school we are taught to decode what appears on the page as finished writing. Writers, however, face a different category of possibility
and responsibility when they read their own drafts. To them the words
on the page are never finished. Each can be changed and rearranged,
can set off a chain reaction of confusion or clarified meaning. This is a
different kind of reading which is possibly more difficult and certainly
more exciting.

Writers must learn to be their own best enemy. They must accept the
criticism of others and be suspicious of it; they must accept the praise of
others and be even more suspicious of it. Writers cannot depend on others. They must detach themselves from their own pages so that they can
apply both their caring and their craft to their own work.

Such detachment is not easy. Science-fiction writer Ray Bradbury
supposedly puts each manuscript away for a year to the day and then
rereads it as a stranger. Not many writers have the discipline or the time
to do this. We must read when our judgment may be at its worst, when
we are close to the euphoric moment of creation.

Then the writer, counsels novelist Nancy Hale, "should be critical
of everything that seems to him most delightful in his style. He should
excise what he most admires, because he wouldn't thus admire it if he
weren't . . . in a sense protecting it from criticism." John Ciardi, the
poet, adds, "The last act of the writing must be to become one's own
reader. It is, I suppose, a schizophrenic process, to begin passionately
and to end critically, to begin hot and to end cold; and, more important, to be passion-hot and critic-cold at the same time."

Most people think that the principal problem is that writers are too
proud of what they have written. Actually, a greater problem for most
professional writers is one shared by the majority of students. They are
overly critical, think everything is dreadful, tear up page after page,
never complete a draft, see the task as hopeless.

The writer must learn to read critically but constructively, to cut
what is bad, to reveal what is good. Eleanor Estes, the children's book
author, explains: "The writer must survey his work critically, coolly, as
though he were a stranger to it. He must be willing to prune, expertly
and hard-heartedly. At the end of each revision, a manuscript may look
. . . worked over, torn apart, pinned together, added to, deleted from,
words changed and words changed back. Yet the book must maintain
its original freshness and spontaneity."

Most readers underestimate the amount of rewriting it usually
takes to produce spontaneous reading. This is a great disadvantage to
the student writer, who sees only a finished product and never watches
the craftsman who takes the necessary step back, studies the work carefully, returns to the task, steps back, returns, steps back, again and

again. Anthony Burgess, one of the most prolific writers in the English-speaking world, admits, "I might revise a page twenty times." Roald Dahl, the popular children's writer, states, "By the time I'm nearing the end of a story, the first part will have been reread and altered and corrected at least 150 times. . . . Good writing is essentially rewriting. I am positive of this."

Rewriting isn't virtuous. It isn't something that ought to be done. It is simply something that most writers find they have to do to discover what they have to say and how to say it. It is a condition of the writer's life.   10

There are, however, a few writers who do little formal rewriting, primarily because they have the capacity and experience to create and review a large number of invisible drafts in their minds before they approach the page. And some writers slowly produce finished pages, performing all the tasks of revision simultaneously, page by page, rather than draft by draft. But it is still possible to see the sequence followed by most writers most of the time in rereading their own work.   11

Most writers scan their drafts first, reading as quickly as possible to catch the larger problems of subject and form, and then move in closer and closer as they read and write, reread and rewrite.   12

The first thing writers look for in their drafts is *information*. They know that a good piece of writing is built from specific, accurate, and interesting information. The writer must have an abundance of information from which to construct a readable piece of writing.   13

Next writers look for *meaning* in the information. The specifics must build to a pattern of significance. Each piece of specific information must carry the reader toward meaning.   14

Writers reading their own drafts are aware of *audience*. They put themselves in the reader's situation and make sure that they deliver information which a reader wants to know or needs to know in a manner which is easily digested. Writers try to be sure that they anticipate and answer the questions a critical reader will ask when reading the piece of writing.   15

Writers make sure that the *form* is appropriate to the subject and the audience. Form, or genre, is the vehicle which carries meaning to the reader, but form cannot be selected until the writer has adequate information to discover its significance and an audience which needs or wants that meaning.   16

Once writers are sure the form is appropriate, they must then look at the *structure*, the order of what they have written. Good writing is built on a solid framework of logic, argument, narrative, or motivation which runs through the entire piece of writing and holds it together. This is the time when many writers find it most effective to outline as a way of visualizing the hidden spine by which the piece of writing is supported.   17

The element on which writers may spend a majority of their time is *development*. Each section of a piece of writing must be adequately developed. It must give readers enough information so that they are satisfied. How much information is enough? That's as difficult as asking how much garlic belongs in a salad. It must be done to taste, but most beginning writers underdevelop, underestimating the reader's hunger for information. 18

As writers solve development problems, they often have to consider questions of *dimension*. There must be a pleasing and effective proportion among all the parts of the piece of writing. There is a continual process of subtracting and adding to keep the piece of writing in balance. 19

Finally, writers have to listen to their own voices. *Voice* is the force which drives a piece of writing forward. It is an expression of the writer's authority and concern. It is what is between the words on the page, what glues the piece of writing together. A good piece of writing is always marked by a consistent, individual voice. 20

As writers read and reread, write and rewrite, they move closer and closer to the page until they are doing line-by-line editing. Writers read their own pages with infinite care. Each sentence, each line, each clause, each phrase, each word, each mark of punctuation, each section of white space between the type has to contribute to the clarification of meaning. 21

Slowly the writer moves from word to word, looking through language to see the subject. As a word is changed, cut, or added, as a construction is rearranged, all the words used before that moment and all those that follow that moment must be considered and reconsidered. 22

Writers often read aloud at this stage of the editing process, muttering or whispering to themselves, calling on the ear's experience with language. Does this sound right—or that? Writers edit, shifting back and forth from eye to page to ear to page. I find I must do this careful editing in short runs, no more than fifteen or twenty minutes at a stretch, or I become too kind with myself. I begin to see what I hope is on the page, not what actually is on the page. 23

This sounds tedious if you haven't done it, but actually it is fun. Making something right is immensely satisfying, for writers begin to learn what they are writing about by writing. Language leads them to meaning, and there is the joy of discovery, of understanding, of making meaning clear as the writer employs the technical skills of language. 24

Words have double meanings, even triple and quadruple meanings. Each word has its own potential of connotation and denotation. And when writers rub one word against the other, they are often rewarded with a sudden insight, an unexpected clarification. 25

The maker's eye moves back and forth from word to phrase to sentence to paragraph to sentence to phrase to word. The maker's eye sees 26 the need for variety and balance, for a firmer structure, for a more appropriate form. It peers into the interior of the paragraph, looking for coherence, unity, and emphasis, which make meaning clear.

I learned something about this process when my first bifocals were   27
prescribed. I had ordered a larger section of the reading portion of the glass because of my work, but even so, I could not contain my eyes within this new limit of vision. And I still find myself taking off my glasses and bending my nose toward the page, for my eyes unconsciously flick back and forth across the page, back to another page, forward to still another, as I try to see each evolving line in relation to every other line.

When does this process end? Most writers agree with the great   28
Russian writer Tolstoy, who said, "I scarcely ever reread my published writings; if by chance I come across a page, it always strikes me: all this must be rewritten; this is how I should have written it."

The maker's eye is never satisfied, for each word has the potential   29
to ignite new meaning. This article has been twice written all the way through the writing process [. . .]. Now it is to be republished in a book. The editors made a few small suggestions, and then I read it with my maker's eye. Now it has been re-edited, re-revised, re-read, and re-re-edited, for each piece of writing to the writer is full of potential and alternatives.

A piece of writing is never finished. It is delivered to a deadline,   30
torn out of the typewriter on demand, sent off with a sense of accomplishment and shame and pride and frustration. If only there were a couple more days, time for just another run at it, perhaps then . . .

THINKING CRITICALLY ABOUT THE TEXT

Murray notes that writers often reach a stage in their editing where they read aloud, "muttering or whispering to themselves, calling on the ear's experience with language" (paragraph 23). What do you think writers are listening for? Try reading several paragraphs of Murray's essay aloud. Discuss what you heard.

DISCUSSING THE CRAFT OF WRITING

1. How does Murray define *information* and *meaning* (paragraphs 13–14)? Why is the distinction between the two terms important?

2. What are the essential differences between revising and editing? What types of language concerns are dealt with at each stage? Why is it important to revise before editing?

3. According to Murray, when in the writing process do writers become concerned about the individual words they are using? What do you think Murray means when he says in paragraph 24 that "language leads [writers] to meaning"?

4. The phrase "the maker's eye" appears in Murray's title and in several places throughout the essay. What do you suppose he means by this? Consider how the maker's eye could be different from the reader's eye.

5. What does Murray see as the connection between reading and writing? How does reading help the writer? What should writers be looking for in their reading?

6. What kinds of writing techniques or strategies does Murray use in his essay? Why should we read a novel or magazine article differently than we would a draft of one of our own essays?

7. According to Murray, writers look for information, meaning, audience, form, structure, development, dimension, and voice in their drafts. What rationale or logic do you see, if any, in the way Murray has ordered these items? Are these the kinds of concerns you have when reading your drafts? Explain.

CHAPTER 4

Narration

WHAT IS NARRATION?

We all love a good story. We want to find out what happens. The tremendous popularity of current fiction and biography reflects our avid interest in stories. Knowing of our interest in stories, many writers and speakers use them to their advantage.

Whenever you recount an event or tell a story or anecdote to illustrate an idea, you are using narration. In its broadest sense, narration includes all writing that gives an account of an event or a series of events in a logical sequence. Although you are already very familiar with narratives, you probably associate narration with novels, short fiction, poetry, and even movies. But narration is effective and useful in most nonfiction writing, such as biography, autobiography, history, and news reporting. A good narrative essay provides a meaningful account of some significant event—anything from an account of recent U.S. involvement in the Middle East to a personal experience that gave you new insight about yourself or others. A narrative may present a straightforward message or moral, or it may make a more subtle point about ourselves and the world we live in.

Consider, for example, the following narrative by E. J. Kahn Jr. about the invention of Coca-Cola as both a medicine and a soft drink, from his book *The Big Drink: The Story of Coca-Cola.*

Writer establishes context for his narrative about Pemberton and Coca-Cola.	The man who invented Coca-Cola was not a native Atlantan, but on the day of his funeral every drugstore in town testimonially shut up shop. He was John Styth Pemberton, born in 1833 in Knoxville, Georgia, eighty

miles away. Sometimes known as Doctor, Pemberton was a pharmacist who, during the Civil War, led a cavalry troop under General Joe Wheeler. He settled in Atlanta in 1869, and soon began brewing such patent medicines as Triplex Liver Pills and Globe of Flower Cough Syrup. In 1885, he registered a trademark for something called French Wine Coca—Ideal Nerve and Tonic Stimulant; a few months later he formed the Pemberton Chemical Company, and recruited the services of a bookkeeper named Frank M. Robinson, who not only had a good head for figures but, attached to it, so exceptional a nose that he could audit the composition of a batch of syrup merely by sniffing it. In 1886—a year in which, as contemporary Coca-Cola officials like to point out, Conan Doyle unveiled Sherlock Holmes and France unveiled the Statue of Liberty— Pemberton unveiled a syrup that he called Coca-Cola. He had taken out the wine and added a pinch of caffeine, and, when the end product tasted awful, had thrown in some extract of cola (or kola) nut and a few other oils, blending the mixture in a three-legged iron pot in his back yard and swishing it around with an oar. He distributed it to soda fountains in used beer bottles, and Robinson, with his flowing bookkeeper's script, presently devised a label on which "Coca-Cola" was written in the fashion that is still employed. Pemberton looked upon his concoction less as a refreshment than as a headache cure, especially for people whose throbbing temples could be traced to overindulgence. On a morning late in 1886, one such victim of the night before dragged himself into an Atlanta drugstore and asked for a dollop of Coca-Cola. Druggists customarily stirred a teaspoonful of syrup into a glass of water, but in this instance the factotum on duty was too lazy to walk to the fresh-water tap, a couple of feet off. Instead, he mixed the syrup with some charged water, which was closer at hand. The suffering customer perked up almost at once, and word quickly spread that the best Coca-Cola was a fizzy one.

Writer uses third-person point of view.

Writer organizes the narrative chronologically, using time markers.

Writer focuses on the discovery that led to Coca-Cola's becoming a popular soft drink.

A good narrative essay, like the paragraph above, has four essential features. The first is *context*: The writer makes clear when the action happened, where it happened, and to whom. The second is *point of view*: The writer establishes and maintains a consistent relationship to the action, either as a participant or as a reporter looking on. The third is *selection of detail*: The writer carefully chooses what to include, focusing on those actions and details that are most important to the story while playing down or even eliminating others. The fourth is *organization*: The writer arranges the events of the narrative in an appropriate sequence, often a strict chronology with a clear beginning, middle, and end.

As you read the selections in this chapter, watch for these features and for how each writer uses them to tell his or her story. Think about how each writer's choices affect the way you react to the selections.

USING NARRATION AS A WRITING STRATEGY

Good stories are compelling; we're hungry for them. We read novels and short stories, and we watch dramatized stories on television, at the movies, and in the theater because we're curious about others' lives. We want to know what happened to other people to gain insights into our own lives. The most basic and most important purpose of narration is to instruct, to share a meaningful experience with readers.

Another important purpose of narration is to report — to give the facts, to tell what happened. Journalists and historians, in reporting events of the near and more distant past, provide us with information that we can use to form opinions about a current issue or to better understand the world around us. A biographer gives us another person's life as a document of an individual's past but also, perhaps, as a portrait of more general human potential. And naturalists recount the drama of encounters between predators and prey in the wild. We expect writers to make these narratives as objective as possible and to distinguish between facts and opinions.

Using Narration across the Disciplines

When writing essays in the academic disciplines, you will have many opportunities to use the strategy of narration to both organize and strengthen the presentation of your ideas. To determine whether or not narration is the right strategy for you in a particular paper, use the four-step method first described in Choosing Strategies across the Disciplines (pages 24–25). Consider the following examples, which illustrate how this four-step method works for typical college papers.

American History

MAIN IDEA: Although Abraham Lincoln was not the chief speaker at Gettysburg on November 19, 1863, the few remarks he made that day shaped the thinking of our nation as perhaps few other speeches have.

QUESTION: What happened at Gettysburg on November 19, 1863, that made Abraham Lincoln's speech so memorable and influential?

(continued on next page)

(continued from previous page)

STRATEGY: Narration. The thrust of the main idea as well as the direction words *what happened* say "tell me the story," and what better way to tell what happened than to narrate the day's events?

SUPPORTING STRATEGY: Cause and Effect Analysis. The story and how it is narrated can be used to explain the impact of this speech on our nation's thinking.

Anthropology

MAIN IDEA: Food-gathering and religious activities account for a large portion of the daily lives of native peoples in rural Thailand.

QUESTION: What happens during a typical day or week in rural Thailand?

STRATEGY: Narration. The direction words in both the statement of the main idea (*account* and *daily*) and the question (*what happens*) cry out for a narration of what does happen during any given day.

SUPPORTING STRATEGY: Illustration. The paper might benefit from specific examples of the various chores related to food-gathering as well as examples of typical religious activities.

Life Science

MAIN IDEA: British bacteriologist Sir Alexander Fleming discovered penicillin quite by accident in 1928, and that discovery changed the world.

QUESTION: How did Fleming happen to discover penicillin, and why was this discovery so important?

STRATEGY: Narration. The direction words *how* and *did happen* call for the story of Fleming's accidental discovery of penicillin.

SUPPORTING STRATEGY: Argument. The claims that Fleming's discovery was *important* and *changed the world* suggest that the story needs to be both compelling and persuasive.

Narration is often used in combination with one or more of the other rhetorical strategies. In an essay that is written primarily to explain a process—reading a book, for example—a writer might find it useful to tell a brief story or anecdote demonstrating an instance when the process worked especially well (Mortimer Adler, "How to

Mark a Book," Chapter 7). In the same way, a writer attempting to define the term *poverty* might tell several stories to illustrate clearly the many facets of poverty (Jo Goodwin Parker, "What Is Poverty?" Chapter 10). Finally, a writer could use narrative examples to persuade—for example, to argue that having a national language would unify the country (Charles Krauthammer, "In Plain English: Let's Make It Official," Chapter 12) or to demonstrate for readers the power and clarity of monosyllabic words (Richard Lederer, "The Case for Short Words," Chapter 12).

SAMPLE STUDENT ESSAY USING NARRATION AS A WRITING STRATEGY

After reading several personal narratives—the selection from Annie Dillard's *An American Childhood* and Malcolm X's "Coming to an Awareness of Language" in particular—Laura LaPierre decided to write one of her own. Only weeks prior to writing this essay Laura had received some very bad news. It was the experience of living with this news that she decided to write about. The writing was painful, and not everyone would feel comfortable with a similar task. Laura, however, welcomed the opportunity because she came to a more intimate understanding of her own fears and feelings as she moved from one draft to the next. What follows is the final draft of Laura's essay.

Title: Asks central question that paper will answer.

Why Are You Here?

Laura LaPierre

Beginning: Engages the reader and establishes context—when, where, to whom.

Details: Creates image of harsh, unfriendly environment.

Point of View: First-person.

Balancing between a crutch on one side and an I.V. pole with wheels on the other, I dragged my stiff leg along the smooth, sterile floor of the hospital hall. All around me nurses, orderlies, and doctors bustled about, dodging well-meaning visitors laden with flowers and candy. The fluorescent lights glared down with a brightness so sharp that I squinted and thought that sunglasses might be in order. Sticking close to the wall, I rounded the corner and paused to rest for a moment. I breathed in the hot, antiseptic-smelling air which I had grown accustomed to and sighed angrily. 1

Organization: Straightforward chronological organization.

Tears of hurt and frustration pricked at the corner of my eyes as the now familiar pain seared my leg. I tugged my bathrobe closer around my shoulder and, hauling my I.V. pole with me, I continued down the hall. One, two—second door on the left, she had said. I opened the heavy metal door, entered, and realized that I must be a little early because no one else was 2

Descriptive details create dominant impression of a dull, uninviting room.

there yet. After glancing at my watch, I sat down and looked around the room, noting with disgust the prevalence of beige. Beige walls, beige ceiling, shiny beige floor tiles. A small cot stood in one corner with a beige bedspread, and in the opposite corner there was a sink, mirror, and beige waste basket. The only relief from the monotony was the circle of six or seven chairs where I sat. They were a vivid rust color and helped to brighten the dull room. The shades were drawn and the lights were much dimmer than they had been in the hall, and my eyes gradually relaxed as I waited.

Organization: Time reference maintains flow.

Details show that people in group are obviously ill, but specifics are not revealed.

People began to drift in until five of the seats were filled. A nurse was the head of the odd-looking group. Three of us were attached by long tubes to I.V. poles, and then there was a social worker. The man to my left wore a slightly faded, royal blue robe. He had a shock of unruly gray hair above an angular face with deeply sunken cheeks. His eyes were sunken, too, and glassy with pain. Yet he smiled and appeared untroubled by his I.V. pole.   3

Wearing a crisp white uniform and a pretty sweater, the nurse, a pleasant-looking woman in her late twenties, appeared friendly and sympathetic, though not to the point of being sappy. My impressions were confirmed as she began to speak.   4

Dialogue adds life to narrative.

Telling details reveal writer's uneasiness—perhaps fear—at being here.

Comparison and Contrast: Describes other patients in the room.

"Okay. I guess we can begin. Welcome to our group, we meet every Monday at . . . ." She went on, but I wasn't paying attention anymore. I looked around the group and my eyes came to rest on the man sitting next to the nurse. In contrast to the other man's shriveled appearance, this man was robust. He was tall, with a protruding belly and a ruddy complexion. Unlike the other man, he seemed at war with his I.V. pole. He constantly fiddled with the tube and with the tape that held the needle in his arm. Eyes darting around the room, he nervously watched everyone.   5

Dialogue continues. Central question of title introduced.

Repetition of "beige" echoes earlier description of room.

I heard the nurse continue, "So, let's all introduce ourselves and tell why we are here." We went around the circle clockwise, starting with the nurse, and when we got to the social worker, I looked up and surveyed her while she talked. Aside from contributing to the beige monotony with her pants, she was agreeable both in appearance and disposition.   6

Dialogue shows writer's fear.

When it was my turn, I took a deep breath and with my voice quivering began, "My name is Laura an—"   7

Cheerful man relieves tension but intensifies drama of the moment.

"Hi, Laura!" interrupted the cheerful man on my left. I turned and smiled weakly at him.

8

Laura faces her fear—her moment of truth.

Fighting back the tears, I continued, "And I have bone cancer."

9

Analyzing Laura LaPierre's Essay of Narration: Questions for Discussion

1. What context does Laura provide for her narrative? What else, if anything, would you have liked to know about the situation? What would have been lost had she told you more?

2. Laura tells her story in the first person. How would the narrative have changed had she used a third-person point of view?

3. For you, what details conveyed Laura's fear at being in the hospital? Are there places where she could have done more "showing" and less "telling"? Explain.

4. Laura uses a straightforward chronological organization for her narrative. Can you see any places where she might have used a flashback? What would have been the effect?

5. What meaning or importance do you think this experience holds for Laura?

SUGGESTIONS FOR USING NARRATION AS A WRITING STRATEGY

As you plan, write, and revise your narrative essay, be mindful of the five-step writing process described in Chapter 2 (pages 14–38). Also, pay particular attention to the basic requirements and essential ingredients for this writing strategy.

Planning Your Essay of Narration

Planning is an essential part of writing a good narrative essay. You can save yourself a great deal of aggravation by taking the time to think about the key components of your essay before you actually begin to write.

Select a Topic That Has Meaning for You. In your writing course, you may have the freedom to choose the story you want to narrate, or your instructor may give you a list of topics from which to choose. Instead of jumping at the first topic that looks good, brainstorm a list of events that have had an impact on your life and that you could write about. For example, such a list might include your first blind date, catching frogs as a child, making a team or a club, the death of a loved one, a graduation celebration, a trip to the Grand Canyon, the loss of a pet, learning to drive a car, or even the breakup of a relationship. As you narrow down your options, look for an event or an incident that is particularly memorable for you. Memorable experiences are memorable for a reason; they offer us important insights into our lives. Such experiences are worth narrating because people want to read about them. Before you begin writing, ask yourself why the experience you have chosen is meaningful to you. What did you learn from it? How are you different as a result of the experience? What has changed?

Determine Your Point and Purpose.   Right from the beginning, ask yourself what the significance is of the event you are narrating and why you are telling your story. Your narrative point (the meaning of your narrative) and purpose in writing will influence which events and details you include and which you leave out. Suppose, for example, you choose to write about how you learned to ride a bicycle. In some neighborhoods, learning to ride a bike is a real rite of passage. If, however, you mean mainly to entertain, you will probably include a number of unusual and amazing incidents unique to your experience. If your purpose is mainly to report or inform, it will make more sense to concentrate on the kinds of details that are common to most people's experience. However, if your purpose is to tell your readers step-by-step how to ride a bicycle, you should use process analysis, a strategy used by writers whose purpose is to give directions for how something is done or to explain how something works (see Chapter 7).

The most successful narrative essays, however, do more than entertain or inform. While narratives do not have a formal thesis statement, readers will more than likely expect your story to make a statement or to arrive at some meaningful conclusion — implied or explicit — about your experience. The student essay by Laura LaPierre, for example, shows how important it was for her to confront the reality of her bone cancer. In addressing her fears, she gains a measure of control over her life. Certainly, you will not be happy if your story is dismissed as essentially "pointless." So as you prepare to write, look for the significance in the story you want to tell — some broader, more instructive points it could make about the ways of the world. Learning to ride a bicycle may not suggest such points to you, and it may therefore not be a very good subject for your narrative essay. However, the subject does have possibilities. Here's one: Learning to master a difficult, even dangerous, but definitely useful skill like riding a bicycle is an important experience to have in life.

Here's another: Learning to ride a bicycle is an opportunity for you to acquire and use some basic physics, such as the laws of gravity and the behavior of a gyroscope. Perhaps you can think of others. If, however, you do not know why you are telling the story and it seems pointless even to you, your readers will pick up on the ambivalence in your writing, and you should probably find another, more meaningful story to tell.

Establish a Context. Early in your essay, perhaps in the opening paragraphs, establish the context, or setting, of your story—the world within which the action took place:

> *When it happened*—morning; afternoon; 11:37 on the dot; 1997; winter
> *Where it happened*—in the street; at Wendy's; in Pocatello, Idaho
> *To whom it happened*—to me; to my father; to the assistant; to Teri Hopper

Without a clear context, your readers can easily get confused or even completely lost. And remember, readers respond well to specific contextual information because such details make them feel as if they are present, ready to witness the narrative.

Choose the Most Appropriate Point of View. Consider what point of view to take in your narrative. Did you take part in the action? If so, it will seem most natural for you to use the first-person (*I, we*) point of view. On the other hand, if you weren't there at all and must rely on other sources for your information, you will probably choose the third-person (*he, she, it, they*) point of view, as did the author writing about the invention of Coca-Cola earlier in this chapter. However, if you were a witness to part or all of what happened but not a participant, then you will need to choose between the more immediate and subjective quality of the first person and the more distanced, objective effect of the third person. Whichever you choose, you should maintain the same point of view throughout your narrative.

Gather Details That "Show, Don't Tell." When writing your essay, you will need enough detail about the action, the people involved, and the context to let your readers understand what is going on. Start collecting details by asking yourself the traditional reporter's questions:

- Who was involved?
- What happened?
- Where did it happen?
- When did it happen?
- Why did it happen?
- How did it happen?

Generate as many details as you can because you never know which ones will prove valuable in developing your narrative point so that your essay *shows* and doesn't *tell* too much. For example, instead of telling readers that she dislikes being in the hospital, Laura LaPierre shows us what she sees, feels, hears, and smells and lets us draw our own conclusion about her state of mind. As you write, you will want to select and emphasize details that support your point, serve your purpose, and show the reader what is happening. Above all, you should not get so carried away with details that your readers become confused or bored by excess information. In good storytelling, deciding what to leave out can be as important as deciding what to include. In his narrative about the discovery of Coca-Cola, E. J. Kahn Jr. gives us just enough information about inventor John Styth Pemberton to make him interesting but not so much as to distract readers from the story.

Organizing Your Essay of Narration

Identify the Sequence of Events in Your Narrative. Storytellers tend to follow an old rule: Begin at the beginning, and go on till you come to the end; then stop. Chronological organization is natural in narration because it is a retelling of the original order of events; it is also easiest for the writer to manage and the reader to understand.

Some narratives, however, are organized using a technique common in movies and theater called *flashback*: The writer may begin midway through the story, or even at the end, with an important or exciting event, then use flashbacks to fill in what happened earlier to lead up to that event. Some authors begin in the present and then use flashbacks to shift to the past to tell the story. Whatever organizational pattern you choose, words and phrases like *for a month, afterward,* and *three days earlier* are examples of devices that will help you and your reader keep the sequence of events straight.

It may help you in organizing to jot down a quick outline before tackling the first draft of your narrative. Here's the outline that Laura LaPierre used to order the events in his narrative chronologically.

Narration about My First Group Meeting at the Hospital
Point: At some point I had to confront the reality of my illness.
Context: Hospital setting

1. Start slow walk down hospital hall attached to IV pole.
2. Sights, sounds, and smells of hospital hallway set scene.
3. Locate destination—first one to arrive for group meeting.
4. Describe "beige" meeting room.
5. Other patients arrive.
6. Young nurse leads our group meeting.

7. We start by introducing ourselves.
8. My turn — my moment of truth.

Such an outline can remind you of your point, your organization, and the emphasis you want when you write your first draft.

Writing Your Essay of Narration

Keep Your Verb Tense Consistent.   Most narratives are in the past tense, and this is logical: They recount events that have already happened, even if very recently. But writers sometimes use the present tense to create an effect of intense immediacy, as if the events were happening as you read about them. The important thing to remember is to be consistent. If you are recounting an event that has already occurred, use the past tense throughout. For an event in the present, use the present tense consistently. If you find yourself jumping from a present event to a past event, as in the case of a flashback, you will need to switch verb tenses to signal the change in time.

Use Narrative Time for Emphasis.   The number of words or pages you devote to an event does not usually correspond to the number of minutes or hours the event took to happen. You may require several pages to recount an important or complex quarter of an hour, but then pass over several hours or days in a sentence or two. Length has less to do with chronological time than with the amount of detail you include, and that's a function of the amount of emphasis you want to give to a particular incident.

Use Transitional Words to Clarify Narrative Sequence.   Transitional words like *after, next, then, earlier, immediately*, and *finally* are useful, as they help your readers smoothly connect and understand the sequence of events that makes up your narrative. Likewise, a specific time mark like *on April 20, two weeks earlier*, and *in 2004* can indicate time shifts and can signal to readers how much time has elapsed between events. But inexperienced writers sometimes overuse these words; this makes their writing style wordy and tiresome. Use these conventional transitions when you really need them, but when you don't — when your readers can follow your story without them — leave them out.

Use Dialogue to Bring Your Narrative to Life.   Having people in a narrative speak is a very effective way of showing rather than telling or summarizing what happened. Snippets of actual dialogue make a story come alive and feel immediate to the reader.

Consider the following passages from a student narrative, an early draft without dialogue:

> I hated having to call a garage, but I knew I couldn't do the work myself and I knew they'd rip me off. Besides, I had to get the car off the street before the police had it towed. I felt trapped without any choices.

Now compare this early draft, in which the writer summarizes and tells us what happened in very general terms, with the revised draft below, in which the situation is revealed through dialogue.

> "University Gulf, Glen speaking. What can I do for ya?"
>
> "Yeah, my car broke down. I think it's the timing belt, and I was wondering if you could give me an estimate."
>
> "What kind of car is it?" asked Glen.
>
> "A Nissan Sentra."
>
> "What year?"
>
> "1995," I said, emphasizing the 95.
>
> "Oh, those are a bitch to work on. Can ya hold on for a second?"
>
> I knew what was coming before Glen came back on the line.

With dialogue, readers can hear the direct exchange between the car owner and the mechanic. You can use dialogue in your own writing to deliver a sense of immediacy to the reader.

Revising and Editing Your Essay of Narration

Share Your Draft with Others. Try sharing the draft of your essay with other students in your writing class to make sure that your narrative makes sense. Ask them if there are any parts that they do not understand. Have them tell you what they think is the point of your narrative. If their answers differ from what you intended, have them indicate the passages that led them to their interpretations so that you can change your text accordingly. To maximize the effectiveness of conferences with your peers, utilize the guidelines presented on pages 27–28. Feedback from these conferences often provides one or more places where you can start revising.

Question Your Own Work While Revising and Editing. Revision is best done by asking yourself key questions about what you have written. Begin by reading, preferably aloud, what you have written. Reading aloud forces you to pay attention to every single word, and you are more likely to catch lapses in the logical flow of thought. After you have read your paper through, answer the following questions for revising and editing, and make the necessary changes.

Questions for Revising and Editing: Narration

1. Is my narrative well focused, or do I try to cover too long a period of time?

2. What is my reason for telling this story? Is that reason clearly stated or implied for readers?

3. Have I established a clear context for my readers? Is it clear when the action happened, where it happened, and to whom?

4. Have I used the most effective point of view to tell my story? How would my story be different had I used another point of view?

5. Have I selected details that help readers understand what is going on in my narrative, or have I included unnecessary details that distract readers or get in the way of what I'm trying to say? Do I give enough examples of the important events in my narrative?

6. Is the chronology of events in my narrative clear? Have I taken advantage of opportunities to add emphasis, drama, or suspense with flashbacks or other complications of the chronological organization?

7. Have I used transitional expressions or time markers to help readers follow the sequencing of events in my narrative?

8. Have I employed dialogue in my narrative to reveal a situation, or have I told about or summarized the situation too much?

9. Have I avoided run-on sentences and comma splices? Have I used sentence fragments only deliberately to convey mood or tone?

10. Have I avoided other errors in grammar, punctuation, and mechanics?

11. Is the meaning of my narrative clear? Or have I left my readers thinking, "So what?"

Coming to an Awareness of Language

Malcolm X

 *In the course of Malcolm X's brief life, he rose from a world of street crime to become one of the most powerful and articulate African American leaders in the United States during the 1960s. On February 21, 1965, his life was cut short at age thirty-nine; he was shot and killed as he addressed an afternoon rally in Harlem. Malcolm X told his life story in* The Autobiography of Malcolm X *(1964), written with the assistance of* Roots *author Alex Haley. The book, a moving account of his life and his struggle for fulfillment, is still read by hundreds of thousands each year. In 1992, the life of this influential African American leader was reexamined in Spike Lee's film* Malcolm X.

The following selection from The Autobiography *refers to a period Malcolm X spent in federal prison. In the selection, Malcolm X explains how he was frustrated by his inability to express his ideas and how this frustration led him to a goal: acquiring the skills of reading and writing.*

PREPARING TO READ

Our educational system places a great emphasis on our having a large and varied working vocabulary. Has anyone ever stressed to you the importance of developing a good vocabulary? What did you think when you heard this advice? In what ways can words be used as powerful tools? How would you judge your own vocabulary?

I've never been one for inaction. Everything I've ever felt strongly about, I've done something about. I guess that's why, unable to do anything else, I soon began writing to people I had known in the hustling world, such as Sammy the Pimp, John Hughes, the gambling house owner, the thief Jumpsteady, and several dope peddlers. I wrote them all about Allah and Islam and Mr. Elijah Muhammad. I had no idea where most of them lived. I addressed their letters in care of the Harlem or Roxbury bars and clubs where I'd known them.

I never got a single reply. The average hustler and criminal was too uneducated to write a letter. I have known many slick, sharp-looking hustlers, who would have you think they had an interest in Wall Street; privately, they would get someone else to read a letter if they received one. Besides, neither would I have replied to anyone writing me something as wild as "the white man is the devil."

What certainly went on the Harlem and Roxbury wires was that Detroit Red was going crazy in stir, or else he was trying some hype to shake up the warden's office.

During the years that I stayed in the Norfolk Prison Colony, never 4
did any official directly say anything to me about those letters,
although, of course, they all passed through the prison censorship. I'm
sure, however, they monitored what I wrote to add to the files which
every state and federal prison keeps on the conversion of Negro
inmates by the teachings of Mr. Elijah Muhammad.

But at that time, I felt that the real reason was that the white man 5
knew that he was the devil.

Later on, I even wrote to the Mayor of Boston, to the Governor of 6
Massachusetts, and to Harry S. Truman. They never answered; they
probably never even saw my letters. I handscratched to them how the
white man's society was responsible for the black man's condition in
this wilderness of North America.

It was because of my letters that I happened to stumble upon start- 7
ing to acquire some kind of a homemade education.

I became increasingly frustrated at not being able to express what I 8
wanted to convey in letters that I wrote, especially those to Mr. Elijah
Muhammad. In the street, I had been the most articulate hustler out
there—I had commanded attention when I said something. But now,
trying to write simple English, I not only wasn't articulate, I wasn't
even functional. How would I sound writing in slang, the way I would
say it, something such as, "Look, daddy, let me pull your coat about a
cat. Elijah Muhammad—"

Many who today hear me somewhere in person, or on television, 9
or those who read something I've said, will think I went to school far
beyond the eighth grade. This impression is due entirely to my prison
studies.

It had really begun back in the Charlestown Prison, when Bimbi 10
first made me feel envy of his stock of knowledge. Bimbi had always
taken charge of any conversation he was in, and I had tried to emulate
him. But every book I picked up had few sentences which didn't contain anywhere from one to nearly all of the words that might as well
have been in Chinese. When I just skipped those words, of course,
I really ended up with little idea of what the book said. So I had come to
the Norfolk Prison Colony still going through only book-reading
motions. Pretty soon, I would have quit even these motions, unless
I had received the motivation that I did.

I saw that the best thing I could do was get hold of a dictionary— 11
to study, to learn some words. I was lucky enough to reason also that
I should try to improve my penmanship. It was sad. I couldn't even
write in a straight line. It was both ideas together that moved me to
request a dictionary along with some tablets and pencils from the
Norfolk Prison Colony school.

I spent two days just riffling uncertainly through the dictionary's 12
pages. I'd never realized so many words existed! I didn't know *which*

words I needed to learn. Finally, just to start some kind of action, I began copying.

In my slow, painstaking, ragged handwriting, I copied into my tablet everything printed on that first page, down to the punctuation marks.   13

I believe it took me a day. Then, aloud, I read back, to myself, everything I'd written on the tablet. Over and over, aloud, to myself, I read my own handwriting.   14

I woke up the next morning, thinking about those words — immensely proud to realize that not only had I written so much at one time, but I'd written words that I never knew were in the world. Moreover, with a little effort, I also could remember what many of these words meant. I reviewed the words whose meanings I didn't remember. Funny thing, from the dictionary first page right now, that "aardvark" springs to my mind. The dictionary had a picture of it, a long-tailed, long-eared, burrowing African mammal, which lives off termites caught by sticking out its tongue as an anteater does for ants.   15

I was so fascinated that I went on — I copied the dictionary's next page. And the same experience came when I studied that. With every succeeding page, I also learned of people and places and events from history. Actually the dictionary is like a miniature encyclopedia. Finally the dictionary's A section had filled a whole tablet — and I went on into the B's. That was the way I started copying what eventually became the entire dictionary. It went a lot faster after so much practice helped me to pick up handwriting speed. Between what I wrote in my tablet, and writing letters, during the rest of my time in prison I would guess I wrote a million words.   16

I suppose it was inevitable that as my word-base broadened, I could for the first time pick up a book and read and now begin to understand what the book was saying. Anyone who has read a great deal can imagine the new world that opened. Let me tell you something: from then until I left that prison, in every free moment I had, if I was not reading in the library, I was reading on my bunk. You couldn't have gotten me out of books with a wedge. Between Mr. Muhammad's teachings, my correspondence, my visitors . . . and my reading of books, months passed without my even thinking about being imprisoned. In fact, up to then, I never had been so truly free in my life.   17

THINKING CRITICALLY ABOUT THE TEXT

We are all to one degree or another prisoners of our own language. Sometimes we lack the ability to communicate as effectively as we would like. Why do you think this happens, and what do you think can be done to remedy it? How can improved language skills also improve a person's life?

QUESTIONS ON SUBJECT

1. In paragraph 8, Malcolm X refers to the difference between being "articulate" and being "functional" in his speaking and writing. What is the distinction he makes? In your opinion, is it a valid one?

2. Malcolm X offers two possible reasons for the warden's keeping track of African American inmates' conversion to the teachings of Elijah Muhammad. What are those two assertions, and what is their effect on the reader?

3. What is the nature of the freedom that Malcolm X refers to in the final sentence? In what sense can language be said to be liberating?

QUESTIONS ON STRATEGY

1. Malcolm X narrates his experiences as a prisoner using the first-person *I*. Why is the first person particularly appropriate? What would be lost or gained had he narrated his story using the third-person pronoun *he*?

2. In the opening paragraph, Malcolm X refers to himself as a man of action and conviction. What details does he include to support this assertion?

3. Many people think of "vocabulary building" as learning strange, multi-syllabic, difficult-to-spell words. But acquiring an effective vocabulary does not have to be so intimidating. How would you characterize Malcolm X's vocabulary in this narrative? Did you find his word choice suited to what he was trying to accomplish in this selection?

4. What is Malcolm X's narrative point in this passage? How do you know? What does he learn about himself as a result of this experience?

5. In reflecting on his years in prison, Malcolm X comes to an understanding of the events that caused him to reassess his life and take charge of his own education. Identify those events, and discuss the changes that resulted from Malcolm X's actions. How does his inclusion of these causal links enhance the overall narrative? (Glossary: *Cause and Effect Analysis*)

QUESTIONS ON DICTION AND VOCABULARY

1. Although Malcolm X taught himself to be articulate, we can still "hear" a street-savvy voice in his writing. Cite examples of his diction that convey a streetwise sound. (Glossary: *Diction*)

2. What do you do when you encounter new words in your reading? Do you skip those words as Malcolm X once did, do you take the time to look them up, or do you try to figure out their meanings from the context? Explain the strategies you use to determine the meaning of a word from its context. Can you think of other strategies?

3. Refer to your desk dictionary to determine the meanings of the following words as Malcolm X uses them in this selection: *hustler* (paragraph 2), *slick* (2), *hype* (3), *frustrated* (8), *emulate* (10), *riffling* (12), *inevitable* (17).

CLASSROOM ACTIVITY USING NARRATION

Good narrative depends on a sense of continuity or flow, a logical ordering of events and ideas. The following sentences, which make up the first paragraph of E. B. White's essay "Once More to the Lake," have been rearranged. Place the sentences in what seems to be a coherent sequence based on such language signals as transitions, repeated words, pronouns, and temporal references. Be prepared to explain your reason for the placement of each sentence.

1. I have since become a salt-water man, but sometimes in summer there are days when the restlessness of the tides and the fearful cold of the sea water and the incessant wind that blows across the afternoon and into the evening make me wish for the placidity of a lake in the woods.

2. We all got ringworm from some kittens and had to rub Pond's Extract on our arms and legs night and morning, and my father rolled over in a canoe with all his clothes on; but outside of that the vacation was a success and from then on none of us ever thought there was any place in the world like that lake in Maine.

3. A few weeks ago this feeling got so strong I bought myself a couple of bass hooks and a spinner and returned to the lake where we used to go, for a week's fishing and to revisit old haunts.

4. One summer, along about 1904, my father rented a camp on a lake in Maine and took us all there for the month of August.

5. We returned summer after summer—always on August 1st for one month.

WRITING SUGGESTIONS

1. Using Malcolm X's essay as a model, write a narrative about some goal you have set and achieved in which you were motivated by a strong inner conflict. What was the nature of your conflict? What feeling did it arouse in you, and how did the conflict help you to accomplish your goal?

2. Malcolm X solved the problems of his own near-illiteracy by carefully studying the dictionary. Would this be a practical solution to the national problem of illiteracy? In your experience, what does it mean to be literate? Write a proposal on what can be done to promote literacy in this country. You might also consider what is being done now in your community.

From *An American Childhood*

Annie Dillard

 *Born in Pittsburgh, Pennsylvania, in 1945, Annie Dillard has written in many genres. Her first two books were both published in 1974, before she was thirty years old; the first was a collection of poems entitled* Tickets for a Prayer Wheel *and the second was* Pilgrim at Tinker Creek, *a Pulitzer Prize–winning book of essays based on her observations of and reflections about nature. She has explored the world of fiction, writing books of criticism—* Living by Fiction *(1982) and* Encounters with Chinese Writers *(1984)—and a novel,* The Living *(1992). In 2000, she published a collection of essays,* For the Time Being. *Her most recent book is* The Maytrees: A Novel *(2007).*

In one of her early essays, Dillard expressed a mistrust of memoirs, saying, "I don't recommend, or even approve, writing personally. It can lead to dreadful writing." By 1987, however, she had put this warning aside to publish an autobiography, An American Childhood, *from which this selection is taken. The book details Dillard's memories of her years growing up in Pittsburgh and is filled with the wonder and joy of living. This selection reflects the tone of the book as a whole.*

PREPARING TO READ

What activity are you passionate about—an activity that makes you give your all? A sport is a good example of a pursuit that demands and rewards total involvement, but you might also want to consider other types of activities. What satisfactions result from wholehearted participation in the activity of your choice?

Some boys taught me to play football. This was fine sport. You thought up a new strategy for every play and whispered it to the others. You went out for a pass, fooling everyone. Best, you got to throw yourself mightily at someone's running legs. Either you brought him down or you hit the ground flat out on your chin, with your arms empty before you. It was all or nothing. If you hesitated in fear, you would miss and get hurt: you would take a hard fall while the kid got away, or you would get kicked in the face while the kid got away. But if you flung yourself wholeheartedly at the back of his knees—if you gathered and joined body and soul and pointed them diving fearlessly—then you likely wouldn't get hurt, and you'd stop the ball. Your fate, and your team's score, depended on your concentration and courage. Nothing girls did could compare with it. 1

Boys welcomed me at baseball, too, for I had, through enthusiastic practice, what was weirdly known as a boy's arm. In winter, in the snow, there was neither baseball nor football, so the boys and I threw 2 snowballs at passing cars. I got in trouble throwing snowballs, and have seldom been happier since.

On one weekday morning after Christmas, six inches of new snow   3
had just fallen. We were standing up to our boot tops in snow on a front yard on trafficked Reynolds Street, waiting for cars. The cars traveled Reynolds Street slowly and evenly; they were targets all but wrapped in red ribbons, cream puffs. We couldn't miss.

I was seven; the boys were eight, nine, and ten. The oldest two   4
Fahey boys were there—Mikey and Peter—polite blond boys who lived near me on Lloyd Street, and who already had four brothers and sisters. My parents approved Mikey and Peter Fahey. Chickie McBride was there, a tough kid, and Billy Paul and Mackie Kean too, from across Reynolds, where the boys grew up dark and furious, grew up skinny, knowing, and skilled. We had all drifted from our houses that morning looking for action, and had found it here on Reynolds Street.

It was cloudy but cold. The cars' tires laid behind them on the   5
snowy street a complex trail of beige chunks like crenellated castle walls. I had stepped on some earlier; they squeaked. We could have wished for more traffic. When a car came, we all popped it one. In the intervals between cars we reverted to the natural solitude of children.

I started making an iceball—a perfect iceball, from perfectly white   6
snow, perfectly spherical, and squeezed perfectly translucent so no snow remained all the way through. (The Fahey boys and I considered it unfair actually to throw an iceball at somebody, but it had been known to happen.)

I had just embarked on the iceball project when we heard tire   7
chains come clanking from afar. A black Buick was moving toward us down the street. We all spread out, banged together some regular snowballs, took aim, and, when the Buick drew nigh, fired.

A soft snowball hit the driver's windshield right before the driver's   8
face. It made a smashed star with a hump in the middle.

Often, of course, we hit our target, but this time, the only time in   9
all of life, the car pulled over and stopped. Its wide black door opened; a man got out of it, running. He didn't even close the car door.

He ran after us, and we ran away from him, up the snowy Reynolds   10
sidewalk. At the corner, I looked back; incredibly, he was still after us. He was in city clothes: a suit and tie, street shoes. Any normal adult would have quit, having sprung us into flight and made his point. This man was gaining on us. He was a thin man, all action. All of a sudden, we were running for our lives.

Wordless, we split up. We were on our turf; we could lose ourselves   11
in the neighborhood backyards, everyone for himself. I paused and considered. Everyone had vanished except Mikey Fahey, who was just rounding the corner of a yellow brick house. Poor Mikey, I trailed him.

The driver of the Buick sensibly picked the two of us to follow. The man apparently had all day.

He chased Mikey and me around the yellow house and up a back-yard path we knew by heart: under a low tree, up a bank, through a hedge, down some snowy steps, and across the grocery store's delivery driveway. We smashed through a gap in another hedge, entered a scruffy backyard and ran around its back porch and tight between houses to Edgerton Avenue; we ran across Edgerton to an alley and up our own sliding woodpile to the Halls' front yard; he kept coming. We ran up Lloyd Street and wound through mazy backyards toward the steep hilltop at Willard and Lang.

He chased us silently, block after block. He chased us silently over picket fences, through thorny hedges, between houses, around garbage cans, and across streets. Every time I glanced back, choking for breath, I expected he would have quit. He must have been as breathless as we were. His jacket strained over his body. It was an immense discovery, pounding into my hot head with every sliding, joyous step, that this ordinary adult evidently knew what I thought only children who trained at football knew: that you have to fling yourself at what you're doing, you have to point yourself, forget yourself, aim, dive.

Mikey and I had nowhere to go, in our own neighborhood or out of it, but away from this man who was chasing us. He impelled us forward; we compelled him to follow our route. The air was cold; every breath tore my throat. We kept running, block after block; we kept improvising, backyard after backyard, running a frantic course and choosing it simultaneously, failing always to find small places or hard places to slow him down, and discovering always, exhilarated, dismayed, that only bare speed could save us—for he would never give up, this man—and we were losing speed.

He chased us through the backyard labyrinths of ten blocks before he caught us by our jackets. He caught us and we all stopped.

We three stood staggering, half blinded, coughing, in an obscure hilltop backyard: a man in his twenties, a boy, a girl. He had released our jackets, our pursuer, our captor, our hero: he knew we weren't going anywhere. We all played by the rules. Mikey and I unzipped our jackets. I pulled off my sopping mittens. Our tracks multiplied in the backyard's new snow. We had been breaking new snow all morning. We didn't look at each other. I was cherishing my excitement. The man's lower pants legs were wet; his cuffs were full of snow, and there was a prow of snow beneath them on his shoes and socks. Some trees bordered the little flat backyard, some messy winter trees. There was no one around: a clearing in a grove, and we the only players.

It was a long time before he could speak. I had some difficulty at first recalling why we were there. My lips felt swollen; I couldn't see out of the sides of my eyes; I kept coughing.

"You stupid kids," he began perfunctorily. 18

We listened perfunctorily indeed, if we listened at all, for the chew- 19
ing out was redundant, a mere formality, and beside the point. The
point was that he had chased us passionately without giving up, and so
he had caught us. Now he came down to earth. I wanted the glory to
last forever.

But how could the glory have lasted forever? We could have run 20
through every backyard in North America until we got to Panama. But
when he trapped us at the lip of the Panama Canal, what precisely
could he have done to prolong the drama of the chase and cap its
glory? I brooded about this for the next few years. He could only have
fried Mikey Fahey and me in boiling oil, say, or dismembered us piece-
meal, or staked us to anthills. None of which I really wanted, and none
of which any adult was likely to do, even in the spirit of fun. He could
only chew us out there in the Panamanian jungle, after months or
years of exalting pursuit. He could only begin, "You stupid kids," and
continue in his ordinary Pittsburgh accent with his normal righteous
anger and the usual common sense.

If in that snowy backyard the driver of the black Buick had cut off 21
our heads, Mikey's and mine, I would have died happy, for nothing has
required so much of me since as being chased all over Pittsburgh in the
middle of winter—running terrified, exhausted—by this sainted,
skinny, furious red-headed man who wished to have a word with us.
I don't know how he found his way back to his car.

THINKING CRITICALLY ABOUT THE TEXT

As a child, did you ever do something exhilarating, satisfying, or fun even
though you knew that it was "wrong"? Compare your experience to
Dillard's. To what extent should children be held responsible for their deliberate misbehavior? What would have been an appropriate consequence for
Dillard and her companions? If you had chased them down, what would you
have done?

QUESTIONS ON SUBJECT

1. In this essay, Dillard separates the behavior of boys from that of both
   girls and adults. What characteristics does she identify that distinguish
   the actions of boys? Why is she able to play with them?

2. What is Dillard's main point? Where does she state it explicitly?

3. Why was the driver "sensible" to choose Mikey and the author as the targets of his chase?

4. What made the chase so unusual and exciting? Why was the end of the
   chase disappointing? Was there any way it could have ended that would
   have been more satisfying to the author? Why or why not?

QUESTIONS ON STRATEGY

1. In an unusual rhetorical strategy, Dillard opens her essay in the first person but immediately switches to second person. (Glossary: *Point of View*) What is her purpose for using two points of view, and especially for shifting from one to the other? In what ways does Dillard's use of the second-person point of view evoke childhood?

2. This narrative essay begins with two nonnarrative introductory paragraphs whose connection to the rest of the story may not be immediately apparent. Note especially the apparently paradoxical sentence that closes the introduction: "I got in trouble throwing snowballs, and have seldom been happier since." (Glossary: *Paradox*) How do these paragraphs, and particularly this sentence, help the reader understand the story that follows?

3. The event that prompted this narrative was in itself small and seemingly insignificant, but Dillard describes it with such intensity that the reader is left in no doubt as to its tremendous significance for her. Show how she uses carefully crafted description to lift her story from the ordinary to the remarkable. (Glossary: *Description*)

QUESTIONS ON DICTION AND VOCABULARY

1. In paragraph 14, Dillard describes the chase using parallel word structures: "He impelled us forward; we compelled him to follow our route." In paragraph 16, find the parallel noun phrases that Dillard uses to characterize the young man who chased them. What is the impact on the reader of these parallel word structures? (Glossary: *Parallelism*) This essay contains numerous examples of parallelism; find several others that add to the impact you have identified.

2. Notice the use of strong verbs (*flung, popped, smashed*) throughout the narrative. How do strong verbs work to enhance a narrative?

3. Dillard uses a great deal of description in her narrative essay. Look up and define these words, vital to her descriptions, as she uses them: *crenellated* (paragraph 5), *reverted* (5), *turf* (11), *impelled* (14), *compelled* (14), *labyrinths* (15), *obscure* (16), *perfunctorily* (18, 19), *exalting* (20). How do these words contribute to the impact of the finished piece?

CLASSROOM ACTIVITY USING NARRATION

The number of words or paragraphs a writer devotes to the retelling of an event does not usually correspond to the number of minutes or hours the event took to happen. A writer may require multiple paragraphs to recount an important or complex ten- or twenty-minute encounter, but then pass over several hours, days, or even years in several sentences. In narration, length has less to do with chronological real time than with the amount of emphasis the writer wants to give to a particular incident. Identify several passages in Dillard's essay where she uses multiple paragraphs to retell a relatively brief encounter and where she uses a paragraph or two to cover a long period of time. Why do you suppose Dillard chose to tell her story in this manner?

WRITING SUGGESTIONS

1. Children know what it means to plunge headlong, fearlessly and eagerly, into a challenging situation. One of the most wonderful encounters a child can have is with an adult who is still able to summon up that child-like enthusiasm—one who can put aside grown-up ideas of respectability and caution in order to accomplish something. In this narrative, Dillard reveres a man who is willing to pursue his young tormentors until he catches them. Recall and write about an enthusiastic adult—a parent, a relative, a teacher, a chance acquaintance—who abandoned grown-up behavior to inspire you as a child. In what way did he or she do so? As Annie Dillard does, make your story lively and detailed.

2. After reading the selection from *An American Childhood*, how accountable do you think children should be for their misconduct or poor performance? Using Dillard's essay and your own experience, write an essay in which you look at the question of holding people responsible for their actions. Your essay could take the form of an argument in which you take a definite position or of a narrative in which you tell the story of a childhood punishment that you received or witnessed. If you choose to narrate a childhood experience, be sure to be clear about your response to the punishment: Was it justified? Appropriate? Effective? Why or why not? You might find it helpful to review what you wrote in response to Thinking Critically about the Text. In addition, it might be useful to exchange "punishment" stories with classmates and discuss the issues that arise before you start writing.

Stranger Than True

Barry Winston

Barry Winston is a practicing attorney in Chapel Hill, North Carolina. He was born in New York City in 1934 and graduated from the University of North Carolina, from which he also received his law degree. His specialty is criminal law.

"Stranger Than True" was published in Harper's *magazine in December 1986. In the story, Winston recounts his experience defending a young college graduate accused of driving while under the influence of alcohol and causing his sister's death. The story is characterized by Winston's energetic and strong voice. In commenting on his use of narrative detail, Winston says, "I could have made it twice as long, but it wouldn't have been as good a story."*

PREPARING TO READ

The American judicial system works on the basis of the presumption of innocence. In short, you are innocent until proven guilty. But what about a situation in which all the evidence seems to point to a person's guilt? What's the purpose of a trial in such a case?

Let me tell you a story. A true story. The court records are all there if anyone wants to check. It's three years ago. I'm sitting in my office, staring out the window, when I get a call from a lawyer I hardly know. Tax lawyer. Some kid is in trouble and would I be interested in helping him out? He's charged with manslaughter, a felony, and driving under the influence. I tell him sure, have the kid call me.

So the kid calls and makes an appointment to see me. He's a nice kid, fresh out of college, and he's come down here to spend some time with his older sister, who's in med school. One day she tells him they're invited to a cookout with some friends of hers. She's going directly from class and he's going to take her car and meet her there. It's way out in the country, but he gets there before she does, introduces himself around, and pops a beer. She shows up after a while and he pops another beer. Then he eats a hamburger and drinks a third beer. At some point his sister says, "Well, it's about time to go," and they head for the car.

And, the kid tells me, sitting there in my office, the next thing he remembers, he's waking up in a hospital room, hurting like hell, bandages and casts all over him, and somebody is telling him he's charged with manslaughter and DUI because he wrecked his sister's car, killed her in the process, and blew fourteen on the Breathalyzer. I ask him what the hell he means by "the next thing he remembers," and he looks me straight in the eye and says he can't remember anything from the time they leave the cookout until he wakes up in the hospital. He tells me the doctors say he has post-retrograde amnesia. I say of course I believe him, but I'm worried about finding a judge who'll believe him.

I agree to represent him and send somebody for a copy of the wreck report. It says there are four witnesses: a couple in a car going the other way who passed the kid and his sister just before their car ran off the road, the guy whose front yard they landed in, and the trooper who investigated. I call the guy whose yard they ended up in. He isn't home. I leave word. Then I call the couple. The wife agrees to come in the next day with her husband. While I'm talking to her, the first guy calls. I call him back, introduce myself, tell him I'm representing the kid and need to talk to him about the accident. He hems and haws and I figure he's one of those people who think it's against the law to talk to defense lawyers. I say the D.A. will tell him it's O.K. to talk to me, but he doesn't have to. I give him the name and number of the D.A. and he says he'll call me back. 4

Then I go out and hunt up the trooper. He tells me the whole story. The kid and his sister are coming into town on Smith Level Road, after it turns from fifty-five to forty-five. The Thornes—the couple—are heading out of town. They say this sports car passes them, going the other way, right after that bad turn just south of the new subdivision. They say it's going like a striped-ass ape, at least sixty-five or seventy. Mrs. Thorne turns around to look and Mr. Thorne watches in the rearview mirror. They both see the same thing: halfway into the curve, the car runs off the road on the right, whips back onto the road, spins, runs off on the left, and disappears. They turn around in the first drive-way they come to and start back, both terrified of what they're going to find. By this time, Trooper Johnson says, the guy whose front yard the car has ended up in has pulled the kid and his sister out of the wreck and started CPR on the girl. Turns out he's an emergency medical technician. Holloway, that's his name. Johnson tells me that Holloway says he's sitting in his front room, watching television, when he hears a hell of a crash in his yard. He runs outside and finds the car flipped over, and so he pulls the kid out from the driver's side, the girl from the other side. She dies in his arms. 5

And that, says Trooper Johnson, is that. The kid's blood/alcohol content was fourteen, he was going way too fast, *and* the girl is dead. He had to charge him. It's a shame, he seems a nice kid, it was his own sister and all, but what the hell can he do, right? 6

The next day the Thornes come in, and they confirm everything Johnson said. By now things are looking not so hot for my client, and 7

I'm thinking it's about time to have a little chat with the D.A. But Holloway still hasn't called me back, so I call him. Not home. Leave word. No call. I wait a couple of days and call again. Finally I get him on the phone. He's very agitated, and won't talk to me except to say that he doesn't have to talk to me.

I know I better look for a deal, so I go to the D.A. He's very sympa- 8
thetic. But. There's only so far you can get on sympathy. A young woman is dead, promising career cut short, all because somebody has too much to drink and drives. The kid has to pay. Not, the D.A. says, with jail time. But he's got to plead guilty to two misdemeanors: death by vehicle and driving under the influence. That means probation, a big fine. Several thousand dollars. Still, it's hard for me to criticize the D.A. After all, he's probably going to have the MADD mothers all over him because of reducing the felony to a misdemeanor.

On the day of the trial, I get to court a few minutes early. There are 9
the Thornes and Trooper Johnson, and someone I assume is Holloway. Sure enough, when this guy sees me, he comes over and introduces himself and starts right in: "I just want you to know how serious all this drinking and driving really is," he says. "If those young people hadn't been drinking and driving that night, that poor young girl would be alive today." Now, I'm trying to hold my temper when I spot the D.A. I bolt across the room, grab him by the arm, and say, "We gotta talk. Why the hell have you got all those people here? That jerk Holloway. Surely to God you're not going to call him as a witness. This is a guilty plea! My client's parents are sitting out there. You don't need to put them through a dog-and-pony show."

The D.A. looks at me and says, "Man, I'm sorry, but in a case like 10
this, I gotta put on witnesses. Weird Wally is on the bench. If I try to go without witnesses, he might throw me out."

The D.A. calls his first witness. Trooper Johnson identifies himself, 11
tells about being called to the scene of the accident, and describes what he found when he got there and what everybody told him. After he fin-ishes, the judge looks at me. "No questions," I say. Then the D.A. calls Holloway. He describes the noise, running out of the house, the upside-down car in his yard, pulling my client out of the window on the left side of the car and then going around to the other side for the girl. When he gets to this part, he really hits his stride. He describes, in minute detail, the injuries he saw and what he did to try and save her life. And then he tells, breath by breath, how she died in his arms.

The D.A. says, "No further questions, your Honor." The judge looks 12
at me. I shake my head, and he says to Holloway, "You may step down."

One of those awful silences hangs there, and nothing happens for a 13
minute. Holloway doesn't move. Then he looks at me, and at the D.A., and then at the judge. He says, "Can I say something else, your Honor?"

All my bells are ringing at once, and my gut is screaming at me, 14
Object! Object! I'm trying to decide in three quarters of a second
whether it'll be worse to listen to a lecture on the evils of drink from
this jerk Holloway or piss off the judge by objecting. But all I say is, "No
objections, your Honor." The judge smiles at me, then at Holloway, and
says, "Very well, Mr. Holloway. What did you wish to say?"

It all comes out in a rush. "Well, you see, your Honor," Holloway 15
says, "it was just like I told Trooper Johnson. It all happened so fast.
I heard the noise, and I came running out, and it was night, and I was
excited, and the next morning, when I had a chance to think about it,
I figured out what had happened, but by then I'd already told Trooper
Johnson and I didn't know what to do, but you see, the car, it was
upside down, and I did pull that boy out of the left-hand window, but
don't you see, the car was upside down, and if you turned it over on its
wheels like it's supposed to be, the left-hand side is really on the right-
hand side, and your Honor, that boy wasn't driving that car at all. It
was the girl that was driving, and when I had a chance to think about it
the next morning, I realized that I'd told Trooper Johnson wrong, and
I was scared and I didn't know what to do, and that's why"—and now
he's looking right at me—"why I wouldn't talk to you."

Naturally, the defendant is allowed to withdraw his guilty plea. The 16
charges are dismissed and the kid and his parents and I go into one of
the back rooms in the courthouse and sit there looking at one another
for a while. Finally, we recover enough to mumble some Oh my Gods
and Thank yous and You're welcomes. And that's why I can stand to
represent somebody when I know he's guilty.

THINKING CRITICALLY ABOUT THE TEXT

Much abuse is heaped on lawyers who defend clients whose guilt seems obvious. How does Winston's story help explain why lawyers need to defend
"guilty" clients?

QUESTIONS ON SUBJECT

1. Why does the D.A. bring in witnesses for a case that has been plea-
   bargained? What is ironic about that decision? (Glossary: *Irony*)

2. Why was Holloway reluctant to be interviewed by Winston about what
   he saw and did in the aftermath of the accident? What might he have
   been afraid of?

3. Why did Holloway finally ask to speak to the court? Why do you suppose
   Winston chose not to object to Holloway's request?

4. What do you think is the point of Winston's narrative?

QUESTIONS ON STRATEGY

1. Winston establishes the context for his story in the first three paragraphs. What basic information does he give readers?

2. What details does Winston choose to include in the story? Why does he include them? Is there other information that you would like to have had? Why do you suppose Winston chose to omit that information?

3. Explain how Winston uses sentence variety to pace his narrative. What effect do his short sentences and sentence fragments have on you?

4. What does Winston gain as a writer by telling us that this is "a true story," one that we can check out in the court records?

5. During the courtroom scene (paragraphs 9–15), Winston relies heavily on dialogue. (Glossary: *Dialogue*) What does he gain by using dialogue? Why do you suppose he uses dialogue sparingly in the other parts of his narrative?

6. How does Winston use description to differentiate the four witnesses to the accident? (Glossary: *Description*) Why is it important for him to give his readers some idea of their differing characters?

QUESTIONS ON DICTION AND VOCABULARY

1. How would you characterize Winston's voice in this story? How is that voice established?

2. What, if anything, does Winston's diction tell you about Winston himself? (Glossary: *Diction*) What effect does his diction have on the tone of his narrative? (Glossary: *Tone*)

3. Refer to your desk dictionary to determine the meanings of the following words as Winston uses them in this selection: *felony* (paragraph 1), *agitated* (7), *misdemeanor* (8), *probation* (8), *bolt* (9).

CLASSROOM ACTIVITY USING NARRATION

Effective narrations use strong verbs—verbs that contribute significantly to the action of the story. Sportswriters, because they must repeatedly narrate the tug and pull of competitive situations, are acutely aware of the need for action verbs. It is not enough for them to say that a team won or lost; they must accurately describe the type of win or loss in vivid language. Thus such verbs as *beats, buries, edges, shocks,* and *trounces* are common in the headlines on the sports page. Each of these verbs not only describes a victory but also makes a statement about the quality of the victory. Like sportswriters, all of us write about actions that are performed daily. If we were restricted to the verbs *eat, drink, sleep,* and *work* for these activities, our writing would be repetitive and monotonous. List as many alternative verbs as you can for each of these four actions. What connotative (subjective) differences do you find in your lists of alternatives? What is the importance of these connotative differences to a writer?

WRITING SUGGESTIONS

1. "Stranger Than True" is a first-person narrative told from the defense lawyer's point of view. Imagine that you are a newspaper reporter covering this case. What changes would you have to make in Winston's narrative to make it a news story? Make a list of the changes you would have to make, and then rewrite the story.

2. Holloway's revelation in the courtroom catches everyone by surprise. Analyze the chain of events in the accident and the assumptions that people made based on the accounts of those events. Write a cause and effect essay in which you explain some of the possible reasons why Holloway's confession is so unexpected. (Glossary: *Cause and Effect Analysis*)

Not Close Enough for Comfort

David P. Bardeen

 *David P. Bardeen was born in 1974 in New Haven, Connecticut, and grew up in Seattle, Washington. He graduated cum laude from Harvard University in 1996 and then worked for J. P. Morgan & Co. as an investment banking analyst. In 2002, he received his J.D. from the New York University School of Law, where he was the managing editor of the* Law Review. *After graduation, he joined the law firm of Cleary, Gottlieb, Steen & Hamilton and became a member of the New York Bar. Bardeen is proficient in Spanish, and his practice focuses on international business transactions involving clients in Latin America.*

In the following article, which appeared in the New York Times Magazine *on February 29, 2004, Bardeen tells the story of a lunch meeting at which he reveals a secret to his twin brother, a secret that had derailed their relationship for almost fifteen years.*

PREPARING TO READ

Recall a time when a parent, sibling, friend, teacher, or some other person close to you kept a secret from you. How did the secret affect your relationship? How did you feel once the secret was revealed? How has the relationship fared since?

I had wanted to tell Will I was gay since I was 12. As twins, we shared everything back then: clothes, gadgets, thoughts, secrets. Everything except this. So when we met for lunch more than a year ago, I thought that finally coming out to him would close the distance that had grown between us. When we were kids, we created our own language, whispering to each other as our bewildered parents looked on. Now, at 28, we had never been further apart.

I asked him about his recent trip. He asked me about work. Short questions. One-word answers. Then an awkward pause.

Will was one of the last to know. Partly it was his fault. He is hard to pin down for brunch or a drink, and this was not the sort of conversation I wanted to have over the phone. I had actually been trying to tell him for more than a month, but he kept canceling at the last minute — a friend was in town, he'd met a girl.

But part of me was relieved. This was the talk I had feared the most. Coming out is, in an unforgiving sense, an admission of fraud. Fraud against yourself primarily, but also fraud against your family and friends. So, once I resolved to tell my secret, I confessed to my most recent "victims" first. I told my friends from law school — those I had met just a few years earlier and deceived the least—then I worked back through college to the handful of high-school friends I still keep in touch with.

Keeping my sexuality from my parents had always seemed permissible, so our sit-down chat did not stress me out as much as it might have. We all mislead our parents. "I'm too sick for school today." "No, I wasn't drinking." "Yes, Mom, I'm fine. Don't worry about me." That deception is understood and, in some sense, expected. But twins expect complete transparency, however romantic the notion.

Although our lives unfolded along parallel tracks—we went to college together, both moved to New York and had many of the same friends—Will and I quietly drifted apart. When he moved abroad for a year, we lost touch almost entirely. Our mother and father didn't think this was strange, because like many parents of twins, they wanted us to follow divergent paths. But friends were baffled when we began to rely on third parties for updates on each other's lives. "How's Will?" someone would ask. "You tell me," I would respond. One mutual friend, sick of playing the intermediary, once sent me an e-mail message with a carbon copy to Will. "Dave, meet Will, your twin," it said. "Will, let me introduce you to Dave."

Now, here we were, at lunch, just the two of us. "There's something I've been meaning to tell you," I said. "I'm gay." I looked at him closely, at the edges of his mouth, the wrinkles around his eyes, for some hint of what he was thinking.

"O.K.," he said evenly.

"I've been meaning to tell you for a while," I said.

"Uh-huh." He asked me a few questions but seemed slightly   10
uneasy, as if he wasn't sure he wanted to hear the answers. Do Mom
and Dad know? Are you seeing anyone? How long have you known
you were gay? I hesitated.

I've known since I was young, and to some degree, I thought Will   11
had always known. How else to explain my adolescent melancholy, my
withdrawal, the silence when the subject changed to girls, sex, and
who was hot. As a teenager I watched, as if from a distance, as my
demeanor went from outspoken to sullen. I had assumed, in the self-
centered way kids often do, that everyone noticed this change—and
that my brother had guessed the reason. To be fair, he asked me once in
our 20's, after I had ended yet another brief relationship with a woman.
"Of course I'm not gay," I told him, as if the notion were absurd.

"How long have you known?" he asked again.   12

"About 15 years," I said. Will looked away.   13

Food arrived. We ate and talked about other things. Mom, Dad, the   14
mayor and the weather. We asked for the check and agreed to get
together again soon. No big questions, no heart to heart. Just disclo-
sure, explanation, follow-up, conclusion. But what could I expect? I
had shut him out for so long that I suppose ultimately he gave up.
Telling my brother I was gay hadn't made us close, as I had naively
hoped it would; instead it underscored just how much we had strayed
apart.

As we left the restaurant, I felt the urge to apologize, not for being   15
gay, of course, but for the years I'd kept him in the dark, for his being
among the last to know. He hailed a cab. It stopped. He stepped inside,
the door still open.

"I'm sorry," I said.   16

He smiled. "No, I think it's great."   17

A nice gesture. Supportive. But I think he misunderstood.   18

A year later, we are still only creeping toward the intimacy every-   19
one expects us to have. Although we live three blocks away from each
other, I can't say we see each other every week or even every two weeks.
But with any luck, next year, I'll be the one updating our mutual
friends on Will's life.

THINKING CRITICALLY ABOUT THE TEXT

How do you think Will felt when David announced that he was gay? Do
you think Will had any clue about David's sexual orientation? What in
Will's response to David's announcement led you to this conclusion? Why
has it been so difficult for them to recapture the "intimacy everyone expects
[them] to have" (paragraph 19) in the year following David's coming out to
Will?

QUESTIONS ON SUBJECT

1. Why do you suppose Bardeen chose to keep his sexual orientation a secret from his brother? Why was this particular "coming-out" so difficult? Was Bardeen realistic in thinking that "Will had always known" (paragraph 11) that he was gay?

2. What does Bardeen mean when he says, "But twins expect complete transparency, however romantic the notion" (paragraph 5)?

3. Why does Bardeen feel the need to apologize to his brother as they part? Do you think his brother understood the meaning of the apology? Why or why not?

4. What do you think Bardeen had hoped would happen after he confided his secret to his brother? Was this hope unrealistic?

5. What harm had Bardeen's secret done to his relationship with his brother? What is necessary to heal the relationship?

QUESTIONS ON STRATEGY

1. Bardeen narrates his coming-out using the first-person pronoun *I*. (Glossary: *Point of View*) Why is the first person particularly appropriate for telling a story such as this one? Explain.

2. How has Bardeen organized his narrative? (Glossary: *Organization*) In paragraphs 3 through 6, Bardeen uses flashbacks to give readers a context for his relationship with his twin. What would have been lost or gained had he begun his essay with paragraphs 3 through 6?

3. During the lunch meeting part of the narrative (paragraphs 7–17), Bardeen uses dialogue. (Glossary: *Dialogue*) What does he gain by doing this? Why do you suppose he uses dialogue sparingly elsewhere?

4. Bardeen uses a number of short sentences and deliberate sentence fragments. What effect do these have on you? Why do you suppose he uses some sentence fragments instead of complete sentences?

5. Bardeen's title plays on the old saying "too close for comfort." What does his title suggest to you? (Glossary: *Title*) How effectively does it capture the essence of his relationship with his brother? Explain.

6. In paragraphs 6 and 11 Bardeen uses comparison and contrast to high light the similarities and differences between himself and Will. (Glossary: *Comparison and Contrast*) Which did you find more interesting and revealing, the similarities or differences? Why?

QUESTIONS ON DICTION AND VOCABULARY

1. How would you describe Bardeen's voice in this narrative? How is that voice established? What, if anything, does Bardeen's diction tell you about him as a person? (Glossary: *Diction*) Explain.

2. Bardeen says that "coming out is, in an unforgiving sense, an admission of fraud" (paragraph 4). Why do you suppose he uses the word *fraud* to

describe how he felt about his coming-out? What does he mean when he says "in an unforgiving sense"? What other words might he have used instead of *fraud*?

3. Refer to your desk dictionary to determine the meanings of the following words as Bardeen uses them in this selection: *baffled* (paragraph 6), *melancholy* (11), *demeanor* (11), *sullen* (11), *intimacy* (19).

CLASSROOM ACTIVITY USING NARRATION

Beginning at the beginning and ending at the end is not the only way to tell a story. Think of the individual incidents or events in a story that you would like to tell or perhaps one that you are already working on. Don't write the story itself; simply make a list of the events that you need to include. Be sure to identify at least six to ten key events in your story. Start by listing the events in chronological order. Now play with the arrangement of those events; try to develop one or two alternative sequences that include the use of flashback. Using your list of events, discuss with other class members how flashback can improve the dramatic impact of your narrative.

WRITING SUGGESTIONS

1. Using your Preparing to Read response for this selection, write an essay about a secret you once had and how it affected relationships with those close to you. What exactly was your secret? Why did you decide to keep this information secret? How did you feel while you kept your secret? What happened when you revealed your secret? What insights into secrets do you have as a result of this experience?

2. In paragraph 4 Bardeen states, "So, once I resolved to tell my secret, I confessed to my most recent 'victims' first. I told my friends from law school—those I had met just a few years earlier and deceived the least—then I worked back through college to the handful of high-school friends I still keep in touch with." Write an essay in which you compare and contrast your level of honesty among your friends or a larger community and your level of honesty among your family or people with whom you are very close. (Glossary: *Comparison and Contrast*) Are there secrets you would be more likely to share with one group than another? If so, how would you classify those secrets? (Glossary: *Classification; Division*) Do you think it is easier to be honest with people who do or do not know you very well? Why?

3. In paragraph 4 Bardeen states, "Coming out is, in an unforgiving sense, an admission of fraud. Fraud against yourself primarily, but also fraud against your family and friends." Do you agree with Bardeen, or do you think he is being too hard on himself? Explain. The "coming out" photograph of college students at a gay rights rally on page 94 was taken on October 11, 2003—National Coming Out Day—in Austin, Texas. How do you "read" this photograph? Why do you suppose viewers' eyes are drawn to the young man's T-shirt? How do you interpret the message on

his T-shirt? What significance, if any, do you attach to his being the only one wearing sunglasses? In your mind, is the young man being forthright or is he holding back? Explain. Using Bardeen's essay, this photograph, and your own observations and experiences, write an essay about the mixed feelings and emotions as well as the misunderstandings involved with "coming out."

Up in Smoke

Mary Winstead

 *A Minnesota-based journalist, Mary Winstead was born in Minneapolis and grew up listening to her father's stories of his boyhood years in rural Mississippi. On several occasions, she joined him on trips to Mississippi, where she learned about her southern roots. Winstead's undergraduate years were interrupted by marriage and the births of her three children: sons, Sam and Joe, and daughter, Sarah. She was a single parent for sixteen years, during which time she returned to college to complete her B.A. in English at the College of St. Catherine in St. Paul. After ten years in the workforce, she went back to school and received her M.F.A. from the University of Minnesota in 2000. Winstead wrote regularly for regional publications during this period, mostly travel features and a column on single parenting for* Minnesota Parent. *Her essays have been published in the* Minneapolis Star Tribune, Minnesota *magazine, and* Modern Maturity *magazine. Winstead's first book,* Back to Mississippi: A Personal Journey through the Events that Changed America in 1964 *(2002), which won the Minnesota Book Award for memoir, draws heavily on her early years in Minneapolis and on her visits to Mississippi. She has taught writing at St. Olaf College, North Hennepin Community College, and the University of Minnesota and is currently employed at the University of Minnesota Foundation as a senior writer. Winstead has been traveling to France ever since she was an au pair in her youth, and her love affair with France is the subject of a memoir she is working on now.*

In the following article, which first appeared in the July-August 2006 issue of Minnesota — *the University of Minnesota's alumni magazine — Winstead tells the story of her struggles with her newly graduated son Sam's change in career plans. She learns that what she as a parent wishes for her son is not the same thing as what the son wants for himself.*

PREPARING TO READ

Have you ever wanted to do something — take a trip with friends, enroll in a course, work a summer job, apply to a certain college, major in a particular subject — that was in conflict with what your parents wanted you to do? What was the conflict? What did you finally decide to do? How did you feel about your decision? Were you able to talk about the decision with your parents?

"Hey, Mom. Smell my hair." 1

Sitting in the living room of my son's apartment this past spring, 2
I obliged and he leaned his freshly shampooed head toward me. "Does it smell like smoke?" It did.

It wasn't the first time he'd asked me this question. Long before 3
smoking bans, Sam had worked his way through college tending bar.

Back then, everyone left the place smelling like smoke. But this time the question had a completely different meaning.

In the summer of 2002, after Sam's graduation from the University of Minnesota with a degree in journalism, my husband and I visited him at work and asked, as parents of new grads do, what he planned to do next—an internship in sports broadcasting, perhaps, as he'd discussed with us earlier. But he calmly told us that he'd changed his mind. 4

"Oh?" I asked. "What kind of change?" 5

"I want to become a firefighter." 6

"A *what?*" My husband and I responded in tandem. Sam, polishing a glass behind the bar, shook his head. "I was afraid you wouldn't understand." 7

Seeing that I needed to process this bit of information, my husband paid our tab, took me gently by the elbow, and led me outside. Sam was right; I didn't understand. All that time working toward his degree, all that effort and money. "He's throwing it all away," I said, my telegenic son's dream of becoming a sports broadcaster going up, literally, in smoke. 8

I didn't object to his becoming a firefighter *per se*. At least I didn't think so. It was a noble profession, albeit one I hadn't given much thought. When Sam and his siblings were young, I'd taken them to the neighborhood fire station to meet the firefighters, climb into the driver's seat of the hook-and-ladder truck, and try on a fireproof helmet— kids looking up to their local heroes, that kind of thing. 9

Many of my reservations had to do with Sam's talent as a writer, his education. Would he be intellectually challenged as a firefighter? And of course there were the dangers. I much preferred to think of him safely ensconced in a press booth covering Major League Baseball than disappearing into the mouth of a hungry inferno of roaring flames and toxic smoke. 10

But as often happens with my grown children, the roles had become reversed. This time Sam had something to teach *me*. When I looked honestly at my concerns, I saw something unattractive that I'd often observed in *other* parents but certainly not in myself: projecting my own agenda onto my children. 11

The truth is, *I* wanted my son to be a writer, like *me*. My worries about his writing talent and intellectual stimulation had more to do with my interests than his. Writing came easily to Sam, but it wasn't a passion. He needed to choose his destiny, and I needed to sit ringside and cheer him on. 12

Powered by his own internal combustion, Sam embarked on a journey that would take three years. It began with an eight-month program to become an emergency medical technician (EMT). He earned his way through by driving an ambulance (Hemingway drove ambulances,

I reminded myself) and tending bar, all the while dedicating himself
to a physically demanding regime of strength training, aerobics, and
bodybuilding. He went from a lithe 180-pound soccer player to a powerful 200-pound weight lifter.

On the nights we could lure him home with the promise of a steak   14
dinner, he told us stories of nursing homes and hospitals, where he
worked with elderly patients and transported sick or injured people
from one facility to the next, offering reassurance along with basic
medical treatment. When the patient was Hispanic, Sam rode in the
back of the ambulance while his partner drove; his minor in Spanish
allowed him to explain what was happening and comfort someone
who might be frightened.

At the same time, he was crisscrossing the country taking the writ-   15
ten firefighter exam wherever a city or county might be hiring, though
only a handful of municipalities were. Due to budget cuts, some were
laying off firefighters, working with skeleton crews, or using a volunteer force. In Los Angeles, 60,000 men and women applied for 500
openings. In Denver, 12,000 applicants for 50 positions.

As Sam held forth at the dinner table, it was impossible for me to   16
ignore that he told a good story, in journalistic style: a pyramid of the
highlights and details with a compelling narrative. It made me wonder
if my son shouldn't revisit his ambitions. Sports journalism, a difficult
field to break into, looked positively promising.

But not to Sam. Since September 11, 2001, a generation of young   17
people, my son included, had undergone a profound change in the
process of coming of age. The firefighters who stormed into the Twin
Towers that day became national heroes and role models, first respond-
ers in the war on terror.

Now, at a time when young Americans were lining up to follow   18
their example, when it seemed that firefighters were needed more than
ever on the home front, cities across the nation were cutting back. But
the odds did not deter him. Sam enrolled in a full-time, 18-month paramedic training program while working a 40-hour week as an EMT. He
went to the gym. He tended bar Thursday nights. When we would stop
in for a beer, the conversation went in one direction: doing what he
needed to do to become a firefighter.

In 2005, the City of St. Paul announced that it would be hiring   19
and 2,500 applicants showed up to take the written exam. There were
27 openings. Sam took the test, scoring in the top 5 percent. He made
it to the next level, a grueling set of tasks that included running up
10 flights of stairs in under three minutes in full firefighter regalia,
carrying 200 extra pounds. All on the hottest day of the summer. Again,
he scored in the top 5 percent.

There were no more steak dinners, and often on Thursday nights   20
Sam had to find someone to cover his shift while he studied for his

paramedic test or went out on a training ride. From time to time he'd check in with me by phone to brief me about his week, telling stories of heart attack patients or triage at the site of a car accident. He even delivered babies in the back of his ambulance. I'd never seen anyone pursue a goal with such dedication and drive.

He made it to the next level, which involved intensive back-ground checks that scrutinized every inch of his life, all the way back to childhood. Then interviews with the field captains. Then a psycho-logical exam. And then, an interview with the chief. There were 35 finalists. 21

By now I was a full-fledged supporter. Having witnessed three years of sleepless nights, the physical demands, the financial and personal sacrifices, the dedication to his medical training, I was completely on board. After all of this, and with the end so tantalizingly in sight, I just had to believe he'd go all the way. 22

When my cell phone rang on my way home from work and Sam's name appeared on the caller ID, I pulled the car over to answer. No matter what he had to say, I didn't want to be on the road. His voice was shaky but clear. He'd made it. I screamed. My strong, stoic grown son began to cry. 23

Twelve weeks of boot camp. His graduation in dress uniform. His assignment to a fire station in North St. Paul. Lots of paramedic calls—cardiac arrests, falls, and accidents—but no fires. 24

Until Easter Sunday 2006. A two-alarm fire, just blocks from the station, shortly after midnight. 25

I came by the next day with a loaf of banana bread, Easter eggs, and a small wrapped gift. I wanted to hear all about his first fire. How it went. What happened. 26

As he ate the hard-boiled eggs and sliced into the banana bread, he told me a harrowing story. A house engulfed in flames. A family with nine children. Sam was the first to go in, the first with the hose. The heat was too intense and the interior was a pressure-cooker, the win-dows in the upstairs bedrooms had already blown and shattered. There was no saving the home, just putting the fire out so it wouldn't spread. It had taken all night. But every family member was safe and accounted for. Hours later, Sam's eyes were still rimmed in red, there was soot under his fingernails, and after two showers, his hair still smelled like smoke. 27

When he opened his present, I felt a little nervous. I'd wondered, when I'd picked it out, if I was buying it for Sam or for me. But I bought it anyway. It was a leather-bound notebook. 28

"What's this for?" he asked. 29

"What you just told me," I replied. "And all the rest. Please. I want you to write it down." 30

THINKING CRITICALLY ABOUT THE TEXT

What did you think when Sam's mother gave him "a leather-bound notebook" at the end? Is the mother still holding on to the dream of her son becoming a journalist, or did she have some other motive? What evidence is there in this narrative that Sam really does have a knack for telling stories?

QUESTIONS ON SUBJECT

1. What is the central conflict in Winstead's story? How is this conflict resolved?
2. Why did Sam's mother find his decision to become a firefighter so difficult to accept?
3. What eventually convinced her to be a "full-fledged supporter" of Sam's career choice?
4. According to Winstead, why are so many young people like her son aspiring to become firefighters?
5. How difficult was the training that Sam went through to become a firefighter? Why was it so difficult for him to secure a job?

QUESTIONS ON STRATEGY

1. In what ways do the first three paragraphs serve to introduce Mary Winstead's essay? (Glossary: *Beginnings/Endings*) How did you respond when you read the sentence, "But this time the question had a completely different meaning"?
2. What is the context for Winstead's story? Where does she answer the questions When did it happen? Where did it happen? and To whom did it happen?
3. How has Winstead organized her narrative? (Glossary: *Organization*) What use does she make of flashback? Did you find this technique effective? Explain.
4. Identify the places where Winstead uses dialogue in her essay. What specifically does the dialogue add to her narrative? What would have been lost had Winstead simply reported what was said instead of letting people speak for themselves? Explain.
5. Winstead uses a number of intentional sentence fragments in her narrative. Identify several of these fragments. Why do you suppose she chose to use them? Explain.

QUESTIONS ON DICTION AND VOCABULARY

1. In paragraphs 11 and 12 Winstead italicizes four words. Why do you think she chose to italicize these words? Explain.

2. Circle the verbs in paragraphs 13 through 18. Which of these verbs would you call "strong verbs"? (Glossary: *Verb*) What do these strong verbs add to Winstead's narrative?

3. Refer to your desk dictionary to determine the meanings of the following words as Winstead uses them in this selection: *tandem* (paragraph 7), *telegenic* (8), *ensconced* (10), *regime* (13), *triage* (20), *stoic* (23).

CLASSROOM ACTIVITY USING NARRATION

Dialogue is an effective way to bring life to your narrative, to let the people in your story speak for themselves. It is important, however, that you create dialogue that flows logically from one speaker to another. The following sentences, which include dialogue, have been scrambled. Using language cues in each of the sentences, rearrange them in chronological order.

1. The sky was gray and gloomy for as far as she could see, and sleet hissed off the glass.

2. "Oh, hi, Sarah, I'm glad you called," she said happily, but her smile dimmed when she looked outside.

3. As Betsy crossed the room, the phone rang, startling her.

4. "No, the weather's awful, so I don't think I want to leave the house today—I'm still nursing that cold, you know," she sighed.

5. "Hello?" she said, and she wandered over to the window, dragging the phone cord behind her.

6. "Thought you might like to get out for a coffee on a day like today," Sarah urged.

WRITING SUGGESTIONS

1. Once Sam set his sights on a career as a firefighter, he "embarked," as his mother tells us, "on a journey that would take three years" to complete. Using Winstead's account of Sam's "training" as a model, write an essay in which you describe the "journey" that awaits you as you pursue your passion.

2. When talking about career plans, school counselors often ask students, "What do you see yourself doing five or ten years down the road?" How would you answer this question now? What is your "dream" job? Does it involve something that you are passionate about? Have you shared this idea with your parents? If so, are they supportive? If not, why haven't you told them yet? How important is it for you to have your parents' support and approval? Write an essay in which you identify your dream job and explain why you believe it is right for you.

WRITING SUGGESTIONS FOR NARRATION

1. Using Malcolm X's, David P. Bardeen's, or Mary Winstead's essay as a model, narrate an experience that gave you a new awareness of yourself. Use enough telling detail in your narrative to help your reader visualize your experience and understand its significance for you. You may find the following suggestions helpful in choosing an experience to narrate in the first person:

   a. my greatest success
   b. my biggest failure
   c. my most embarrassing moment
   d. my happiest moment
   e. a truly frightening experience
   f. an experience that, in my eyes, turned a hero or idol into an ordinary person
   g. an experience that turned an ordinary person I know into one of my heroes
   h. the experience that was the most important turning point in my life

2. Each of us can tell of an experience that has been unusually significant in teaching us about our relationship to society or to life's institutions — schools, social or service organizations, religious groups, government. Think about your past, and identify one experience that has been especially important for you in this way. After you have considered this event's significance, write an essay recounting it. In preparing to write your narrative, you might enjoy reading George Orwell's account of acting against his better judgment in "Shooting an Elephant" (000–000). To bring your experience into focus and to help you decide what to include in your essay, ask yourself, Why is this experience important to me? What details are necessary for me to re-create the experience in an interesting and engaging way? How can my narrative be most effectively organized? What point of view will work best?

3. As a way of gaining experience with third-person narration, write an article intended for your school or community newspaper in which you report on what happened at one of the following:

   a. the visit of a state or national figure to your campus or community
   b. a dormitory meeting
   c. a current event of local, state, or national significance
   d. an important sports event
   e. a current research project of one of your professors
   f. a campus gathering or performance
   g. an important development at a local business or at your place of employment

4. Imagine that you are a member of a campus organization that is seeking volunteers for a community project. Your job is to write a piece for the school newspaper to solicit help for your organization. To build support

for the project, narrate one or more stories about the rewards of lending a hand to others within the community.

5. Many people love to tell stories (that is, they use narration!) to illustrate an abstract point, to bring an idea down to a personal level, or to render an idea memorable. Often, the telling of such stories can be entertaining as well as instructive. Think about a belief or position that you hold dear (e.g., every individual deserves respect, recycling matters, voluntarism creates community, people need artistic outlets, nature renews the individual), and try to capture that belief in a sentence or two. Then, narrate a story that illustrates your thesis.

6. Like Annie Dillard in the selection from *An American Childhood*, we have all done something we know we should not have done. Sometimes we have gotten away with our transgressions, sometimes not. Sometimes our actions have no repercussions; sometimes they have very serious ones. Tell the story of one of your escapades, and explain why you have remembered it so well.

CHAPTER 5

Description

WHAT IS DESCRIPTION?

The strategy of description enables us to convey, through words, the perceptions of our five senses. We see, hear, smell, taste, and feel; and through description we try to re-create those sensations to share them with others.

It is often said that to describe is to paint a verbal picture—of a thing, a place, a person—and the analogy is a helpful one. Both description and painting seek to transform fleeting perceptions into lasting images—through words in the case of description, oils or water-colors in the case of a painting. Although the original perception may have taken place in a flash, both description and painting are created bit by bit, word by word, or brushstroke by brushstroke. Yet while we can view a painting in a single glance (though appreciation may take longer), we take in a description only piece by piece, or word by word, just as the writer created it, and draw on all of our sense perceptions, evoking not just sight, but also sound, texture, taste, and smell.

Consider, for example, the following description by Bernd Heinrich from his book *One Man's Owl* (1987). In this selection, Heinrich describes trekking through the woods in search of owls. First, allow the words of his description to build up a concrete mental image. Try to see, hear, smell, and feel Heinrich's words. Form the jigsaw puzzle of words and details into a complete experience. Once you've built this mental image, define the dominant impression Heinrich creates.

Writer sets the scene with description of the landscape.

By mid-March in Vermont, the snow from the winter storms has already become crusty as the first midday thaws refreeze during the cold nights. A solid white cap compacts the snow, and you can walk on it without breaking through to your waist. The maple sap is starting to run on warm days, and one's blood quickens.

Writer describes the sights and sounds of the birds in early spring.

Spring is just around the corner, and the birds act as if they know. The hairy and downy woodpeckers drum on dry branches and on the loose flakes of maple bark, and purple finches sing merrily from the spruces. This year the reedy voices of the pine siskins can be heard everywhere on the ridge where the hemlocks grow, as can the chickadees' two-note, plaintive song. Down in the bog, the first red-winged blackbirds have just returned, and they can be heard yodeling from the tops of dry cattails. Flocks of rusty blackbirds fly over in long skeins, heading north.

Writer reveals his position and relies on auditory details as night approaches.

From where I stand at the edge of the woods overlooking Shelburne Bog, I feel a slight breeze and hear a moaning gust sweeping through the forest behind me. It is getting dark. There are eery creaking and scraping noises. Inside the pine forest it is becoming black, pitch black. The songbirds are silent. Only the sound of the wind can be heard above the distant honks of Canada geese flying below the now starry skies. Suddenly I hear a booming hollow "hoo-hoo-*hoo*-hoo—." The deep resonating hoot can send a chill down any spine, as indeed it has done to peoples of many cultures. But I know what the sound is, and it gives me great pleasure.

Heinrich could have described the scene with far fewer words, but that description would likely not have conveyed his dominant impression—one of comfort with the natural surroundings. Heinrich reads the landscape with subtle insight; he knows all the different birds and understands their springtime habits. The reader can imagine the smile on Heinrich's face when he hears the call of the owl.

USING DESCRIPTION AS A WRITING STRATEGY

Writers often use the strategy of description to inform—to provide readers with specific data. You may need to describe the results of a chemical reaction for a lab report; the style of a Renaissance painting for an art history term paper; the physical capabilities and limitations of a stroke patient for a case study; or the acting of Halle Berry in a movie you want your friends to see. Such descriptions will sometimes be scientifically objective, sometimes intensely impressionistic. The approach you use will depend on the subject itself, the information you want to communicate about it, and the format in which the description appears.

Another important use of description is to create a mood or atmosphere or even to convey your own views—to develop a *dominant impression*. Edward Abbey uses the strategy of description to capture the beauty and mystery of the twelve-mile-long Aravaipa Canyon in Arizona:

> The walls bristle with spiky rock gardens of formidable desert vegetation. Most prominent is the giant saguaro cactus, growing five to fifty feet tall out of crevices in the stone you might think could barely lodge a flower. The barrel cactus, with its pink fishhook thorns, thrives here on the sunny side; and clusters of hedgehog cactus, and prickly pear with names like clockface and cows-tongue, have wedged roots into the rock. Since most of the wall is vertical, parallel to gravity, these plants grow first outward then upward, forming right-angled bends near the base. It looks difficult but they do it. They like it here.

Each of the descriptions in this chapter, whether informative, entertaining, or both, is distinguished by the strong dominant impression the writer creates.

There are essentially two types of description: objective and subjective. *Objective description* is as factual as possible, emphasizing the actual qualities of the subject being described while subordinating the writer's personal responses. For example, a holdup witness would try to give authorities a precise, objective description of the assailant, unaffected by emotional responses, so that positive identification could be made and an innocent person would not be arrested by mistake. In the excerpt from his book, Bernd Heinrich objectively describes what he sees: "The hairy and downy woodpeckers drum on dry branches and on the loose flakes of maple bark, and purple finches sing merrily from the spruces." *Subjective* or *impressionistic description*, on the other hand, conveys the writer's personal opinion or impression of the object, often in language rich in modifiers and figures of speech. A food critic describing a memorable meal would inevitably write about it impressionistically, using colorful or highly subjective language; in fact, relatively few words in English can describe the subtleties of smell and taste in neutral terms. In "Aravaipa Canyon," Edward Abbey uses subjective description to capture the subtle beauty that he witnesses when walking through a desert canyon in America's Southwest. Notice that with objective description, it is usually the person, place, or thing being described that stands out, whereas with subjective description the response of the person doing the describing is the most prominent feature. Most subjects, however, lend themselves to both objective and subjective description, depending on the writer's purpose. You could write, for example, that you had "exactly four weeks" to finish a history term paper (objective) or that you had "all the time in the world" or "an outrageously short amount of time" (subjective). Each type of description can be accurate and useful in its own way.

Although descriptive writing can stand alone, and often does, it is also used with other types of writing. In a narrative, for example, descriptions provide the context for the story—and make the characters, settings, and events come alive. Description may also help to define an unusual object or thing, such as a giraffe, or to clarify the steps of a process, such as diagnosing an illness. Wherever it is used, good description creates vivid and specific pictures that clarify, create a mood, build a dominant impression, inform, and entertain.

Using Description across the Disciplines

When writing essays in the academic disciplines, you will have many opportunities to use the strategy of description to both organize and strengthen the presentation of your ideas. To determine whether or not description is the right strategy for you in a particular paper, use the four-step method first described in Choosing Strategies across the Disciplines (pages 24–25). Consider the following examples:

History

MAIN IDEA: Roman medicine, while primitive in some ways, was in general very advanced.

QUESTION: What primitive beliefs and advanced thinking characterize Roman medicine?

STRATEGY: Description. The direction word *characterize* signals the need to describe Roman medical practices and beliefs.

SUPPORTING STRATEGY: Comparison and contrast might be used to set off Roman practices and beliefs from those in later periods of history.

Chemistry

MAIN IDEA: The chemical ingredients in acid rain are harmful to humans and the environment.

QUESTION: What are the components of acid rain?

STRATEGY: Description. The direction word *components* suggests the need for a description of acid rain, including as it does sulfuric acid, carbon monoxide, carbon dioxide, chlorofluorocarbons, and nitric acid.

SUPPORTING STRATEGY: Cause and effect might be used to show the harmful effects caused by acid rain. Process analysis might be used to explain how acid rain develops.

Psychology

MAIN IDEA: Law enforcement officers who are under abnormal stress manifest certain symptoms.

QUESTION: What comprises the symptoms?

STRATEGY: Description. The direction words *comprises* suggests the need for a picture or description of the *symptoms*.

SUPPORTING STRATEGY: Comparison and contrast might be used to differentiate those officers suffering from stress. Process analysis might be used to explain how to carry out examination to identify the symptoms of stress. Argumentation might be used to indicate the need for programs to test for excessive stress on the job.

SAMPLE STUDENT ESSAY USING DESCRIPTION AS A WRITING STRATEGY

James Blake Wilson wrote the following essay while he was a student at the University of California–Riverside. Drawing details from his teenage memories of Crenshaw Boulevard in South Central Los Angeles, where he grew up, Wilson gives an insightful view of an infamous place—a place that has gotten much media attention, mostly negative and sensational. His observations offer readers a unified picture of the region that they won't see on the eleven o'clock news or on the front page of the *Los Angeles Times*.

The "Shaw"

James Blake Wilson

Thesis: Idea that this is "my home" controls rest of essay.

Dominant impression: The sensory impressions that add up to "Neighborhood Pride"

Ah yes, my home. It feels good to be back. It's just another Sunday afternoon in the beautiful city of Los Angeles. As I walk down the street I see all the little things that make me remember all of the good times I have had out here on this street, and all the bad things that I wish I could put in the back of my memory. I'm standing on the corner of Slauson Avenue and Crenshaw Boulevard, the center of liveliness here on the "Shaw." As I stand here and close my eyes, I can hear many different noises and sounds that would convince anyone that they were

1

Organization: Focus on sounds of the "Shaw"

Sentences: Repetition of "I hear"

in the big city. I hear the diesel exhaust of the "108" metro bus line throttle up to take its passengers up and down Crenshaw every twenty minutes. I hear the mingling of car horns honking from impatient drivers trying to get from point A to point B in a matter of minutes, squeaking wheels of a homeless man's shopping cart that he uses to collect cans. These cans, which to me conveniently hold soda, are a source of income for him. It's amazing to see that what one man takes for granted, another man may cherish.

Organization: Focus on sight

I open my eyes and see street vendors of all shapes and 2 sizes. I see little children trying to sell ten dollar cutlery sets to every motorist that stops at a street light, and grown adults selling the latest in scandal fashion. With clothes bearing slogans such as "Let the Juice Loose" or "Free O.J.," you can't help but think that people will try to make money off of anything these days. Alongside the street vendors, you can see members of The Nation of Islam, dressed in their single breasted suits with afrocentric bowties, selling bean pies for five dollars and copies of the *Final Call* for fifty cents. I walk up the street and see Willie

Organization: Focus on movement

on the corner of Crenshaw and 54th Street. It is here that Willie waits for his bus with a Walkman and his hyperactive body which dances, slides, and gyrates to the music that he hears in his own world. People watch and laugh at the zany actions of a man we call crazy. But who are we to call someone crazy?

I look up the block and see the paint on the Crenshaw 3 "Wall of Fame" fading from the sun. This wall symbolizes those in the Black community who have struggled, fought, and sometimes died for the Black race in America. With portraits of Martin

Well-selected details of the "Wall of Fame"

Luther King Jr., Malcolm X, Louis Farrakhan, Frederick Douglass, and many others, this wall is highly respected and remains untouched by graffiti and vandalism all year round. Of course

Paragraph: Development relies on comparison and contrast—pros and cons.

Description is used to depict emotion.

with every pro, there's a con. It only takes a glimpse down the street to see gang colors on the white walls of a neighborhood liquor store. It's heartbreaking to know that hundreds of kids, male and female, mark up, fight and die over territory that isn't even theirs. I wonder what these kids could accomplish if their efforts were taken away from gang violence and put into something more productive. Maybe their efforts could go towards cleaning up the infamous Leimert Park, a home to many homeless people. The park is a truly diverse landmark, where one day you might see an organized marketplace of vendors selling clothing and food, and the next day the sirens and lights of police cars at the scene of a drug deal gone bad.

Paragraph/ sentence: Two-sentence paragraph explains how thumping bass turns Crenshaw Boulevard into the "Shaw."

As the sun goes down, and the moon illuminates the dark gray, almost black, asphalt of the street, Crenshaw Boulevard turns into the "Shaw." It all starts with the first sonic thumps of bass extending from the oversized speakers of a car stereo. 4

"The name of the game is . . . Boom-Boom." 5

I hear the two thundering thumps muffle out the lyrics and hit me in my chest. Ten-, twelve-, or fifteen-inch diameter speakers can be commonly found in the trunks of these attention hungry motorists. Out here there's no telling what kind of car you'll see: anything from a new Lexus to a fully restored 1964 Chevrolet Impala with hydraulic lifts on every wheel and axle. 6

Paragraph: Conclusion returns to idea of "home" in thesis.

I've seen a lot of things on this street, some good, some bad. But no matter how hard I try, I can never repress my inner feeling that this is my home.

Analyzing James Blake Wilson's Essay of Description: Questions for Discussion

1. What senses does Wilson call on to describe the "Shaw"?
2. Why is it significant that no graffiti mar the "Wall of Fame"? What does much of the graffiti elsewhere symbolize to Wilson?
3. Why is the "Shaw" a paradoxical place for Wilson? How does his description serve to strengthen his conflicted emotions about the place?

SUGGESTIONS FOR USING DESCRIPTION AS A WRITING STRATEGY

As you plan, write, and revise your essay of description, be mindful of the five-step writing process described in Chapter 2 (see pages 14–31). Pay particular attention to the basic requirements and essential ingredients of this writing strategy.

Planning Your Essay of Description

Planning is an essential part of writing a good essay of description. You can save yourself a deal of aggravation by taking the time to think about key building blocks of your essay before you actually begin to write.

Determine a Purpose. Begin by determining your purpose: Are you trying to inform, express your emotions, or persuade? While it is not necessary, or even desirable, to state your purpose explicitly, it is necessary that you have one that your readers recognize. If your readers do not see a purpose in your writing they may be tempted to respond by asking, "So what?" Making your reason for writing clear in the first place will help you avoid this pitfall.

Use Description in the Service of an Idea. Your readers will appreciate your description of an object, event, person, or experience, but what they really want to know is why you chose to describe what you did. You would not describe a person, a horse, or a canoe trip and let it go at that because you write description with a thesis in mind, an idea you want to convey to your readers. For example, you would describe the canoe trip as one of both serenity and exhilarating danger, which you came to realize symbolizes the contrasting aspects of nature. In his essay, Cherokee Paul McDonald uses description in the service of an idea, and that idea is description itself. McDonald needs to describe a fish so that a blind boy can "see" it. Description works here because it is a practical necessity and it advances the action. In the process of describing, the author comes to an epiphany, a deeper insight into the power of description. As McDonald is compelled to describe the fish, he comes closer to the essence of it. He realizes then that he has received from the boy more than he has given, and for that he is grateful.

Organizing Your Essay of Description

Create a Dominant Impression. From the catalog of details that you have collected, select those that will be most helpful in developing a dominant impression. Suppose that you wish to depict the hospital emergency room as a place of great tension. You will then naturally choose details to reinforce that sense of tension: the worried looks on the faces of a couple sitting in the corner, the quick movements of the medical staff as they tend a patient on a wheeled stretcher, the urgent whisperings of two interns out in the hallway, the incessant paging of Dr. Thomas. If the dominant impression you want to create is of the emergency room's sterility, however, you will choose different details: the smell of disinfectant, the spotless white uniforms of the staff members, the stainless steel tables and chairs, the gleaming instruments the nurse hands to the physician. Building a convincing dominant impression depends on the selection of such details.

Of course, it is equally important to omit any details that conflict with the dominant impression. Perhaps there was an orderly lounging in a corner, chewing gum and reading a magazine, who did not feel the tension of the emergency room; perhaps the room's sterility was marred by several used Styrofoam coffee cups left on a corner table. Deciding which details to include and which to exclude is up to you.

Organize Your Details to Create a Vivid Picture. A photographer can capture a large, complicated scene with the press of a button. The writer has to put descriptive details down on paper one at a time. It's not enough to decide which details to include and which to leave out; you also need to arrange your chosen details in a particular order, one that serves your purpose and is easy for the reader to follow.

Imagine what the reader would experience first. A description of an emergency room could begin at the entrance, move through the waiting area, pass the registration desk, and proceed into the treatment cubicles. A description of a restaurant kitchen might conjure up the smells and sounds that escape through the swinging doors even before moving on to the first glimpse inside the kitchen.

Other patterns of organization include moving from general to specific, from smallest to largest, from least to most important, or from the usual to the unusual. Keep in mind that the last details you present will probably stay in the reader's mind the longest and that the first details will also have special force. Those in the middle of your description, though they will have their effect, may not have the same impact as those before and after them.

Before you begin your first draft, you may find it useful to sketch out an outline of your description. Here's a sample outline for Bernd Heinrich's description earlier in this introduction:

Description of Shelburne Bog

Dominant impression: Comfort with the natural surroundings

Paragraph 1: Snow-crusted landscape in mid-March

Paragraph 2: Activity and sounds of the birds (e.g., woodpeckers, finches, chickadees, and red-winged blackbirds) described from the edge of the woods

Paragraph 3: Activity and sounds inside the pine forest behind the speaker, culminating with the call of the familiar owl

Such an outline can remind you of the dominant impression you want to create and can suggest which specific details may be most useful to you.

Revising and Editing Your Essay of Description

Share Your Work with Others. Try sharing your drafts with other students in your writing class to make sure that your description makes sense. Ask them if there are any parts that they do not understand. Have them tell you what they think is the point of your description. If their answers differ from what you intended, have them indicate the passages that led them to their interpretations so that you can change your text accordingly. To maximize the effectiveness of conferences with your peers, utilize the guidelines presented on pages 27–28. Feedback from these conferences often provides one or more places where you can start revising.

Show, Don't Tell: Use Specific Nouns and Action Verbs.   Inexperienced writers often believe that adjectives and adverbs are the basis for effective descriptions. They're right in one sense, but not wholly so. Although strong adjectives and adverbs are crucial, description also depends on well-chosen nouns and verbs. *Vehicle* is not nearly as descriptive as something more specific—*Jeep, snowmobile,* or *Honda Civic.* Why write *see* when what you mean is *glance, stare, spy, gaze, peek, examine,* or *witness*? The more specific and strong you make your nouns and verbs, the more lively and interesting your descriptions will be.

When you have difficulty thinking of specific action nouns and verbs to use, reach for a thesaurus—but only if you are sure you can discern the best word for your purpose. Inexpensive paperback editions are available at any bookstore, and most word-processing programs have a thesaurus utility. A thesaurus will help you keep your descriptions from getting repetitive and will be invaluable when you need to find a specific word with just the right meaning.

Question Your Own Work While Revising and Editing.   Revision is best done by asking yourself key questions about what you have written. Begin by reading, preferably aloud, what you have written. Reading aloud forces you to pay attention to every single word, and you are more likely to catch lapses in the logical flow of thought. After you have read your paper through, answer the following questions for revising and editing, and make the necessary changes.

Questions for Revising and Editing: Description

1. Do I have a clear purpose for my description? Have I answered the "so what" question?
2. Is the subject of my description interesting and relevant to my audience?
3. What senses have I chosen to use to describe it? For example, what does it look like, sound like, or smell like? Does it have a texture or taste that is important to mention?
4. Which details must I include in my essay? Which are irrelevant or distracting to my purpose and should be discarded?

5. Have I achieved the dominant impression I wish to leave with my audience?

6. Does the organization I have chosen for my essay make it easy for the reader to follow my description?

7. How carefully have I chosen my descriptive words? Are my nouns and verbs strong and specific?

8. Have I used figurative language, if appropriate, to further strengthen my description?

9. Does my paper contain any errors in grammar, punctuation, or mechanics?

A View from the Bridge

Cherokee Paul McDonald

 *A fiction writer and journalist, Cherokee Paul McDonald was raised and schooled in Fort Lauderdale, Florida. In 1970, he returned home from a tour of duty in Vietnam and joined the Fort Lauderdale Police Department, where he remained until 1980, resigning with the rank of sergeant. During this time, McDonald received a degree in criminal science from Broward Community College. He left the police department to become a writer and worked a number of odd jobs before publishing his first book,* The Patch, *in 1986. McDonald has said that almost all of his writing comes from his police work, and his common themes of justice, balance, and fairness reflect his life as part of the "thin blue line" (the police department). In 1991, he published* Blue Truth, *a memoir. His first novel,* Summer's Reason, *was released in 1994. His most recent book is a memoir of his three years as an artillery forward observer in Vietnam,* Into the Green: A Reconnaissance by Fire *(2001).*

"A View from the Bridge" was originally published in Sunshine *magazine in 1990. The essay shows McDonald's usual expert handling of fish and fishermen, both in and out of water, and reminds us that things are not always as they seem.*

PREPARING TO READ

There's an old saying that "familiarity breeds contempt." We've all had the experience of becoming numb to sights or experiences that once struck us with wonderment; but sometimes, with luck, something happens to renew our appreciation. Think of an example from your own experience. What are some ways we can retain or recover our appreciation of the remarkable things we have come to take for granted?

I was coming up on the little bridge in the Rio Vista neighborhood of Fort Lauderdale, deepening my stride and my breathing to negotiate the slight incline without altering my pace. And then, as I neared the crest, I saw the kid.

He was a lumpy little guy with baggy shorts, a faded T-shirt and heavy sweat socks falling down over old sneakers.

Partially covering his shaggy blond hair was one of those blue baseball caps with gold braid on the bill and a sailfish patch sewn onto the peak. Covering his eyes and part of his face was a pair of those stupid-looking '50s-style wrap-around sunglasses.

He was fumbling with a beat-up rod and reel, and he had a little bait bucket by his feet. I puffed on by, glancing down into the empty bucket as I passed.

"Hey, mister! Would you help me, please?"   5

The shrill voice penetrated my jogger's concentration, and I was   6
determined to ignore it. But for some reason, I stopped.

With my hands on my hips and the sweat dripping from my nose   7
I asked, "What do you want, kid?"

"Would you please help me find my shrimp? It's my last one and   8
I've been getting bites and I know I can catch a fish if I can just find
that shrimp. He jumped outta my hand as I was getting him from the
bucket."

Exasperated, I walked slowly back to the kid, and pointed.   9

"There's the damn shrimp by your left foot. You stopped me for   10
that?"

As I said it, the kid reached down and trapped the shrimp.   11

"Thanks a lot, mister," he said.   12

I watched as the kid dropped the baited hook down into the canal.   13
Then I turned to start back down the bridge.

That's when the kid let out a "Hey! Hey!" and the prettiest tarpon   14
I'd ever seen came almost six feet out of the water, twisting and turning
as he fell through the air.

"I got one!" the kid yelled as the fish hit the water with a loud   15
splash and took off down the canal.

I watched the line being burned off the reel at an alarming rate.   16
The kid's left hand held the crank while the extended fingers felt for
the drag setting.

"No, kid!" I shouted. "Leave the drag alone . . . just keep that damn   17
rod tip up!"

Then I glanced at the reel and saw there were just a few loops of   18
line left on the spool.

"Why don't you get yourself some decent equipment?" I said, but   19
before the kid could answer I saw the line go slack.

"Ohhh, I lost him," the kid said. I saw the flash of silver as the fish   20
turned.

"Crank, kid, crank! You didn't lose him. He's coming back toward   21
you. Bring in the slack!"

The kid cranked like mad, and a beautiful grin spread across his   22
face.

"He's heading in for the pilings," I said. "Keep him out of those   23
pilings!"

The kid played it perfectly. When the fish made its play for the   24
pilings, he kept just enough pressure on to force the fish out. When the
water exploded and the silver missile hurled into the air, the kid kept
the rod tip up and the line tight.

As the fish came to the surface and began a slow circle in the middle   25
of the canal, I said, "Whooee, is that a nice fish or what?"

The kid didn't say anything, so I said, "Okay, move to the edge of the bridge and I'll climb down to the seawall and pull him out." 26

When I reached the seawall I pulled in the leader, leaving the fish lying on its side in the water. 27

"How's that?" I said. 28

"Hey, mister, tell me what it looks like." 29

"Look down here and check him out," I said, "He's beautiful." 30

But then I looked up into those stupid-looking sunglasses and it hit me. The kid was blind. 31

"Could you tell me what he looks like, mister?" he said again. 32

"Well, he's just under three, uh, he's about as long as one of your arms," I said. "I'd guess he goes about 15, 20 pounds. He's mostly silver, but the silver is somehow made up of *all* the colors, if you know what I mean." I stopped. "Do you know what I mean by colors?" 33

The kid nodded. 34

"Okay. He has all these big scales, like armor all over his body. They're silver too, and when he moves they sparkle. He has a strong body and a large powerful tail. He has big round eyes, bigger than a quarter, and a lower jaw that sticks out past the upper one and is very tough. His belly is almost white and his back is a gunmetal gray. When he jumped he came out of the water about six feet, and his scales caught the sun and flashed it all over the place." 35

By now the fish had righted itself, and I could see the bright-red gills as the gill plates opened and closed. I explained this to the kid, and then said, more to myself, "He's a beauty." 36

"Can you get him off the hook?" the kid asked. "I don't want to kill him." 37

I watched as the tarpon began to slowly swim away, tired but still alive. 38

By the time I got back up to the top of the bridge the kid had his line secured and his bait bucket in one hand. 39

He grinned and said, "Just in time. My mom drops me off here, and she'll be back to pick me up any minute." 40

He used the back of one hand to wipe his nose. 41

"Thanks for helping me catch that tarpon," he said, "and for helping me to see it." 42

I looked at him, shook my head, and said, "No, my friend, thank you for letting *me* see that fish." 43

I took off, but before I got far the kid yelled again. 44

"Hey, mister!" 45

I stopped. 46

"Someday I'm gonna catch a sailfish and a blue marlin and a giant tuna and *all* those big sportfish!" 47

As I looked into those sunglasses I knew he probably would. I wished I could be there when it happened. 48

THINKING CRITICALLY ABOUT THE TEXT

The jogger and the kid are very different from each other, but they share an interest in fishing. What role does the tarpon play in this story? What can a shared interest do for a relationship between two people?

QUESTIONS ON SUBJECT

1. Why is the narrator angry with the kid at the beginning of the story?

2. What clues lead up to the revelation that the kid is blind? Why does it take the narrator so long to realize it?

3. "Why don't you get yourself some decent equipment?" the narrator asks the kid (paragraph 19). Why does McDonald include this question? Speculate about the answer.

4. Near the end of the story, why does the narrator say to the kid, "No, my friend, thank you for letting *me* see that fish" (paragraph 43)?

5. The boy boasts that one day he will catch big sport fish, too. Why does the narrator say he "wished [he] could be there when it happened" (paragraph 48)?

QUESTIONS ON STRATEGY

1. Notice the way the narrator chooses and actually adjusts some of the words he uses to describe the fish to the kid. Why does he do this? What is McDonald's desired effect?

2. By the end of the essay, we know much more about the kid than the fact that he is blind, but, after the initial description, McDonald characterizes him only indirectly. As the essay unfolds, what do we learn about the kid, and by what techniques does the author convey this knowledge?

3. Reread the description of the kid (paragraphs 2 and 3). Which details gain significance as events unfold over the course of the essay?

4. McDonald is able to move his story along rather quickly by being selective about what he tells the reader. For example, examine paragraphs 9–13 and explain how the author moves the action forward.

5. This essay, descriptive in theme and intent, is structured as a narrative. (Glossary: *Narration*) What makes the combination of story and description effective? Suppose McDonald had started his essay with a statement like this: "If you really want to see something clearly, try describing it to a blind child." How would such an opening change the impact of the essay? Which other rhetorical strategies might McDonald have used along with the new opening?

QUESTIONS ON DICTION AND VOCABULARY

1. What is the metaphor in paragraph 24? Why is it apt? How does this metaphor enhance McDonald's description? (Glossary: *Figures of Speech*)

2. What is the connotation of the word *view* in the title? Of the word *bridge*? (Glossary: *Connotation/Denotation*)

3. You may be unfamiliar with some of the fishing-related vocabulary in this essay. What sort of fish is a tarpon? In the context of fishing, define *drag* (paragraph 16), *pilings* (23), *seawall* (26), *leader* (27).

CLASSROOM ACTIVITY USING DESCRIPTION

Write a brief, objective description of a common object that you can observe close at hand while sitting in your writing class, such as a pencil, paper clip, piece of clothing, pair of glasses, or coin. Once you have completed your objective description, try to describe the same object in a subjective manner, infusing your description with personal feelings and emotional reactions to it.

WRITING SUGGESTIONS

1. Divide the class into groups of three or four. In your group, take turns describing some specific beautiful or remarkable thing to the others as if they were blind. You may actually want to bring an object to observe while your classmates cover their eyes. Help each other find the best words to create a vivid verbal picture. Write your description in a couple of brief paragraphs, retaining the informal style of your speaking voice.

2. McDonald's "A View from the Bridge" is yet another in the long line of historical anecdotes and tales about the sport of fishing known as "fish stories." The theme, or *motif* as folklorists would put it, is characterized by exaggeration about the size of a fish, its special features, or a description of the tremendous battle that took place in landing it. Most of these tales "grow" with each retelling — the fish becomes bigger and the battle more ferocious — but always the tales are highly entertaining for both storyteller and listener. In McDonald's case the fish is extraordinarily beautiful and the battle very challenging given the boy's blindness. The story is not funny, but it is entertaining for its descriptive passages. It is, moreover, highly instructive in a number of ways. Write an essay in which you tell a "fish story" of your own, using passages of description about the fish as well as the task of catching it. Make sure your essay also reveals some larger, significant truth or life lesson beyond simply the catching of a fish.

Aravaipa Canyon

Edward Abbey

Edward Abbey (1927–1989) wrote numerous novels, including two that were adapted for film: The Brave Cowboy *(1958), which was released as a film in 1962 under the title* Lonely Are the Brave, *and* Fire on the Mountain *(1962). He is best known, however, for his many volumes of nature writings. Variously called an ecologist, a naturalist, and an environmental activist, Abbey described himself simply as "one who loves the unfenced country." He had a particular love for the American Southwest, where he worked for many years as a ranger in the National Park Service. In his collections of nonfiction essays,* including Desert Solitaire *(1968),* The Journey Home *(1977), and* Abbey's Road *(1979), Abbey celebrated the Southwest and made a passionate case for the preservation of its natural wonders.*

"Aravaipa Canyon," first published in Down River *(1982), is a strong example of the rich descriptive prose in which he expressed his belief in the sacred power of the landscape.*

PREPARING TO READ

Recall a natural setting that you found particularly beautiful, impressive, or awe-inspiring. Describe this setting using rich and evocative details.

Southeast of Phoenix and northeast of Tucson, in the Pinal Mountains, is a short deep gorge called Aravaipa Canyon. It is among the few places in Arizona with a permanent stream of water and in popular estimation one of the most beautiful. I am giving away no secrets here: Aravaipa Canyon has long been well known to hikers, campers, horsemen, and hunters from the nearby cities. The federal Bureau of Land Management (BLM), charged with administration of the canyon, recently decreed it an official Primitive Area, thus guaranteeing its fame. Demand for enjoyment of the canyon is so great that the BLM has been obliged to institute a rationing program: no one camps here without a permit and only a limited number of such permits are issued.

Two friends and I took a walk into Aravaipa Canyon a few days ago. We walked because there is no road. There is hardly even a foot trail. Twelve miles long from end to end, the canyon is mostly occupied by the little river which gives it its name, and by stream banks piled with slabs of fallen rock from the cliffs above, the whole overgrown with cactus, trees, and riparian desert shrubbery.

Aravaipa is an Apache name (some say Pima, some say Papago) and the commonly accepted meaning is "laughing waters." The name fits. The stream is brisk, clear, about a foot deep at normal flow levels,

1

2

3

churning its way around boulders, rippling over gravelbars, plunging into pools with bright and noisy vivacity. Schools of loach minnow, roundtail chub, spike dace, and Gila mudsuckers—rare and endemic species—slip and slither past your ankles as you wade into the current. The water is too warm to support trout or other varieties of what are called game fish; the fish here live out their lives undisturbed by anything more than horses' hooves and the sneaker-shod feet of hikers. (PLEASE DO NOT MOLEST THE FISH.)

The Apaches who gave the name to this water and this canyon are   4
not around anymore. Most of that particular band—unarmed old men, women, children—huddled in a cave near the mouth of Aravaipa Canyon, were exterminated in the 1880s by a death squad of American pioneers, aided by Mexicans and Papagos, from the nearby city of Tucson. The reason for this vigilante action is obscure (suspicion of murder and cattle stealing) but the results were clear. No more Apaches in Aravaipa Canyon. During pauses in the gunfire, as the pioneers reloaded their rifles, the surviving Indians could have heard the sound of laughing waters. One hundred and twenty-five were killed, the remainder relocated in the White Mountain Reservation to the northeast. Since then those people have given us no back talk at all.

Trudging upstream and over rocky little beaches, we are no more   5
troubled by ancient history than are the mudsuckers in the pools. We prefer to enjoy the scenery. The stone walls stand up on both sides, twelve hundred feet high in the heart of the canyon. The rock is of volcanic origin, rosy-colored andesites and buff, golden, consolidated tuff. Cleavages and fractures across the face of the walls form perfect stairways and sometimes sloping ramps, slick as sidewalks. On the beaches lie obsidian boulders streaked with veins of quartzite and pegmatite.

The walls bristle with spiky rock gardens of formidable desert vege-   6
tation. Most prominent is the giant saguaro cactus, growing five to fifty feet tall out of crevices in the stone you might think could barely lodge a flower. The barrel cactus, with its pink fishhook thorns, thrives here on the sunny side; and clusters of hedgehog cactus, and prickly pear with names like clockface and cows-tongue, have wedged roots into the rock. Since most of the wall is vertical, parallel to gravity, these plants grow first outward then upward, forming right-angled bends near the base. It looks difficult but they do it. They like it here.

Also present are tangles of buckhorn, staghorn, chainfruit, and   7
teddybear cholla; the teddybear cholla is a cactus so thick with spines it glistens under the sun as if covered with fur. From more comfortable niches in the rock grow plants like the sotol, a thing with sawtooth leaves and a flower stalk ten feet tall. The agave, a type of lily, is even bigger, and its leaves are long, rigid, pointed like bayonets. Near the summit of the cliffs, where the moisture is insufficient to support

cactus, we see gray-green streaks of lichen clinging to the stone like a mold.

The prospect at streamside is conventionally sylvan, restful to desert-weary eyes. Great cottonwoods and sycamores shade the creek's stony shores; when we're not wading in water we're wading through a crashing autumn debris of green-gold cottonwood and dusty-red sycamore leaves. Other trees flourish here—willow, salt cedar, alder, desert hackberry, and a kind of wild walnut. Cracked with stones, the nuts yield a sweet but frugal meat. At the water's edge is a nearly continuous growth of peppery-flavored watercress. The stagnant pools are full of algae; and small pale frogs, treefrogs, and leopard frogs leap from the bank at our approach and dive into the water; they swim for the deeps with kicking legs, quick breaststrokes. 8

We pass shadowy, intriguing side canyons with names like Painted Cave (ancient pictographs), Iceberg (where the sun seldom shines), and Virgus (named in honor of himself by an early settler in the area). At midday we enter a further side canyon, one called Horse-camp, and linger here for a lunch of bread, cheese, and water. We contemplate what appears to be a bottomless pool. 9

The water in this pool has a dark clarity, like smoked glass, transparent but obscure. We see a waterlogged branch six feet down resting on a ledge but cannot see to the bottom. The water feels intensely cold to hand and foot; a few tadpoles have attached themselves to the stony rim of the pool just beneath the surface of the water. They are sluggish, barely animate. One waterbug, the kind called boatman, propels itself with limp oars down toward darkness when I extend my hand toward it. 10

Above the pool is a thirty-foot bluff of sheer, vesiculated, fine-grained, monolithic gray rock with a glossy chute carved down its face. Flash floods, pouring down that chute with driving force, must have drilled this basin in the rock below. The process would require a generous allowance of time—ten thousand, twenty thousand years—give or take a few thousand. Only a trickle of water from a ring of seeps enters the pool now, on this hot still blazing day in December. Feels like 80°F; a month from now it may be freezing; in June 110°. In the silence I hear the rasping chant of locusts—that universal lament for mortality and time—here in this canyon where winter seldom comes. 11

The black and bottomless pool gleams in the shining rock—a sinister paradox, to a fanciful mind. To any man of natural piety this pool, this place, this silence, would suggest reverence, even fear. But I'm an apostate Presbyterian from a long-ago Pennsylvania: I shuck my clothes, jump in, and touch bottom only ten feet down. Bedrock bottom, as I'd expected, and if any Grendels dwell in this inky pool they're not inclined to reveal themselves today. 12

We return to the Aravaipa. Halfway back to camp and the canyon 13
entrance we pause to inspect a sycamore that seems to be embracing a
boulder. The trunk of the tree has grown around the rock. Feeling the
tree for better understanding, I hear a clatter of loose stones, look up,
and see six, seven, eight bighorn sheep perched on the rimrock a hundred feet above us. Three rams, five ewes. They are browsing at the local
salad bar—brittlebush, desert holly, bursage, and jojoba—aware of us
but not alarmed. We watch them for a long time as they move casually
along the rim and up a talus slope beyond, eating as they go, halting
now and then to stare back at the humans staring up at them.

Once, years before, I had glimpsed a mountain lion in this canyon, 14
following me through the twilight. It was the only mountain lion I had
ever seen, so far, in the wild. I stopped, the big cat stopped, we peered at
each other through the gloom. Mutual curiosity: I felt more wonder
than fear. After a minute, or perhaps it was five minutes, I made a move
to turn. The lion leaped up into the rocks and melted away.

We see no mountain lions this evening. Nor any of the local deer, 15
either Sonoran whitetail or the desert mule deer, although the little
heart-shaped tracks of the former are apparent in the sand. Javelina, or
peccary, too, reside in this area; piglike animals with tusks, oversized
heads, and tapering bodies, they roam the slopes and gulches in family
bands (like the Apaches), living on roots, tubers, and innards of barrel
cactus, on grubs, insects, and carrion. Omnivorous, like us, and equally
playful, if not so dangerous. Any desert canyon with permanent water,
like Aravaipa, will be as full of life as it is beautiful.

We stumble homeward over the stones and through the ankle- 16
bone-chilling water. The winter day seems alarmingly short; it is.

We reach the mouth of the canyon and the old trail uphill to the 17
roadhead in time to see the first stars come out. Barely in time. Nightfall
is quick in this arid climate and the air feels already cold. But we have
earned enough memories, stored enough mental-emotional images in
our heads, from one brief day in Aravaipa Canyon, to enrich the urban
days to come. As Thoreau found a universe in the woods around Concord, any person whose senses are alive can make a world of any natural
place, however limited it might seem, on this subtle planet of ours.

"The world is big but it is comprehensible," says R. Buckminster 18
Fuller. But it seems to me that the world is not nearly big enough and
that any portion of its surface, left unpaved and alive, is infinitely rich
in details and relationships, in wonder, beauty, mystery, comprehensible only in part. The very existence of existence is itself suggestive of
the unknown—not a problem but a mystery.

We will never get to the end of it, never plumb the bottom of it, 19
never know the whole of even so small and trivial and useless and precious a place as Aravaipa. Therein lies our redemption.

THINKING CRITICALLY ABOUT THE TEXT

Aravaipa Canyon is under the protection of the Bureau of Land Management. For what reasons should the government restrict land use in a nation with a relatively unrestricted economy? Given Abbey's commentary in this essay, how might he answer that question? What are some aspects of the question that he doesn't address?

QUESTIONS ON SUBJECT

1. Abbey writes that he and his companions "are no more troubled by ancient history than are the mudsuckers in the pools" (paragraph 5). Why not? What does he mean by this statement? If his assertion is true, why does he include a long paragraph about the canyon's ancient history? Why is his tone in paragraph 4 ironic? (Glossary: *Irony*)

2. What happened to the Apaches who used to live in Aravaipa Canyon, according to Abbey?

3. What does Abbey mean when he writes "any person whose senses are alive can make a world of any natural place, however limited it might seem, on this subtle planet of ours" (paragraph 17)?

4. Why, in your opinion, does Abbey dive into the pool? (Before answering, consider the final sentence of paragraph 18.)

5. What does the last paragraph mean, particularly in regard to the word *redemption*? How does this paragraph contradict the Buckminster Fuller quotation in paragraph 18?

QUESTIONS ON STRATEGY

1. How does Abbey use his first paragraph to establish a context for his later description?

2. Abbey gives a chronological account of his explorations of Aravaipa Canyon; that is, he recounts the events of the day in the order in which they happened. How does he organize his descriptions of what he experienced?

3. Much of this essay is composed of objective, factual description, but Abbey also shares with the reader some subjective thoughts inspired by his exploration of Aravaipa Canyon. (Glossary: *Objective/Subjective*) Note the places where he expresses his own opinions. As a writer, what effect does he achieve through the contrast between objective and subjective detail?

4. This primarily descriptive essay makes clear the author's opinion about the relationship of humans to nature. What is his argument? Does it take the form of a thesis statement? Explain.

5. Why does Abbey place the direct argument at the end of the piece rather than at the beginning, where arguments are usually stated?

QUESTIONS ON DICTION AND VOCABULARY

1. What, for Abbey, is both appropriate and ironic about the fact that the commonly accepted meaning of Aravaipa is "laughing waters" (Glossary: *Irony*)?

2. Paragraph 3 ends with an unexpected warning: "(PLEASE DO NOT MOLEST THE FISH.)" Why is it written in capitals and parenthesized? What is the effect on the reader?

3. Abbey pays close attention to the sounds of words, using techniques such as the alliteration found in this sentence in paragraph 5: "Cleavages and fractures across the face of the walls form perfect stairways and sometimes sloping ramps, slick as sidewalks." How does the repeated sound of *s* add to the effectiveness of his description? Find other instances where the author uses repetition of sound to good effect.

4. The words *obscure* (paragraph 10) and *comprehensible* (18) bring strong connotations to the passages in which they are used. What multiple meanings are implied?

5. Abbey uses a great deal of precise terminology in naming what he sees. The following descriptive words, all equally important to the essay, are not restricted to the land and wildlife of Aravaipa Canyon. Be sure you know their meanings to appreciate the description fully: *riparian* (paragraph 2), *vivacity* (3), *endemic* (3), *vigilante* (4), *formidable* (6), *sylvan* (8), *vesiculated* (11), *apostate* (12), *Grendel* (12).

CLASSROOM ACTIVITY USING DESCRIPTION

Think about your topic—the person, place, thing, or concept that lies at the center of your descriptive essay. Make a long list of all the details that you gather through your five senses as well as those that simply come to mind when you consider your topic. Determine a dominant impression that you would like to create, and then choose those details from your list that will best help you form the dominant impression you have in mind. Your instructor may wish to have students go over the items on their lists in class and discuss how effective the items will be in building the dominant impressions.

WRITING SUGGESTIONS

1. Write about a trip you have taken into a natural setting. Using "Aravaipa Canyon" as a model, tell about the trip in chronological order, describing in detail what you saw and experienced. In your writing, make sure you convey the impact the natural setting had on you.

2. Refer to your Thinking Critically about the Text answer. Land-use restrictions are a matter of considerable controversy in America today. Which is more important, the development of natural resources or the preservation of wilderness? To reach a decision about any particular piece of land, what issues should be taken into consideration? Who should have the right to decide? Write an essay in support of your own stance toward land use.

Remembering Lobo

Pat Mora

Pat Mora was born in El Paso, Texas, in 1942. She grew up in a mostly Spanish-speaking household greatly influenced by her four grandparents, who had fled to El Paso during the Mexican Revolution in the early part of the twentieth century. Speaking Spanish at home and English in public school, Mora received her B.A. from Texas Western College in 1963 and her M.A. from the University of Texas at El Paso in 1967. As a writer, lecturer, teacher, university administrator, and literacy advocate, Mora has spent her career speaking and writing about the value of family, Mexican-American culture, and the desert. She is the author of twenty works of fiction and nonfiction for children and adults, among them collections of poetry such as Chants (1984), Borders (1986), and Communion (1991) that explore bicultural and bilingual themes. House of Houses (1997), perhaps her most important work, is a family memoir that uses the metaphor of a house to tell the generational story of her family in the span of a single year.

In "Remembering Lobo," taken from Nepantla: Essays from the Middle (1993), Mora offers us a poignant portrait of her Aunt Ignacia, better known to family members as Lobo. With telling details and touching devotion, Mora describes her aunt and shows how Lobo "taught [her] much about one of our greatest challenges as human beings: loving well."

PREPARING TO READ

Think about one of your favorite aunts or uncles. What makes that person someone special for you? Is it that the person has a special affection for you? Is it because the person has special character traits that you'd like to emulate or think are in some way strange but appealing? Or is it that the person shares some family traits with your parents? Explain.

We called her *Lobo*. The word means "wolf" in Spanish, an odd name for a generous and loving aunt. Like all names it became synonymous with her, and to this day returns me to my childself. Although the name seemed perfectly natural to us and to our friends, it did cause frowns from strangers throughout the years. I particularly remember one hot afternoon when on a crowded streetcar between the border cities of El Paso and Juarez, I momentarily lost sight of her. "Lobo! Lobo!" I cried in panic. Annoyed faces peered at me, disappointed at such disrespect to a white-haired woman. 1

Actually the fault was hers. She lived with us for years, and when she arrived home from work in the evening, she'd knock on our front door and ask, "*¿Dónde están mis lobitos?*" "Where are my little wolves?" 2

Gradually she became our *lobo*, a spinster aunt who gathered the 3
four of us around her, tying us to her for life by giving us all she had.
Sometimes to tease her we would call her by her real name. *"¿Dónde
está Ignacia?"* we would ask. Lobo would laugh and say, "She is a ghost."

To all of us in nuclear families today, the notion of an extended 4
family under one roof seems archaic, complicated. We treasure our private space. I will always marvel at the generosity of my parents, who
opened their door to both my grandmother and Lobo. No doubt I am
drawn to the elderly because I grew up with two entirely different
white-haired women who worried about me, tucked me in at night,
made me tomato soup or hot *hierbabuena* (mint tea) when I was ill.

Lobo grew up in Mexico, the daughter of a circuit judge, my grand- 5
father. She was a wonderful storyteller and over and over told us about
the night her father, a widower, brought his grown daughters on a
flatbed truck across the Rio Grande at the time of the Mexican Revolution. All their possessions were left in Mexico. Lobo had not been
wealthy, but she had probably never expected to have to find a job and
learn English.

When she lived with us, she worked in the linens section of a local 6
department store. Her area was called "piece goods and bedding." Lobo
never sewed, but she would talk about materials she sold, using words I
never completely understood, such as *pique* and *broadcloth*. Sometimes
I still whisper such words just to remind myself of her. I'll always savor
the way she would order "sweet milk" at restaurants. The precision of a
speaker new to the language.

Lobo saved her money to take us out to dinner and a movie, to take 7
us to Los Angeles in the summer, to buy us shiny black shoes for Christmas. Though she never married and never bore children, Lobo taught
me much about one of our greatest challenges as human beings: loving
well. I don't think she ever discussed the subject with me, but through
the years she lived her love, and I was privileged to watch.

She died at ninety-four. She was no sweet, docile Mexican woman 8
dying with perfect resignation. Some of her last words before drifting
into semiconsciousness were loud words of annoyance at the incompetence of nurses and doctors.

"No sirven." "They're worthless," she'd say to me in Spanish. 9

"They don't know what they're doing. My throat is hurting and 10
they're taking X rays. Tell them to take care of my throat first."

I was busy striving for my cherished middle-class politeness. "Shh, 11
shh," I'd say. "They're doing the best they can."

"Well, it's not good enough," she'd say, sitting up in anger. 12

Lobo was a woman of fierce feelings, of strong opinions. She was a 13
woman who literally whistled while she worked. The best way to cheer
her when she'd visit my young children was to ask for her help. Ask her
to make a bed, fold laundry, set the table or dry dishes, and the

whistling would begin as she moved about her task. Like all of us, she loved being needed. Understandable, then, that she muttered in annoyance when her body began to fail her. She was a woman who found self-definition and joy in visibly showing her family her love for us by bringing us hot *té de canela* (cinnamon tea) in the middle of the night to ease a cough, by bringing us comics and candy whenever she returned home. A life of giving.

One of my last memories of her is a visit I made to her on November 2, *El Día de los Muertos*, or All Souls' Day. She was sitting in her rocking chair, smiling wistfully. The source of the smile may seem a bit bizarre to a U.S. audience. She was fondly remembering past visits to the local cemetery on this religious feast day.   14

"What a silly old woman I have become," she said. "Here I sit in my rocking chair all day on All Souls' Day, sitting when I should be out there. At the cemetery. Taking good care of *mis muertos*, my dead ones.   15

"What a time I used to have. I'd wake while it was still dark outside. I'd hear the first morning birds, and my fingers would almost itch to begin. By six I'd be having a hot bath, dressing carefully in black, wanting *mis muertos* to be proud of me, proud to have me looking respectable and proud to have their graves taken care of. I'd have my black coffee and plenty of toast. You know the way I like it. Well browned and well buttered. I wanted to be ready to work hard.   16

"The bus ride to the other side of town was a long one, but I'd say a rosary and plan my day. I'd hope that my perfume wasn't too strong and yet would remind others that I was a lady.   17

"The air at the cemetery gates was full of chrysanthemums: that strong, sharp, fall smell. I'd buy tin cans full of the gold and wine flowers. How I liked seeing aunts and uncles who were also there to care for the graves of their loved ones. We'd hug. Happy together.   18

"Then it was time to begin. The smell of chrysanthemums was like a whiff of pure energy. I'd pull the heavy hose and wash the gravestones over and over, listening to the water pelting away the desert sand. I always brought newspaper. I'd kneel on the few patches of grass, and I'd scrub and scrub, shining the gray stones, leaning back on my knees to rest for a bit and then scrubbing again. Finally a relative from nearby would say, 'Ya, ya, Nacha,' and laugh. Enough. I'd stop, blink my eyes to return from my trance. Slightly dazed, I'd stand slowly, place a can of chrysanthemums before each grave.   19

"Sometimes I would just stand there in the desert sun and listen. I'd hear the quiet crying of people visiting new graves; I'd hear families exchanging gossip while they worked.   20

"One time I heard my aunt scolding her dead husband. She'd sweep his gravestone and say, '¿Porqué? Why did you do this, you thoughtless man? Why did you go and leave me like this? You know I don't like to be alone. Why did you stop living?' Such a sight to see my   21 aunt with her proper black hat and her fine dress and her carefully polished shoes muttering away for all to hear.

"To stifle my laughter, I had to cover my mouth with my hands."

THINKING CRITICALLY ABOUT THE TEXT

Mora grew up living with an extended family that included her grandmother and aunt. Why does she "marvel at the generosity of [her] parents" in this regard (paragraph 4)? What concessions might her parents have made to help make their living arrangement work? What were the benefits of the arrangement for Mora in particular?

QUESTIONS ON SUBJECT

1. Why do you think Mora's aunt Ignacia wanted to be called "Lobo"?
2. What does Mora mean when she writes in paragraph 1 about the name Lobo: "Like all names it became synonymous with her, and to this day returns me to my childself" (paragraph 1)?
3. Mora writes in paragraph 13 that Lobo "found self-definition and joy in visibly showing her family her love." In what acts did Lobo specifically, according to Mora, exhibit her love?
4. Why was All Souls' Day so important to Lobo? Why was it important for her to go to the cemetery on this day?
5. When she was dying, Lobo became annoyed at her nurses. What was her problem? How does Mora inform us of Lobo's problem with her nurses? (Glossary: *Dialogue*)

QUESTIONS ON STRATEGY

1. How does Mora show us Lobo's playful side?
2. How does the image of the "wolf" work in furthering Mora's purpose? (Glossary: *Figures of Speech*)
3. What advantage does Mora gain by using food, particularly drink, to help her describe Lobo? (Glossary: *Figures of Speech*)
4. Mora writes in paragraph 8 that Lobo was "no sweet, docile Mexican woman dying with perfect resignation." How does Mora show us this side of Lobo?
5. How does Mora show us Lobo's respect for All Souls' Day? (Glossary: *Illustration, Dialogue*)

QUESTIONS ON DICTION AND VOCABULARY

1. Why do you suppose Mora invents the term "childself" instead of using the word *childhood* (paragraph 1)? How does the new term help Mora accomplish her purpose?

2. What does Mora accomplish by adding some Spanish words and phrases to her description of Lobo?

3. Mora says in paragraph 6 that Lobo used words in referring to her job that she [Mora] "never completely understood." What were those words and why did she not bother to find out their meanings? What magic qualities might they have had for Mora?

CLASSROOM ACTIVITY USING DESCRIPTION

Once you have made a list of all the characteristics and features of the object of your descriptive essay, whether it be a person, place, thing, or concept, you need to present the features according to some organizing principle that gives them shape and power. Depending on your purpose you could present the same set of details and order them in several different ways. Suppose, for example, you wanted to describe a favorite teacher you had in high school. You could present your teacher's qualities according to a logical plan ranging from the least important to the most important, or you could describe her qualities in a chronological manner from the time you first met her to the time you had to leave her class. You could also organize your description according to her obvious physical attributes and then move on to describe the more complex parts of her personality, in effect moving from the outer to the inner person.

Organizational possibilities are many and varied, reflecting your purpose and the subject or object you are attempting to describe. In order to see how this works, first make a list of descriptive features for an object of your choice and then organize them according to any two of the following principles:

Smallest to largest

Least to most important

Outside to inside

Far to near

Left to right

Easiest to most difficult to understand

Specific to general

WRITING SUGGESTIONS

1. Using Mora's essay as a model and the questions in the Preparing to Read prompt for this essay, write a description of one of your favorite aunts or uncles. Keep in mind that effective description requires examples drawn from sense perceptions, telling details, thoughtful organization, showing and not telling, and the use of concrete nouns and strong action verbs, as well as figurative language. Above all, think about the dominant impression you wish to create and your larger purpose in describing the person you choose as your subject.

2. Mora returned the gift of love that her aunt bestowed on her by writing about Lobo and, in a sense, immortalized her. In similar fashion, describe

a relative, friend, or perhaps stranger who has given you a character-building gift, whether it be perseverance, courage, dedication, honesty, or some other intangible trait—and how that gift was passed on to you by your subject. Describe how your subject was able to influence you so importantly and how you have put that gift to good use in your own life.

The Barrio

Robert Ramírez

Robert Ramírez was born in 1949 and was raised in Edinburg, Texas, near the Mexican border. He graduated from the University of Texas–Pan American and then worked in several communications-related jobs before joining KGBT-TV in Harlingen, Texas, where he was an anchor. He then moved to finance and worked for a time in banking and as a development officer responsible for alumni fund-raising for his alma mater.

Ramírez's knowledge of the barrio allows him to paint an affectionate portrait of barrio life that nevertheless has a hard edge. His barrio is colorful but not romantic, and his description raises important societal issues as it describes the vibrant community.

PREPARING TO READ

Describe the neighborhood in which you grew up or the most memorable neighborhood you ever encountered. Did you like it? Why or why not? How strong was the sense of community between neighbors? How did it contrast with other neighborhoods nearby?

The train, its metal wheels squealing as they spin along the silvery tracks, rolls slower now. Through the gaps between the cars blinks a streetlamp, and this pulsing light on a barrio streetcorner beats slower, like a weary heartbeat, until the train shudders to a halt, the light goes out, and the barrio is deep asleep. 1

Throughout Aztlán (the Nahuatl term meaning "land to the north"), trains grumble along the edges of a sleeping people. From Lower California, through the blistering Southwest, down the Rio Grande to the muddy Gulf, the darkness and mystery of dreams engulf communities fenced off by railroads, canals, and expressways. Paradoxical communities, isolated from the rest of the town by concrete columned monuments of progress, yet stranded in the past. They are surrounded by change. It eludes their reach, in their own backyards, and the people, unable and unwilling to see the future, or even touch the present, perpetuate the past. 2

Leaning from the expressway or jolting across the tracks, one enters a different physical world permeated by a different attitude. The physical dimensions are impressive. It is a large section of town which extends for fifteen blocks north and south along the tracks, and then advances eastward, thinning into nothingness beyond the city limits. Within the invisible (yet sensible) walls of the barrio, are many, many 3 people living in too few houses. The homes, however, are much more numerous than on the outside.

Members of the barrio describe the entire area as their home. It is a home, but it is more than this. The barrio is a refuge from the harshness and the coldness of the Anglo world. It is a forced refuge. The leprous people are isolated from the rest of the community and contained in their section of town. The stoical pariahs of the barrio accept their fate, and from the angry seeds of rejection grow the flowers of closeness between outcasts, not the thorns of bitterness and the mad desire to flee. There is no want to escape, for the feeling of the barrio is known only to its inhabitants, and the material needs of life can also be found here.   4

The *tortillería* fires up its machinery three times a day, producing steaming, round, flat slices of barrio bread. In the winter, the warmth of the tortilla factory is a wool *sarape* in the chilly morning hours, but in the summer, it unbearably toasts every noontime customer.   5

The *panadería* sends its sweet messenger aroma down the dimly lit street, announcing the arrival of fresh, hot sugary *pan dulce*.   6

The small corner grocery serves the meal-to-meal needs of customers, and the owner, a part of the neighborhood, willingly gives credit to people unable to pay cash for foodstuffs.   7

The barbershop is a living room with hydraulic chairs, radio, and television, where old friends meet and speak of life as their salted hair falls aimlessly about them.   8

The pool hall is a junior level country club where 'chucos, strangers in their own land, get together to shoot pool and rap, while veterans, unaware of the cracking, popping balls on the green felt, complacently play dominoes beneath rudely hung *Playboy* foldouts.   9

The *cantina* is the night spot of the barrio. It is the country club and the den where the rites of puberty are enacted. Here the young become men. It is in the taverns that the young dude shows his *machismo* through the quantity of beer he can hold, the stories of *rucas* he has had, and his willingness and ability to defend his image against hardened and scarred old lions.   10

No, there is no frantic wish to flee. It would be absurd to leave the familiar and nervously step into the strange and cold Anglo community when the needs of the Chicano can be met in the barrio.   11

The barrio is closeness. From the family living unit, familial relationships stretch out to immediate neighbors, down the block, around the corner, and to all parts of the barrio. The feeling of family, a rare and treasurable sentiment, pervades and accounts for the inability of the people to leave. The barrio is this attitude manifested on the countenances of the people, on the faces of their homes, and in the gaiety of their gardens.   12

The color-splashed homes arrest your eyes, arouse your curiosity, and make you wonder what life scenes are being played out in them.   13

The flimsy, brightly colored, wood-frame houses ignore no neon-brilliant color. Houses trimmed in orange, chartreuse, lime-green, yellow, and mixtures of these and other hues beckon the beholder to reflect on the peculiarity of each home. Passing through this land is refreshing like Brubeck, not narcotizing like revolting rows of similar houses, which neither offend nor please.

In the evenings, the porches and front yards are occupied with men   14
calmly talking over the noise of children playing baseball in the unpaved extension of the living room, while the women cook supper or gossip with female neighbors as they water their *jardines*. The gardens mutely echo the expressive verses of the colorful houses. The denseness of multicolored plants and trees gives the house the appearance of an oasis or a tropical island hideaway, sheltered from the rest of the world.

Fences are common in the barrio, but they are fences and not the   15
walls of the Anglo community. On the western side of town, the high wooden fences between houses are thick, impenetrable walls, built to keep the neighbors at bay. In the barrio, the fences may be rusty, wire contraptions or thick green shrubs. In either case you can see through them and feel no sense of intrusion when you cross them.

Many lower-income families of the barrio manage to maintain a   16
comfortable standard of living through the communal action of family members who contribute their wages to the head of the family. Economic need creates interdependence and closeness. Small barefooted boys sell papers on cool, dark Sunday mornings, deny themselves pleasantries, and give their earnings to *mamá*. The older the child, the greater the responsibility to help the head of the household provide for the rest of the family.

There are those, too, who for a number of reasons have not achieved   17
a relative sense of financial security. Perhaps it results from too many children too soon, but it is the homes of these people and their situation that
numbs rather than charms. Their houses, aged and bent, oozing children,
are fissures in the horn of plenty. Their wooden homes may have brick-
pattern asbestos tile on the outer walls, but the tile is not convincing.

Unable to pay city taxes or incapable of influencing the city to live   18
up to its duty to serve all the citizens, the poorer barrio families remain
trapped in the nineteenth century and survive as best they can. The
backyards have well-worn paths to the outhouses, which sit near the
alley. Running water is considered a luxury in some parts of the barrio.
Decent drainage is usually unknown, and when it rains, the water
stands for days, an incubator of health hazards and an avoidable nui-
sance. Streets, costly to pave, remain rough, rocky trails. Tires do not
last long, and the constant rattling and shaking grind away a car's life
and spread dust through screen windows.

The houses and their *jardines*, the jollity of the people in an adverse   19
world, the brightly feathered alarm clock pecking away at supper and
cautiously eyeing the children playing nearby, produce a mystifying
sensation at finding the noble savage alive in the twentieth century. It
is easy to look at the positive qualities of life in the barrio, and look at
them with a distantly envious feeling. One wishes to experience the
feelings of the barrio and not the hardships. Remembering the illness,
the hunger, the feeling of time running out on you, the walls, both real
and imagined, reflecting on living in the past, one finds his envy
becoming more elusive, until it has vanished altogether.

Back now beyond the tracks, the train creaks and groans, the cars   20
jostle each other down the track, and as the light begins its pulsing, the
barrio, with all its meanings, greets a new dawn with yawns and restless
stretchings.

THINKING CRITICALLY ABOUT THE TEXT

Does Ramírez's essay leave you with a positive or negative image of the barrio? Is it a place you would like to live in, visit, or avoid? Explain your answer.

QUESTIONS ON SUBJECT

1. Based on Ramírez's essay, what is the barrio? Why do you think that
   Ramírez uses the image of the train to introduce and close his essay
   about the barrio?

2. Why does Ramírez refer to the barrios of the Southwest as "paradoxical
   communities" (paragraph 2)?

3. In paragraph 4, Ramírez states that residents consider the barrio something more than a home. What does he mean? In what ways is it more
   than just a place where they live?

4. Why are the color schemes of the houses in the barrio striking? How do they contrast with houses in other areas of town? (Glossary: *Comparison and Contrast*)

5. Many of the barrio residents are able to achieve financial security. How are they able to do this? What is life like for those who cannot?

QUESTIONS ON STRATEGY

1. Explain Ramírez's use of the imagery of walls and fences to describe a sense of cultural isolation. What might this imagery symbolize?

2. Ramírez uses several metaphors throughout his essay. (Glossary: *Figures of Speech*) Identify them, and discuss how they contribute to the essay.

3. Ramírez begins his essay with a relatively positive picture of the barrio but ends on a more disheartening note. (Glossary: *Beginnings/Endings*) Why has he organized his essay this way? What might the effect have been if he had reversed the images?

4. Ramírez goes into detail about the many groups living in the barrio. How does his subtle use of division and classification add to his description of the barrio? (Glossary: *Classification; Division*) In what ways do the groups he identifies contribute to the unity of life in the barrio?

5. Ramírez invokes such warm images of the barrio that his statement that its inhabitants do not wish to leave seems benign. In the end, however, it has a somewhat ominous ring. How does the description of the barrio have two components, one good and one bad? What are the two sides of the barrio's embrace for the residents?

QUESTIONS ON DICTION AND VOCABULARY

1. Ramírez uses Spanish phrases throughout his essay. Why do you suppose he uses them? What is their effect on the reader? He also uses the words *home, refuge, family*, and *closeness*. In what ways, if any, are they essential to his purpose? (Glossary: *Purpose*)

2. Ramírez calls barrio residents "the leprous people" (paragraph 4). What does the word *leprous* connote in the context of this essay? (Glossary: *Connotation/Denotation*) Why do you think Ramírez chose to use such a strong word to communicate the segregation of the community?

3. In paragraph 6, Ramírez uses personification when he calls the aroma of freshly baked sweet rolls a "messenger" who announces the arrival of the baked goods. Cite other words or phrases that Ramírez uses to give human characteristics to the barrio.

CLASSROOM ACTIVITY USING DESCRIPTION

1. Using action verbs can make a major difference in the quality of your writing. Instead of the weak verb *talk*, it is more descriptive to use a strong verb like *mutter, ramble, chatter, sputter, tattle, yell*, or *scream*, assuming the word you choose is appropriate to your context. Review a

draft of a descriptive essay that you have written and look for at least three weak verbs you have used—verbs that do not add very much descriptive punch—and make a list of at least three alternatives you could replace them with. Be sure that the meaning of each of your alternative action verbs supports your meaning and fits the context in which you use it.

2. The photo on page 137 depicts a contemporary daytime street scene in a small-town setting or a neighborhood of a bigger urban area. Examine the photo carefully. It may be a barrio as such or it may simply be a particular area of a city. Based on the visual details in the photograph, what can you say about the community of people who live in the neighborhood? Which details suggest the area's ethnicity and socioeconomic status? What can you say about the pace of life as depicted in the photograph? From what you see, is this an appealing neighborhood, in your judgment? How does this scene differ from the portrait of a barrio that Ramírez paints in his essay?

WRITING SUGGESTIONS

1. Ramírez frames his essay with the image of a train rumbling past the sleeping residents. Using Ramírez's essay as a model, write a descriptive essay about the place you currently live, whether it is a dorm, an apartment, or a neighborhood with an identity, such as a barrio. (Glossary: *Description*) Use a metaphorical image to frame your essay. (Glossary: *Figures of Speech*) What image is both a part of life where you live and an effective metaphor for the life you lead there?

2. Write a comparison and contrast essay in which you compare where you live now with another residence. (Glossary: *Comparison and Contrast*) Where are you the most comfortable? What about your current surroundings do you like? What do you dislike? How does it compare with your hometown, your first apartment, or another place you have lived? If and when you move on, where do you hope to go?

Sister Flowers

Maya Angelou

Best-selling author and poet Maya Angelou was born in 1928. She is an educator, historian, actress, playwright, civil rights activist, producer, and director. She is best known as the author of I Know Why the Caged Bird Sings *(1970), the first book in a series that constitutes her recently completed autobiography, and for "On the Pulse of the Morning," a characteristically optimistic poem on the need for personal and national renewal that she read at President Clinton's inauguration in 1993. Starting with her beginnings in St. Louis in 1928, Angelou's autobiography presents a joyful triumph over hardships that test her courage and threaten her spirit. It includes the titles* All God's Children Need Traveling Shoes *(1986),* Wouldn't Take Anything for My Journey Now *(1993), and* Heart of a Woman *(1997). The sixth and final book in the series,* A Song Flung Up to Heaven, *was published in 2002. Several volumes of her poetry were collected in* Complete Collected Poems of Maya Angelou *in 1994.*

In the following excerpt from I Know Why the Caged Bird Sings, *Angelou describes a family friend who had a major impact on her early life. As you read, notice the way Angelou describes Sister Flowers's physical presence, her stately manners, and the guidance she offered her as a youngster.*

PREPARING TO READ

Think about a major crisis you have had to face in your life thus far. Is there someone who has come to your aid, offering solid advice and comforting support? How would you describe that person? What physical and personality traits characterize that person?

For nearly a year [after I was raped], I sopped around the house, the Store, the school and the church, like an old biscuit, dirty and inedible. Then I met, or rather got to know, the lady who threw me my first life line.

Mrs. Bertha Flowers was the aristocrat of Black Stamps. She had the grace of control to appear warm in the coldest weather, and on the Arkansas summer days it seemed she had a private breeze which swirled around, cooling her. She was thin without the taut look of wiry people, and her printed voile dresses and flowered hats were as right for her as denim overalls for a farmer. She was our side's answer to the richest white woman in town.

Her skin was a rich black that would have peeled like a plum if snagged, but then no one would have thought of getting close enough to Mrs. Flowers to ruffle her dress, let alone snag her skin. She didn't encourage familiarity. She wore gloves too.

1

2

3

I don't think I ever saw Mrs. Flowers laugh, but she smiled often. A 4
slow widening of her thin black lips to show even, small white teeth,
then the slow effortless closing. When she chose to smile on me, I
always wanted to thank her. The action was so graceful and inclusively
benign.

She was one of the few gentlewomen I have ever known, and has 5
remained throughout my life the measure of what a human being
can be.

Momma had a strange relationship with her. Most often when she 6
passed on the road in front of the Store, she spoke to Momma in that
soft yet carrying voice, "Good day, Mrs. Henderson." Momma
responded with "How you, Sister Flowers?"

Mrs. Flowers didn't belong to our church, nor was she Momma's 7
familiar. Why on earth did she insist on calling her Sister Flowers?
Shame made me want to hide my face. Mrs. Flowers deserved better
than to be called Sister. Then, Momma left out the verb. Why not ask,
"How *are* you, *Mrs.* Flowers?" With the unbalanced passion of the
young, I hated her for showing her ignorance to Mrs. Flowers. It didn't
occur to me for many years that they were as alike as sisters, separated
only by formal education.

Although I was upset, neither of the women was in the least shaken 8
by what I thought an unceremonious greeting. Mrs. Flowers would
continue her easy gait up the hill to her little bungalow, and Momma
kept on shelling peas or doing whatever had brought her to the front
porch.

Occasionally, though, Mrs. Flowers would drift off the road and 9
down to the Store and Momma would say to me, "Sister, you go on and
play." As she left I would hear the beginning of an intimate conversation. Momma persistently using the wrong verb, or none at all.

"Brother and Sister Wilcox is sho'ly the meanest —" "Is," Momma? 10
"Is"? Oh, please, not "is," Momma, for two or more. But they talked,
and from the side of the building where I waited for the ground to open
up and swallow me, I heard the soft-voiced Mrs. Flowers and the tex-
tured voice of my grandmother merging and melting. They were interrupted from time to time by giggles that must have come from Mrs.
Flowers (Momma never giggled in her life). Then she was gone.

She appealed to me because she was like people I had never met 11
personally. Like women in English novels who walked the moors
(whatever they were) with their loyal dogs racing at a respectful distance. Like the women who sat in front of roaring fireplaces, drinking
tea incessantly from silver trays full of scones and crumpets. Women
who walked over the "heath" and read morocco-bound books and had
two last names divided by a hyphen. It would be safe to say that she
made me proud to be Negro, just by being herself.

She acted just as refined as whitefolks in the movies and books and she was more beautiful, for none of them could have come near that warm color without looking gray by comparison. 12

It was fortunate that I never saw her in the company of powhite-folks. For since they tend to think of their whiteness as an evenizer, I'm certain that I would have had to hear her spoken to commonly as Bertha, and my image of her would have been shattered like the unmendable Humpty-Dumpty. 13

One summer afternoon, sweet-milk fresh in my memory, she stopped at the Store to buy provisions. Another Negro woman of her health and age would have been expected to carry the paper sacks home in one hand, but Momma said, "Sister Flowers, I'll send Bailey up to your house with these things." 14

She smiled that slow dragging smile, "Thank you, Mrs. Henderson. I'd prefer Marguerite, though." My name was beautiful when she said it. "I've been meaning to talk to her, anyway." They gave each other age-group looks. 15

Momma said, "Well, that's all right then. Sister, go and change your dress. You going to Sister Flowers's." 16

The chifforobe was a maze. What on earth did one put on to go to Mrs. Flowers's house? I knew I shouldn't put on a Sunday dress. It might be sacrilegious. Certainly not a house dress, since I was already wearing a fresh one. I chose a school dress, naturally. It was formal without suggesting that going to Mrs. Flowers's house was equivalent to attending church. 17

I trusted myself back into the Store. 18

"Now, don't you look nice." I had chosen the right thing, for once. . . . 19

There was a little path beside the rocky road, and Mrs. Flowers walked in front swinging her arms and picking her way over the stones. 20

She said, without turning her head, to me, "I hear you're doing very good school work, Marguerite, but that it's all written. The teachers report that they have trouble getting you to talk in class." We passed the triangular farm on our left and the path widened to allow us to walk together. I hung back in the separate unasked and unanswerable questions. 21

"Come and walk along with me, Marguerite." I couldn't have refused even if I wanted to. She pronounced my name so nicely. Or more correctly, she spoke each word with such clarity that I was certain a foreigner who didn't understand English could have understood her. 22

"Now no one is going to make you talk—possibly no one can. But bear in mind, language is man's way of communicating with his fellow man and it is language alone which separates him from the lower animals." That was a totally new idea to me, and I would need time to think about it. 23

"Your grandmother says you read a lot. Every chance you get. 24
That's good, but not good enough. Words mean more than what is set
down on paper. It takes the human voice to infuse them with the
shades of deeper meaning."

I memorized the part about the human voice infusing words. It 25
seemed so valid and poetic.

She said she was going to give me some books and that I not only 26
must read them, I must read them aloud. She suggested that I try to
make a sentence sound in as many different ways as possible.

"I'll accept no excuse if you return a book to me that has been 27
badly handled." My imagination boggled at the punishment I would
deserve if in fact I did abuse a book of Mrs. Flowers's. Death would be
too kind and brief.

The odors in the house surprised me. Somehow I had never con- 28
nected Mrs. Flowers with food or eating or any other common experience of common people. There must have been an outhouse, too, but
my mind never recorded it.

The sweet scent of vanilla had met us as she opened the door. 29

"I made tea cookies this morning. You see, I had planned to invite 30
you for cookies and lemonade so we could have this little chat. The
lemonade is in the icebox."

It followed that Mrs. Flowers would have ice on an ordinary 31
day, when most families in our town bought ice late on Saturdays only
a few times during the summer to be used in the wooden ice-cream
freezers.

She took the bags from me and disappeared through the kitchen 32
door. I looked around the room that I had never in my wildest fantasies
imagined I would see. Browned photographs leered or threatened from
the walls and the white, freshly done curtains pushed against themselves and against the wind. I wanted to gobble up the room entire and
take it to Bailey, who would help me analyze and enjoy it.

"Have a seat, Marguerite. Over there by the table." She carried a 33
platter covered with a tea towel. Although she warned that she hadn't
tried her hand at baking sweets for some time, I was certain that like
everything else about her the cookies would be perfect.

They were flat round wafers, slightly browned on the edges and 34
butter-yellow in the center. With the cold lemonade they were sufficient for childhood's lifelong diet. Remembering my manners, I took
nice little lady-like bites off the edges. She said she had made them
expressly for me and that she had a few in the kitchen that I could take
home to my brother. So I jammed one whole cake in my mouth and
the rough crumbs scratched the insides of my jaws, and if I hadn't had
to swallow, it would have been a dream come true.

As I ate she began the first of what we later called "my lessons in 35
living." She said that I must always be intolerant of ignorance but

understanding of illiteracy. That some people, unable to go to school, were more educated and even more intelligent than college professors. She encouraged me to listen carefully to what country people called mother wit. That in those homely sayings was couched the collective wisdom of generations.

When I finished the cookies she brushed off the table and brought a thick, small book from the bookcase. I had read *A Tale of Two Cities* and found it up to my standards as a romantic novel. She opened the first page and I heard poetry for the first time in my life.

"It was the best of times and the worst of times . . ." Her voice slid in and curved down through and over the words. She was nearly singing. I wanted to look at the pages. Were they the same that I had read? Or were there notes, music, lined on the pages, as in a hymn book? Her sounds began cascading gently. I knew from listening to a thousand preachers that she was nearing the end of her reading, and I hadn't really heard, heard to understand, a single word.

"How do you like that?"

It occurred to me that she expected a response. The sweet vanilla flavor was still on my tongue and her reading was a wonder in my ears. I had to speak.

I said, "Yes, ma'am." It was the least I could do, but it was the most also.

"There's one more thing. Take this book of poems and memorize one for me. Next time you pay me a visit, I want you to recite."

I have tried often to search behind the sophistication of years for the enchantment I so easily found in those gifts. The essence escapes but its aura remains. To be allowed, no, invited, into the private lives of strangers, and to share their joys and fears, was a chance to exchange the Southern bitter wormwood for a cup of mead with Beowulf or a hot cup of tea and milk with Oliver Twist. When I said aloud, "It is a far, far better thing that I do, than I have ever done . . ." tears of love filled my eyes at my selflessness.

On that first day, I ran down the hill and into the road (few cars ever came along it) and had the good sense to stop running before I reached the Store.

I was liked, and what a difference it made. I was respected not as Mrs. Henderson's grandchild or Bailey's sister but for just being Marguerite Johnson.

Childhood's logic never asks to be proved (all conclusions are absolute). I didn't question why Mrs. Flowers had singled me out for attention, nor did it occur to me that Momma might have asked her to give me a little talking to. All I cared about was that she had made tea cookies for *me* and read to *me* from her favorite book. It was enough to prove that she liked me.

THINKING CRITICALLY ABOUT THE TEXT

In paragraph 44 Marguerite indicates how important it was for her to be respected and liked for "just being Marguerite Johnson." Why do you suppose she, in particular, feels that way? Why is it important for anyone to feel that way?

QUESTIONS ON SUBJECT

1. What is Angelou's main point in describing Sister Flowers? Why was Sister Flowers so important to her?

2. What does Angelou mean when she writes that Sister Flowers did not "encourage familiarity" (paragraph 3)?

3. Why does Sister Flowers think that reading is "good, but not good enough" for Marguerite (paragraph 24)?

4. What revelations about race relations in her community growing up does Angelou impart in this selection? What do those revelations add to the point Angelou is trying to make?

5. Why is being liked by Sister Flowers important to Marguerite?

QUESTIONS ON STRATEGY

1. What dominant impression of Sister Flowers does Angelou create in this selection? (Glossary: *Dominant Impression*)

2. To which of the reader's senses does Angelou appeal in describing Sister Flowers? To which senses does she appeal in describing Sister Flowers's house?

3. At the end of her description of Sister Flowers, Angelou implies that at the time it did not occur to her that Sister Flowers might have been asked to give her "a little talking to" (paragraph 45). What clues in the description suggest that Momma asked Sister Flowers to befriend and draw out Marguerite? Why didn't Momma take on that task herself?

4. Why does Angelou have Marguerite imagine the conversations that Momma and Sister Flowers have on several occasions instead of reporting them directly (paragraph 10)?

QUESTIONS ON DICTION AND VOCABULARY

1. Angelou uses figures of speech in paragraphs 1 and 3. Explain how they work and what they add to her description of herself and Sister Flowers. (Glossary: *Figures of Speech*)

2. How do Momma and Sister Flowers differ in their manner of speaking? What annoys Marguerite about the way Momma speaks? Does Momma's speech annoy Sister Flowers? Why, or why not?

3. What do you think Sister Flowers means when she tells Marguerite that "words mean more than what is set down on paper" (paragraph 24)? Why is it important for Sister Flowers to tell Marguerite about this difference between reading and speaking?

CLASSROOM ACTIVITY USING DESCRIPTION

One of the best ways to make a description memorable is to use figurative language such as a simile (making a comparison using *like* or *as*) or a metaphor (making a comparison without the use of *like* or *as*). Create a simile or metaphor that would be helpful in describing each item in the following list. To illustrate the assignment, the first one has been completed for you.

1. a skyscraper: The skyscraper sparkled like a huge glass needle.
2. a huge explosion
3. an intelligent student
4. a crowded bus
5. a slow-moving car
6. a pillow
7. a narrow alley
8. a thick milkshake
9. hot sun
10. a dull knife

WRITING SUGGESTIONS

1. Sister Flowers is an excellent example of a person with grace, charm, spirit, intelligence, generosity, and high-mindedness—personality traits we ourselves might possess or are capable of possessing. Describe someone you know who has similar personality traits and try to imagine what might account for such traits. Can such qualities be learned from a role model? Can they be taught in the abstract?

2. Review your response to the Preparing to Read prompt for this selection. How would you describe the person who came along at just the right time to help you when you were having a personal crisis? Write a description of that person's physical and character traits. Be sure to select the details of your description carefully so that you create a dominant impression rather than simply offering a series of loosely related descriptive details.

WRITING SUGGESTIONS FOR DESCRIPTION

1. Most description is predominantly visual; that is, it appeals to our sense of sight. Good description, however, often goes beyond the visual; it appeals as well to one or more of the other senses—hearing, smell, taste, and touch. One way to heighten your awareness of these other senses is to purposefully deemphasize the visual impressions you receive. For example, while standing on a busy street corner, sitting in a classroom, or shopping in a supermarket, carefully note what you hear, smell, taste, or feel. (It may help if you close your eyes to eliminate visual distractions as you carry out this experiment.) Use these sense impressions to write a brief description of the street corner, the classroom, the supermarket, or another spot of your choosing.

2. Select one of the following topics, and write an objective description of it. Remember that your task in writing an objective description is to inform the reader about the object, not to convey to the reader the mood or feeling that the object evokes in you.

   a. a pine tree
   b. a personal computer
   c. a café
   d. a dictionary
   e. a fast-food restaurant
   f. a basketball
   g. the layout of your campus
   h. a stereo system
   i. a houseplant
   j. your room

3. Writers of description often rely on factual information to make their writing more substantial and interesting. Using facts, statistics, or other information found in standard reference works in your college library (encyclopedias, dictionaries, almanacs, atlases, biographical dictionaries, or yearbooks), write an essay of several paragraphs describing one of the people, places, or things in the following list. Be sure that you focus your description, that you have a purpose for your description, and that you present your facts in an interesting manner.

   a. the Statue of Liberty
   b. the telephone
   c. Bono
   d. the Grand Canyon
   e. the Great Wall of China
   f. Al Gore
   g. Aretha Franklin
   h. the Tower of London
   i. the sun
   j. Disney World
   k. the Hubble Space Telescope
   l. Maya Angelou
   m. Tom Brokaw
   n. a local landmark

4. Select one of the following places, and write a multiparagraph description that captures your subjective sense impressions of that particular place.

   a. a busy intersection
   b. a bakery
   c. a dorm room
   d. a factory
   e. a service station
   f. a zoo
   g. a cafeteria
   h. a farmers' market
   i. a concert hall
   j. a locker room
   k. a bank
   l. a library

5. At college you have the opportunity to meet many new people, students as well as teachers; perhaps you would like to share your impressions of these people with a friend or family member. In a letter to someone back home, describe one of your new acquaintances. Try to capture the essence of the person you choose and to explain why this person stands out from all the other people you have met at school.

6. As a way of getting to know your campus, select a building, statue, sculpture, or other familiar landmark and research it. What's its significance or meaning to your college or university? Are there any ceremonies or rituals associated with the object? What are its distinctive or unusual features? When was it erected? Who sponsored it? Is it currently being used as originally intended? Once you have completed your informal research, write a description of your subject in which you create a dominant impression of your landmark's importance to the campus community.

    You and your classmates may wish to turn this particular assignment into a collaborative class project: the compilation of a booklet of essays that introduces readers to the unique physical and historic features of your campus. To avoid duplication, the class should make a list of campus landmarks, and students should sign up for the one that they would like to write about.

CHAPTER 6

Illustration

WHAT IS ILLUSTRATION?

The strategy of illustration uses examples—facts, opinions, samples, and anecdotes or stories—to make a generalization more vivid, understandable, and persuasive.

In the following paragraph from "Wandering through Winter," notice how naturalist Edwin Way Teale uses examples to illustrate his generalization that "country people" have many superstitions about how harsh the coming winter will be.

Topic sentence about weather superstitions frames the entire paragraph.

Series of examples amplify and elucidate the topic sentence.

In the folklore of the country, numerous superstitions relate to winter weather. Back-country farmers examine their husks—the thicker the husk, the colder the winter. They watch the acorn crop—the more acorns, the more severe the season. They observe where white-faced hornets place their paper nests—the higher they are, the deeper will be the snow. They examine the size and shape and color of the spleens of butchered hogs for clues to the severity of the season. They keep track of the blooming of the dogwood in the spring—the more abundant the blooms, the more bitter the cold in January. When chipmunks carry their tails high and squirrels have heavier fur, the superstitious gird themselves for a long, hard winter. Without any specific basis, a wider-than-usual black band on a woolly-bear caterpillar is accepted as a sign that winter will arrive early and stay late. Even the way a cat sits beside the stove carries its message to the credulous. According to the belief once widely held in the Ozarks, a

ILLUSTRATION | 151

cat sitting with its tail to the fire indicates very cold weather is on the way.

Teale uses nine separate examples to illustrate and explain his topic sentence about weather-related superstitions. These examples both demonstrate his knowledge of folk traditions and entertain us. As readers, we come away from Teale's paragraph thinking that he is an authority on his subject.

Teale's examples are a series of related but varied illustrations of his main point. Not only are there many examples, but the examples are representative because they illustrate the main generalization and are typical or characteristic of the topic. Sometimes just one sustained example is more effective if the example is representative and the writer develops it well. Here is one such example by basketball legend Bill Russell from his autobiographical *Second Wind*:

Topic sentence focuses on athletes slipping into an unknown gear.

Extended example of Bob Beamon's record-shattering day exemplifies Russell's topic sentence.

Every champion athlete has a moment when everything goes so perfectly for him he slips into a gear that he didn't know was there. It's easy to spot that perfect moment in a sport like track. I remember watching the 1968 Olympics in Mexico City, where the world record in the long jump was just under 27 feet. Then Bob Beamon flew down the chute and leaped out over the pit in a majestic jump that I have seen replayed many times. There was an awed silence when the announcer said that Beamon's jump measured 29 feet 2¼ inches. Generally world records are broken by fractions of inches, but Beamon had exceeded the existing record by more than two feet. On learning what he had done, Beamon slumped down on the ground and cried. Most viewers' image of Beamon ends with the picture of him weeping on the ground, but in fact

Example illustrates that even Beamon did not anticipate his own performance.

he got up and took some more jumps that day. I like to think that he did so because he had jumped for so long at his best that *even then* he didn't know what might come out of him. At the end of the day he wanted to be absolutely sure that he'd had his perfect day.

Few readers have experienced that "extra gear" that Russell describes, so he illustrates what he means with a single, extended example—in this case, an anecdote that gives substance to the idea he wants his readers to understand. Russell's example of Bob Beamon's record-breaking jump is not only concrete and specific; it is memorable because it so aptly captures the essence of his topic sentence about athletic perfection. Without this extended example, Russell's claim that every great athlete "slips into a gear that he didn't know was there" would simply be a hollow statement.

USING ILLUSTRATION AS A WRITING STRATEGY

Illustrating a point with examples is a basic strategy of human communication, and it serves several purposes for writers. First, examples make writing more vivid and interesting. Writing that consists of loosely strung together generalizations is lifeless and difficult to read, regardless of the believability of the generalizations or our willingness to accept them. Good writers try to provide just the right kind and number of examples to make their ideas clear and convincing. For example, an essay about television bloopers will be dull and pointless without some examples of on-screen blunders—accidents, pratfalls, and "tips of the slongue," as one writer calls them. Likewise, a more serious essay on the dangers of drunk driving will have more impact if it is illustrated with descriptive examples of the victims' suffering and the grief and outrage of their family and friends.

Writers also use illustration to explain or clarify their ideas. All readers want specific information and feel that it is the writer's responsibility to provide it. Even if readers can provide examples themselves, they want to see what kind of evidence the writer can present. In an essay on political leadership for a history or political science class, for instance, the assertion "Successful leaders are often a product of their times" will certainly require further explanation. Such explanation could be provided effectively through examples: Franklin D. Roosevelt, Winston Churchill, Charles de Gaulle, Corazon Aquino, and Nelson Mandela all rose to power because their people were looking for leadership in a time of national crisis. Keep in mind, however, that the use of these specific examples paints a different picture of the term "successful leaders" than a different set of examples would; unlike leaders like Joseph Stalin, Adolf Hitler, and Benito Mussolini, who rose to power under similar circumstances, the first group of leaders exercised their power in the interest of the people. The importance of carefully selected examples cannot be overemphasized. Good examples always clearly illustrate the writer's point or idea.

Illustration is so useful and versatile a strategy that it is found in many different kinds of writing such as reports, cover letters, editorials, applications, proposals, law briefs, and reviews. In fact, there is hardly an essay in this book that does not use illustration in one way or another.

Using Illustration across the Disciplines

When writing essays in the academic disciplines, you will have many opportunities to use the strategy of illustration to both organize and strengthen the presentation of your ideas. To determine whether or not illustration is the right strategy for you in

ILLUSTRATION | 153

a particular paper, use the four-step method first described in Choosing Strategies across the Disciplines (pages 24–25). Consider the following examples, which illustrate how this four-step method works for typical college papers.

American Literature

MAIN IDEA: Mark Twain uses irony to speak out against racism in *The Adventures of Huckleberry Finn.*

QUESTION: Where does Mark Twain use irony to combat racism in *The Adventures of Huckleberry Finn?*

STRATEGY: Illustration. The direction words *uses* and *where* say "show me," and what better way to show than with solid, representative examples from the novel of Twain's use of irony to speak out against racism?

SUPPORTING STRATEGY: Argument. The examples can be used to argue in favor of a particular interpretation of Twain's work.

Criminal Justice

MAIN IDEA: America's criminal justice system neglects the families of capital offenders.

QUESTION: How has America's criminal justice system neglected the families of capital offenders?

STRATEGY: Illustration. Both the statement of the main idea and the question cry out for proof or evidence, and the best evidence would be a series of examples of the claimed neglect.

SUPPORTING STRATEGY: Process analysis. The paper might conclude with a possible remedy or solution—a step-by-step process for eliminating the current neglect.

Biology

MAIN IDEA: Cloning and other biotechnical discoveries give rise to serious moral and ethical issues that need our attention.

QUESTION: What are some of the moral and ethical issues raised by recent biotechnical discoveries that we need to address?

STRATEGY: Illustration. The direction words *what* and *some* call for examples of the moral and ethical issues raised by biotechnical discoveries.

SUPPORTING STRATEGY: Argument. The direction word *need* suggests that the examples should be both compelling and persuasive so that readers will want to address these issues.

SAMPLE STUDENT ESSAY USING ILLUSTRATION AS A WRITING STRATEGY

Family photographs fascinated Carrie White, and she sought in one of her essays to explain why she valued them so much. She started by making a list of information, memories, and specific family pictures she might include in her essay. Soon Carrie discovered that the entries on her list clustered into several key groups or categories that helped explain why she treasured family photographs. On the basis of these groupings, she was able to develop the following preliminary thesis: "Photographs have played an extremely important role in my life by allowing me to learn about my past and to stay connected with my family in the present." This thesis, with its emphasis on both past and present, helped Carrie decide to organize her examples chronologically, starting with her grandparents' and parents' lives before she was born and moving through her own childhood into the present. What follows is the final draft of Carrie White's essay.

Title: Introduces the topic of the paper.

Family Portraits

Carrie White

Beginning: Engages the reader — we can all remember annoying photo sessions.

I haven't always liked photographs. I can still remember squinting into the sun's glare, annoyed as my Mom straightened my shirt and said, "Hold still." In spite of such annoyances, I have to admit that photographs have incredible capabilities: to document history, to tell the absolute truth, to capture a moment. But to me they mean more. By allowing me to learn about my past and that of my family before, during, and after I was born, photographs have played an extremely important role in my life. Only recently have I appreciated the immeasurable value of photographs.

Thesis: Announces the focus of the essay and signals chronological organization.

Topic Sentence: Indicates focus of the paragraph.

Photographs can take you to places you've never been and times before you were born. I can visit my grandmother's childhood home in Vienna, Austria, and walk down the high-ceilinged, iron staircase by looking through the small, white album my Grandma treasures. I also know of the tomboy she once was, wearing Lederhosen instead of the Dirndls worn by her friends. I have seen the beautiful young woman who traveled with the Red Cross during the war, uncertain of her future. It is the photograph that rests in a red leather frame on my Grandma's nightstand that has allowed me to meet the man she would later marry. He died before I was born, but I've been told that I would have loved his calm manner, and I can see for myself his gentle smile and tranquil expression.

Organization: Starts with photographs from distant past — grandparents' generation.

Examples from her grandparents' past make this period come alive.

1

2

ILLUSTRATION | **155**

Topic Sentence: Indicates focus on parents.

Photographs have let me know my parents before they 3
were married, as the carefree college students they were, in love
and awaiting the rest of their lives. I have seen the light blue
Volkswagen van my dad used to take down the coast of California

Relevant and representative examples illustrate the many facets of her parents' lives.

when he went surfing, and the silver dress my mom wore to her
senior prom. Through pictures I am able to witness their
wedding, which has shown me that there is much in their
relationship that goes beyond their children. I am able to see the
look in their eyes as they hold their first, newborn daughter, as

Telling details reveal the "magical" something about early family photographs.

well as my sister's jealous expression at my birth a few years
later. There is something almost magical about viewing an image
of yourself that you are too young to remember, such as a second
birthday or a first trip to the beach.

Topic Sentence: Focuses on elementary-school photographs as documents of change.

School portraits can be a painful reminder of the past, but 4
they undoubtedly document growth and change. I distinctly
remember school portrait day each year in elementary school. I
can still hear the "One-two, one-two-three . . . smile" of Sterling,
the photographer who dutifully came back year after year to take

Unified Paragraph: Examples "document growth and change" during early school years.

our pictures, always telling each of us how much we'd grown.
Each portrait of mine represents a phase in my life, often one that
I'd otherwise forget about. Catching a glimpse of the faded green
corduroy jumper in my second-grade school picture reminds me of
the time I was first allowed to dress myself each day, wearing the
same outfit three days a week if I chose to do so. Most of us
probably have certain periods in our lives which make us shake
our heads when we reflect on them. Whether it is an awkward
growth phase or a unique fashion statement, a picture shows you
as you were then and reminds you of the progress you've made.

Transitions: Sentence shifts focus to family trip.

The summer after I was in fifth grade my family went to 5
Greece. My Mom carefully documented the trip and took her
camera wherever we went. There is not a single picture in which
my older sister, Jamie, is smiling. Instead she displays an
unpleasant scowl in each one. I distinctly remember that "non-
smiling" stage in her life, when she was a teenager, unsure of the

Details about sister make this paragraph memorable.

way she felt about anything. While she may not like to remember
that particular time, the pictures serve as an honest reminder.

Organization: Shift to present time.

Often, photographs are all that there is to go on. 6
I never realized this until coming to college here in Vermont, over
five thousand miles from home. At first I felt like I was living in
two completely separate worlds. The only bridge I had to connect
the two places was photography. It was very important to me for
the people at college to know my family and friends at home, and

Examples of current photographs from Carrie's two worlds.

for everyone at home to know my friends here at school. Documenting the first snowfall of freshman year on film, for which purpose I excitedly ran outside in my pajamas, allowed my family at home to feel as if they had experienced it, too. Similarly, showing my friends at school photographs of my dad's sailboat or the white sand of Lanikai Beach gives them an idea of what my home is like. I have done my best to capture both places through pictures, and by sharing them I feel as though my worlds have been brought closer together. When my family came to Vermont for Christmas this year, my friends told me that my family was "just as they had imagined from the pictures."

Conclusion summarizes the reasons for valuing photographs, especially the way they capture the past and keep it alive.

Some of my most prized possessions are photo albums, not because of the material objects they contain, but because of all they represent. Photographs have documented my life and serve as reminders of so many things I have done, people I've met, and places I've been. They capture my birthday party in first grade, my awkward stage in sixth grade, and my first experience making a snowball, and they allow me to share these moments with the people in my life—those I grew up with, as well as those who came later. When I look at my photo albums, I well up with an overwhelming feeling of both pride in all I have accomplished and sadness that so much of my life has passed, leaving little behind but the photos.

7

One of the few truly irreplaceable things in this world is the past. The more time goes by, the fainter memories and feelings become. So much can be learned from our pasts if we will only recollect them. Old mistakes can be avoided. Experiences and their lessons can be remembered. By sharing our experiences with others, we can aid in their understanding of us, and shared memories grant us a deep and unique understanding of those we love.

8

The past should never be forgotten. Photographs help us remember.

9

Analyzing Carrie White's Essay of Illustration: Questions for Discussion

1. What points do Carrie's examples serve to illustrate or support?
2. Do you consider her examples relevant and representative? Explain why, or why not.

ILLUSTRATION | **157**

3. Which examples did you find most effective? Least effective? Why?

4. How does Carrie conclude her essay? In what ways is her conclusion connected to her beginning? Explain.

SUGGESTIONS FOR USING ILLUSTRATION AS A WRITING STRATEGY

As you plan, write, and revise your essay of illustration, be mindful of the five-step writing process described in Chapter 2 (see pages 14–38). Also, pay particular attention to the basic requirements and essential ingredients for this writing strategy.

Planning Your Essay of Illustration

Planning is an essential part of writing a good essay of illustration. You can save yourself a great deal of aggravation by taking the time to think about the key building blocks of your essay before you actually begin to write.

Focus on Your Thesis or Main Idea.   Begin by thinking of ideas and generalizations about your topic that you can make clearer and more persuasive by illustrating them with examples—facts, anecdotes, and specific details. Eventually, you should focus primarily on your thesis, the main point that you will develop in your essay. Once you have established your thesis—a statement of what you intend to say in your essay—you will find that examples add clarity, color, and authority.

Consider the following thesis:

> Americans are a pain-conscious people who would rather get rid of pain than seek and cure its root causes.

This assertion is broad and general; it cries out for evidence or support. As a writer, you could make this thesis statement stronger and more meaningful through illustration. You might support this thesis statement by pointing to the sheer number of over-the-counter painkillers available and the different types of pain they address, or by citing specific situations in which people you know have gone to the drugstore instead of to a doctor. In addition, you might cite sales figures for painkillers in the United States and compare them with sales figures in other countries.

Gather More Examples Than You Can Use.   Before you begin to write, bring together as many examples as you can that are related to your subject—more than you can possibly use. An example may be anything from a fact or a statistic to an anecdote or a story; it may be stated in a few words—"India's population is now approaching 1.2 billion people"—or it may go on for several pages of elaborate description or explanation.

The kinds of examples you look for and where you look for them will depend, of course, on your subject and the point you want to make about it. If you plan to write about all the quirky, fascinating people who make up your family, you can gather your examples without leaving your room: descriptions of their habits and clothing, stories about their strange adventures, facts about their backgrounds, quotations from their conversations. If, however, you are writing an essay on book censorship in American public schools, you will need to do research in the library or on the Internet and read many sources to supply yourself with examples. Your essay might well include accounts drawn from newspapers; statistics published by librarians' or teachers' professional organizations; court transcripts and judicial opinions on censorship; and interviews with school board members, parents, book publishers, and even the authors whose work has been pulled off library shelves or kept out of the classroom.

The range of sources and the variety of examples are limited only by your imagination and the time you can spend on research. One student who was trying to answer the question "Do diets really work?" remembers her research in the library very clearly: "It's really not that difficult if you stay organized. I started with *The Readers' Guide to Periodical Literature*. I also thought it was wise to use a variety of magazines, starting with popular newsmagazines such as *Time* and *U.S. News & World Report*. After this, I consulted scholarly journals in order to get a better understanding of the short- and long-term effects of diets." As she puts it, "I collected all kinds of examples because I did not know at that point which ones would be most useful when I got to actually writing my paper, and I wanted to make sure that I had more than enough to choose from."

Collecting an abundance of examples will allow you to choose the strongest and most representative ones for your essay, not merely the first ones that come to mind. Having enough material will also make it less likely that you will have to stop in mid-draft and hunt for further examples, losing the rhythm of your work or the thread of your ideas. Moreover, the more examples you gather, the more you will learn about your subject and the easier it will be to write about it with authority.

Choose Relevant Examples.   You must make sure that your examples are relevant. Do they clarify and support the points you want to make?

ILLUSTRATION | 159

Suppose the main point of your planned essay is that censorship runs rampant in American public education. A newspaper story about the banning of *Catcher in the Rye* and *The Merchant of Venice* from the local high school's English curriculum would clearly be relevant because it concerns book censorship at a public school. The fact that James Joyce's novel *Ulysses* was first banned as obscene and then vindicated in a famous trial, although a landmark case of censorship in American history, has nothing to do with books in public schools. While the case of *Ulysses* might be a useful example for other discussions of censorship, it would not be relevant to your essay.

Sometimes more than one of your examples will be relevant. In such cases, choose the examples that are most closely related to your thesis or main idea. If you were working on the pain essay mentioned earlier, a statistic indicating the sales of a particular drug in a given year might be interesting; however, a statistic showing that over the past ten years painkiller sales in America have increased more rapidly than the population would be relevant to the idea that Americans are a pain-conscious people, and so this statistic could be used to support your assertion. In other words, examples may be interesting in and of themselves, but they only come alive when they illustrate and link important ideas that the writer is trying to promote.

Be Sure Your Examples Are Representative. Besides being relevant, to be most effective an example should also be representative. The story it tells or the fact it presents should be typical of the main point or concept, an example indicative of a larger pattern rather than an uncommon or isolated occurrence. Figures showing how many people use aspirin, and for what purposes, would be representative because aspirin is the most widely used painkiller in America. Statistics about a newly developed barbiturate (a highly specialized kind of painkiller) might show a tremendous increase in its use compared with other barbiturates, but the example would not be very representative because not many people use barbiturates compared with other kinds of painkillers. In fact, giving the barbiturate example might even cause readers to wonder why aspirin, which is better known, was not used as an example.

If, while working on the censorship paper, you found reports on a dozen quiet administrative hearings and orderly court cases, but only one report of a sensational incident in which books were actually burned in a school parking lot, the latter incident, however dramatic, is clearly not a representative example. You might want to mention the book burning in your essay as an extremist viewpoint, but you should not present it as typical of how censorship is handled.

What if your examples do not support your point? Perhaps you have missed some important information and need to look further. It may be, though, that the problem is with the point itself. For example, suppose you intend your censorship paper to illustrate the following thesis: "Book censorship has seriously impacted American public education." However, you have not found very many examples in which specific books were actually censored or banned outright. While many attempts at censorship have been made, most were ultimately prevented or overturned in the courts. You might then have to revise your original thesis: "Although there have been many well-publicized attempts to censor books in public schools, actual censorship is relatively rare."

Organizing Your Essay of Illustration

Sequence Your Examples Logically.   It is important to arrange your examples in an order that serves your purpose, is easy for readers to follow, and will have maximum effect. Some possible patterns of organization include chronological order and spatial order. Others include moving from the least to the most controversial, as in Martin Luther King Jr.'s "The Ways of Meeting Oppression" (page 000); or from the least to the most important, as in Jo Goodwin Parker's "What Is Poverty?" (page 000). Or you may hit upon an order that "feels right" to you, as Edwin Way Teale did in his paragraph about winter superstitions (page 150–51). How many examples you include depends, of course, on the length and nature of the assignment. Before starting the first draft, you may find it helpful to work out your organization in a rough outline, using only enough words so that you can tell which example each entry refers to.

Use Transitions.   While it is important to give the presentation of your examples an inherent logic, it is also important to link your examples to the topic sentences in your paragraphs and, indeed, to the thesis of your entire essay by using transitional words and expressions such as *for example, for instance, therefore, afterward, in other words, next*, and *finally*. Such structural devices will make the sequencing of the examples easy to follow.

Revising and Editing Your Essay of Illustration

Share Your Work with Others.   You may find it particularly helpful to share the drafts of your essays with other students in your writing class. One of our students commented, "In total, I probably wrote five or six different versions of this essay. I shared them with members of the class, and their comments were extremely insightful. I remember one student's question in particular because she really got me to focus on the problems with fad diets. The students also helped me to see where I needed examples to explain what I was talking about. The very

ILLUSTRATION | **161**

first draft that I wrote is completely different from the one I submitted in class." To maximize the effectiveness of peer conferences, utilize the suggestions on pages 27–28. Feedback from these conferences often provides one or more places where you can start writing.

Question Your Own Work While Revising and Editing. Revision is best done by asking yourself key questions about what you have written. Begin by reading your paper, preferably aloud. Reading aloud forces you to pay attention to every single word. You are more likely to catch lapses in the logical flow of thought. After you have read your paper through, answer the following questions for revising and editing, and make the necessary changes.

Questions for Revising and Editing: Illustration

1. Is my topic well focused?
2. Does my thesis statement clearly identify my topic and make an assertion about it?
3. Are my examples well chosen to support my thesis? Are there other examples that might work better?
4. Are my examples representative? That is, are they typical of the main point or concept, rather than bizarre or atypical?
5. Do I have enough examples to be convincing, or do I have too many examples?
6. Have I developed my examples in enough detail so as to be clear to readers?
7. Have I organized my examples in some logical pattern, and is that pattern clear to readers?
8. Does the essay accomplish my purpose?
9. Are my topic sentences strong? Are my paragraphs unified?
10. Does my paper contain any errors in grammar, punctuation, or mechanics?

Be Specific

Natalie Goldberg

Author Natalie Goldberg has made a specialty of writing about writing. Her first and best-known work, Writing Down the Bones: Freeing the Writer Within, *was published in 1986. Goldberg's advice to would-be writers is, on the one hand, practical and pithy; on the other, it is almost mystical in its call to know and appreciate the world. "Be Specific," the excerpt that appears below, is representative of the book as a whole. Amid widespread acclaim for the book, one critic commented, "Goldberg teaches us not only how to write better, but how to live better."* Writing Down the Bones *was followed by three more successful books about writing:* Wild Mind: Living the Writer's Life *(1990),* Living Color: A Writer Paints Her World *(1996), and* Thunder and Lightning: Cracking Open the Writer's Craft *(2000). Altogether, more than three-quarters of a million copies of these books are now in print. Goldberg has also written fiction; her first novel,* Banana Rose, *was published in 1994. Her most recent books are* Top of My Lungs *(2002), a collection of poetry and paintings, and* The Great Failure: A Bartender, a Monk, and My Unlikely Path to Truth *(2004), a memoir.*

Notice the way in which Goldberg demonstrates her advice to be specific in the following selection.

PREPARING TO READ

Suppose someone says to you, "I walked in the woods." What do you envision? Write down what you see in your mind's eye. Now suppose someone says, "I walked in the redwood forest." Again, write what you see. What's different about your two descriptions, and why?

B e specific. Don't say "fruit." Tell what kind of fruit—"It is a pome- 1
granate." Give things the dignity of their names. Just as with human beings, it is rude to say, "Hey, girl, get in line." That "girl" has a name. (As a matter of fact, if she's at least twenty years old, she's a woman, not a "girl" at all.) Things, too, have names. It is much better to say "the geranium in the window" than "the flower in the window." "Geranium"—that one word gives us a much more specific picture. It penetrates more deeply into the beingness of that flower. It immediately gives us the scene by the window—red petals, green circular leaves, all straining toward sunlight.

About ten years ago I decided I had to learn the names of plants 2
and flowers in my environment. I bought a book on them and walked down the tree-lined streets of Boulder, examining leaf, bark, and seed,

trying to match them up with their descriptions and names in the book. Maple, elm, oak, locust. I usually tried to cheat by asking people working in their yards the names of the flowers and trees growing there. I was amazed how few people had any idea of the names of the live beings inhabiting their little plot of land.

When we know the name of something, it brings us closer to the ground. It takes the blur out of our mind; it connects us to the earth. If I walk down the street and see "dogwood," "forsythia," I feel more friendly toward the environment. I am noticing what is around me and can name it. It makes me more awake.

If you read the poems of William Carlos Williams, you will see how specific he is about plants, trees, flowers—chicory, daisy, locust, poplar, quince, primrose, black-eyed Susan, lilacs—each has its own integrity. Williams says, "Write what's in front of your nose." It's good for us to know what is in front of our noses. Not just "daisy," but how the flower is in the season we are looking at it—"The dayseye hugging the earth / in August . . . brownedged, / green and pointed scales / armor his yellow."[1] Continue to hone your awareness: to the name, to the month, to the day, and finally to the moment.

Williams also says: "No idea, but in things." Study what is "in front of your nose." By saying "geranium" instead of "flower," you are penetrating more deeply into the present and being there. The closer we can get to what's in front of our nose, the more it can teach us everything. "To see the World in a Grain of Sand, and a heaven in a Wild Flower . . ."[2]

In writing groups and classes too, it is good to quickly learn the names of all the other group members. It helps to ground you in the group and make you more attentive to each other's work.

Learn the names of everything: birds, cheese, tractors, cars, buildings. A writer is all at once everything—an architect, French cook, farmer—and at the same time, a writer is none of these things.

THINKING CRITICALLY ABOUT THE TEXT

Natalie Goldberg found that she wasn't the only one in her neighborhood who didn't know the names of local trees and flowers. Are you unable to name individual members of some categories of things that you encounter often? What are these categories? What are some that would be pleasing or useful for you to learn? How might you go about learning them? (Consider

---

[1]William Carlos Williams, "Daisy," in *The Collected Earlier Poems* (New York: New Directions, 1938).

[2]William Blake, "The Auguries of Innocence."

why Goldberg says it was "cheating" to ask people the names of their flowers and trees.) What would you gain by knowing them?

QUESTIONS ON SUBJECT

1. In paragraphs 3, 5, and 6, Goldberg cites a number of advantages to be gained by knowing the names of things. Review these advantages. What are they? Do they ring true?

2. Throughout the essay, Goldberg instructs readers to be specific and to be aware of the world around them. Of what besides names are the readers advised to be aware? Why?

QUESTIONS ON STRATEGY

1. How does Goldberg "specifically" follow the advice she gives writers in this essay?

2. Goldberg makes several lists of the names of things. What purpose do these lists serve? How does she use these specifics to illustrate her point?

3. What specific audience is Goldberg addressing in this essay? (Glossary: *Audience*) How do you know?

4. The strategies of definition and illustration are closely intertwined in this essay; to name a thing precisely, after all, is to take the first step in defining it. (Glossary: *Definition*) What central concept is defined by Goldberg's many illustrations of naming? How might a writer use illustration to make definitions richer and more meaningful?

QUESTIONS ON DICTION AND VOCABULARY

1. Goldberg says that to name an object gives it dignity (paragraph 1) and integrity (4). What does she mean in each case?

2. In paragraph 1, Goldberg writes, "It [the word *geranium*] penetrates more deeply into the beingness of that flower." The word *beingness* does not appear in the dictionary. Where does it come from? Why does Goldberg use it, and what does she mean by her statement?

3. In his poem "Daisy," quoted in paragraph 4, William Carlos Williams calls the flower "dayseye." How does this spelling reinforce the central idea of the paragraph? Of the essay as a whole?

4. Refer to your desk dictionary to determine the meanings of the following words as Goldberg uses them in this selection: *pomegranate* (paragraph 1), *integrity* (4).

CLASSROOM ACTIVITY USING ILLUSTRATION

Specific examples are always more effective and convincing than general ones. A useful exercise in learning to be specific is to see the words we use for people, places, objects, and ideas as being positioned somewhere on a continuum of specificity. In the following chart, notice how the words become more specific as you move from left to right:

More General	General	Specific	More Specific
Organism	Reptile	Snake	Coral Snake
Food	Sandwich	Corned beef sandwich	Reuben

Fill in the missing part for each of the following lists:

More General	General	Specific	More Specific
Writing instrument	_____	Fountain pen	Waterman fountain pen
Vehicle	Car	_____	1958 Chevrolet Impala
Book	Reference book	Dictionary	_____
American	_____	Navaho	Laguna Pueblo
_____	Oral medicine	Gel capsule	Tylenol Gel Caps
School	High school	Technical high school	_____
Celebrity	Male celebrity	_____	Brad Pitt

WRITING SUGGESTIONS

1. Write a brief essay advising your readers of something they should do. Title your essay, as Goldberg does, with a directive ("Be Specific"). Tell your readers how they can improve their lives by taking your advice, and give strong examples of the behavior you are recommending.

2. Goldberg likes William Carlos Williams's statement, "No idea, but in things" (paragraph 5). Using this line as both a title and a thesis, write your own argument for the use of the specific over the general in a certain field—journalism, history, political science, biology, or literature, for example. (Glossary: *Argument*) Be sure to support your argument with relevant, representative examples.

If You Had One Day with Someone Who's Gone

Mitch Albom

Journalist and author Mitch Albom was born in Passaic, New Jersey, in 1958. He earned a degree in sociology from Brandeis University in 1979 and master's degrees in journalism and business administration from Columbia University in 1981 and 1982. Starting in 1985, after working for newspapers in New York and Florida, Albom landed a staff position at the Detroit Free Press, *where he writes a regular sports column. Over the years he has earned a loyal following of Detroit sports fans both in print and as a host of radio and television sports talk shows. His reputation as a sportswriter blossomed with the publication of* The Live Albom: The Best of *Detroit Free Press* Sports *(1988–1995), four volumes of his sports column. With the University of Michigan's legendary football coach Bo Schembechler, he wrote* Bo: The Bo Schembechler Story *(1989) and, when Michigan won the national championship in basketball, he authored* Fab Five: Basketball, Trash Talk, and the American Dream *(1993). But it was the publication of* Tuesdays with Morrie: An Old Man, a Young Man, and Life's Greatest Lesson *(1997), the story of Albom's weekly visits with his former sociology professor Morrie Schwartz, that catapulted Albom onto the national stage. Albom followed this work of nonfiction with the two novels* The Five People You Meet in Heaven *(2003) and* For One More Day *(2006), both of which have been national best-sellers. In addition to numerous sportswriting awards, Albom has received humanitarian awards for his work with Dream Team, A Time to Help, Caring Athletes Team for Children's and Henry Ford Hospitals, Forgotten Harvest, and National Hospice.*

In "If You Had One Day with Someone Who's Gone," an essay first published in Parade *magazine on September 17, 2006, Albom uses the illustrative stories of five people to find out what they would do if they were granted one more day with a loved one. His examples lead him to a surprising life lesson.*

PREPARING TO READ

Have you ever lost or become disconnected from someone you loved or were close to—a family member or childhood friend? What were the circumstances that separated you? What would you most like to do with this person if you could be reconnected for a whole day?

H er world shattered in a telephone call. My mother was 15 years old. "Your father is dead," her aunt told her. 1

Dead? How could he be dead? Hadn't she seen him the night before, when she kissed him goodnight? Hadn't he given her two new words to look up in the dictionary? Dead? 2

"You're a liar," my mother said. 3

But it wasn't a lie. Her father, my grandfather, had collapsed that 4
morning from a massive heart attack. No final hugs. No goodbye. Just a
phone call. And he was gone.

Have you ever lost someone you love and wanted one more con- 5
versation, one more day to make up for the time when you thought
they would be here forever? I wrote that sentence as part of a new
novel. Only after I finished did I realize that, my whole life, I had wondered this question of my mother.

So, finally, I asked her. 6

"One more day with my father?" she said. Her voice seemed to tum- 7
ble back into some strange, misty place. It had been six decades since
their last day together. Murray had wanted his little girl, Rhoda, to be a
doctor. He had wanted her to stay single and go to medical school. But
after his death, my mother had to survive. She had to look after a
younger brother and a depressed mother. She finished high school and
married the first boy she ever dated. She never finished college.

"I guess, if I saw my father again, I would first apologize for not 8
becoming a doctor," she answered. "But I would say that I became a different kind of doctor, someone who helped the family whenever they
had problems.

"My father was my pal, and I would tell him I missed having a pal 9
around the house after he was gone. I would tell him that my mother
lived a long life and was comfortable at the end. And I would show him
my family—his grandchildren and his great-grandchildren—of which
I am the proudest. I hope he'd be proud of me too."

My mother admitted that she cried when she first saw the movie 10
Ghost, where Patrick Swayze "comes back to life" for a few minutes to
be with his girlfriend. She couldn't help but wish for time like that with
her father. I began to pose this scenario to other people—friends, colleagues, readers. How would they spend a day with a departed loved
one? Their responses said a lot about what we long for.

Almost everyone wanted to once again "tell them how much I 11
loved them"—even though these were people they had loved their
whole lives on Earth.

Others wanted to relive little things. Michael Carroll, from San 12
Antonio, Tex., wrote that he and his departed father "would head for
the racetrack, then off to Dad's favorite hamburger place to eat and
chat about old times."

Cathy Koncurat of Bel Air, Md., imagined a reunion with her best 13
friend, who died after mysteriously falling into an icy river. People had
always wondered what happened. "But if I had one more day with her,
those questions wouldn't be important. Instead, I'd like to spend it the
way we did when we were girls—shopping, seeing a movie, getting our
hair done."

Some might say, "That's such an ordinary day." 14
Maybe that's the point. 15

Rabbi Gerald Wolpe has spent nearly 50 years on the pulpit and is a 16
senior fellow at the University of Pennsylvania's Center for Bioethics.
Yet, at some moment every day, he is an 11-year-old boy who lost his
dad to a sudden heart attack in 1938.

"My father is a prisoner of my memory," he said. "Would he even 17
recognize me today?" Rabbi Wolpe can still picture the man, a former
vaudevillian, taking him to Boston Braves baseball games or singing
him a bedtime prayer.

Help me always do the right
Bless me every day and night.

If granted one more day, Rabbi Wolpe said, he "would share the good 18
and the bad. My father needed to know things. For example, as a boy, he
threw a snowball at his brother and hit him between the eyes. His
brother went blind. My father went to his death feeling guilty for that.

"But we now know his brother suffered an illness that made him 19
susceptible to losing his vision. I would want to say, 'Dad, look. It wasn't
your fault.'"

At funerals, Rabbi Wolpe often hears mourners lament missed 20
moments: "I never apologized. My last words were in anger. *If only I*
could have one more chance."

Maury De Young, a pastor in Kentwood, Mich., hears similar things 21
in his church. But De Young can sadly relate. His own son, Derrick, was
killed in a car accident a few years ago, at age 16, the night before
his big football game. There was no advance notice. No chance for
goodbye.

"If I had one more day with him?" De Young said, wistfully. "I'd 22
start it off with a long, long hug. Then we'd go for a walk, maybe to our
cottage in the woods."

De Young had gone to those woods after Derrick's death. He'd sat 23
under a tree and wept. His faith had carried him through. And it eases
his pain now, he said, "because I know Derrick is in heaven."

Still, there are questions. Derrick's football number was 42. The day 24
after his accident, his team, with heavy hearts, won a playoff game by
scoring 42 points. And the next week, the team won the state title by
scoring—yes—42 points.

"I'd like to ask my son," De Young whispered, "if he had something 25
to do with that."

We often fantasize about a perfect day—something exotic and far 26
away. But when it comes to those we miss, we desperately want one
more familiar meal, even one more argument. What does this teach us?
That the ordinary is precious. That the normal day is a treasure.

Think about it. When you haven't seen a loved one in a long time, 27
the first few hours of catching up feel like a giddy gift, don't they?
That's the gift we wish for when we can't catch up anymore. That
feeling of connection. It could be a bedside chat, a walk in the woods,
even a few words from the dictionary.

I asked my mother if she still recalled those two words her father 28
had assigned her on the last night of his life.

"Oh, yes," she said quickly. "They were 'detrimental' and 'incul- 29
cate.' I'll never forget them."

Then she sighed, yearning for a day she didn't have and words she 30
never used. And it made me want to savor every day with her even more.

THINKING CRITICALLY ABOUT THE TEXT

Albom shares with us the stories of five people who lost a loved one. In each
case, the loss was sudden and unexpected. How did the suddenness of the
loss affect each of the survivors? In what ways do you think sudden loss is different from losing someone to a terminal illness or old age? Explain.

QUESTIONS ON SUBJECT

1. Why did Albom's mother cry when she first viewed the movie *Ghost*?

2. When asked how they would spend a day with a departed loved one—if
   that were possible—how did people respond? What life lesson does
   Albom draw from these responses in his conclusion?

3. What do you think Rabbi Wolpe meant when he said, "My father is a
   prisoner of my memory" (paragraph 17)?

4. What does it say about Albom's mother and the relationship she had
   with her father when it's revealed that she still remembers the two
   vocabulary words her father gave her the night before he died six decades
   ago? Explain.

QUESTIONS ON STRATEGY

1. Albom opens his essay with the story of his mother losing her father
   when she was fifteen years old. How effective did you find this beginning? How is Albom's conclusion connected to this beginning? (Glossary: *Beginnings/Endings*)

2. Paragraph 5 starts with the rhetorical question "Have you ever lost someone you love and wanted one more conversation, one more day to make
   up for the time when you thought they would be here forever?" (Glossary: *Rhetorical Question*) How does this question function in the context
   of Albom's essay?

3. How did Albom find the examples he uses in this essay? In what ways are
   Albom's examples both relevant and representative?

4. Albom often repeats key words or ideas to make the transition from one
   paragraph to the next. Identify several places where he has done this

particularly well. What other transitional devices or expressions does he use? (Glossary: *Transitions*)

5. Why do you suppose Albom uses several one-sentence paragraphs? What would be lost had he tacked the sentence "So, finally, I asked her" (paragraph 6) on the end of the previous paragraph?

QUESTIONS ON DICTION AND VOCABULARY

1. Albom lets most of the people in his examples speak for themselves. What does he gain by letting people tell their own stories instead of telling us what they said? Explain.

2. What, if anything, does Albom's diction tell you about Albom himself? (Glossary: *Diction*) Do you think Albom's diction and tone are appropriate for his subject? (Glossary: *Tone*) Explain.

3. Refer to your desk dictionary to determine the meanings of the following words as Albom uses them in this selection: *scenario* (paragraph 10), *vaudevillian* (17), *lament* (20), *wistfully* (22), *giddy* (27), *detrimental* (29), *inculcate* (29).

CLASSROOM ACTIVITY USING ILLUSTRATION

Suppose you are writing an essay about the career choices that members of your extended family have made to see what trends or influences you could discover. Using your own extended family (great-grandparents, grandparents, parents, aunts and uncles, siblings) as potential material, make several lists of examples—for instance, one for family members who worked in agriculture or one of the trades, a second for those who worked in education, a third for those worked in one of the professions, and a fourth for those who worked in the service sector.

WRITING SUGGESTIONS

1. Has someone close to you—a parent, grandparent, relative, or friend—died, or has someone moved away so that you no longer see that person whom you would like to see again if only for a day? Write an essay in which you first tell us something about your relationship with the person you are missing and then describe what you would do with that person for one whole day.

2. What do you value most about your relationships with family members? Like Albom's mother, who considered her father "my pal," do you have a special relationship with one particular parent? Or maybe for you it's a special sibling, aunt or uncle, or grandparent. How would you describe the relationship you have with this special person? What specifically do you get from him or her? Write an essay about your relationship with this family member, using relevant and representative examples to illustrate why you value having the person in your life.

How to Give Orders Like a Man

Deborah Tannen

 *Deborah Tannen, professor of linguistics at Georgetown University, was born in 1945 in Brooklyn, New York. Tannen received her B.A. in English from the State University of New York at Binghamton in 1966 and taught English in Greece until 1968. She then earned an M.A. in English literature from Wayne State University in 1970. While pursuing her Ph.D. in linguistics at the University of California–Berkeley, she received several prizes for her poetry and short fiction. Her work has appeared in* New York, Vogue, *and the* New York Times Magazine. *In addition, she has authored three best-selling books on how people communicate:* You Just Don't Understand *(1990)*, That's Not What I Meant *(1991), and* Talking from Nine to Five *(1994). The success of these books attests to the public's interest in language, especially when it pertains to gender differences. Tannen's most recent books include* The Argument Culture: Stopping America's War of Words *(1998)*, I Only Say This Because I Love You: Talking to Your Parents, Partners, Sibs, and Kids When You're All Adults *(2002), and* You're Wearing That? Mothers and Daughters in Conversation *(2006).*

In this essay, first published in the New York Times Magazine *in August 1994, Tannen looks at the variety of ways in which orders are given and received. Interestingly, she concludes that, contrary to popular belief, directness is not necessarily logical or effective and indirectness is not necessarily manipulative or insecure.*

PREPARING TO READ

Write about a time in your life when you were ordered to do something. Who gave you the order—a friend, a parent, maybe a teacher? Did the person's relationship to you affect how you carried out the order? Did it make a difference to you whether the order giver was male or female? Why?

A university president was expecting a visit from a member of the board of trustees. When her secretary buzzed to tell her that the board member had arrived, she left her office and entered the reception area to greet him. Before ushering him into her office, she handed her secretary a sheet of paper and said: "I've just finished drafting this letter. Do you think you could type it right away? I'd like to get it out before lunch. And would you please do me a favor and hold all calls while I'm meeting with Mr. Smith?" 1

When they sat down behind the closed door of her office, Mr. Smith began by telling her that he thought she had spoken inappropriately to her secretary. "Don't forget," he said. "*You're* the president!" 2

Putting aside the question of the appropriateness of his admonishing the president on her way of speaking, it is revealing—and representative 3 of many Americans' assumptions—that the indirect way in which the university president told her secretary what to do struck him as self-deprecating. He took it as evidence that she didn't think she had the right to make demands of her secretary. He probably thought he was giving her a needed pep talk, bolstering her self-confidence.

I challenge the assumption that talking in an indirect way neces- 4 sarily reveals powerlessness, lack of self-confidence or anything else about the character of the speaker. Indirectness is a fundamental element in human communication. It is also one of the elements that varies most from one culture to another, and one that can cause confusion and misunderstanding when speakers have different habits with regard to using it. I also want to dispel the assumption that American women tend to be more indirect than American men. Women and men are both indirect, but in addition to differences associated with their backgrounds—regional, ethnic and class—they tend to be indirect in different situations and in different ways.

At work, we need to get others to do things, and we all have differ- 5 ent ways of accomplishing this. Any individual's ways will vary depending on who is being addressed—a boss, a peer or a subordinate. At one extreme are bald commands. At the other are requests so indirect that they don't sound like requests at all, but are just a statement of need or a description of a situation. People with direct styles of asking others to do things perceive indirect requests—if they perceive them as requests at all—as manipulative. But this is often just a way of blaming others for our discomfort with their styles.

The indirect style is no more manipulative than making a tele- 6 phone call, asking "Is Rachel there?" and expecting whoever answers the phone to put Rachel on. Only a child is likely to answer "Yes" and continue holding the phone—not out of orneriness but because of inexperience with the conventional meaning of the question. (A mischievous adult might do it to tease.) Those who feel that indirect orders are illogical or manipulative do not recognize the conventional nature of indirect requests.

Issuing orders indirectly can be the prerogative of those in power. 7 Imagine, for example, a master who says "It's cold in here" and expects a servant to make a move to close a window, while a servant who says the same thing is not likely to see his employer rise to correct the situation and make him more comfortable. Indeed, a Frenchman raised in Brittany tells me that his family never gave bald commands to their servants but always communicated orders in indirect and highly polite ways. This pattern renders less surprising the finding of David Bellinger and Jean Berko Gleason that fathers' speech to their young children had a higher incidence than mothers' of both direct imperatives like "Turn the bolt with the wrench" *and* indirect orders like "The wheel is going to fall off."

The use of indirectness can hardly be understood without the 8
cross-cultural perspective. Many Americans find it self-evident that
directness is logical and aligned with power while indirectness is akin
to dishonesty and reflects subservience. But for speakers raised in most
of the world's cultures, varieties of indirectness are the norm in communication. This is the pattern found by a Japanese sociolinguist,
Kunihiko Harada, in his analysis of a conversation he recorded between
a Japanese boss and a subordinate.

The markers of superior status were clear. One speaker was a Japan- 9
ese man in his late 40's who managed the local branch of a Japanese
private school in the United States. His conversational partner was a
Japanese-American woman in her early 20's who worked at the school.
By virtue of his job, his age and his native fluency in the language
being taught, the man was in the superior position. Yet when he
addressed the woman, he frequently used polite language and almost
always used indirectness. For example, he had tried and failed to find a
photography store that would make a black-and-white print from a
color negative for a brochure they were producing. He let her know
that he wanted her to take over the task by stating the situation and
allowed her to volunteer to do it: (This is a translation of the Japanese
conversation.)

> On this matter, that, that, on the leaflet? This photo, I'm thinking of
> changing it to black-and-white and making it clearer. . . . I went to a
> photo shop and asked them. They said they didn't do black-and-white.
> I asked if they knew any place that did. They said they didn't know. They
> weren't very helpful, but anyway, a place must be found, the negative
> brought to it, the picture developed.

Harada observes, "Given the fact that there are some duties to be 10
performed and that there are two parties present, the subordinate is
supposed to assume that those are his or her obligation." It was precisely because of his higher status that the boss was free to choose
whether to speak formally or informally, to assert his power or to play it
down and build rapport—an option not available to the subordinate,
who would have seemed cheeky if she had chosen a style that
enhanced friendliness and closeness.

The same pattern was found by a Chinese sociolinguist, Yuling 11
Pan, in a meeting of officials involved in a neighborhood youth program. All spoke in ways that reflected their place in the hierarchy.
A subordinate addressing a superior always spoke in a deferential way,
but a superior addressing a subordinate could either be authoritarian,
demonstrating his power, or friendly, establishing rapport. The ones in
power had the option of choosing which style to use. In this spirit,
I have been told by people who prefer their bosses to give orders

indirectly that those who issue bald commands must be pretty insecure; otherwise why would they have to bolster their egos by throwing their weight around?

I am not inclined to accept that those who give orders directly are   12
really insecure and powerless, any more than I want to accept that judgment of those who give indirect orders. The conclusion to be drawn is that ways of talking should not be taken as obvious evidence of inner psychological states like insecurity or lack of confidence. Considering the many influences on conversational style, individuals have a wide range of ways of getting things done and expressing their emotional states. Personality characteristics like insecurity cannot be linked to ways of speaking in an automatic, self-evident way.

Those who expect orders to be given indirectly are offended when   13
they come unadorned. One woman said that when her boss gives her instructions, she feels she should click her heels, salute, and say "Yes, boss!" His directions strike her as so imperious as to border on the militaristic. Yet I received a letter from a man telling me that indirect orders were a fundamental part of his military training. He wrote:

> Many years ago, when I was in the Navy, I was training to be a radio technician. One class I was in was taught by a chief radioman, a regular Navy man who had been to sea, and who was then in his third hitch. The students, about 20 of us, were fresh out of boot camp, with no sea duty and little knowledge of real Navy life. One day in class the chief said it was hot in the room. The students didn't react, except perhaps to nod in agreement. The chief repeated himself: "It's hot in this room." Again there was no reaction from the students.
>
> Then the chief explained. He wasn't looking for agreement or discussion from us. When he said that the room was hot, he expected us to do something about it—like opening the window. He tried it one more time, and this time all of us left our workbenches and headed for the windows. We had learned. And we had many opportunities to apply what we had learned.

This letter especially intrigued me because "It's cold in here" is the   14
standard sentence used by linguists to illustrate an indirect way of getting someone to do something—as I used it earlier. In this example, it is the very obviousness and rigidity of the military hierarchy that makes the statement of a problem sufficient to trigger corrective action on the part of subordinates.

A man who had worked at the Pentagon reinforced the view that the   15
burden of interpretation is on subordinates in the military—and he noticed the difference when he moved to a position in the private sector. He was frustrated when he'd say to his new secretary, for example, "Do we have a list of invitees?" and be told, "I don't know; we probably do" rather than "I'll get it for you." Indeed, he explained, at the Pentagon,

such a question would likely be heard as a reproach that the list was not already on his desk.

The suggestion that indirectness is associated with the military   16
must come as a surprise to many. But everyone is indirect, meaning more than is put into words and deriving meaning from words that are never actually said. It's a matter of where, when and how we each tend to be indirect and look for hidden meanings. But indirectness has a built-in liability. There is a risk that the other will either miss or choose to ignore your meaning.

On January 13, 1982, a freezing cold, snowy day in Washington,   17
Air Florida Flight 90 took off from National Airport, but could not get the lift it needed to keep climbing. It crashed into a bridge linking Washington to the state of Virginia and plunged into the Potomac. Of the 79 people on board, all but 5 perished, many floundering and drowning in the icy water while horror-stricken bystanders watched helplessly from the river's edge and millions more watched, aghast, on their television screens. Experts later concluded that the plane had waited too long after deicing to take off. Fresh buildup of ice on the wings and engine brought the plane down. How could the pilot and co-pilot have made such a blunder? Didn't at least one of them realize it was dangerous to take off under these conditions?

Charlotte Linde, a linguist at the Institute for Research on Learning   18
in Palo Alto, Calif., has studied the "black box" recordings of cockpit conversations that preceded crashes as well as tape recordings of conversations that took place among crews during flight simulations in which problems were presented. Among the black box conversations she studied was the one between the pilot and co-pilot just before the Air Florida crash. The pilot, it turned out, had little experience flying in icy weather. The co-pilot had a bit more, and it became heartbreakingly clear on analysis that he had tried to warn the pilot, but he did so indirectly.

The co-pilot repeatedly called attention to the bad weather and to   19
ice building up on other planes:

> Co-pilot: Look how the ice is just hanging on his, ah, back, back there, see that?
> . . .
> Co-pilot: See all those icicles on the back there and everything?
> Captain: Yeah.

He expressed concern early on about the long waiting time   20
between deicing:

> Co-pilot: Boy, this is a, this is a losing battle here on trying to de-ice those things, it [gives] you a false feeling of security, that's all that does.

Shortly after they were given clearance to take off, he again   21
expressed concern:

> Co-pilot: Let's check these tops again since we been setting here
> awhile.
> Captain: I think we get to go here in a minute.

When they were about to take off, the co-pilot called attention to   22
the engine instrument readings, which were not normal:

> Co-pilot: That don't seem right, does it? [three-second pause] Ah,
> that's not right. . . .
> Captain: Yes, it is, there's 80.
> Co-pilot: Naw, I don't think that's right. [seven-second pause] Ah,
> maybe it is.
> Captain: Hundred and twenty.
> Co-pilot: I don't know.

The takeoff proceeded, and 37 seconds later the pilot and co-pilot   23
exchanged their last words.

The co-pilot had repeatedly called the pilot's attention to danger-   24
ous conditions but did not directly suggest they abort the takeoff. In
Linde's judgment, he was expressing his concern indirectly, and the
captain didn't pick up on it—with tragic results.

That the co-pilot was trying to warn the captain indirectly is sup-   25
ported by evidence from another airline accident—a relatively minor
one—investigated by Linde that also involved the unsuccessful use of
indirectness.

On July 9, 1978, Allegheny Airlines Flight 453 was landing at Mon-   26
roe County Airport in Rochester, when it overran the runway by 728
feet. Everyone survived. This meant that the captain and co-pilot could
be interviewed. It turned out that the plane had been flying too fast for
a safe landing. The captain should have realized this and flown around
a second time, decreasing his speed before trying to land. The captain
said he simply had not been aware that he was going too fast. But the
co-pilot told interviewers that he "tried to warn the captain in subtle
ways, like mentioning the possibility of a tail wind and the slowness of
flap extension." His exact words were recorded in the black box. The
crosshatches indicate words deleted by the National Transportation
Safety Board and were probably expletives:

> Co-pilot: Yeah, it looks like you got a tail wind here.
> Captain: Yeah.
> [?]: Yeah [it] moves awfully # slow.
> Co-pilot: Yeah the # flaps are slower than a #.

Captain: We'll make it, gonna have to add power.
Co-pilot: I know.

The co-pilot thought the captain would understand that if there   27
was a tail wind, it would result in the plane going too fast, and if the
flaps were slow, they would be inadequate to break the speed sufficiently for a safe landing. He thought the captain would then correct
for the error by not trying to land. But the captain said he didn't interpret the co-pilot's remarks to mean they were going too fast.

Linde believes it is not a coincidence that the people being indirect   28
in these conversations were the co-pilots. In her analyses of flight-crew
conversations she found it was typical for the speech of subordinates to
be more mitigated—polite, tentative or indirect. She also found that
topics broached in a mitigated way were more likely to fail, and that
captains were more likely to ignore hints from their crew members
than the other way around. These findings are evidence that not only
can indirectness and other forms of mitigation be misunderstood, but
they are also easier to ignore.

In the Air Florida case, it is doubtful that the captain did not realize   29
what the co-pilot was suggesting when he said, "Let's check these tops
again since we been setting here awhile" (though it seems safe to
assume he did not realize the gravity of the co-pilot's concern). But the
indirectness of the co-pilot's phrasing certainly made it easier for the
pilot to ignore it. In this sense, the captain's response, "I think we get to
go here in a minute," was an indirect way of saying, "I'd rather not."
In view of these patterns, the flight crews of some airlines are now
given training to express their concerns, even to superiors, in more
direct ways.

The conclusion that people should learn to express themselves more   30
directly has a ring of truth to it—especially for Americans. But direct
communication is not necessarily always preferable. If more direct
expression is better communication, then the most direct-speaking crews
should be the best ones. Linde was surprised to find in her research that
crews that used the most mitigated speech were often judged the best
crews. As part of the study of talk among cockpit crews in flight simulations, the trainers observed and rated the performances of the simulation
crews. The crews they rated top in performance had a higher rate of
mitigation than crews they judged to be poor.

This finding seems at odds with the role played by indirectness in   31
the examples of crashes that we just saw. Linde concluded that since
every utterance functions on two levels—the referential (what it says)
and the relational (what it implies about the speaker's relationships),
crews that attend to the relational level will be better crews. A similar
explanation was suggested by Kunihiko Harada. He believes that the

secret of successful communication lies not in teaching subordinates to be more direct, but in teaching higher-ups to be more sensitive to indirect meaning. In other words, the crashes resulted not only because the co-pilots tried to alert the captains to danger indirectly but also because the captains were not attuned to the co-pilots' hints. What made for successful performance among the best crews might have been the ability — or willingness — of listeners to pick up on hints, just as members of families or longstanding couples come to understand each other's meaning without anyone being particularly explicit.

It is not surprising that a Japanese sociolinguist came up with this   32
explanation; what he described is the Japanese system, by which good communication is believed to take place when meaning is gleaned without being stated directly — or at all.

While Americans believe that "the squeaky wheel gets the grease"   33
(so it's best to speak up), the Japanese say, "The nail that sticks out gets hammered back in" (so it's best to remain silent if you don't want to be hit on the head). Many Japanese scholars writing in English have tried to explain to bewildered Americans the ethics of a culture in which silence is often given greater value than speech, and ideas are believed to be best communicated without being explicitly stated. Key concepts in Japanese give a flavor of the attitudes toward language that they reveal — and set in relief the strategies that Americans encounter at work when talking to other Americans.

Takie Sugiyama Lebra, a Japanese-born anthropologist, explains   34
that one of the most basic values in Japanese culture is *omoiyari*, which she translates as "empathy." Because of *omoiyari*, it should not be necessary to state one's meaning explicitly; people should be able to sense each other's meaning intuitively. Lebra explains that it is typical for a Japanese speaker to let sentences trail off rather than complete them because expressing ideas before knowing how they will be received seems intrusive. "Only an insensitive, uncouth person needs a direct, verbal, complete message," Lebra says.

Sasshi, the anticipation of another's message through insightful   35
guesswork, is considered an indication of maturity.

Considering the value placed on direct communication by Americans   36
in general, and especially by American business people, it is easy to imagine that many American readers may scoff at such conversational habits. But the success of Japanese businesses makes it impossible to continue to maintain that there is anything inherently inefficient about such conversational conventions. With indirectness, as with all aspects of conversational style, our own habitual style seems to make sense — seems polite, right and good. The light cast by the habits and assumptions of another culture can help us see our way to the flexibility and respect for other styles that is the only best way of speaking.

THINKING CRITICALLY ABOUT THE TEXT

In her essay, Tannen states that "indirectness is a fundamental element in human communication" (paragraph 4). Do you agree with Tannen on this point? What does she mean when she says that it is just as important to notice what we do not say as what we actually say?

QUESTIONS ON SUBJECT

1. How does Tannen define indirect speech? What does she see as the built-in liability of indirect speech? Do you see comparable liability inherent in direct speech?

2. Tannen doesn't contest a finding that fathers had a higher incidence of both direct imperatives and indirect orders than mothers. How does she interpret these results?

3. Why do you think Tannen doesn't tell her audience how to deal with an insecure boss?

4. Why is it typical for Japanese speakers to let their sentences trail off?

QUESTIONS ON STRATEGY

1. What is Tannen's thesis, and where does she present it? (Glossary: *Thesis*)

2. Tannen mostly uses examples in which men give direct orders. In what ways do these examples support her thesis?

3. For what audience has Tannen written this essay? Does this help to explain why she focuses primarily on indirect communication? Why or why not? (Glossary: *Audience*)

4. Tannen gives two examples of flight accidents that resulted from indirect speech, and yet she then explains that top-performing flight teams used indirect speech more often than poorly performing teams. How do these seemingly contradictory examples support the author's argument?

5. Explain how Tannen uses comparison and contrast to document the assertion that "indirectness is a fundamental element in human communication. It is also one of the elements that varies most from one culture to another, and one that can cause confusion and misunderstanding when speakers have different habits with regard to using it" (paragraph 4). (Glossary: *Comparison and Contrast*) How does this strategy enhance or support the dominant strategy of illustration in the essay?

QUESTIONS ON DICTION AND VOCABULARY

1. In paragraph 13, what irony does Tannen point out in the popular understanding of the word *militaristic*? (Glossary: *Irony*)

2. How would you describe Tannen's diction in this essay? (Glossary: *Diction*) Does she ever get too scientific for the general reader? If so, where do you think her language gets too technical? Why do you think she uses such language?

3. Refer to your desk dictionary to determine the meanings of the following words as Tannen uses them in this selection: *admonishing* (paragraph 3), *self-deprecating* (3), *manipulative* (5), *prerogative* (7), *subservience* (8), *cheeky* (10), *deferential* (11), *imperious* (13), *liability* (16), *mitigated* (28), *broached* (28), *gleaned* (32), *relief* (33), *empathy* (34).

CLASSROOM ACTIVITY USING ILLUSTRATION

Once you have established what examples you will use in a paper, you need to decide how you will organize them. Here are some major patterns of organization you may want to use:

- Chronological (oldest to newest, or the reverse)
- Spatial (top to bottom, left to right, inside to outside, and so forth)
- Most familiar to least familiar, or the reverse
- Easiest to most difficult to comprehend
- Easiest to most difficult to accept or carry out
- According to similarities or differences

Use one or more of these patterns to organize the examples in the paper you are currently working on, or to organize the lists of examples of career choice in your extended family that you generated for the classroom activity accompanying the Albom essay on page 170.

WRITING SUGGESTIONS

1. Tannen concludes that "the light cast by the habits and assumptions of another culture can help us see our way to the flexibility and respect for other styles that is the only best way of speaking" (paragraph 36). Write an essay in which you use concrete examples from your own experience, observation, or readings to agree or disagree with her conclusion.

2. Write an essay comparing the command styles of two people—either people you know or fictional characters. You might consider your parents, professors, coaches, television characters, or characters from movies or novels. What conclusions can you draw from your analysis? (Glossary: *Comparison and Contrast*) Illustrate your essay with clear examples of the two command styles.

Those Crazy Ideas

Isaac Asimov

Born in Russia in 1920, Isaac Asimov immigrated to the United States three years later. His death in 1992 ended a long career as a science-fiction and nonfiction writer. Asimov was uniquely talented at making topics from Shakespeare to physics not only comprehensible but entertaining to the average reader. He grew up in Brooklyn, New York, and went to Columbia University, earning his doctorate in 1948. At the time of his death, he had published more than five hundred books. It's Been a Good Life, *published in 2002, was compiled from selections from Asimov's three previous autobiographical volumes and contains "A Way of Thinking," Asimov's four-hundredth essay for the* Magazine of Fantasy and Science Fiction. *His science fiction includes the novels* The Gods Themselves *(1972) and* Foundation's Edge *(1982), and two of his short stories—* "Nightfall" *and* "Bicentennial Man"*—are sci-fi classics.*

When a Boston consulting firm contacted Asimov to learn where his futuristic ideas came from, Asimov's response was the essay "Those Crazy Ideas," which was subsequently published in the Magazine of Fantasy and Science Fiction *in January 1960. The example of Darwin's principles of evolution and natural selection spell out Asimov's theory of creativity.*

PREPARING TO READ

For you, what are the characteristics of a creative person? Do you consider yourself creative? Why or why not? What is it that separates a creative idea from an ordinary one? Explain.

Time and time again I have been asked (and I'm sure others who have, in their time, written science fiction have been asked too): "Where do you get your crazy ideas?" 1

Over the years, my answers have sunk from flattered confusion to a shrug and a feeble smile. Actually, I don't really know, and the lack of knowledge doesn't really worry me, either, as long as the ideas keep coming. 2

But then some time ago, a consultant firm in Boston, engaged in a sophisticated space-age project for the government, got in touch with me. 3

What they needed, it seemed, to bring their project to a successful conclusion were novel suggestions, startling new principles, conceptual breakthroughs. To put it into the nutshell of a well-turned phrase, they needed "crazy ideas." 4

Unfortunately, they didn't know how to go about getting crazy ideas, but some among them had read my science fiction, so they 5 looked me up in the phone book and called me to ask (in essence), "Dr. Asimov, where do you get your crazy ideas?"

Alas, I still didn't know, but as speculation is my profession, I am perfectly willing to think about the matter and share my thoughts with you. 6

The question before the house, then, is: How does one go about creating or inventing or dreaming up or stumbling over a new and revolutionary scientific principle? 7

For instance—to take a deliberately chosen example—how did Darwin come to think of evolution? 8

To begin with, in 1831, when Charles Darwin was twenty-two, he joined the crew of a ship called the *Beagle*. This ship was making a five-year voyage about the world to explore various coast lines and to increase man's geographical knowledge. Darwin went along as ship's naturalist, to study the forms of life in far-off places. 9

This he did extensively and well, and upon the return of the *Beagle* Darwin wrote a book about his experiences (published in 1840) which made him famous. In the course of this voyage, numerous observations led him to the conclusion that species of living creatures changed and developed slowly with time; that new species descended from old. This, in itself, was not a new idea. Ancient Greeks had had glimmerings of evolutionary notions. Many scientists before Darwin, including Darwin's own grandfather, had theories of evolution. 10

The trouble, however, was that no scientist could evolve an explanation for the *why* of evolution. A French naturalist, Jean-Baptiste de Lamarck, had suggested in the early 1800s that it came about by a kind of conscious effort or inner drive. A tree-grazing animal, attempting to reach leaves, stretched its neck over the years and transmitted a longer neck to its descendants. The process was repeated with each generation until a giraffe in full glory was formed. 11

The only trouble was that acquired characteristics are not inherited and this was easily proved. The Lamarckian explanation did not carry conviction. 12

Charles Darwin, however, had nothing better to suggest after several years of thinking about the problem. 13

But in 1798, eleven years before Darwin's birth, an English clergyman named Thomas Robert Malthus had written a book entitled *An Essay on the Principle of Population*. In this book Malthus suggested that the human population always increased faster than the food supply and that the population had to be cut down by either starvation, disease, or war; that these evils were therefore unavoidable. 14

In 1838 Darwin, still puzzling over the problem of the development of species, read Malthus's book. It is hackneyed to say "in a flash" but that, apparently, is how it happened. In a flash, it was clear to Darwin. Not only human beings increased faster than the food supply; 15

all species of living things did. In every case, the surplus population had to be cut down by starvation, by predators, or by disease. Now no two members of any species are exactly alike; each has slight individual variations from the norm. Accepting this fact, which part of the population was cut down?

Why—and this was Darwin's breakthrough—those members of the species who were less efficient in the race for food, less adept at fighting off or escaping from predators, less equipped to resist disease, went down.   16

The survivors, generation after generation, were better adapted, on the average, to their environment. The slow changes toward a better fit with the environment accumulated until a new (and more adapted) species had replaced the old. Darwin thus postulated the reason for evolution as being the action of *natural selection*. In fact, the full title of his book is *On the Origin of Species by Means of Natural Selection, or the Preservation of Favored Races in the Struggle for Life*. We just call it *The Origin of Species* and miss the full flavor of what it was he did.   17

It was in 1838 that Darwin received this flash and in 1844 that he began writing his book, but he worked on for fourteen years gathering evidence to back up his thesis. He was a methodical perfectionist and no amount of evidence seemed to satisfy him. He always wanted more. His friends read his preliminary manuscripts and urged him to publish. In particular, Charles Lyell (whose book *Principles of Geology*, published in 1830–1833, first convinced scientists of the great age of the earth and thus first showed there was *time* for the slow progress of evolution to take place) warned Darwin that someone would beat him to the punch.   18

While Darwin was working, another and younger English naturalist, Alfred Russel Wallace, was traveling in distant lands. He too found copious evidence to show that evolution took place and he too wanted to find a reason. He did not know that Darwin had already solved the problem.   19

He spent three years puzzling, and then in 1858, he too came across Malthus's book and read it. I am embarrassed to have to become hackneyed again, but in a flash he saw the answer. Unlike Darwin, however, he did not settle down to fourteen years of gathering and arranging evidence.   20

Instead, he grabbed pen and paper and at once wrote up his theory. He finished this in two days.   21

Naturally, he didn't want to rush into print without having his notions checked by competent colleagues, so he decided to send it to some well-known naturalist. To whom? Why, to Charles Darwin. To whom else?   22

I have often tried to picture Darwin's feeling as he read Wallace's essay which, he afterward stated, expressed matters in almost his own   23 words. He wrote to Lyell that he had been forestalled "with a vengeance."

Darwin might easily have retained full credit. He was well-known and there were many witnesses to the fact that he had been working on his project for a decade and a half. Darwin, however, was a man of the highest integrity. He made no attempt to suppress Wallace. On the contrary, he passed on the essay to others and arranged to have it published along with a similar essay of his own. The year after, Darwin published his book.

Now the reason I chose this case was that here we have two men making one of the greatest discoveries in the history of science independently and simultaneously and under precisely the same stimulus. Does that mean *anyone* could have worked out the theory of natural selection if they had but made a sea voyage and combined that with reading Malthus?

Well, let's see. Here's where the speculation starts.

To begin with, both Darwin and Wallace were thoroughly grounded in natural history. Each had accumulated a vast collection of facts in the field in which they were to make their breakthrough. Surely this is significant.

Now every man in his lifetime collects facts, individual pieces of data, items of information. Let's call these "bits" (as they do, I think, in information theory). The "bits" can be of all varieties: personal memories, girls' phone numbers, baseball players' batting averages, yesterday's weather, the atomic weights of the chemical elements.

Naturally, different men gather different numbers of different varieties of "bits." A person who has collected a larger number than usual of those varieties that are held to be particularly difficult to obtain—say, those involving the sciences and the liberal arts—is considered "educated."

There are two broad ways in which the "bits" can be accumulated. The more common way, nowadays, is to find people who already possess many "bits" and have them transfer those "bits" to your mind in good order and in predigested fashion. Our schools specialize in this transfer of "bits" and those of us who take advantage of them receive a "formal education."

The less common way is to collect "bits" with a minimum amount of live help. They can be obtained from books or out of personal experience. In that case you are "self-educated." (It often happens that "self-educated" is confused with "uneducated." This is an error to be avoided.)

In actual practice, scientific breakthroughs have been initiated by those who were formally educated, as for instance by Nicolaus Copernicus, and by those who were self-educated, as for instance by Michael Faraday.

To be sure, the structure of science has grown more complex over the years and the absorption of the necessary number of "bits" has become more and more difficult without the guidance of someone who has already absorbed them. The self-educated genius is therefore becoming rarer, though he has still not vanished. 33

However, without drawing any distinction according to the manner in which "bits" have been accumulated, let's set up the first criterion for scientific creativity: 34

1) The creative person must possess as many "bits" of information as possible; i.e., he must be educated. 35

Of course, the accumulation of "bits" is not enough in itself. We have probably all met people who are intensely educated, but who manage to be abysmally stupid, nevertheless. They have the "bits," but the "bits" just lie there. 36

But what is there one can do with "bits"? 37

Well, one can combine them into groups of two or more. Everyone does that; it is the principle of the string on the finger. You tell yourself to remember *a* (to buy bread) when you observe *b* (the string). You enforce a combination that will not let you forget *a* because *b* is so noticeable. 38

That, of course, is a conscious and artificial combination of "bits." It is my feeling that every mind is, more or less unconsciously, continually making all sorts of combinations and permutations of "bits," probably at random. 39

Some minds do this with greater facility than others; some minds have greater capacity for dredging the combinations out of the unconscious and becoming consciously aware of them. This results in "new ideas," in "novel outlooks." 40

The ability to combine "bits" with facility and to grow consciously aware of the new combinations is, I would like to suggest, the measure of what we call "intelligence." In this view, it is quite possible to be educated and yet not intelligent. 41

Obviously, the creative scientist must not only have his "bits" on hand but he must be able to combine them readily and more or less consciously. Darwin not only observed data, he also made deductions — clever and far-reaching deductions — from what he observed. That is, he combined the "bits" in interesting ways and drew important conclusions. 42

So the second criterion of creativity is: 43

2) The creative person must be able to combine "bits" with facility and recognize the combinations he has formed; i.e., he must be intelligent. 44

Even forming and recognizing new combinations is insufficient in itself. Some combinations are important and some are trivial. How do you tell which are which? There is no question but that a person who 45 cannot tell them apart must labor under a terrible disadvantage. As he plods after each possible new idea, he loses time and his life passes uselessly.

There is also no question but that there are people who somehow have the gift of seeing the consequences "in a flash" as Darwin and Wallace did; of feeling what the end must be without consciously going through every step of the reasoning. This, I suggest, is the measure of what we call "intuition."

46

Intuition plays more of a role in some branches of scientific knowledge than others. Mathematics, for instance, is a deductive science in which, once certain basic principles are learned, a large number of items of information become "obvious" as merely consequences of those principles. Most of us, to be sure, lack the intuitive powers to see the "obvious."

47

To the truly intuitive mind, however, the combination of the few necessary "bits" is at once extraordinarily rich in consequences. Without too much trouble they see them all, including some that have not been seen by their predecessors.

48

It is perhaps for this reason that mathematics and mathematical physics has seen repeated cases of first-rank breakthroughs by youngsters. Evariste Galois evolved group theory at twenty-one. Isaac Newton worked out calculus at twenty-three. Albert Einstein presented the theory of relativity at twenty-six, and so on.

49

In those branches of science which are more inductive and require larger numbers of "bits" to begin with, the average age of the scientists at the time of the breakthrough is greater. Darwin was twenty-nine at the time of his flash, Wallace was thirty-five.

50

But in any science, however inductive, intuition is necessary for creativity. So:

51

3) The creative person must be able to see, with as little delay as possible, the consequences of the new combinations of "bits" which he has formed; i.e., he must be intuitive.

52

But now let's look at this business of combining "bits" in a little more detail. "Bits" are at varying distances from each other. The more closely related two "bits" are, the more apt one is to be reminded of one by the other and to make the combination. Consequently, a new idea that arises from such a combination is made quickly. It is a "natural consequence" of an older idea, a "corollary." It "obviously follows."

53

The combination of less related "bits" results in a more startling idea; if for no other reason than that it takes longer for such a combination to be made, so that the new idea is therefore less "obvious." For a scientific breakthrough of the first rank, there must be a combination of "bits" so widely spaced that the random chance of the combination being made is small indeed. (Otherwise, it will be made quickly and be

54

considered but a corollary of some previous idea which will then be considered the "breakthrough.")

But then, it can easily happen that two "bits" sufficiently widely   55
spaced to make a breakthrough by their combination are not present in the same mind. Neither Darwin nor Wallace, for all their education, intelligence, and intuition, possessed the key "bits" necessary to work out the theory of evolution by natural selection. Those "bits" were lying in Malthus's book, and both Darwin and Wallace had to find them there.

To do this, however, they had to read, understand, and appreciate   56
the book. In short, they had to be ready to incorporate other people's "bits" and treat them with all the ease with which they treated their own.

It would hamper creativity, in other words, to emphasize intensity   57
of education at the expense of broadness. It is bad enough to limit the nature of the "bits" to the point where the necessary two would not be in the same mind. It would be fatal to mold a mind to the point where it was incapable of accepting "foreign bits."

I think we ought to revise the first criterion of creativity, then,   58
to read:

1) The creative person must possess as many "bits" as possible,   59
falling into as wide a variety of types as possible; i.e., he must be broadly educated.

As the total amount of "bits" to be accumulated increases with the   60
advance of science, it is becoming more and more difficult to gather enough "bits" in a wide enough area. Therefore, the practice of "brain-busting" is coming into popularity; the notion of collecting thinkers into groups and hoping that they will cross-fertilize one another into startling new breakthroughs.

Under what circumstances could this conceivably work? (After   61
all, anything that will stimulate creativity is of first importance to humanity.)

Well, to begin with, a group of people will have more "bits" on   62
hand than any member of the group singly since each man is likely to have some "bits" the others do not possess.

However, the increase in "bits" is not in direct proportion to the   63
number of men, because there is bound to be considerable overlapping. As the group increases, the smaller and smaller addition of completely new "bits" introduced by each additional member is quickly out-weighed by the added tensions involved in greater numbers; the longer wait to speak, the greater likelihood of being interrupted, and so on. It is my (intuitive) guess that five is as large a number as one can stand in such a conference.

Now of the three criteria mentioned so far, I feel (intuitively) that   64
intuition is the least common. It is more likely that none of the group

will be intuitive than that none will be intelligent or none educated. If no individual in the group is intuitive, the group as a whole will not be intuitive. You cannot add non-intuition and form intuition.

If one of the group is intuitive, he is almost certain to be intelligent and educated as well, or he would not have been asked to join the group in the first place. In short, for a brain-busting group to be creative, it must be quite small and it must possess at least one creative individual. But in that case, does that one individual need the group? Well, I'll get back to that later.   65

Why did Darwin work fourteen years gathering evidence for a theory he himself must have been convinced was correct from the beginning? Why did Wallace send his manuscript to Darwin first instead of offering it for publication at once?   66

To me it seems that they must have realized that any new idea is met by resistance from the general population who, after all, are not creative. The more radical the new idea, the greater the dislike and distrust it arouses. The dislike and distrust aroused by a first-class breakthrough are so great that the author must be prepared for unpleasant consequences (sometimes for expulsion from the respect of the scientific community; sometimes, in some societies, for death).   67

Darwin was trying to gather enough evidence to protect himself by convincing others through a sheer flood of reasoning. Wallace wanted to have Darwin on his side before proceeding.   68

It takes courage to announce the results of your creativity. The greater the creativity, the greater the necessary courage in much more than direct proportion. After all, consider that the more profound the breakthrough, the more solidified the previous opinions; the more "against reason" the new discovery seems, the more against cherished authority.   69

Usually a man who possesses enough courage to be a scientific genius seems odd. After all, a man who has sufficient courage or irreverence to fly in the face of reason or authority must be odd, if you define "odd" as "being not like most people." And if he is courageous and irreverent in such a colossally big thing, he will certainly be courageous and irreverent in many small things so that being odd in one way, he is apt to be odd in others. In short, he will seem to the non-creative, conforming people about him to be a "crackpot."   70

So we have the fourth criterion: 71

4) The creative person must possess courage (and to the general public may, in consequence, seem a crackpot).   72

As it happens, it is the crackpottery that is most often most noticeable about the creative individual. The eccentric and absentminded professor is a stock character in fiction; and the phrase "mad scientist" is almost a cliché.   73

(And be it noted that I am never asked where I get my interesting or   74
effective or clever or fascinating ideas. I am invariably asked where I get
my *crazy* ideas.)

Of course, it does not follow that because the creative individual is   75
usually a crackpot, that any crackpot is automatically an unrecognized
genius. The chances are low indeed, and failure to recognize that
the proposition cannot be so reversed is the cause of a great deal of
trouble.

Then, since I believe that combinations of "bits" take place quite at   76
random in the unconscious mind, it follows that it is quite possible
that a person may possess all four of the criteria I have mentioned in
superabundance and yet may never happen to make the necessary
combination. After all, suppose Darwin had never read Malthus. Would
he ever have thought of natural selection? What made him pick up
the copy? What if someone had come in at the crucial time and interrupted him?

So there is a fifth criterion which I am at a loss to phrase in any   77
other way than this:

5) A creative person must be lucky.   78

To summarize: 79

A creative person must be 1) broadly educated, 2) intelligent, 3) intu-   80
itive, 4) courageous, and 5) lucky.

How, then, does one go about encouraging scientific creativity? For   81
now, more than ever before in man's history, we must; and the need
will grow constantly in the future.

Only, it seems to me, by increasing the incidence of the various cri-   82
teria among the general population.

Of the five criteria, number 5 (luck) is out of our hands. We can   83
only hope; although we must also remember Louis Pasteur's famous
statement that "Luck favors the prepared mind." Presumably, if we
have enough of the four other criteria, we shall find enough of number
five as well.

Criterion 1 (broad education) is in the hands of our school system.   84
Many educators are working hard to find ways of increasing the quality
of education among the public. They should be encouraged to continue doing so.

Criteria 2 (intelligence) and 3 (intuition) are inborn and their inci-   85
dence cannot be increased in the ordinary way. However, they can be
more efficiently recognized and utilized. I would like to see methods
devised for spotting the intelligent and intuitive (particularly the latter)
early in life and treating them with special care. This, too, educators are
concerned with.

To me, though, it seems that it is criterion 4 (courage) that receives   86
the least concern, and it is just the one we may most easily be able to

handle. Perhaps it is difficult to make a person more courageous than he is, but that is not necessary. It would be equally effective to make it sufficient to be less courageous; to adopt an attitude that creativity is a permissible activity.

Does this mean changing society or changing human nature? I   87
don't think so. I think there are ways of achieving the end that do not involve massive change of anything, and it is here that brain-busting has its greatest chance of significance.

Suppose we have a group of five that includes one creative individ-   88
ual. Let's ask again what that individual can receive from the non-creative four.

The answer to me, seems to be just this: Permission!   89

They must permit him to create. They must tell him to go ahead   90
and be a crackpot.[1]

How is this permission to be granted? Can four essentially non-   91
creative people find it within themselves to grant such permission? Can the one creative person find it within himself to accept it?

I don't know. Here, it seems to me, is where we need experimenta-   92
tion and perhaps a kind of creative breakthrough about creativity. Once we learn enough about the whole matter, who knows—I may even find out where I get those crazy ideas.

THINKING CRITICALLY ABOUT THE TEXT

Asimov notes, "I am never asked where I get my interesting or effective or clever or fascinating ideas. I am invariably asked where I get my *crazy* ideas" (paragraph 74). Why do you suppose people react to Asimov this way? What does this tell you about society's willingness to accept potentially innovative or breakthrough thinking?

QUESTIONS ON SUBJECT

1. For Asimov, what are the five criteria for a creative person? Which criteria separate intelligent from creative people?

2. Asimov uses the example of Charles Darwin and Alfred Russel Wallace to illustrate the discovery of a "new and revolutionary scientific principle" (paragraph 7). What principle did these men discover, and how did each make his discovery?

---

[1]Always with the provision, of course, that the crackpot creation that results survives the test of hard inspection. Though many of the products of genius seem crackpot at first, very few of the creations that seem crackpot turn out, after all, to be products of genius.

3. How did Darwin react when he read Wallace's manuscript, which articulated the same theory Darwin himself had first discovered twenty years earlier?

4. Asimov believes that an educated person is one who has accumulated many pieces of information, which he calls "bits." According to Asimov, what are the two ways people accumulate "bits"?

5. What advice does Asimov offer concerning the practice of "brain-busting"? What does Asimov think are the essential ingredients of an effective group?

QUESTIONS ON STRATEGY

1. What is Asimov's purpose in writing this essay? (Glossary: *Purpose*)

2. Asimov takes care to tell us that the example of Charles Darwin was "deliberately chosen" (paragraph 8). How effective did you find this example? How does it illustrate each of the points that Asimov makes about creativity?

3. Asimov informs us that a creative person must be educated, intelligent, and intuitive—and then, after some discussion, he decides to "revise the first criterion for creativity" (paragraph 58). What does Asimov gain by adding the stipulation that the education should be "broad" at this point in his essay? Why do you think he organized his essay this way? (Glossary: *Organization*)

4. Asimov carefully compares how Darwin and Wallace made "one of the greatest discoveries in the history of science independently and simultaneously" (paragraph 25). What about these two scientists' careers does he compare? What insights into the creative person does this yield? (Glossary: *Comparison and Contrast*)

5. Asimov tells us that in "mathematics and mathematical physics" there have been a number of "first-rank breakthroughs by youngsters" (paragraph 49). What examples does he provide to document his case? Are they convincing? Explain.

6. How effective did you find Asimov's beginning and ending? How are the two linked? Explain.

QUESTIONS ON DICTION AND VOCABULARY

1. In talking about creativity's fourth criterion, courage, Asimov uses the words *crackpot* and *crackpottery*. Why do you suppose he chose these particular words? What alternatives might he have used? When noncreative, conforming people use the label *crackpot* to describe genius, what does Asimov imply they are saying about themselves?

2. Refer to your desk dictionary to determine the meanings of the following words as Asimov uses them in this selection: *evolution* (paragraph 8), *hackneyed* (15), *postulated* (17), *copious* (19), *stimulus* (25), *permutations* (39), *intuition* (47), *inductive* (50).

CLASSROOM ACTIVITY USING ILLUSTRATION

Some writers, like Edwin Way Teale on pages 150–51, use a series of short examples to illustrate the point they wish to make, while others, like Bill Russell on page 151 or Isaac Asimov in the essay under consideration, use a single, well-developed example to illustrate their generalizations. Using the first generalization with its example as a model, think of a single extended example that might be used to best illustrate each of the following generalizations:

> **Model**
>
> Generalization: Seat belts save lives.
>
> Example: Describe an automobile accident in which a friend's or relative's life was saved because the person was wearing a seat belt.
>
> Loud music can damage a person's hearing.
>
> Reading the directions for a new product you have just purchased can save time and aggravation.
>
> Humor can often make a bad situation more tolerable.
>
> Good study skills can improve a person's grades.

WRITING SUGGESTIONS

1. Asimov writes, "A creative person must be lucky" (paragraph 78). Is there more to creativity than just "dumb luck"? Is luck ever "dumb"? Is creativity something that happens passively or something one works at actively? Write an essay based on examples from your own experience, observation, and reading to agree or disagree with Asimov's assertion.

2. As Asimov reminds us, "it does not follow that because the creative individual is usually a crackpot, that any crackpot is automatically an unrecognized genius" (paragraph 75). What for you constitutes real genius? Using examples from your own experience and reading, write an essay in which you compare and contrast your thinking about creativity and genius with Asimov's. (Glossary: *Comparison and Contrast*) Before you start to write, you may find it helpful to refer to your Preparing to Read response for this selection.

In Search of Our Mothers' Gardens

Alice Walker

 *Best known for her Pulitzer Prize–winning novel* The Color Purple, *Alice Walker is a prolific writer of poetry, essays, and fiction. Walker was born in Georgia in 1944, the youngest of eight children in a sharecropping family. She took advantage of educational opportunities to escape a life of poverty and servitude, attending Spelman College in Georgia and then graduating from the prestigious Sarah Lawrence College in New York. An African American activist and feminist, Walker often deals with controversial subjects in her writing;* The Color Purple *(1982), the novel* Possessing the Secret of Joy *(1992), and the nonfiction* Warrior Marks *(1993) are known for this characteristic. Other widely acclaimed works by Walker include her collected poems,* Her Blue Body Everything We Know: Earthling Poems, 1965–1990 *(1991); a memoir entitled* The Same River Twice: Honoring the Difficult *(1996); a collection of essays,* Anything We Love Can Be Saved: A Writer's Activism *(1997); and a collection of stories,* The Way Forward Is with a Broken Heart *(2000). Walker's most recent work includes* Now Is the Time to Open Your Heart: A Novel *(2004), and* We Are the Ones We Have Been Waiting For: Light in a Time of Darkness *(2006), a collection of essays. Although much of her writing deals with pain and life's hardships, her work is not pessimistic; in the words of one reviewer, Walker's writing represents a "quest for peace and joy in a difficult world."*

In the following essay, the title piece from a collection of essays published in 1983, she explores what it has meant in the past—and, by implication, what it means today—to be a black woman in America.

PREPARING TO READ

Is everyone born with creative impulses, with the urge to indulge artistic expression of some kind, or is creativity a special gift granted only to a few? Are there ways to satisfy creativity other than with art? What happens to a person whose artistic drive is discouraged? Explain.

> I described her own nature and temperament. Told how they needed a larger life for their expression. . . . I pointed out that in lieu of proper channels, her emotions had overflowed into paths that dissipated them. I talked, beautifully I thought, about an art that would be born, an art that would open the way for women the likes of her. I asked her to hope, and build up an inner life against the coming of that day. . . . I sang, with a strange quiver in my voice, a promise song.
>
> —Jean Toomer,
> *"Avey,"* Cane

The poet speaking to a prostitute who falls asleep while he's talking — 1

When the poet Jean Toomer walked through the South in the early 2 twenties, he discovered a curious thing: black women whose spirituality was so intense, so deep, so *unconscious*, that they were themselves unaware of the richness they held. They stumbled blindly through their lives: creatures so abused and mutilated in body, so dimmed and confused by pain, that they considered themselves unworthy even of hope. In the selfless abstractions their bodies became to the men who used them, they became more than "sexual objects," even more than mere women: they became "Saints." Instead of being perceived as whole persons, their bodies became shrines, what was thought to be their minds became temples suitable for worship. These crazy Saints stared out at the world, wildly, like lunatics — or quietly, like suicides; and the "God" that was in their gaze was as mute as a great stone.

Who were these Saints? These crazy, loony, pitiful women? 3

Some of them, without a doubt, were our mothers and grandmothers. 4

In the still heat of the post-Reconstruction South, this is how they 5 seemed to Jean Toomer: exquisite butterflies trapped in an evil honey, toiling away their lives in an era, a century, that did not acknowledge them, except as "the *mule* of the world." They dreamed dreams that no one knew — not even themselves, in any coherent fashion — and saw visions no one could understand. They wandered or sat about the countryside crooning lullabies to ghosts, and drawing the mother of Christ in charcoal on courthouse walls.

They forced their minds to desert their bodies and their striving 6 spirits sought to rise, like frail whirlwinds from the hard red clay. And when those frail whirlwinds fell, in scattered particles, upon the ground, no one mourned. Instead, men lit candles to celebrate the emptiness that remained, as people do who enter a beautiful but vacant space to resurrect a God.

Our mothers and grandmothers, some of them: moving to music 7 not yet written. And they waited.

They waited for a day when the unknown thing that was in them 8 would be made known; but guessed, somehow in their darkness, that on the day of their revelation they would be long dead. Therefore to Toomer they walked, and even ran, in slow motion. For they were going nowhere immediate, and the future was not yet within their grasp. And men took our mothers and grandmothers, "but got no pleasure from it." So complex was their passion and their calm.

To Toomer, they lay vacant and fallow as autumn fields, with har- 9 vest time never in sight: and he saw them enter loveless marriages, without joy; and become prostitutes, without resistance, and become mothers of children, without fulfillment.

For these grandmothers and mothers of ours were not Saints, but   10
Artists; driven to a numb and bleeding madness by the springs of creativity in them for which there was no release. They were Creators, who
lived lives of spiritual waste, because they were so rich in spirituality—
which is the basis of Art—that the strain of enduring their unused and
unwanted talent drove them insane. Throwing away this spirituality
was their pathetic attempt to lighten the soul to a weight their work-
worn, sexually abused bodies could bear.

What did it mean for a black woman to be an artist in our grand-   11
mothers' time? In our great-grandmothers' day? It is a question with an
answer cruel enough to stop the blood.

Did you have a genius of a great-great-grandmother who died under   12
some ignorant and depraved white overseer's lash? Or was she required to
bake biscuits for a lazy backwater tramp, when she cried out in her soul to
paint watercolors of sunsets, or the rain falling on the green and peaceful
pasturelands? Or was her body broken and forced to bear children (who
were more often than not sold away from her)—eight, ten, fifteen,
twenty children—when her one joy was the thought of modeling heroic
figures of rebellion, in stone or clay?

How was the creativity of the black woman kept alive, year after   13
year and century after century, when for most of the years black people
have been in America, it was a punishable crime for a black person to
read or write? And the freedom to paint, to sculpt, to expand the mind
with an action did not exist. Consider, if you can bear to imagine it,
what might have been the result if singing, too, had been forbidden by
law. Listen to the voices of Bessie Smith, Billie Holiday, Nina Simone,
Roberta Flack, and Aretha Franklin, among others, and imagine those
voices muzzled for life. Then you may begin to comprehend the lives of
our "crazy," "Sainted" mothers and grandmothers. The agony of the
lives of women who might have been Poets, Novelists, Essayists, and
Short-Story Writers (over a period of centuries), who died with their
real gifts stifled within them.

And, if this were the end of the story, we would have cause to cry   14
out in my paraphrase of Okot p'Bitek's great poem:

O, my clanswomen
Let us all cry together!
Come,
Let us mourn the death of our mother,
The death of a Queen
The ash that was produced
By a great fire!
O, this homestead is utterly dead
Close the gates
With *lacari* thorns,

For our mother
The creator of the Stool is lost!
And all the young women
Have perished in the wilderness!

But this is not the end of the story, for all the young women — our
mothers and grandmothers, *ourselves* — have not perished in the
wilderness. And if we ask ourselves why, and search for and find the
answer, we will know beyond all efforts to erase it from our minds, just
exactly who, and of what, we black American women are.

One example, perhaps the most pathetic, most misunderstood one,
can provide a backdrop for our mothers' work: Phillis Wheatley,[1] a
slave in the 1700s.

Virginia Woolf,[2] in her book *A Room of One's Own*, wrote that in
order for a woman to write fiction she must have two things, certainly:
a room of her own (the key and lock) and enough money to support
herself.

What then are we to make of Phillis Wheatley, a slave, who owned
not even herself? This sickly, frail black girl who required a servant of
her own at times — her health was so precarious — and who, had she
been white, would have been easily considered the intellectual superior
of all women and most of the men in the society of her day.

Virginia Woolf wrote further, speaking of course not of our Phillis,
that "any woman born with a great gift in the sixteenth century [insert
"eighteenth century," insert "black woman," insert "born or made a
slave"] would certainly have gone crazed, shot herself, or ended her
days in some lonely cottage outside the village, half witch, half wizard
[insert "Saint"], feared and mocked at. For it needs little skill and psychology to be sure that a highly gifted girl who had tried to use her gift
for poetry would have been so thwarted and hindered by contrary
instincts [add "chains, guns, the lash, the ownership of one's body by
someone else, submission to an alien religion"], that she must have lost
her health and sanity to a certainty."

The key words, as they relate to Phillis, are "contrary instincts." For
when we read the poetry of Phillis Wheatley — and when we read the
novels of Nella Larsen or the oddly false-sounding autobiography of
that freest of all black women writers, Zora Hurston[3] — evidence of

15

16

17

18

19

20

---

[1]Wheatley (1753–1784) published several volumes of poetry and is considered the first important African American writer in the United States.

[2]Woolf (1882–1941) was an acclaimed English essayist and novelist.

[3]Larsen (1891–1964) wrote realistic novels about the relationships between
different races; Hurston (1903–1960) is known for her folklore research, novels,
and stories that convey the nuances of southern black speech.

"contrary instincts" is everywhere. Her loyalties were completely divided, as was, without question, her mind.

But how could this be otherwise? Captured at seven, a slave of wealthy, doting whites who instilled in her the "savagery" of the Africa they "rescued" her from . . . one wonders if she was even able to remember her homeland as she had known it, or as it really was.   21

Yet, because she did not try to use her gift for poetry in a world that made her a slave, she was "so thwarted and hindered by . . . contrary instincts, that she . . . lost her health. . . ." In the last years of her brief life, burdened not only with the need to express her gift but also with a penniless, friendless "freedom" and several small children for whom she was forced to do strenuous work to feed, she lost her health, certainly. Suffering from malnutrition and neglect and who knows what mental agonies, Phillis Wheatley died.   22

So torn by "contrary instincts" was black, kidnapped, enslaved Phillis that her description of "the Goddess"—as she poetically called the Liberty she did not have—is ironically, cruelly humorous. And, in fact, has held Phillis up to ridicule for more than a century. It is usually read prior to hanging Phillis's memory as that of a fool. She wrote: 23

> The Goddess comes, she moves divinely fair,
> Olive and laurel binds her *golden* hair.
> Wherever shines this native of the skies,
> Unnumber'd charms and recent graces rise. [My italics]

It is obvious that Phillis, the slave, combed the "Goddess's" hair every morning; prior, perhaps, to bringing in the milk, or fixing her mistress's lunch. She took her imagery from the one thing she saw elevated above all others.   24

With the benefit of hindsight we ask, "How could she?"   25

But at last, Phillis, we understand. No more snickering when your stiff, struggling, ambivalent lines are forced on us. We know now that you were not an idiot or a traitor; only a sickly little black girl, snatched from your home and country and made a slave; a woman who still struggled to sing the song that was your gift, although in a land of barbarians who praised you for your bewildered tongue. It is not so much what you sang, as that you kept alive, in so many of our ancestors, *the notion of song.*   26

Black women are called, in the folklore that so aptly identifies one's status in society, "the *mule* of the world," because we have been handed the burdens that everyone else—*everyone* else—refused to carry. We have also been called "Matriarchs," "Superwomen," and "Mean and Evil Bitches." Not to mention "Castrators" and "Sapphire's Mama." When we have pleaded for understanding, our character has been distorted; when we have asked for simple caring, we have been handed   27 empty inspirational appellations, then stuck in the farthest corner. When we have asked for love, we have been given children. In short, even our plainer gifts, our labors of fidelity and love, have been knocked down our throats. To be an artist and a black woman, even today, lowers our status in many respects, rather than raises it: and yet, artists we will be.

Therefore we must fearlessly pull out of ourselves and look at   28
and identify with our lives the living creativity some of our great-grandmothers were not allowed to know. I stress *some* of them because it is well known that the majority of our great-grandmothers knew, even without "knowing" it, the reality of their spirituality, even if they didn't recognize it beyond what happened in the singing at church— and they never had any intention of giving it up.

How they did it—those millions of black women who were not   29
Phillis Wheatley, or Lucy Terry or Frances Harper or Zora Hurston or Nella Larsen or Bessie Smith; or Elizabeth Catlett, or Katherine Dunham,[4] either—brings me to the title of this essay, "In Search of Our Mothers' Gardens," which is a personal account that is yet shared, in its theme and its meaning, by all of us. I found, while thinking about the far-reaching world of the creative black woman, that often the truest answer to a question that really matters can be found very close.

In the late 1920s my mother ran away from home to marry my   30
father. Marriage, if not running away, was expected of seventeen-year-old girls. By the time she was twenty, she had two children and was pregnant with a third. Five children later, I was born. And this is how I came to know my mother: she seemed a large, soft, loving-eyed woman who was rarely impatient in our home. Her quick, violent temper was on view only a few times a year when she battled with the white landlord who had the misfortune to suggest to her that her children did not need to go to school.

She made all the clothes we wore, even my brothers' overalls. She   31
made all the towels and sheets we used. She spent the summers canning vegetables and fruits. She spent the winter evenings making quilts enough to cover all our beds.

During the "working" day, she labored beside—not behind—my   32
father in the fields. Her day began before sunup, and did not end until late at night. There was never a moment for her to sit down, undisturbed, to unravel her own private thoughts; never a time free from interruption—by work or the noisy inquiries of her many children. And

[4]Accomplished African American female artists; the first five were writers, Smith was a singer and songwriter, Catlett a sculptor, and Dunham a choreographer and dancer.

yet, it is to my mother—and all our mothers who were not famous—
that I went in search of the secret of what has fed that muzzled and
often mutilated, but vibrant, creative spirit that the black woman has
inherited, and that pops out in wild and unlikely places to this day.

But when, you will ask, did my overworked mother have time to   33
know or care about feeding the creative spirit?

The answer is so simple that many of us have spent years discover-   34
ing it. We have constantly looked high, when we should have looked
high—and low.

For example: in the Smithsonian Institution in Washington, D.C.,   35
there hangs a quilt unlike any other in the world. In fanciful, inspired,
and yet simple and identifiable figures, it portrays the story of the Cru-
cifixion. It is considered rare, beyond price. Though it follows no
known pattern of quilt-making, and though it is made of bits and
pieces of worthless rags, it is obviously the work of a person of powerful
imagination and deep spiritual feeling. Below this quilt I saw a note
that says it was made by "an anonymous Black woman in Alabama, a
hundred years ago."

If we could locate this "anonymous" black woman from Alabama,   36
she would turn out to be one of our grandmothers—an artist who left
her mark in the only materials she could afford, and in the only
medium her position in society allowed her to use.

As Virginia Woolf wrote further, in *A Room of One's Own:*   37

> Yet genius of a sort must have existed among women as it must have
> existed among the working class. [Change this to "slaves" and "the wives
> and the daughters of sharecroppers."] Now and again an Emily Brontë or a
> Robert Burns [change this to "a Zora Hurston or a Richard Wright"] blazes
> out and proves its presence. But certainly it never got itself on to paper.
> When, however, one reads of a witch being ducked, of a woman possessed

by devils [or "Sainthood"], of a wise woman selling herbs [our root workers], or even a very remarkable man who had a mother, then I think we are on the track of a lost novelist, a suppressed poet, of some mute and inglorious Jane Austen. . . . Indeed, I would venture to guess that Anon, who wrote so many poems without signing them, was often a woman. . . .

And so our mothers and grandmothers have, more often than not   38
anonymously, handed on the creative spark, the seed of the flower they themselves never hoped to see: or like a sealed letter they could not plainly read.

And so it is, certainly, with my own mother. Unlike "Ma" Rainey's[5]   39
songs, which retained their creator's name even while blasting forth from Bessie Smith's mouth, no song or poem will bear my mother's name. Yet so many of the stories that I write, that we all write, are my mother's stories. Only recently did I fully realize this: that through years of listening to my mother's stories of her life, I have absorbed not only the stories themselves, but something of the manner in which she spoke, something of the urgency that involves the knowledge that her stories—like her life—must be recorded. It is probably for this reason that so much of what I have written is about characters whose counterparts in real life are so much older than I am.

But the telling of these stories, which came from my mother's lips   40
as naturally as breathing, was not the only way my mother showed herself as an artist. For stories, too, were subject to being distracted, to dying without conclusion. Dinners must be started, and cotton must be gathered before the big rains. The artist that was and is my mother showed itself to me only after many years. This is what I finally noticed:

Like Mem, a character in *The Third Life of Grange Copeland*, my   41
mother adorned with flowers whatever shabby house we were forced to live in. And not just your typical straggly country stand of zinnias, either. She planted ambitious gardens—and still does—with over fifty different varieties of plants that bloom profusely from early March until late November. Before she left home for the fields, she watered her flowers, chopped up the grass, and laid out new beds. When she returned from the fields she might divide clumps of bulbs, dig a cold pit, uproot and replant roses, or prune branches from her taller bushes or trees—until night came and it was too dark to see.

Whatever she planted grew as if by magic, and her fame as a grower   42
of flowers spread over three counties. Because of her creativity with her flowers, even my memories of poverty are seen through a screen of blooms—sunflowers, petunias, roses, dahlias, forsythia, spirea, delphiniums, verbena . . . and on and on.

---

[5]Rainey (1886–1939) was a famous blues singer and songwriter.

And I remember people coming to my mother's yard to be given 43
cuttings from her flowers; I hear again the praise showered on her
because whatever rocky soil she landed on, she turned into a garden. A
garden so brilliant with colors, so original in its design, so magnificent
with life and creativity, that to this day people drive by our house in
Georgia—perfect strangers and imperfect strangers—and ask to stand
or walk in my mother's art.

I notice that it is not only when my mother is working in her flowers 44
that she is radiant, almost to the point of being invisible—except as Creator: hand and eye. She is involved in work her soul must have. Ordering
the universe in the image of her personal conception of Beauty.

Her face, as she prepares the Art that is her gift, is a legacy of respect 45
she leaves to me, for all that illuminates and cherishes life. She has
handed down respect for the possibilities—and the will to grasp them.

For her, so hindered and intruded upon in so many ways, being 46
an artist has still been a daily part of her life. This ability to hold on,
even in very simple ways, is work black women have done for a very
long time.

This poem is not enough, but it is something, for the woman who 47
literally covered the holes in our walls with sunflowers:

They were women then
My mama's generation
Husky of voice—Stout of
Step
With fists as well as
Hands
How they battered down
Doors
And ironed
Starched white
Shirts
How they led
Armies
Headragged Generals
Across mined
Fields
Booby-trapped
Kitchens
To discover books
Desks
A place for us
How they knew what we
Must know
Without knowing a page
Of it
Themselves.

Guided by my heritage of a love of beauty and a respect for   48
strength — in search of my mother's garden, I found my own.

And perhaps in Africa over two hundred years ago, there was just such   49
a mother; perhaps she painted vivid and daring decorations in oranges
and yellows and greens on the walls of her hut; perhaps she sang — in a
voice like Roberta Flack's — *sweetly* over the compounds of her village;
perhaps she wove the most stunning mats or told the most ingenious stories of all the village storytellers. Perhaps she was herself a poet — though
only her daughter's name is signed to the poems that we know.

Perhaps Phillis Wheatley's mother was also an artist.   50

Perhaps in more than Phillis Wheatley's biological life is her   51
mother's signature made clear.

THINKING CRITICALLY ABOUT THE TEXT

Walker finds art in a quilt and a garden. Where have you encountered examples
of artistic expression in unusual forms or in everyday places? Describe one or
two. What do they suggest to you about the nature and motivation of their
creators?

QUESTIONS ON SUBJECT

1. Why does Walker open her essay with a quote from Jean Toomer? What
   surprising discovery did he make many years ago about black women in
   America? Where did his understanding of them fall short?

2. Who was Phillis Wheatley? Why might modern blacks consider her a
   "traitor"? What is Walker's opinion of her?

3. Walker gives two examples of her mother's artistry. What are these
   examples? What is the impact of each upon Walker herself?

QUESTIONS ON STRATEGY

1. Near the end of the essay, Walker includes a poem of her own, written in
   tribute to her mother and other black women of her mother's generation. Why is it appropriate here? What central idea does it support and
   exemplify? How does mixing two forms, prose and poetry, emphasize
   her main point?

2. Paragraph 11 uses a rhetorical question to introduce a turning point in
   the essay: "What did it mean for a black woman to be an artist in our
   grandmothers' time?" (Glossary: *Rhetorical Question*) What shift of
   emphasis does this question bring about? Although Walker says the
   answer is "cruel enough to stop the blood," she does not state it directly.
   In your own words, what is the answer?

3. Examples and illustrations have a purpose; usually they support an argument. (Glossary: *Argument*) Walker uses different types of examples

throughout this essay. Find and identify several different kinds of examples. What idea or argument does each support?

4. Walker tells of her mother's natural gift for narrative. (Glossary: *Narration*) The only brief examples of narrative in this essay occur when Walker tells about her mother. Find these examples, and explain why they are effective in their context.

5. Walker quotes Virginia Woolf, a white author, to support her vision of the suppressed female artist, but she also draws a contrast between Woolf's ancestors and her own. (Glossary: *Comparison and Contrast*) How does she make the contrast explicit? Why does Walker use Woolf as an example?

QUESTIONS ON DICTION AND VOCABULARY

1. In paragraph 44, what does Walker imply when she describes her mother as "radiant, almost to the point of being invisible"? What is the metaphor in this paragraph, and how does it relate to the earlier description of black women as "Saints"? Through these metaphors, what is Walker trying to express about the process of art? (Glossary: *Figures of Speech*)

2. What does Walker mean, in paragraph 34, when she says that "we should have looked high—and low" to find examples of the creative spirit? What kinds of places does she mean?

3. Walker, a poet, chooses words precisely. Be sure you know the meanings of these words as she uses them: *abstractions* (paragraph 2), *post-Reconstruction* (5), *revelation* (8), *depraved* (12), *precarious* (18), *doting* (21), *ambivalent* (26), *matriarchs* (27), *appellations* (27), *vibrant* (32).

CLASSROOM ACTIVITY USING ILLUSTRATION

Consider the following paragraph from the rough draft of a student paper on Americans' obsession with losing weight. The student writer wanted to show the sometimes bizarre extremes that people would go to in an effort to improve their appearances.

> Americans have long been obsessed with thinness—even at the risk of dying. In the 1930s, people took di-nitrophenol, an industrial poison, to lose weight. It boosted metabolism but caused blindness and some deaths. Since that time dieters have experimented with any number of bizarre schemes that seem to work wonders in the short term but often end in disappointment or disaster in the long term. Some weight loss strategies have even led to life-threatening eating disorders.

Try your hand at revising this paragraph, supplying specific examples as needed to illustrate and support the central idea contained in the writer's topic sentence.

WRITING SUGGESTIONS

1. Walker equates creative artistry with spirituality. Do you agree with the connection she makes? What does she mean by these two terms? How would you define them? What do you believe to be the wellspring of art? Write an essay in which you use numerous illustrations to define and exemplify the creative spirit. You might find it helpful to refer to your Preparing to Read and Responding to the Text entries.

2. Consider the photograph of the quilt maker and the young child on page 199. How do you "read" this photograph; what do you see happening in it? What do you think is the relationship between the two people? What is the young girl watching so intently? How would you describe the quilt that the woman is creating? What similarities and differences do you see between it and the one that is hanging in the background? Write an essay in which you discuss this photograph in the context of what Alice Walker is saying about black women in "In Search of Our Mothers' Gardens."

WRITING SUGGESTIONS FOR ILLUSTRATION

1. Write an essay on one of the following statements, using examples to illustrate your ideas. You should be able to draw some of your examples from personal experience and firsthand observations.

   a. Fads never go out of style.
   b. Television has produced a number of "classic" programs.
   c. Every college campus has its own unique slang terms.
   d. Making excuses sometimes seems like a national pastime.
   e. A liberal arts education can have many practical applications.
   f. All good teachers (or doctors, secretaries, auto mechanics, sales representatives) have certain traits in common.
   g. Television talk shows are an accurate (or inaccurate) reflection of our society.
   h. Good literature always teaches us something about our humanity.
   i. Grades are not always a good indication of what has been learned.
   j. Recycling starts with the individual.

2. Write an essay on one of the following statements, using examples to illustrate your ideas. Draw your examples from a variety of sources: your library's print and Internet resources, interviews, and information gathered from lectures and the media. As you plan your essay, consider whether you will want to use a series of short examples or one or more extended examples.

   a. Much has been (or should still be) done to eliminate barriers for the physically handicapped.
   b. Nature's oddities are numerous.
   c. Throughout history, dire predictions have been made about the end of the world.
   d. Boxing should be outlawed.
   e. The past predictions of science fiction are today's realities.
   f. The world has not seen an absence of warfare since World War II.
   g. Young executives have developed many innovative management strategies.
   h. A great work of art may come out of an artist's most difficult period.
   i. The misjudgments of our presidents can be useful lessons in leadership.
   j. Genius is 10 percent talent and 90 percent hard work.
   k. Drugs have taken an economic toll on American business.
   l. Democracy has attracted renewed interest in countries outside of the United States.

3. College students are not often given credit for the community volunteer work they do. Write a letter to the editor of your local newspaper in which you demonstrate, with several extended examples, the beneficial impact that you and your fellow students have had on the community.

4. How do advertisers portray older people in their advertisements? Based on your analysis of some real ads, how fair are advertisers to senior citizens? What tactics do advertisers use to sell their products to senior

citizens? Write an essay in which you use actual ads to illustrate two or three such tactics.

5. Most students would agree that in order to be happy and "well adjusted," people need to learn how to relieve stress and to relax. What strategies do you and your friends use to relax? What have been the benefits of these relaxation techniques for you? Write an article for the school newspaper in which you give examples of several of these techniques and encourage your fellow students to try them.

6. The Internet has profoundly altered the way people around the world communicate and share information. One area in which significant change is especially evident is education. While having so much information at your fingertips can be exciting, such technology is not with out its problems. What are the advantages and disadvantages of the Internet for teachers and students? Write an essay in which you analyze the Internet's educational value. Document your assessment with specific examples.

7. Some people think it's important to look their best and, therefore, give careful attention to the clothing they wear. Others do not seem to care. How much stock do you put in the old saying, "Clothes make the person"? Use examples of the people on your own campus or in your community to argue your position.

CHAPTER 7

Process Analysis

WHAT IS PROCESS ANALYSIS?

The strategy of process analysis involves separating an event, an operation, or a cycle of development into distinct steps, describing each step precisely, and arranging the steps in their proper order.

Whenever you explain how something occurs or how it can (and should) be done—how plants create oxygen, how to make ice cream, or merely how to get to your house—you are using process analysis. Each year, thousands of books and magazine articles tell us how to make home repairs, how to lose weight and get physically fit, how to improve our memories, how to play better tennis, how to manage our money. They try to satisfy our curiosity about how television shows are made, how jet airplanes work, and how monkeys, bees, or whales mate. People simply want to know how things work and how to do things for themselves, so it's not surprising that process analysis is one of the most widespread and popular forms of writing today.

Process analysis resembles narration because both strategies present a series of events occurring over time. But a narration is the story of how things happened in a particular way, during one particular period of time; process analysis relates how things always happen—or always should happen—in essentially the same way time after time.

Here is a process analysis written by Bernard Gladstone to explain how to light a fire in a fireplace.

First sentence establishes purpose: how to build a fire in a fireplace. Though "experts" differ as to the best technique to follow when building a fire, one generally accepted method consists of first laying a generous amount of crumpled

First paragraph takes us through six steps: the result is a wood-and-paper structure.

newspaper on the hearth between the andirons. Kindling wood is then spread generously over this layer of newspaper and one of the thickest logs is placed across the back of the andirons. This should be as close to the back of the fireplace as possible, but not quite touching it. A second log is then placed an inch or so in front of this, and a few additional sticks of kindling are laid across these two. A third log is then placed on top to form a sort of pyramid with air space between all logs so that flames can lick freely up between them.

The next three paragraphs present three common mistakes.

A mistake frequently made is in building the fire too far forward so that the rear wall of the fireplace does not get properly heated. A heated back wall helps increase the draft and tends to suck smoke and flames rearward with less chance of sparks or smoke spurting out into the room.

Another common mistake often made by the inexperienced fire-tender is to try to build a fire with only one or two logs, instead of using at least three. A single log is difficult to ignite properly, and even two logs do not provide an efficient bed with adequate fuel burning capacity.

Conclusion reinforces his directions for building a fire.

Use of too many logs, on the other hand, is also a common fault and can prove hazardous. Building too big a fire can create more smoke and draft than the chimney can safely handle, increasing the possibility of sparks or smoke being thrown out into the room. For best results, the homeowner should start with three medium-sized logs as described above, then add additional logs as needed if the fire is to be kept burning.

USING PROCESS ANALYSIS AS A WRITING STRATEGY

There are essentially two major reasons for writing a process analysis: to give directions, known as *directional process analysis*, and to inform, known as *informational process analysis*. Writers often combine one of these reasons with other rhetorical strategies to evaluate the process in question; this is known as *evaluative process analysis*. Let's take a look at each of these forms of process analysis more closely.

Directional Process Analysis

Writers use directional process analysis to provide readers with the necessary steps to achieve a desired result. The directions may be as simple as the instructions on a frozen-food package ("Heat in microwave on high for six to eight minutes. Rotate one-quarter turn halfway through cooking time, stir, and serve") or as complex as the operator's manual for a personal computer. Mortimer Adler proposes a method for getting the most out of reading in his essay "How to Mark a Book." First he compares what he sees as the "two ways in which one can own a book" and classifies book lovers into three categories. Then he presents his directions for how one should make marginal comments to get the most out of a book. In his "How to Say Nothing in 500 Words," Paul Roberts lays out the steps by which a writer can turn a dull subject into a lively, interesting one. No matter their length or complexity, however, all directions have the same purpose: to guide the reader through a clear and logically ordered series of steps toward a particular goal.

Informational Process Analysis

This strategy deals not with processes that readers are able to perform for themselves, but with processes that readers are curious about or would like to understand better: how presidents are elected, how plants reproduce, how an elevator works, how the brain processes and generates language. In the following selection from his *Lives Around Us*, Alan Devoe explains what happens to an animal when it goes into hibernation.

> The woodchuck's hibernation usually starts about the middle of September. For weeks he has been foraging with increased appetite among the clover blossoms and has grown heavy and slow-moving. Now, with the coming of mid-September, apples and corn and yarrow tops have become less plentiful, and the nights are cool. The woodchuck moves with slower gait, and emerges less and less frequently for feeding trips. Layers of fat have accumulated around his chest and shoulders, and there is thick fat in the axils of his legs. He has extended his summer burrow to a length of nearly thirty feet, and has fashioned a deep nest-chamber at the end of it, far below the level of the frost. He has carried in, usually, a little hay. He is ready for the Long Sleep.
>
> When the temperature of the September days falls below 50 degrees or so, the woodchuck becomes too drowsy to come forth from his burrow in the chilly dusk to forage. He remains in the deep nest-chamber, lethargic, hardly moving. Gradually, with the passing of hours or days, his coarse-furred body curls into a semicircle, like a fetus, nose-tip touching tail. The small legs are tucked in, the hand-like clawed forefeet folded. The woodchuck has become a compact ball. Presently the temperature of his body begins to fall.
>
> In normal life the woodchuck's temperature, though fluctuant, averages about 97 degrees. Now, as he lies tight-curled in a ball with the winter sleep stealing over him, this body heat drops ten degrees, twenty degrees, thirty. Finally, by the time the snow is on the ground and the woodchuck's winter dormancy has become complete, his temperature is only 38 or 40. With the falling of the body heat there is a slowing of his heartbeat and his respiration. In normal life he breathes thirty or forty times each minute; when he is excited, as many as a hundred times. Now he breathes slower and slower: ten times a minute, five times a minute, once a minute, and at

last only ten or twelve times in an hour. His heartbeat is a twentieth of normal. He has entered fully into the oblivion of hibernation.

The process Devoe describes is natural to woodchucks but not to humans, so obviously he cannot be giving instructions. Rather, he has created an informational process analysis to help us understand what happens during the remarkable process of hibernation. As Devoe's analysis reveals, hibernation is not a series of well-defined steps but a long, slow change from the activity of late summer to the immobility of a deep winter's sleep. The woodchuck does not suddenly stop feeding, nor do his temperature, pulse, and rate of respiration plummet at once. Using transitional expressions and time markers, Devoe shows us that the process lasts for weeks, even months. He connects the progress of hibernation with changes in the weather because the woodchuck's body responds to the dropping temperature as autumn sets in rather than to the passage of specific periods of time.

Evaluative Process Analysis

People often want to understand processes in order to evaluate them — to make improvements in how things are done, to better understand how events occur — and usually to improve those processes or to profit from their increased understanding. They want to improve processes by making them simpler, quicker, safer, or more efficient. They may also wish to analyze processes to understand them more deeply or accurately in order to base subsequent actions on more reliable information. An evaluative process analysis might give the reader insight into the writer's thinking about the pros and cons, the pitfalls, and the rewards of altering a widely understood and accepted process. In other words, an evaluative process analysis may offer a reconsideration of our understanding of a known process. If we look at Paul Roberts's "How to Say Nothing in 500 Words," we see that throughout the essay he describes an ineffective writing process used by some students and then compares and contrasts it with a more effective process. Whether used to direct, inform, or evaluate, process analysis is an invaluable critical thinking skill.

Using Process Analysis across the Disciplines

When writing essays in the academic disciplines, you will have many opportunities to use the strategy of process analysis to both organize and strengthen the presentation of your ideas. To determine whether or not process analysis is the right strategy for you in a particular paper, use the four-step method first described in

"Determining Your Strategy" (pages 24–25). Consider the following examples, which illustrate how this four-step method works for typical college papers:

Psychology

MAIN IDEA: Most people go through a rather predictable grief process when a friend or loved one dies.

QUESTION: What are the steps in the grieving process?

STRATEGY: Process Analysis. The word *steps* signals the need to list the stages of the grieving process.

SUPPORTING STRATEGY: Description. Each step might be described and be accompanied by descriptions of the subject's behavior throughout the process.

Biology

MAIN IDEA: Human blood samples can be tested to determine their blood groups.

QUESTION: What steps are followed in typing human blood?

STRATEGY: Process Analysis. The words *steps* suggests a sequence of activities that is to be followed in testing blood.

SUPPORTING STRATEGY: Comparison and Contrast. Comparison and contrast might be used to differentiate blood characteristics and chemistry. Classification might be used to place samples in various categories.

Folklore

MAIN IDEA: Folklorists uses several main methods for gathering their data.

QUESTION: How do folklorists go about collecting data?

STRATEGY: Process Analysis. The words *how do* and *go about* suggest process analysis.

SUPPORTING STRATEGY: Illustration and Argumentation. Illustration can give examples of particular data and how it is collected. Argumentation might support one method over others.

SAMPLE STUDENT ESSAY USING PROCESS ANALYSIS AS A WRITING STRATEGY

Shoshanna Lew was born in Pinetop, Arizona, and was a double major in English and music at the University of Vermont. After graduation, she continued her studies in graduate school as a musicologist. In this informative essay, Lew explains the process for selecting people to serve on juries in New York City. Notice, as you read, how she manages to explain clearly the steps in the process, as well as accommodate two audiences, those who would welcome jury duty and those who would rather be doing just about anything else.

Title: Introduces mixed feelings about the prospect of jury duty

How (Not) to Be Selected
for Jury Duty
Shoshanna Lew

Sentence: Effective one-word sentence

"SUMMONS." The red-lettered envelope slipped out from behind the junk mail and magazines. At first, I thought it must be for one of my parents, but, when I looked closer, I realized that it was *my* name on the jury duty notice. I didn't even know eighteen-year-old college students were *eligible* for jury duty, but a quick Google search told me otherwise. Great, for my summer vacation, I'd be trapped inside a jury box listening to dull testimony, or worse, examining grotesque photos of bullet wounds à la a *CSI* episode. On the upside, the $44 a day for serving was more than what I was making at my summer internship.

1

Thesis: Jury selection is a multi-step process.

Exemption process is explained.

Jury selection in New York City is a multi-step process. It starts bright and early with a video extolling the virtues of the justice system in which each potential juror is participating by simply showing up on the appointed day and time. After the video finishes, the bailiff in charge of the jury pool collects everyone's cards and fields the requests of people to postpone or be exempt from their civic duty. Doctors' letters appear out of handbags and suited business people wave their Blackberries to show that they are far too busy to be on a jury. As the bailiff — who determines the fate of each potential juror — dismisses people, the crowd thins down to those who will be eligible to be called to juries in the next three days. Since it is summer, my full-time student status doesn't let me off the hook. Once this process is complete, the remaining people begin doing what they will do for most of their time: they wait.

2

From the jury room, the courthouse looks nothing like the ones on television. Presumably — according to our introductory video — somewhere in the building lawyers are making arguments before judges, settling cases out of court, or succeeding in getting charges dropped. But in the jury room, folks read, watch television (CNN only), or nap. Suddenly, an announcement comes

3

over the intercom. A case has been called; jury members will be empaneled — meaning a select group from the jury pool will be questioned, and some selected to sit on the jury — in fifteen minutes.

Bailiff presents jurors' cards.

Once the bailiff is informed that a jury is being called, he brings out a bin containing cards, one for each potential juror. Just like the bins used in raffles at county fairs, the bailiff turns the crank several times and begins to pull out names. The bailiff assigns each person a number, and the lucky raffle winners are escorted into the jury room where they sit in the order they were called and fill out questionnaires. Beyond the basics of name and address, jurists provide level of education, place of birth, and employment information, and disclose whether or not they have relatives working in medical, legal, or insurance professions. (Bring a family tree with you on jury duty day. You'll be asked to explain jobs of any relation!)

Organization: Paragraph addresses general questions asked of all jurors.

Unity: Paragraph stays on topic of questions asked of all jurors.

Unlike John Grisham legal thrillers, in which a dramatic jury questioning occurs in a courtroom with a judge and court reporter (and some rhetorical fireworks), a real jury selection may or may not happen in front of a judge. After the lawyers acquaint themselves with the potential jurists' questionnaires, they ask all the jurors if they have any philosophical objections to the American legal system and the role of a jury in it. These questions focus on beliefs about the justice system, but are phrased to weed out only those people with the strongest opinions *against* the American justice system. (This is a good time to find your inner anarchist.) The lawyers also want to make sure that no panelist has any connection to a party to the case — be it the plaintiff, the defendant, the lawyers in the case, or others affiliated with the attorneys' firms.

Organization: Plaintiff's lawyer's questions

Once these preliminaries have been dealt with, the actual questioning begins. First, the lawyer for the plaintiff — the person with the legal complaint — presents the basis for the lawsuit. Then, the plaintiff's lawyer questions the jurors. He asks questions to the entire group, and he also addresses jurors about specific information on their questionnaires. Much of the questioning is meant to illuminate potential biases that jury members might harbor. For instance, doctors can expect to face intense scrutiny if they are being considered for a malpractice case. Jurors will also be questioned about their ability to put aside connections they have to the participants in the case — such as a shared profession or common alma mater — and be objective in weighing evidence.

Organization: Defense attorney's questions

When the plaintiff's lawyer has finished posing questions, the defense attorney — who represents the person being sued — takes her turn. Again, the potential jurors hear a short summary of the case but from the defense's perspective. Once more, the lawyer asks specific jurors about their background and directs inquiries to the entire group. During this part of the process people begin to be dismissed from the case. At this point, you'll probably also wish for some courtroom drama to break up the monotony of the day, but you're not likely to see a war of words. Despite the numerous jokes intimating otherwise, lawyers tend to remain polite, if not cordial, during jury selection. If you are lucky enough to be one of the later jurors to be questioned, you'll have plenty of time to figure out what answers will give you the best chance of being dismissed from or accepted to — if that's you're goal — the jury.   7

Organization: Final jury selection is made.

Finally, the lawyers pick their jury. Even though they dismiss some people based on their answers to questions as the inquiries are made, they make their final "picks" only after the defense finishes its part. After conferring privately, the lawyers provide a bailiff with their list of jurors and the bailiff announces the final outcome to the panel. In the reverse of a playground kickball game, the bailiff first names the people who will not be on the jury. Those who are left at the end make up Team Jury.   8

Conclusion: Why attorneys may have chosen as they did

It's difficult to know why the lawyers choose who they do. My guess is that they look for people who seem the least likely to let their emotions play a part in weighing evidence and for people with the stamina to spend more than a week listening to dense testimony. Jury selection doesn't have the theatricality of *Law and Order*, but it is clear that the lawyers are invested in assembling the fairest jury possible — not simply the one most likely to rule in their favor — out of the candidates pulled from that raffle bin.   9

Analyzing Shoshanna Lew's Essay
of Process Analysis: Questions for Discussion

1. Lew shifts from the past tense (paragraph 1) to the present tense (paragraphs 2–9) in her essay. Why is it important for her to put the actual jury selection process in the present tense?

2. Try explaining Lew's analysis of the jury selection process to a friend. Is it more or less complex than you first thought? Did you leave any parts of the process out? Did you get the activities out of order? Explain.

3. Lew's title indicates that some people may want to serve on a jury while others may not. Serving on a jury is an important civic responsibility, so why do you think there are mixed feelings about it? How do you feel about the prospect of serving on a jury?

SUGGESTIONS FOR USING PROCESS ANALYSIS AS A WRITING STRATEGY

As you plan and revise your essay of process analysis, be mindful of the five-step writing process described in Chapter 2 (see pages 14–31). Pay particular attention to the basic requirements and essential ingredients of this strategy.

Planning Your Essay of Process Analysis

Know the Process You Are Writing About.   There's no substitute for thorough knowledge of your subject. Be sure that you have more than a vague or general grasp of the process you are writing about. Make sure you analyze it fully, from beginning to end. You can sometimes convince yourself that you understand an entire process when, in fact, your understanding is somewhat superficial. If you were analyzing the process by which children learn language, you wouldn't want to rely on only one expert's account. Instead, it would be a good idea to read explanations by several authorities on the subject. Turning to more than one account not only reinforces your understanding of key points in the process, but also points out various ways the process is performed; you may want to consider these alternatives in your writing.

Have a Clear Purpose.   Giving directions for administering cardiopulmonary resuscitation and explaining how the El Niño phenomenon unfolds are worthy purposes for writing a process analysis paper. Many process analysis papers go beyond these fundamental purposes, however. They lay out processes to evaluate them, to suggest alternative steps, to point out shortcomings in generally accepted practices, and to suggest improvements. In short, process analysis papers are frequently persuasive or argumentative; they use an understanding and discussion of process analysis to achieve another goal: to persuade readers that there is a better way of doing or understanding a given process.

Organizing and Writing Your Essay of Process Analysis

Organize the Process into Steps.   As much as possible, make each step a simple and well-defined action, preferably a single action. To guide yourself in doing so, write a scratch outline listing the steps. Here, for example, is an outline of Bernard Gladstone's directions for building a fire.

Process Analysis of Building a Fire in a Fireplace

1. Put down crumpled newspaper.
2. Lay kindling.
3. Place back log near rear wall but not touching.
4. Place front log an inch forward.
5. Bridge logs with kindling.
6. Place third log on top of kindling bridge.

Next, check your outline to make sure that the steps are in the right order and that none has been omitted. Then analyze your outline more carefully. Are any steps so complex that they need to be described in some detail—or perhaps divided into more steps? Will you need to explain the purpose of a certain step because the reason for it is not obvious? Especially in an informational process analysis, two steps may take place at the same time; perhaps they are performed by different people or different parts of the body. Does your outline make this clear? (One solution is to assign both steps the same number but divide them into substeps by labeling one of them "A" and the other "B.") When you feel certain that the steps of the process are complete and correct, ask yourself two more questions. Will the reader need any other information to understand the process—definitions of unusual terms, for example, or descriptions of special equipment? Should you anticipate common mistakes or misunderstandings and discuss them, as Gladstone does? If so, be sure to add an appropriate note or two to your scratch outline as a reminder.

Use Transitions to Link the Steps.   Transitional words and phrases like *then*, *next*, *after doing this*, and *during the summer months* can both emphasize and clarify the sequence of steps in your process analysis. The same is true of sequence markers like *first*, *second*, *third*, and so on. Devoe uses such words to make clear which stages in the hibernation process are simultaneous and which are not; Gladstone includes an occasional *first* or *then* to alert us to shifts from one step to the next. But both writers are careful not to overuse these words, and you should exercise the same caution. Transitional words are a resource of language, but they should not be used arbitrarily.

Revising and Editing Your Essay of Process Analysis

Energize Your Writing: Use the Active Voice and Strong Action Verbs. Writers prefer the active voice because it stresses the doer of an action, is lively and emphatic, and uses strong descriptive verbs. The passive voice, on the other hand, stresses what was done rather than who did it and uses forms of the weak verb *to be.*

ACTIVE   The coaches analyzed the game film, and the fullback decided to rededicate herself to playing defense.

PASSIVE   A game film analysis was performed by the coaches, and a rededication to playing defense was decided upon by the fullback.

Sometimes, however, the doer of an action is unknown or less important than the recipient of an action. In this case, it is acceptable to use the passive voice:

The Earth's moon was formed more than 4 billion years ago.

When you revise your drafts, scan your sentences for passive constructions and weak verbs. Put your sentences into the active voice and find strong action verbs to replace weak verbs. Instead of the weak verb *run,* use *fly, gallop, hustle, jog, race, rush, scamper, scoot, scramble, tear,* or *trot,* for example. Instead of the weak verb *say,* use *declare, express, muse, mutter, pronounce, report, respond, recite, reply, snarl,* or *utter,* for example. Forms of the verb *to be* (*is, are, was, were, will be, should be*) are weak and nondescriptive and, therefore, should be avoided whenever possible. If you can't form a picture of a verb's action in your mind, it is most likely a weak verb. Here are some common weak verbs you should replace with strong action verbs in your writing:

have, had, has	get
make	involve
concern	determine
reflect	become
provide	go
do	appear
use	

Use Consistent Verb Tense.   A verb's tense indicates when an action is taking place: some time in the past, right now, or in the future. Using verb tense consistently helps your readers understand time changes in your writing. Inconsistent verb tenses — or *shifts* — within a sentence confuse readers and are especially noticeable in narration and process analysis writing, which are sequence and time oriented. Generally, you should write in the past or present tense and maintain that tense throughout your sentence:

INCONSISTENT   I mixed the eggs and sugar and then add the flour.

Mixed is past tense; *add* is present tense.

CORRECTED   I mix the eggs and sugar and then add the flour.

The sentence is now consistently in the present tense. The sentence can also be revised to be consistently in the past tense:

CORRECTED   I mixed the eggs and sugar and then added the flour.

Here's another example:

INCONSISTENT   The painter studied the scene and pulls a fan brush decisively from her cup.

Studied is past tense, indicating an action that has already taken place; *pulls* is present tense, indicating an action taking place now.

CORRECTED   The painter studies the scene and pulls a fan brush decisively from her cup.
CORRECTED   The painter studied the scene and pulled a fan brush decisively from her cup.

Share Your Drafts with Others.   Try sharing the drafts of your essays with other students in your writing class to make sure that your process analysis works, that it makes its point. Ask them if there are any steps in the process that they do not understand. Have them tell you what they think is the point of your essay. If their answers differ from what you intended, have them indicate the passages that led them to their interpretations so that you can change your text accordingly. To maximize the effectiveness of conferences with your peers, utilize the guidelines presented on pages 27–28. Feedback from these conferences often provides one or more places where you can start revising.

Question Your Own Work While Revising and Editing. Revision is best done by asking yourself key questions about what you have written. Begin by reading, preferably aloud, what you have written. Reading aloud forces you to pay attention to every single word, and you are more likely to catch lapses in the logical flow of thought. After you have read your paper through, answer the following questions for revising and editing and make the necessary changes.

Questions for Revising and Editing: Process Analysis

1. Do I have a thorough knowledge of the process I chose to write about?
2. Have I clearly informed readers about how to perform the process (directional process analysis), or have I explained how a process occurs (informational process analysis)? Does my choice reflect the overall purpose of my process analysis paper?
3. Have I divided the process into clear, readily understandable steps?
4. Did I pay particular attention to transitional words to take readers from one step to the next?
5. Are all my sentences in the active voice?
6. Have I used strong action verbs, and is my tense consistent?
7. Have I succeeded in tailoring my diction to my audience's familiarity with the subject?
8. Are my pronoun antecedents clear?
9. How did my test reader respond to my essay? Did he or she find any confusing passages or any missing steps?
10. Have I avoided errors in grammar, punctuation, and mechanics?

How to Mark a Book

Mortimer Adler

Writer, editor, and educator Mortimer Adler (1902–2001) was born in New York City. A high school dropout, Adler completed the undergraduate program at Columbia University in three years, but he did not graduate because he refused to take the mandatory swimming test. Adler is recognized for his editorial work on the Encyclopaedia Britannica *and for his leadership of the Great Books Program at the University of Chicago, where adults from all walks of life gathered twice a month to read and discuss the classics.*

In the following essay, which first appeared in the Saturday Review of Literature *in 1940, Adler offers a timeless lesson: He explains how to take full ownership of a book by marking it up, by making it "a part of yourself."*

PREPARING TO READ

When you read a book that you must understand thoroughly and remember for a class or for your own purposes, what techniques do you use to help you understand what you are reading? What helps you remember important parts of the book and improve your understanding of what the author is saying?

1   You know you have to read "between the lines" to get the most out of anything. I want to persuade you to do something equally important in the course of your reading. I want to persuade you to "write between the lines." Unless you do, you are not likely to do the most efficient kind of reading.

2   I contend, quite bluntly, that marking up a book is not an act of mutilation but of love.

3   You shouldn't mark up a book which isn't yours. Librarians (or your friends) who lend you books expect you to keep them clean, and you should. If you decide that I am right about the usefulness of marking books, you will have to buy them. Most of the world's great books are available today in reprint editions.

4   There are two ways in which one can own a book. The first is the property right you establish by paying for it, just as you pay for clothes and furniture. But this act of purchase is only the prelude to possession. Full ownership comes only when you have made it a part of yourself, and the best way to make yourself a part of it is by writing in it. An illustration may make the point clear. You buy a beefsteak and transfer it from the butcher's icebox to your own. But you do not own the beefsteak in the most important sense until you consume it and get it into

your bloodstream. I am arguing that books, too, must be absorbed in your bloodstream to do you any good.

Confusion about what it means to *own* a book leads people to a false reverence for paper, binding, and type—a respect for the physical thing—the craft of the printer rather than the genius of the author. They forget that it is possible for a man to acquire the idea, to possess the beauty, which a great book contains, without staking his claim by pasting his bookplate inside the cover. Having a fine library doesn't prove that its owner has a mind enriched by books; it proves nothing more than that he, his father, or his wife, was rich enough to buy them.

There are three kinds of book owners. The first has all the standard sets and best-sellers—unread, untouched. (This deluded individual owns woodpulp and ink, not books.) The second has a great many books—a few of them read through, most of them dipped into, but all of them as clean and shiny as the day they were bought. (This person would probably like to make books his own, but is restrained by a false respect for their physical appearance.) The third has a few books or many—every one of them dog-eared and dilapidated, shaken and loosened by continual use, marked and scribbled in from front to back. (This man owns books.)

Is it false respect, you may ask, to preserve intact and unblemished a beautifully printed book, an elegantly bound edition? Of course not. I'd no more scribble all over a first edition of *Paradise Lost* than I'd give my baby a set of crayons and an original Rembrandt! I wouldn't mark up a painting or a statue. Its soul, so to speak, is inseparable from its body. And the beauty of a rare edition or of a richly manufactured volume is like that of a painting or a statue.

But the soul of a book *can* be separated from its body. A book is more like the score of a piece of music than it is like a painting. No great musician confuses a symphony with the printed sheets of music. Arturo Toscanini reveres Brahms, but Toscanini's score of the C-minor Symphony is so thoroughly marked up that no one but the maestro himself can read it. The reason why a great conductor makes notations on his musical scores—marks them up again and again each time he returns to study them—is the reason why you should mark your books. If your respect for magnificent binding or typography gets in the way, buy yourself a cheap edition and pay your respects to the author.

Why is marking up a book indispensable to reading? First, it keeps you awake. (And I don't mean merely conscious; I mean wide awake.) In the second place, reading, if it is active, is thinking, and thinking tends to express itself in words, spoken or written. The marked book is usually the thought-through book. Finally, writing helps you remember the thoughts you had, or the thoughts the author expressed. Let me develop these three points.

If reading is to accomplish anything more than passing time, it 10 must be active. You can't let your eyes glide across the lines of a book and come up with an understanding of what you have read. Now an ordinary piece of light fiction, like say, *Gone with the Wind*, doesn't require the most active kind of reading. The books you read for pleasure can be read in a state of relaxation, and nothing is lost. But a great book, rich in ideas and beauty, a book that raises and tries to answer great fundamental questions, demands the most active reading of which you are capable. You don't absorb the ideas of John Dewey[1] the way you absorb the crooning of Mr. Vallee.[2] You have to reach for them. That you cannot do while you're asleep.

If, when you've finished reading a book, the pages are filled with 11 your notes, you know that you read actively. The most famous active reader of great books I know is President Hutchins, of the University of Chicago. He also has the hardest schedule of business activities of any man I know. He invariably reads with a pencil, and sometimes, when he picks up a book and pencil in the evening, he finds himself, instead of making intelligent notes, drawing what he calls "caviar factories" on the margins. When that happens, he puts the book down. He knows he's too tired to read, and he's just wasting time.

But, you may ask, why is writing necessary? Well, the physical act 12 of writing, with your own hand, brings words and sentences more sharply before your mind and preserves them better in your memory. To set down your reaction to important words and sentences you have read, and the questions they have raised in your mind, is to preserve those reactions and sharpen those questions.

Even if you wrote on a scratch pad, and threw the paper away 13 when you had finished writing, your grasp of the book would be surer. But you don't have to throw the paper away. The margins (top and bottom, as well as side), the end-papers, the very space between the lines, are all available. They aren't sacred. And, best of all, your marks and notes become an integral part of the book and stay there forever. You can pick up the book the following week or year, and there are all your points of agreement, disagreement, doubt, and inquiry. It's like resuming an interrupted conversation with the advantage of being able to pick up where you left off.

And that is exactly what reading a book should be: a conversation 14 between you and the author. Presumably he knows more about the

---

[1]John Dewey (1859–1952) was an educational philosopher who had a profound influence on learning through experimentation.

[2]Rudy Vallee (1901–1986) was a popular singer of the 1920s, famous for his crooning high notes.

subject than you do; naturally, you'll have the proper humility as you approach him. But don't let anybody tell you that a reader is supposed to be solely on the receiving end. Understanding is a two-way operation; learning doesn't consist in being an empty receptacle. The learner has to question himself and question the teacher. He even has to argue with the teacher, once he understands what the teacher is saying. And marking a book is literally an expression of your differences, or agreements of opinion, with the author.

There are all kinds of devices for marking a book intelligently and   15
fruitfully. Here's the way I do it:

1. *Underlining*: of major points, of important or forceful statements.   16

2. *Vertical lines at the margin*: to emphasize a statement already   17
underlined.

3. *Star, asterisk, or other doo-dad at the margin*: to be used sparingly,   18
to emphasize the ten or twenty most important statements in the book. (You may want to fold the bottom corner of each page on which you use such marks. It won't hurt the sturdy paper on which most modern books are printed, and you will be able to take the book off the shelf at any time and, by opening it at the folded-corner page, refresh your recollection of the book.)

4. *Numbers in the margin*: to indicate the sequence of points the   19
author makes in developing a single argument.

5. *Numbers of other pages in the margin*: to indicate where else in the   20
book the author made points relevant to the point marked; to tie up the ideas in a book, which, though they may be separated by many pages, belong together.

6. *Circling*: of key words or phrases.   21

7. *Writing in the margin, or at the top or bottom of the page, for the sake*   22
of: recording questions (and perhaps answers) which a passage raised in your mind; reducing a complicated discussion to a simple statement; recording the sequence of major points right through the book. I use the end-papers at the back of the book to make a personal index of the author's points in the order of their appearance.

The front end-papers are, to me, the most important. Some people   23
reserve them for a fancy bookplate. I reserve them for fancy thinking. After I have finished reading the book and making my personal index on the back end-papers, I turn to the front and try to outline the book, not page by page, or point by point (I've already done that at the back), but as an integrated structure, with a basic unity and an order of parts. This outline is, to me, the measure of my understanding of the work.

If you're a die-hard anti-book-marker, you may object that the   24
margins, the space between the lines, and the end-papers don't give you room enough. All right. How about using a scratch pad slightly smaller than the page-size of the book—so that the edges of the sheets won't protrude? Make your index, outlines, and even your notes on the

pad, and then insert these sheets permanently inside the front and back covers of the book.

Or, you may say that this business of marking books is going to slow up your reading. It probably will. That's one of the reasons for doing it. Most of us have been taken in by the notion that speed of reading is a measure of our intelligence. There is no such thing as the right speed for intelligent reading. Some things should be read quickly and effortlessly, and some should be read slowly and even laboriously. The sign of intelligence in reading is the ability to read different things differently according to their worth. In the case of good books, the point is not to see how many of them you can get through, but rather how many can get through you—how many you can make your own. A few friends are better than a thousand acquaintances. If this be your aim, as it should be, you will not be impatient if it takes more time and effort to read a great book than it does a newspaper. 25

You may have one final objection to marking books. You can't lend them to your friends because nobody else can read them without being distracted by your notes. Furthermore, you won't want to lend them because a marked copy is a kind of intellectual diary, and lending it is almost like giving your mind away. 26

If your friend wishes to read your *Plutarch's Lives*, *Shakespeare*, or *The Federalist Papers*, tell him gently but firmly to buy a copy. You will lend him your car or your coat—but your books are as much a part of you as your head or your heart. 27

THINKING CRITICALLY ABOUT THE TEXT

After you have read Adler's essay, compare your answer to the Preparing to Read prompt with Adler's guidelines for reading. What are the most significant differences between Adler's guidelines and your own? How can you better make the books you read part of yourself?

QUESTIONS ON SUBJECT

1. What are the three kinds of book owners Adler identifies? What are their differences?

2. According to Adler, why is marking up a book indispensable to reading? Do you agree with his three arguments? (Glossary: *Argumentation*) Why or why not?

3. What does Adler mean when he writes "the soul of a book *can* be separated from its body" (paragraph 8)? Is the separation a good thing? Explain.

4. Adler says that reading a book should be a conversation between the reader and the author. What characteristics does he say the conversation

should have? How does marking a book help in carrying on and preserving the conversation?

5. What kinds of devices do you use for "marking a book intelligently and fruitfully" (paragraph 15)? How useful do you find these devices?

QUESTIONS ON STRATEGY

1. In the first paragraph, Adler writes, "I want to persuade you to do something equally important in the course of your reading. I want to persuade you to 'write between the lines.'" What assumptions does Adler make about his audience when he chooses to use the parallel structure of "I want to persuade you . . ."? (Glossary: *Audience; Parallelism*) Is stating his intention so blatantly an effective way of presenting his argument? (Glossary: *Argumentation*) Why or why not?

2. Adler expresses himself very clearly throughout the essay, and his topic sentences are carefully crafted. (Glossary: *Topic Sentence*) Reread the topic sentences for paragraphs 3–6, and identify how each introduces the main idea for the paragraph and unifies it.

3. Throughout the essay, Adler provides the reader with a number of verbal cues ("There are two ways," "Let me develop these three points"). What do these verbal cues indicate about the organizational connections of the essay? (Glossary: *Organization*) Explain how Adler's organization creates an essay that logically follows from sentence to sentence and from paragraph to paragraph.

4. Summarize in your own words Adler's process analysis about how one should mark a book. Explain how Adler's process analysis is also an argument for the correct way to read. (Glossary: *Argumentation*)

5. Adler's process analysis is also a description of an event or a sequence of events (how to read). Does he claim that his recommended reading process will aid the reader's understanding, increase the reader's interest, or both?

QUESTIONS ON DICTION AND VOCABULARY

1. Adler makes an analogy that links reading books with the statement "A few friends are better than a thousand acquaintances" (paragraph 25). (Glossary: *Analogy*) Explain how this analogy works. Why is this analogy important to Adler's overall argument?

2. Throughout the essay, Adler uses the personal pronoun *I* to describe his reading experience. (Glossary: *Point of View*) How does this personalized voice help or hinder the explanation of the process of reading?

3. What does Adler mean by the phrase "active reading"?

CLASSROOM ACTIVITY USING PROCESS ANALYSIS

This exercise requires that you work in pairs. Draw a simple geometric design similar to one of the following without letting your partner see your drawing:

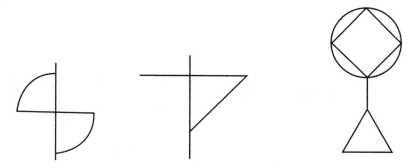

With the finished design in front of you, write a set of directions that will allow your partner to reproduce it accurately. Before writing your directions, ask yourself how you will convey the context for your instructions, where you will begin, and how what you write may help your partner or lead your partner astray. As your partner attempts to draw the design from your instructions, do not offer any verbal advice. Let your directions speak for themselves. Once you have finished, compare your drawing to the one your partner has produced. Discuss the results with your partner and, if time allows, with the entire class.

WRITING SUGGESTIONS

1. Write a directional process analysis in which you present your techniques for getting the most enjoyment out of a common activity. For example, perhaps you have a set routine you follow for spending an evening watching television—preparing popcorn, checking the program listings, clearing off the coffee table, finding the remote control, settling into your favorite chair, and so on. Choose from the following topics:

   How to listen to music
   How to eat an ice-cream cone
   How to reduce stress
   How to wash a dog
   How to play a sport or game

2. Adler devotes a large portion of his essay to persuading his audience that marking books is a worthwhile task. (Glossary: *Persuasion*) Write an essay in which you instruct your audience about how to do something they do not necessarily wish to do or they do not think they need to do. For instance, before explaining how to buy the best MP3 player, you may need to convince readers that they *should* buy an MP3 player. Write your directional process analysis after making a convincing argument for the validity of the process you wish to present. (Glossary: *Argument*)

How to Say Nothing in 500 Words

Paul Roberts

Paul Roberts (1917–1967) was a linguist, a teacher, and a writer at San Jose State College from 1946 to 1960 and at Cornell University from 1962 to 1964. His books on writing, including English Syntax *(1954) and* Patterns of English *(1956), have helped generations of high school and college students become better writers.*

"How to Say Nothing in 500 Words" is taken from his best-known book, Understanding English *(1958). Although written almost fifty years ago, the essay is still relevant for student writers today. Good writing, Roberts tells us, is not simply a matter of filling up a page; rather, the words have to hold the reader's interest, and they must say something. In this essay, Roberts uses lively prose and a step-by-step process to guide the student from the blank page to the finished essay. His bag of writing strategies holds good advice for anyone who wants to write well.*

PREPARING TO READ

How do you feel about writing? Do you find writing difficult? What are some of your most memorable experiences with writing in school or during your free time? How have these experiences affected your current attitude toward writing? Explain.

Nothing About Something

It's Friday afternoon, and you have almost survived another week of classes. You are just looking forward dreamily to the weekend when the English instructor says: "For Monday you will turn in a five-hundred word composition on college football." 1

Well, that puts a good big hole in the weekend. You don't have any strong views on college football one way or the other. You get rather excited during the season and go to all the home games and find it rather more fun than not. On the other hand, the class has been reading Robert Hutchins in the anthology and perhaps Shaw's "Eighty-Yard Run," and from the class discussion you have got the idea that the instructor thinks college football is for the birds. You are no fool, you. You can figure out what side to take. 2

After dinner you get out the portable typewriter that you got for high school graduation. You might as well get it over with and enjoy Saturday and Sunday. Five hundred words is about two double-spaced 3 pages with normal margins. You put in a sheet of paper, think up a title, and you're off:

WHY COLLEGE FOOTBALL SHOULD
BE ABOLISHED

College football should be abolished because it's bad for the school and also bad for the players. The players are so busy practicing that they don't have any time for their studies.

This, you feel, is a mighty good start. The only trouble is that it's only thirty-two words. You still have four hundred and sixty-eight to go, and you've pretty well exhausted the subject. It comes to you that you do your best thinking in the morning, so you put away the type-writer and go to the movies. But the next morning you have to do your washing and some math problems, and in the afternoon you go to the game. The English instructor turns up too, and you wonder if you've taken the right side after all. Saturday night you have a date, and Sunday morning you have to go to church. (You shouldn't let English assignments interfere with your religion.) What with one thing and another, it's ten o'clock Sunday night before you get out the typewriter again. You make a pot of coffee and start to fill out your views on college football. Put a little meat on the bones.

WHY COLLEGE FOOTBALL SHOULD
BE ABOLISHED

In my opinion, it seems to me that college football should be abolished. The reason why I think this to be true is because I feel that football is bad for the colleges in nearly every respect. As Robert Hutchins says in his article in our anthology in which he discusses college football, it would be better if the colleges had race horses and had races with one another, because then the horses would not have to attend classes. I firmly agree with Mr. Hutchins on this point, and I am sure that many other students would agree too.

One reason why it seems to me that college football is bad is that it has become too commercial. In the olden times when people played football just for the fun of it, maybe college football was all right, but they do not play football just for the fun of it now as they used to in the old days. Nowadays college football is what you might call a big business. Maybe this is not true at all schools, and I don't think it is especially true here at State, but certainly this is the case at most colleges and universities in America nowadays, as Mr. Hutchins points out in his very interesting article. Actually the coaches and alumni go around to the high schools and offer the high school stars large salaries to come to their colleges and play football for them. There was one case where a high school star was offered a convertible if he would play football for a certain college.

Another reason for abolishing college football is that it is bad for the players. They do not have time to get a college education, because they are so busy playing football. A football player has to practice every afternoon from three to six, and then he is so tired that he can't concentrate on his studies. He just feels like dropping off to sleep after dinner, and then the next day he goes to his classes without having studied and maybe he fails the test.

(Good ripe stuff so far, but you're still a hundred and fifty-one words from home. One more push.)

Also I think college football is bad for the colleges and the universities because not very many students get to participate in it. Out of a college of ten thousand students only seventy-five or a hundred play football, if that many. Football is what you might call a spectator sport. That means that most people go to watch it but do not play it themselves.

(Four hundred and fifteen. Well, you still have the conclusion, and when you retype it, you can make the margins a little wider.)

These are the reasons why I agree with Mr. Hutchins that college football should be abolished in American colleges and universities.

On Monday you turn it in, moderately hopeful, and on Friday it   5
comes back marked "weak in content" and sporting a big "D."

This essay is exaggerated a little, not much. The English instructor   6
will recognize it as reasonably typical of what an assignment on college football will bring in. He knows that nearly half of the class will contrive in five hundred words to say that college football is too commercial and bad for the players. Most of the other half will inform him that college football builds character and prepares one for life and brings prestige to the school. As he reads paper after paper all saying the same thing in almost the same words, all bloodless, five hundred words dripping out of nothing, he wonders how he allowed himself to get trapped into teaching English when he might have had a happy and interesting life as an electrician or a confidence man.

Well, you may ask, what can you do about it? The subject is one on   7
which you have few convictions and little information. Can you be expected to make a dull subject interesting? As a matter of fact, this is precisely what you are expected to do. This is the writer's essential task. All subjects, except sex, are dull until somebody makes them interesting. The writer's job is to find the argument, the approach, the angle, the wording that will take the reader with him. This is seldom easy, and it is particularly hard in subjects that have been much discussed: College Football, Fraternities, Popular Music, Is Chivalry Dead?, and the like. You will feel that there is nothing you can do with such subjects

except repeat the old bromides. But there are some things you can do which will make your papers, if not throbbingly alive, at least less insufferably tedious than they might otherwise be.

Avoid the Obvious Content

Say the assignment is college football. Say that you've decided to be against it. Begin by putting down the arguments that come to your mind: it is too commercial, it takes the students' minds off their studies, it is hard on the players, it makes the university a kind of circus instead of an intellectual center, for most schools it is financially ruinous. Can you think of any more arguments just off hand? All right. Now when you write your paper, *make sure that you don't use any of the material on this list.* If these are the points that leap to your mind, they will leap to everyone else's too, and whether you get a "C" or a "D" may depend on whether the instructor reads your paper early when he is fresh and tolerant or late, when the sentence "In my opinion, college football has become too commercial," inexorably repeated, has brought him to the brink of lunacy. 8

Be against college football for some reason or reasons of your own. If they are keen and perceptive ones, that's splendid. But even if they are trivial or foolish or indefensible, you are still ahead so long as they are not everybody else's reasons too. Be against it because the colleges don't spend enough money on it to make it worthwhile, because it is bad for the characters of spectators, because the players are forced to attend classes, because the football stars hog all the beautiful women, because it competes with baseball and is therefore un-American and possibly Communist inspired. There are lots of more or less unused reasons for being against college football. 9

Sometimes it is a good idea to sum up and dispose of the trite and conventional points before going on to your own. This has the advantage of indicating to the reader that you are going to be neither trite nor conventional. Something like this: 10

> We are often told that college football should be abolished because it has become too commercial or because it is bad for the players. These arguments are no doubt very cogent, but they don't really go to the heart of the matter.

Then you go to the heart of the matter.

Take the Less Usual Side

One rather simple way of getting interest into your paper is to take the side of the argument that most of the citizens will want to avoid. If the assignment is an essay on dogs, you can, if you choose, explain that dogs 11 are faithful and lovable companions, intelligent, useful as guardians of the house and protectors of children, indispensable in police work—in short, when all is said and done, man's best friends. Or you can suggest that those big brown eyes conceal, more often than not, a vacuity of mind and an inconstancy of purpose; that the dogs you have known most intimately have been mangy, ill-tempered brutes, incapable of instruction; and that only your nobility of mind and fear of arrest prevent you from kicking the flea-ridden animals when you pass them on the street.

Naturally, personal convictions will sometimes dictate your approach. If the assigned subject is "Is Methodism Rewarding to the Individual?" and you are a pious Methodist, you have really no choice. But few assigned subjects, if any, will fall in this category. Most of them will lie in broad areas of discussion with much to be said on both sides. They are intellectual exercises and it is legitimate to argue now one way and now another, as debaters do in similar circumstances. Always take the side that looks to you hardest, least defensible. It will almost always turn out to be easier to write interestingly on that side. 12

This general advice applies where you have a choice of subjects. If you are to choose among "The Value of Fraternities" and "My Favorite High School Teacher" and "What I Think about Beetles," by all means plump for the beetles. By the time the instructor gets to your paper, he will be up to his ears in tedious tales about the French teacher at Bloombury High and assertions about how fraternities build character and prepare one for life. Your views on beetles, whatever they are, are bound to be a refreshing change. 13

Don't worry too much about figuring out what the instructor thinks about the subject so that you can cuddle up with him. Chances are his views are no stronger than yours. If he does have convictions and you oppose them, his problem is to keep from grading you higher than you deserve in order to show he is not biased. This doesn't mean that you should always cantankerously dissent from what the instructor says; that gets tiresome too. And if the subject assigned is "My Pet Peeve," do not begin, "My pet peeve is the English instructor who assigns papers on 'my pet peeve.'" This was still funny during the War of 1812, but it has sort of lost its edge since then. It is in general good manners to avoid personalities. 14

Slip Out of Abstraction

If you will study the essay on college football . . . you will perceive that one reason for its appalling dullness is that it never gets down to particulars. It is just a series of not very glittering generalities: "football is bad for the colleges," "it has become too commercial," "football is a big business," "it is bad for the players," and so on. Such round phrases thudding against the reader's brain are unlikely to convince him, though they may well render him unconscious. 15

If you want the reader to believe that college football is bad for the players, you have to do more than say so. You have to display the evil. Take your roommate, Alfred Simkins, the second-string center. Picture poor old Alfy coming home from football practice every evening, bruised and aching, agonizingly tired, scarcely able to shovel the mashed potatoes into his mouth. Let us see him staggering up to the room, getting out his econ textbook, peering desperately at it with his good eye, falling asleep and failing the test in the morning. Let us share his unbearable tension as Saturday draws near. Will he fail, be demoted, lose his monthly allowance, be forced to return to the coal mines? And if he succeeds, what will be his reward? Perhaps a slight ripple of applause when the third-string center replaces him, a moment of elation in the locker room if the team wins, of despair if it loses. What will he look back on when he graduates from college? Toil and torn ligaments. And what will be his future? He is not good enough for pro football, and he is too obscure and weak in econ to succeed in stocks and bonds. College football is tearing the heart from Alfy Simkins and, when it finishes with him, will callously toss aside the shattered hulk. 16

This is no doubt a weak enough argument for the abolition of college football, but it is a sight better than saying, in three or four variations, that college football (in your opinion) is bad for the players. 17

Look at the work of any professional writer and notice how constantly he is moving from the generality, the abstract statement, to the concrete example, the facts and figures, the illustration. If he is writing on juvenile delinquency, he does not just tell you that juveniles are (it seems to him) delinquent and that (in his opinion) something should be done about it. He shows you juveniles being delinquent, tearing up movie theatres in Buffalo, stabbing high school principals in Dallas, smoking marijuana in Palo Alto. And more than likely he is moving toward some specific remedy, not just a general wringing of the hands. 18

It is no doubt possible to be *too* concrete, too illustrative or anecdotal, but few inexperienced writers err this way. For most the soundest advice is to be seeking always for the picture, to be always turning general remarks into seeable examples. Don't say, "Sororities teach girls the social graces." Say, "Sorority life teaches a girl how to carry on a conversation while pouring tea, without sloshing the tea into the saucer." Don't say, "I like certain kinds of popular music very much." Say, "Whenever I hear Gerber Spinklittle play 'Mississippi Man' on the trombone, my socks creep up my ankles." 19

Get Rid of Obvious Padding

The student toiling away at his weekly English theme is too often tormented by a figure: five hundred words. How, he asks himself, is he 20 to achieve this staggering total? Obviously by never using one word when he can somehow work in ten.

He is therefore seldom content with a plain statement like "Fast driving is dangerous." This has only four words in it. He takes thought, and the sentence becomes: 21

> In my opinion, fast driving is dangerous.

Better, but he can do better still:

> In my opinion, fast driving would seem to be rather dangerous.

If he is really adept, it may come out:

> In my humble opinion, though I do not claim to be an expert on this complicated subject, fast driving, in most circumstances, would seem to be rather dangerous in many respects, or at least so it would seem to me.

Thus four words have been turned into forty, and not an iota of content has been added.

Now this is a way to go about reaching five hundred words, and if you are content with a "D" grade, it is as good a way as any. But if you aim higher, you must work differently. Instead of stuffing your sentences with straw, you must try steadily to get rid of the padding, to make your sentences lean and tough. If you are really working at it, your first draft will greatly exceed the required total, and then you will work it down, thus: 22

> It is thought in some quarters that fraternities do not contribute as much as might be expected to campus life.
> Some people think that fraternities contribute little to campus life.

> The average doctor who practices in small towns or in the country must toil night and day to heal the sick.
> Most country doctors work long hours.

> When I was a little girl, I suffered from shyness and embarrassment in the presence of others.
> I was a shy little girl.

> It is absolutely necessary for the person employed as a marine fireman to give the matter of steam pressure his undivided attention at all times.
> The fireman has to keep his eye on the steam gauge.

You may ask how you can arrive at five hundred words at this rate. Simply. You dig up more real content. Instead of taking a couple of obvious points off the surface of the topic and then circling warily around them for six paragraphs, you work in and explore, figure out   23 the details. You illustrate. You say that fast driving is dangerous, and then you prove it. How long does it take to stop a car at forty and at eighty? How far can you see at night? What happens when a tire blows? What happens in a head-on collision at fifty miles an hour? Pretty soon your paper will be full of broken glass and blood and headless torsos, and reaching five hundred words will not really be a problem.

Call a Fool a Fool

Some of the padding in freshman themes is to be blamed not on anxiety about the word minimum but on excessive timidity. The student writes, "In my opinion, the principal of my high school acted in ways that I believe every unbiased person would have to call foolish." This isn't exactly what he means. What he means is, "My high school principal was a fool." If he was a fool, call him a fool. Hedging the thing about with "in-my-opinion's" and "it-seems-to-me's" and "as-I-see-it's" and "at-least-from-my-point-of-view's" gains you nothing. Delete these phrases whenever they creep into your paper. 24

The student's tendency to hedge stems from a modesty that in other circumstances would be commendable. He is, he realizes, young and inexperienced, and he half suspects that he is dopey and fuzzy-minded beyond the average. Probably only too true. But it doesn't help to announce your incompetence six times in every paragraph. Decide what you want to say and say it as vigorously as possible, without apology and in plain words. 25

Linguistic diffidence can take various forms. One is what we call *euphemism*. This is the tendency to call a spade "a certain garden implement" or women's underwear "unmentionables." It is stronger in some eras than others and in some people than others but it always operates more or less in subjects that are touchy or taboo: death, sex, madness, and so on. Thus we shrink from saying, "He died last night" but say instead, "passed away," "left us," "joined his Maker," "went to his reward." Or we try to take off the tension with a lighter cliché: "kicked the bucket," "cashed in his chips," "handed in his dinner pail." We have found all sorts of ways to avoid saying *mad*: "mentally ill," "touched," "not quite right upstairs," "feeble-minded," "innocent," "simple," "off his trolley," "not in his right mind." Even such a now plain word as *insane* began as a euphemism with the meaning "not healthy." 26

Modern science, particularly psychology, contributes many polysyllables in which we can wrap our thoughts and blunt their force. To many writers there is no such thing as a bad schoolboy. Schoolboys are maladjusted or unoriented or misunderstood or in need of guidance or lacking in continued success toward satisfactory integration of the personality as a social unit, but they are never bad. Psychology no doubt makes us better men or women, more sympathetic and tolerant, but 27 it doesn't make writing any easier. Had Shakespeare been confronted with psychology, "To be or not to be" might have come out, "To continue as a social unit or not to do so. That is the personality problem. Whether 'tis a better sign of integration at the conscious level to display a psychic tolerance toward the maladjustments and repressions induced by one's lack of orientation in one's environment or—" But Hamlet would never have finished the soliloquy.

Writing in the modern world, you cannot altogether avoid modern jargon. Nor, in an effort to get away from euphemism, should you salt your paper with four-letter words. But you can do much if you will mount guard against those roundabout phrases, those echoing polysyllables that tend to slip into your writing to rob it of its crispness and force. 28

Beware of the Pat Expression

Other things being equal, avoid phrases like "other things being equal." Those sentences that come to you whole, or in two or three doughy lumps, are sure to be bad sentences. They are no creation of yours but pieces of common thought floating in the community soup. 29

Pat expressions are hard, often impossible, to avoid, because they come too easily to be noticed and seem too necessary to be dispensed with. No writer avoids them altogether, but good writers avoid them more often than poor writers. 30

By "pat expressions" we mean such tags as "to all practical intents and purposes," "the pure and simple truth," "from where I sit," "the time of his life," "to the ends of the earth," "in the twinkling of an eye," "as sure as you're born," "over my dead body," "under cover of darkness," "took the easy way out," "when all is said and done," "told him time and time again," "parted the best of friends," "stand up and be counted," "gave him the best years of her life," "worked her fingers to the bone." Like other clichés, these expressions were once forceful. Now we should use them only when we can't possibly think of anything else. 31

Some pat expressions stand like a wall between the writer and thought. Such a one is "the American way of life." Many student writers feel that when they have said that something accords with the American way of life or does not they have exhausted the subject. Actually, they have stopped at the highest level of abstraction. The American way of life is the complicated set of bonds between a hundred and eighty million ways. All of us know this when we think about it, but the tag phrase too often keeps us from thinking about it. 32

So with many another phrase dear to the politician: "this great land of ours," "the man in the street," "our national heritage." These may prove our patriotism or give a clue to our political beliefs, but otherwise they add nothing to the paper except words. 33

Colorful Words

The writer builds with words, and no builder uses a raw material more slippery and elusive and treacherous. A writer's work is a constant struggle to get the right word in the right place, to find that particular word that will convey his meaning exactly, that will persuade the reader or soothe him or startle or amuse him. He never succeeds altogether—sometimes he feels that he scarcely succeeds at all—but such successes as he has are what make the thing worth doing. 34

There is no book of rules for this game. One progresses through everlasting experiment on the basis of ever-widening experience. There are few useful generalizations that one can make about words as words, but there are perhaps a few. 35

Some words are what we call "colorful." By this we mean that they are calculated to produce a picture or induce an emotion. They are dressy instead of plain, specific instead of general, loud instead of soft. Thus, in place of "Her heart beat," we may write "Her heart *pounded, throbbed, fluttered, danced.*" Instead of "He sat in his chair," we may say, "He *lounged, sprawled, coiled.*" Instead of "It was hot," we may say, "It was *blistering, sultry, muggy, suffocating, steamy, wilting.*" 36

However, it should not be supposed that the fancy word is always better. Often it is as well to write "Her heart beat" or "It was hot" if that is all it did or all it was. Ages differ in how they like their prose. The nineteenth century liked it rich and smoky. The twentieth has usually preferred it lean and cool. The twentieth-century writer, like all writers, is forever seeking the exact word, but he is wary of sounding feverish. He tends to pitch it low, to understate it, to throw it away. He knows that if he gets too colorful, the audience is likely to giggle. 37

See how this strikes you: "As the rich, golden glow of the sunset died away along the eternal western hills, Angela's limpid blue eyes looked softly and trustingly into Montague's flashing brown ones, and her heart pounded like a drum in time with the joyous song surging in her soul." Some people like that sort of thing, but most modern readers would say, "Good grief," and turn on the television. 38

Colored Words

Some words we would call not so much colorful as colored—that is, loaded with associations, good or bad. All words—except perhaps structure words—have associations of some sort. We have said that the meaning of a word is the sum of the contexts in which it occurs. When we hear a word, we hear with it an echo of all the situations in which we have heard it before. 39

In some words, these echoes are obvious and discussable. The word *mother*, for example, has, for most people, agreeable associations. 40

When you hear *mother* you probably think of home, safety, love, food, and various other pleasant things. If one writes, "She was like a mother to me," he gets an effect which he would not get in "She was like an aunt to me." The advertiser makes use of the associations of *mother* by working it in when he talks about his product. The politician works it in when he talks about himself.

So also with such words as *home, liberty, fireside, contentment, patriot,* 41 *tenderness, sacrifice, childlike, manly, bluff, limpid.* All of these words are loaded with favorable associations that would be rather hard to indicate in a straightforward definition. There is more than a literal difference between "They sat around the fireside" and "They sat around the stove." They might have been equally warm and happy around the stove, but *fireside* suggests leisure, grace, quiet tradition, congenial company, and *stove* does not.

Conversely, some words have bad associations. *Mother* suggests 42 pleasant things, but *mother-in-law* does not. Many mothers-in-law are heroically lovable and some mothers drink gin all day and beat their children insensible, but these facts of life are beside the point. The thing is that *mother* sounds good and *mother-in-law* does not.

Or consider the word *intellectual.* This would seem to be a compli- 43 mentary term, but in point of fact it is not, for it has picked up associations of impracticality and ineffectuality and general dopiness. So also with such words as *liberal, reactionary, Communist, Socialist, capitalist, radical, schoolteacher, truck driver, undertaker, operator, salesman, huckster, speculator.* These convey meanings on the literal level, but beyond that — sometimes, in some places — they convey contempt on the part of the speaker.

The question of whether to use loaded words or not depends on 44 what is being written. The scientist, the scholar, try to avoid them; for the poet, the advertising writer, the public speaker, they are standard equipment. But every writer should take care that they do not substitute for thought. If you write, "Anyone who thinks that is nothing but a Socialist (or Communist or capitalist)" you have said nothing except that you don't like people who think that, and such remarks are effective only with the most naïve readers. It is always a bad mistake to think your readers more naïve than they really are.

Colorless Words

But probably most student writers come to grief not with words that are 45 colorful or those that are colored but with those that have no color at all. A pet example is *nice,* a word we would find it hard to dispense with in casual conversation but which is no longer capable of adding much to a description. Colorless words are those of such general meaning that in a particular sentence they mean nothing. Slang adjectives, like *cool* ("That's real cool.") tend to explode all over the language. They are applied to everything, lose their original force, and quickly die.

Beware also of nouns of very general meaning, like *circumstances*, *cases, instances, aspects, factors, relationships, attitudes, eventualities*, etc. In most circumstances you will find that those cases of writing which contain too many instances of words like these will in this and other aspects have factors leading to unsatisfactory relationships with the reader resulting in unfavorable attitudes on his part and perhaps other eventualities, like a grade of "D." Notice also what "etc." means. It means "I'd like to make this list longer, but I can't think of any more examples." 46

THINKING CRITICALLY ABOUT THE TEXT

In this essay, Roberts points out certain features, positive and negative, found in the work of many writers. Does your writing exhibit any of these features? How would you rate your writing with respect to each of these features?

QUESTIONS ON SUBJECT

1. What, for you, is the most important advice Roberts has to offer?

2. According to Roberts, what is the job of the writer? Why, in particular, is it difficult for college students to do this job well? Discuss how your college experience leads you to agree or disagree with Roberts.

3. The author offers several "tricks" or techniques of good writing in his essay. What are they? Do you find them more useful than other techniques? Explain.

4. If, according to Roberts, a good writer never uses unnecessary words, then what are the legitimate ways a student can reach the goal of the five-hundred-word essay?

5. According to Roberts, how has modern psychology made it more difficult to write well?

QUESTIONS ON STRATEGY

1. What is Roberts's thesis in this essay? (Glossary: *Thesis*)

2. Make a scratch outline of Roberts's essay. What are the similarities between his organization of material and the process analysis he outlines for students? (Glossary: *Organization*) Explain.

3. What kind of information does the title of Roberts's essay lead you to expect? (Glossary: *Title*) Does the author deliver what the title promises? Why do you think he chose this title?

4. What are Roberts's main points? How do his examples help him explain and clarify his main points? (Glossary: *Illustration*)

5. Roberts's writing style is well-suited to his student audience; he includes examples that would be familiar to many students. How would you describe his writing style? What are some of the ways he uses narration and illustration to make the process analysis easy to follow? (Glossary: *Illustration; Narration*)

QUESTIONS ON DICTION AND VOCABULARY

1. Roberts wrote this essay almost fifty years ago, and at some points the facts he cites indicate this; he gives the population of the United States as 180 million (paragraph 32), whereas today it is over 300 million. Is there anything in his diction or word choice that makes Roberts's writing seem dated, or does it sound contemporary? Choose examples from the text to support your answer. (Glossary: *Diction*)

2. What does Roberts mean by "colorful words," "colored words," and "colorless words"?

3. What is Roberts's tone in this essay? What words does he use to create this tone? Explain how the tone affects you as a reader. (Glossary: *Tone*)

CLASSROOM ACTIVITY USING PROCESS ANALYSIS

Before class, find a how-to article that interests you on the Web site for Wiki-HOW at http://www.wikihow.com/Main-Page. Bring a copy of the article to class and be prepared to discuss why you think the article is incomplete or inaccurate and how you might revise it.

WRITING SUGGESTIONS

1. In paragraph 16, Roberts explains how a brief but good essay on college football might be written. He obeys a major rule of good writing—show, don't tell. Thus, instead of a dry lump of words, his brief "essay" uses humor, exaggeration, and concrete details to breathe life into the football player. Review Roberts's strategies for good writing. Then choose one of the dull topics he suggests or one of your own, and following the steps he lays out, write a five-hundred-word essay.

2. Roberts's essay was first published in 1958—before personal computers and word processing programs became ubiquitous. Write an essay in which you compare and contrast the process of writing an essay on a typewriter and on a computer. (Glossary: *Comparison and Contrast*) How is the process similar? How is it different? What equipment and supplies does each require? Which do you prefer? Why?

How Dictionaries Are Made

S. I. Hayakawa

Samuel Ichiye Hayakawa (1906–1992) was born to Japanese parents in Vancouver, Canada. Educated at the University of Manitoba, McGill University, and the University of Wisconsin at Madison, Hayakawa had a distinguished career as a professor of linguistics and was considered a pioneer in semantics, the formal study of meanings. He authored several books on language theory, including Our Language and Our World *(1959). During his last teaching position, at San Francisco State University, he was introduced to the political arena when he was named interim president of the college to deal with student rioters in 1968. His strict suppression of the uprising endeared him to conservatives throughout the country, and he went on to serve as a U.S. senator from California for one term (1977–1983).*

In the following selection taken from Hayakawa's highly regarded textbook Language in Thought and Action *(4th ed., 1978), the linguist dispels some rather popular misconceptions about the role dictionaries play in our society by explaining the process of making them.*

PREPARING TO READ

How do you use dictionaries? Do you regard dictionaries as the final word on the meanings of words? How do you think dictionaries are made?

It is an almost universal belief that every word has a "correct meaning," that we learn these meanings principally from teachers and grammarians (except that most of the time we don't bother to, so that we ordinarily speak "sloppy English"), and that dictionaries and grammars are the "supreme authority" in matters of meaning and usage. Few people ask by what authority the writers of dictionaries and grammars say what they say. The docility with which most people bow down to the dictionary is amazing, and the person who says, "Well, the dictionary is wrong!" is looked upon with smiles of pity and amusement which say plainly, "Poor fellow! He's really quite sane otherwise."

Let us see how dictionaries are made and how the editors arrive at definitions. What follows applies, incidentally, only to those dictionary offices where first-hand, original research goes on — not those in which editors simply copy existing dictionaries. The task of writing a dictionary begins with the reading of vast amounts of the literature of the period or subject that it is intended to cover. As the editors read, they copy on cards every interesting or rare word, every unusual or peculiar occurrence of a common word, a large number of common words in

1

2

their ordinary uses, and also the sentences in which each of these words appears, thus:

---

pail
The dairy *pails* bring home increase of milk
Keats, Endymion
I, 44–45

That is to say, the context of each word is collected, along with the word itself. For a really big job of dictionary writing, such as the *Oxford English Dictionary* (usually bound in about twenty-five volumes), millions of such cards are collected, and the task of editing occupies decades. As the cards are collected, they are alphabetized and sorted. When the sorting is completed, there will be for each word anywhere from two or three to several hundred illustrative quotations, each on its card. 3

To define a word, then, the dictionary editor places before him the stack of cards illustrating that word; each of the cards represents an actual use of the word by a writer of some literary or historical importance. He reads the cards carefully, discards some, re-reads the rest, and divides up the stack according to what he thinks are the several senses of the word. Finally, he writes his definitions, following the hard-and-fast rule that each definition must be based on what the quotations in front of him reveal about the meaning of the word. The editor cannot be influenced by what he thinks a given word ought to mean. He must work according to the cards, or not at all. 4

The writing of a dictionary, therefore, is not a task of setting up authoritative statements about the "true meanings" of words, but a task of recording, to the best of one's ability, what various words have meant to authors in the distant or immediate past. The writer of a dictionary is a historian, not a law-giver. If, for example, we had been writing a dictionary in 1890, or even as late as 1919, we could have said that the word "broadcast" means "to scatter," seed and so on; but we could not have decreed that from 1921 on, the commonest meaning of the word should become "to disseminate audible messages, etc., by wireless telephony." To regard the dictionary as an "authority," therefore, is to credit the dictionary writer with gifts of prophecy which neither he nor anyone else possesses. In choosing our words when we speak or write, we can be guided by the historical record afforded us by the dictionary, but we cannot be bound by it, because new situations, new experiences, new inventions, new feelings, are always compelling us to give new uses to old words. Looking under a "hood," we should ordinarily have found, five hundred years ago, a monk; today, we find a motorcar engine. 5

THINKING CRITICALLY ABOUT THE TEXT

How did your reading of this selection change your thinking — if it did — about the way dictionaries are made and the way many people in our society regard them? How might you explain what you have learned to someone who uses a dictionary as "lawgiver," not as a historical document?

QUESTIONS ON SUBJECT

1. What misconceptions, according to Hayakawa, surround dictionaries and their definitions?

2. What is Hayakawa's purpose in this essay? (Glossary: *Purpose*)

3. Why do the meanings of words change over time? What one sentence in the essay illustrates this role of history better than all others? (Glossary: *Illustration*)

4. Is there a paradox in Hayakawa's saying in paragraph 4 that an editor's own thinking should not interfere with the choices of a word's meanings, while at the same time he says that the editor decides which cards to keep and which to discard? (Glossary: *Paradox*) Explain.

5. Is Hayakawa's information about dictionaries helpful to you in any way? Explain.

QUESTIONS ON STRATEGY

1. What is Hayakawa's thesis in this essay? (Glossary: *Thesis*)

2. How has Hayakawa organized his essay? (Glossary: *Organization*) Identify his introduction, developing paragraphs, and conclusion.

3. What point is Hayakawa trying to make in his introduction? Is his introduction appropriate to the rest of his essay?

4. Briefly restate in your own words the way dictionaries are made.

5. How helpful are Hayakawa's illustrative examples? (Glossary: *Illustration*) How much do they help to establish him as an authority on the English language? (Glossary: *Evidence*)

QUESTIONS ON DICTION AND VOCABULARY

1. What is Hayakawa's tone in this essay? (Glossary: *Tone*) Is it forceful? Easygoing? Egocentric or boastful? Businesslike? What words and phrases help him establish his tone?

2. Hayakawa was a leading expert in the field of semantics, the formal study of meanings. Use the Web to investigate the field more deeply. What kinds of investigations do semanticists carry out?

3. What does Hayakawa mean when he writes in paragraph 1 that "we ordinarily speak 'sloppy English'"?

CLASSROOM ACTIVITY USING PROCESS ANALYSIS

As a classroom exercise, try organizing a set of directions. Let's say, for example, that you want to tell someone how to get from your classroom to the college or university library circulation desk or to the nearest gas station. Establish a context for the directions and then sequence the steps so that someone unfamiliar with your campus could arrive at the desired location. Your instructor will want to share one or two sets of directions and have the members of your class discuss their accuracy. Classroom discussion should focus on what, if anything, is incomplete or inaccurate about the directions and how they might be improved.

WRITING SUGGESTIONS

1. Hayakawa explains how dictionaries are made and helps us understand how we should use them. However, how does one go about accomplishing the larger and more fundamental task of learning to read? In your college library or on the Internet, research phonics or whole-language learning. Choose one of these methods and write an informational process analysis essay in which you explain how it works.

2. Write a directional process essay in which you explain the steps that should be followed in writing a term paper. What kinds of preparation and tools are necessary, and what pitfalls are common in accomplishing the task?

Why Leaves Turn Color in the Fall

Diane Ackerman

 *Diane Ackerman was born in Waukegan, Illinois, in 1948. She received her B.A. from Pennsylvania State University and her M.F.A., M.A., and Ph.D. from Cornell University. Ackerman has worked as a writer-in-residence at several major universities, has directed the Writer's Program at Washington University in St. Louis, and has been a staff writer at the New Yorker. She has written several books of poetry and several collections of essays, among them* The Moon by Whale Light, and Other Adventures among Bats, Penguins, Croc-odilians, and Whales *(1991);* A Natural History of Love *(1994);* The Rarest of the Rare: Vanishing Animals, Timeless Worlds *(1995);* The Curious Naturalist *(1998); and* A Natural History of My Garden *(2001).*

The following selection is from Ackerman's acclaimed A Natural History of the Senses *(1990). Notice the way she shares her enthusiasm for the natural world as she explains the process by which autumn leaves assume their brilliant colors.*

PREPARING TO READ

What is your favorite season? What is it about this season that makes it your favorite — the weather, the activities and memories, the time of year, or a combination of these factors? Is there something about your particular geo-graphic region that makes this season different there than in other parts of the country?

The stealth of autumn catches one unaware. Was that a goldfinch perching in the early September woods, or just the first turning leaf? A red-winged blackbird or a sugar maple closing up shop for the winter? Keen-eyed as leopards, we stand still and squint hard, looking for signs of movement. Early-morning frost sits heavily on the grass, and turns barbed wire into a string of stars. On a distant hill, a small square of yellow appears to be a lighted stage. At last the truth dawns on us: Fall is staggering in, right on schedule, with its baggage of chilly nights, macabre holidays, and spectacular, heart-stoppingly beautiful leaves. Soon the leaves will start cringing on the trees, and roll up in clenched fists before they actually fall off. Dry seedpods will rattle like tiny gourds. But first there will be weeks of gushing color so bright, so pastel, so confettilike, that people will travel up and down the East Coast just to stare at it — a whole season of leaves.

Where do the colors come from? Sunlight rules most living things with its golden edicts. When the days begin to shorten, soon after the summer solstice on June 21, a tree reconsiders its leaves. All summer it feeds them so they can process sunlight, but in the dog days of summer the tree begins pulling nutrients back into its trunk and roots, pares down, and gradually chokes off its leaves. A corky layer of cells forms at the leaves' slender petioles, then scars over. Undernourished, the leaves stop producing the pigment chlorophyll, and photosynthesis ceases. Animals can migrate, hibernate, or store food to prepare for winter. But where can a tree go? It survives by dropping its leaves, and by the end of autumn only a few fragile threads of fluid-carrying xylem hold leaves to their stems.

A turning leaf stays partly green at first, then reveals splotches of 3 yellow and red as the chlorophyll gradually breaks down. Dark green seems to stay longest in the veins, outlining and defining them. During the summer, chlorophyll dissolves in the heat and light, but it is also being steadily replaced. In the fall, on the other hand, no new pigment is produced, and so we notice the other colors that were always there, right in the leaf, although chlorophyll's shocking green hid them from view. With their camouflage gone, we see these colors for the first time all year, and marvel, but they were always there, hidden like a vivid secret beneath the hot glowing greens of summer.

The most spectacular range of fall foliage occurs in the northeastern 4 United States and in eastern China, where the leaves are robustly colored, thanks in part to a rich climate. European maples don't achieve the same flaming reds as their American relatives, which thrive on cold nights and sunny days. In Europe, the warm, humid weather turns the leaves brown or mildly yellow. Anthocyanin, the pigment that gives apples their red and turns leaves red or red-violet, is produced by sugars that remain in the leaf after the supply of nutrients dwindles. Unlike the carotenoids, which color carrots, squash, and corn, and turn leaves orange and yellow, anthocyanin varies from year to year, depending on the temperature and amount of sunlight. The fiercest colors occur in years when the fall sunlight is strongest and the nights are cool and dry (a state of grace scientists find vexing to forecast). This is also why leaves appear dizzyingly bright and clear on a sunny fall day: The anthocyanin flashes like a marquee.

Not all leaves turn the same colors. Elms, weeping willows, and the 5 ancient ginkgo all grow radiant yellow, along with hickories, aspens, bottlebrush buckeyes, cottonweeds, and tall, keening poplars. Basswood turns bronze, birches bright gold. Water-loving maples put on a symphonic display of scarlets. Sumacs turn red, too, as do flowering dogwoods, black gums, and sweet gums. Though some oaks yellow, most turn a pinkish brown. The farmlands also change color, as tepees of cornstalks and bales of shredded-wheat-textured hay stand drying in the fields. In some spots, one slope of a hill may be green and the other already in bright color, because the hillside facing south gets more sun and heat than the northern one.

An odd feature of the colors is that they don't seem to have any 6 special purpose. We are predisposed to respond to their beauty, of course.

They shimmer with the colors of sunset, spring flowers, the tawny buff of a colt's pretty rump, the shuddering pink of a blush. Animals and flowers color for a reason—adaptation to their environment—but there is no adaptive reason for leaves to color so beautifully in the fall any more than there is for the sky or ocean to be blue. It's just one of the haphazard marvels the planet bestows every year. We find the sizzling colors thrilling, and in a sense they dupe us. Colored like living things, they signal death and disintegration. In time, they will become fragile and, like the body, return to dust. They are as we hope our own fate will be when we die: Not to vanish, just to sublime from one beautiful state into another. Though leaves lose their green life, they bloom with urgent colors, as the woods grow mummified day by day, and Nature becomes more carnal, mute, and radiant.

We call the season "fall," from the Old English *feallan*, to fall, which leads back through time to the Indo-European *phol*, which also means to fall. So the word and the idea are both extremely ancient, and haven't really changed since the first of our kind needed a name for fall's leafy abundance. As we say the word, we're reminded of that other Fall, in the garden of Eden, when fig leaves never withered and scales fell from our eyes. Fall is the time when leaves fall from the trees, just as spring is when flowers spring up, summer is when we simmer, and winter is when we whine from the cold.

Children love to play in piles of leaves, hurling them into the air like confetti, leaping into soft unruly mattresses of them. For children, leaf fall is just one of the odder figments of Nature, like hailstones or snowflakes. Walk down a lane overhung with trees in the never-never land of autumn, and you will forget about time and death, lost in the sheer delicious spill of color. Adam and Eve concealed their nakedness with leaves, remember? Leaves have always hidden our awkward secrets.

But how do the colored leaves fall? As a leaf ages, the growth hormone, auxin, fades, and cells at the base of the petiole divide. Two or three rows of small cells, lying at right angles to the axis of the petiole, react with water, then come apart, leaving the petioles hanging on by only a few threads of xylem. A light breeze, and the leaves are airborne. They glide and swoop, rocking in invisible cradles. They are all wing and may flutter from yard to yard on small whirlwinds or updrafts, swiveling as they go. Firmly tethered to earth, we love to see things rise up and fly—soap bubbles, balloons, birds, fall leaves. They remind us that the end of a season is capricious, as is the end of life. We especially like the way leaves rock, careen, and swoop as they fall. Everyone knows the motion. Pilots sometimes do a maneuver called a "falling leaf," in which the plane loses altitude quickly and on purpose, by slipping first to the right, then to the left. The machine weighs a ton or more, but in one pilot's mind it is a weightless thing, a falling leaf. She has seen the motion before, in the Vermont woods where she played as a child. Below her the trees radiate gold, copper, and red. Leaves are falling, although she can't see them fall, as she falls, swooping down for a closer view.

At last the leaves leave. But first they turn color and thrill us for weeks on end. Then they crunch and crackle underfoot. They *shush*, as children drag their small feet through leaves heaped along the curb. Dark, slimy mats of leaves cling to one's heels after a rain. A damp, stuccolike mortar of semidecayed leaves protects the tender shoots with a roof until spring, and makes a rich humus. An occasional bulge or ripple in the leafy mounds signals a shrew or a field mouse tunneling out of sight. Sometimes one finds in fossil stones the imprint of a leaf, long since disintegrated, whose outlines remind us how detailed, vibrant, and alive are the things of this earth that perish.

10

THINKING CRITICALLY ABOUT THE TEXT

In paragraphs 2 and 6 Ackerman attributes some human qualities to Nature and to the trees. What effect does her personification have on you as a reader? Why do you think she chose to use these figures of speech in a process analysis essay? (Glossary: *Figures of Speech*)

QUESTIONS ON SUBJECT

1. What causes leaves to change color?

2. Could it be said that leaves do not actually turn color in the fall? Explain.

3. Why do we call the season "fall"? Why do you suppose Ackerman chooses to give us this language lesson in paragraph 7?

4. What does Ackerman mean when she says, "Leaves have always hidden our awkward secrets" (paragraph 8)? Explain.

5. What, according to Ackerman, is the function of leaves underfoot? Does her assertion make sense to you? Explain.

QUESTIONS ON STRATEGY

1. How has Ackerman organized her essay? (Glossary: *Organization*) Explain why this organization seems most appropriate for her subject.

2. Ackerman is fond of asking questions. (Glossary: *Rhetorical Question*) Locate four or five questions, and explain the different functions they serve within this essay.

3. Reread Ackerman's concluding sentence. What does she mean? Why do you suppose she has chosen to end her essay by discussing "fossil stones" and things that perish? In what ways is this a particularly appropriate ending? (Glossary: *Beginnings/Endings*)

4. When discussing the process of leaves changing colors, Ackerman adds some personal associations, yet remains in the third-person point of view. (Glossary: *Point of View*) How would the essay differ if she wrote in the first person? How would this affect the scientific information in the essay?

5. Ackerman uses several strategies to support her process analysis. For example, she uses cause and effect analysis to explain why leaves are bright in certain years and dull in others, why trees change color at different rates, and why leaves finally fall to earth. (Glossary: *Cause and Effect Analysis*) She also uses description throughout her process analysis. (Glossary: *Description*) How effective would Ackerman's essay be without these supporting strategies? What do they add to your appreciation for her process analysis?

QUESTIONS ON DICTION AND VOCABULARY

1. Identify several similes and metaphors that Ackerman uses, and explain how each functions in this essay. (Glossary: *Figures of Speech*)

2. What is Ackerman's attitude toward her subject? (Glossary: *Attitude*) Cite examples from her essay to support your answer.

3. How would you describe the level of Ackerman's diction in this essay? (Glossary: *Diction*) Does she ever get too scientific for the average reader? If so, where?

CLASSROOM ACTIVITY USING PROCESS ANALYSIS

Most do-it-yourself jobs require that you follow a set process to achieve the best results.

Make a list of the steps involved in doing one of the following household activities and then share your list with other students:

baking chocolate-chip cookies

transplanting a plant

cleaning a swimming pool

replacing a lock

packing a suitcase

doing laundry

WRITING SUGGESTIONS

1. Write an essay using directional process analysis for a "simple" task that could prove disastrous if not explained precisely—for example, changing a tire, driving a standard-shift car, packing for a camping trip, or loading film into a camera. Be sure to explain why your directions are the best and what could happen if readers did not follow them exactly.

2. There are a number of famous writers such as Henry David Thoreau, Aldo Leopold, and Janisse Ray who have made careers out of writing about the processes of the natural world. Read several essays by a nature writer. How does his or her writing compare with Ackerman's? (Glossary: *Comparison and Contrast*) Write an essay in which you compare and contrast two nature writers with respect to their style, tone, organization, or theme. (Glossary: *Organization; Style; Tone*)

Campus Racism 101

Nikki Giovanni

Yolanda Cornelia "Nikki" Giovanni was born in Knoxville, Tennessee, in 1943 and was raised in Ohio. After graduating from Fisk University, she organized the Black Arts Festival in Cincinnati and then entered graduate school at the University of Pennsylvania. Her first book of poetry, Black Feeling, Black Talk, *was published in 1968 and began a lifetime of writing that reflects on the African American identity. Recent books of poetry include the anthologies* Selected Poems of Nikki Giovanni *(1996),* Love Poems *(1997),* Blues for All the Changes: New Poems *(1999),* Quilting the Black-Eyed Pea: Poems and Not Quite Poems *(2002),* The Collected Poetry of Nikki Giovanni *(2003), and* Acolytes: Poems *(2007). Her honors include the Langston Hughes Award for Distinguished Contributions to Arts and Letters in 1996, the NAACP Image Award for Literature in 1998, and Woman of the Year awards from several magazines, including* Essence, Mademoiselle, *and* Ladies Home Journal. *She is currently professor of English and Gloria D. Smith Professor of Black Studies at Virginia Tech.*

The following selection, taken from her nonfiction work Racism 101, *instructs Black students about how to succeed at predominantly white colleges.*

PREPARING TO READ

How would you characterize race relations at your school? How much do white and minority students interact, and what, in your experience, is the tone of those interactions? What is being done within the institution to address any problems or to foster greater respect and understanding?

There is a bumper sticker that reads: TOO BAD IGNORANCE ISN'T PAINFUL. I like that. But ignorance is. We just seldom attribute the pain to it or even recognize it when we see it. Like the postcard on my corkboard. It shows a young man in a very hip jacket smoking a cigarette. In the background is a high school with the American flag waving. The caption says: "Too cool for school. Yet too stupid for the real world." Out of the mouth of the young man is a bubble enclosing the words "Maybe I'll start a band." There could be a postcard showing a jock in a uniform saying. "I don't need school. I'm going to the NFL or NBA." Or one showing a young man or woman studying and a group of young people saying, "So you want to be white." Or something equally demeaning. We need to quit it. 1

I am a professor of English at Virginia Tech. I've been here for four years, though for only two years with academic rank. I am tenured, which 2 means I have a teaching position for life, a rarity on a predominantly white campus. Whether from malice or ignorance, people who think I should be at a predominantly Black institution will ask, "Why are you at Tech?" Because it's here. And so are Black students. But even if Black students weren't here, it's painfully obvious that this nation and this world cannot allow white students to go through higher education without interacting with Blacks in authoritative positions. It is equally clear that predominantly Black colleges cannot accommodate the numbers of Black students who want and need an education.

Is it difficult to attend a predominantly white college? Compared with what? Being passed over for promotion because you lack credentials? Being turned down for jobs because you are not college-educated? Joining the armed forces or going to jail because you cannot find an alternative to the streets? Let's have a little perspective here. Where can you go and what can you do that frees you from interacting with the white American mentality? You're going to interact; the only question is, will you be in some control of yourself and your actions, or will you be controlled by others? I'm going to recommend self-control. 3

What's the difference between prison and college? They both prescribe your behavior for a given period of time. They both allow you to read books and develop your writing. They both give you time alone to think and time with your peers to talk about issues. But four years of prison doesn't give you a passport to greater opportunities. Most likely that time only gives you greater knowledge of how to get back in. Four years of college gives you an opportunity not only to lift yourself but to serve your people effectively. What's the difference when you are called nigger in college from when you are called nigger in prison? In college you can, though I admit with effort, follow procedures to have those students who called you nigger kicked out or suspended. You can bring issues to public attention without risking your life. But mostly, college is and always has been the future. We, neither less nor more than other people, need knowledge. There are discomforts attached to attending predominantly white colleges, though no more so than living in a racist world. Here are some rules to follow that may help: 4

Go to class. No matter how you feel. No matter how you think the professor feels about you. It's important to have a consistent presence in the classroom. If nothing else, the professor will know you care enough and are serious enough to be there. 5

Meet your professors. Extend your hand (give a firm handshake) and tell them your name. Ask them what you need to do to make an A. You may never make an A, but you have put them on notice that you are serious about getting good grades. 6

Do assignments on time. Typed or computer-generated. You have the 7
syllabus. Follow it, and turn those papers in. If for some reason you
can't complete an assignment on time, let your professor know before
it is due and work out a new due date—then meet it.

Go back to see your professor. Tell him or her your name again. If an 8
assignment received less than an A, ask why, and find out what you
need to do to improve the next assignment.

Yes, your professor is busy. So are you. So are your parents who are 9
working to pay or help with your tuition. Ask early what you need to
do if you feel you are starting to get into academic trouble. Do not wait
until you are failing.

Understand that there will be professors who do not like you; there may 10
even be professors who are racist or sexist or both. You must discriminate among your professors to see who will give you the help you need.
You may not simply say, "They are all against me." They aren't. They
mostly don't care. Since you are the one who wants to be educated,
find the people who want to help.

Don't defeat yourself. Cultivate your friends. Know your enemies. 11
You cannot undo hundreds of years of prejudicial thinking. Think for
yourself and speak up. Raise your hand in class. Say what you believe
no matter how awkward you may think it sounds. You will improve in
your articulation and confidence.

Participate in some campus activity. Join the newspaper staff. Run for 12
office. Join a dorm council. Do something that involves you on campus. You are going to be there for four years, so let your presence be
known, if not felt.

You will inevitably run into some white classmates who are troubling 13
because they often say stupid things, ask stupid questions—and expect
an answer. Here are some comebacks to some of the most common
inquiries and comments:

Q: What's it like to grow up in a ghetto? 14
A: I don't know. 15

Q: (from the teacher) Can you give us the Black perspective on Toni 16
Morrison, Huck Finn, slavery, Martin Luther King, Jr., and others?
A: I can give you *my* perspective. (Do not take the burden of 22 million 17
people on your shoulders. Remind everyone that you are an individual,
and don't speak for the race or any other individual within it.)

Q: Why do all the Black people sit together in the dining hall? 18
A: Why do all the white students sit together? 19

Q: Why should there be an African-American studies course?   20
A: Because white Americans have not adequately studied the contribu-   21
tions of Africans and African-Americans. Both Black and white students
need to know our total common history.

Q: Why are there so many scholarships for "minority" students?   22
A: Because they wouldn't give my great-grandparents their forty acres   23
and the mule.

Q: How can whites understand Black history, culture, literature, and so   24
forth?
A: The same way we understand white history, culture, literature, and   25
so forth. That is why we're in school: to learn.

Q: Should whites take African-American studies courses? 26
A: Of course. We take white-studies courses, though the universities 27
don't call them that.

Comment: When I see groups of Black people on campus, it's really 28
intimidating.
Comeback: I understand what you mean. I'm frightened when I see 29
white students congregating.

Comment: It's not fair. It's easier for you guys to get into college than 30
for other people.
Comeback: If it's so easy, why aren't there more of us? 31

Comment: It's not our fault that America is the way it is. 32
Comeback: It's not our fault, either, but both of us have a responsibil- 33
ity to make changes.

It's really very simple. Educational progress is a national concern; 34
education is a private one. Your job is not to educate white people; it is
to obtain an education. If you take the racial world on your shoulders,
you will not get the job done. Deal with yourself as an individual worthy of respect, and make everyone else deal with you the same way.
College is a little like playing grown-up. Practice what you want to be.
You have been telling your parents you are grown. Now is your chance to
act like it.

THINKING CRITICALLY ABOUT THE TEXT

Giovanni concludes her essay by pointing out the nature of the "job" black
students have undertaken, focusing on what it does *not* involve for them. For
you, does the "job" of being a student involve more than just getting an education? If so, what other priorities do you have, and what additional challenges do they present? If not, explain your situation. How well are you able
to put other things aside to achieve your educational goals?

QUESTIONS ON SUBJECT

1. Who is Giovanni's audience? Where does the intended audience first
   become clear? (Glossary: *Audience*)
2. Why does Giovanni dismiss the notion that it is difficult being a black
   student at a predominantly white college? What contexts does she use to
   support her contention?
3. The rules Giovanni presents to help black students succeed at white
   colleges offer a lot of sound advice for any student at any college. Why does
   Giovanni use what could be considered general information in her essay?

4. On what topic does Giovanni provide sample questions and answers for her readers? Why is the topic important to her readers?

5. In paragraph 34, Giovanni makes the point that there is a difference between "educational progress" and "education." What is that difference?

QUESTIONS ON STRATEGY

1. What is Giovanni arguing for in this essay? (Glossary: *Argumentation*) What is her thesis? (Glossary: *Thesis*)

2. Giovanni begins her essay with staccato rhythm. Short sentences appear throughout the essay, but they are emphasized in the beginning. (Glossary: *Beginnings/Endings*) Reread paragraph 1. What does Giovanni accomplish with her rapid-fire delivery? Why is it appropriate for the subject matter?

3. What does Giovanni gain by including her short personal narrative in paragraph 2? (Glossary: *Narration*) Why is it necessary to know her personal history and current situation?

4. After beginning her essay with straight prose, Giovanni uses a list with full explanations and a series of Q&A examples to outline strategies to help black students cope at predominantly white colleges. Why did Giovanni use these techniques to convey her material? How might they add to the usefulness of the essay for the reader?

5. What does Giovanni mean when she says, "Educational progress is a national concern; education is a private one" (paragraph 34)? In what ways is this point important to her purpose? (Glossary: *Purpose*)

QUESTIONS ON DICTION AND VOCABULARY

1. How did you first react to Giovanni's title, "Campus Racism 101"? What did it connote to you? (Glossary: *Connotation/Denotation*) After reading the essay, do you think the title is appropriate? Explain your answer.

2. Giovanni uses the word *stupid* on two occasions. The first use (paragraph 1), "too stupid for the real world," provides a context for how she views the word, while the second characterizes what white students sometimes ask or say to black students. The second use (paragraph 13) is a little jarring—often these days the characterization is softened to "insensitive" or "thoughtless." The use of *stupid* implies a more active ignorance on the part of the questioner. What does Giovanni gain by using the word? Do you think it is meant to be pejorative toward the white students? Explain your answer.

3. How would you describe the author's tone in this essay? Is it angry, firm, moderate, instructional, or something else? Explain.

CLASSROOM ACTIVITY USING PROCESS ANALYSIS

After finishing the first draft of your process analysis essay, have someone else in your writing class read it. If you are writing a directional analysis, ask your reader to follow the instructions and then tell you whether he or she was able to understand each step and, if possible, perform it satisfactorily. Was the desired result achieved? If not, examine your process step by step, looking for errors and omissions that would explain the unsatisfactory result.

WRITING SUGGESTIONS

1. What specific strategies do you employ to do well in your classes? Do you ask the professor what is needed for an A and make sure you attend every class, as Giovanni suggests in her essay? Do you take meticulous notes, study every day, just cram the night before exams, or have a lucky shirt for test days? Write a process analysis in which you present your method for success in school in a way that others could emulate—should they so choose.

2. In Giovanni's Q&A section, she replies to the question, "Why are there so many scholarships for 'minority' students?" with the answer, "Because they wouldn't give my great-grandparents their forty acres and the mule" (paragraphs 22–23). Write an argumentative essay in which you react to both Giovanni's answer and the situation as a whole. Do you think qualified minority students should receive preferential treatment for admissions and financial aid? If you argue no, what other strategies would you support to address the current educational inequities between whites and blacks?

3. Giovanni's essay covers a subject—African Americans attending pre-dominantly white colleges—that has a relatively short history in many areas of the country. Although African Americans have a long history of success in higher education in the Northeast, where they were admitted to some schools as early as the 1820s, it has only been in the last five decades that the final barriers to college attendance have been removed nationwide. The battle over education rights became one of the most important components of the civil rights movement and led to some of the most contentious showdowns.

   The photograph on page 252 shows James Meredith as he attempts to become the first African American to enter the University of Mississippi on October 1, 1962. His efforts resulted in riots that caused two deaths and 160 injuries. Meredith graduated from Ole Miss in 1964 and then went on to Columbia University and earned a degree in law.

   What evidence of determination do you see on the faces and in the body language of both those who wished to keep James Meredith from entering the university and those who were his supporters? Notice that the photograph reveals a sort of mirror image, with the opposing sides reflecting each other's confrontational attitudes.

   Research the background and precipitating circumstances of Meredith's admittance to the University of Mississippi, and write an essay explaining the process he went through to make his case heard and accepted by authorities in the civil rights movement, the federal government, the state of Mississippi, and the university.

WRITING SUGGESTIONS FOR PROCESS ANALYSIS

1. Write a directional or evaluative process analysis on one of the following topics:

    a. how to make chocolate-chip cookies
    b. how to adjust brakes on a bicycle
    c. how to change a tire
    d. how to throw a party
    e. how to use the memory function on a calculator
    f. how to add, drop, or change a course
    g. how to play a specific card game
    h. how to wash a sweater
    i. how to develop black-and-white film
    j. how to make a pizza
    k. how to build a Web page
    l. how to select a major course of study
    m. how to winterize a car
    n. how to rent an apartment
    o. how to develop confidence
    p. how to start and operate a small business
    q. how to run for student government office
    r. how to do a magic trick

2. Write an informational or evaluative process analysis on one of the following topics:

    a. how your heart functions
    b. how a U.S. president is elected
    c. how ice cream is made
    d. how a hurricane forms
    e. how hailstones form
    f. how a volcano erupts
    g. how the human circulatory system works
    h. how a camera works
    i. how photosynthesis takes place
    j. how an atomic bomb or reactor works
    k. how fertilizer is made
    l. how a refrigerator works
    m. how water evaporates
    n. how flowers bloom
    o. how a recession occurs
    p. how an automobile is made
    q. how a bill becomes law in your state
    r. how a caterpillar becomes a butterfly

3. Think about your favorite pastime or activity. Write an essay in which you explain one or more of the processes you follow in participating in that activity. For example, if basketball is your hobby, how do you go

about making a layup? If you are a photographer, how do you develop and print a picture? If you are an actor, how do you go about learning your lines? Do you follow standard procedures, or do you personalize the process in some way?

4. Although each of us hopes never to be in an automobile accident, many of us have been or will be. Accidents are unsettling, and it is important that people know what to do if they ever find themselves in a collision. Write an essay in which you explain the steps that a person should follow to protect life and property in the aftermath of the accident.

5. All college students have to register for courses each term. What is the registration process like at your college? Do you find any part of the process unnecessarily frustrating or annoying? In a letter to your campus newspaper or an appropriate administrator, evaluate your school's current registration procedure, offering suggestions for making the process more efficient and pleasurable.

6. Writing to a person who is a computer novice, explain how to do a Web search. Be sure to define key terms and to illustrate the steps in your process with screen shots of search directories and search results.

CHAPTER 8

Comparison and Contrast

WHAT ARE COMPARISON AND CONTRAST?

A comparison presents two or more subjects (people, ideas, or objects), considers them together, and shows in what ways they are alike; a contrast shows how they differ. These two perspectives, apparently in contradiction to each other, actually work so often in conjunction that they are commonly considered a single strategy, called comparison and contrast or simply comparison for short.

Comparison and contrast are so much a part of daily life that we are often not aware of using them. Whenever you make a choice — what to wear, where to eat, what college to attend, what career to pursue — you implicitly use comparison and contrast to evaluate your options and arrive at your decision.

The strategy of comparison and contrast is most commonly used in writing when the subjects under discussion belong to the same class or general category: four makes of car, for example, or two candidates for Senate. (See Chapter 9, "Division and Classification," for a more complete discussion of classes.) Such subjects are said to be *comparable*, or to have a strong basis for comparison.

Point-by-Point and Block Comparison

There are two basic ways to organize an essay of comparison and contrast. In the first, *point-by-point comparison*, the author starts by comparing both subjects in terms of a particular point, then moves on to a second point and compares both subjects, then moves on to a third point, and so on. The other way to organize a comparison is called *block comparison.* In this pattern, the information about one subject is gathered into a block, which is followed by a block of comparable information about the second subject. Each pattern of comparison has advantages and disadvantages. Point-by-point comparison allows the reader to grasp fairly easily the specific points of comparison the author is making; it may be harder, though, to pull together the details and convey a distinct impression of what each subject is like. The block comparison guarantees that each subject will receive a more unified discussion; however, the points of comparison between them may be less clear.

The first of the following two annotated passages illustrates a point-by-point comparison. This selection, a comparison of President Franklin Roosevelt and his vice-presidential running mate Harry Truman of Missouri, is from historian David McCullough's Pulitzer Prize–winning biography *Truman* (1992).

Point-by-point comparison identifies central similarities between the two men.

Point-by-point contrast introduces several differences, alternating between Roosevelt and Truman.

Both were men of exceptional determination, with great reserves of personal courage and cheerfulness. They were alike too in their enjoyment of people. (The human race, Truman once told a reporter, was an "excellent outfit.") Each had an active sense of humor and was inclined to be dubious of those who did not. But Roosevelt, who loved stories, loved also to laugh at his own, while Truman was more of a listener and laughed best when somebody else told "a good one." Roosevelt enjoyed flattery, Truman was made uneasy by it. Roosevelt loved the subtleties of human relations. He was a master of the circuitous solution to problems, of the pleasing if ambiguous answer to difficult questions. He was sensitive to nuances in a way Harry Truman never was and never would be. Truman, with his rural Missouri background, and partly,

Development of key difference

too, because of the limits of his education, was inclined to see things in far simpler terms, as right or wrong, wise or foolish. He dealt little in abstractions. His answers to questions, even complicated questions, were nearly always direct and assured, plainly said, and followed often by a conclusive "And that's all there is to it," an old Missouri expression, when in truth there may have been a great deal more "to it."

Point-by-point comparison and contrast— Roosevelt's and Truman's life struggles and experiences

Each of them had been tested by his own painful struggle, Roosevelt with crippling polio, Truman with debt, failure, obscurity, and the heavy stigma of the Pendergasts. Roosevelt liked to quote the admonition of his old headmaster at Groton, Dr. Endicott Peabody: "Things in life will not always run smoothly. Sometimes we will be rising toward the heights — then all will seem to reverse itself and start downward. The great fact to remember is that the trend of civilization is forever upward. . . ." Assuredly Truman would have subscribed to the same vision. They were two optimists at heart, each in his way faithful to the old creed of human progress. But there had been nothing in Roosevelt's experience like the night young Harry held the lantern as his mother underwent surgery, nothing like the Argonne, or Truman's desperate fight for political survival in 1940.

In the following example from *Harper's* magazine, Otto Friedrich uses a block format to contrast a newspaper story with a newsmagazine story.

Subjects of comparison: Newspaper story and magazine story belong to the same class.

There is an essential difference between a news story, as understood by a newspaperman or a wire-service writer, and a newsmagazine story. The chief purpose of the conventional news story is to tell what happened. It starts with the most important information and continues into increasingly inconsequential details, not only because the reader may not read beyond the first paragraph, but because an editor working on galley proofs a few minutes before press time likes to be able to cut freely from the end of the story.

Block comparison: Each paragraph deals with one type of story.

A newsmagazine is very different. It is written to be read consecutively from beginning to end, and each of its stories is designed, following the critical theories of Edgar Allan Poe, to create one emotional effect. The news, what happened that week, may be told in the beginning, the middle, or the end; for the purpose is not to throw information at the reader but to seduce him into reading the whole story, and into accepting the dramatic (and often political) point being made.

In this selection, Friedrich has two purposes: to offer information that explains the differences between a newspaper story and a newsmagazine story, and to persuade readers that magazine stories tend to be more biased than newspaper stories.

Analogy: A Special Form of Comparison and Contrast

When the subject under discussion is unfamiliar, complex, or abstract, the resourceful writer may use a special form of comparison called *analogy* to help readers understand the difficult subject. An analogy compares two largely dissimilar subjects to look for illuminating similarities. Most comparisons analyze items within the same class. For example, an exploration of the similarities and differences between short stories and novels—two forms of fiction—would constitute a logical comparison. Short stories and novels belong to the same class, and your purpose would be to tell something about both. In contrast, analogy pairs things of different classes. In analogy, the only basis for comparison lies in the writer's imagination. In addition, while the typical comparison seeks to illuminate specific features of both subjects, the primary purpose of analogy is to clarify one subject that is complex or unfamiliar by pointing out its similarities to a more familiar or concrete subject. If, for example, your purpose were to explain the craft of fiction writing, you might note its similarities to the craft of carpentry. In this case, you would be drawing an analogy, because the two subjects clearly belong to different classes. Your imagination will suggest many ways in which the concrete work of the carpenter can be used to help readers understand the more abstract work of the novelist. You can use analogy in one or two paragraphs to clarify a particular aspect of the larger topic, or you can use it as the organizational strategy for an entire essay.

In the following example from *The Mysterious Sky* (1960), observe how Lester Del Rey explains the functions of the Earth's atmosphere (a subject that people have difficulty with because they can't "see" it) by making an analogy with an ordinary window.

> The atmosphere of Earth acts like any window in serving two very important functions. It lets light in and it permits us to look out. It also serves as a shield to keep out dangerous or uncomfortable things. A normal glazed window lets us keep our houses warm by keeping out cold air, and it prevents rain, dirt, and unwelcome insects and animals from coming in. As we have already seen, Earth's atmospheric window also helps to keep our planet at a comfortable temperature by holding back radiated heat and protecting us from dangerous levels of ultraviolet light.
>
> Lately, we have discovered that space is full of a great many very dangerous things against which our atmosphere guards us. It is not a perfect shield, and sometimes one of these dangerous objects does get through. There is even some evidence that a few of these messengers from space contain life, though this has by no means been proved yet.

You'll notice that Del Rey's analogy establishes no direct relationship between the subjects under comparison. The analogy is effective precisely because it enables the reader to visualize the atmosphere, which is unobservable, by comparing it to something quite different — a window — that is familiar and concrete.

USING COMPARISON AND CONTRAST AS A WRITING STRATEGY

To compare one thing or idea with another, to discover the similarities and differences between them, is one of the most basic human strategies for learning, evaluating, and making decisions. Because it serves so many fundamental purposes, comparison and contrast is a particularly useful strategy for the writer. It may be the primary mode for essay writers who seek to educate or persuade the reader; to evaluate things, people, or events; and to differentiate between apparently similar subjects or to reconcile the differences between dissimilar ones.

Comparison and contrast may be combined readily with other writing strategies and often serves to sharpen, clarify, and add interest to essays written in a different primary mode. For example, an essay of argumentation gains credibility when the writer contrasts desirable and undesirable reasons or examples. In the Declaration of Independence (page 474), Thomas Jefferson effectively contrasts the actual behavior of the English king with the ideals of a democratic society. In "I Have a Dream" (page 486), Martin Luther King Jr. compares 1960s America with the promise of what ought to be to argue that the realization of the dream of freedom for all American citizens is long overdue. Likewise, Richard Lederer, in "The Case for Short Words" (page 480), uses comparison and contrast to showcase the virtues of one-syllable words when measured against their multisyllabic counterparts.

Many descriptive essays rely heavily on comparison and contrast; one of the most effective ways to describe any person, place, or thing is to show how it is like another model of the same class and how it differs. Robert Ramírez ("The Barrio," page 135) describes his Hispanic neighborhood against "the harshness and the coldness of the Anglo world." Definition is also clarified and enriched by the use of comparison and contrast. Virtually all the essays in Chapter 10 employ this strategy to some degree.

Using Comparison and Contrast across the Disciplines

When writing essays in the academic disciplines, you will have many opportunities to use the strategy of comparison and contrast to both organize and strengthen the presentation of your ideas. To determine whether or not comparison and contrast is the right strategy for you in a particular paper, use the four-step method first described in "Determining Your Strategy" (pages 24–25). Consider the following examples, which illustrate how this four-step method works for typical college papers:

Music

MAIN IDEA: The music of the Romantic period sharply contrasts with the music of the earlier Classical period.

QUESTION: What are the key differences between the music of the Romantic and Classical periods?

STRATEGY: Comparison and Contrast. The direction words *contrasts* and *differences* call for a discussion distinguishing characteristics of the two periods in music history.

SUPPORTING STRATEGIES: Definition and Illustration. It might be helpful to define the key terms *romanticism* and *classicism* and to illustrate each of the differences with examples from representative Romantic composers (Brahms, Chopin, Schubert, and Tchaikovsky) and Classical composers (Beethoven, Haydn, and Mozart).

Political Science

MAIN IDEA: Though very different people, Winston Churchill and Franklin D. Roosevelt shared many larger-than-life leadership qualities during World War II, a period of doubt and crisis.

QUESTION: What are the similarities between Winston Churchill and Franklin D. Roosevelt as world leaders?

STRATEGY: Comparison and Contrast. The direction words *shared* and *similarities* require a discussion of the leadership traits displayed by both men.

SUPPORTING STRATEGY: Definition. It might prove helpful to define *leader* and/or *leadership* to establish a context for this comparison.

Physics

MAIN IDEA: Compare and contrast the three classes of levers, simple machines used to amplify force.

QUESTION: What are the similarities and differences among the three classes of levers?

STRATEGY: Comparison and Contrast. The direction words *compare, contrast, similarities*, and *differences* say it all.

SUPPORTING STRATEGY: Illustration. Readers will certainly appreciate familiar examples — pliers, nutcracker, and tongs — of the three classes of levers, examples that both clarify and emphasize the similarities and differences.

SAMPLE STUDENT ESSAY USING COMPARISON AND CONTRAST AS A WRITING STRATEGY

A studio art major from Pittsburgh, Pennsylvania, Barbara Bowman has a special interest in photography. In her writing courses, Bowman has discovered many similarities between the writing process and the process that an artist follows. Her essay "Guns and Cameras," however, explores similarities of another kind: those between hunting with a gun and hunting with a camera.

Guns and Cameras

Barbara Bowman

Introduction of the objects being compared

With a growing number of animals heading toward extinction, and with the idea of protecting such animals on game reserves increasing in popularity, photographic safaris are replacing hunting safaris. This may seem odd because of the obvious differences between guns and cameras. Shooting is aggressive, photography is passive; shooting eliminates, photography preserves. However, some hunters are willing to trade their guns for cameras because of similarities in the way the equipment is used, as well as in the relationship among equipment, user, and "prey."

1

Brief point-by-point contrast

Thesis

Block organization: first block about the hunter

The hunter has a deep interest in the apparatus he uses to kill his prey. He carries various types of guns, different kinds of ammunition, and special sights and telescopes to increase his chances of success. He knows the mechanics of his guns and understands how and why they work. This fascination with the hardware of his sport is practical — it helps him achieve his goal — but it frequently becomes an end, almost a hobby in itself.

2

Point A: equipment

Point B: stalking

Not until the very end of the long process of stalking an animal does a game hunter use his gun. First he enters into the animal's world. He studies his prey, its habitat, its daily habits, its watering holes and feeding areas, its migration patterns, its enemies and allies, its diet and food chain. Eventually the hunter himself becomes animal-like, instinctively sensing the habits and moves of his prey. Of course, this instinct gives the hunter a better chance of killing the animal; he knows where and when he will get the best shot. But it gives him more than that. Hunting is not just pulling the trigger and killing the prey. Much of it is a multifaceted and ritualistic identification with nature.

3

Point C: the result

After the kill, the hunter can do a number of things with his trophy. He can sell the meat or eat it himself. He can hang the animal's head on the wall or lay its hide on the floor or even sell these objects. But any of these uses is a luxury, and its cost is high. An animal has been destroyed; a life has been eliminated.

4

Second block about the photographer

Like the hunter, the photographer has a great interest in the tools he uses. He carries various types of cameras, lenses, and film to help him get the picture he wants. He understands the way cameras work, the uses of telephoto and micro lenses, and often the technical procedures of printing and developing.

5

Point A: equipment

Of course, the time and interest a photographer invests in these mechanical aspects of his art allow him to capture and produce the image he wants. But as with the hunter, these mechanics can and often do become fascinating in themselves.

Point B: stalking

The wildlife photographer also needs to stalk his "prey" 6 with knowledge and skill in order to get an accurate "shot." Like the hunter, he has to understand the animal's patterns, characteristics, and habitat; he must become animal-like in order to succeed. And like the hunter's, his pursuit is much more prolonged and complicated than the shot itself. The stalking processes are almost identical and give many of the same satisfactions.

Point C: the result

The successful photographer also has something tangible 7 to show for his efforts. A still picture of an animal can be displayed in a home, a gallery, a shop; it can be printed in a publication, as a postcard, or as a poster. In fact, a single photograph can be used in all these ways at once; it can be reproduced countless times. And despite all these ways of using his "trophies," the photographer continues to preserve his prey.

Conclusion: The two activities are similar and give the same satisfaction, so why kill?

Photography is obviously the less violent and to me the 8 more acceptable method for obtaining a trophy of a wild animal. We no longer need to hunt in order to feed or clothe ourselves, and hunting for "sport" seems to be barbaric. Luckily, the excitement of pursuing an animal, learning its habits and patterns, outsmarting it on its own level, and finally "getting" it can all be done with a camera. So why use guns?

Analyzing Barbara Bowman's Essay of Comparison and Contrast: Questions for Discussion

1. What is Bowman's thesis in this essay?
2. What are her main points of comparison between hunting with a gun and hunting with a camera?
3. How has Bowman organized her comparison? Why do you suppose she decided on this option? Explain.
4. How else could she have organized her essay? Would this alternative organization have been as effective as the one she used? Explain.
5. How does Bowman conclude her essay? In what ways is her conclusion a reflection of her thesis?

SUGGESTIONS FOR USING COMPARISON AND CONTRAST AS A WRITING STRATEGY

As you plan, write, and revise your essay of comparison and contrast, be mindful of the five-step writing process described in Chapter 2 (see pages 14–31). Also, pay particular attention to the basic requirements and essential ingredients for this writing strategy.

Planning Your Essay of Comparison and Contrast

Planning is an essential part of writing a good essay of comparison and contrast. You can save yourself a great deal of aggravation by taking the time to think about the key components of your essay before you actually begin to write.

Many assignments in college ask you to use the strategy of comparison and contrast. As you read an assignment, look for one or more of the words that suggest the use of this strategy. When you are asked to *compare* and *contrast* one item with another or to identify the *similarities* and *differences* between two items, you should use comparison and contrast. Other assignments might ask you to determine which of two options is *better* or to select the *best* solution to a particular problem. Again, the strategy of comparison and contrast will help you make this evaluation and arrive at a sound, logical conclusion. As you start planning and writing an essay of comparison and contrast, keep in mind the basic requirements of this writing strategy.

Compare Subjects from the Same Class.　Remember that the subjects of your comparison should be in the same class or general category, so that you can establish a clear basis for comparison. (There are any number of possible classes, such as particular types of persons, places, and things, as well as occupations, activities, philosophies, points in history, and even concepts and ideas.) If your subject is difficult, complex, or unobservable, you may find that analogy, a special form of comparison, is the most effective strategy to explain that subject. Remember, also, that if the similarities and differences between the subjects are obvious, your reader is certain to lose interest quickly.

Determine Your Purpose, and Focus on It.　Suppose you choose to compare and contrast solar energy with wind energy. It is clear that both are members of the same class—energy—so there is a basis for comparing them; there also seem to be enough interesting differences to make a comparison and contrast possible. But before going any further, you must ask yourself why you want to compare and contrast these particular subjects. What audience do you seek to address? Do you want to inform, to emphasize, to explain, to evaluate, to persuade?

Do you have more than one purpose? Whatever your purpose, it will influence the content and organization of your comparison.

In comparing and contrasting solar and wind energy, you will certainly provide factual information; yet you will probably also want to evaluate the two energy sources to determine whether either is a practical means of producing energy. You may also want to persuade your readers that one technology is superior to the other.

Formulate a Thesis Statement.   Once you have your purpose clearly in mind, formulate a preliminary thesis statement. At this early stage in the writing process, the thesis statement is not cast in stone; you may well want to modify it later on, as a result of research and further consideration of your subject. A preliminary thesis statement has two functions: First, it fixes your direction so that you will be less tempted to stray into byways while doing research and writing drafts; second, establishing the central point of the essay makes it easier for you to gather supporting material and to organize your essay.

Suppose, for example, that you live in the Champlain Valley of Vermont, one of the cloudiest areas of the country, where the wind whistles along the corridor between the Green Mountains and the Adirondacks. If you were exploring possible alternative energy sources for the area, your purpose might be to persuade readers of a local environmental journal that wind is preferable to sun as a source of energy for this region. The thesis statement for this essay will certainly differ from that of a writer for a national newsmagazine whose goal is to offer general information about alternative energy sources to a broad readership.

Choose the Points of Comparison.   *Points of comparison* are the qualities and features of your subjects on which you base your comparison. For some comparisons, you will find the information you need in your own head; for others, you will have to search for that information in the library or on the Internet. At this stage, if you know only a little about the subjects of your comparison, you may have only a few hazy ideas for points of comparison. Perhaps wind energy means no more to you than an image of giant windmills lined up on a California ridge, and solar energy brings to mind only the reflective, glassy roof on a Colorado ski lodge. Even so, it is possible to list points of comparison that will be relevant to your subjects and your purpose. Here, for example, are important points of comparison in considering energy sources:

Cost
Efficiency
Convenience
Environmental impact

As you learn more about your subjects and think about what you are learning, you may want to change some of these points or add new ones. Meanwhile, a tentative list will help you by suggesting the kind of information you need to gather for your comparison and contrast. Let your tentative points of comparison be your guide, but remain alert for others you may not have thought of. For example, as you conduct research, you may find that maintenance requirements are another important factor in considering energy systems, and thus you might add that point to your list.

Organizing and Writing Your Essay of Comparison and Contrast

Choose an Organizational Pattern That Fits Your Material.   Once you have gathered the necessary information, you should decide which organizational pattern, block or point-by-point, will best serve your purpose. In deciding which pattern to use, you may find it helpful to jot down a scratch outline before beginning your draft.

Block organization works best when the two objects of comparison are relatively straightforward and when the points of comparison are rather general, few in number, and can be stated succinctly. As a scratch outline illustrates, block organization makes for a unified discussion of each object, which can help your readers understand the information you have to give them.

Block Organization Outline
BLOCK ONE   **Solar Energy**
   Point 1. Cost
   Point 2. Efficiency
   Point 3. Convenience
   Point 4. Maintenance requirements
   Point 5. Environmental impact

BLOCK TWO   **Wind Energy**
   Point 1. Cost
   Point 2. Efficiency
   Point 3. Convenience
   Point 4. Maintenance requirements
   Point 5. Environmental impact

If your essay will be more than two or three pages long, however, block organization may be a poor choice. By the time your readers come to your discussion of the costs of wind energy, they may well have forgotten what you had to say about solar energy costs several pages earlier and may have to flip back and forth to grasp the comparison. If such difficulties are a possibility, you would do better to use point-by-point organization, in which comparisons are made immediately as each point is raised.

Point-by-Point Outline

Point One **Cost**
Subject 1. Solar energy
Subject 2. Wind energy

Point Two **Efficiency**
Subject 1. Solar energy
Subject 2. Wind energy

Point Three **Convenience**
Subject 1. Solar energy
Subject 2. Wind energy

Point Four **Maintenance Requirements**
Subject 1. Solar energy
Subject 2. Wind energy

Point Five **Environmental Impact**
Subject 1. Solar energy
Subject 2. Wind energy

Use Parallel Constructions for Emphasis. Use parallel grammatical structures to emphasize the similarities and differences between the items being compared. Parallelism is the repetition of word order or grammatical form either within a single sentence or in several sentences that develop the same central idea. As a rhetorical device, parallel structure can aid coherence and add emphasis. Franklin Roosevelt's famous Depression-era statement "I see one-third of a nation *ill-housed*, *ill-clad*, and *ill-nourished*" illustrates effective parallelism. Look for opportunities to use parallel constructions with 1) paired items or items in a series, 2) correlative conjunctions, and 3) the words *as* or *than*.

Draw a Conclusion from Your Comparison. Only after you have gathered your information and made your comparisons will you be ready to decide on a conclusion. When drawing the conclusion to your essay, remember your purpose in writing, the claim made in your thesis statement, and your audience and emphasis. Perhaps, having presented information about both technologies, your comparison shows that solar and wind energy are both feasible, with solar energy having a slight edge on most points. If your purpose has been evaluation for a general audience, you might conclude, "Both solar and wind energy are practical alternatives to conventional energy sources." If you asserted in your thesis statement that one of the technologies is superior to the other, your comparison will support a more persuasive conclusion. For the general audience, you might say, "While both solar and wind energy are practical technologies, solar energy now seems the better investment." However, for a readership made up of residents of the cloudy Champlain Valley, you might conclude, "While both solar and wind energy are practical technologies, wind energy makes more economic sense for investors in northwest Vermont."

Revising and Editing Your Essay of Comparison and Contrast

Share Your Drafts with Others. Try sharing the drafts of your essays with other students in your writing class to make sure that your comparison and contrast works, that it makes its point. Ask them if there are any parts that they do not understand. Have them tell you what they think is the point of your essay. If their answers differ from what you intended, have them indicate the passages that led them to their interpretations so that you can change your text accordingly. To maximize the effectiveness of conferences with your peers, utilize the guidelines presented on pages 27–28. Feedback from these conferences often provides one or more places where you can start revising.

Question Your Own Work While Revising and Editing. Revision is best done by asking yourself key questions about what you have written. Begin by reading, preferably aloud, what you have written. Reading aloud forces you to pay attention to every single word, and you are more likely to catch lapses in the logical flow of thought. After you have read your paper through, answer the following questions for revising and editing and make the necessary changes.

Questions for Revising and Editing: Comparison and Contrast

1. Are the subjects of my comparison comparable; that is, do they belong to the same class of items (for example, two cars, two advertisements, two landscape paintings) so that there is a clear basis for comparison?

2. Are there any complex or abstract concepts that might be clarified by using an analogy, in which I convey what the concept has in common with a more familiar or concrete subject?

3. Is the purpose of my comparison clearly stated?

4. Have I presented a clear thesis statement?

5. Have I chosen my points of comparison well? Have I avoided obvious points of comparison, concentrating instead on similarities between obviously different items or differences between essentially similar items?

6. Have I developed my points of comparison in sufficient detail so that my readers can appreciate my thinking?

7. Have I chosen the best pattern—block or point-by-point—to organize my information?

8. Have I drawn a conclusion that is in line with my thesis and purpose?

9. Have I used parallel constructions correctly in my sentences?

10. Have I avoided errors in grammar, punctuation, and mechanics?

Two Ways of Seeing a River

Mark Twain

 *Mark Twain, the pen name of Samuel L. Clemens (1835–1910), was born in Florida, Missouri, and raised in Hannibal, Missouri. He created* Tom Sawyer *(1876),* The Prince and the Pauper *(1882),* Huckleberry Finn *(1884), and* A Connecticut Yankee in King Arthur's Court *(1889), among other classics. One of America's most popular writers, Twain is generally regarded as the most important practitioner of the realistic school of writing, a style that emphasizes observable details.*

The following passage is taken from Life on the Mississippi *(1883), Twain's study of the great river and his account of his early experiences learning to be a river steamboat pilot. As you read the passage, notice how Twain uses figurative language in describing two quite different ways of seeing the Mississippi River.*

PREPARING TO READ

Our way of seeing an event or a place in our life often changes over time. Recall an important event or a place you visited in the past. Tell a story based on your memories. Has your view of this event or place changed over time? How?

N ow when I had mastered the language of this water and had come to   1
know every trifling feature that bordered the great river as familiarly as I knew the letters of the alphabet, I had made a valuable acquisition. But I had lost something, too. I had lost something which could never be restored to me while I lived. All the grace, the beauty, the poetry, had gone out of the majestic river! I still kept in mind a certain wonderful sunset which I witnessed when steamboating was new to me. A broad expanse of the river was turned to blood; in the middle distance the red hue brightened into gold, through which a solitary log came floating, black and conspicuous; in one place a long, slanting mark lay sparkling upon the water; in another the surface was broken by boiling, tumbling rings that were as many-tinted as an opal; where the ruddy flush was faintest was a smooth spot that was covered with graceful circles and radiating lines, ever so delicately traced; the shore on our left was densely wooded, and the somber shadow that fell from this forest was broken in one place by a long, ruffled trail that shone like silver; and high above the forest wall a clean-stemmed dead tree waved a single leafy bough that glowed like a flame in the unobstructed splendor that was flowing from the sun. There were graceful curves, reflected images, woody heights, soft distances, and over the whole scene, far and near, the dissolving lights drifted steadily, enriching it every passing moment with new marvels of coloring.

I stood like one bewitched. I drank it in, in a speechless rapture. 2
The world was new to me and I had never seen anything like this at
home. But as I have said, a day came when I began to cease from noting
the glories and the charms which the moon and the sun and the twilight wrought upon the river's face; another day came when I ceased
altogether to note them. Then, if that sunset scene had been repeated,
I should have looked upon it without rapture and should have commented upon it inwardly after this fashion: "This sun means that we
are going to have wind tomorrow; that floating log means that the river
is rising, small thanks to it; that slanting mark on the water refers to a
bluff reef which is going to kill somebody's steamboat one of these
nights, if it keeps on stretching out like that; those tumbling 'boils'
show a dissolving bar and a changing channel there; the lines and circles in the slick water over yonder are a warning that that troublesome
place is shoaling up dangerously; that silver streak in the shadow of the
forest is the 'break' from a new snag and he has located himself in the
very best place he could have found to fish for steamboats; that tall
dead tree, with a single living branch, is not going to last long, and
then how is a body ever going to get through this blind place at night
without the friendly old landmark?"

No, the romance and beauty were all gone from the river. All the 3
value any feature of it had for me now was the amount of usefulness it
could furnish toward compassing the safe piloting of a steamboat.
Since those days, I have pitied doctors from my heart. What does the
lovely flush in a beauty's cheek mean to a doctor but a "break" that rip-
ples above some deadly disease? Are not all her visible charms sown
thick with what are to him the signs and symbols of hidden decay?
Does he ever see her beauty at all, or doesn't he simply view her profes-
sionally and comment upon her unwholesome condition all to himself? And doesn't he sometimes wonder whether he has gained most or
lost most by learning his trade?

THINKING CRITICALLY ABOUT THE TEXT

In the essay, Twain points to a change of attitude he underwent as a result of
seeing the river from a new perspective, that of a steamboat pilot. Why and
how do you think perspectives change? How would you characterize Twain's
change of perspective?

QUESTIONS ON SUBJECT

1. What points of contrast does Twain refer to between his two ways of seeing
   the river?
2. What point does Twain make regarding the difference between appearance
   and reality, between romance and practicality? What role does knowledge
   play in Twain's inability to see the river as he once did?

3. Now that he has learned the trade of steamboating, does Twain feel he has "gained most or lost most" (paragraph 3)? What has he gained, and what has he lost?

QUESTIONS ON STRATEGY

1. What method of organization does Twain use in this selection? (Glossary: *Organization*) What alternative methods might he have used? What would have been gained or lost?

2. Explain the analogy that Twain uses in paragraph 3. (Glossary: *Analogy*) What is his purpose in using this analogy?

3. Reread Twain's conclusion. (Glossary: *Beginnings/Endings*) How effective do you find it? Why does he switch the focus to a doctor's perspective?

4. In reflecting on his two ways of seeing the river, Twain relies on a combination of subjective and objective descriptions. (Glossary: *Description*) Identify places in the essay where Twain uses description. How does the inclusion of these descriptions enhance his overall comparison and contrast?

QUESTIONS ON DICTION AND VOCABULARY

1. Twain uses a number of similes and metaphors in this selection. (Glossary: *Figures of Speech*) Identify three of each, and explain what is being compared in each case. What do these figures add to Twain's writing?

2. What effect do the italicized words have in each of the following quotations from this selection? What do these words contribute to Twain's description?
   a. "ever so *delicately* traced" (paragraph 1)
   b. "shadow that *fell* from this forest" (1)
   c. "*wrought* upon the river's face" (2)
   d. "show a *dissolving* bar" (2)
   e. "get through this *blind* place at night" (2)
   f. "lovely *flush* in a beauty's cheek" (3)

3. Refer to your desk dictionary to determine the meanings of the following words as Twain uses them in this selection: *acquisition* (paragraph 1), *hue* (1), *opal* (1), *rapture* (2), *romance* (3).

CLASSROOM ACTIVITY USING COMPARISON AND CONTRAST

Imagine that you have been asked to compare two places that have the same purpose. For example, you could compare your college cafeteria with your dining room at home, the classroom you are in now with another one on campus, or your dormitory lounge with your living room or den at home. What do you like about each place? What do you dislike? Compile a list of distinctive features for each place. Which features do the two places have in common? Which of these shared features offer solid opportunities for comparison? What did you learn about these two places from this exercise? Discuss your conclusions with your classmates.

WRITING SUGGESTIONS

1. Having read Twain's essay, you now understand how it is possible for a person to have two different views of a single scene, event, or issue. How might experience or perspective change the way we view something? Write an essay modeled on Twain's in which you offer two different views of a scene, an event, or an issue. You might consider a reporter's view compared with a victim's view, a teacher's view compared with a student's view, or a customer's view compared with a salesclerk's view.

2. Write an essay in which you use comparison and contrast to help you describe one of the following places or another place of your choice. (Glossary: *Description*)

   a. a place of worship
   b. a fast-food restaurant
   c. your dormitory
   d. your college library
   e. your favorite place
   f. your college student center
   g. your hometown

Neat People vs. Sloppy People

Suzanne Britt

Born in Winston-Salem, North Carolina, Suzanne Britt now makes her home in Raleigh. She graduated from Salem College and Washington University, where she received her M.A. in English. A freelance writer, Britt has a regular column in North Carolina Gardens and Homes. *Her work has appeared in the* New York Times, Newsweek, *and the* Boston Globe. *Her essays have been collected in two books,* Skinny People Are Dull and Crunchy Like Carrots *and* Show and Tell. *Currently, she teaches English at Meredith College in North Carolina and continues to write.*

In the following essay taken from Show and Tell, *Britt takes a humorous look at the differences between neat and sloppy people by giving us some insights about several important personality traits.*

PREPARING TO READ

Many people in our society are fond of comparing people, places, and things. Often, these comparisons are premature and even damaging. Consider the ways people judge others based on clothes, appearance, or hearsay. Write about a time in your life when you made such a comparison about someone or something. Did your initial judgment hold up? If not, why did it change?

I've finally figured out the difference between neat people and sloppy people. The distinction is, as always, moral. Neat people are lazier and meaner than sloppy people. 1

Sloppy people, you see, are not really sloppy. Their sloppiness is merely the unfortunate consequence of their extreme moral rectitude. Sloppy people carry in their mind's eye a heavenly vision, a precise plan, that is so stupendous, so perfect, it can't be achieved in this world or the next. 2

Sloppy people live in Never-Never Land. Someday is their métier.[1] Someday they are planning to alphabetize all their books and set up home catalogs. Someday they will go through their wardrobes and mark certain items for tentative mending and certain items for passing on to relatives of similar shape and size. Someday sloppy people will make family scrapbooks into which they will put newspaper clippings, postcards, locks of hair, and the dried corsage from their senior prom. Someday they will file everything on the surface of their desks, including the cash receipts from coffee purchases at the snack shop. Someday they will sit down and read all the back issues of *The New Yorker*. 3

---

[1] Activity or work for which a person is especially suited.

For all these noble reasons and more, sloppy people never get neat.   4
They aim too high and wide. They save everything, planning someday
to file, order, and straighten out the world. But while these ambitious
plans take clearer and clearer shape in their heads, the books spill from
the shelves onto the floor, the clothes pile up in the hamper and closet,
the family mementos accumulate in every drawer, the surface of the
desk is buried under mounds of paper and the unread magazines
threaten to reach the ceiling.

Sloppy people can't bear to part with anything. They give loving   5
attention to every detail. When sloppy people say they're going to
tackle the surface of the desk, they really mean it. Not a paper will go
unturned; not a rubber band will go unboxed. Four hours or two weeks
into the excavation, the desk looks exactly the same, primarily because
the sloppy person is meticulously creating new piles of papers with new
headings and scrupulously stopping to read all of the old book catalogs
before he throws them away. A neat person would just bulldoze the desk.

Neat people are bums and clods at heart. They have cavalier atti-   6
tudes toward possessions, including family heirlooms. Everything is
just another dust-catcher to them. If anything collects dust, it's got to
go and that's that. Neat people will toy with the idea of throwing the
children out of the house just to cut down on the clutter.

Neat people don't care about process. They like results. What they   7
want to do is get the whole thing over with so they can sit down and
watch the rasslin' on TV. Neat people operate on two unvarying principles: never handle any item twice, and throw everything away.

The only thing messy in a neat person's house is the trash can. The   8
minute something comes to a neat person's hand, he will look at it, try
to decide if it has immediate use and, finding none, throw it in the trash.

Neat people are especially vicious with mail. They never go through   9
their mail unless they are standing directly over a trash can. If the trash
can is beside the mailbox, even better. All ads, catalogs, pleas for charitable
contributions, church bulletins and money-saving coupons go straight
into the trash can without being opened. All letters from home, postcards
from Europe, bills and paychecks are opened, immediately responded to,
then dropped in the trash can. Neat people keep their receipts only for tax
purposes. That's it. No sentimental salvaging of birthday cards or the last
letter a dying relative ever wrote. Into the trash it goes.

Neat people place neatness above everything, even economics. They   10
are incredibly wasteful. Neat people throw away several toys every time
they walk through the den. I knew a neat person once who threw away a
perfectly good dish drainer because it had mold on it. The drainer was
too much trouble to wash. And neat people sell their furniture when they
move. They will sell a La-Z-Boy recliner while you are reclining in it.

Neat people are no good to borrow from. Neat people buy every-   11
thing in expensive little single portions. They get their flour and sugar

in two-pound bags. They wouldn't consider clipping a coupon, saving a leftover, reusing plastic nondairy whipped cream containers or rinsing off tin foil and draping it over the unmoldy dish drainer. You can never borrow a neat person's newspaper to see what's playing at the movies. Neat people have the paper all wadded up and in the trash by 7:05 A.M.

Neat people cut a clean swath through the organic as well as the   12
inorganic world. People, animals, and things are all one to them. They are so insensitive. After they've finished with the pantry, the medicine cabinet, and the attic, they will throw out the red geranium (too many leaves), sell the dog (too many fleas), and send the children off to boarding school (too many scuff marks on the hardwood floors).

THINKING CRITICALLY ABOUT THE TEXT

Suzanne Britt reduces people to two types: sloppy and neat. What does she see as the defining characteristics of each type? Do you consider yourself a sloppy or a neat person? Perhaps you are neither. If this is the case, make up your own category, and explain why Britt's categories are not broad enough.

QUESTIONS ON SUBJECT

1. Why do you suppose Britt characterizes the distinction between sloppy and neat people as a "moral" one (paragraph 1)? What is she really poking fun at with this reference? (Glossary: *Irony*)

2. In your own words, what is the "heavenly vision," the "precise plan," Britt refers to in paragraph 2? How does Britt use this idea to explain why sloppy people can never be neat?

3. Exaggeration, as Britt uses it, is only effective if it is based on some shared idea of the truth. What commonly understood ideas about sloppy and neat people does Britt rely on? Do you agree with her? Why or why not?

QUESTIONS ON STRATEGY

1. Note Britt's use of transitions as she moves from trait to trait. (Glossary: *Transitions*) How well does she use transitions to achieve unity in her essay? Explain.

2. One of the ways Britt achieves a sense of the ridiculous in her essay is to switch the commonly accepted attributes of sloppy and neat people. Cite examples of this technique, and discuss the ways in which it adds to her essay. What does it reveal to the reader about her purpose in writing the essay? (Glossary: *Purpose*)

3. Britt uses block comparison to point out the differences between sloppy and neat people. Make a side-by-side list of the traits of sloppy and neat people. After reviewing your list, determine any ways in which sloppy and neat people may be similar. Why do you suppose Britt does not include any of the ways in which they are the same?

4. Why do you think Britt has chosen to use a block comparison? What would have been gained or lost had she used a point-by-point system of contrast?

5. Throughout the essay, Britt uses numerous examples to show the differences between sloppy and neat people. (Glossary: *Illustration*) Cite five examples that Britt uses to exemplify these points. How effective do you find Britt's use of examples? What do they add to her essay of comparison and contrast?

QUESTIONS ON DICTION AND VOCABULARY

1. Cite examples of Britt's diction that indicate her change of tone when she is talking about either sloppy or neat people. (Glossary: *Diction; Tone*)

2. How would you characterize Britt's vocabulary in the essay—easy or difficult? What does her choice of vocabulary say about her intended audience? In which places does Britt use precise word choice to particularly good effect?

3. Refer to your desk dictionary to determine the meanings of the following words as Britt uses them in this selection: *rectitude* (paragraph 2), *tentative* (3), *meticulously* (5), *heirlooms* (6), *salvaging* (9), *swath* (12).

CLASSROOM ACTIVITY USING COMPARISON AND CONTRAST

Prepare both block and point-by-point outlines for one of the following topics:

1. dogs and cats as pets
2. print media and electronic media
3. an economy car and a luxury car
4. your local newspaper and the *New York Times*
5. a high school teacher and a college teacher

Explain any advantages of one organizational plan over the other.

WRITING SUGGESTIONS

1. Write an essay in which you describe yourself as either sloppy or neat. In what ways does your behavior compare or contrast with the traits Britt offers? You may follow Britt's definition of sloppy and neat, or you may come up with your own.

2. Take some time to reflect on a relationship in your life—perhaps one with a friend, a family member, or a teacher. Write an essay in which you discuss what it is about you and that other person that makes the relationship work. You may find it helpful to think of a relationship that doesn't work to better understand why the relationship you're writing about does work. What discoveries about yourself did you make while working on this essay? Explain. (Glossary: *Description*)

Of Weirdos and Eccentrics

Pico Iyer

 *Pico Iyer is one of the most popular travel writers at work today. "Travel," writes Iyer, "is how we put a face on the Other and step a little beyond our secondhand images of the alien." Born in 1957 to Indian parents, Iyer graduated from Eton, England's most famous preparatory school, and took both his bachelor's and master's degrees from Oxford University in 1978 and 1982, respectively. He also has a master's degree from Harvard University. What is particularly note-worthy about Iyer's travel writing is that he crosses ethnic and cultural barriers with an easy and natural style, taking note of both the borders and the essences of the countries he visits. Critics hailed his first travel book,* Video Night in Kathmandu and Other Reports from the Not-So-Distant Far East *(1989), for its humor, perception, and personal reflection. This success was followed by* The Lady and the Monk: Four Seasons in Kyoto *(1991);* Falling Off the Map: Some Lonely Places of the World *(1993);* Tropical Classi-cal: Essays from Several Directions *(1998);* The Global Soul: Jet Lag, Shopping Malls, and the Search for Home *(2000); and* Sun After Dark: Flights into the Foreign *(2004). Iyer is also the author of two novels —* Cuba and the Night *(1995) and* Abandon: A Romance *(2003).*

While many people are quick to lump eccentrics and weirdos into the category of "strange" people, Pico Iyer does not agree. In the following essay, which first appeared in Time *on January 18, 1988, Iyer explores the essential differences between* eccentrics *and* weirdos *and what these characters can tell us about society at large.*

PREPARING TO READ

Identify someone you know or have read about whom you would label an "eccentric" and another whom you would label a "weirdo." What, for you, are the essential similarities or differences between these two people? Explain.

Charles Waterton was just another typical eccentric. In his 80s the eminent country squire was to be seen clambering around the upper branches of an oak tree with what was aptly described as the agility of an "adolescent gorilla." The beloved 27th lord of Walton Hall also devoted his distinguished old age to scratching the back part of his head with his right big toe. Such displays of animal high spirits were not, however, confined to the gentleman's later years. When young, Waterton made four separate trips to South America, where he sought the wourali poison (a cure, he was convinced, for hydrophobia), and once spent months on end with one foot dangling from his hammock in the quixotic hope of having his toe sucked by a vampire bat.

James Warren Jones, by contrast, was something of a weirdo. As a   2
boy in the casket-making town of Lynn, Ind., he used to conduct elaborate funeral services for dead pets. Later, as a struggling preacher, he
went from door to door, in bow tie and tweed jacket, selling imported
monkeys. After briefly fleeing to South America (a shelter, he believed,
from an imminent nuclear holocaust), the man who regarded himself
as a reincarnation of Lenin settled in Northern California and opened
some convalescent homes. Then, one humid day in the jungles of
Guyana, he ordered his followers to drink a Kool-Aid-like punch soured
with cyanide. By the time the world arrived at Jonestown, 911 people
were dead.

The difference between the eccentric and the weirdo is, in its way,   3
the difference between a man with a teddy bear in his hand and a
man with a gun. We are also, of course, besieged by other kinds of
deviants—crackpots, oddballs, fanatics, quacks and cranks. But the
weirdo and the eccentric define between them that invisible line at
which strangeness acquires an edge and oddness becomes menace.

The difference between the two starts with the words themselves: 4
eccentric, after all, carries a distinguished Latin pedigree that refers,
quite reasonably, to anything that departs from the center; weird, by
comparison, has its mongrel origins in the Old English *wyrd*, meaning
fate or destiny; and the larger, darker forces conjured up by the term —
Macbeth's weird sisters and the like—are given an extra twist with the
slangy, bastard suffix -o. Beneath the linguistic roots, however, we feel
the difference on our pulses. The eccentric we generally regard as something of a donny, dotty, harmless type, like the British peer who threw
over his Cambridge fellowship in order to live in a bath. The weirdo is
an altogether more shadowy figure—Charles Manson acting out his
messianic visions. The eccentric is a distinctive presence; the weirdo
something of an absence, who casts no reflection in society's mirror.
The eccentric raises a smile; the weirdo leaves a chill.

All too often, though, the two terms are not so easily distinguished.   5
Many a criminal trial, after all, revolves around precisely that gray area
where the two begin to blur. Was Bernhard Goetz just a volatile Every-
man, ourselves pushed to the limit, and then beyond? Or was he in fact
an aberration? Often, besides, eccentrics may simply be weirdos in possession of a VIP pass, people rich enough or powerful enough to live
above convention, amoral as Greek gods. Elvis Presley could afford to
pump bullets into silhouettes of humans and never count the cost.
Lesser mortals, however, must find another kind of victim.

To some extent too, we tend to think of eccentricity as the preroga-   6
tive, even the hallmark, of genius. And genius is its own vindication. Who
cared that Glenn Gould sang along with the piano while playing Bach, so
long as he played so beautifully? Even the Herculean debauches of Babe
Ruth did not undermine so much as confirm his status as a legend.

Indeed, the unorthodox inflections of the exceptional can lead to 7
all kinds of dangerous assumptions. If geniuses are out of the ordinary
and psychopaths are out of the ordinary, then geniuses are psychopaths
and vice versa, or so at least runs the reasoning of many dramatists who
set their plays in loony bins. If the successful are often strange, then
being strange is a way of becoming successful, or so believe all those
would-be artists who work on eccentric poses. And if celebrity is its own
defense, then many a demagogue or criminal assures himself that he
will ultimately be redeemed by the celebrity he covets.

All these distortions, however, ignore the most fundamental dis- 8
tinction of all: the eccentric is strange because he cares too little about
society, the weirdo because he cares too much. The eccentric generally
wants nothing more than his own attic-like space in which he can live
by his own peculiar lights. The weirdo, however, resents his outcast status and constantly seeks to get back into society, or at least get back at
it. His is the rage not of the bachelor but the divorcé.

Thus the eccentric hardly cares if he is seen to be strange; that in a 9
sense is what makes him strange. The weirdo, however, wants desperately to be taken as normal and struggles to keep his strangeness to
himself. "He was always such a nice man," the neighbors ritually tell
reporters after a sniper's rampage. "He always seemed so normal."

And because the two mark such different tangents to the norm, 10
their incidence can, in its way, be an index of a society's health. The
height of British eccentricity, for example, coincided with the height of
British power, if only, perhaps, because Britain in its imperial heyday
presented so strong a center from which to depart. Nowadays, with the
empire gone and the center vanishing, Britain is more often associated
with the maladjusted weirdo—the orange-haired misfit or the soccer
hooligan.

At the other extreme, the relentless and ritualized normalcy of a 11
society like Japan's — there are only four psychiatrists in all of Tokyo —
can, to Western eyes, itself seem almost abnormal. Too few eccentrics
can be as dangerous as too many weirdos. For in the end, eccentricity
is a mark of confidence, accommodated best by a confident society,
whereas weirdness inspires fear because it is a symptom of fear and
uncertainty and rage. A society needs the eccentric as much as it needs
a decorated frame for the portrait it fashions of itself; it needs the
weirdo as much as it needs a hole punched through the middle of the
canvas.

THINKING CRITICALLY ABOUT THE TEXT

At the end of his essay, Iyer claims that the incidence of eccentrics and
weirdos "can, in its way, be an index of a society's health." What do you think
he means by this statement? Has he convinced you that "too few eccentrics
can be just as dangerous as too many weirdos"? Explain.

QUESTIONS ON SUBJECT

1. What, for Iyer, is the essential difference between an eccentric and a weirdo?

2. Out of the whole cast of "deviants — crackpots, oddballs, fanatics, quacks and cranks" (paragraph 3), why does Iyer say he chose to explain the differences between eccentrics and weirdos? Do you agree with his assessment of the important differences between these two personality types? Why, or why not?

3. Iyer believes that the terms *eccentric* and *weirdo* can be difficult to distinguish at times, that there is a "gray area where the two begin to blur" (paragraph 5). What are some of the problems that come up when we try to categorize "people rich enough or powerful enough to live above convention" or "geniuses"?

4. How does Iyer resolve the "distortions" of wealth, power, and genius? Explain.

QUESTIONS ON STRATEGY

1. What is Iyer's thesis, and where does he present it? (Glossary: *Thesis*)

2. Iyer begins his essay with two paragraphs about Charles Waterton and James Warren Jones. How do these two paragraphs serve to both introduce the essay and show the essential differences between eccentrics and weirdos? (Glossary: *Beginnings/Endings; Examples*)

3. Iyer uses a point-by-point organization for his essay. What would have been gained or lost had he chosen to use a block-by-block organization? Explain.

4. In addition to the examples in the opening two paragraphs, Iyer uses other examples to illustrate the critical differences between eccentrics and weirdos. Identify five or six of these examples, and explain how they work in the context of the essay. (Glossary: *Examples*) Which examples worked best for you? Explain why.

5. How does Iyer use the strategy of definition in support of his comparison and contrast? (Glossary: *Definition*) Explain.

QUESTIONS ON DICTION AND VOCABULARY

1. In discussing the etymology or history of the words *eccentric* and *weird* in paragraph 4, Iyer contrasts the former's "distinguished Latin pedigree" with the latter's "mongrel origins." What point is Iyer making here? What does he mean when he says "the larger, darker forces conjured up by the term [weird] . . . are given an extra twist with the slangy, bastard suffix -o"?

2. Make a list of at least six to ten words Iyer uses to describe an eccentric and another list of words for a weirdo. In what ways do the connotations of these words reinforce Iyer's central distinction between these two personality types? (Glossary: *Connotation/Denotation*)

3. Refer to your desk dictionary to determine the meanings of the following words as Iyer uses them in this selection: *eminent* (paragraph 1),

hydrophobia (1), *imminent* (2), *conjured* (4), *prerogative* (6), *vindication* (6), *debauches* (6), *demagogue* (7), *tangents* (10).

CLASSROOM ACTIVITY USING COMPARISON AND CONTRAST

Consider the following topics for an essay of comparison and contrast:

1. two close friends
2. two entertainers
3. two professional athletes
4. *Time* and *Newsweek* magazines
5. two cities you have visited

Select one topic, and then write out short answers to the following questions:

Who/what could I compare and contrast?

What is my purpose in this comparison and contrast?

Are the similarities or differences more interesting?

What specific points of comparison should I discuss?

What organizational pattern will best suit my purpose: point-by-point or block comparison?

What do your answers to these questions tell you about the importance of planning for any writing project? Compare your answers with those of your classmates, and discuss.

WRITING SUGGESTIONS

1. Using Iyer's statement "If the successful are often strange, then being strange is a way of becoming successful" (paragraph 7) as your thesis, write an essay in which you explore America's fascination with success. Do you see a connection between strange dress or behavior and success? Have you or has anyone you know behaved strangely to enhance the chances for success? In this age of celebrities, many actors, entertainers, and sports figures seem to thrive on bizarre behavior. How much of this behavior are Americans willing to tolerate? How many of these celebrities do you think, as Iyer suggests, are adopting "eccentric poses" and how many are downright weird?

2. Iyer believes that one way to determine the health of a given society at any particular time is to look at the incidence of eccentrics and weirdos as a starting point. Write an essay in which you assess the "health" of American society today. Do you think that America is a "confident society" or one controlled by "fear and uncertainty and rage"? Use specific examples from your own experience, observation, or reading to support your assessment. You may find it helpful to reread your response to the "Thinking Critically about the Text" question for this selection before you begin writing.

Grant and Lee: A Study in Contrasts

Bruce Catton

Bruce Catton (1899–1978) was born in Petoskey, Michigan, and attended Oberlin College. Early in his career, Catton worked as a reporter for various newspapers, among them the Cleveland Plain Dealer. Having an interest in history, Catton became a leading authority on the Civil War and wrote a number of books on the subject. These include Mr. Lincoln's Army (1951), Glory Road (1952), A Stillness at Appomattox (1953), This Hallowed Ground (1956), The Coming Fury (1961), Never Call Retreat (1965), and Gettysburg: The Final Fury (1974). Catton won both the Pulitzer Prize and the National Book Award in 1954.

The following selection was included in The American Story, a collection of historical essays edited by Earl Schenk Miers. In this essay, Cotton considers "two great Americans, Grant and Lee—very different, yet under everything very much alike."

PREPARING TO READ

What do you know about America's Civil War and the roles played by Ulysses S. Grant and Robert E. Lee in that monumental struggle? For you, what does each of these men represent? Do you consider either of them to be an American hero? Explain.

When Ulysses S. Grant and Robert E. Lee met in the parlor of a modest house at Appomattox Court House, Virginia, on April 9, 1865, to work out the terms for the surrender of Lee's Army of Northern Virginia, a great chapter in American life came to a close, and a great new chapter began. 1

These men were bringing the Civil War to its virtual finish. To be sure, other armies had yet to surrender, and for a few days the fugitive Confederate government would struggle desperately and vainly, trying to find some way to go on living now that its chief support was gone. But in effect it was all over when Grant and Lee signed the papers. And the little room where they wrote out the terms was the scene of one of the poignant, dramatic contrasts in American history. 2

They were two strong men, these oddly different generals, and they represented the strengths of two conflicting currents that, through them, had come into final collision. 3

Back of Robert E. Lee was the notion that the old aristocratic concept might somehow survive and be dominant in American life. 4

Lee was tidewater Virginia, and in his background were family, culture, and tradition . . . the age of chivalry transplanted to a New World which was making its own legends and its own myths. He embodied a 5 way of life that had come down through the age of knighthood and the English country squire. America was a land that was beginning all over again, dedicated to nothing much more complicated than the rather hazy belief that all men had equal rights and should have an equal chance in the world. In such a land Lee stood for the feeling that it was

Robert E. Lee

somehow of advantage to human society to have a pronounced inequality in the social structure. There should be a leisure class, backed by ownership of land; in turn, society itself should be keyed to the land as the chief source of wealth and influence. It would bring forth (according to this ideal) a class of men with a strong sense of obligation to the community; men who lived not to gain advantage for themselves, but to meet the solemn obligations which had been laid on them by the very fact that they were privileged. From them the country would get its leadership; to them it could look for the higher values—of thought, of conduct, of personal deportment—to give it strength and value.

Lee embodied the noblest elements of this aristocratic ideal. 6 Through him, the landed nobility justified itself. For four years, the Southern states had fought a desperate war to uphold the ideals for which Lee stood. In the end, it almost seemed as if the Confederacy fought for Lee; as if he himself was the Confederacy . . . the best thing that the way of life for which the Confederacy stood could ever have to offer. He had passed into legend before Appomattox. Thousands of tired, underfed, poorly clothed Confederate soldiers, long since past the simple enthusiasm of the early days of the struggle, somehow considered Lee the symbol of everything for which they had been willing to die. But they could not quite put this feeling into words. If the Lost Cause, sanctified by so much heroism and so many deaths, had a living justification, its justification was General Lee.

Grant, the son of a tanner on the Western frontier, was everything 7 Lee was not. He had come up the hard way and embodied nothing in particular except the eternal toughness and sinewy fiber of the men who grew up beyond the mountains. He was one of a body of men who owed reverence and obeisance to no one, who were self-reliant to a fault, who cared hardly anything for the past but who had a sharp eye for the future.

These frontier men were the precise opposite of the tidewater aristo- 8 crats. Back of them, in the great surge that had taken people over the Alleghenies and into the opening Western country, there was a deep, implicit dissatisfaction with a past that had settled into grooves. They stood for democracy, not from any reasoned conclusion about the proper ordering of human society, but simply because they had grown up in the middle of democracy and knew how it worked. Their society might have privileges, but they would be privileges each man had won for himself. Forms and patterns meant nothing. No man was born to anything, except perhaps to a chance to show how far he could rise. Life was competition.

Yet along with this feeling had come a deep sense of belonging to a 9 national community. The Westerner who developed a farm, opened a shop, or set up in business as a trader, could hope to prosper only as his own community prospered—and his community ran from the Atlantic to the Pacific and from Canada down to Mexico. If the land was settled, with towns and highways and accessible markets, he could better himself.

Ulysses S. Grant

He saw his fate in terms of the nation's own destiny. As its horizons expanded, so did his. He had, in other words, an acute dollars-and-cents stake in the continued growth and development of his country.

And that, perhaps, is where the contrast between Grant and Lee   10
becomes most striking. The Virginia aristocrat, inevitably, saw himself in relation to his own region. He lived in a static society which could endure almost anything except change. Instinctively, his first loyalty would go to the locality in which that society existed. He would fight to the limit of endurance to defend it, because in defending it he was defending everything that gave his own life its deepest meaning.

The Westerner, on the other hand, would fight with an equal tenac-   11
ity for the broader concept of society. He fought so because everything he

lived by was tied to growth, expansion and a constantly widening horizon. What he lived by would survive or fall with the nation itself. He could not possibly stand by unmoved in the face of an attempt to destroy the Union. He would combat it with everything he had, because he could only see it as an effort to cut the ground out from under his feet.

So Grant and Lee were in complete contrast, representing two diametrically opposed elements in American life. Grant was the modern man emerging; beyond him, ready to come on the stage, was the great age of steel and machinery, of crowded cities and a restless burgeoning vitality. Lee might have ridden down from the old age of chivalry, lance in hand, silken banner fluttering over his head. Each man was the perfect champion of his cause, drawing both his strengths and his weaknesses from the people he led. 12

Yet it was not all contrast, after all. Different as they were—in background, in personality, in underlying aspiration—these two great soldiers had much in common. Under everything else, they were marvelous fighters. Furthermore, their fighting qualities were really very much alike. 13

Each man had, to begin with, the great virtue of utter tenacity and fidelity. Grant fought his way down the Mississippi Valley in spite of acute personal discouragement and profound military handicaps. Lee hung on in the trenches at Petersburg after hope itself had died. In each man there was an indomitable quality . . . the born fighter's refusal to give up as long as he can still remain on his feet and lift his two fists. 14

Daring and resourcefulness they had, too; the ability to think faster and move faster than the enemy. These were the qualities which gave Lee the dazzling campaigns of Second Manassas and Chancellorsville and won Vicksburg for Grant. 15

Lastly, and perhaps greatest of all, there was the ability, at the end, to turn quickly from war to peace once the fighting was over. Out of the way these two men behaved at Appomattox came the possibility of a peace of reconciliation. It was a possibility not wholly realized, in the years to come, but which did, in the end, help the two sections to become one nation again . . . after a war whose bitterness might have seemed to make such a reunion wholly impossible. No part of either man's life became him more than the part he played in their brief meeting in the McLean house at Appomattox. Their behavior there put all succeeding generations of Americans in their debt. Two great Americans, Grant and Lee—very different, yet under everything very much alike. Their encounter at Appomattox was one of the great moments of American history. 16

THINKING CRITICALLY ABOUT THE TEXT

Catton concludes with the claim that Grant and Lee's "encounter at Appomattox was one of the great moments of American history" (paragraph 16). How does Catton prepare readers for this claim? What, for Catton, do these two Civil War generals represent, and what does he see as the implications for the country of Lee's surrender?

QUESTIONS ON SUBJECT

1. In paragraphs 10 through 12, Catton discusses what he considers to be the most striking contrast between Grant and Lee. What is that difference?

2. List the similarities that Catton sees between Grant and Lee. Which similarity does Catton believe is most important? Why?

3. What attitudes and ideas does Catton describe to support his view that the culture of tidewater Virginia was a throwback to the "age of chivalry" (paragraph 5)?

4. Catton says that Grant was "the modern man emerging" (paragraph 12). How does he support that statement? Do you agree?

QUESTIONS ON STRATEGY

1. What would have been lost had Catton looked at the similarities between Grant and Lee before looking at the differences? Would anything have been gained?

2. How does Catton organize the body of his essay (paragraphs 3 to 16)? When answering this question, you may find it helpful to summarize the point of comparison in each paragraph and to label whether the paragraph concerns Lee, Grant, or both. (Glossary: *Organization*)

3. Catton makes clear transitions between paragraphs. Identify the transitional devices he uses to lead readers from one paragraph to the next throughout the essay. As a reader, how do these transitions help you? (Glossary: *Transitions*) Explain.

4. How does Catton use both description and cause and effect analysis to enhance his comparison and contrast of Grant and Lee? In what ways does description serve to sharpen the differences between these generals? How does Catton use cause and effect analysis to explain their respective natures? Cite several examples of Catton's use of each strategy to illustrate your answer.

QUESTIONS ON DICTION AND VOCABULARY

1. Identify at least two metaphors that Catton uses, and explain what each contributes to his comparison. (Glossary: *Figures of Speech*)

2. Refer to your desk dictionary to determine the meanings of the following words as Catton uses them in this selection: *poignant* (paragraph 2), *chivalry* (5), *sanctified* (6), *sinewy* (7), *obeisance* (7), *tidewater* (8), *tenacity* (11), *aspiration* (13).

CLASSROOM ACTIVITY USING COMPARISON AND CONTRAST

Carefully read and analyze the following paragraphs from Stephen E. Ambrose's book *Crazy Horse and Custer: The Parallel Lives of Two American Warriors* (1975). Then answer the questions that follow.

> It was bravery, above and beyond all other qualities, that Custer and Crazy Horse had in common. Each man was an outstanding warrior in war-mad societies. Thousands upon thousands of Custer's fellow whites had as much opportunity as he did to demonstrate their courage, just as all of Crazy Horse's associates had countless opportunities to show that they equaled him in bravery. But no white warrior, save his younger brother, Tom, could outdo Custer, just as no Indian warrior, save his younger brother, Little Hawk, could outdo Crazy Horse. And for both white and red societies, no masculine virtue was more admired than bravery. To survive, both societies felt they had to have men willing to put their lives on the line. For men who were willing to do so, no reward was too great, even though there were vast differences in the way each society honored its heroes.
>
> Beyond their bravery, Custer and Crazy Horse were individualists, each standing out from the crowd in his separate way. Custer wore outlandish uniforms, let his hair fall in long, flowing golden locks across his shoulders, surrounded himself with pet animals and admirers, and in general did all he could to draw attention to himself. Crazy Horse's individualism pushed him in the opposite direction — he wore a single feather in his hair when going into battle, rather than a war bonnet. Custer's vast energy set him apart from most of his fellows; the Sioux distinguished Crazy Horse from other warriors because of Crazy Horse's quietness and introspection. Both men lived in societies in which drugs, especially alcohol, were widely used, but neither Custer nor Crazy Horse drank. Most of all, of course, each man stood out in battle as a great risk taker.

What is Ambrose's point in these two paragraphs? How does he use comparison and contrast to make this point? How has Ambrose organized his paragraphs?

WRITING SUGGESTIONS

1. Catton gives readers few details of the physical appearance of Grant and Lee, but the portraits that accompany this essay do show us what these men looked like. Write a brief essay in which you compare and contrast the men you see in the portraits. How closely does your assessment of each general match the "picture" Catton presents in his essay? How would you describe the appearance — both dress and posture — of these

two generals? What details in the photographs are most telling for you? Explain why. In what ways can Grant and Lee be said to represent the way of life associated with the side each commanded? Explain.

2. In the persons of Grant and Lee, Catton sees the "final collision" (paragraph 3) between two ways of living and thinking—the "age of steel and machinery" (12) conquering the "age of chivalry" (5). What do you see as the dominant ways of living and thinking in the current "age of information"? Do today's lifestyles appear to be on a collision course with one another, or do you think they can all coexist? Write an essay in which you present your position and defend it using appropriate examples.

Sex, Lies, and Conversation

Deborah Tannen

Deborah Tannen, professor of linguistics at Georgetown University, was born in 1945 in Brooklyn, New York. Tannen received her B.A. in English from the State University of New York at Binghamton in 1966 and taught English in Greece until 1968. She then earned an M.A. in English literature from Wayne State University in 1970. While pursuing her Ph.D. in linguistics at the University of California–Berkeley, she received several prizes for her poetry and short fiction. Her work has appeared in New York *magazine,* Vogue, *and the* New York Times Magazine. *In addition, she has authored three best-selling language books:* You Just Don't Understand *(1990),* That's Not What I Meant *(1991), and* Talking from Nine to Five *(1994). The success of these books attests to the public's interest in language, especially when it pertains to gender differences. Tannen's most recent books include* The Argument Culture: Stopping America's War of Words *(1998),* I Only Say This Because I Love You: Talking to Your Parents, Partners, Sibs, and Kids When You're All Adults *(2002), and* You're Wearing That?: Mothers and Daughters in Conversation *(2006).*

In this essay, which first appeared in the Washington Post *in 1990, Tannen examines the differences between men's and women's public and private speech. Interestingly, she concludes that cross-gender conversation, when seen as cross-cultural communication, "allows us to understand the problem and forge solutions without blaming either party."*

PREPARING TO READ

How important is it for people to be aware of gender and cultural differences when interacting with others? What are some of the potential benefits of such awareness?

I was addressing a small gathering in a suburban Virginia living room—a women's group that had invited men to join them. Throughout the evening, one man had been particularly talkative, frequently offering ideas and anecdotes, while his wife sat silently beside him on the couch. Toward the end of the evening, I commented that women frequently complain that their husbands don't talk to them. This man quickly concurred. He gestured toward his wife and said, "She's the talker in our family." The room burst into laughter; the man looked puzzled and hurt. "It's true," he explained. "When I come home from work I have nothing to say. If she didn't keep the conversation going, we'd spend the whole evening in silence."

This episode crystallizes the irony that although American men tend to talk more than women in public situations, they often talk less at home. And this pattern is wreaking havoc with marriage.

The pattern was observed by political scientist Andrew Hacker in the late '70s. Sociologist Catherine Kohler Riessman reports in her new book *Divorce Talk* that most of the women she interviewed — but only a few of the men — gave lack of communication as the reason for their divorces. Given the current divorce rate of nearly 50 percent, that amounts to millions of cases in the United States every year — a virtual epidemic of failed conversation. 3

In my own research, complaints from women about their husbands most often focused not on tangible inequities such as having given up the chance for a career to accompany a husband to his, or doing far more than their share of daily life-support work like cleaning, cooking, social arrangements, and errands. Instead, they focused on communication: "He doesn't listen to me," "He doesn't talk to me." I found, as Hacker observed years before, that most wives want their husbands to be, first and foremost, conversational partners, but few husbands share this expectation of their wives. 4

In short, the image that best represents the current crisis is the stereotypical cartoon scene of a man sitting at the breakfast table with a newspaper held up in front of his face, while a woman glares at the back of it, wanting to talk. 5

Linguistic Battle of the Sexes

How can women and men have such different impressions of communication in marriage? Why the widespread imbalance in their interests and expectations? 6

In the April issue of *American Psychologist*, Stanford University's Eleanor Maccoby reports the results of her own and others' research showing that children's development is most influenced by the social structure of peer interactions. Boys and girls tend to play with children of their own gender, and their sex-separate groups have different organizational structures and interactive norms. 7

I believe these systematic differences in childhood socialization make talk between women and men like cross-cultural communication, heir to all the attraction and pitfalls of that enticing but difficult enterprise. My research on men's and women's conversations uncovered patterns similar to those described for children's groups. 8

For women, as for girls, intimacy is the fabric of relationships, and talk is the thread from which it is woven. Little girls create and maintain friendships by exchanging secrets; similarly, women regard conversation as the cornerstone of friendship. So a woman expects her husband to be a new and improved version of a best friend. What is important is not the individual subjects that are discussed but the sense of closeness, of a life shared, that emerges when people tell their thoughts, feelings, and impressions. 9

Bonds between boys can be as intense as girls', but they are based less on talking, more on doing things together. Since they don't assume talk is the cement that binds a relationship, men don't know what kind of talk women want, and they don't miss it when it isn't there. 10

Boys' groups are larger, more inclusive, and more hierarchical, so boys must struggle to avoid the subordinate position in the group. This may play a role in women's complaints that men don't listen to them. Some men really don't like to listen, because being the listener makes them feel one-down, like a child listening to adults or an employee to a boss. 11

But often when women tell men, "You aren't listening," and the men protest, "I am," the men are right. The impression of not listening results from misalignments in the mechanics of conversation. The misalignment begins as soon as a man and a woman take physical positions. This became clear when I studied videotapes made by psychologist Bruce Dorval of children and adults talking to their same-sex best friends. I found that at every age, the girls and women faced each other directly, their eyes anchored on each other's faces. At every age, the boys and men sat at angles to each other and looked elsewhere in the room, periodically glancing at each other. They were obviously attuned to each other, often mirroring each other's movements. But the tendency of men to face away can give women the impression they aren't listening even when they are. A young woman in college was frustrated: Whenever she told her boyfriend she wanted to talk to him, he would lie down on the floor, close his eyes, and put his arm over his face. This signaled to her, "He's taking a nap." But he insisted he was listening extra hard. Normally, he looks around the room, so he is easily distracted. Lying down and covering his eyes helped him concentrate on what she was saying. 12

Analogous to the physical alignment that women and men take in conversation is their topical alignment. The girls in my study tended to talk at length about one topic, but the boys tended to jump from topic to topic. The second-grade girls exchanged stories about people they knew. The second-grade boys teased, told jokes, noticed things in the room, and talked about finding games to play. The sixth-grade girls talked about problems with a mutual friend. The sixth-grade boys talked about 55 different topics, none of which extended over more than a few turns. 13

Listening to Body Language

Switching topics is another habit that gives women the impression men aren't listening, especially if they switch to a topic about themselves. But the evidence of the 10th-grade boys in my study indicates otherwise. The 10th-grade boys sprawled across their chairs with bodies parallel and eyes straight ahead, rarely looking at each other. They 14 looked as if they were riding in a car, staring out the windshield. But they were talking about their feelings. One boy was upset because a girl had told him he had a drinking problem, and the other was feeling alienated from all his friends.

Now, when a girl told a friend about a problem, the friend responded by asking probing questions and expressing agreement and understanding. But the boys dismissed each other's problems. Todd assured Richard that his drinking was "no big problem" because "sometimes you're funny when you're off your butt." And when Todd said he felt left out, Richard responded, "Why should you? You know more people than me." 15

Women perceive such responses as belittling and unsupportive. But the boys seemed satisfied with them. Whereas women reassure each other by implying, "You shouldn't feel bad because I've had similar experiences," men do so by implying, "You shouldn't feel bad because your problems aren't so bad." 16

There are even simpler reasons for women's impression that men don't listen. Linguist Lynette Hirschman found that women make more listener-noise, such as "mhm," "uhuh," and "yeah," to show "I'm with you." Men, she found, more often give silent attention. Women who expect a stream of listener-noise interpret silent attention as no attention at all. 17

Women's conversational habits are as frustrating to men as men's are to women. Men who expect silent attention interpret a stream of listener-noise as overreaction or impatience. Also, when women talk to each other in a close, comfortable setting, they often overlap, finish each other's sentences, and anticipate what the other is about to say. This practice, which I call "participatory listenership," is often perceived by men as interruption, intrusion, and lack of attention. 18

A parallel difference caused a man to complain about his wife, "She just wants to talk about her own point of view. If I show her another view, she gets mad at me." When most women talk to each other, they assume a conversationalist's job is to express agreement and support. But many men see their conversational duty as pointing out the other side of an argument. This is heard as disloyalty by women, and refusal to offer the requisite support. It is not that women don't want to see other points of view, but that they prefer them phrased as suggestions and inquiries rather than as direct challenges. 19

In his book *Fighting for Life*, Walter Ong points out that men use "agonistic" or warlike, oppositional formats to do almost anything; thus discussion becomes debate, and conversation a competitive sport. In contrast, women see conversation as a ritual means of establishing rapport. If Jane tells a problem and June says she has a similar one, they walk away feeling closer to each other. But this attempt at establishing rapport can backfire when used with men. Men take too literally 20 women's ritual "troubles talk," just as women mistake men's ritual challenges for real attack.

The Sounds of Silence

These differences begin to clarify why women and men have such different expectations about communication in marriage. For women, talk creates intimacy. Marriage is an orgy of closeness: you can tell your feelings and thoughts, and still be loved. Their greatest fear is being pushed away. But men live in a hierarchical world, where talk maintains independence and status. They are on guard to protect themselves from being put down and pushed around. 21

This explains the paradox of the talkative man who said of his silent wife, "She's the talker." In the public setting of a guest lecture, he felt challenged to show his intelligence and display his understanding of the lecture. But at home, where he has nothing to prove and no one to defend against, he is free to remain silent. For his wife, being home means she is free from the worry that something she says might offend someone, or spark disagreement, or appear to be showing off; at home she is free to talk. 22

The communication problems that endanger marriage can't be fixed by mechanical engineering. They require a new conceptual framework about the role of talk in human relationships. Many of the psychological explanations that have become second nature may not be helpful, because they tend to blame either women (for not being assertive enough) or men (for not being in touch with their feelings). A sociolinguistic approach by which male–female conversation is seen as cross-cultural communication allows us to understand the problem and forge solutions without blaming either party. 23

Once the problem is understood, improvement comes naturally, as it did to the young woman and her boyfriend who seemed to go to sleep when she wanted to talk. Previously, she had accused him of not listening, and he had refused to change his behavior, since that would be admitting fault. But then she learned about and explained to him the differences in women's and men's habitual ways of aligning themselves in conversation. The next time she told him she wanted to talk, he began, as usual, by lying down and covering his eyes. When the familiar negative reaction bubbled up, she reassured herself that he really was listening. But then he sat up and looked at her. Thrilled, she asked why. He said, "You like me to look at you when we talk, so I'll try to do it." Once he saw their differences as cross-cultural rather than right and wrong, he independently altered his behavior. 24

Women who feel abandoned and deprived when their husbands won't listen to or report daily news may be happy to discover their 25 husbands trying to adapt once they understand the place of small talk in women's relationships. But if their husbands don't adapt, the women may still be comforted that for men, this is not a failure of intimacy. Accepting the difference, the wives may look to their friends or family for that kind of talk. And husbands who can't provide it shouldn't feel their wives have made unreasonable demands. Some couples will still decide to divorce, but at least their decisions will be based on realistic expectations.

In these times of resurgent ethnic conflicts, the world desperately needs cross-cultural understanding. Like charity, successful cross-cultural communication should begin at home.   26

THINKING CRITICALLY ABOUT THE TEXT

Consider the times in your life when you have experienced problems in conversation. Do you think that these problems might have occurred as a result of gender or cultural differences, as Tannen explains?

QUESTIONS ON SUBJECT

1. In paragraph 8, Tannen compares conversational problems between men and women to the problems of "cross-cultural communication." What does she mean by this comparison?

2. In paragraph 7, Tannen reports on a study that shows boys' and girls' conversational development follows different patterns. How does she think these patterns carry over into adult conversational patterns?

3. Throughout the essay, Tannen makes a conscious effort to treat both her male and female readers fairly. In what ways has she sought to encourage understanding rather than attach blame?

QUESTIONS ON STRATEGY

1. How does Tannen organize her essay—point-by-point or block organization? (Glossary: *Organization*) Why do you think she makes this choice, and is it effective?

2. In hopes of explaining conversational differences between men and women, Tannen employs the analogy of cross-cultural communication. (Glossary: *Analogy*) How well does the analogy work? Did it help you gain a better understanding of her topic? Explain.

3. In keeping with her role as a popularizer of linguistic research, Tannen assumes an informal, almost conversational tone in the essay. (Glossary: *Tone*) Why do you think she chose to keep her own experiences out of the essay? What could she have gained or lost by including personal experience?

4. In discussing speech differences, Tannen attempts to explain the causes of our different approaches to conversation. How does a knowledge of

these causes help us better understand their effects on cross-gender conversations? Explain how Tannen's use of cause and effect strengthens her overall argument. (Glossary: *Cause and Effect Analysis*)

QUESTIONS ON DICTION AND VOCABULARY

1. Tannen's essay appeals to a wide audience because of her informal, conversational diction. (Glossary: *Audience; Diction*) Is there anything in her choice of words that reveals her academic background?

2. In paragraph 18, Tannen introduces her term "participatory listenership." What does she mean by it? (Glossary: *Definition*) How does Tannen's use of this term point to the larger problem of gender miscommunication?

3. Refer to your desk dictionary to determine the meanings of the following words as Tannen uses them in this selection: *fabric* (paragraph 9), *hierarchical* (11), *mechanics* (12), *rapport* (20), *paradox* (22), *framework* (23).

CLASSROOM ACTIVITY USING COMPARISON AND CONTRAST

After reviewing the discussion of analogy in the introduction to this chapter (pages 260–261), create an analogy to explain your relationship with

1. one of your parents;
2. a boyfriend or girlfriend;
3. a pet or other object; or
4. your bedroom at home or at college.

WRITING SUGGESTIONS

1. Write an essay modeled on Tannen's in which you analyze the characteristics of conversation she has labeled as particularly "masculine" or "feminine," using examples from your own experience. How does your own experience of what men and women do when they converse compare with Tannen's explanation?

2. Imagine that your college is considering the adoption of a course entitled "Language, Gender, and Communication." As a concerned student, position yourself to argue for or against such a course. (Glossary: *Argument*) Present your argument as an essay or as a letter to the editor of your school newspaper.

WRITING SUGGESTIONS FOR COMPARISON AND CONTRAST

1. Write an essay in which you compare and contrast two objects, people, or events to show at least one of the following.

   a. their important differences
   b. their significant similarities
   c. their relative value
   d. their distinctive qualities

2. Select a topic from the list that follows. Write an essay using comparison and contrast as your primary means of development. Be sure that your essay has a definite purpose and a clear direction.

   a. two methods of dieting
   b. two television situation comedies
   c. two types of summer employment
   d. two people who display different attitudes toward responsibility
   e. two restaurants
   f. two courses in the same subject area
   g. two friends who exemplify different lifestyles
   h. two network television or local news programs
   i. two professional quarterbacks
   j. two ways of studying for an exam
   k. two rooms in which you have classes
   l. two of your favorite magazines
   m. two attitudes toward death
   n. two ways to heat a home

3. Use one of the following "before and after" situations as the basis for an essay of comparison and contrast.

   a. before and after an examination
   b. before and after seeing a movie
   c. before and after reading an important book
   d. before and after dieting
   e. before and after a long trip

4. Most of us have seen something important in our lives—a person, place, or thing—undergo a significant change, either in the subject itself or in our own perception of it. Write an essay comparing and contrasting the person, place, or thing before and after the change. First, reread Mark Twain's "Two Ways of Seeing a River" in this chapter (page 272) and Malcolm X's "Coming to an Awareness of Language" in Chapter 4 (page 76), and then consider your topic. There are many possibilities to consider. Perhaps a bucolic vista of open fields has become a shopping mall; perhaps a favorite athletic team has gone from glory to shame; perhaps a loved one has been altered by decisions, events, or illness.

5. Interview a professor who has taught for many years at your college or university. Ask the professor to compare and contrast the college as it was

when he or she first taught there with the way it is now; encourage reminiscence and evaluation. Combine strategies of description, comparison and contrast, and possibly definition as you write your essay. (Glossary: *Definition; Description*)

6. Six of the essays in this book deal, more or less directly, with issues related to the definition, achievement, or nature of manhood in America. The essays are "How to Give Orders Like a Man" (page 171) and "Sex, Lies, and Conversation" (page 293), both by Deborah Tannen; "Up in Smoke" by Mary Winstead (page 99); "Grant and Lee: A Study in Contrasts" by Bruce Catton (page 285); "How Boys Become Men" by Jon Katz (page 421); and "Shooting an Elephant" by George Orwell (page 588). Read these essays, and discuss with classmates the broad issues they raise. Choose one topic of particular interest to you, and study the three or four essays that seem to bear most directly on this topic. Write an essay in which you compare, contrast, and evaluate the assertions in these essays.

CHAPTER 9

Division and Classification

WHAT ARE DIVISION AND CLASSIFICATION?

Like comparison and contrast, division and classification are separate yet closely related operations. Division involves breaking down a single large unit into smaller subunits or separating a group of items into discrete categories. Classification, on the other hand, entails placing individual items into established categories. Division, then, takes apart, whereas classification groups together. But even though the two processes can operate separately, writers tend to use them together.

Division can be the most effective method for making sense of one large, complex, or multifaceted entity. Consider, for example, the following passage from E. B. White's *Here Is New York*, in which he discusses New Yorkers and their city.

Division into categories occurs in the opening sentence.　There are roughly three New Yorks. There is, first, the New York of the man or woman who was born here, who takes the city for granted and accepts its size and its turbulence as natural and inevitable. Second, there is the New York of the commuter—the city that is devoured by locusts each day and spat out each night. Third, there is the New York of the person who was born somewhere else and came to New York in quest of something. Of these three trembling cities the greatest is the last—the city of final destination, the city that is a goal. It is this third city that accounts for New York's highstrung disposition, its poetical deportment, its dedication to the arts, and its incomparable achievements. Commuters give the city its tidal restlessness;

Author explains the nature of people in each category.

natives give it solidarity and continuity; but the settlers give it passion. And whether it is a farmer arriving from Italy to set up a small grocery store in a slum, or a young girl arriving from a small town in Mississippi to escape the indignity of being observed by her neighbors, or a boy arriving from the Corn Belt with a manuscript in his suitcase and a pain in his heart, it makes no difference: each embraces New York with the intense excitement of first love, each absorbs New York with the fresh eyes of an adventurer, each generates heat and light to dwarf the Consolidated Edison Company.

In his opening sentences, White suggests a principle for dividing the population of New York, establishing his three categories on the basis of a person's relationship to the city. There is the New York of the native, the New York of the commuter, and the New York of the immigrant. Although White gives specific examples for only his third grouping, it is easy to see where any individual would be classified. The purpose and result of White's divisions are clear and effective. They help him make a point about the character of New York City, depicting its restlessness, its solidarity, and its passion.

In contrast to breaking a large idea into parts, classification can be used to draw connections between disparate elements based on a common category—price, for example. Often, classification is used in conjunction with another rhetorical strategy, such as comparison and contrast. Consider, for example, how in the following passage from Toni Cade Bambara's "The Lesson" she classifies a toy in F.A.O. Schwarz and other items in the $35 category to compare the relative value of things in the life of two girls, Sylvia and Sugar.

Same thing in the store. We all walkin on tiptoe and hardly touchin the games and puzzles and things. And I watched Miss Moore who is steady watchin us like she waitin for a sign. Like Mama Drewery watches the sky and sniffs the air and takes note of just how much slant is in the bird formation. Then me and Sugar bump smack into each other, so busy gazing at the toys, 'specially the sailboat. But we don't laugh and go into our fat-lady bump-stomach routine. We

First mention of price

just stare at that price tag. Then Sugar run a finger over the whole boat. And I'm jealous and want to hit her. Maybe not her, but I sure want to punch somebody in the mouth.

"Whatcha bring us here for, Miss Moore?"

"You sound angry, Sylvia. Are you mad about something?" Givin me one of them grins like she tellin a grown-up joke that never turns out to be funny. And she's lookin very closely at me like maybe she plannin to do my portrait from memory. I'm mad, but I won't give her that satisfaction. So I slouch around the store being very bored and say, "Let's go."

Me and Sugar at the back of the train watchin the tracks whizzin by large then small then getting gobbled up in the dark. I'm thinkin about this tricky toy I saw in the store. A clown that somersaults on a bar then does chin-ups just cause you yank lightly at his leg. Cost $35. I could see me askin my mother for a $35 birthday clown. "You wanna who that costs what?" she'd say, cocking her head to the side to get a better view of the hole in my head.

Classification used along with comparison and contrast

Thirty-five dollars could buy new bunk beds for Junior and Gretchen's boy. Thirty-five dollars and the whole household could go visit Grand-daddy Nelson in the country. Thirty-five dollars would pay for the rent and the piano bill too. Who are these people that spend that much for performing clowns and $1000 for toy sailboats? What kinda work they do and how they live and how come we ain't in on it?

Another example may help clarify how division and classification work hand in hand. Suppose a sociologist wants to determine whether the socioeconomic status of the people in a particular neighborhood has any influence on their voting behavior. Having decided on her purpose, the sociologist chooses as her subject the fifteen families living on Maple Street. Her goal then becomes to group these families in a way that will be relevant to her purpose. She immediately knows that she wants to divide the neighborhood in two ways: (1) according to socioeconomic status (low-income earners, middle-income earners, and high-income earners) and (2) according to voting behavior (voters and nonvoters). However, her process of division won't be complete until she can classify individual families into her various groupings.

In confidential interviews with each family, the sociologist learns first its income and then whether any member of the household has voted in a state or federal election during the last four years. Based on this information, she begins to classify each family according to her established categories and at the same time to divide the neighborhood into the subclasses crucial to her study. Her work leads her to construct the following diagram of her divisions/classifications. This diagram allows the sociologist to visualize her division and classification system and its essential components: subject, basis or principle of division, subclasses or categories, and conclusion. It is clear that her ultimate conclusion depends on her ability to work back and forth between the potential divisions or subclasses and the actual families to be classified.

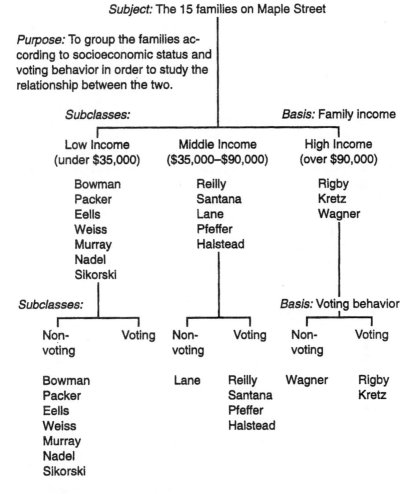

Subject: The 15 families on Maple Street

Purpose: To group the families according to socioeconomic status and voting behavior in order to study the relationship between the two.

Subclasses: | *Basis:* Family income

Low Income (under $35,000)	Middle Income ($35,000–$90,000)	High Income (over $90,000)
Bowman	Reilly	Rigby
Packer	Santana	Kretz
Eells	Lane	Wagner
Weiss	Pfeffer	
Murray	Halstead	
Nadel		
Sikorski		

Subclasses: | *Basis:* Voting behavior

Non-voting	Voting	Non-voting	Voting	Non-voting	Voting
Bowman		Lane	Reilly	Wagner	Rigby
Packer			Santana		Kretz
Eells			Pfeffer		
Weiss			Halstead		
Murray					
Nadel					
Sikorski					

Conclusion: On Maple Street there seems to be a relationship between socioeconomic status and voting behavior: The low-income families are nonvoters.

USING DIVISION AND CLASSIFICATION AS A WRITING STRATEGY

As the work of the Maple Street sociologist shows, division and classification are used primarily to demonstrate a particular point about the subject under discussion. In a paper about the emphasis a television network places on reaching various audiences, you could begin by dividing prime-time programming into suitable subclasses: shows primarily for adults, shows for families, shows for children, and so forth. You could then classify each of that network's individual programs into one of these categories. Ultimately, you would want to analyze how the programs are divided among the various categories; in this way you could make a point about which audiences the network tries hardest to reach.

Another purpose of division and classification is to help writers and readers make choices. A voter may classify politicians on the basis of their attitudes toward nuclear energy or abortion; *Consumer Reports* classifies laptop computers on the basis of available memory, screen size, processor speed, repair record, and warranty; high school seniors classify colleges and universities on the basis of prestige, geographic location, programs available, and tuition fees. In such cases, division and classification have an absolutely practical end: making a decision about whom to vote for, which laptop to buy, and where to apply for admission to college.

Finally, writers use division and classification as a basic organizational strategy, one that brings a sense of order to a large amorphous whole. As you'll see later in this chapter, for example, Rosalind Wiseman's system of classification in "The Queen Bee and Her Court" establishes seven categories of roles played by young girls in school cliques to help us better understand how those cliques function.

Using Division and Classification across the Disciplines

When writing essays in the academic disciplines, you will have many opportunities to use the strategy of division and classification to both organize and strengthen the presentation of your ideas. To determine whether or not division and classification is the right strategy for you in a particular paper, use the four-step method first described in "Determining Your Strategy" (pages 24–25). Consider the following examples, which illustrate how this four-step method works for typical college papers:

Earth Sciences

MAIN IDEA: Pollution is a far-reaching and unwieldy subject.

QUESTION: On what basis can we divide pollution into its various categories and what examples of pollution can we place into each category?

STRATEGY: Division and Classification. This strategy involves two activities: dividing into categories and placing items in their appropriate categories. The word *divide* signals the need to separate pollution into manageable groupings. The word *examples* and the phrase *place into each category* signal the need to classify types of pollution into appropriate categories.

SUPPORTING STRATEGY: Argumentation is often used to support both the rationale for categorization and classification itself.

Education

MAIN IDEA: Children's learning disabilities fall into three major groups.

QUESTION: What are the major types of learning disabilities into which children fall?

STRATEGY: Division and Classification. The words *major types* suggest the need to divide learning problems into major categories. The words *fall into* suggest that every learning disability can be classified into one of the three categories.

SUPPORTING STRATEGY: Argumentation could be used to persuade readers that the categories of problems discussed are major and to persuade them that a knowledge of these three major types of problems can be useful to teachers and parents in helping a child.

Political Science

MAIN IDEA: There are four types of U.S. presidents.

QUESTION: On what basis or bases do we group U.S. presidents?

STRATEGY: Division and Classification. The words *basis* or *bases* signals the need to establish criteria for dividing all our presidents. The word *group* suggests the need to classify the presidents according to the established groupings.

SUPPORTING STRATEGY: Illustration can be used to provide examples of various presidents.

SAMPLE STUDENT ESSAY USING DIVISION AND CLASSIFICATION AS A WRITING STRATEGY

Gerald Cleary studied mathematics as an undergraduate and later attended law school at Cornell University. He spent his last two years of high school in West Germany as a military dependent. During that time, Cleary sold stereo equipment at a large post exchange. In this well-unified essay, Cleary has fun dividing and classifying the different types of customers he dealt with in his job.

How Loud? How Good? How Much? How Pretty?
Gerald Cleary

As stereo equipment gets better and prices go down,   1
stereo systems are becoming household necessities rather than
luxuries. People are buying stereos by the thousands. During
my year as a stereo salesman, I witnessed this boom firsthand.
I dealt with hundreds of customers, and it didn't take long for me
to learn that people buy stereos for different reasons. Eventually,
though, I was able to divide all the stereo buyers into four basic
categories: the looks buyer, the wattage buyer, the price buyer,
and the quality buyer.

Thesis: Division of stereo buyers into four categories. Labels make for ease of reference.

The looks buyer cannot be bothered with the question   2
of how the stereo will sound. The only concern is how the stereo
looks, making the buyer least respected by the stereo salesperson.
The looks buyer has an irresistible attraction to flashing lights,
knobs, switches, and frivolous features. Even the loudspeakers
are chosen on the basis of appearance — the looks buyer always
removes the grille to make sure a couple of knobs are present.
Enjoyment for him is watching the output meters flash on his
amplifier, or playing with his cassette deck's remote control.
No matter what the component, the looks buyer always decides
on the flashiest, exclaiming, "Wait 'til my friends see this!"

Organization: Least appealing buyer to salesperson is discussed.

Illustration: Typical statement used as example

Slightly more respected is the wattage buyer, who is most   3
easily identified by his trademark question: "How many watts
does it put out?" He will not settle for less than 100 watts from
his amp, and his speakers must be able to handle all this power.
He is interested only in the volume level his stereo can produce,
for the wattage buyer always turns it up loud — so loud that
most would find it painful. The wattage buyer genuinely enjoys
his music — either rap or heavy metal — at this volume. He is
actually proud of his stereo's ability to put out deafening noise.
As a result, the wattage buyer becomes as well-known to his
neighbors as he is to the salesperson. His competitive nature
makes him especially obvious as he pays for his new system,
telling his friend, "Man, this is gonna blow Jones's stereo away!"

Organization: Second, more appealing, buyer is discussed.

Illustration: Typical statement used as example

In this money-conscious world, the price buyer has the   4
understanding, if not the respect, of the salesperson. Often, she
is ashamed of her budget limitations and will try to disguise
herself as one of the other types of buyers, asking, "What's the
loudest receiver I can buy for $200?" Or, "What's the best

Organization: Third, still more appealing, buyer is discussed.

Sentence: Dialogue

turntable for under $150?" It is always obvious that price is this buyer's greatest worry — she doesn't really want the "loudest" or the "best." The price buyer can be spotted looking over the sale items or staring open-mouthed at the price tag of an expensive unit. After asking the salesperson where the best deal in the store can be found, she cringes at the standard reply: "You usually get what you pay for." But the price buyer still picks the cheapest model, telling her friends, "You won't believe the deal I got on this!"

Illustration: Typical statement used as example

Organization: Fourth, and most appealing, buyer is discussed.

Only one category remains: the quality buyer. He is the buyer most respected by the salesperson, although he is often not even in the store to buy — he may simply want to listen to the new compact-disc player tested in his latest issue of *High Fidelity*. The quality buyer never buys on impulse; he has already read about and listened to any piece of equipment he finally buys. But along with high quality comes high price. The quality buyer can often be seen fingering the price tag of that noise-reduction unit he just has to own but can't yet afford. He never considers a cheaper model, preferring to wait until he can afford the high standard of quality he demands. The quality buyer shuns salespeople, believing that he knows more than they do anyway. Asking him "May I help you?" is the greatest insult of all.

5

Conclusion: How classifying buyers helped the author do his job

Recognizing the kind of buyer I was dealing with helped me steer her to the right corner of the store. I took looks buyers to the visually dazzling working displays, and wattage buyers into the soundproof speaker rooms. I directed price buyers to the sale items and left quality buyers alone. By the end of the year, I was able to identify the type of buyer almost instantly. My expertise paid off, making me the most successful salesperson in the store.

6

Analyzing Gerald Cleary's Essay of Division and Classification: Questions for Discussion

1. What categories does Cleary use to classify his subject? Brainstorm about other categories of stereo shoppers that might exist. Could these alternate categories be used to make a similar point?

(continued on next page)

(continued from previous page)

2. How did Cleary organize the categories in his essay? Is his organization effective, or could he have chosen a better way?
3. What other strategies might Cleary have used to strengthen his essay? Be specific about the benefits of each strategy.

SUGGESTIONS FOR USING DIVISION AND CLASSIFICATION AS A WRITING STRATEGY

As you plan, write, and revise your essay of division and classification, be mindful of the five-step writing process described in Chapter 2 (see pages 14–31). Pay particular attention to the basic requirements and essential ingredients of this writing strategy.

Planning Your Essay of Division and Classification

Planning is an essential part of writing a good essay of division and classification. You can save yourself a great deal of aggravation by taking the time to think about the key building blocks of your essay before you actually begin to write.

Determine Your Purpose, and Focus on It.   The principle you use to divide your subject into categories depends on your larger purpose. It is crucial, then, that you determine a clear purpose for your division and classification before you begin to examine your subject in detail. For example, in studying the student body at your school, you might have any number of purposes: to discover how much time your classmates spend in the library during the week, to explain how financial aid is distributed, to discuss the most popular movies or music on campus, to describe styles of dorm-room decor. The categories into which you divide the student body will vary according to your chosen purpose.

Let's say, for example, that you are in charge of writing an editorial for your school newspaper that will make people aware of how they might reduce the amount of trash going to the landfill. How might you approach such a task using division and classification? Having established your purpose, your next task might be to identify the different ways objects can be handled to avoid sending them to the landfill. For instance, you might decide that there are four basic ways to prevent things from ending up in the trash. Then you could establish a sequence or order of importance in which they should be addressed. Your first draft might start something like the following.

Over the course of the last semester, more trash was removed from our campus than in any semester in history. But was it all trash that had to go to the landfill? For example, many of us love to wear fleece vests, but did you know that they are made from recycled plastic bottles? Much of what is considered trash need not go to the landfill at all. There are four ways we can prevent trash from being sent to the landfill. I call them the four R's. First, we can all reduce the amount of individually packaged goods that we send to the landfill by buying frequently used items in family-size or bulk containers. Next, we can reuse those containers, as well as other items, either for their original purpose or for another. Be creative. After a while, though, things will wear out after repeated use. Then it's a good time to try to restore them. If that, too, can no longer be done, then they should be recycled. Only after these options have failed should items be considered "real" trash and be removed to the landfill. Using the four R's — Reduce, Reuse, Restore, Recycle — we can reduce the amount of trash our campus sends to the landfill every semester.

This introduction should make the purpose of the editorial clear. In the editorial the author attempts to change readers' behavior and to reduce the amount of trash they throw out. Once items have been divided or classified, the classification can be used to persuade readers toward or away from certain types of actions. As we will see in the essay "The Ways of Meeting Oppression" later in this chapter, Martin Luther King Jr., by identifying three categories of protest, is able to cite historical precedents to argue against violent forms of protest and in favor of nonviolent ones. Argumentation, especially in conjunction with other strategies, can be one of the most powerful rhetorical modes and will be explained in detail in Chapter 12.

Formulate a Thesis Statement. When writing a division and classification essay, be sure that your thesis statement presents clearly both the type and the number of categories that you will be using to make your point. Here are two examples from this chapter.

- "Eventually, though, I was able to divide all the stereo buyers into four basic categories: the looks buyer, the wattage buyer, the price buyer, and the quality buyer." This thesis statement, from the annotated student essay by Gerald Cleary, presents the subject — stereo buyers — and the four different categories into which they fall. This statement makes it clear to the reader what the essay will be about and what points the author will make.
- "Because girls' social hierarchies are complicated and overwhelming in their detail, I'm going to take you through a general breakdown of the different positions in the clique." This thesis statement is from Rosalind Wiseman's "The Queen Bee and Her Court" later in

this chapter. From this opening statement, the reader knows exactly what Wiseman intends to discuss and how.

When you begin to formulate your thesis statement, keep these examples in mind. You could also look for other examples of thesis statements in the essays throughout this book. As you begin to develop your thesis statement, ask yourself, "What is my point?" Next ask yourself, "What categories will be most useful in making my point?" If you can't answer these questions, write some ideas down, and try to determine your main point from these ideas.

Once you have settled on an idea, go back to the two questions above, and write down your answers to them. Then combine the answers into a single thesis statement like the examples above. Your thesis statement does not necessarily have to be one sentence; making it one sentence, though, can be an effective way of focusing both your point and your categories.

Organizing and Writing Your Essay of Division and Classification

Establish Valid Categories. When establishing categories, make sure that they meet three criteria:

- *The categories must be appropriate to your purpose.* In determining the factors affecting financial aid distribution, you might consider family income, academic major, and athletic participation, but obviously you would not consider style of dress or preferred brand of toothpaste.
- *The categories must be consistent and mutually exclusive.* For example, dividing the student body into the classes of men, women, and athletes would be illogical because athletes can be either male or female. Instead, you could divide the student body into male athletes, female athletes, male nonathletes, and female nonathletes.
- *The categories must be complete, and they must account for all the members or aspects of your subject.* In dividing the student body according to place of birth, it would be inaccurate to consider only states in the United States; such a division would not account for foreign students or citizens born outside the country.

You may often find that a diagram (such as the one of families on Maple Street), a chart, or a table can help you visualize your organization and help you make sure that your categories meet the three criteria. It can help you determine whether your classes are appropriate, mutually exclusive, and complete. Essays of division and classification, when sensibly planned, can generally be organized with little trouble; the essay's chief divisions will reflect the classes into which the subject itself has been divided. A scratch outline can help you see those divisions and plan your order or presentation. For example, here is an outline of student Gerald Cleary's essay "How Loud? How Good? How Much? How Pretty?"

Four Types of Stereo Shoppers

1. The Looks Buyer
   a. Least respected by salespeople
   b. Appearance of stereo paramount
2. The Wattage Buyer
   a. More respected
   b. Volume level capability paramount
3. The Price Buyer
   a. Not respected but understood
   b. Cost concerns paramount
4. The Quality Buyer
   a. Most respected
   b. Quality and sound reproduction paramount

Such an outline clearly reveals the essay's overall structure.

State Your Conclusion.   Your essay's purpose will determine the kinds of conclusions you reach. For example, a study of the student body of your college might show that 35 percent of male athletes are receiving scholarships, compared with 20 percent of female athletes, 15 percent of male nonathletes, and 10 percent of female nonathletes. These facts could provide a conclusion in themselves, or they might be the basis for a more controversial assertion about your school's athletic program. A study of dorm-room decor might conclude with the observation that juniors and seniors tend to have more elaborate rooms than first-year students. Your conclusion will depend on the way you work back and forth between the various classes you establish and the individual items available for you to classify.

Revising and Editing Your Essay of Division and Classification

Listen to What Your Classmates Have to Say.   The importance of student peer conferences cannot be stressed enough, particularly as you revise and edit your essay. Often, others in your class will easily see that the basis for your classification needs adjustment or that there are inconsistencies in your division and classification categories and sub-classes that can easily be corrected—problems that you can't see your-self because you are too close to your essay. Or perhaps you need more and better transitions to link the discussions of your categories; or you may even need more examples. So take advantage of suggestions where you know them to be valid, and make revisions accordingly. For questions on peer conferences, see pages 27–28.

Question Your Own Work While Revising and Editing.   Revision is best done by asking yourself key questions about what you have written. Begin by reading, preferably aloud, what you have written. Reading aloud forces you to pay attention to every single word, and you are more likely to catch lapses in the logical flow of thought. After you have read your paper through, answer the following questions for revising and editing and make the necessary changes.

Questions for Revising and Editing: Division and Classification

1. Is my subject a coherent entity that readily lends itself to analysis by division and classification?
2. Does the manner in which I divide my subject into categories help me achieve my purpose in writing the essay?
3. Does my thesis statement clearly identify the number and type of categories I will be using in my essay?
4. Do I stay focused on my subject and stay within the limits of my categories throughout my essay?
5. Do my categories meet the following three criteria: Are they appropriate to my purpose, consistent and mutually exclusive, and complete?
6. Have I organized my essay in a way that makes it easy for the reader to understand my categories and how they relate to my purpose?
7. Are there other rhetorical strategies that I can use to help me achieve my purpose?
8. Is my use of headings and subheadings consistent? Could I use headings and subheadings to clarify the organization of my essay?

The Queen Bee and Her Court

Rosalind Wiseman

Rosalind Wiseman was born in 1969 in Philadelphia, Pennsylvania. She received her B.A. in political science from Occidental College in Los Angeles, California, in 1988. Wiseman is the cofounder and president of the Empower Program, a nonprofit organization whose "mission is to work with youth to end the culture of violence" and is certified through the Program for Young Negotiators at Harvard University. Her articles have appeared in Principal Leadership Magazine, Educational Digest, *and* New York Newsday, *and she has spoken extensively in the media about young people and violence. Wiseman's books include* Defending Ourselves: A Guide to Prevention, Self-Defense, and Recovery from Rape *(1995);* Queen Bees and Wannabees: Helping Your Daughter Survive Cliques, Gossip, Boyfriends, and Other Realities of Adolescence *(2002), on which the film* Mean Girls *(2004) is based; and* Queen Bee Moms and Kingpin Dads *(2007), a book about the social pecking orders of parents.*

In "The Queen Bee and Her Court," an excerpt from Queen Bees and Wannabees, *Wiseman divides and classifies young schoolgirls into various hierarchical social classes dominated by the "Queen Bee."*

PREPARING TO READ

How did the various cliques work in your elementary school and high school? What roles did you play within those cliques? Did the existence of cliques bother you, or did you regard them as merely a reflection of society as a whole?

We need to give girls credit for the sophistication of their social structures. Our best politicians and diplomats couldn't do better than a teen girl does in understanding the social intrigue and political landscape that lead to power. Cliques are sophisticated, complex, and multilayered, and every girl has a role within them. However, positions in cliques aren't static. Especially from the sixth to eighth grade, a girl can lose her position to another girl, and she can move up and down the social totem pole. Also, your daughter doesn't have to be in the "popular" group to have these roles within her group of friends. Because girls' social hierarchies are complicated and overwhelming in their detail, I'm going to take you through a general breakdown of the different positions in the clique. However, when you talk to your daughter about cliques, encourage her to come up with her own names and create roles she thinks I've missed. If you can answer yes to the

1

majority of items for each role, you've identified your daughter. So, here are the different roles that your daughter and her friends might play:

Queen Bee
Sidekick
Banker
Floater
Torn Bystander
Pleaser/Wannabe/Messenger
Target

The Queen Bee

For the girl whose popularity is based on fear and control, think of a   2
combination of the Queen of Hearts in *Alice in Wonderland* and Barbie.
I call her the Queen Bee. Through a combination of charisma, force,
money, looks, will, and manipulation, this girl reigns supreme over the
other girls and weakens their friendships with others, thereby strengthening her own power and influence. Indeed, she appears omnipotent.
Never underestimate her power over other girls (and boys as well). She
can and will silence her peers with a look. If your daughter's the Queen
Bee and you could spy on her, you would (or should) be mortified by
how she treats other girls.

Your Daughter Is a Queen Bee If . . .

- Her friends do what she wants to do.   3
- She isn't intimidated by any other girl in her class.
- Her complaints about other girls are limited to the lame things
  they did or said.
- When she's young, you have to convince her to invite everyone to
  her birthday party. When she does invite everyone you want, she
  ignores and excludes some of her guests. (When she's older, you
  lose your privilege to tell her who she can invite.)
- She can persuade her peers to do just about anything she wants.
- She can argue anyone down, including friends, peers, teachers, and
  parents.
- She's charming to adults, a female Eddie Haskell.
- She can make another girl feel "anointed" by declaring her a special
  friend.

- She's affectionate, but often that affection is deployed to demonstrate her rejection of another girl. For example, she sees two girls in her group, one she's pleased with and one she isn't. When she sees them, she'll throw her arms around one and insist that they sit together and barely say anything to the other.
- She won't (or is very reluctant to) take responsibility when she hurts someone's feelings.
- If she thinks she's been wronged she feels she has the right to seek revenge. She has an eye-for-an-eye worldview.

> *She thinks she's better than everyone else. She's in control, intimidating, smart, caring, and has the power to make others feel good or bad. She'll make stuff up about people and everyone will believe her.* 4
>
> —Anne, 15

Who was the Queen Bee in your junior and/or high school? (If you 5 were the Queen Bee, it's okay to admit it.) Remember how much power she had? Keep in mind that Queen Bees are good at slipping under adults' radar (including parents, teachers, and myself). Some of the nicest girls in my classes, who speak the most eloquently about how terrible they feel when girls are mean to each other, turn out to be the most cruel.

> *We're like an army.* 6
>
> —Amanda, 13

Most Queen Bees aren't willing to recognize the cruelty of their actions. 7 They believe their behavior is justified because of something done to them first. Justifications usually begin with, "For no reason, this girl got really upset about not being in the group. I mean we told her nicely and she just wasn't getting the hint. We tried to be nice but she just wasn't listening." When a Queen Bee does this, she's completely bypassing what she did and defining right and wrong by whether the individual was loyal (i.e., not challenging her authority).

If that sinking feeling in your stomach is because you just realized 8 your daughter is a Queen Bee, congratulate yourself. Honesty is the first step to parenting an adolescent successfully.

What Does She Gain by Being a Queen Bee?

She feels power and control over her environment. She's the center of 9 attention and people pay homage to her.

Stefanie Felix—Susie Fitzhugh Photography

What Does She Lose by Being a Queen Bee?

A real sense of self. She's so busy maintaining her image that she loses 10
herself in the process. She can be incredibly cynical about her friendships
with both boys and girls ("They're only sucking up to me because I'm
popular; they don't really like me."). She's vulnerable to having intimate relationships where she believes her image is dependent on the
relationship. She may easily feel that she can't admit to anyone when

she's in over her head because her reputation dictates that she always has everything and everyone in control.

The Sidekick

She's the lieutenant or second in command, the girl who's closest to the Queen Bee and will back her no matter what because her power depends on the confidence she gets from the Queen Bee. All girls in a clique tend to dress similarly, but the Sidekick wears the most identical clothes and shares the mannerisms and overall style closest to the Queen Bee. Together they appear to other girls as an impenetrable force. They commonly bully and silence other girls to forward their own agenda. These girls are usually the first to focus on boys and are often attracted to older boys. This is particularly true in seventh and eighth grade (and their behavior is even worse if they're physically mature and going to high school parties). The difference between the two is if you separate the Sidekick from the Queen Bee, the Sidekick can alter her behavior for the better, while the Queen Bee would be more likely to find another Sidekick and begin again. 11

Your Daughter Is a Sidekick If . . .

- She has a best friend (the Queen Bee) who tells her what to do, think, dress, etc. 12
- The best friend is your daughter's authority figure, not you.
- She feels like it's the two of them and everyone else is a Wannabe.
- You think her best friend pushes her around.

> *She notices everything about the Queen Bee. She will do everything the Queen Bee says and wants to be her. She lies for the Queen Bee but she isn't as pretty as the Queen Bee.* 13
>
> —MADELINE, 14

What Does She Gain by Being a Sidekick?

Power over other girls that she wouldn't have without the Queen Bee. She also gains a close friend (whom you may not like) who makes her feel popular and included. 14

What Does She Lose by Being a Sidekick?

The right to express her personal opinions. If she sticks around the Queen Bee too long, she may forget she even has her own opinion. 15

The Banker

Information about each other is currency in Girl World. The Banker creates chaos everywhere she goes by banking information about girls in her social sphere and dispensing it at strategic intervals for her own benefit. For instance, if a girl has said something negative about another girl, the Banker will casually mention it to someone in conversation because she knows it's going to cause a conflict and strengthen her status as someone "in the know." She can get girls to trust her because when she pumps them for information it doesn't seem like gossip; instead, she does it in an innocent, I'm-trying-to-be-your-friend way.

> *Her power lies in getting girls to confide in her. Once they figure out she can't be trusted, it's too late because she already has information on them, and in order to keep her from revealing things, girls will be nice to her.*
>
> —Leigh, 17

The Banker is almost as powerful as the Queen Bee, but it's easy to mistake her for the Messenger. She's usually quiet and withdrawn in front of adults and can be physically immature in comparison to her friends. This is the girl who sneaks under adult radar all the time because she seems so cute and harmless.

Your Daughter Is a Banker If . . .

- She is extremely secretive.
- She thinks in complex, strategic ways.
- She seems to be friends with everyone; some girls even treat her like a pet.
- She's rarely the subject of fights.
- She's rarely excluded from the group.

What Does She Gain by Being a Banker?

Power and security. The Banker is very confusing to other girls because she seems harmless and yet everyone is afraid of her.

What Does She Lose by Being a Banker?

Once other girls figure out what she's doing, they don't trust her. With her utilitarian mind-set, she can forget to look to other girls as a trusted resource.

> *The girls can't oust the Banker from the clique because she has informa-* 22
> *tion on everyone and could make or break reputations based on the information*
> *she knows.*
>
> —CHARLOTTE, 15

The Floater

You can usually spot this girl because she doesn't associate with only one 23
clique. She has friends in different groups and can move freely among
them. She usually has protective characteristics that shield her from
other girls' cruelty—for example, she's beautiful but not too beautiful,
nice, not terribly sophisticated, and avoids conflicts. She's more likely to
have higher self-esteem because she doesn't base her self-worth on how
well she's accepted by one group. Because she has influence over other
girls but doesn't use it to make them feel bad, I call her the Floater. Girls
want to be the Floater because she has confidence, people genuinely like
her, and she's nice to everyone. She has the respect of other girls because
she doesn't rule by meanness. When backed into a corner, the Floater is
one of the few girls who will actually stand up to the Queen Bee. While
Floaters have some power, they don't have the same influence and impact
as Queen Bees. Why? Because Floaters don't gain anything by sowing
seeds of discontent and insecurity among the other girls; Queen Bees do.

> *I have always felt that many potential Floaters are either swallowed up* 24
> *by the popular crowd or choose not to identify with popular people at all and*
> *instead create their own groups. In every girl there is a Floater who wants to*
> *get out.*
>
> —JOANNA, 17

> *I don't think there are* real *Floaters. Maybe I'm just bitter, but most of the* 25
> *time they are too good to be true.*
>
> —LIZA, 17

Your Daughter Is a Floater If . . .

- She doesn't want to exclude people; you aren't always having 26
  fights with her about spending time with people she considers
  "losers."
- Her friends are comfortable around her and don't seem intimidated; she's not "winning" all the conversations.
- She's not exclusively tied to one group of friends; she may have a
  jock group she hangs with, then the kids in the band, then her
  friends in the neighborhood.

- She can bring another person into a group on her own with some success.

What Does She Gain by Being a Floater?

Her peers like her for who she is as a person. She'll be less likely to sacrifice herself to gain and keep social status. 27

What Does She Lose by Being a Floater?

Nothing! Count yourself truly blessed that she's your daughter. 28

If you're thinking this is your daughter, wait. It isn't that I don't believe you, but please read all the roles before making your final decision. We all want to believe the best about the people we love, but sometimes our love blinds us to reality. I've met countless parents who truly believe their daughters are Floaters, and they're not. It should go without saying that just because your daughter isn't a Floater doesn't mean she won't become an amazing young woman and/or that you haven't done a good job raising her. But if you insist on seeing her in a way that she isn't, you won't be able to be as good a parent as she needs you to be. 29

The Torn Bystander

She's constantly conflicted between doing the right thing and her allegiance to the clique. As a result, she's the one most likely to be caught in the middle of a conflict between two girls or two groups of girls. She'll often rationalize or apologize for the Queen Bee and Sidekick's behavior, but she knows it's wrong. She often feels more uncomfortable around boys, but can be very easily influenced by the clique to do what it wants (for example, getting together with a boy they decide is right for her). The status she gets from the group is very important, and the thought of standing up to the more powerful girls in the clique is terrifying. She's honest enough with herself (and maybe with you as well) to know that she doesn't like what the Queen Bee does but feels powerless to stop it. 30

Your Daughter Is a Torn Bystander If . . .

- She's always finding herself in situations where she has to choose between friends. 31
- She tries to accommodate everyone.
- She's not good at saying no to her friends.

- She wants everyone "to get along."
- She can't imagine standing up to anyone she has a conflict with; she goes along to get along.

> *She's confused and insecure because her reputation is over if she doesn't stick with the Queen Bee, but she can be really cool when she's alone.*
>
> —ANNE, 13

32

What Does She Gain by Being a Torn Bystander?

By associating herself with more powerful girls, she has access to popularity, high social status, and boys.

33

What Does She Lose by Being a Torn Bystander?

She has to sacrifice a great deal. She may not try new things or she may stop doing things she's interested in (plays, band, "geeky" clubs, etc.) because her friends make fun of her. She may dumb herself down to get along with others. This doesn't mean her grades will suffer, although they could. Lots of girls hide their academic accomplishments from their peers for this reason. ("I know I totally failed that test.") It more likely means that she presents herself as less intelligent than she is. This is merely irritating when she's a teen, but literally stupid when she's an adult in a job interview.

34

The Pleaser/Wannabe/Messenger

Almost all girls are pleasers and wannabes; some are just more obvious than others. This is one of the more fascinating roles. She can be in the clique or on the perimeter trying to get in. She will do anything to be in the good graces of the Queen Bee and the Sidekick. She'll enthusiastically back them up no matter what. She'll mimic their clothes, style, and anything else she thinks will increase her position in the group. She's a careful observer, especially of the girls in power. She's motivated above all else to please the person who's standing above her on the social totem pole. She can easily get herself into messy conflicts with other people because she'll change her mind depending on who she's interacting with.

35

As a Pleaser/Wannabe/Messenger her security in the clique is precarious and depends on her doing the Queen Bee's "dirty work," such as spreading gossip about a Target. While the Banker gathers information to further her own causes, the Pleaser/Wannabe/Messenger does it to

36

service the Queen Bee and get in her good graces and feel important. But she can easily be dropped and ridiculed if she's seen as trying too hard to fit in. (One of the worst accusations you can make of a teen is to say she's trying too hard. In Girl World, all actions must appear effortless.) The Queen Bee and Sidekick enjoy the convenience of making her their servant, but they love talking behind her back. ("Can you believe what a suck-up she is? That's so pathetic.")

When there's a fight between two girls or two groups of girls, she 37 often serves as a go-between. Her status immediately rises when she's in active duty as a Messenger. It's also the most powerful position she can attain, which means she has a self-interest in creating and maintaining conflicts between girls so she doesn't get laid off.

Your Daughter Is a Pleaser/Wannabe/ Messenger If . . .

- Other girls' opinions and wants are more important than her own. 38
- Her opinions on dress, style, friends, and "in" celebrities constantly change.
- She can't tell the difference between what she wants and what the group wants.
- She's desperate to have the "right" look (clothes, hair, etc.).
- She'll stop doing things she likes because she fears the clique's disapproval.
- She's always in the middle of a conflict.
- She feels better about herself when the other girls are coming to her for help, advice, or when she's doing their dirty work.
- She loves to gossip—the phone and e-mail are her lifeline.

What Does She Gain by Being a Pleaser?

The feeling that she belongs; she's in the middle of the action and has 39 power over girls.

What Does She Lose by Being a Pleaser?

Personal authenticity—she hasn't figured out who she is or what she 40 values. She's constantly anticipating what people want from her and doesn't ask herself what she wants in return. She feels insecure about her friendships—do girls really like her, or do they only value her for the gossip she trades in? She has trouble developing personal boundaries and the ability to communicate them to others.

> *She's insecure and you can't trust her.* 41
>
> —Carrie, 14

The Target

She's the victim, set up by the other girls to be humiliated, made fun of, 42
excluded. Targets are assumed to be out of the clique, one of the class
"losers." While this is sometimes true, it's not always the case. Just
because a girl is in the clique doesn't mean she can't be targeted by the
other members. Often the social hierarchy of the clique is maintained
precisely by having someone clearly at the bottom of the group's totem
pole. Girls outside the clique tend to become Targets because they've
challenged the clique or because their style of dress, behavior, and such
are outside the norms acceptable to the clique. Girls inside the clique
tend to become Targets if they've challenged someone higher on the
social totem pole (i.e., the Queen Bee, Sidekick, or Banker) and need to
be taken down a peg.

Your Daughter Is a Target If . . .

- She feels helpless to stop the girls' behavior. 43
- She feels she has no allies. No one will back her up.
- She feels isolated.
- She can mask her hurt by rejecting people first, saying she doesn't like anyone.

This role can be harder to figure out than you would think, and your 44
daughter may be too embarrassed to tell you. She might admit she feels
excluded, or she might just withdraw from you and "not want to talk
about it."

> *Targets don't want to tell their parents because they don't want their* 45
> *parents to think they're a loser or a nobody.*
>
> —Jennifer, 16

What Does She Gain by Being a Target?

This may seem like an odd question, but being a Target can have some 46
hidden benefits. There's nothing like being targeted to teach your

daughter about empathy and understanding for people who are bullied and/or discriminated against. Being a Target can also give her objectivity. She can see the costs of fitting in and decide she's better off outside the clique because at least she can be true to herself and/or find good friends who like her for who she is, not for her social standing.

What Does She Lose by Being a Target?

She feels totally helpless in the face of other girls' cruelty. She feels ashamed of being rejected by the others girls because of who she is. She'll be tempted to change herself in order to fit in. She feels vulnerable and unable to affect the outcome of her situation. She could become so anxious that she can't concentrate on schoolwork. 47

> *I didn't understand why I was so unhappy in sixth grade. I couldn't have told my parents that girls were being mean to me.* 48
>
> — ERIN, 17

> *Girls will almost always withdraw instead of telling a parent.* 49
>
> — CLAIRE, 14

> *If a girl's stuck in a degrading clique, it's the same as when she's later in a bad relationship. She doesn't expect to be treated any better.* 50
>
> — ELLEN, 15

OK, now you know the different roles girls play in cliques. The next questions are: How were these roles created in the first place? Who and what determine these positions and power plays? Why are girls able to get away with treating each other so badly? 51

It isn't really that big a secret. As girls become teens, the world becomes a much bigger, scarier place. Many girls go from a small elementary school to a much larger, more impersonal institutional school. 52

In elementary school, students are usually based in one room, with one teacher. The principal sees them on a daily basis and parents are often active in the school's activities, going on field trips, bringing food for bake sales, and volunteering in after-school programs. By the end of fifth or sixth grade, girls are beginning to prepare to leave this safe, comfy haven of elementary school. They alternatively look forward to and dread moving on to middle school or junior high. 53

Then comes the first day at the middle school or junior high — and everything changes. Adults, in our profound wisdom, place them in a setting where they're overwhelmed by the number of students, and they become nameless faces with ID security cards. If you ever want to remember what it feels like, go to your daughter's school and hang 54 out in the hall when the bell rings right before a lunch period (you probably have lots of times to choose from since most schools have so many students that they need multiple lunch periods, which means some students eat their midday meal at ten A.M.). When the bell rings, walk from one end of the hall to the other. It's hard enough simply navigating through this noisy throng. Now imagine navigating the same hallway and caring what each person thinks of you as you walk by.

We put our girls in this strange new environment at exactly the same time that they're obsessively microanalyzing social cues, rules, and regulations and therefore are at their most insecure. Don't underestimate how difficult and frightening this is for girls, and give your daughter credit for getting out of bed in the morning.

55

THINKING CRITICALLY ABOUT THE TEXT

How real for you is the social classification system that Wiseman establishes in this piece? As a young woman, where would you place yourself in the hierarchy? Were you a Queen Bee, a Banker, a Floater? If you are a young man, do you think Wiseman's classification of girls would work for boys as well? Explain.

QUESTIONS ON SUBJECT

1. What characteristics does the Queen Bee possess, according to Wiseman? Would you agree or disagree with her assessment of the girl at the top of the social totem pole? Would you add or subtract any characteristics? Explain.

2. Throughout her essay, Wiseman includes quoted passages in which young girls offer their own accounts of the characters. How effective do you find these passages? What do they add, if anything, to Wiseman's classification system?

3. For every character type Wiseman includes a formulaic set of questions: "What does she gain by being an X?" and "What does she lose by being an X?" Why do you suppose she uses that formula? (Glossary: *Cause and Effect Analysis*)

4. Wiseman states that each character in the hierarchy gains from her position — even the Target. Do you agree? Explain.

5. What explanation does Wiseman give for the development of cliques? (Glossary: *Cause and Effect Analysis*)

QUESTIONS ON STRATEGY

1. What does Wiseman mean when she writes that "cliques are sophisticated, complex, and multilayered, and every girl has a role within them" (paragraph 1)? Is that statement her thesis? (Glossary: *Thesis*)

2. What does Wiseman hope to gain when she advises that "when you talk to your daughter about cliques, encourage her to come up with her own

names and create roles she thinks I've missed" (paragraph 1)? Why is her advice a useful strategy, given her subject and audience? (Glossary: *Audience; Subject*)

3. Into what classes does Wiseman divide all young girls in her classification system?

4. Explain how Wiseman has organized her essay. (Glossary: *Organization*) Is that organizational pattern effective? Explain.

5. Wiseman's division and classification is supported by her use of definition, illustration, and comparison and contrast. (Glossary: *Comparison and Contrast; Definition; Illustration*) How do these supporting strategies strengthen Wiseman's essay?

QUESTIONS ON DICTION AND VOCABULARY

1. How effective is Wiseman's title? (Glossary: *Title*) How effective are the names she gives each class in her classification? Would you change any of those names? If so, why?

2. What is Wiseman's attitude toward cliques? (Glossary: *Attitude*) What in her diction indicates that attitude? (Glossary: *Diction*)

3. Refer to your desk dictionary to determine the meanings of the following words as Wiseman uses them in this selection: *clique* (paragraph 1), *omnipotent* (2), *mortified* (2), *anointed* (3), *cynical* (10), *agenda* (11), *utilitarian* (21), *oust* (22), *rationalize* (30), *perimeter* (35), *precarious* (36).

CLASSROOM ACTIVITY USING DIVISION AND CLASSIFICATION

Think about how you might classify people in one of the following groups:

athletes
dieters
television addicts
sports fans
college students

Compare your method of classification with the method used by others in your class who chose the same category. What conclusions can you draw from the differences?

WRITING SUGGESTIONS

1. Rosalind Wiseman offers her classification system for the roles that young girls play in cliques. Her system is based on interviews with young girls, their friends, their teachers, and their mothers. But girls are not the only ones who belong to cliques. What about boys' cliques? Write a classification essay in which you divide and classify schoolboys on the basis

of their behavioral characteristics and the roles they play within cliques. Review Wiseman's organization. Model your organization on hers, modify her design, or create an entirely new approach.

2. What about parents? Can we classify them into some recognizable and meaningful classes and subclasses? Jim Faye of the Love and Logic Institute in Boulder, Colorado, thinks so. He classifies parents into three groups: the Consultant who "provides guidance," the Helicopter "who hovers over children and rescues them from the hostile world in which they live," and the Drill Sargeant "who commands and directs the lives of children." Think about your parents and talk to your friends, the students in your dormitory, and others to gather opinions about the various parenting approaches that people demonstrate. Use the information to write an essay in which you classify parents. Be sure to define each class clearly and provide examples of their members' behavior. (Glossary: *Definition; Illustration*)

3. The photograph on page 318 depicts a common scene of a group of girls sitting, talking, and passing the time together. How do you "read" this photograph? What might the girls' facial expressions, body language, hairstyles, and dress tell you about them as individuals? As members of the group? What does their configuration on the steps tell you about the girls as a group? About their roles in the group? Write an essay in which you analyze the photograph and theorize about this group of girls and the dynamics that may hold them together as well as separate them.

Diving into the Gene Pool

Carolina A. Miranda

Carolina A. Miranda was born in 1971 in Casper, Wyoming, and attended Smith College, where she majored in Latin American studies. Now a freelance writer, she authored arti- cles on such diverse topics as Al Gore, food and cooking classes, gas prices, the playwright Eve Ensler, the actors Adam Beach and Alan Arkin, and The Da Vinci Code *while a reporter for* Time. *In addition, she wrote the Lonely Planet guide to Costa Rica and contributed chapters on food and cul- ture to Lonely Planet's Peru and Puerto Vallarta guidebooks. Miranda offers the following advice to writers: "The most important thing you can do to improve your writing is to read a lot and to read all kinds of things. By reading a wide variety of subject matter you increase your knowl- edge base and also experience many different styles, all of which will broaden your range and skill as a writer."*

In the following essay, which first appeared in Time *on August 6, 2006, Miranda explains what happened when she submitted her own DNA to one of the new upstart Internet services offering to provide a genetic analysis of her ancestry and geographic origins. The results will surprise you no less than they did Miranda.*

PREPARING TO READ

Do you ever wonder who your ancestors were and where they came from? Perhaps you know something about your origins already. Maybe your family has kept a genealogical history, but what about records that go back not just hundreds of years but thousands of years? Would you like to learn more about your genetic history? Do you think that knowing more about your origins would change your view of yourself?

I f they held a convention for racial purity, I would never make the guest list. Like most other Latin American families, mine is a multi- ethnic stew that has left me with the generic black-eyed and olive- skinned look typical of large swaths of the world's population. My father's family is from Peru, my mother's from Chile. Their parents were born and reared in South America. Beyond that, I know nothing about my ancestors. That was fine by me—until the new and growing industry of personal DNA analysis created a need I never knew I had.

Today at least half a dozen companies will, for about $200 a pop, take your spittle, analyze the heck out of it and tell you who and what you are. The tests are popular among adoptees, armchair genealogists and high school seniors praying that a link to some underrepresented ethnic group will help get them into the Ivies. Already a card-carrying minority, I thought a test might help me figure out a thing or two about my forebears—and my mixed-up identity.

So I hit the Internet and quickly found a couple of companies that looked promising. The first, DNA Tribes in Arlington, Va., filled its website with glossy shots of ethnic types. The next, DNAPrint in Sarasota, Fla., offered a cool Flash movie of a rotating double helix. I was doubly sold. I ordered a test from each and within a couple of days was scraping the inside of my cheek with swabs and depositing my cells into prepaid envelopes ready to be sent off to the labs.

Then I set about trying to predict the results. On my father's side, I figured, high cheekbones and almond eyes probably showed evidence of native-Andean blood. The aquiline profiles and curly hair on my mother's side, on the other hand, are common on Mediterranean shores. My best guess: I was mostly European, a bit of native South American and perhaps a dash of Middle Eastern. But like most other people who do this sort of thing, I also secretly hoped I would be related to an American Indian tribe with a lucrative casino operation. Anything that would justify the tests on my next expense account.

Within a few weeks, I received my first results, from DNA Tribes. As I had guessed, the genetic indicators showed both European and American Indian roots. But No. 1 on the list of places I was supposed to be from was—to my great surprise—sub-Saharan Africa. What's more, No. 1 on the list of the top 10 regional populations with which I was most likely to share a piece of genetic code was Belorussia, followed closely by southeast Poland and Mozambique.

That's when I began to wonder whether there had been some kind of DNA mix-up. Fond as I am of stuffed cabbage, Poland and Belorussia are not places I had ever identified with. The sub-Saharan African connection was also puzzling. Any physical evidence of black Africa has apparently been diluted beyond recognition in my murky gene pool. And while heavy traces of African blood are not unusual in Latin America, they tend to be linked to West Africa, where much of the slave trade to the Americas originated. Clearly, my ancestors got around.

My mother, when I finally told her about all this, thought I was joking. My father asked me to ring back during halftime. And none of us even want to think about how my more persnickety aunts—the ones convinced they're descendants of Spanish nobility—will react when they read about our Afro-Polish roots.

I was in for yet another surprise when, a few days later, the results from DNAPrint came in. The basic elements were similar, but the blend was different: 71% European, 26% Native American and 3% sub-Saharan African. Beyond a few inscrutable charts, there was little specific information.

In fact, there were a lot of things the tests didn't tell me. Unlike a pregnancy test, with its emphatic yes or no, ancestral-DNA testing gives you only a "statistical likelihood" of membership in a certain 10 group. I don't know how many generations ago those ethnicities appeared in my family tree, nor (without further tests) on which side. Moreover, the gene test hasn't been invented that can unravel the improbable chain of events that connected Belorussians with Mozambicans, and American Indians with Poles—ultimately to produce me, a Latina living and working in New York City.

Did the tests change my view of myself? Not really. I'll still put my 11 check in the Latino box, imperfect as it is. If the process proved anything, it's that we're all a messy amalgam of centuries of mixing and migration. True identity, it seems, resides not in our genes but in our mind.

THINKING CRITICALLY ABOUT THE TEXT

What do you conclude from Miranda's essay about the usefulness of the DNA analyses she received from services on the Internet? Were the services fraudulent? What did she really want to know? Did she have unrealistic expectations? Can anyone actually provide what she was looking for? Explain.

QUESTIONS ON SUBJECT

1. What does Miranda mean when she says that the "new and growing industry of personal DNA analysis created a need I never knew I had" (paragraph 1)?

2. How did Miranda submit her cellular material in order to get her DNA analysis?

3. What predictable results came back from the DNA Tribes and DNAPrint companies?

4. What surprises were in the test results from both companies?

5. What didn't the tests tell Miranda? Why didn't they tell her more?

QUESTIONS ON STRATEGY

1. What is Miranda's purpose in this essay? (Glossary: *Purpose*)

2. How did the methods of division and classification help Miranda develop her essay? What specifically is being divided and classified in the essay?

3. What is the basis of classification as set up by the DNA companies? Is the basis of classification clear-cut? Explain.

4. How does Miranda use humor in her essay? Point out several instances of her use of humor. What effect did this have on you as a reader?

5. Assess the effectiveness of the beginning and ending paragraphs of Miranda's essay. (Glossary: *Beginnings/Endings*) Would you have begun and ended the essay differently? Explain.

QUESTIONS ON DICTION AND VOCABULARY

1. Miranda's language is rather matter-of-fact, maybe at times a little flippant. What in her diction contributes to her tone? (Glossary: *Tone*)

2. What does Miranda mean by a "statistical likelihood" (paragraph 9)?

3. Miranda uses a metaphor in her title. Analyze how well it works. (Glossary: *Figures of Speech*)

CLASSROOM ACTIVITY USING DIVISION AND CLASSIFICATION

Visit a local supermarket and select one of the many product areas (frozen foods, dairy products, cereals, soft drinks, meat, produce) for an exercise in classification. First, establish the general class of products in the area you have selected by determining the features that distinguish one subclass from another. Next, place the products from your selected area in appropriate subclasses within your classification system. Finally, share your classification system and how it works with members of your class. Be prepared to answer questions they may have about the decisions you have made.

WRITING SUGGESTIONS

1. Write an essay in which you categorize yourself according to your interests, the qualities of your heart and mind, and the things you do and are interested in rather than your ethnicity. Are you a lover of art, do you love movies, do you play sports or are you a sports fan, are you concerned about the environment, do you like to read and write, do you think it's important to give something to your community rather than simply ask what it can do for you? What are the various characteristics that best represent you?

2. Write an essay using Miranda's "Diving into the Gene Pool" as a model, not of genealogical searching but for the way she handles her subject with a lighthearted tone, all the while arriving at a rather important message: "True identity, it seems, resides not in our genes but in our mind."

The Truth about Lying

Judith Viorst

Judith Viorst, poet, journalist, author of children's books, and novelist, was born in 1931. She has chronicled her life in such books as It's Hard to Be Hip Over Thirty and Other Tragedies of Married Life *(1968),* How Did I Get to Be Forty and Other Atrocities *(1976), and* When Did I Stop Being Twenty and Other Injustices: Selected Prose from Single to Mid-Life *(1987). In 1981, she went back to school, taking courses at the Washington Psychoanalytic Institute. This study, along with her personal experience of psychoanalysis, helped to inspire* Necessary Losses *(1986), a popular and critical success. Combining theory, poetry, interviews, and anecdotes, Viorst approaches personal growth as a shedding of illusions. Her recent work includes* I'm Too Young to Be Seventy: And Other Delusions *(2005).*

In this essay, first published in the March 1981 issue of Redbook, *the author approaches lying with delicacy and candor as she carefully classifies the different types of lies we all encounter.*

PREPARING TO READ

Lying happens every day in our society, whether it is a politician hiding behind a subtly worded statement or a guest fibbing to a host about the quality of a meal. What, for you, constitutes lying? Are all lies the same? In other words, are there different degrees or types of lying?

I 've been wanting to write on a subject that intrigues and challenges me: the subject of lying. I've found it very difficult to do. Everyone I've talked to has a quite intense and personal but often rather intolerant point of view about what we can—and can never *never*—tell lies about. I've finally reached the conclusion that I can't present any ultimate conclusions, for too many people would promptly disagree. Instead, I'd like to present a series of moral puzzles, all concerned with lying. I'll tell you what I think about them. Do you agree? 1

Social Lies

Most of the people I've talked with say that they find social lying 2 acceptable and necessary. They think it's the civilized way for folks to behave. Without these little white lies, they say, our relationships would be short and brutish and nasty. It's arrogant, they say, to insist on being so incorruptible and so brave that you cause other people unnecessary embarrassment or pain by compulsively assailing them with your honesty. I basically agree. What about you?

Will you say to people, when it simply isn't true, "I like your new hairdo," "You're looking much better," "It's so nice to see you," "I had a wonderful time"? 3

Will you praise hideous presents and homely kids? 4

Will you decline invitations with "We're busy that night—so sorry we can't come," when the truth is you'd rather stay home than dine with the So-and-sos? 5

And even though, as I do, you may prefer the polite evasion of "You really cooked up a storm" instead of "The soup"—which tastes like warmed-over coffee—"is wonderful," will you, if you must, proclaim it wonderful? 6

There's one man I know who absolutely refuses to tell social lies. "I can't play that game," he says; "I'm simply not made that way." And his answer to the argument that saying nice things to someone doesn't cost anything is, "Yes, it does—it destroys your credibility." Now, he won't, unsolicited, offer his views on the painting you just bought, but you don't ask his frank opinion unless you want *frank*, and his silence at those moments when the rest of us liars are muttering, "Isn't it lovely?" is, for the most part, eloquent enough. My friend does not indulge in what he calls "flattery, false praise and mellifluous comments." When others tell fibs he will not go along. He says that social lying is lying, that little white lies are still lies. And he feels that telling lies is morally wrong. What about you? 7

Peace-Keeping Lies

Many people tell peace-keeping lies; lies designed to avoid irritation or argument; lies designed to shelter the liar from possible blame or pain; lies (or so it is rationalized) designed to keep trouble at bay without hurting anyone. 8

I tell these lies at times, and yet I always feel they're wrong. I understand why we tell them, but still they feel wrong. And whenever I lie so that someone won't disapprove of me or think less of me or holler at me, I feel I'm a bit of a coward, I feel I'm dodging responsibility, I feel . . . guilty. What about you? 9

Do you, when you're late for a date because you overslept, say that you're late because you got caught in a traffic jam? 10

Do you, when you forget to call a friend, say that you called several times but the line was busy? 11

Do you, when you didn't remember that it was your father's birthday, say that his present must be delayed in the mail? 12

And when you're planning a weekend in New York City and you're 13
not in the mood to visit your mother, who lives there, do you conceal—
with a lie, if you must—the fact that you'll be in New York? Or do you
have the courage—or is it the cruelty?—to say, "I'll be in New York,
but sorry—I don't plan on seeing you"?

(Dave and his wife Elaine have two quite different points of view 14
on this very subject. He calls her a coward. She says she's being wise. He
says she must assert her right to visit New York sometimes and not see
her mother. To which she always patiently replies: "Why should we
have useless fights? My mother's too old to change. We get along much
better when I lie to her.")

Finally, do you keep the peace by telling your husband lies on the 15
subject of money? Do you reduce what you really paid for your shoes?
And in general do you find yourself ready, willing and able to lie to him
when you make absurd mistakes or lose or break things?

"I used to have a romantic idea that part of intimacy was confessing 16
every dumb thing that you did to your husband. But after a couple of
years of that," says Laura, "have I changed my mind!"

And having changed her mind, she finds herself telling peace- 17
keeping lies. And yes, I tell them too. What about you?

Protective Lies

Protective lies are lies folks tell—often quite serious lies—because 18
they're convinced that the truth would be too damaging. They lie
because they feel there are certain human values that supersede the
wrong of having lied. They lie, not for personal gain, but because they
believe it's for the good of the person they're lying to. They lie to those
they love, to those who trust them most of all, on the grounds that
breaking this trust is justified.

They may lie to their children on money or marital matters. 19

They may lie to the dying about the state of their health. 20

They may lie about adultery, and not—or so they insist—to save 21
their own hide, but to save the heart and the pride of the men they are
married to.

They may lie to their closest friend because the truth about her tal- 22
ents or son or psyche would be—or so they insist—utterly devastating.

I sometimes tell such lies, but I'm aware that it's quite presumptu- 23
ous to claim I know what's best for others to know. That's called playing God. That's called manipulation and control. And we never can be
sure, once we start to juggle lies, just where they'll land, exactly where
they'll roll.

And furthermore, we may find ourselves lying in order to back up 24
the lies that are backing up the lie we initially told.

And furthermore—let's be honest—if conditions were reversed, we certainly wouldn't want anyone lying to us. 25

Yet, having said all that, I still believe that there are times when protective lies must nonetheless be told. What about you? 26

If your Dad had a very bad heart and you had to tell him some bad family news, which would you choose: to tell him the truth or lie? 27

If your former husband failed to send his monthly child-support check and in other ways behaved like a total rat, would you allow your children—who believed he was simply wonderful—to continue to believe that he was wonderful? 28

If your dearly beloved brother selected a wife whom you deeply disliked, would you reveal your feelings or would you fake it? 29

And if you were asked, after making love, "And how was that for you?" would you reply, if it wasn't too good, "Not too good"? 30

Now, some would call a sex lie unimportant, little more than social lying, a simple act of courtesy that makes all human intercourse run smoothly. And some would say all sex lies are bad news and unacceptably protective. Because, says Ruth, "a man with an ego that fragile doesn't need your lies—he needs a psychiatrist." Still others feel that sex lies are indeed protective lies, more serious than simple social lying, and yet at times they tell them on the grounds that when it comes to matters sexual, everybody's ego is somewhat fragile. 31

"If most of the time things go well in sex," says Sue, "I think you're allowed to dissemble when they don't. I can't believe it's good to say, 'Last night was four stars, darling, but tonight's performance rates only a half.'" 32

I'm inclined to agree with Sue. What about you? 33

Trust-Keeping Lies

Another group of lies are trust-keeping lies, lies that involve triangulation, with A (that's you) telling lies to B on behalf of C (whose trust you'd promised to keep). Most people concede that once you've agreed not to betray a friend's confidence, you can't betray it, even if you must lie. But I've talked with people who don't want you telling them anything that they might be called on to lie about. 34

"I don't tell lies for myself," says Fran, "and I don't want to have to tell them for other people." Which means, she agrees, that if her best friend is having an affair, she absolutely doesn't want to know about it. 35

"Are you saying," her best friend asks, "that if I went off with a lover and I asked you to tell my husband I'd been with you, that you wouldn't lie for me, that you'd betray me?" 36

Fran is very pained but very adamant. "I wouldn't want to betray you, so . . . don't ask me." 37

Fran's best friend is shocked. What about you? 38

Do you believe you can have close friends if you're not prepared to receive their deepest secrets? 39

Do you believe you must always lie for your friends? 40

Do you believe, if your friend tells a secret that turns out to be quite immoral or illegal, that once you've promised to keep it, you must keep it? 41

And what if your friend were your boss—if you were perhaps one of the President's men—would you betray or lie for him over, say, Watergate? 42

As you can see, these issues get terribly sticky. 43

It's my belief that once we've promised to keep a trust, we must tell lies to keep it. I also believe that we can't tell Watergate lies. And if these two statements strike you as quite contradictory, you're right— they're quite contradictory. But for now they're the best I can do. What about you? 44

Some say that truth will out and thus you might as well tell the truth. Some say you can't regain the trust that lies lose. Some say that even though the truth may never be revealed, our lies pervert and damage our relationships. Some say . . . well, here's what some of them have to say. 45

"I'm a coward," says Grace, "about telling close people important, difficult truths. I find that I'm unable to carry it off. And so if something is bothering me, it keeps building up inside till I end up just not seeing them anymore." 46

"I lie to my husband on sexual things, but I'm furious," says Joyce, "that he's too insensitive to know I'm lying." 47

"I suffer most from the misconception that children can't take the truth," says Emily. "But I'm starting to see that what's harder and more damaging for them is being told lies, is not being told the truth." 48

"I'm afraid," says Joan, "that we often wind up feeling a bit of contempt for the people we lie to." 49

And then there are those who have no talent for lying. 50

"Over the years, I tried to lie," a friend of mine explained, "but I always got found out and I always got punished. I guess I gave myself away because I feel guilty about any kind of lying. It looks as if I'm stuck with telling the truth." 51

For those of us, however, who are good at telling lies, for those of us who lie and don't get caught, the question of whether or not to lie can be a hard and serious moral problem. I liked the remark of a friend of mine who said, "I'm willing to lie. But just as a last resort—the truth's always better." 52

"Because," he explained, "though others may completely accept the lie I'm telling, I don't." 53

I tend to feel that way too. 54

What about you? 55

THINKING CRITICALLY ABOUT THE TEXT

The title of the essay plays with the relationship between lies and the truth. Viorst discusses lies that help to conceal the truth, but she's quick to point out that not all lies are malicious. Look at her subsections about "protective lies" (paragraphs 18–33) and "trust-keeping lies" (34–44). Do you think that these lies are necessary? Or would it be easier to tell the truth? Explain.

QUESTIONS ON SUBJECT

1. Why is Viorst wary of giving advice on the subject of lying?

2. Viorst admits to contradicting herself in her section on "trust-keeping lies." Where else do you see her contradicting herself?

3. In telling a "protective lie," what assumption about the person hearing the lie does Viorst make? Would you make the same assumption? Why or why not?

4. What's the difference between a "peace-keeping lie" and a "protective lie"?

QUESTIONS ON STRATEGY

1. Into what main categories does Viorst divide lying? Do you agree with her division or do some of her categories seem to overlap? Explain.

2. Viorst recognizes that many people have steadfast views on lying. What accommodations does she make for this audience? (Glossary: *Audience*) How does she challenge this audience?

3. There are at least two parties involved in a lie—the liar and the listener. How much significance does the author give to each of these parties? How does she make the distinction?

4. Viorst presents the reader with a series of examples or moral puzzles. How do these puzzles encourage further thought on the subject of lying? Are they successful? Why or why not?

5. Viorst chooses an unconventional way to conclude her essay by showing different people's opinions of lying. What do you think she's doing in this last section, beginning in paragraph 45? Does this ending intensify any of the points she has made? Explain. (Glossary: *Beginnings/Endings*)

6. Viorst wants us to see that a lie is not a lie is not a lie is not a lie (i.e., that not all lies are the same). To clarify the various types of lies, she uses division and classification. She also uses illustration to illustrate the ways in which people lie. (Glossary: *Illustration*) Using several of the examples that work best for you, discuss how Viorst's use of illustration strengthens and enhances her classification.

QUESTIONS ON DICTION AND VOCABULARY

1. How would you characterize Viorst's diction in this essay? (Glossary: *Diction*) Consider the essay's subject and audience. (Glossary: *Audience; Subject*) Cite specific examples of her word choice to support your conclusions.

2. Refer to your desk dictionary to determine the meanings of the following words as Viorst uses them in this selection: *mellifluous* (paragraph 7), *supersede* (18), *dissemble* (32).

CLASSROOM ACTIVITY USING DIVISION AND CLASSIFICATION

Consider the following classes of items and determine at least two principles of division that could be used for each class. Then write a paragraph or two in which you classify one of the groups of items according to a single principle of division. For example, in discussing crime one could use the seriousness of the crime or the type of crime as principles of division. If the seriousness of the crime were used, this might yield two categories: felonies and misdemeanors. If the types of crime were used, this would yield categories such as burglary, murder, larceny, and embezzlement.

movies
college professors
social sciences
roommates
professional sports

WRITING SUGGESTIONS

1. Viorst wrote this essay for *Redbook*, which is usually considered a women's magazine. If you were writing this essay for a male audience, would you change the examples? If so, how would you change them? If not, why not? Do you think men are more likely to tell lies of a certain category? Explain. Write an essay in which you discuss whether men and women share similar perspectives about lying. (Glossary: *Comparison and Contrast*)

2. Write an essay of division and classification on the subject of friends. How many different types of friends do you recognize? On what basis do you differentiate them? Do you make distinctions among them on the basis of gender? Are some friends more important, more useful, more intimate, more convenient, more trustworthy, more reliable, more lasting than others? Are you more willing to share your most personal thoughts and feelings with some friends than with others? Be sure to establish a context for why you are writing about friends and putting forth an essay that divides and classifies them. Conclude with an insightful statement drawn from your thesis, the division and classification you establish, and the examples you provide.

Weasel Words: The Art of Saying Nothing at All

William Lutz

William Lutz was born in 1941 in Racine, Wisconsin. He is Professor of English at Rutgers University in Camden, New Jersey. In addition to a Ph.D. in English, he holds a Doctor of Law degree and is a member of the Pennsylvania Bar. Lutz is the author of seventeen books, including Doublespeak Defined *(1999) and* The New Doublespeak: Why No One Knows What Anyone's Saying Anymore *(1996), the sequel to his best-selling* Doublespeak: From Revenue Enhancement to Terminal Living *(1989), and* The Cambridge Thesaurus of American English *(1994). The term doublespeak comes from the Newspeak vocabulary of George Orwell's novel* Nineteen Eighty-Four. *It refers to speech or writing that presents two or more contradictory ideas in such a way that an unsuspecting audience is not consciously aware of the contradiction and is likely to be deceived.*

In the following excerpt from his book Doublespeak, *Lutz analyzes weasel words — words that "appear to say one thing when in fact that they say the opposite, or nothing at all." Notice how Lutz divides and classifies examples of advertising slogans that use weasel words so that we are better able to see and understand and, possibly, avoid being taken in by their deceptiveness.*

PREPARING TO READ

Imagine what it would be like if you were suddenly transported to a world in which there were no advertisements and no one trying to sell you a product. Think about how you would decide what to buy. How would you learn about new products? Would you prefer to live in such a world? Why or why not?

Weasel Words

One problem advertisers have when they try to convince you that the product they are pushing is really different from other, similar products is that their claims are subject to some laws. Not a lot of laws, but there are some designed to prevent fraudulent or untruthful claims in advertising. Even during the happy years of nonregulation under President Ronald Reagan, the FTC did crack down on the more blatant abuses in advertising claims. Generally speaking, advertisers have to be careful in what they say in their ads, in the claims they make for the products they advertise. Parity claims are safe because they are legal and supported by a number of court decisions. But beyond parity claims there are weasel words.

1

Advertisers use weasel words to appear to be making a claim for a 2
product when in fact they are making no claim at all. Weasel words get
their name from the way weasels eat the eggs they find in the nests of
other animals. A weasel will make a small hold in the egg, suck out the
insides, then place the egg back in the nest. Only when the egg is examined closely is it found to be hollow. That's the way it is with weasel
words in advertising: Examine weasel words closely and you'll find that
they're as hollow as any egg sucked by a weasel. Weasel words appear to
say one thing when in fact they say the opposite, or nothing at all.

"Help" — The Number One Weasel Word. The biggest weasel word 3
used in advertising doublespeak is "help." Now "help" only means to
aid or assist, nothing more. It does not mean to conquer, stop, eliminate, end, solve, heal, cure, or anything else. But once the ad says
"help," it can say just about anything after that because "help" qualifies everything coming after it. The trick is that the claim that comes
after the weasel word is usually so strong and so dramatic that you forget the word "help" and concentrate only on the dramatic claim. You
read into the ad a message that the ad does not contain. More importantly, the advertiser is not responsible for the claim that you read into
the ad, even though the advertiser wrote the ad so you would read that
claim into it.

The next time you see an ad for a cold medicine that promises that 4
it "helps relieve cold symptoms fast," don't rush out to buy it. Ask yourself what this claim is really saying. Remember, "help" means only that
the medicine will aid or assist. What will it aid to assist in doing? Why,
"relieve" your cold "symptoms." "Relieve" only means to ease, alleviate, or mitigate, not to stop, end or cure. Nor does the claim say how
much relieving this medicine will do. Nowhere does this ad claim it
will cure anything. In fact, the ad doesn't even claim it will *do* anything
at all. The ad only claims that it will aid in relieving (not curing) your
cold symptoms, which are probably a runny nose, watery eyes, and a
headache. In other words, this medicine probably contains a standard
decongestant and some aspirin. By the way, what does "fast" mean?
Ten minutes, one hour, one day? What is fast to one person can be very
slow to another. Fast is another weasel word.

Ad claims using "help" are among the most popular ads. One says, 5
"Helps keep you young looking," but then a lot of things will help keep
you young looking, including exercise, rest, good nutrition, and a
facelift. More importantly, this ad doesn't say the product will keep you
young, only "young *looking*." Someone may look young to one person
and old to another.

A toothpaste ad says, "Helps prevent cavities," but it doesn't say it 6
will actually prevent cavities. Brushing your teeth regularly, avoiding
sugars in food, and flossing daily will also help prevent cavities. A liquid

cleaner ad says, "Helps keep your home germ free," but it doesn't say it actually kills germs, nor does it even specify which germs it might kill.

"Help" is such a useful weasel word that it is often combined with other action-verb weasel words such as "fight" and "control." Consider the claim, "Helps control dandruff symptoms with regular use." What does it really say? It will assist in controlling (not eliminating, stopping, ending, or curing) the *symptoms* of dandruff, not the cause of dandruff nor the dandruff itself. What are the symptoms of dandruff? The ad deliberately leaves that undefined, but assume that the symptoms referred to in the ad are the flaking and itching commonly associated with dandruff. But just shampooing with *any* shampoo will temporarily eliminate these symptoms, so this shampoo isn't any different from any other. Finally, in order to benefit from this product, you must use it regularly. What is "regular use" — daily, weekly, hourly? Using another shampoo "regularly" will have the same effect. Nowhere does this advertising claim say this particular shampoo stops, eliminates, or cures dandruff. In fact, this claim says nothing at all, thanks to all the weasel words.

Look at ads in magazines and newspapers, listen to ads on radio and television, and you'll find the word "help" in ads for all kinds of products. How often do you read or hear such phrases as "helps stop . . . ," "helps overcome . . . ," "helps eliminate . . . ," "helps you feel . . . ," or "helps you look . . ."? If you start looking for this weasel word in advertising, you'll be amazed at how often it occurs. Analyze the claims in the ads using "help," and you will discover that these ads are really saying nothing.

There are plenty of other weasel words used in advertising. But, in order to identify the doublespeak of advertising and understand the real meaning of an ad, you have to be aware of the most popular weasel words in advertising today.

Virtually Spotless. One of the most powerful weasel words is "virtually," a word so innocent that most people don't pay any attention to it when it is used in an advertising claim. But watch out. "Virtually" is used in advertising claims that appear to make specific, definite promises when there is no promise. After all, what does "virtually" mean? It means "in essence or effect, although not in fact." Look at that definition again. "Virtually" means *not in fact*. It does *not* mean "almost" or "just about the same as," or anything else. And before you dismiss all this concern over such a small word, remember that small words can have big consequences.

In 1971 a federal court rendered its decision on a case brought by a woman who became pregnant while taking birth control pills. She sued the manufacturer, Eli Lilly and Company, for breach of warranty. The woman lost her case. Basing its ruling on a statement in the pamphlet accompanying the pills, which stated that, "When taken as directed, the tablets offer virtually 100 percent protection," the court ruled that there was no warranty, expressed or implied, that the pills were absolutely effective. In its ruling, the court pointed out that, according to *Webster's Third New International Dictionary*, "virtually" means "almost entirely" and clearly does not mean "absolute" (*Whittington* v. *Eli Lilly and Company*, 333 F. Supp. 98). In other words, the Eli Lilly company was really saying that its birth control pill, even when taken as directed, *did not in fact* provide 100 percent protection against pregnancy. But Eli Lilly didn't want to put it that way because then many women might not have bought Lilly's birth control pills.

The next time you see the ad that says that this dishwasher deter- 12 gent "leaves dishes virtually spotless," just remember how advertisers twist the meaning of the weasel word "virtually." You can have lots of spots on your dishes after using this detergent and the ad claim will still be true, because what this claim really means is that this detergent does not *in fact* leave your dishes spotless. Whenever you see or hear an ad claim that uses the word "virtually," just translate that claim into its real meaning. So the television set that is "virtually trouble free" becomes the television set that is not in fact trouble free, the "virtually foolproof operation" of any appliance becomes an operation that is in fact not foolproof, and the product that "virtually never needs service" becomes the product that is not in fact service free.

New and Improved. If "new" is the most frequently used word on a 13 product package, "improved" is the second most frequent. In fact, the two words are almost always used together. It seems just about everything sold these days is "new and improved." The next time you're in the supermarket, try counting the number of times you see these words on products. But you'd better do it while you're walking down just one aisle, otherwise you'll need a calculator to keep track of your counting.

Just what do these words mean? The use of the word "new" is 14 restricted by regulations, so an advertiser can't just use the word on a product or in an ad without meeting certain requirements. For example, a product is considered new for about six months during a national advertising campaign. If the product is being advertised only in a limited test market area, the word can be used longer, and in some instances has been used for as long as two years.

What makes a product "new"? Some products have been around 15 for a long time, yet every once in a while you discover that they are being advertised as "new." Well, an advertiser can call a product new if there has been "a material functional change" in the product. What is "a material functional change," you ask? Good question. In fact it's such a good question it's being asked all the time. It's up to the manufacturer to prove that the product has undergone such a change. And if the manufacturer isn't challenged on the claim, then there's no one to stop it. Moreover, the change does not have to be an improvement in the product. One manufacturer added an artificial lemon scent to a cleaning product and called it "new and improved," even though the product did not clean any better than without the lemon scent. The manufacturer defended the use of the word "new" on the grounds that the artificial scent changed the chemical formula of the product and therefore constituted "a material functional change."

Which brings up the word "improved." When used in advertising, "improved" does not mean "made better." It only means "changed" or "different from before." So, if the detergent maker puts a plastic pour spout on the box of detergent, the product has been "improved," and away we go with a whole new advertising campaign. Or, if the cereal maker adds more fruit or a different kind of fruit to the cereal, there's an improved product. Now you know why manufacturers are constantly making little changes in their products. Whole new advertising campaigns, designed to convince you that the product has been changed for the better, are based on small changes in superficial aspects of a product. The next time you see an ad for an "improved" product, ask yourself what was wrong with the old one. Ask yourself just how "improved" the product is. Finally, you might check to see whether the "improved" version costs more than the unimproved one. After all, someone has to pay for the millions of dollars spent advertising the improved product.

Of course, advertisers really like to run ads that claim a product is "new and improved." While what constitutes a "new" product may be subject to some regulation, "improved" is a subjective judgment. A manufacturer changes the shape of its stick deodorant, but the shape doesn't improve the function of the deodorant. That is, changing the shape doesn't affect the deodorizing ability of the deodorant, so the manufacturer calls it "improved." Another manufacturer adds ammonia to its liquid cleaner and calls it "new and improved." Since adding ammonia does affect the cleaning ability of the product, there has been a "material functional change" in the product, and the manufacturer can now call its cleaner "new," and "improved" as well. Now the weasel words "new and improved" are plastered all over the package and are the basis for a multimillion-dollar ad campaign. But after six months the word "new" will have to go, until someone can dream up another change in the product. Perhaps it will be adding color to the liquid, or changing the shape of the package, or maybe adding a new dripless pour spout, or perhaps a ____. The "improvements" are endless, and so are the new advertising claims and campaigns.

"New" is just too useful and powerful a word in advertising for advertisers to pass it up easily. So they use weasel words that say "new" without really saying it. One of their favorites is "introducing," as in, "Introducing improved Tide," or "Introducing the stain remover." The first is simply saying, here's our improved soap; the second, here's our new advertising campaign for our detergent. Another favorite is "now," as in, "Now there's Sinex," which simply means that Sinex is available. Then there are phrases like "Today's Chevrolet," "Presenting Dristan," and "A fresh way to start the day." The list is really endless because advertisers are always finding new ways to say "new" without really saying it. If there is a second edition of [my] book, I'll just call it the "new and improved" edition. Wouldn't you really rather have a "new and improved" edition of [my] book rather than a "second" edition?

Acts Fast.   "Acts" and "works" are two popular weasel words in adver-   19
tising because they bring action to the product and to the advertising claim. When you see the ad for the cough syrup that "Acts on the cough control center," ask yourself what this cough syrup is claiming to do. Well, it's just claiming to "act," to do something, to perform an action. What is it that the cough syrup does? The ad doesn't say. It only claims to perform an action or do something on your "cough control center." By the way, what and where is your "cough control center"? I don't remember learning about that part of the body in human biology class.

Ads that use such phrases as "acts fast," "acts against," "acts to pre-   20
vent," and the like are saying essentially nothing, because "act" is a word empty of any specific meaning. The ads are always careful not to specify exactly what "act" the product performs. Just because a brand of aspirin claims to "act fast" for headache relief doesn't mean this aspirin is any better than any other aspirin. What is the "act" that this aspirin performs? You're never told. Maybe it just dissolves quickly. Since aspirin is a parity product, all aspirin is the same and therefore functions the same.

Works Like Anything Else.   If you don't find the word "acts" in an   21
ad, you will probably find the weasel word "works." In fact, the two words are almost interchangeable in advertising. Watch out for ads that say a product "works against," "works like," "works for," or "works longer." As with "acts," "works" is the same meaningless verb used to make you think that this product really does something, and maybe even something special or unique. But "works," like "acts," is basically a word empty of any specific meaning.

Like Magic.   Whenever advertisers want you to stop thinking about the   22
product and to start thinking about something bigger, better, or more attractive than the product, they use that very popular weasel word "like." The word "like" is the advertiser's equivalent of a magician's use of

misdirection. "Like" gets you to ignore the product and concentrate on the claim the advertiser is making about it. "For skin like peaches and cream" claims the ad for a skin cream. What is this ad really claiming? It doesn't say this cream will give you peaches-and-cream skin. There is no verb in this claim, so it doesn't even mention using the product. How is skin ever like "peaches and cream"? Remember, ads must be read literally and exactly, according to the dictionary definition of words. (Remember "virtually" in the Eli Lilly case.) The ad is making absolutely no promise or claim whatsoever for this skin cream. If you think this cream will give you soft, smooth, youthful-looking skin, you are the one who has read that meaning into the ad.

The wine that claims "It's like taking a trip to France" wants you to   23
think about a romantic evening in Paris as you walk along the boulevard after a wonderful meal in an intimate little bistro. Of course, you don't really believe that a wine can take you to France, but the goal of the ad is to get you to think pleasant, romantic thoughts about France and not about how the wine tastes or how expensive it may be. That little word "like" has taken you away from crushed grapes into a world of your own imaginative making. Who knows, maybe the next time you buy wine, you'll think those pleasant thoughts when you see this brand of wine, and you'll buy it. Or, maybe you weren't even thinking about buying wine at all, but now you just might pick up a bottle the next time you're shopping. Ah, the power of "like" in advertising.

How about the most famous "like" claim of all, "Winston tastes   24
good like a cigarette should"? Ignoring the grammatical error here, you might want to know what this claim is saying. Whether a cigarette tastes good or bad is a subjective judgment because what tastes good to one person may well taste horrible to another. Not everyone likes fried snails, even if they are called escargot. (*De gustibus non est disputandum*, which was probably the Roman rule for advertising as well as for defending the games in the Colosseum.) There are many people who say all cigarettes taste terrible, other people who say only some cigarettes taste all right, and still others who say all cigarettes taste good. Who's right? Everyone, because taste is a matter of personal judgment.

Moreover, note the use of the conditional, "should." The complete   25
claim is, "Winston tastes good like a cigarette should taste." But should cigarettes taste good? Again, this is a matter of personal judgment and probably depends most on one's experiences with smoking. So, the Winston ad is simply saying that Winston cigarettes are just like any other cigarette: Some people like them and some people don't. On that statement R. J. Reynolds conducted a very successful multimillion-dollar advertising campaign that helped keep Winston the number-two-selling cigarette in the United States, close behind number one, Marlboro.

Can It Be Up to the Claim?

Analyzing ads for doublespeak requires that you pay attention to every word in the ad and determine what each word really means. Advertisers try to wrap their claims in language that sounds concrete, specific, and objective, when in fact the language of advertising is anything but. Your job is to read carefully and listen critically so that when the announcer says that "Crest can be of significant value . . ." you know immediately that this claim says absolutely nothing. Where is the doublespeak in this ad? Start with the second word.   26

Once again, you have to look at what words really mean, not what you think they mean or what the advertiser wants you to think they mean. The ad for Crest only says that using Crest "can be" of "significant value." What really throws you off in this ad is the brilliant use of "significant." It draws your attention to the word "value" and makes you forget that the ad only claims that Crest "can be." The ad doesn't say that Crest *is* of value, only that it is "able" or "possible" to be of value, because that's all that "can" means.   27

It's so easy to miss the importance of those little words, "can be." Almost as easy as missing the importance of the words "up to" in an ad. These words are very popular in sale ads. You know, the ones that say, "Up to 50% Off!" Now, what does that claim mean? Not much, because the store or manufacturer has to reduce the price of only a few items by 50 percent. Everything else can be reduced a lot less, or not even reduced. Moreover, don't you want to know 50 pecent off of what? Is it 50 percent off the "manufacturer's suggested list price," which is the highest possible price? Was the price artificially inflated and then reduced? In other ads, "up to" expresses an ideal situation. The medicine that works "up to ten times faster," the battery that lasts "up to twice as long," and the soap that gets you "up to twice as clean" all are based on ideal situations for using those products, situations in which you can be sure you will never find yourself.   28

Unfinished Words

Unfinished words are a kind of "up to" claim in advertising. The claim that a battery lasts "up to twice as long" usually doesn't finish the comparison — twice as long as what? A birthday candle? A tank of gas? A cheap battery made in a country not noted for its technological achievements? The implication is that the battery lasts twice as long as batteries made by other battery makers, or twice as long as earlier model batteries made by the advertiser, but the ad doesn't really make these claims. You read these claims into the ad, aided by the visual images the advertiser so carefully provides.   29

Unfinished words depend on you to finish them, to provide the words the advertisers so thoughtfully left out of the ad. Pall Mall   30 cigarettes were once advertised as "A longer finer and milder smoke." The question is, longer, finer, and milder than what? The aspirin that claims it contains "Twice as much of the pain reliever doctors recommend most" doesn't tell you what pain reliever it contains twice as much of. (By the way, it's aspirin. That's right; it just contains twice the amount of aspirin. And how much is twice the amount? Twice of what amount?) Panadol boasts that "nobody reduces fever faster," but, since Panadol is a parity product, this claim simply means that Panadol isn't any better than any other product in its parity class. "You can be sure if it's Westinghouse," you're told, but just exactly what it is you can be sure of is never mentioned. "Magnavox gives you more" doesn't tell you what you get more of. More value? More television? More than they gave you before? It sounds nice, but it means nothing, until you fill in the claim with your own words, the words the advertiser didn't use. Since each of us fills in the claim differently, the ad and the product can become all things to all people, and not promise a single thing.

Unfinished words abound in advertising because they appear to promise so much. More importantly, they can be joined with powerful visual images on television to appear to be making significant promises about a product's effectiveness without really making any promises. In a television ad, the aspirin product that claims fast relief can show a person with a headache taking the product and then, in what appears to be a matter of minutes, claiming complete relief. This visual image is far more powerful than any claim made in unfinished words. Indeed, the visual image completes the unfinished words for you, filling in with pictures what the words leave out. And you thought that ads didn't affect you. What brand of aspirin do you use?

Some years ago, Ford's advertisements proclaimed "Ford LTD — 700 percent quieter." Now, what do you think Ford was claiming with these unfinished words? What was the Ford LTD quieter than? A Cadillac? A Mercedes Benz? A BMW? Well, when the FTC asked Ford to substantiate this unfinished claim, Ford replied that it meant that the inside of the LTD was 700 percent quieter than the outside. How did you finish those unfinished words when you first read them? Did you even come close to Ford's meaning?

Combining Weasel Words

A lot of ads don't fall neatly into one category or another because they use a variety of different devices and words. Different weasel words are often combined to make an ad claim. The claim, "Coffee-Mate gives coffee more body, more flavor," uses unfinished words ("more" than what?) and also uses words that have no specific meaning ("body" and "flavor"). Along with "taste" (remember the Winston ad and its claim to taste good), "body" and "flavor" mean nothing because their mean-ing is entirely subjective. To you, "body" in coffee might mean thick, black, almost bitter coffee, while I might take it to mean a light brown, delicate coffee. Now, if you think you understood that last sentence, read it again, because it said nothing of objective value; it was filled with weasel words of no specific meaning: "thick," "black," "bitter," "light brown," and "delicate." Each of those words has no specific, objective meaning, because each of us can interpret them differently.

Try this slogan: "Looks, smells, tastes like ground-roast coffee." So, are 34 you now going to buy Taster's Choice instant coffee because of this ad? "Looks," "smells," and "tastes" are all words with no specific meaning and depend on your interpretation of them for any meaning. Then there's that great weasel word "like," which simply suggests a comparison but does not make the actual connection between the product and the quality. Besides, do you know what "ground-roast" coffee is? I don't, but it sure sounds good. So, out of seven words in this ad, four are definite weasel words, two are quite meaningless, and only one has clear meaning.

Remember the Anacin ad—"Twice as much of the pain reliever 35 doctors recommend most"? There's a whole lot of weaseling going on in this ad. First, what's the pain reliever they're talking about in this ad? Aspirin, of course. In fact, any time you see or hear an ad using those words "pain reliever," you can automatically substitute the word "aspirin" for them. (Makers of acetaminophen and ibuprofen pain relievers are careful in their advertising to identify their products as nonaspirin products.) So, now we know that Anacin has aspirin in it. Moreover, we know that Anacin has twice as much aspirin in it, but we don't know twice as much as what. Does it have twice as much aspirin as an ordinary aspirin tablet? If so, what is a ordinary aspirin tablet, and how much aspirin does it contain? Twice as much as Excedrin or Bufferin? Twice as much as a chocolate chip cookie? Remember those unfinished words and how they lead you on without saying anything.

Finally, what about those doctors who are doing all that recom- 36 mending? Who are they? How many of them are there? What kind of doctors are they? What are their qualifications? Who asked them about recommending pain relievers? What other pain relievers did they rec-ommend? And there are a whole lot more questions about this "poll" of doctors to which I'd like to know the answers, but you get the point. Sometimes, when I call my doctor, she tells me to take two aspirin and call her office in the morning. Is that where Anacin got this ad?

THINKING CRITICALLY ABOUT THE TEXT

Before reading Lutz's essay did you have any idea that the language advertis-ers use can be so deceiving? Explain. Are weasel words simply annoying, or are they, in fact, harmful in some ways? Explain.

QUESTIONS ON SUBJECT

1. What are weasel words? How, according to Lutz, did they get their name?

2. According to Lutz, why is *help* the biggest weasel word used by advertisers (paragraphs 3–8)? In what ways does the word *help* aid advertisers in presenting their products without having to make promises about actual performance?

3. Why is *virtually* a particularly effective weasel word (paragraphs 10–12)? Why can advertisers get away with using words that literally mean the opposite of what they want to convey?

4. What kinds of claims fit into Lutz's "unfinished words" category (paragraphs 29–32)? Why are they weasels? What makes them so difficult to detect?

5. Is Lutz being too negative about weasel words? Is there something that might be said in their defense?

QUESTIONS ON STRATEGY

1. What is Lutz's purpose in writing this essay? (Glossary: *Purpose*)

2. Lutz is careful to illustrate each of the various kinds of weasel words with examples of actual usage. (Glossary: *Examples*) What do these examples add to his essay? Which ones do you find most effective? Explain.

3. For what audience do you think Lutz wrote this essay? (Glossary: *Audience*) Do you consider yourself part of this audience?

4. Lutz uses the strategy of division and classification to develop his essay. Explain how he uses this strategy.

5. Why do you suppose Lutz felt the need to create the "Combining Weasel Words" category? Did the headings in the essay help you follow his discussion? What would be lost had he not included them?

QUESTIONS ON DICTION AND VOCABULARY

1. Do you find Lutz's diction and tone appropriate for his audience? (Glossary: *Tone*) Explain.

2. Analyze the following slogan used to sell motor oil: "Works like liquid ball bearings." What are the weasel words? Why does this authoritative-sounding slogan actually say nothing at all? Base your answer on Lutz's arguments.

3. Does Lutz himself use any weasel words? Explain.

CLASSROOM ACTIVITY USING DIVISION AND CLASSIFICATION

Divide each item in the following list into at least three different categories, and be prepared to explain the principle of division. Also, provide a few examples that might be placed in each category. For example, newspapers can be divided into these categories: the time of day they are published (morning or evening), how conventional they are (mainstream or alternative), the coverage they give (general or localized, or both); their cost (more or less than a dollar); their degree of specialization (sports, financial, foreign language); and so forth.

pets
restaurants
discount stores
soft drinks
checking accounts

WRITING SUGGESTIONS

1. As is readily apparent in "Weasel Words," advertisers depend on language ploys to win you over. Yet they use other techniques, including simple dissemination of information and misinformation, side-by-side comparisons, logical argumentation, and so on. Watch a couple of hours of television, and note the techniques used in each commercial. Then write a division and classification essay in which you present the different types of techniques and describe how advertisers use them.

2. Pay attention to the ads for companies that offer rival products or services (for example, Apple and IBM, Coca-Cola and Pepsi-Cola, Burger King and McDonald's, Charles Schwab and Smith Barney, and AT&T and MCI). Focusing on a single pair of ads, analyze the different appeals that companies make when comparing their products or services to those of the competition. To what audience does each ad appeal? How many weasel words can you detect? Based on your analysis, write an essay about the advertising strategies companies use when in head-to-head competition with the products of other companies.

The Ways of Meeting Oppression
Martin Luther King Jr.

Martin Luther King Jr. (1929–1968) was the son of a Baptist minister. Ordained at the age of eighteen, King went on to study at Morehouse College, Crozer Theological Seminary, Boston University, and Chicago Theological Seminary. He came to prominence in 1955 in Montgomery, Alabama, when he led a successful boycott against the city's segregated bus system. A powerful orator and writer, King went on to become the leading spokesman for the civil rights movement during the 1950s and 1960s. In 1964, he was awarded the Nobel Peace Prize for his policy of nonviolent resistance to racial injustice, a policy that he explains in the following selection. King was assassinated in April 1968 after speaking at a rally in Memphis, Tennessee.

This selection is excerpted from the book Stride Toward Freedom *(1958). Notice how King classifies the three ways oppressed people throughout history have reacted to their oppressors and how his organization prepares the reader for his conclusion.*

PREPARING TO READ

Summarize what you know about the civil rights movement of the late 1950s and early 1960s. What tactics did its leaders use? How successful were those tactics? How did this movement change American society?

Oppressed people deal with their oppression in three characteristic ways. One way is acquiescence: the oppressed resign themselves to their doom. They tacitly adjust themselves to oppression, and thereby become conditioned to it. In every movement toward freedom some of the oppressed prefer to remain oppressed. Almost 2800 years ago Moses set out to lead the children of Israel from the slavery of Egypt to the freedom of the promised land. He soon discovered that slaves do not always welcome their deliverers. They become accustomed to being slaves. They would rather bear those ills they have, as Shakespeare pointed out, than flee to others that they know not of. They prefer the "fleshpots of Egypt" to the ordeals of emancipation. 1

There is such a thing as the freedom of exhaustion. Some people are so worn down by the yoke of oppression that they give up. A few years ago in the slum areas of Atlanta, a Negro guitarist used to sing almost daily: "Been down so long that down don't bother me." This is the type of negative freedom and resignation that often engulfs the life of the oppressed. 2

But this is not the way out. To accept passively an unjust system is to cooperate with that system; thereby the oppressed become as evil as 3 the oppressor. Noncooperation with evil is as much a moral obligation as is cooperation with good. The oppressed must never allow the conscience of the oppressor to slumber. Religion reminds every man that he is his brother's keeper. To accept injustice or segregation passively is to say to the oppressor that his actions are morally right. It is a way of allowing his conscience to fall asleep. At this moment the oppressed fails to be his brother's keeper. So acquiescence—while often the easier way—is not the moral way. It is the way of the coward. The Negro cannot win the respect of his oppressor by acquiescing; he merely increases the oppressor's arrogance and contempt. Acquiescence is interpreted as proof of the Negro's inferiority. The Negro cannot win the respect of the white people of the south or the peoples of the world if he is willing to sell the future of his children for his personal and immediate comfort and safety.

A second way that oppressed people sometimes deal with oppression is to resort to physical violence and corroding hatred. Violence often brings about momentary results. Nations have frequently won their independence in battle. But in spite of temporary victories, violence never brings permanent peace. It solves no social problem; it merely creates new and more complicated ones.   4

Violence as a way of achieving racial justice is both impractical and immoral. It is impractical because it is a descending spiral ending in destruction for all. The old law of an eye for an eye leaves everybody blind. It is immoral because it seeks to humiliate the opponent rather than win his understanding; it seeks to annihilate rather than to convert. Violence is immoral because it thrives on hatred rather than love. It destroys community and makes brotherhood impossible. It leaves society in monologue rather than dialogue. Violence ends by defeating itself. It creates bitterness in the survivors and brutality in the destroyers. A voice echoes through time saying to every potential Peter, "Put up your sword." History is cluttered with the wreckage of nations that failed to follow this command.   5

If the American Negro and other victims of oppression succumb to the temptation of using violence in the struggle for freedom, future generations will be the recipients of a desolate night of bitterness, and our chief legacy to them will be an endless reign of meaningless chaos. Violence is not the way.   6

The third way open to oppressed people in their quest for freedom is the way of nonviolent resistance. Like the synthesis in Hegelian philosophy, the principle of nonviolent resistance seeks to reconcile the truths of two opposites—the acquiescence and violence—while avoiding the extremes and immoralities of both. The nonviolent resister agrees with the person who acquiesces that one should not be physically aggressive toward his opponent; but he balances the equation by agreeing with the person of violence that evil must be resisted. He avoids the nonresistance   7 of the former and the violent resistance of the latter. With nonviolent resistance, no individual or group need submit to any wrong, nor need anyone resort to violence in order to right a wrong.

It seems to me that this is the method that must guide the actions of the Negro in the present crisis in race relations. Through nonviolent resistance the Negro will be able to rise to the noble height of opposing the unjust system while loving the perpetrators of the system. The Negro must work passionately and unrelentingly for full stature as a citizen, but he must not use inferior methods to gain it. He must never come to terms with falsehood, malice, hate, or destruction. 8

Nonviolent resistance makes it possible for the Negro to remain in the South and struggle for his rights. The Negro's problem will not be solved by running away. He cannot listen to the glib suggestion of those who would urge him to migrate en masse to other sections of the country. By grasping his great opportunity in the South he can make a lasting contribution to the moral strength of the nation and set a sublime example of courage for generations yet unborn. 9

By nonviolent resistance, the Negro can also enlist all men of good will in his struggle for equality. The problem is not a purely racial one, with Negroes set against whites. In the end, it is not a struggle between people at all, but a tension between justice and injustice. Nonviolent resistance is not aimed against oppressors but against oppression. Under its banner consciences, not racial groups, are enlisted. 10

THINKING CRITICALLY ABOUT THE TEXT

Find the definition of *oppress* or *oppression* in the dictionary. Exactly what does King mean when he speaks of people being "oppressed" in the South in twentieth-century America? Do you think that people are still being oppressed in America today? Explain.

QUESTIONS ON SUBJECT

1. What does King mean by the term "freedom of exhaustion" (paragraph 2)? Why is he scathing in his assessment of people who succumb to such a condition in response to oppression?
2. According to King, what is the role of religion in the battle against oppression?
3. Why does King advocate the avoidance of violence in fighting oppression, despite the short-term success violence often achieves for the victors? How do such victories affect the future?
4. According to King, how does nonviolent resistance transform a racial issue into one of conscience?

QUESTIONS ON STRATEGY

1. King's essay is easy to read and understand, and everything in it relates to his purpose. (Glossary: *Purpose*) What is that purpose? Summarize how

each paragraph supports his purpose. How does the essay's organization help King achieve his purpose? (Glossary: *Organization*)

2. King says that "nonviolent resistance is not aimed against oppressors but against oppression" (paragraph 10). What does he mean by this? Why does he deflect anger and resentment away from a concrete example, the oppressors, to an abstract concept, oppression? (Glossary: *Concrete/ Abstract*) How does this choice support his purpose? (Glossary: *Purpose*)

3. King evokes the names of Moses, Shakespeare, and Hegel in his essay. What does this tell you about his intended audience? (Glossary: *Audience*) Why does King address the audience in this way?

4. King uses division and classification to help him argue his point in this essay. What other rhetorical strategies does King use? How does each strategy, including division and classification and argument, contribute to the effectiveness of the essay?

QUESTIONS ON DICTION AND VOCABULARY

1. In his discussion about overcoming oppression with violence, King says that "future generations will be the recipients of a desolate night of bitterness" (paragraph 6). What image do his words evoke for you? Why do you think he chooses to use a striking metaphor here, instead of a less poetic statement? (Glossary: *Figures of Speech*)

2. King urges Negroes to avoid "falsehood, malice, hate, or destruction" (paragraph 8) in their quest to gain full stature as citizens. How does each of these terms relate to his earlier argument about avoiding violence? How does each enhance or add new meaning to his earlier argument?

3. Refer to your desk dictionary to determine the meanings of the following words as King uses them in this selection: *acquiescence* (paragraph 1), *tacitly* (1), *yoke* (2), *perpetrators* (8), *glib* (9), *sublime* (9).

CLASSROOM ACTIVITY USING DIVISION AND CLASSIFICATION

Be prepared to discuss in class why you believe division and classification are important strategies or ways of thinking in everyday life. Be prepared to explain why, and how useful the two complementary strategies are for you as you go shopping in the supermarket for items on your shopping list or look for particular textbooks in your college bookstore.

WRITING SUGGESTIONS

1. Write a division and classification essay in which you follow King's model by arguing for or advocating one of the categories. Identify three methods that you can use to achieve a goal—study for a test, apply to graduate school, or interview for a job, for example. Choose one method to advocate; then frame your essay so that the division and classification strategy helps you make your point.

2. Toward the end of his essay, King states, "By grasping his great opportunity in the South [the Negro] can make a lasting contribution to the moral strength of the nation and set a sublime example of courage for generations yet unborn" (paragraph 9). With your classmates, discuss whether the movement that King led achieved its goal of solving many of the underlying racial tensions and inequities in the United States. In terms of equality, what has happened in the United States since King's famous "I Have a Dream" speech (page 486)? Write a paper in which you argue for or against the idea that King's "dream" is still intact. (Glossary: *Argumentation*)

WRITING SUGGESTIONS FOR DIVISION AND CLASSIFICATION

1. To write a meaningful classification essay, you must analyze a body of unorganized material, arranging it for a particular purpose. (Glossary: *Purpose*) For example, to identify for a buyer the most economical cars currently on the market, you might initially determine which cars can be purchased for under $20,000 and which cost between $20,000 and $30,000. Then, using a second basis of selection—fuel economy—you could determine which cars have the best gas mileage within each price range.

    Select one of the following subjects, and write a classification essay. Be sure that your purpose is clearly explained and that your bases of selection are chosen and ordered in accordance with your purpose.

    a. attitudes toward physical fitness
    b. contemporary American music
    c. reading materials
    d. reasons for going to college
    e. attitudes toward the religious or spiritual side of life
    f. choosing a hobby
    g. television comedies
    h. college professors
    i. local restaurants
    j. choosing a career
    k. college courses
    l. recreational activities
    m. ways of financing a college education
    n. parties or other social events

2. We sometimes resist classifying other people because it can seem like "pigeonholing" or stereotyping individuals unfairly. In an essay, compare and contrast two or more ways of classifying people, including at least one that you would call legitimate and one that you would call misleading. (Glossary: *Comparison and Contrast*) What conclusions can you draw about the difference between useful classifications and damaging stereotypes?

3. Use division and classification to explain your school or town. What categories might you use? Would you divide your subject into different types of people? Would you classify people by their spending habits? What are the other ways in which you might explain your school or town? What other rhetorical strategies might you incorporate to strengthen your presentation? You might want to look at the Web site of your school or town to find out what categories it uses to present itself.

4. Write an essay about the types of presidents that have been elected since the invention of television. How would you organize the different presidents and elections? Would you divide the presidents by political party? By age? By their geographic origins? By their political programs—domestic, international, military, economic, and so forth? What other rhetorical strategies might you use to develop and explain your categories?

CHAPTER 10

Definition

WHAT IS DEFINITION?

A definition explains the meaning of a word or phrase; if you have ever used a dictionary, you will be familiar with the concept of definition. We can only communicate with one another properly when all of us define the words we use in the same way—and that is not always easy. What one person believes he or she is saying might be construed differently by the listener. For example, if someone told you to be *discriminatory*, you might understand the word in a manner not intended by the speaker. Let's look at how Robert Keith Miller attempts to define *discrimination* in his essay called "Discrimination Is a Virtue," which first appeared in *Newsweek*.

> We have a word in English which means "the ability to tell differences." That word is *discrimination*. But within the last [fifty] years, this word has been so frequently misused that an entire generation has grown up believing that "discrimination" means "racism." People are always proclaiming that "discrimination" is something that should be done away with. Should that ever happen, it would prove to be our undoing.
>
> Discrimination means discernment; it means the ability to perceive the truth, to use good judgment and to profit accordingly. The *Oxford English Dictionary* traces this meaning of the word back to 1648 and demonstrates that for the next 300 years, "discrimination" was a virtue, not a vice. Thus, when a character in a nineteenth-century novel makes a happy marriage, Dickens has another character remark, "It does credit to your discrimination that you should have found such a very excellent young woman."

Of course, "the ability to tell differences" assumes that differences exist, and this is unsettling for a culture obsessed with the notion of equality. The contemporary belief that discrimination is a vice stems from the compound "discriminate against." What we need to remember, however, is that some things deserve to be judged harshly: We should not leave our kingdoms to the selfish and the wicked.

Discrimination is wrong only when someone or something is discriminated against because of prejudice. But to use the word in that sense, as so many people do, is to destroy its true meaning. If you discriminate against something because of general preconceptions rather than particular insights, then you are not discriminating—bias has clouded the clarity of vision that discrimination demands.

How does Miller define *discrimination*? He mainly uses a technique called *extended definition*, a definition that requires a full discussion. This is only one of many types of definition that you could use to explain what a word or an idea means to you. The following paragraphs identify and explain several types of definition; see if you can find examples of them in Miller's article.

A *formal definition*—a definition such as that found in a dictionary—explains the meaning of a word by assigning it to a class and then differentiating it from other members of that class.

Term		Class	Differentiation
Music	is	sound	made by voices or instruments and characterized by melody, harmony, or rhythm.

Note how crucial the differentiation is here: There are many sounds—from the roar of a passing jet airplane to the fizz of soda in a glass—that must be excluded for the definition to be precise and useful. Dictionary entries often follow the class-differentiation pattern of the formal definition.

A *synonymous definition* explains a word by pairing it with another word of similar but perhaps more limited meaning.

Music is melody.

Synonymous definition is almost never as precise as formal definition because few words share exactly the same meaning. But when the word being defined is reasonably familiar and somewhat broad, a well-chosen synonym can provide readers with a surer sense of its meaning in context.

A *negative definition* explains a word by saying what it does not mean.

> Music is not silence, and it is not noise.

Such a definition must obviously be incomplete: There are sounds that are neither silence nor noise and yet are not music—quiet conversation, for example. But specifying what something is *not* often helps to clarify other statements about what it is.

An *etymological definition* also seldom stands alone, but by tracing a word's origins it helps readers understand its meaning. *Etymology* itself is defined as the study of the history of a linguistic form—the history of words.

> Music is descended from the Greek word *mousikē*, meaning literally "the art of the Muse."

The Muses, according to Greek mythology, were deities and the sources of inspiration in the arts. Thus the etymology suggests why we think of music as an art and as the product of inspiration. Etymological definitions often reveal surprising sources that suggest new ways of looking at ideas or objects.

A *stipulative definition* is a definition invented by a writer to convey a special or unexpected sense of an existing and often familiar word.

> Music is a language, but a language of the intangible, a kind of soul-language.
>
> —EDWARD MACDOWELL

> Music is the arithmetic of sounds.   —CLAUDE DEBUSSY

Although these two examples seem to disagree with each other, and perhaps also with your idea of what music is, note that neither is arbitrary. (That is, neither assigns to the word *music* a completely foreign meaning, as Humpty Dumpty did in *Through the Looking-Glass* when he defined *glory* as "a nice knock-down argument.") The stipulative definitions by MacDowell and Debussy help explain each composer's conception of the subject and can lead, of course, to further elaboration. Stipulative definitions almost always provide the basis for a more complex discussion. These definitions are often the subjects of an extended definition.

Sometimes a word, or the idea it stands for, requires more than a sentence of explanation. Such a longer definition—called, naturally enough, *extended definition*—may go on for a paragraph, a page, an essay, or even an entire book. It may employ any of the techniques already mentioned in this chapter, as well as the various strategies discussed throughout the text. An extended definition tends to differ greatly from a formal definition; writers use extended definition to make a specific, and often unusual, point about an idea. An extended definition of music might provide *examples*, ranging from African drumming to a Bach fugue to a Bruce Springsteen song, to develop a fuller and more vivid sense of what music is. A writer might *describe* music in detail by showing its characteristic features, or explain the *process* of composing music, or *compare and contrast* music with language (according to MacDowell's stipulative definition) or arithmetic (according to Debussy's). Each of these strategies, and others too, helps make the meaning of a writer's words and ideas clear.

Robert Keith Miller primarily used an extended definition to explain his understanding of the word *discrimination*. What other types did you find in his brief essay? Let's go through the essay again to see the various definitions that he used. To begin with, Miller used a very brief formal definition of *discrimination* [term]: "the ability [class] to tell differences [differentiation]". He then offered a negative definition (discrimination is not racism) and a synonymous definition (discrimination is discernment). Next he cited the entry in a great historical dictionary of English to support his claim, and he quoted an example to illustrate his definition. He concluded by contrasting the word *discrimination* with the compound "discriminate against." Each of these techniques helped make the case that the most precise meaning of *discrimination* is in direct opposition to its common usage today.

USING DEFINITION AS A WRITING STRATEGY

Since most readers have dictionaries, it might seem that writers would hardly ever have to define their terms with formal definitions. In fact, writers don't necessarily do so all the time, even when using an unusual word like *tergiversation*, which few readers have in their active vocabularies; if readers don't know it, the reasoning goes, let them look it up. But there are times when a definition is quite necessary. One of these times is when a writer uses a word so specialized or so new that it simply won't be in dictionaries; another is when a writer must use a number of unfamiliar technical terms within only a few sentences. Also, when a word has several different meanings or may mean different things to different people, writers will often state exactly the sense in which they are using the word. In each of these cases, definition serves the purpose of achieving clarity.

But writers also sometimes use definition, particularly extended definition, to explain the essential nature of the things and ideas they write about. For example, consider E. B. White's definition of *democracy*, which first appeared in the *New Yorker* on July 3, 1943.

> We received a letter from the Writers' War Board the other day asking for a statement on "The Meaning of Democracy." It presumably is our duty to comply with such a request, and it is certainly our pleasure.
>
> Surely the Board knows what democracy is. It is the line that forms on the right. It is the don't in don't shove. It is the hole in the stuffed shirt through which the sawdust slowly trickles; it is the dent in the high hat. Democracy is the recurrent suspicion that more than half of the people are right more than half of the time. It is the feeling of privacy in the voting booths, the feeling of communion in the libraries, the feeling of vitality everywhere. Democracy is a letter to the editor. Democracy is the score at the beginning of the ninth. It is an idea which hasn't been disproved yet, a song the words of which have not gone bad. It's the mustard on the hot dog and the cream in the rationed coffee. Democracy is a request from a War Board, in the middle of a morning in the middle of a war, wanting to know what democracy is.

Such writing goes beyond answering the question, "What does _____ mean exactly?" to tackle the much broader and deeper question "What is _____, and what does it represent?"

Although exploring a term and what it represents is often the primary object of such a definition, sometimes writers go beyond giving a formal definition; they also use extended definitions to make persuasive points. Take the Miller essay, for example (page 359). The subject of Miller's extended definition is clearly the word *discrimination*. His purpose, however, is less immediately obvious. At first it appears that he wants only to explain what the word means. But by the third sentence he is distinguishing what it does not mean, and at the end it's clear he's trying to persuade readers to use the word correctly and thus to discriminate more sharply and justly themselves.

Using Definition across the Disciplines

When writing essays in the academic disciplines, you will have many opportunities to use the strategy of definition to both organize and strengthen the presentation of your ideas. To determine whether or not definition is the right strategy for you in a

(continued on next page)

(continued from previous page)

particular paper, use the four-step method first described in "Determining Your Strategy" (pages 24–25). Consider the following examples, which illustrate how this four-step method works for typical college papers:

Philosophy

MAIN IDEA: A person of integrity is more than just an honest person.

QUESTION: What does it mean to have *integrity*?

STRATEGY: Definition. The direction words *mean* and *is more than* call for a complete explanation of the meaning of the word *integrity*.

SUPPORTING STRATEGY: Comparison and Contrast. To clarify the definition of *integrity*, it might be helpful to differentiate a person of integrity from a moral person or an ethical person.

Economics

MAIN IDEA: One way to understand the swings in the United States economy is to know the meaning of inflation.

QUESTION: What is inflation?

STRATEGY: Definition. The direction words *meaning* and *is* point us toward the strategy of definition—the word *inflation* needs to be explained.

SUPPORTING STRATEGY: Cause and Effect Analysis. In explaining the meaning of *inflation*, it would be interesting to explore economic factors that cause inflation as well as the effects of inflation on the economy.

Astronomy

MAIN IDEA: With the demotion of Pluto from planet to asteroid, astronomers have given new attention to the definition of *planet*.

QUESTION: What is a planet?

STRATEGY: Definition. The direction words *definition* and *is* call for an extended definition of the word *planet*. For clarification purposes, it would be helpful to define *asteroid* as well.

SUPPORTING STRATEGIES: Illustration and Cause and Effect Analysis. The definition of *planet* could be supported with several concrete examples of planets as well as an explanation of why astronomers thought a new definition was necessary.

SAMPLE STUDENT ESSAY USING DEFINITION AS A WRITING STRATEGY

Originally a native of New York City, Howard Solomon Jr. studied in France as part of the American Field Services Intercultural Program in high school, and he majored in French at the University of Vermont. Solomon's other interests include foreign affairs, languages, photography, and cycling; in his wildest dreams, he imagines becoming an international lawyer. For the following essay, Solomon began by interviewing students in his dormitory, collecting information and opinions that he eventually brought together with his own experiences to develop a definition of *best friends*.

Best Friends
Howard Solomon Jr.

Introduction: Writer provides brief definition of best friend.

Purpose: In defining best friend, writer comes to new understanding of self and relationships.

Organization: Sequence of interview questions

Three-part answer to question 1: What qualities do you value in a best friend?

Defines "reciprocity" between best friends

Defines "honesty" between best friends

Best friends, even when they are not a part of our day-to-day lives, are essential to our well-being. They supply the companionship, help, security, and love that we all need. It is not easy to put into words exactly what a best friend is, because the matter is so personal. From time to time, however, we may think about our best friends — who they are, what characteristics they share, and why they are so important to us — in order to gain a better understanding of ourselves and our relationships.

I recently asked several people for their opinions on the subject, beginning with a question about the qualities they valued in their own best friends. They all agreed on three traits: reciprocity, honesty, and love. Reciprocity means that one can always rely on a best friend in times of need. A favor doesn't necessarily have to be returned; but best friends will return it anyway, because they want to. Best friends are willing to help each other for the sake of helping and not just for personal gain. One woman said that life seemed more secure because she knew her best friend was there if she ever needed help.

Honesty in a best friendship is the sharing of feelings openly and without reserve. The people I interviewed said they could rely on their best friends as confidants: They could share problems with their best friends and ask for advice. They also felt that, even if best friends were critical of each other, they would never be hurtful or spiteful.

1

2

3

Love is probably the most important quality of a best friend relationship, according to the people I interviewed. They very much prized the affection and enjoyment they felt in the company of their best friends. One man described it as a "gut reaction," and all said it was a different feeling from being with other friends. Private jokes, looks, and gestures create personal communication between best friends that is at a very high level—many times one person knows what the other is thinking without anything being said. The specifics differ, but almost everyone I talked to agreed that a special feeling exists, which is best described as love.

I next asked who could be a best friend and who could not. My sources all felt it was impossible for parents, other relatives, and people of the opposite sex (especially husbands or wives) to be best friends. One woman said such people were "too inhibitive." Personally, I disagree—I have two best friends who are women. However, I may be an exception, and most best friends may fit the above requirements. There could be a good reason for this, too: Most of the people I interviewed felt that their best friends were not demanding, while relatives and partners of the opposite sex can be very demanding.

To the question of how many best friends one can have, some in my sample responded that it is possible to have several best friends, although very few people can do so; others said it was possible to have only a very few best friends; and still others felt they could have just one—that single friend who is most outstanding. It was interesting to see how ideas varied on this question. Although best friends may be no less special for one person than another, people do define the concept differently.

Regarding how long it takes to become best friends and how long the relationship lasts, all were in agreement. "It is a long hard process which takes a lot of time," one woman explained. "It isn't something that can happen overnight," suggested another. One man said, "You usually know the person very well before you consider him your best friend. In fact you know everything about him, his bad points as well as his good points, so there is little likelihood that you can come into conflict with him." In addition, everyone thought that once a person has become a best friend, he or she remains so for the rest of one's life.

During the course of the interviews I discovered one important and unexpected difference between men and women regarding the qualities of their best friends. The men all said that a

4

5

6

7

8

best friend usually possessed one quality that stood out above all others—an easygoing manner or humor or sympathy, for example. One of them told me that he looked not for loyalty but for honesty, for someone who was truthful, because it was so rare to find this quality in anyone. The women I surveyed, however, all responded that they looked for a well-rounded person who had many good qualities. One said that a person who had just one good quality and not several would be "too boring to associate with." Does this difference hold true beyond my sample? If so, it means that men and women have quite different definitions of their best friends.

Personal example: Writer tells what he learned about best friends at the time of his father's death.

I have always wondered why my own best friends were 9 so important to me; but it wasn't until recently that something happened to make me really understand my relationship with my best friends. My father died, and this was a crisis for me. Most of my friends gave me their condolences. But my best friends did more than that: they actually supported me. They called long distance to see how I was and what I needed, to try to help me work out my problems, or simply to talk. Two of my best friends even took time from their spring break and, along with two other best friends, attended my father's memorial service; none of my other friends came. Since then, these are the only people who have continued to worry about me and talk to me about my father. I know that whenever I need someone they will be there and willing to help me. I know also that whenever they need help I will be ready to do the same for them.

Conclusion: Writer gives personal definition of best friend.

Thesis

Yet, I don't value my best friends so much just for what 10 they do for me. I simply enjoy their company more than anyone else's. We talk, joke, play sports, and do all kinds of things when we are together. I never feel ill at ease, even after we've been apart for a while. However, the most important thing for me about best friends is the knowledge that I am never alone, that there are others in the world who care about my well-being as much as I do about theirs. Surely this is a comforting feeling for everyone.

Analyzing Howard Solomon Jr.'s Essay of Definition: Questions for Discussion

1. How does Solomon define best friend in his opening paragraph?
2. According to the people Solomon surveyed, what three qualities are valued most in a best friend?

(continued on next page)

(continued from previous page)

3. Which of these qualities is considered the most important? Why?

4. How do men's and women's definitions of a best friend differ? Do you agree with Solomon's informants?

5. In what ways do Solomon's interviews enhance his own definition of best friend?

6. In the final analysis, why does Solomon think people value their best friends so much?

SUGGESTIONS FOR USING DEFINITION AS A WRITING STRATEGY

As you plan, write, and revise your essay of definition, be mindful of the five-step writing process described in Chapter 2 (see pages 14–31). Also, pay particular attention to the basic requirements and essential ingredients for this writing strategy.

Planning Your Essay of Definition

Planning is an essential part of writing a good essay of definition. You can save yourself a great deal of aggravation by taking the time to think about the key components of your essay before you actually begin to write.

Determine Your Purpose. Whatever your subject, make sure you have a clear sense of your purpose. Why are you writing a definition? If it's only to explain what a word or phrase means, you'll probably run out of things to say in a few sentences, or you'll find that a good dictionary has already said them for you. An effective extended definition should attempt to explain the essential nature of a thing or an idea, whether it be *photosynthesis* or *spring fever* or *Republicanism* or *prison* or *common sense*.

Often the challenge of writing a paper using the rhetorical strategy of definition is in getting your audience to understand your particular perception of the term or idea you are trying to define and explain. Take, for example, the selection below from a student essay. For many years, the citizens of Quebec, one of Canada's ten provinces, have been debating and voting on the issue of secession from Canada. At the core of this volatile issue is the essential question of Canadian identity. As you will see from the student's introduction, the Quebecois define Canadian identity very differently from the way other Canadians define it.

Quebecois Are Canadians

The peaceful formation of Canada as an independent nation has led to the current identity crisis in Quebec. The Quebecois perceive themselves to be different from all other Canadians because of their French ancestry and their unique history as both rulers and minorities in Canada. In an attempt to create a unified Canada the government has tried to establish a common Canadian culture through the building of a transcontinental railroad, a nationalized medical system, a national arts program, a national agenda, and the required use of both French and English in all publications and on all signs. As the twenty-first century begins, however, Canadians, especially the Quebecois, continue to grapple with the issue of what it means to be a Canadian, and unless some consensus can be reached on the definition of the Canadian identity, Quebec's attempt to secede from Canada may succeed.

This introductory paragraph establishes the need to define the terms *Canadians* and *Quebecois*. Implicit in any discussion of the meanings for these two terms is another rhetorical strategy: comparison and contrast. The writer might go on to use other strategies, such as description or illustration, to highlight common characteristics or differences of the Canadians and Quebecois. Judging from the title, it is clear that an argument (see Chapter 12) will be made that, based on the definitions, Quebecois are Canadians.

When you decide on your topic, consider an idea or term that you would like to clarify or explain to someone. For example, Howard Solomon Jr. hit on the idea of defining what a best friend is. He recalls that "a friend of mine had become a best friend, and I was trying to figure out what had happened, what was different. So I decided to explore what was on my mind." At the beginning, you should have at least a general idea of what your subject means to you, as well as a sense of the audience you are writing your definition for and the impact you want your definition to achieve. The following advice will guide you as you plan and draft your essay.

Formulate a Thesis Statement. A strong, clear thesis statement is critical in any essay. When writing an essay using extended definition, you should formulate a thesis statement that states clearly both the word or idea that you want to define or explain and the way in which you are going to present your thoughts. Here are two examples from this chapter.

THESIS We have a word in English which means "the ability to tell differences." That word is *discrimination*. But within the last [fifty] years, this word has been so frequently misused that an entire generation has grown up believing that "discrimination" means "racism."
[Robert Keith Miller's thesis statement tells us that he will be discussing the word *discrimination* and how it is not the same as racism.]

THESIS As the twenty-first century begins, however, Canadians, especially the Quebecois, continue to grapple with the issue of what it means to be a Canadian, and unless some consensus can be reached on the definition of the Canadian identity, Quebec's attempt to secede from Canada may succeed.
[The student writer makes it clear that the identity of both the Canadians and the Quebecois will be defined. The thesis statement also conveys a sense of the urgency for discussing these definitions.]

As you begin to develop your thesis statement, ask yourself, "What is my point?" Next ask yourself, "What types of definitions will be most useful in making my point?" If you can't answer these questions yet, write some ideas down and try to determine your main point from these ideas.

Once you have settled on an idea, go back to the two questions above and write down your answers to them. Then combine the answers into a single-sentence thesis statement. Your eventual thesis statement does not have to be one sentence, but this exercise can be an effective way of focusing your point.

Consider Your Audience.   What do your readers know? If you're an economics major in an undergraduate writing course, you can safely assume that you know your subject better than most of your readers do, and so you will have to explain even very basic terms and ideas. If, however, you're writing a paper for your course in econometrics, your most important reader—the one who grades your paper—won't even slow down at your references to *monetary aggregates* and *Philips Curves*—provided, of course, that you obviously know what they mean.

Choose a Type of Definition That Fits Your Subject.   How you choose to develop your definition depends on your subject, your purpose, and your readers. Many inexperienced writers believe that any extended definition, no matter what the subject, should begin with a formal "dictionary" definition or should at least introduce one before the essay has proceeded very far. This is not necessarily so; you will find that most of the essays in this chapter include no such formal definition. Assume that your readers have dictionaries and know how to use them. If, however, you think your readers do require a short, formal definition at some point, don't simply quote from a dictionary. Unless you have some very good reason for doing otherwise, put the definition into your own words—words that suit your approach and the probable readers of your essay. (Certainly, in an essay about photosynthesis, nonscientists would be baffled by an opening such as this: "The dictionary defines *photosynthesis* as 'the process by which chlorophyll-containing cells in green plants convert incident light to chemical energy and synthesize organic compounds from inorganic compounds, especially carbohydrates from carbon dioxide and water, with the simultaneous release of oxygen.'") There's another advantage to using your own words: You won't have to write "The dictionary defines . . ." or "According to *Webster's* . . ."; stock phrases like these almost immediately put the reader's mind to sleep.

Certain subjects, such as liberalism and discrimination, lend themselves to different interpretations, depending on the writer's point of view. While readers may agree in general about what such subjects mean, there will be much disagreement over particulars and therefore room for you to propose and defend your own definitions.

Solomon remembers the difficulties he had getting started with his essay on best friends. "The first draft I wrote was nothing. I tried to get a start with the dictionary definition, but it didn't help—it just put into two words what really needs hundreds of words to explain, and the words it used had to be defined, too. My teacher suggested I might get going better if I talked about my topic with other people. I decided to make it semiformal, so I made up a list of a few specific questions— five questions—and went to about a dozen people I knew and asked them. Questions like, 'What qualities do your best friends have?' and 'What are some of the things they've done for you?' And I took notes on the answers. I was surprised when so many of them agreed. It isn't a scientific sampling, but the results helped me get started."

Organizing and Writing Your Essay of Definition

Develop an Organizational Plan.   Once you have gathered all the information you will need for your essay of extended definition, you will want to settle on an organizational plan that suits your purpose and your materials. If you want to show that one definition of *family* is better than others, for example, you might want to lead with the definitions you plan to discard and end with the one you want your readers to accept.

Howard Solomon Jr. can trace several distinct stages that his paper went through before he settled on the plan of organizing his examples around the items on his interview questionnaire. "Doing this paper showed me that writing isn't all that easy. Boy, I went through so many copies—adding some things, taking out some things, reorganizing. At one point half the paper was a definition of friends, so I could contrast them with best friends. That wasn't necessary. Then the personal stuff came in late. In fact, my father died after I'd begun writing the paper, so that paragraph came in almost last of all. On the next-to-last draft everything was there, but it was put together in a sort of random way—not completely random, one idea would lead to the next and then the next—but there was a lot of circling around. My teacher pointed this out and suggested I outline what I'd written and work on the outline. So I tried it, and I saw what the problem was and what I had to do. It was just a matter of getting my examples into the right order, and finally everything clicked into place."

Use Other Rhetorical Strategies to Support Your Definition. Although definition can be used effectively as a separate rhetorical strategy, it is generally used alongside other writing strategies. Photosynthesis, for example, is a natural process, so one logical strategy for defining it would be *process analysis*; readers who know little about biology may better understand photosynthesis if you draw an *analogy* with the eating and breathing of human beings. Common sense is an abstract concept, so its meaning could certainly be *illustrated* with concrete *examples*; in addition, its special nature might emerge more sharply through *comparison and contrast* with other ways of thinking. To define a salt marsh, you might choose a typical marsh and *describe* it. To define economic inflation or a particular disease, you might discuss its *causes and effects*. Solomon builds his essay of definition around the many examples he garnered from his interviews with other students and his own personal experiences. Before you combine strategies, however, consider the purpose of your essay and the tone that you wish to adopt. Only two requirements limit your choice of rhetorical strategy: The strategy must be appropriate to your subject, and it must help you explain your subject's essential nature.

As you read the essays in this chapter, consider all of the writing strategies that the authors have used to support their definitions. How do you think these other strategies have added to or changed the style of the essay? Are there strategies that you might have added or taken out? What strategies, if any, do you think you might use to strengthen your definition essay?

Revising and Editing Your Essay of Definition

Share Your Drafts with Others.   Try sharing the drafts of your essay with other students in your writing class to make sure that your definition works, that it makes its point. Ask them if there are any parts that they do not understand. Have them tell you what they think is the point of your essay. If their answers differ from what you intended, have them indicate the passages that led them to their interpretations so that you can change your text accordingly. To maximize the effectiveness of conferences with your peers, utilize the guidelines presented on pages 27–28. Feedback from these conferences often provides one or more places where you can start revising.

Select Words That Accurately Denote and Connote What You Want to Say. The *denotation* of a word is its literal meaning or dictionary definition. Most of the time you will have no trouble with denotation, but problems can occur when words are close in meaning or sound a lot alike.

accept	v., to receive
except	prep., to exclude
affect	v., to influence
effect	n., the result; v., to produce, bring into existence
anecdote	n., a short narrative
antidote	n., a medicine for countering effects of poison
coarse	adj., rough; crude
course	n., a route, a program of instruction
disinterested	adj., free of self-interest or bias
uninterested	adj., without interest
eminent	adj., outstanding, as in reputation
immanent	adj., remaining within, inherent
imminent	adj., about to happen
principal	n., a school official; in finance, a capital sum; adj., most important
principle	n., a basic law or rule of conduct
than	conj., used in comparisons
then	adv., at that time

Consult your desk dictionary if you are not sure you are using the correct word.

Words have connotative values as well as denotative meanings. *Connotations* are the associations or emotional overtones that words have acquired. For example, the word *hostage* denotes a person who is given or held as security for the fulfillment of certain conditions or terms, but it connotes images of suffering, loneliness, torture, fear, deprivation, starvation, anxiety, and other private images based on our individual associations. Because many words in English are synonyms or have the same meanings — *strength, potency, force,* and *might* all denote "power" — your task as a writer in any given situation is to choose the word with the connotations that best suit your purpose.

Use Specific and Concrete Words. Words can be classified as relatively general or specific, abstract or concrete. *General words* name groups or classes of objects, qualities, or actions. *Specific words* name individual objects, qualities, or actions within a class or group. For examples, *dessert* is more specific than *food,* but more general than *pie.* And *pie* is more general than *blueberry pie.*

Abstract words refer to ideas, concepts, qualities, and conditions — *love, anger, beauty, youth, wisdom, honesty, patriotism,* and *liberty,* for example. *Concrete words,* on the other hand, name things you can see, hear, taste, touch, or smell. *Cornbread, rocking chair, sailboat, nitrogen, computer, rain, horse,* and *coffee* are all concrete words.

General and abstract words generally fail to create in the reader's mind the kind of vivid response that concrete, specific words do. Always question the words you choose. Notice how Jo Goodwin Parker uses concrete, specific diction in the opening sentences of many paragraphs in her essay "What Is Poverty?" to paint a powerful verbal picture of what poverty is:

> Poverty is getting up every morning from a dirt- and illness-stained mattress.
> Poverty is being tired.
> Poverty is dirt.
> Poverty is staying up all night on cold nights to watch the fire, knowing one spark on the newspaper covering the walls means your sleeping children die in flames.

—Jo Goodwin Parker
"What Is Poverty?," pages 376–79

Collectively, these specific and concrete words create a memorable definition of the abstraction *poverty.*

Question Your Own Work While Revising and Editing. Revision is best done by asking yourself key questions about what you have written. Begin by reading, preferably aloud, what you have written. Reading aloud forces you to pay attention to every single word, and you are more likely to catch lapses in the logical flow of thought. After you have read your paper through, answer the following questions for revising and editing, and make the necessary changes.

Questions for Revising and Editing: Definition

1. Have I selected a subject in which there is some controversy or at least a difference of opinion about the definitions of key words?
2. Is the purpose of my definition clearly stated?
3. Have I presented a clear thesis statement?
4. Have I considered my audience? Do I oversimplify material for knowledgeable people or complicate material for beginners?
5. Have I used the types of definitions (*formal definition, synonymous definition, negative definition, etymological definition, stipulative definition,* and *extended definition*) that are most useful in making my point?
6. Is my essay of definition easy to follow? That is, is there a clear organizational principle (chronological or logical, for example)?
7. Have I used other rhetorical strategies—such as illustration, comparison and contrast, and cause and effect analysis—as needed and appropriate to enhance my definition?
8. Does my conclusion stem logically from my thesis statement and purpose?
9. Have I used precise language to convey my meaning? Have I used words that are specific and concrete?
10. Have I avoided errors in grammar, punctuation, and mechanics?

What Is Poverty?

Jo Goodwin Parker

All we know about Jo Goodwin Parker is that when George Henderson, a professor at the University of Oklahoma, was preparing his 1971 book America's Other Children: Public Schools Outside Suburbia, *the following essay was mailed to him from West Virginia under Parker's name. Henderson included Parker's essay in his book, and according to him, the piece was an unpublished speech given in De Land, Florida, on December 27, 1965. Perhaps Parker is, as her essay says, one of the rural poor who eke out a difficult living just beyond view of America's middle-class majority; or perhaps she is a spokesperson for them, writing not from her own experience but from long and sympathetic observation. In either case, her definition of poverty is so detailed and forceful that it conveys, even to those who have never known it, the nature of poverty.*

PREPARING TO READ

What does it mean to you to be poor? What do you see as some of the effects of poverty on people?

You ask me what is poverty? Listen to me. Here I am, dirty, smelly,   1
and with no "proper" underwear on and with the stench of my
rotting teeth near you. I will tell you. Listen to me. Listen without pity.
I cannot use your pity. Listen with understanding. Put yourself in my
dirty, worn out, ill-fitting shoes, and hear me.

Poverty is getting up every morning from a dirt- and illness-stained   2
mattress. The sheets have long since been used for diapers. Poverty is
living in a smell that never leaves. This is a smell of urine, sour milk,
and spoiling food sometimes joined with the strong smell of long-
cooked onions. Onions are cheap. If you have smelled this smell, you
did not know how it came. It is the smell of the outdoor privy. It is the
smell of young children who cannot walk the long dark way in the
night. It is the smell of the mattresses where years of "accidents" have
happened. It is the smell of the milk which has gone sour because the
refrigerator long has not worked, and it costs money to get it fixed. It is
the smell of rotting garbage. I could bury it, but where is the shovel?
Shovels cost money.

Poverty is being tired. I have always been tired. They told me at the   3
hospital when the last baby came that I had chronic anemia caused
from poor diet, a bad case of worms, and that I needed a corrective operation. I listened politely—the poor are always polite. The poor always
listen. They don't say that there is no money for iron pills, or better
food, or worm medicine. The idea of an operation is frightening and
costs so much that, if I had dared, I would have laughed. Who takes care

of my children? Recovery from an operation takes a long time. I have three children. When I left them with "Granny" the last time I had a job, I came home to find the baby covered with fly specks, and a diaper that had not been changed since I left. When the dried diaper came off, bits of my baby's flesh came with it. My other child was playing with a sharp bit of broken glass, and my oldest was playing alone at the edge of a lake. I made twenty-two dollars a week, and a good nursery school costs twenty dollars a week for three children. I quit my job.

Poverty is dirt. You say in your clean clothes coming from your clean house, "Anybody can be clean." Let me explain about housekeeping with no money. For breakfast I give my children grits with no oleo or cornbread without eggs and oleo. This does not use up many dishes. What dishes there are, I wash in cold water and with no soap. Even the cheapest soap has to be saved for the baby's diapers. Look at my hands, so cracked and red. Once I saved for two months to buy a jar of Vaseline for my hands and the baby's diaper rash. When I had saved enough, I went to buy it and the price had gone up two cents. The baby and I suffered on. I have to decide every day if I can bear to put my cracked, sore hands into the cold water and strong soap. But you ask, why not hot water? Fuel costs money. If you have a wood fire it costs money. If you burn electricity, it costs money. Hot water is a luxury. I do not have luxuries. I know you will be surprised when I tell you how young I am. I look so much older. My back has been bent over the wash tubs for so long, I cannot remember when I ever did anything else. Every night I wash every stitch my school age child has on and just hope her clothes will be dry by morning.

Poverty is staying up all night on cold nights to watch the fire, knowing one spark on the newspaper covering the walls means your sleeping children die in flames. In summer poverty is watching gnats and flies devour your baby's tears when he cries. The screens are torn and you pay so little rent you know they will never be fixed. Poverty means insects in your food, in your nose, in your eyes, and crawling over you when you sleep. Poverty is hoping it never rains because diapers won't dry when it rains and soon you are using newspapers. Poverty is seeing your children forever with runny noses. Paper handkerchiefs cost money and all your rags you need for other things. Even more costly are antihistamines. Poverty is cooking without food and cleaning without soap.

Poverty is asking for help. Have you ever had to ask for help, knowing your children will suffer unless you get it? Think about asking for a loan from a relative, if this is the only way you can imagine asking for help. I will tell you how it feels. You find out where the office is that you are supposed to visit. You circle that block four or five times. Thinking of your children, you go in. Everyone is very busy. Finally, someone comes out and you tell her that you need help. That never is the person you need to see. You go see another person, and after spilling the whole shame of your poverty all over the desk between you, you find that this isn't the right office after all—you must repeat the whole process, and it never is any easier at the next place.

You have asked for help, and after all it has a cost. You are again told to wait. You are told why, but you don't really hear because of the red cloud of shame and the rising black cloud of despair.   7

Poverty is remembering. It is remembering quitting school in junior high because "nice" children had been so cruel about my clothes and my smell. The attendance officer came. My mother told him I was pregnant. I wasn't but she thought that I could get a job and help out. I had jobs off and on, but never long enough to learn anything. Mostly I remember being married. I was so young then. I am still young. For a time, we had all the things you have. There was a little house in another town, with hot water and everything. Then my husband lost his job. There was unemployment insurance for a while and what few jobs I could get. Soon, all our nice things were repossessed and we moved back here. I was pregnant then. This house didn't look so bad when we first moved in. Every week it gets worse. Nothing is ever fixed. We now had no money. There were a few odd jobs for my husband, but everything went for food then, as it does now. I don't know how we lived through three years and three babies, but we did. I'll tell you something, after the last baby I destroyed my marriage. It had been a good one, but could you keep on bringing children in this dirt? Did you ever think how much it costs for any kind of birth control? I knew my husband was leaving the day he left, but there were no good-byes between us. I hope he has been able to climb out of this mess somewhere. He never could hope with us to drag him down.   8

That's when I asked for help. When I got it, you know how much it was? It was, and is, seventy-eight dollars a month for the four of us; that is all I ever can get. Now you know why there is no soap, no needles and thread, no hot water, no aspirin, no worm medicine, no hand cream, no shampoo. None of these things forever and ever and ever. So that you can see clearly, I pay twenty dollars a month rent, and most of the rest goes for food. For grits and cornmeal, and rice and milk and beans. I try my best to use only the minimum electricity. If I use more, there is that much less for food.   9

Poverty is looking into a black future. Your children won't play with my boys. They will turn to other boys who steal to get what they want. I can already see them behind the bars of their prison instead of behind the bars of my poverty. Or they will turn to the freedom of alcohol or drugs, and find themselves enslaved. And my daughter? At best, there is for her a life like mine.   10

But you say to me, there are schools. Yes, there are schools. My children have no extra books, no magazines, no extra pencils, or crayons,   11 or paper and the most important of all, they do not have health. They have worms, they have infections, they have pinkeye all summer. They do not sleep well on the floor, or with me in my one bed. They do not suffer from hunger, my seventy-eight dollars keeps us alive, but they do suffer from malnutrition. Oh yes, I do remember what I was taught about health in school. It doesn't do much good. In some places there is a surplus commodities program. Not here. The county said it cost too much. There is a school lunch program. But I have two children who will already be damaged by the time they get to school.

But, you say to me, there are health clinics. Yes, there are health clinics and they are in the towns. I live out here eight miles from town. I can walk that far (even if it is sixteen miles both ways), but can my little children? My neighbor will take me when he goes; but he expects to get paid, *one way or another.* I bet you know my neighbor. He is that large man who spends his time at the gas station, the barbershop, and the corner store complaining about the government spending money on the immoral mothers of illegitimate children.

Poverty is an acid that drips on pride until all pride is worn away. Poverty is a chisel that chips on honor until honor is worn away. Some of you say that you would do *something* in my situation, and maybe you would, for the first week or the first month, but for year after year after year?

Even the poor can dream. A dream of a time when there is money. Money for the right kinds of food, for worm medicine, for iron pills, for toothbrushes, for hand cream, for a hammer and nails and a bit of screening, for a shovel, for a bit of paint, for some sheeting, for needles and thread. Money to pay *in money* for a trip to town. And, oh, money for hot water and money for soap. A dream of when asking for help does not eat away the last bit of pride. When the office you visit is as nice as the offices of other governmental agencies, when there are enough workers to help you quickly, when workers do not quit in defeat and despair. When you have to tell your story to only one person, and that person can send you for other help and you don't have to prove your poverty over and over and over again.

I have come out of my despair to tell you this. Remember I did not come from another place or another time. Others like me are all around you. Look at us with an angry heart, anger that will help you help me. Anger that will let you tell of me. The poor are always silent. Can you be silent too?

THINKING CRITICALLY ABOUT THE TEXT

Throughout the essay, Parker describes the feelings and emotions associated with her poverty. Have you ever witnessed or observed people in Parker's situation? What was your reaction?

QUESTIONS ON SUBJECT

1. Why didn't Parker have the operation that was recommended for her? Why did she quit her job?

2. In Parker's view, what makes asking for help such a difficult and painful experience? What compels her to do so anyway?

3. Why did Parker's husband leave her? How does she justify her attitude toward his leaving? (Glossary: *Attitude*)

4. In paragraph 12, Parker says the following about a neighbor giving her a ride to the nearest health clinic: "My neighbor will take me when he goes; but he expects to get paid, *one way or another.* I bet you know my neighbor." What is she implying in these sentences and in the rest of the paragraph?

5. What are the chances that the dreams described in paragraph 14 will come true? What do you think Parker would say?

QUESTIONS ON STRATEGY

1. What is Parker's purpose in defining poverty as she does? (Glossary: *Purpose*) Why has she cast her essay in the form of an extended definition? What effect does this have on the reader?

2. What techniques of definition does Parker use? What is missing that you would expect to find in a more general and impersonal definition of poverty? Why does Parker leave such information out?

3. Parker repeats words and phrases throughout this essay. Choose several examples, and explain their impact on you. (Glossary: *Coherence*)

4. In depicting poverty, Parker uses description to create vivid verbal pictures, and she illustrates the various aspects of poverty with examples drawn from her experience. (Glossary: *Description; Illustration*) What are the most striking details she uses? How do you account for the emotional impact of the details and images she has selected? In what ways do description and illustration enhance her definition of poverty?

QUESTIONS ON DICTION AND VOCABULARY

1. Although her essay is written for the most part in simple, straightforward language, Parker does make use of an occasional striking figure of speech. (Glossary: *Figures of Speech*) Identify at least three such figures—you might begin with those in paragraph 13 (for example, "Poverty is an acid")—and explain their effect on the reader.

2. In paragraph 10, Parker states that "poverty is looking into a black future." How does she use language to characterize her children's future?

3. How would you characterize Parker's tone and her style? (Glossary: *Style; Tone*) How do you respond to her use of the pronoun *you*? Point to specific examples of her diction and descriptions as support for your view. (Glossary: *Diction*)

4. Refer to your desk dictionary to determine the meanings of the following words as Parker uses them in this selection: *chronic* (paragraph 3), *anemia* (3), *grits* (4), *oleo* (4), *antihistamines* (5).

CLASSROOM ACTIVITY USING DEFINITION

Without consulting a dictionary, try writing a formal definition for one of the following terms by putting it in a class and then differentiating it from other words in the class. See page 360 for a discussion of formal definitions together with examples.

tortilla chips	trombone
psychology	*American Idol*
robin	Catholicism
anger	secretary

Once you have completed your definition, compare it with the definition found in a dictionary. What conclusions can you draw? Explain.

WRITING SUGGESTIONS

1. Using Parker's essay as a model, write an extended definition of a topic about which you have some expertise. Choose as your subject a particular environment (suburbia, the inner city, a dormitory, a shared living area), a way of living (the child of divorce, the physically handicapped, the working student), or a topic of your own choosing. If you prefer, you can adopt a persona instead of writing from your own perspective.

2. Write a proposal or a plan of action that would make people aware of poverty or some other social problem in your community. What is the problem? What needs to be done to increase awareness? What practical steps would you propose be undertaken once the public is made aware of the situation?

Caring for Your Introvert

Jonathan Rauch

Jonathan Rauch was born in 1960 in Phoenix, Arizona. He earned his B.A. at Yale University in 1982 and then took a job as an education reporter for the Winston-Salem Journal *in North Carolina. He later moved to Washington, D.C., to work for the* National Journal, *where he continues as a columnist and contributing editor. In addition, he is a correspondent for the* Atlantic Monthly *and a writer-in-residence at the Brookings Institution. His books include* The Outnation: A Search for the Soul of Japan *(1992),* Kindly Inquisitors: The New Attacks on Free Thought *(1993),* Demosclerosis: The Silent Killer of American Government *(1994),* Government's End: Why Washington Stopped Working *(1999), and most recently* Gay Marriage: Why It Is Good for Gays, Good for Straights, and Good for America *(2003). Rauch is a frequent contributor to the* Los Angeles Times, *the* New York Times, *and the* Washington Post.

First published in the March 2003 issue of the Atlantic Monthly, *"Caring for Your Introvert" explores the habits and needs of a little-understood group— introverts. Notice how Rauch uses both illustration and comparison and contrast as he develops his definition.*

PREPARING TO READ

What do you think of when you hear the words *introvert* and *extrovert*? Make a list of five or six characteristics that come to mind for each personality type. Compare your lists with those of others in your class.

Do you know someone who needs hours alone every day? Who loves quiet conversations about feelings or ideas, and can give a dynamite presentation to a big audience, but seems awkward in groups and maladroit at small talk? Who has to be dragged to parties and then needs the rest of the day to recuperate? Who growls or scowls or grunts or winces when accosted with pleasantries by people who are just trying to be nice?

If so, do you tell this person he is "too serious," or ask if he is okay? Regard him as aloof, arrogant, rude? Redouble your efforts to draw him out?

If you answered yes to these questions, chances are that you have an introvert on your hands—and that you aren't caring for him properly. Science has learned a good deal in recent years about the habits and requirements of introverts. It has even learned, by means of brain scans, that introverts process information differently from other people (I am not making this up). If you are behind the curve on this important matter, be reassured that you are not alone. Introverts may be common, but they are also among the most misunderstood and aggrieved groups in America, possibly the world.

I know. My name is Jonathan, and I am an introvert.   4

Oh, for years I denied it. After all, I have good social skills. I am not   5 morose or misanthropic. Usually, I am far from shy. I love long conversations that explore intimate thoughts or passionate interests. But at last I have self-identified and come out to my friends and colleagues. In doing so, I have found myself liberated from any number of damaging misconceptions and stereotypes. Now I am here to tell you what you need to know in order to respond sensitively and supportively to your own introverted family members, friends, and colleagues. Remember, someone you know, respect, and interact with every day is an introvert, and you are probably driving this person nuts. It pays to learn the warning signs.

What is introversion? In its modern sense, the concept goes back to   6 the 1920s and the psychologist Carl Jung. Today it is a mainstay of personality tests, including the widely used Myers-Briggs Type Indicator. Introverts are not necessarily shy. Shy people are anxious or frightened or self-excoriating in social settings; introverts generally are not. Introverts are also not misanthropic, though some of us do go along with Sartre as far as to say "Hell is other people at breakfast." Rather, introverts are people who find other people tiring.

Extroverts are energized by people, and wilt or fade when alone.   7 They often seem bored by themselves, in both senses of the expression. Leave an extrovert alone for two minutes and he will reach for his cell phone. In contrast, after an hour or two of being socially "on," we introverts need to turn off and recharge. My own formula is roughly two hours alone for every hour of socializing. This isn't antisocial. It isn't a sign of depression. It does not call for medication. For introverts, to be alone with our thoughts is as restorative as sleeping as nourishing as eating. Our motto: "I'm okay, you're okay—in small doses."

How many people are introverts? I performed exhaustive   8 research on this question, in the form of a quick Google search. The answer: About 25 percent. Or: Just under half. Or—my favorite— "a minority in the regular population but a majority in the gifted population."

Are introverts misunderstood? Wildly. That, it appears, is our lot in   9 life. "It is very difficult for an extrovert to understand an introvert," write the education experts Jill D. Burruss and Lisa Kaenzig. (They are also the source of the quotation in the previous paragraph.) Extroverts are easy for introverts to understand, because extroverts spend so much of their time working out who they are in voluble, and frequently inescapable, interaction with other people. They are as inscrutable as puppy dogs. But the street does not run both ways. Extroverts have little or no grasp of introversion. They assume that company, especially their own, is always welcome. They cannot imagine why someone would need to be alone; indeed, they often take umbrage at the suggestion. As often as I have tried to explain the matter to extroverts, I have never sensed that any of them really understood. They listen for a moment and then go back to barking and yipping.

Are introverts oppressed? I would have to say so. For one thing, extroverts are overrepresented in politics, a profession in which only the garrulous are really comfortable. Look at George W. Bush. Look at Bill Clinton. They seem to come fully to life only around other people. To think of the few introverts who did rise to the top in politics — Calvin Coolidge, Richard Nixon — is merely to drive home the point. With the possible exception of Ronald Reagan, whose fabled aloofness and privateness were probably signs of a deep introverted streak (many actors, I've read, are introverts, and many introverts, when socializing, feel like actors), introverts are not considered "naturals" in politics.

Extroverts therefore dominate public life. This is a pity. If we introverts ran the world, it would no doubt be a calmer, saner, more peaceful sort of place. As Coolidge is supposed to have said, "Don't you know that four fifths of all our troubles in this life would disappear if we would just sit down and keep still?" (He is also supposed to have said, "If you don't say anything, you won't be called on to repeat it." The only thing a true introvert dislikes more than talking about himself is repeating himself.)

With their endless appetite for talk and attention, extroverts also dominate social life, so they tend to set expectations. In our extrovertist society, being outgoing is considered normal and therefore desirable, a mark of happiness, confidence, leadership. Extroverts are seen as big-hearted, vibrant, warm, empathic. "People person" is a compliment. Introverts are described with words like "guarded," "loner," "reserved," "taciturn," "self-contained," "private" — narrow, ungenerous words, words that suggest emotional parsimony and smallness of personality. Female introverts, I suspect, must suffer especially. In certain circles, particularly in the Midwest, a man can still sometimes get away with being what they used to call a strong and silent type; introverted women, lacking that alternative, are even more likely than men to be perceived as timid, withdrawn, haughty.

Are introverts arrogant? Hardly. I suppose this common misconception has to do with our being more intelligent, more reflective, more independent, more level-headed, more refined, and more sensitive than extroverts. Also, it is probably due to our lack of small talk, a lack that extroverts often mistake for disclaim. We tend to think before talking, whereas extroverts tend to think *by* talking, which is why their meetings never last less than six hours. "Introverts," writes a perceptive fellow named Thomas P. Crouser, in an online review of a recent book

10

11

12

13

called *Why Should Extroverts Make All the Money?* (I'm not making *that* up, either), "are driven to distraction by the semi-internal dialogue extroverts tend to conduct. Introverts don't outwardly complain, instead roll their eyes and silently curse the darkness." Just so.

The worst of it is that extroverts have no idea of the torment they 14 put us through. Sometimes, as we gasp for air amid the fog of their 98-percent-content-free talk, we wonder if extroverts even bother to listen to themselves. Still, we endure stoically, because the etiquette books — written, no doubt, by extroverts — regard declining to banter as rude and gaps in conversation as awkward. We can only dream that someday, when our condition is more widely understood, when perhaps an Introverts' Rights movement has blossomed and borne fruit, it will not be impolite to say "I'm an introvert. You are a wonderful person and I like you. But now please shush."

How can I let the introvert in my life know that I support him and 15 respect his choice? First, recognize that it's not a choice. It's not a lifestyle. It's an *orientation*.

Second, when you see an introvert lost in thought, don't say 16 "What's the matter?" or "Are you all right?"

Third, don't say anything else, either. 17

THINKING CRITICALLY ABOUT THE TEXT

In paragraph 12 Rauch states that "in our extrovertist society, being outgoing is considered normal and therefore desirable, a mark of happiness, confidence, leadership." Do you agree with Rauch's assessment? Do you think that if "introverts ran the world, it would no doubt be a calmer, saner, more peaceful sort of place"(11)? Explain.

QUESTIONS ON SUBJECT

1. According to Rauch, what is an introvert? What is an extrovert?

2. In paragraph 4, Rauch announces that he is an introvert. Why do think he "denied it" for so long? What has he gained by having "self-identified and come out to my friends and colleagues"(5)?

3. According to Rauch, why are introverts so misunderstood? How does he dispel the misconception that introverts are arrogant? What does he mean when he says that introversion is "an *orientation*"(paragraph 15)?

4. Why do introverts find it so easy to understand extroverts, according to Rauch?

5. Why does Rauch think female introverts must suffer more than their male counterparts?

6. What advice does Rauch offer for dealing with the introvert in your life?

QUESTIONS ON STRATEGY

1. Rauch begins his essay with a series of questions. Did you find this beginning effective? (Glossary: *Beginnings*) Why or why not? In what ways do these questions help Rauch define *introvert*? Explain.

2. What is Rauch's purpose in this essay? Where does Rauch state his purpose? (Glossary: *Purpose*)

3. How has Rauch organized his essay? In what ways is this organizational plan related to his purpose? Explain.

4. In paragraph six, Rauch uses negative definition to explain what introverts are not. What other types of definition does he use to explain the meaning of *introvert*?

5. How does Rauch use the strategy of comparison and contrast to sharpen his definition of *introvert*?

QUESTIONS ON DICTION AND VOCABULARY

1. What does Rauch mean when he uses the simile "as inscrutable as puppy dogs" (paragraph 9) to describe extroverts? In what ways is their talk just so much "barking and yipping"(9)?

2. Rauch claims that "words that suggest emotional parsimony and smallness of personality" are used to describe introverts. What words can you add to the list of introvert descriptors he gives in paragraph 12? What connotations do these words share? (Glossary: *Connotations*)

3. What is Rauch's tone in this essay? (Glossary: *Tone*) Cite examples of his diction that led you to this conclusion.

4. Be sure that you know the meanings of these words as Rauch uses them in his essay: *maladroit* (paragraph 1), *winces* (1), *accosted* (1), *aggrieved* (3), *morose* (5), *misanthropic* (5), *self-excoriating* (6), *umbrage* (9), *haughty* (12), *stoically* (14).

CLASSROOM ACTIVITY USING DEFINITION

One way to approach definition is through negative definition— explaining a word or phrase by what it does not mean. For example, in paragraph 6 notice how Rauch uses negative definition to eliminate several popular misconceptions about introverts and thus clarify his statement about what they are— "introverts are people who find other people tiring." Try your hand at negative definition, using one or more of the following words. Be sure that when you specify what something is not, you help clarify what it is.

freedom	patriotism
marriage	trust
friendship	secret
loyalty	lie

WRITING SUGGESTIONS

1. In paragraph 11, Rauch bemoans the fact that "extroverts . . . dominate public life." He believes that "if we introverts ran the world, it would no doubt be a calmer, saner, more peaceful sort of place." From your own experience in school and local town living, do you think he is right? What examples do you have that either support or refute his claim? What do you think would happen if introverts ran your student or local town government? Write an essay in which you explore Rauch's idea, using specifics from your own experience, observation, or reading.

2. Other interesting personality types include the procrastinator, workaholic, obsessive-compulsive, liar, and addict. Write an essay modeled on Rauch's that uses a series of thoughtful questions to help you explain the defining characteristics for one of these interesting personality types or for one of your own choosing.

Steal This MP3 File: What Is Theft?

G. Anthony Gorry

G. Anthony Gorry is a medical educator and information technology specialist. He received his B.S. from Yale University in 1962 and pursued graduate study at the University of California–Berkeley, where he earned his M.S. in 1964, and at MIT, where he received his Ph.D. in 1967. Gorry has taught at Baylor College of Medicine and is currently a professor of management and computer science at Rice University. He is the author of numerous journal articles on management information systems and problem identification.

In the following article, which first appeared in the Chronicle of Higher Education *on May 23, 2003, Gorry recounts an experience he had in one of his information technology courses to demonstrate how technology might be shaping the attitude of today's youth. He senses that the meaning of theft may be shifting in our ever-changing world.*

PREPARING TO READ

What for you constitutes theft? Do you recall ever stealing anything? Did you get caught? Did you have to return the item or make restitution? How did you feel about the incident at the time? How do you feel about it now?

Sometimes when my students don't see life the way I do, I recall the   1
complaint from *Bye Bye Birdie*, "What's the matter with kids today?"
Then I remember that the "kids" in my class are children of the information age. In large part, technology has made them what they are, shaping their world and what they know. For my students, the advance of technology is expected, but for me, it remains both remarkable and somewhat unsettling.

In one course I teach, the students and I explore the effects of infor-   2
mation technology on society. Our different perspectives on technology lead to engaging and challenging discussions that reveal some of the ways in which technology is shaping the attitudes of young people. An example is our discussion of intellectual property in the information age, of crucial importance to the entertainment business.

In recent years, many users of the Internet have launched an   3
assault on the music business. Armed with tools for "ripping" music from compact discs and setting it "free" in cyberspace, they can disseminate online countless copies of a digitally encoded song. Music companies, along with some artists, have tried to stop this perceived pillaging of intellectual property by legal and technical means. The industry has had some success with legal actions against companies that provide the

infrastructure for file sharing, but enthusiasm for sharing music is growing, and new file-sharing services continue to appear.

The Recording Industry Association of America recently filed law-   4
suits against four college students, seeking huge damages for "an emporium of music piracy" run on campus networks. However, the industry
settled those lawsuits less than a week after a federal judge in California
ruled against the association in another case, affirming that two of the
Internet's most popular music-swapping services are not responsible for
copyright infringements by their users. (In the settlement, the students
admitted no wrongdoing but agreed to pay amounts ranging from
$12,000 to $17,500 in annual installments over several years and to
shut down their file-sharing systems.)

With so many Internet users currently sharing music, legal maneu-   5
vers alone seem unlikely to protect the industry's way of doing business. Therefore, the music industry has turned to the technology itself,
seeking to create media that cannot be copied or can be copied only
in prescribed circumstances. Finding the right technology for such a
defense, however, is not easy. Defensive technology must not prevent
legitimate uses of the media by customers, yet it must somehow ward
off attacks by those seeking to "liberate" the content to the Internet.
And each announcement of a defensive technology spurs development
of means to circumvent it.

In apparent frustration, some companies have introduced defective   6
copies of their music into the file-sharing environment of the Internet,
hoping to discourage widespread downloading of music. But so far, the
industry's multifaceted defense has failed. Sales of CDs continue to
decline. And now video ripping and sharing is emerging on the Internet, threatening to upset another industry in the same way.

Music companies might have more success if they focused on the   7
users instead of the courts and technology. When they characterize file
sharing as theft, they overlook the interplay of technology and behavior that has altered the very idea of theft, at least among young people.
I got a clear demonstration of that change in a class discussion that
began with the matter of a stolen book.

During the '60s, I was a graduate student at a university where   8
student activism had raised tensions on and around the campus. In
the midst of debates, demonstrations, and protests, a football player
was caught leaving the campus store with a book he had not bought.
Because he was well known, his misadventure made the school newspaper. What seemed to be a simple case of theft, however, took on
greater significance. A number of groups with little connection to ath-
letics rose to his defense, claiming that he had been entrapped: The
university required that he have the book, the publisher charged an
unfairly high price, and the bookstore put the book right in front of
him, tempting him to steal it. So who could blame him?

Well, my students could. They thought it was clear that he had 9
stolen the book. But an MP3 file played from my laptop evoked a different response. Had I stolen the song? Not really, because a student had
given me the file as a gift. Well, was that file stolen property? Was it like
the book stolen from the campus bookstore so many years ago? No
again, because it was a copy, not the original, which presumably was
with the student. But then what should we make of the typical admonition on compact-disc covers that unauthorized duplication is illegal?
Surely the MP3 file was a duplication of the original. To what extent is
copying stealing?

The readings for the class amply demonstrated the complexity of 10
the legal, technical, and economic issues surrounding intellectual
property in the information age and gave the students much to talk
about. Some students argued that existing regulations are simply inadequate at a time when all information "wants to be free" and when liberating technology is at hand. Others pointed to differences in the
economics of the music and book businesses. In the end, the students
who saw theft in the removal of the book back in the '60s did not see
stealing in the unauthorized copying of music. For me, that was the
most memorable aspect of the class because it illustrates how technology affects what we take to be moral behavior.

The technology of copying is closely related to the idea of theft. For 11
example, my students would not take books from a store, but they do
not consider photocopying a few pages of a book to be theft. They
would not copy an entire book, however, perhaps because they vaguely
acknowledge intellectual-property rights but probably more because
copying would be cumbersome and time-consuming. They would buy
the book instead. In that case, the very awkwardness of the copying
aligns their actions with moral guidelines and legal standards.

But in the case of digital music, where the material is disconnected 12
from the physical moorings of conventional stores and copying is so
easy, many of my students see matters differently. They freely copy and
share music. And they copy and share software, even though such copying is often illegal. If their books were digital and thus could be copied
with comparable ease, they most likely would copy and share them.

Of course, the Digital Millennium Copyright Act, along with other 13
laws, prohibits such copying. So we could just say that theft is theft,
and complain with the song, "Why can't they be like we were, perfect
in every way? . . . Oh, what's the matter with kids today?" But had we
had the same digital technology when we were young, we probably
would have engaged in the same copying and sharing of software, digital music, and video that are so common among students today. We
should not confuse lack of tools with righteousness.

The music industry would be foolish to put its faith in new protec- 14
tive schemes and devices alone. Protective technology cannot undo the

changes that previous technology has caused. Should the industry aggressively pursue legal defenses like the suits against the four college students? Such highly publicized actions may be legally sound and may even slow music sharing in certain settings, but they cannot stop the transformation of the music business. The technology of sharing is too widespread, and my students (and their younger siblings) no longer agree with the music companies about right and wrong. Even some of the companies with big stakes in recorded music seem to have recognized that lawsuits and technical defenses won't work. Sony, for example, sells computers with "ripping and burning" capabilities, MP3 players, and other devices that gain much of their appeal from music sharing. And the AOL part of AOL Time Warner is promoting its new broadband service for faster downloads, which many people will use to share music sold by the Warner part of the company.

The lesson from my classroom is that digital technology has unal- 15 terably changed the way a growing number of customers think about recorded music. If the music industry is to prosper, it must change, too — perhaps offering repositories of digital music for downloading (like Apple's newly announced iTunes Music Store), gaining revenue from the scope and quality of its holdings, and from a variety of new products and relationships, as yet largely undefined. Such a transformation will be excruciating for the industry, requiring the abandonment of previously profitable business practices with no certain prospect of success. So it is not surprising that the industry has responded aggressively, with strong legal actions, to the spread of file sharing. But by that response, the industry is risking its relationship with a vital segment of its market. Treating customers like thieves is a certain recipe for failure.

THINKING CRITICALLY ABOUT THE TEXT

Where do you stand on file sharing? Like Gorry's students, do you freely copy and share music or software? Do you consider all such sharing acceptable, or is there some point where it turns into theft? Explain.

QUESTIONS ON SUBJECT

1. What is intellectual property, and how is it different from other types of property?
2. How has the music industry tried to stop "music piracy" on the Internet? What has been the success of their efforts?
3. Do you think the football player caught leaving the campus store with a book was guilty of stealing, or are you persuaded by the argument that "he had been entrapped" (paragraph 8)? Explain.
4. What does Gorry mean when he says that "the technology of copying is closely related to the idea of theft" (11)?

5. What advice do Gorry and his students have for the music industry? Is this advice realistic? Explain. What suggestions would you like to add?

QUESTIONS ON STRATEGY

1. What is Gorry's thesis, and where is it stated? (Glossary: *Thesis*)

2. Gorry's purpose is to show that there has recently been a shift in what the Internet generation believes constitutes theft. (Glossary: *Purpose*) How well does he accomplish his purpose?

3. What examples does Gorry use to develop his definition of theft? (Glossary: *Illustration*) How does he use these examples to illustrate the shift in meaning that he believes has occurred?

4. With what authority does Gorry write on the subjects of intellectual property, technology, and theft?

5. Gorry uses lyrics from the movie *Bye Bye Birdie* to introduce his essay and start his conclusion. (Glossary: *Beginnings/Endings*) Are these just gimmicky quotations or do they contribute to the substance of Gorry's essay?

6. Gorry ends paragraph 8 with the question "So who could blame him?" and then begins paragraph 9 with the response "Well, my students could," thus making a smooth transition from one paragraph to the next. (Glossary: *Transitions*) What other transitional devices does Gorry use to add coherence to his essay? (Glossary: *Coherence*)

QUESTIONS ON DICTION AND VOCABULARY

1. Who is Gorry's intended audience? (Glossary: *Audience*) To whom does the pronoun *we* in paragraph 13 refer? What other evidence in Gorry's diction do you find to support your conclusion about his audience?

2. How would you describe Gorry's diction—formal, objective, conversational, jargon-filled? (Glossary: *Technical Language*) Point out specific words and phrases that led you to this conclusion.

3. Refer to your desk dictionary to determine the meanings of the following words as Gorry uses them in this selection: *disseminate* (paragraph 3), *encoded* (3), *emporium* (4), *infringements* (4), *repositories* (15).

CLASSROOM ACTIVITY USING DEFINITION

Definitions are often dependent on one's perspective, as Gorry illustrates with the word *theft* in his essay. Discuss with your classmates other words or terms—such as *success, failure, wealth, poverty, cheap, expensive, happiness, loneliness, want, need*—whose definitions often are dependent on one's perspective. Write brief definitions for several of these words from your perspective. Share your definitions with other members of your class. What perspective differences, if any, are apparent in the definitions?

WRITING SUGGESTIONS

1. Although it is not always immediately apparent, English is constantly changing because it is a living language. New words come into the lexicon, and others become obsolete. Some words like *theft* change over time to reflect society's thinking and behavior. Another word whose definition has ignited recent debate is *marriage*. Using Gorry's essay as a model, write a paper in which you define a word whose meaning has changed over the past decade.

2. Gorry is very aware of how information technology is shaping our attitudes about the world. We're living at a time when digital technology makes it not only possible but also surprisingly easy for us to copy and share software, music, and video. Gorry does not condemn such behavior out of hand; instead, he warns that "we should not confuse lack of tools with righteousness" (paragraph 13). Write an essay in which you explore some of the ways today's technology has shaped your attitudes, especially as it "affects what we take to be moral behavior" (10). Be sure to support your key points with examples from your own reading or experience. (Glossary: *Illustration*)

Ain't I a Woman?

Sojourner Truth

 *Sojourner Truth was born a slave named Isabella in Ulster County, New York, in 1797. After her escape from slavery in 1827, she went to New York City and underwent a profound religious transformation. She worked as a domestic servant, and as an evangelist she tried to reform prostitutes. Adopting the name Sojourner Truth in 1843, she became a travel- ing preacher and abolitionist, frequently appearing with Frederick Douglass. Although she never learned to write, Truth's compelling presence gripped her audience as she spoke eloquently about emancipation and women's rights. After the Civil War and until her death in 1883, she worked to provide education and employment for emancipated slaves.*

At the Women's Rights Convention in Akron, Ohio, in May 1851, Truth extemporaneously delivered the following speech, as transcribed by Elizabeth Cady Stanton, to a nearly all-white audience.

PREPARING TO READ

What comes to mind when you hear the word *speech*? Have you ever attended a rally or convention and heard speeches given on behalf of a social cause or political issue? What were your impressions of the speakers and their speeches?

Well, children, where there is so much racket there must be some- 1 thing out of kilter. I think that 'twixt the Negroes of the South and the women of the North, all talking about rights, the white men will be in a fix pretty soon. But what's all this here talking about?

That man over there says that women need to be helped into car- 2 riages, and lifted over ditches, and to have the best place everywhere. Nobody ever helps me into carriages, or over mud-puddles, or gives me any best place! And ain't I a woman? Look at me! Look at my arm! I have ploughed and planted, and gathered into barns, and no man could head me! And ain't I a woman? I could work as much and eat as much as a man—when I could get it—and bear the lash as well! And ain't I a woman? I have borne thirteen children, and seen them most all sold off to slavery, and when I cried out with my mother's grief, none but Jesus heard me! And ain't I a woman?

Then they talk about this thing in the head; what's this they call it? 3 [Intellect, someone whispers.] That's it, honey. What's that got to do with women's rights or negro's rights? If my cup won't hold but a pint, and yours holds a quart, wouldn't you be mean not to let me have my little half-measure full?

Then that little man in black there, he says women can't have as 4
much rights as men, 'cause Christ wasn't a woman! Where did your
Christ come from? Where did your Christ come from? From God and a
woman! Man had nothing to do with Him.

If the first woman God ever made was strong enough to turn the 5
world upside down all alone, these women together ought to be able to
turn it back, and get it right side up again! And now they is asking to do
it, the men better let them.

Obliged to you for hearing me, and now old Sojourner ain't got 6
nothing more to say.

THINKING CRITICALLY ABOUT THE TEXT

What are your immediate impressions of Truth's speech? Now take a minute
to read her speech again, this time aloud. What are your impressions now?
Are they different, and if so, how and why? What aspects of her speech are
memorable?

QUESTIONS ON SUBJECT

1. What does Truth mean when she says, "Where there is so much racket there must be something out of kilter" (paragraph 1)? Why does Truth believe that white men are going to find themselves in a "fix" (1)?

2. What does Truth put forth as her "credentials" as a woman?

3. How does Truth counter the argument that "women can't have as much rights as men, 'cause Christ wasn't a woman" (paragraph 4)?

QUESTIONS ON STRATEGY

1. What is Truth's purpose in this essay? (Glossary: *Purpose*) Why is it important for her to define what a woman is for her audience? (Glossary: *Audience*)

2. How does Truth use the comments of "that man over there" (paragraph 2) and "that little man in black" (4) to help her establish her definition of *woman*?

3. What, for you, is the effect of Truth's repetition of the question "And ain't I a woman?" four times? (Glossary: *Rhetorical Question*) What other questions does she ask? Why do you suppose Truth doesn't provide answers to the questions in paragraph 3, but does for the question in paragraph 4?

4. How would you characterize Truth's tone in this speech? (Glossary: *Tone*) What phrases in the speech suggest that tone to you?

5. Explain how Truth uses comparison and contrast to help establish her definition of *woman*, especially in paragraph 2. (Glossary: *Comparison and Contrast*)

QUESTIONS ON DICTION AND VOCABULARY

1. How would you describe Truth's diction in this speech? What does her diction reveal about her character and background?

2. Refer to your desk dictionary to determine the meanings of the following words as Truth uses them in this selection: *kilter* (paragraph 1), *ditches* (2), *intellect* (3), *obliged* (6).

CLASSROOM ACTIVITY USING DEFINITION

In a letter to the editor of the *New York Times*, Nancy Stevens, president of a small New York City advertising agency, argues against using the word *guys* to address women. She believes that the "use of *guy* to mean 'person' is so insidious that I'll bet most women don't notice they are being called 'guys,' or, if they do, find it somehow flattering to be one of them." Do you find such usage objectionable? Why or why not? How is the use of *guy* to mean "person" different from using *gal* to mean "person"? How do you think Truth would react to the use of the word *guys* to refer to women? What light does your dictionary shed on this issue of definition?

WRITING SUGGESTIONS

1. Sojourner Truth spoke out against the injustice she saw around her. In arguing for the rights of women, she found it helpful to define *woman* in order to make her point. What social cause do you find most compelling today? Human rights? AIDS awareness? Domestic abuse? Alcoholism? Gay marriage? Racism? Select an issue about which you have strong feelings. Now carefully identify all key terms that you must define before arguing your position. Write an essay in which you use definition to make your point convincingly.

2. Sojourner Truth's speech holds out hope for the future. She envisions a future in which women join together to take charge and "turn [the world] back, and get it right side up again" (paragraph 5). What she envisioned has, to some extent, come to pass. For example, today the distinction between "women's work" and "men's work" has blurred or even vanished in some fields. Write an essay in which you speculate about how Truth would react to the world as we know it, and, more specifically, to the world depicted in the photograph on page 395. What do you think would please her? What would disappoint her? What do you think she would want to change about our society? Explain your reasoning.

What Is the Quarterlife Crisis?

Alexandra Robbins and Abby Wilner

Childhood friends and classmates at Walt Whitman High School in Bethesda, Maryland, Alexandra Robbins and Abby Wilner were both born in 1976. Robbins studied at Yale University and Wilner at Washington University of St. Louis, and soon after graduating they joined forces on Quarterlife Crisis: The Unique Challenges of Life in Your Twenties *(2001), a book that draws heavily on the interviews that Wilner had with over two hundred recent college graduates as well as on their own experiences in the first years after college. The book's message resonated with America's twentysomethings, and Robbins and Wilner soon found themselves on the talk show circuit, appearing on* The Oprah Winfrey Show *and* Today, *among others. Wilner co-authored* Quarterlifer's Companion *(2005) with Catherine Stocker, and together they administer a quarterlife crisis Web site and conduct workshops and seminars on this topic throughout the United States. Since 2001 Robbins has authored three books that investigate modern college life and its more sordid aspects:* Secrets of the Tomb: Skull and Bones, the Ivy League, and the Hidden Paths of Power *(2002),* Pledged: The Secret Life of Sororities *(2004), and* The Overachievers: The Secret Lives of Driven Kids *(2006). Robbins and Wilner currently live in Washington, D.C.*

In the following selection, the first chapter from the book Quarterlife Crisis, *Robbins and Wilner identify a new phenomenon — the quarterlife crisis — define it, and explain why we need to understand its causes and sometimes devastating effects.*

PREPARING TO READ

What do you see yourself doing five years after graduation from college? How did you arrive at this choice? What other career choices are you still considering? Do you have any concerns about what might be in store for you after graduation? If so, what are they?

Jim, the neighbor who lives in the three-story colonial down the block, has recently turned 50. You know this because Jim's wife threw him a surprise party about a month ago. You also know this because, since then, Jim has dyed his hair blond, purchased a leather bomber jacket, traded in his Chevy Suburban for a sleek Miata, and ditched the wife for a girlfriend half her size and age. 1

Yet, aside from the local ladies' group's sympathetic clucks for the scorned wife, few neighbors are surprised at Jim's instant lifestyle change. Instead, they nod their heads understandingly. "Oh, Jim," they say. "He's just going through a midlife crisis. Everyone goes through it." Friends, colleagues, and family members excuse his weird behavior as 2 an inevitable effect of reaching this particular stage of life. Like millions of other middle-aged people, Jim has reached a period during which he believes he must ponder the direction of his life—and then alter it.

Chances are . . . you're not Jim. You know this because you can't   3
afford a leather bomber jacket, you drive your parents' Volvo (if you drive a car at all), and, regardless of your gender, you would happily marry Jim's wife if she gets to keep the house. But Jim's midlife crisis is relevant to you nonetheless, because it is currently the only age-related crisis that is widely recognized as a common, inevitable part of life. This is pertinent because, despite all of the attention lavished on the midlife crisis, despite the hundreds of books, movies, and magazine articles dedicated to explaining the sometimes traumatic transition through middle age and the ways to cope with it, the midlife crisis is not the only age-related crisis that we experience. As Yoda whispered to Luke Skywalker, "There is another."

This other crisis can be just as, if not more, devastating than the   4
midlife crisis. It can throw someone's life into chaotic disarray or para-lyze it completely. It may be the single most concentrated period during which individuals relentlessly question their future and how it will follow the events of their past. It covers the interval that encompasses the transition from the academic world to the "real" world—an age group that can range from late adolescence to the mid-thirties but is usually most intense in twentysomethings. It is what we call the quar-terlife crisis, and it is a real phenomenon.

The quarterlife crisis and the midlife crisis stem from the same   5
basic problem, but the resulting panic couldn't be more opposite. At their cores, both the quarterlife and the midlife crisis are about a major life change. Often, for people experiencing a midlife crisis, a sense of stagnancy sparks the need for change. During this period, a middle-aged person tends to reflect on his past, in part to see if his life to date measures up to the life he had envisioned as a child (or as a twen-tysomething). The midlife crisis also impels a middle-aged person to look forward, sometimes with an increasing sense of desperation, at the time he feels he has left.

In contrast, the quarterlife crisis occurs precisely because there is   6
none of that predictable stability that drives middle-aged people to do unpredictable things. After about twenty years in a sheltered school setting—or more if a person has gone on to graduate or professional school—many graduates undergo some sort of culture shock. In the academic environment, goals were clear-cut and the ways to achieve them were mapped out distinctly. To get into a good college or graduate school, it helped if you graduated with honors; to graduate with hon-ors, you needed to get good grades; to get good grades, you had to study hard. If your goals were athletic, you worked your way up from junior varsity or walk-on to varsity by practicing skills, working out in

the weight room and gelling with teammates and coaches. The better you were, the more playing time you got, the more impressive your statistics could become.

But after graduation, the pathways blur. In that crazy, wild nexus that people like to call the "real world," there is no definitive way to get from point A to point B, regardless of whether the points are related to a career, financial situation, home, or social life (though we have found through several unscientific studies that offering to pay for the next round of drinks can usually improve three out of the four). The extreme uncertainty that twentysomethings experience after graduation occurs because what was once a solid line that they could follow throughout their series of educational institutions has now disintegrated into millions of different options. The sheer number of possibilities can certainly inspire hope—that is why people say that twentysomethings have their whole lives ahead of them. But the endless array of decisions can also make a recent graduate feel utterly lost. 7

So while the midlife crisis revolves around a doomed sense of stagnancy, of a life set on pause while the rest of the world rattles on, the quarterlife crisis is a response to overwhelming instability, constant change, too many choices, and a panicked sense of helplessness. Just as the monotony of a lifestyle stuck in idle can drive a person to question himself intently, so, too, can the uncertainty of a life thrust into chaos. The transition from childhood to adulthood—from school to the world beyond—comes as a jolt for which many of today's twentysomethings simply are not prepared. The resulting overwhelming senses of helplessness and cluelessness, of indecision and apprehension, make up the real and common experience we call the quarterlife crisis. Individuals who are approaching middle age at least know what is coming. Because the midlife crisis is so widely acknowledged, people who undergo it are at the very least aware that there are places where they can go for help, such as support groups, books, movies, or Internet sites. Twentysomethings, by contrast, face a crisis that hits them with a far more powerful force than they ever expected. The slam is particularly painful because today's twentysomethings believe that they are alone and that they are having a much more difficult transition period than their peers—because the twenties are supposed to be "easy," because no one talks about these problems, and because the difficulties are therefore so unexpected. And at the fragile, doubt-ridden age during which the quarterlife crisis occurs, the ramifications can be extremely dangerous. 8

Why Worry about a Quarterlife Crisis?

The whirlwind of new responsibilities, new liberties, and new choices can be entirely overwhelming for someone who has just emerged from the shelter of twenty years of schooling. We don't mean to make 9 graduates sound as if they have been hibernating since they emerged from the womb; certainly it is not as if they have been slumbering throughout adolescence (though some probably tried). They have in a sense, however, been encased in a bit of a cocoon, where someone or something—parents or school, for example—has protected them from a lot of the scariness of their surroundings. As a result, when graduates are let loose into the world, their dreams and desires can be tinged with trepidation. They are hopeful, but at the same time they are also, to put it simply, scared silly.

Some might say that because people have had to deal with the rite 10 of passage from youth to adulthood since the beginning of time, this crisis is not really a "crisis" at all, given that historically this transitional period has, at various times, been marked with ceremonial rituals involving things like spears and buffalo dung. Indeed, it may not always have been a crisis.

But it has become one . . . 11

Although hope is a common emotion for twentysomethings, hope- 12 lessness has become just as widespread. The revelation that life simply isn't easy—a given for some twentysomethings, a mild inconvenience for others, but a shattering blow for several—is one of the most distressing aspects of the quarterlife crisis, particularly for individuals who do not have large support networks or who doubt themselves often. It is in these situations that the quarterlife crisis becomes not just a common stage—it can become hazardous. Not everyone at the age of the quarterlife encounters some sort of depression. . . . But we are addressing depression as one common result of the quarterlife crisis here so that we can illustrate why it is so important to acknowledge this transition period.

After interviewing dozens of twentysomethings who said they were 13 depressed because of the transition, we ran our conclusions by Robert DuPont, a Georgetown Medical School professor of psychology who wrote *The Anxiety Cure*. "Based on my experience," DuPont said, "I have found that there is a high rate of all forms of disorder in this age group, including addiction, anxiety, depression, and many other kinds of problems because of the high stress associated with the transition from being a child to being an adult. And that has gotten more stressful as the road map has become less used. The old way of doing this was to get out and get it done right away. There was an economic imperative to doing it. It's not like that anymore. And as the road map has disappeared, the stress has gone up. People have to invent their own road map. It used to be that it came with the college graduation. Now you have to go out and figure it out yourself."

These high rates of disorders, however, have gone virtually unac- 14 knowledged. That's why we can't bog you down with statistics on this age group. They don't exist. Psychological research on twentysomethings, including statistics on depression and suicide, has not been performed. We asked major national mental health associations such as the National Institutes of Mental Health, the American Psychiatric Association, and the National Depressive and Manic Depressive Association for any information they had on people in their twenties. They didn't have any. As one psychologist told us, associations don't cut the data to incorporate this age group. "It's not a subject that's interesting to them. They just lump everybody together," he said. . . .

Another way the quarterlife crisis can show up, particularly in the mid- to late twenties, is in a feeling of disappointment, of "This is all there is?" Maybe the job turns out to be not so glamorous after all, or maybe it just doesn't seem to lead anywhere interesting. Perhaps the year of travel in Europe was more of a wallet buster than previously imagined—even with nights in youth hostels and meals of ramen. Or maybe the move to a hip, new city just didn't turn out to be as fabulous a relocation as expected. 15

While these are, according to older generations, supposed to be the best years of their lives, twentysomethings also feel that the choices they make during this period will influence their thirties, forties, fifties, and on, in an irreparable domino effect. As a result, twentysomethings frequently have the unshakable belief that this is the time during which they have to nail down the meaning in their lives, which explains why they often experience a nagging feeling that somehow they need to make their lives more fulfilling. This is why there are so many drastic life changes at this point in life: an investment banker breaks off his engagement and volunteers for the Peace Corps; a consultant suddenly frets that consulting may not really have that much influence on other people's lives; a waiter chucks the steady paycheck to live in his car and try to make it in Hollywood; a law school graduate decides she doesn't want to be a lawyer after all and seeks a job in technology. 16

The changes hurtling toward a young adult, as well as the potential for more changes ahead, can be excruciatingly overwhelming for someone who is trying so hard to figure out how to feel fulfilled. A lot of people don't realize just how suffocating this pressure can be. The prevalent belief is that twentysomethings have it relatively easy because they do not have as many responsibilities as older individuals. But it is precisely this reduced responsibility that renders the vast array of decisions more difficult to make. For instance, if there were, say, a family to consider, a mother might not be as inclined to take a risk on the stock market. If a guy's elderly father were sick, he probably wouldn't take that year off to travel in South America. Twentysomethings, for the most part, just aren't at those stages yet, which is why they are sometimes envied. But because their choices aren't narrowed down for them by responsibilities, they have more decisions to make. And while this isn't necessarily bad, it can make things pretty complex. Figuring out which changes to make in order to make life more fulfilling is hard enough. 17

But deciding to make a change and then following through with it requires an extraordinary amount of strength, which is sometimes hard to come by for a recent graduate who has not had to rely solely on himself for very long.

The most widespread, frightening, and quite possibly the most difficult manifestation of the quarterlife crisis is a feeling that can creep up on a twentysomething whether he is unemployed, living at home, and friendless, or in an interesting job, with a great apartment, and dozens of buddies. Regardless of their levels of self-esteem, confidence, and overall well-being, twentysomethings are particularly vulnerable to doubts. They doubt their decisions, their abilities, their readiness, their past, present, and future . . . but most of all, they doubt themselves. The twenties comprise a period of intense questioning—of introspection and self-development that young adults often feel they are not ready for. The questions can range from seemingly trivial choices—"Should I really have spent $100 to join that fantasy baseball league?"—to irrefutably mammoth decisions—"When is the right time for me to start a family?" It is healthy, of course, for people to question themselves some; an occasional self-assessment or life inventory is a natural part of the quest for improvement. But if the questioning becomes constant and the barrage of doubts never seems to cease, twentysomethings can feel as if it is hard to catch their breath, as if they are spiraling downward. Many times the doubts increase because twentysomethings think it is abnormal to have them in the first place. No one talks about having doubts at this age, so when twentysomethings do find that they are continuously questioning themselves, they think something is wrong with them.

THINKING CRITICALLY ABOUT THE TEXT

For most people, choice is a good thing. But Robbins and Wilner are quick to point out that "the extreme uncertainty that twentysomethings experience after graduation occurs because what was once a solid line that they could follow throughout their series of educational institutions has now disintegrated into millions of different options" (paragraph 7). How do you feel about having choices? Do you think it is possible to have too many choices? Have you ever been in such a situation? How did you feel when presented with more options/choices than you knew what to do with? Discuss.

QUESTIONS ON SUBJECT

1. According to Robbins and Wilner, what is the quarterlife crisis, and why is it important for us to understand it?
2. What age group is typically affected by the quarterlife crisis?
3. What characteristics does the quarterlife crisis share with the midlife crisis? How are they different?

4. What do Robbins and Wilner see as the relationship between choice and responsibility? Do you agree with their assessment? Explain.

5. Robbins and Wilner believe that "twentysomethings are particularly vulnerable to doubts" (paragraph 18). How do they account for these doubts, and at what point do they think doubt ceases to be "healthy" and starts to be a difficult problem?

QUESTIONS ON STRATEGY

1. Robbins and Wilner begin their essay with the story of Jim's midlife crisis. How do they use Jim's story to introduce the topic of quarterlife crisis? Explain.

2. For what audience did Robbins and Wilner write their essay? (Glossary: *Audience*) How do you know?

3. What do you see as Robbins and Wilner's purpose in writing this extended definition of *quarterlife crisis*? (Glossary: *Purpose*) Explain.

4. Identify passages in which Robbins and Wilner use the strategies of comparison and contrast as well as cause and effect analysis to develop their definition. (Glossary: *Comparison and Contrast; Cause and Effect Analysis*) What does each strategy add to the definition of *quarterlife crisis*?

5. In paragraph 13, Robbins and Wilner quote Robert DuPont, author of *The Anxiety Cure* and professor of psychology at Georgetown Medical School. What light do DuPont's words shed on the widespread hopelessness and depression among America's twentysomethings? What is gained by quoting an authority on this subject?

6. Writers often use repeated words and phrases, transitional expressions, pronouns that refer to a specific antecedent, and repeated key ideas to connect one paragraph to another. (Glossary: *Transitions*) What types of transitional devices do Robbins and Wilner use to enhance the coherence of their essay? Cite specific examples of each type.

QUESTIONS ON DICTION AND VOCABULARY

1. In paragraph 10, Robbins and Wilner discuss "the rite of passage from youth to adulthood." What exactly is a "rite of passage"? What rites of passage have you gone through, and what others do you see in your future?

2. What is Robbins and Wilner's tone in this essay? (Glossary: *Tone*) How does their choice of words lead you to this conclusion? (Glossary: *Diction*) What does the parenthetical comment in paragraph 7 contribute to this tone?

3. Refer to your dictionary to determine the meanings of the following words as Robbins and Wilner have used them in this selection: *pertinent* (paragraph 3), *disarray* (4), *stagnancy* (5), *impels* (5), *nexus* (7), *sheer* (7), *trepidation* (9), *imperative* (13), *excruciatingly* (17), *manifestation* (18), *introspection* (18).

CLASSROOM ACTIVITY USING DEFINITION

Dictionary makers often have to write definitions for new words based on the ways those words are used by people. After examining the following six sentences, write a brief (fewer than twenty-five words) definition of a *lasto*.

The blades of a *lasto* must be bent for it to work well.

A *lasto* can be purchased at most hardware or housewares stores.

A *lasto* is sometimes difficult to clean.

Sofia put too much food into her *lasto*, and it overflowed.

A knife will do many of the jobs that a *lasto* will do but cannot do them as efficiently.

Some *lastos* have only three speeds, whereas others have as many as ten speeds.

WRITING SUGGESTIONS

1. In this selection and in their book *Quarterlife Crisis: The Unique Challenges of Life in Your Twenties*, Robbins and Wilner define the problem of quarterlife crisis, analyze several causes for it, and discuss its sometimes devastating effects on young people. What do you think can or should be done to minimize or eliminate the effects of quarterlife crisis? How can parents and schools better prepare young people for the liberties, choices, decisions, and responsibilities that await them in the so-called "real world"? Should college-age people take on more responsibility for their lives and education? What kinds of experiences and information do they need to have before they graduate? Write an essay in which you propose a plan or a program that will help college students prepare for their transition to adulthood.

2. How do you define the word *crisis*? Have you ever experienced any event—personal, family, or community—that you would call a crisis? If so, what were the defining characteristics of that crisis? Do you think that "quarterlife crisis," as Robbins and Wilner define it, qualifies as a real crisis, or is it just a flashy label for a period of uncertain transition that everyone experiences to one degree or another? Write an essay in which you first define the term *crisis* and then compare your crisis experience with the one described by Robbins and Wilner.

WRITING SUGGESTIONS FOR DEFINITION

1. Some of the most pressing social issues in American life today are further complicated by imprecise definitions of critical terms. Various medical cases, for example, have brought worldwide attention to the legal and medical definitions of the word *death*. Debates continue about the meanings of other controversial words, such as these:

a. values	i. remedial
b. minority (ethnic)	j. insanity
c. alcoholism	k. forgiveness
d. cheating	l. sex
e. pornography	m. success
f. kidnapping	n. happiness
g. lying	o. life
h. censorship	p. equality

    Select one of these words, and write an essay in which you discuss not only the definition of the term but also the problems associated with defining it.

2. Write an essay in which you define one of the words listed below by telling not only what it is, but also what it is *not*. (For example, one could say that "poetry is that which cannot be expressed in any other way.") Remember, however, that defining by negation does not relieve you of the responsibility of defining the term in other ways as well.

a. intelligence	g. family
b. leadership	h. style
c. fear	i. loyalty
d. patriotism	j. selflessness
e. wealth	k. creativity
f. failure	l. humor

3. Karl Marx defined *capitalism* as an economic system in which the bourgeois owners of the means of production exploit the proletariat, who lack the means of production, for their own selfish gain. How would you define *capitalism*? Write an essay defining *capitalism* that includes all six types of definition: formal, synonymous, negative, etymological, stipulative, and extended.

4. *Marriage* is a word that often means different things to different people. What does *marriage* mean to you? How would you define it? Write a definition essay to explain your understanding of marriage and what it means to be married. To make your definition clearer to your reader, you might consider describing a marriage with which you are personally familiar. Perhaps it would be helpful to compare and contrast two or more different marriages. (Glossary: *Comparison and Contrast*) You could also incorporate some narration or illustration to make your definition more powerful. (Glossary: *Illustration; Narration*)

5. Consider the sample introduction to the essay defining Quebecois and Canadian identity (page 369). Think about your school, town, or country's identity. How would you define its essential character? Choose a place that is important in your life, and write an essay defining its character and its significance to you.

CHAPTER 11

Cause and Effect Analysis

WHAT IS CAUSE AND EFFECT ANALYSIS?

People exhibit their natural curiosity about the world by asking questions. These questions represent a fundamental human need to find out how things work. Whenever a question asks *why*, answering it will require discovering a *cause* or a series of causes for a particular *effect*; whenever a question asks *what if*, its answer will point out the effect or effects that can result from a particular cause. Cause and effect analysis, then, explores the relationship between events or circumstances and the outcomes that result from them.

You will have frequent opportunity to use cause and effect analysis in your college writing. For example, a history instructor might ask you to explain the causes of the Six-Day War between Israel and its neighbors. In a paper for an American literature course, you might try to determine why *Huckleberry Finn* has sparked so much controversy in a number of schools and communities. On an environmental studies exam, you might have to speculate about the long-term effects acid rain will have on the ecology of northeastern Canada and the United States. Demonstrating an understanding of cause and effect is crucial to the process of learning.

One common use of the strategy is for the writer to identify a particular causal agent or circumstance and then discuss the consequences or effects it has had or may have. In the following passage from *The Telephone* by John Brooks, it is clear from the first sentence that the author is primarily concerned with the effects that the telephone has had or may have had on modern life.

First sentence establishes purpose in the form of a question.

What has the telephone done to us, or for us, in the hundred years of its existence? A few effects suggest themselves at once. It has saved lives by getting rapid word of illness, injury, or famine from remote places. By joining with the elevator to make possible the multistory residence or office building, it has made possible—for better or worse—the modern city. By bringing about a quantum leap in the speed and ease with which information moves from place to place, it has greatly accelerated the rate of scientific and technological change and growth in industry. Beyond doubt it has crippled if not killed the ancient art of letter writing. It has made living alone possible for persons with normal social impulses; by so doing, it has played a role in one of the greatest social changes of this century, the breakup of the multigenerational household. It has made the waging of war chillingly more efficient than formerly. Perhaps (though not provably) it has prevented wars that might have arisen out of international misunderstanding caused by written communication. Or perhaps—again not provably—by magnifying and extending irrational personal conflicts based on voice contact, it has caused wars. Certainly it has extended the scope of human conflicts, since it impartially disseminates the useful knowledge of scientists and the babble of bores, the affection of the affectionate and the malice of the malicious.

A series of effects with the telephone as cause.

The bulk of Brooks's paragraph is devoted to answering the very question he poses in his opening sentence: "What has the telephone done to us, or for us, in the hundred years of its existence?" Notice that even though many of the effects Brooks discusses are verifiable or probable, he is willing to admit that he is speculating about those effects that he cannot prove.

A second common use of the strategy is to reverse the forms by first examining the effect; the writer describes an important event or problem (effect) and then examines the possible reasons (causes) for it. For example, experts might trace the causes of poverty to any or all of the following: poor education, a nonprogressive tax system, declining commitment to social services, inflation, discrimination, or even the welfare system that is designed to help those most in need.

A third use of the strategy is for the writer to explore a complex causal chain. In this selection from his book *The Politics of Energy*, Barry Commoner examines the series of malfunctions that led to the near disaster at the Three Mile Island nuclear facility in Harrisburg, Pennsylvania.

On March 28, 1979, at 3:53 A.M., a pump at the Harrisburg plant failed. Because the pump failed, the reactor's heat was not drawn off in the heat exchanger and the very hot water in the primary loop overheated. The pressure in the loop increased, opening a release valve that was supposed to counteract such an event. But the valve stuck open and the primary loop system lost so much water (which ended up as a highly radioactive pool, six feet deep, on the floor of the reactor building) that it was unable to carry off all the heat generated within the reactor core. Under these circumstances, the intense heat held within the reactor could, in theory, melt its fuel rods, and the resulting "meltdown" could then carry a hugely radioactive mass through the floor of the reactor. The reactor's emergency cooling system, which is designed to prevent this disaster, was then automatically activated, but when it was, apparently, turned off too soon, some of the fuel rods overheated. This produced a bubble of hydrogen gas at the top of the reactor. (The hydrogen is dissolved in the water in order to react with oxygen that is produced when the intense reactor radiation splits water molecules into their atomic constituents. When heated, the dissolved hydrogen bubbles out of the solution.) This bubble blocked the flow of cooling water so that despite the action of the emergency cooling system the reactor core was again in danger of melting down. Another danger was that the gas might contain enough oxygen to cause an explosion that could rupture the huge containers that surround the reactor and release a deadly cloud of radioactive material into the surrounding countryside. Working desperately, technicians were able to gradually reduce the size of the gas bubble using a special apparatus brought in from the atomic laboratory at Oak Ridge, Tennessee, and the danger of a catastrophic release of radioactive materials subsided. But the sealed-off plant was now so radioactive that no one could enter it for many months—or, according to some observers, for years—without being exposed to a lethal dose of radiation.

Tracing a causal chain, as Commoner does here, is similar to narration. The writer must organize the events sequentially to show clearly how each event leads to the next.

In a causal chain, an initial cause brings about a particular effect, which in turn becomes the immediate cause of a further effect, and so on, bringing about a series of effects that also act as new causes. The so-called domino effect is a good illustration of the idea of a causal chain; the simple tipping over of a domino (initial cause) can result in the toppling of any number of dominoes down the line (series of effects). For example, before a salesperson approaches an important client about a big sale, she prepares extensively for the meeting (initial cause). Her preparation causes her to impress the client (effect A), which guarantees her the big sale (effect B), which in turn results in her promotion to district sales manager (effect C). The sale she made is the most immediate and the most obvious cause of her promotion, but it is possible to trace the chain back to its more essential cause: her hard work preparing for the meeting.

While the ultimate purpose of cause and effect analysis may seem simple—to know or to understand why something happens—determining causes and effects is often a thought-provoking and complex strategy. One reason for this complexity is that some causes are less obvious than others. *Immediate causes* are readily apparent because they are closest in time to the effect; the immediate cause of a flood, for example, may be the collapse of a dam. However, *remote causes* may be just as important, even though they are not as apparent and are perhaps even hidden. The remote (and, in fact, primary) cause of the flood might have been an engineering error or the use of substandard building materials or the failure of personnel to relieve the pressure on the dam caused by unseasonably heavy rains. In many cases, it is necessary to look beyond the most immediate causes to discover the true underlying sources of an event.

A second reason for the complexity of this strategy is the difficulty of distinguishing between possible and actual causes, as well as between possible and actual effects. An upset stomach may be caused by spoiled food, but it may also be caused by overeating, by flu, by nervousness, by pregnancy, or by a combination of factors. Similarly, an increase in the cost of electricity may have multiple effects: higher profits for utility companies, fewer sales of electrical appliances, higher prices for other products that depend on electricity in their manufacture, even the development of alternative sources of energy. Making reasonable choices among the various possibilities requires thought and care.

USING CAUSE AND EFFECT ANALYSIS AS A WRITING STRATEGY

Writers may use cause and effect analysis for three essential purposes: to inform, to speculate, and to argue. Most commonly, they will want to inform — to help their readers understand some identifiable fact. A state wildlife biologist, for example, might wish to tell the public about the effects severe winter weather has had on the state's deer herds. Similarly, in a newsletter, a member of Congress might explain to his or her constituency the reasons changes are being made in the Social Security system.

Cause and effect analysis may also allow writers to speculate — to consider what might be or what might have been. To satisfy the board of trustees, for example, a university treasurer might discuss the impact an increase in tuition will have on the school's budget. A columnist for *People* magazine might speculate about the reasons for a new singer's sudden popularity. Similarly, pollsters estimate the effects that various voter groups will have on future elections, and historians evaluate how the current presidency will continue to influence American government in the coming decades.

Finally, cause and effect analysis provides an excellent basis from which to argue a given position or point of view. An editorial writer, for example, could argue that bringing a professional basketball team into the area would have many positive effects on the local economy and on the community as a whole. Educators who think that video games are a cause of delinquency and poor school performance have argued in newspapers and professional journals against the widespread acceptance of such games.

Using Cause and Effect Analysis across the Disciplines

When writing essays in the academic disciplines, you will have many opportunities to use the strategy of cause and effect analysis to both organize and strengthen the presentation of your ideas. To determine whether or not cause and effect analysis is the right strategy for you in a particular paper, use the four-step method first described in "Determining Your Strategy" (pages 24–25). Consider the following examples, which illustrate how this four-step method works for typical college papers:

Native American History

MAIN IDEA: Treaties between Native American groups and the United States government had various negative effects on the Native Americans involved.

QUESTION: What have been some of the most harmful results for Native Americans of treaties between Native American groups and the United States government?

STRATEGY: Cause and Effect Analysis. The word *results* signals that this study needs to examine the harmful effects of the provisions of the treaties.

SUPPORTING STRATEGY: Illustration. Examples need to be given of both treaties and their consequences.

Nutrition

MAIN IDEA: A major factor to be considered when examining why people suffer from poor nutrition is poverty.

QUESTION: What is the relationship between poverty and nutrition?

STRATEGY: Cause and Effect Analysis. The word *relationship* signals a linkage between poverty and nutrition. The writer will have to determine what is meant by poverty and poor nutrition in this country and/or in the countries examined.

SUPPORTING STRATEGY: Definition. Precise definitions will first be necessary in order for the writer to make valid judgments concerning the causal relationship in question.

Nursing

MAIN IDEA: Alzheimer's disease is the progressive loss of brain nerve cells, causing gradual loss of memory, concentration, understanding, and in some cases sanity.

QUESTION: What role does the overproduction of a protein that destroys nerve cells play in the development of Alzheimer's disease, and what causes the overproduction in the first place?

STRATEGY: Cause and Effect Analysis. The words *role*, *play*, and *causes* signal that the issue here is determining and explaining how Alzheimer's disease originates.

SUPPORTING STRATEGY: Process Analysis. Describing how Alzheimer's operates will be essential to making the reader understand its causes and effects.

SAMPLE STUDENT ESSAY USING CAUSE AND EFFECT ANALYSIS AS A WRITING STRATEGY

Born in Brooklyn, New York, Kevin Cunningham spent most of his life in Flemington, New Jersey. While enrolled in the mechanical engineering program at the University of Vermont, Cunningham shared an apartment near the Burlington waterfront with several other students. There he became interested in the effects that upscale real estate development—or gentrification—would have on his neighborhood. Such development is not unique to Burlington; it is happening in the older sections of cities across the country. After gathering information for his essay by talking with people who live in the neighborhood, Cunningham found it useful to discuss both the causes and the effects of gentrification in his well-unified essay.

Gentrification

Kevin Cunningham

Epigram sets forth theme and raises central question— why?

I went back to Ohio, and my city was gone. . . .

—Chrissie Hynde, of the Pretenders

My city is in Vermont, not Ohio, but soon my neighborhood will probably be gone, too. Or maybe it's I who   1 will be gone. My street, Lakeview Terrace, lies unobtrusively in the old northwest part of Burlington and is notable, as its name suggests, for spectacular views of Lake Champlain framed by the Adirondacks. It's not that the neighborhood is going to seed — no, quite the contrary. Recently it has been discovered, and now it is on the verge of being gentrified. For some of us who live here, that's bad.

Thesis

Well-organized and unified paragraph: Description of life cycle of city neighborhoods

Cities are often assigned human characteristics, one of which is a life cycle: they have a birth, a youth, a middle age, and an old age. A neighborhood is built and settled by young, vibrant people, proud of their sturdy new homes. Together, residents and houses mature, as families grow larger and extensions get built on. Eventually, though, the neighborhood begins to show its age. Buildings sag a little, houses aren't repainted as quickly, and maintenance slips. The neighborhood may grow poorer, as the young and upwardly mobile find new jobs and move away, while the older and less successful inhabitants remain.

2

Decay, renewal, or redevelopment awaits aging neighborhoods.

One of three fates awaits the aging neighborhood. Decay may continue until the neighborhood becomes a slum. It may face urban renewal, with old buildings being razed, and ugly, new apartment houses taking their place. Or it may undergo redevelopment, in which government encourages the upgrading of existing housing stock by offering low-interest loans or outright grants; thus, the original character of the neighborhood may be retained or restored, allowing the city to keep part of its identity.

3

Organization: Example of Hoboken, New Jersey

An example of redevelopment at its best is Hoboken, New Jersey. In the early 1970s Hoboken was a dying city, with rundown housing and many abandoned buildings. However, low-interest loans enabled some younger residents to begin to refurbish their homes, and soon the area began to show signs of renewed vigor. Even outsiders moved in and rebuilt some of the abandoned houses. Today, whole blocks have been restored, and neighborhood life is active again. The city does well too, because property values are higher and so are property taxes. And there, at least for my neighborhood, is the rub.

4

Effects of redevelopment on Hoboken

Transition: Writer moves from example of Hoboken to his Lakeview Terrace neighborhood.

Lakeview Terrace is a demographic potpourri of students and families, young professionals and elderly retirees, homeowners and renters. It's a quiet street where kids can play safely and the neighbors know each other. Most of the houses are fairly old and look it, but already some redevelopment has

5

Describes "gentrification" to date

begun. Recently, several old houses were bought by a real estate company, rebuilt, and sold as condominiums; the new residents drive BMWs and keep to themselves. The house where I live is owned by a Young Urban Professional couple — he's an architect — and they have renovated the place to what it must have looked like when it was new. They did a nice job, too. These two kinds of development are the main forms of gentrification, and so far they have done no real harm.

Redevelopment causes property values to increase, which will cause property taxes to rise.

But the city is about to start a major property tax reappraisal. Because of the renovations, the houses on Lakeview Terrace are currently worth more than they used to be; soon there will be a big jump in property taxes. And then a lot of people will be hurt — even dispossessed from their own neighborhood.

6

Organization: Effects of gentrification on local property owners

Clem is a retired General Electric employee who has lived on Lakeview for over thirty years and who owns his home. About three years ago some condos were built on the lot next door, which didn't please Clem — he says they just don't fit in. But with higher property taxes, it may be Clem who no longer fits in. At the very least, since he's on a fixed income, he will have to make sacrifices in order to stay. Ryan works as a mailman and also owns his Lakeview Terrace home, which is across the street from the houses that were converted into condos: same cause, same effect.

7

Organization: Effects of gentrification on renters

Then there are those of us who rent. As our landlords have to pay higher property taxes, they will naturally raise rents at least as much (and maybe more, if they've spent money on renovations of their own). Some of us won't be able to afford the increase and will have to leave. "Some of us" almost certainly includes me, as well as others who have lived on Lakeview Terrace much longer than I have. In fact, the exodus has already begun, with the people who were displaced by the condo conversions.

8

Conclusion

Of course, many people would consider what's happening on Lakeview Terrace a genuine improvement in every way, resulting not only in better-looking houses but also in a better class of people. I dispute that. The new people may be more affluent than those they displace, but certainly not "better,"

9

Restatement of thesis

not by any standard that counts with me. Gentrification may do wonders for a neighborhood's aesthetics, but it certainly can be hard on its soul.

> ### Analyzing Kevin Cunningham's Essay of Cause and Effect Analysis: Questions for Discussion
>
> 1. According to Cunningham, in what way are cities like humans? What does he describe as the three possible outcomes for aging neighborhoods?
> 2. Cunningham presents this causal chain: Redevelopment (cause) increases property values (effect), which in turn increases property taxes upon reassessment by the city (effect), which leads to the displacement of poorer residents (effect). What other effects of redevelopment can you think of?
> 3. Cunningham decries the gentrification of the neighborhood, but a neighborhood descending into disrepair is not a desirable alternative. What do you think Cunningham would like to see happen on Lakeview Terrace? How can a neighborhood fend off decay while still maintaining its "soul"?
> 4. Would the essay have benefited if Cunningham had proposed and speculated about a viable alternative to gentrification? Explain.

SUGGESTIONS FOR USING CAUSE AND EFFECT ANALYSIS AS A WRITING STRATEGY

As you plan, write, and revise your essay of cause and effect, be mindful of the five-step writing process described in Chapter 2 (see pages 14–31). Pay particular attention to the basic requirements and essential ingredients of this writing strategy.

Planning Your Essay of Cause and Effect Analysis

Establish Your Focus. Decide whether your essay will propose causes, talk about effects, or analyze both causes and effects. Any research you do and any questions you ask will depend on how you wish to concentrate your attention. For example, let's say that as a reporter for the school paper, you are writing a story about a fire that destroyed an apartment building in the neighborhood, killing four people. In planning your story, you might focus on the cause of the fire: Was there more than one cause? Was carelessness to blame? Was the fire of suspicious origin? You might focus on the effects of the fire: How much damage was done to the building? How many people were left homeless? What was the impact on the families of the four victims? Or you might cover both the reasons for this tragic event and its ultimate effects, setting up a sort of causal chain. Such a focus is crucial as you gather information. For example, student Kevin Cunningham decided early on that he wanted to explore what would happen (the effects) if gentrification continued on his street.

Determine Your Purpose.   Once you begin to draft your essay and as you continue to refine it, make sure your purpose is clear. Do you wish your cause and effect analysis to be primarily informative, speculative, or argumentative? An informative essay allows readers to say, "I learned something from this. I didn't know that the fire was caused by faulty wiring." A speculative essay suggests to readers new possibilities: "That never occurred to me before. The apartment house could indeed be replaced by an office building." An argumentative essay convinces readers that some sort of action should be taken: "I have to agree—fire inspections should occur more regularly in our neighborhood." In his essay on gentrification, Cunningham uses cause and effect analysis to question the value of redevelopment by examining what it does to the soul of a neighborhood. Whatever your purpose, be sure to provide the information necessary to carry it through.

Formulate a Thesis Statement.   All essays need a strong, clear thesis statement. When you are writing an essay using cause and effect, your thesis statement should clearly present either a cause and its effect(s) or an effect and its cause(s). As a third approach, your essay could focus on a complex causal chain of events. Here are a few examples from this chapter.

- "What has the telephone done to us, or for us, in the hundred years of its existence?" John Brooks's opening sentence makes it easy for the reader to know that he has chosen the telephone as his cause and that he will be exploring its effects in the essay.
- "On March 28, 1979, at 3:53 A.M., a pump at the Harrisburg plant failed." Here, Barry Commoner has chosen the failure of the pump to introduce the causal chain of events that led to the near–nuclear disaster at Three Mile Island.
- "Recently [our neighborhood] has been discovered, and now it is on the verge of being gentrified. For some of us who live here, that's bad."

When you begin to formulate your thesis statement, keep these examples in mind. You can find other examples of thesis statements in the essays throughout this book. As you begin to develop your thesis statement, ask yourself, "What is my point?" Next, ask yourself, "What approach to a cause and effect essay will be most useful in making my point?" If you can't answer these questions yet, write some ideas down and try to determine your main point from these ideas.

Organizing and Writing Your Essay of Cause and Effect Analysis

Avoid Oversimplification and Errors of Logic.   Sound and thoughtful reasoning, while present in all good writing, is central to any analysis of cause and effect. Writers of convincing cause and effect analysis must examine their material objectively and develop their essays carefully, taking into account any potential objections that readers might raise. Therefore, do not jump to conclusions or let your prejudices interfere with the logic of your interpretation or the completeness of your presentation. In gathering information for his essay, Kevin Cunningham discovered that he had to watch himself—that he had to distinguish between cause and effect and mere coincidence. "You have to know your subject, and you have to be honest. For example, my downstairs neighbors moved out last month because the rent was raised. Somebody who didn't know the situation might say, 'See? Gentrification.' But that wasn't the reason—it's that heating costs went up. This is New England, and we had a cold winter; gentrification had nothing to do with it. It's something that is just beginning to happen, and it's going to have a big effect, but we haven't actually felt many of the effects here yet."

Be sure that you do not oversimplify the cause and effect relationship you are writing about. A good working assumption is that most important matters cannot be traced to a single verifiable cause; similarly, a cause or set of causes rarely produces a single isolated effect. To be believable, your analysis of your topic must demonstrate a thorough understanding of the surrounding circumstances; there is nothing less convincing than the single-minded determination to show one particular connection. For example, someone writing about how the passage of a tough new crime bill (cause) has led to a decrease in arrests in a particular area (effect) will have little credibility unless other possible causes—socioeconomic conditions, seasonal fluctuations in crime, the size and budget of the police force, and so on—are also examined and taken into account. Of course, to achieve coherence, you will want to emphasize the important causes or the most significant effects. But be careful not to lose your reader's trust by insisting on an oversimplified "X leads to Y" relationship.

The other common problem in cause and effect analysis is lack of evidence in establishing a cause or effect. This error is known as the "after this, therefore because of this" fallacy (in Latin, *post hoc, ergo propter hoc*). In attempting to discover an explanation for a particular event or circumstance, a writer may point to something that merely preceded it in time, assuming a causal connection where none has in fact been proven. If you have dinner out one evening and the next day come down with stomach cramps, you may blame your illness on the restaurant where you ate the night before; but you do so without justification if your only proof is the fact that you ate there beforehand.

More evidence would be required to establish a causal relationship. The *post hoc, ergo propter hoc* fallacy is often harmlessly foolish ("I failed the exam because I lost my lucky key chain"). It can, however, lead writers into serious errors of judgment and blind them to more reasonable explanations of cause and effect. And, like oversimplification, such mistakes in logic can undercut a reader's confidence. Make sure that the causal relationships you cite are, in fact, based on demonstrable evidence and not merely on a temporal connection.

Use Other Rhetorical Strategies. Although cause and effect analysis can be used effectively as a separate writing strategy, it is more common for essays to combine different strategies. For example, in an essay about a soccer team's victories, you might use comparison and contrast to highlight the differences between the team's play in the two losses and in five victories. Narration from interviews might also be used to add interest and color. An essay about the Internet might incorporate the strategy of argumentation as well as definition to defend the openness and effectiveness of the Internet. The argument could analyze exactly how the benefits outweigh the drawbacks, while definition could be ued to focus the subject matter to better achieve your purpose. By combining strategies, you can gain both clarity and forcefulness in your writing.

You must always keep the purpose of your essay and the tone you wish to adopt in the front of your mind when combining strategies. Without careful planning, using more than one rhetorical strategy can alter both the direction and the tone of your essay in ways that detract from, rather than contribute to, your ability to achieve your purpose.

As you read the essays in this chapter, consider all of the writing strategies the authors have used to support their cause and effect analysis. How have these other strategies added to or changed the style of the essay? Are there strategies that you might have added or taken out? What strategies, if any, do you think you might use to strengthen your cause and effect essay? Although some essays are developed using a single rhetorical strategy, more often good writing takes advantage of several strategies to develop the writer's purpose and thesis to produce a stronger essay that is more informative, persuasive, and entertaining.

Revising and Editing Your Essay of Cause and Effect Analysis

Select Words That Strike a Balanced Tone. Be careful to neither overstate nor understate your position. Avoid exaggerations like "there can be no question" and "the evidence speaks for itself." Such diction is usually annoying and undermines your interpretation. Instead, allow your analysis of the facts to convince readers of the cause and effect relationship you wish to suggest. Do not be afraid to admit the possibility of other viewpoints. At the same time, no analytical writer convinces by understating or qualifying information with words and phrases such as *it seems that, perhaps, maybe, I think, sometimes, most often, nearly always,* or *in my opinion.* While it may be your intention to appear reasonable, overusing such qualifying words can make you sound unclear or indecisive, and it renders your analysis less convincing. Present your case forcefully, but do so honestly and sensibly.

Questions for Revising and Editing: Cause and Effect Analysis

1. Why do I want to use cause and effect: to inform, to speculate, or to argue? Does my analysis help me achieve my purpose?
2. Is my topic manageable for the essay I wish to write? Have I effectively established my focus?
3. Does my thesis statement clearly state either the cause and its effects or the effect and its causes?
4. Have I identified the nature of my cause and effect scenario? Is there a causal chain? Have I identified immediate and remote causes? Have I distinguished between possible and actual causes and effects?
5. Have I been able to avoid oversimplifying the cause and effect relationship I am writing about? Are there any errors in my logic?
6. Is my tone balanced, neither overstating nor understating my position?
7. Is there another rhetorical strategy that I can use with cause and effect to assist me in achieving my purpose? If so, have I been able to implement it with care so that I have not altered either the direction or the tone of my essay?
8. Have I taken every opportunity to use words and phrases that signal cause and effect relationships?
9. Have I used *affect* and *effect* properly?
10. Have I avoided the phrase *the reason is because*?
11. Have I avoided errors in grammar, punctuation, and mechanics?

How Boys Become Men

Jon Katz

Journalist and novelist Jon Katz was born in 1947. He writes with a keen understanding of life in contemporary suburban America. Each of his four mystery novels is a volume in the Suburban Detective Mystery *series:* The Family Stalker *(1994),* Death by Station Wagon *(1994),* The Father's Club *(1996), and* The Last Housewife *(1996). The best known of these novels,* The Last Housewife, *won critical praise for its insights into the pressures and conflicts experienced by young professional couples in their efforts to achieve the American dream. Katz is also the author of* Media Rants: Postpolitics in the Digital Nation *(1997), a collection of his newspaper columns dealing primarily with the role and influence of the media in the public life of modern America;* Virtuous Reality: How Americans Surrendered Discussion of Moral Values to Opportunists, Nitwits, and Blockheads Like William Bennett *(1998); and* Geeks: How Two Lost Boys Rode the Internet Out of Idaho *(2000). Since 2000, he has written six books about dogs.*

In the following essay, first published in January 1993 in Glamour, *Katz explains why many men appear insensitive.*

PREPARING TO READ

How important are childhood experiences to the development of identity? How do the rituals of the playground, the slumber party, and the neighborhood gang help mold us as men and women? Write about one or two examples from your own experience.

Two nine-year-old boys, neighbors and friends, were walking home from school. The one in the bright blue windbreaker was laughing and swinging a heavy-looking book bag toward the head of his friend, who kept ducking and stepping back. "What's the matter?" asked the kid with the bag, whooshing it over his head. "You chicken?"

His friend stopped, stood still and braced himself. The bag slammed into the side of his face, the thump audible all the way across the street where I stood watching. The impact knocked him to the ground, where he lay mildly stunned for a second. Then he struggled up, rubbing the side of his head. "See?" he said proudly. "I'm no chicken."

No. A chicken would probably have had the sense to get out of the way. This boy was already well on the road to becoming a *man*, having learned one of the central ethics of his gender: Experience pain rather than show fear.

Women tend to see men as a giant problem in need of solution. They tell us that we're remote and uncommunicative, that we need to demonstrate less machismo and more commitment, more humanity. But if you don't understand something about boys, you can't understand why men are the way we are, why we find it so difficult to make friends or to acknowledge our fears and problems.

Boys live in a world with its own Code of Conduct, a set of ruthless, unspoken, and unyielding rules: 5

> Don't be a goody-goody.
> Never rat. If your parents ask about bruises, shrug.
> Never admit fear. Ride the roller coaster, join the fistfight, do what you have to do. Asking for help is for sissies.
> Empathy is for nerds. You can help your best buddy, under certain circumstances. Everyone else is on his own.
> Never discuss anything of substance with anybody. Grunt, shrug, dump on teachers, laugh at wimps, talk about comic books. Anything else is risky.

Boys are rewarded for throwing hard. Most other activities— reading, befriending girls, or just thinking—are considered weird. And if there's one thing boys don't want to be, it's weird. 6

More than anything else, boys are supposed to learn how to handle themselves. I remember the bitter fifth-grade conflict I touched off by elbowing aside a bigger boy named Barry and seizing the cafeteria's last carton of chocolate milk. Teased for getting aced out by a wimp, he had to reclaim his place in the pack. Our fistfight, at recess, ended with my knees buckling and my lip bleeding while my friends, sympathetic but out of range, watched resignedly. 7

When I got home, my mother took one look at my swollen face and screamed. I wouldn't tell her anything, but when my father got home I cracked and confessed, pleading with them to do nothing. Instead, they called Barry's parents, who restricted his television for a week. 8

The following morning, Barry and six of his pals stepped out from behind a stand of trees. "It's the rat," said Barry. 9

I bled a little more. *Rat* was scrawled in crayon across my desk. 10

They were waiting for me after school for a number of afternoons to follow. I tried varying my routes and avoiding bushes and hedges. It usually didn't work. 11

I was as ashamed for telling as I was frightened. "You did ask for it," said my best friend. Frontier Justice has nothing on Boy Justice. 12

In panic, I appealed to a cousin who was several years older. He followed me home from school, and when Barry's gang surrounded me, he came barreling toward us. "Stay away from my cousin," he shouted, "or I'll kill you." 13

After they were gone, however, my cousin could barely stop laughing. "You were afraid of *them?*" he howled. "They barely came up to my waist." 14

Men remember receiving little mercy as boys; maybe that's why it's 15
sometimes difficult for them to show any.

"I know lots of men who had happy childhoods, but none who 16
have happy memories of the way other boys treated them," says a
friend. "It's a macho marathon from third grade up, when you start
butting each other in the stomach."

"The thing is," adds another friend, "you learn early on to hide 17
what you feel. It's never safe to say, 'I'm scared.' My girlfriend asks me
why I don't talk more about what I'm feeling. I've gotten better at it,
but it will *never* come naturally."

You don't need to be a shrink to see how the lessons boys learn 18
affect their behavior as men. Men are being asked, more and more, to
show sensitivity, but they dread the very word. They struggle to build
their increasingly uncertain work lives but will deny they're in trouble.
They want love, affection, and support but don't know how to ask for
them. They hide their weaknesses and fears from all, even those they
care for. They've learned to be wary of intervening when they see others in trouble. They often still balk at being stigmatized as weird.

Some men get shocked into sensitivity—when they lose their jobs, 19
their wives, or their lovers. Others learn it through a strong marriage, or
through their own children.

It may be a long while, however, before male culture evolves to the 20
point that boys can learn more from one another than how to hit curve
balls. Last month, walking my dog past the playground near my house,
I saw three boys encircling a fourth, laughing and pushing him. He was
skinny and rumpled, and he looked frightened. One boy knelt behind
him while another pushed him from the front, a trick familiar to any
former boy. He fell backward.

When the others ran off, he brushed the dirt off his elbows and 21
walked toward the swings. His eyes were moist and he was struggling
for control.

"Hi," I said through the chain-link fence. "How ya doing?" 22

"Fine," he said quickly, kicking his legs out and beginning his 23
swing.

THINKING CRITICALLY ABOUT THE TEXT

Do you agree with Katz that men in general are less communicative, less sensitive, and less sympathetic in their behavior than women? Why or why not?
Where does "Boy Justice" originate?

QUESTIONS ON SUBJECT

1. Why, according to Katz, do "women tend to see men as a giant problem
in need of solution" (paragraph 4)?

2. In paragraph 3, Katz states that one of the "central ethics" of his gender is "Experience pain rather than show fear." Would you agree with Katz?

3. What is it that boys are supposed to learn "more than anything else" (paragraph 7)? What do you think girls are supposed to learn more than anything else?

4. In paragraph 12, what does Katz mean when he says, "Frontier Justice has nothing on Boy Justice"?

5. How, according to Katz, do some men finally achieve sensitivity? Can you think of other softening influences on adult males?

QUESTIONS ON STRATEGY

1. This essay was originally published in *Glamour* magazine. Can you find any places where Katz addresses himself specifically to an audience of young women? Where? (Glossary: *Audience*)

2. Early in the essay, Katz refers to men as "we," but later he refers to men as "they." What is the purpose of this change?

3. Notice that in paragraphs 16 and 17, Katz quotes two friends on the nature of male development. Why is the location of these quotes crucial to the structure of the essay?

4. Katz illustrates his thesis with three anecdotes. Identify each of them. Where in the essay is each located? How do they differ? How does each enhance the author's message? (Glossary: *Narration*)

5. What irony is expressed by the boy's answer "Fine" in paragraph 23? (Glossary: *Irony*)

QUESTIONS ON DICTION AND VOCABULARY

1. In paragraph 3, Katz identifies what he describes as "one of the central ethics" of his gender. Why does he call it an ethic rather than a rule?

2. What connotations do the words *chicken* and *weird* have for you? (Glossary: *Connotation/Denotation*)

3. Are you familiar with the word "rat" as Katz uses it? What does it mean? Check your desk dictionary for what it says about *rat* as a noun and as a verb.

CLASSROOM ACTIVITY USING CAUSE AND EFFECT ANALYSIS

Think about what might be necessary to write an essay similar to Katz's entitled "How Girls Become Women." If we assume, as Katz does, that who men are is the product of their early experiences as boys, what in a woman's character (as determined by each member of the class) might be caused by the experiences girls have in growing up in our society? Share your response with others in your class.

WRITING SUGGESTIONS

1. Discuss with classmates the expectations that shape women; in your discussion you might find it useful to share anecdotes from your own experience. It may be helpful to review your response to the Preparing to Read prompt as well as ideas generated by the Classroom Activity for this selection. Write an essay patterned on "How Boys Become Men," showing the causes and effects surrounding females growing up in American culture. You might come to the conclusion that women do not have a standard way of growing up; you could also write a cause and effect essay supporting this idea. Either way, be sure to include forceful examples.

2. The subject of the differences between men and women perpetually spawns a lot of discussion and debate, and a spate of recently published and widely read books have commented seriously on relationship issues. Read one of these books. (*Men Are from Mars, Women Are from Venus* by John Gray and *You Just Don't Understand* by Deborah Tannen are good examples.) Write a review presenting and evaluating the major thesis of the book you have chosen. Other than evolution, what issues make male-female relations so problematic? What can be done to bridge the "gender gap" that many of us seem to need experts, books, and teaching to understand?

How Reading Changed My Life

Anna Quindlen

Anna Quindlen was born in Philadelphia, Pennsylvania, in 1953. After graduating from Barnard College in 1974, she became a reporter for the New York Times *and later a columnist, winning the Pulitzer Prize for her "Public and Private" column in 1992. Quindlen left the* Times *in 1994 to concentrate on writing fiction and her new column at* Newsweek. *Quindlen's novels include* Object Lessons *(1991),* One True Thing *(1995),* Black and Blue *(1998), and* Rise and Shine *(2006). Her nonfiction books—* How Reading Changed My Life *(1998),* A Short Guide to the Happy Life *(2000), and* Being Perfect *(2005)—focus on everyday life issues.*

In the following excerpt, taken from How Reading Changed My Life, *Quindlen shares with us the nature of her passion for reading as well as some of the wondrous effects that reading has had on her knowledge of herself and her world.*

PREPARING TO READ

The ability to read is an important life skill, one that enriches far beyond simply conveying information about the world around you. For example, have you ever thought about how your ability to read and what you have read have affected your sense of who you are and the person you want to be? Think about the reading you have done and how it may have changed your life and maybe even "saved" your life.

It still seems infinitely mysterious to me that there are some of us who 1 have built not a life but a self, based largely on our hunger for what are a series of scratches on a piece of paper. There remain in the world, six millennia after a list of livestock on a clay tablet created reading, cultures in which the written word is a mystery, a luxury, even a redundancy. Stories are still told beside fires and streams by people bent almost double from working in the fields, told as richly as the ones my father and his brothers tell when they have a meal together and set to work embroidering the ever-changing tapestry of their past. There is something both magical and natural about the told story, the wise man spinning a tale at a table in medieval Europe giving way to the mother talking about family history in the kitchen with her children in a small apartment in Chicago. That power of the spoken word was even given a new kind of life at the tail end of the twentieth century, when publishing houses began as a matter of course to do what beforehand only libraries for the blind had done: to release audio versions of books, although audio books sometimes seem to me to have more to do with saving time and alleviating the tedium of travel by car than they do with the need to hear the syllables of a sentence caressed by the human voice.

But the act of reading, the act of seeing a story on the page as opposed to hearing it told—of translating story into specific and immutable language, putting that language down in concrete form with the aid of the arbitrary handful of characters our language offers, of then handing the story on to others in a transactional relationship— that is infinitely more complex, and stranger, too, as though millions of us had felt the need, over the span of centuries, to place messages in bottles, to ameliorate the isolation of each of us, each of us a kind of desert island made less lonely by words. Or, not simply by words, but by words without the evanescence of speech, words that would always be the same, only the reader different each time, so that today, or next year, or a hundred years from now, someone could pick up *A Tale of Two Cities,* turn to the last page, and see that same final sentence, that coda that Dickens first offered readers in 1859: "It is a far, far better thing . . ."

The Sumerians first used the written word to make laundry lists, to keep track of cows and slaves and household goods. But even in such primitive form, the writing down of symbols told of something hugely and richly revolutionary: the notion that one person could have a thought, even if that thought was only about the size of his flocks, and that that thought could be retained and then accessed—rethought, really—by another person in another place and time. The miraculous and transformative quality of this was immediately apparent to some and denied by others: Aristotle turned Alexander the Great into a great reader and champion of books, which led Alexander's successor, Ptolemy I, to create the world's first great library in Alexandria. But Socrates thought books were a waste of time, since they could only "remind one of what one already knows."

Perhaps, seeing his disdain rekindled on the printed page 2500 years after he first felt it—and understanding, surely, that some readers, reading his words, were indeed learning something about Socrates that they had never known before—the great thinker would change his mind. The clay tablet gave way to the scroll and then to the codex, the folded sheets that prefigured the book we hold and sell and treasure today. Wealthy households had books of prayers hand lettered and illuminated by monks; great soldiers kept their dispatches on paper. The French and English modified Gutenberg's press and then mechanized it to set down religious texts and the books of the Bible. Martin Luther nailed his written manifesto against the excesses of the Catholic hierarchy to the door of a church in Wittenberg and began a war of words that led to the Reformation and, eventually, to Protestantism; the Declaration of Independence was set in type and fomented, in relatively few words, a new way for men and women to look at their own government.

And soon publishers had the means, and the will, to publish   5
anything—cookbooks, broadsides, newspapers, novels, poetry, pornog-
raphy, picture books for children—and to publish them in a form that
many people could afford and most could find at the library. Reading
became a democratic act, making it possible for the many to teach
themselves what the few had once learned from tutors. The president
could quote Mark Twain because he had read *The Adventures of Huckleberry Finn,* and the postman could understand the reference because he
had read it, too. The Big Lies of demagoguery required more stealth and
cleverness, for careful reading of books and newspapers could reveal
their flaws to ordinary people. Not for nothing did the Nazis light up the
night skies in their cities with the burning of books. Not for nothing
were free white folks in America prohibited from teaching slaves to read,
and slaves in South Carolina threatened with the loss of the first joint of
their forefingers if they were caught looking at a book; books became
the greatest purveyors of truth, and the truth shall make you free.

But there was much more than freedom. Reading became the path-   6
way to the world, a world without geographic boundaries or even the
steep risers of time. There was a time machine in our world, but not the
contraption of metal and bolts and motors imagined even by a man as
imaginative as H. G. Wells. Socrates was wrong: a reader learns what he
or she does not know from books, what has passed and yet is forever
present through print. The mating rituals of the Trobriand Islanders.
The travails of the Donner Party. The beaches at Normandy. The smoke
from the stacks at Auschwitz. Experience, emotion, landscape: the world
is as layered as the earth, life cumulative with books. The eyewitnesses
die; the written word lives forever. So does the antipathy that ties two
brothers together in *East of Eden,* and the female search for independent
identity in *The Golden Notebook.* How is it that, a full two centuries after
Jane Austen finished her manuscript, we come to the world of *Pride
and Prejudice* and find ourselves transcending customs, strictures, time,
mores, to arrive at a place that educates, amuses, and enthralls us? It is
a miracle. We read in bed because reading is halfway between life and
dreaming, our own consciousness in someone else's mind. "To completely analyse what we do when we read," wrote E. B. Huey, "would
almost be the acme of the psychologist's achievements, for it would be
to describe very many of the most intricate workings of the human
mind." Yet we take it so for granted, the ability to simply flip the pages
and to know what the daughter of a parson, now long dead, once
thought of the conventions of matrimony in Regency England, and,
certainly, of the relations between men and women into perpetuity.

It is like the rubbing of two sticks together to make a fire, the act   7
of reading, an improbable pedestrian task that leads to heat and light.
Perhaps this only becomes clear when one watches a child do it. Dulled
to the mystery by years of STOP signs, recipes, form letters, package

instructions, suddenly it is self-evident that this is a strange and difficult thing, this making symbols into words, into sentences, into sentiments and scenes and a world imagined in the mind's eye. The children's author Lois Lowry recalled it once: "I remember the feeling of excitement that I had, the first time that I realized each letter had a sound, and the sounds went together to make words; and the words became sentences, and the sentences became stories." The very beginning of a child's reading is even more primal than that, for it is not so much reading but writing, learning to form the letters that make her own name. Naming the world: it is what we do with words from that moment on. All of reading is really only finding ways to name ourselves, and, perhaps, to name the others around us so that they will no longer seem like strangers. Crusoe and Friday. Ishmael and Ahab. Daisy and Gatsby. Pip and Estella. Me. Me. Me. I am not alone. I am surrounded by words that tell me who I am, why I feel what I feel. Or maybe they just help me while away the hours as the rain pounds down on the porch roof, taking me away from the gloom and on to somewhere sunny, somewhere else.

THINKING CRITICALLY ABOUT THE TEXT

Think about the nature of the written word. What can you say about its symbolic nature, its composition as arbitrary, squiggly marks on a page that in combination make up yet other arbitrary but well-agreed-upon words and meanings, that themselves can be combined into an infinite variety of sentences? In what ways can this symbolic layering be thought of as magical?

QUESTIONS ON SUBJECT

1. In paragraph 2 Quindlen sees words on the page, "words without the evanescence of speech," to have a special virtue. What for her is that virtue?

2. What difference in their attitudes toward books does Quindlen see between Alexander the Great and Socrates? Why does she think that Socrates was wrong about books?

3. Why does Quindlen think that watching a child read gives so much insight into the mysteries of the act of reading itself?

4. Why does Quindlen think we don't value reading?

5. In paragraph 6, Quindlen writes that "reading is halfway between life and dreaming, our own consciousness in someone else's mind." What does she mean?

QUESTIONS ON STRATEGY

1. What is Quindlen's thesis in this essay?

2. Make a list of at least six effects that reading has had on Quindlen.

3. In paragraph 5, Quindlen refers to a number of events caused by the production of texts. Does she establish a causal chain in any of these events?

4. Is your understanding of Quindlen's argument hampered in any way by not recognizing or understanding all of the citations to literary works that she makes? Explain.

5. Why, in paragraph 7, do you think that Quindlen turns to the role of writing in discussing the importance of reading?

QUESTIONS ON DICTION AND VOCABULARY

1. What does the sound of speech, the told story, offer us that the written story does not? What does Quindlen believe the written story offers us that the spoken story does not?

2. In paragraph 7 Quindlen relates the beginning of a child's reading to the naming process. In what ways are words themselves the result of the naming process?

3. Consult your dictionary for the following print-related terms that Quindlen uses if you do not know their meanings: *scroll* (paragraph 4), *codex* (4), *illuminated* (4), *dispatches* (4), *broadsides* (5).

CLASSROOM ACTIVITY USING CAUSE AND EFFECT ANALYSIS

Discuss at least six possible effects stemming from any one of the following innovations:

Laser surgery
iPods
blogs
satellite radio
Wi-Fi
magnetic resonance imaging (MRI)
Hubbell telescope

WRITING SUGGESTIONS

1. Using Quindlen's essay as a model, write an essay of your own that is entitled "How Writing Changed My Life." Tell how the cause (writing) results in the effects you want to highlight. In your experience, was writing a remote cause or an immediate one? Did writing cause you to become a keen observer of the world around you, to be more critical and analytical? Did writing cause you to analyze and then synthesize from your own perspective the people, ideas, and circumstances of your life? How did writing change your thinking and the way you go about knowing and sharing your world?

2. Popular media today often refer to the "YouTube influence." This is usually taken to mean a quick, fragmented way of presenting things that,

detractors say, gives us a shallow sound-bite understanding of an issue, rather than an in-depth exploration of the topic. Do you feel comfortable with the frenetic pace of communication these days? Write an essay in which you explore the effects of new ways of communicating information and entertainment that have moved us away from what some would call the relaxing, thoughtful, in-depth process that we know as reading.

3. Quindlen's thesis that reading changed her life relies for its support on her catalog of the traditional books that have influenced her. There are a number of people, however, who can imagine that books as physical objects may become a thing of the past. One argument for this is that books "imprison" information, making it difficult, if not impossible, to transfer the information they contain across various platforms. Write an essay in which you explore the idea that while books may change their physical form and morph into ebooks, or audiobooks, or hypertext, the act of reading and the benefits we derive from it will endure.

iPod World: The End of Society?

Andrew Sullivan

Andrew Sullivan was born in 1963 in South Godstone, Surrey, England, to Irish parents. He earned his B.A. degree in modern history at Magdalene College, Oxford, and his master's degree and Ph.D. in government at Harvard. Sullivan began his career in journalism at the New Republic *and later wrote* for the New York Times Magazine. *A gay, Catholic, conservative, and often controversial commentator, Sullivan has made history as a blogger. His* The Daily Dish *became very popular post–9/11 and was receiving over 50,000 hits a day by 2005. After nearly five years of blogging and writing books and articles, he decided to take a break from journalism. Later, in 2007, he accepted an editorial position with the* Atlantic. *Sullivan has written several books:* Virtually Normal: An Argument about Homosexuality *(1995);* Love Undetectable: Notes on Friendship, Sex and Survival *(1998); and* The Conservative Soul: How We Lost It, How to Get It Back *(2006).*

In "iPod World: The End of Society?," which was first published in the New York Times Magazine *on February 20, 2005, Sullivan examines the effects, both positive and negative, of the proliferation of iPods in our society.*

PREPARING TO READ

If you are an iPod owner, what is attractive to you about the device? What does it allow you to do? What does it prevent you from having to do? Do you feel any sense of isolation in using your iPod? Do you think that your use of an iPod represents anything unique in our history? If so, what? If you do not have an iPod, what has prevented you from entering "iPod World"?

I was visiting New York City last week and noticed something I'd never thought I'd say about the big city. Yes, nightlife is pretty much dead (and I'm in no way the first to notice that). But daylife—that insane mishmash of yells, chatter, clatter, hustle and chutzpah that makes New York the urban equivalent of methamphetamine—was also a little different. It was just a little quieter. Yes, the suburbanization of Manhattan is now far-gone, its downtown a Disney-like string of malls, riverside parks, and pretty upper-middle-class villages. But there was something else as well. And as I looked across the throngs on the pavements, I began to see why. There were little white wires hanging down from their ears, tucked into pockets or purses or jackets. The eyes were a little vacant. Each was in his or her own little musical world, walking to their own soundtrack, stars in their own music video, almost oblivious to the world around them. These are the iPod people.

1

The "i" Stands for ISOLATION.

iPod

10,000 songs in your pocket. Mac or PC.

Even without the white wires, you can tell who they are. They walk   2
down the street in their own MP3 cocoon, bumping into others, deaf to
small social cues, shutting out anyone not in their bubble. Every now
and again, some start unconsciously emitting strange tuneless
squawks, like a badly-tuned radio, and their fingers snap or their arms
twitch to some strange soundless rhythm. When others say, "Excuse
me," there's no response. "Hi." Ditto. It's strange to be among so much
people and hear so little. Except that each one is hearing so much.

Yes, I might as well fess up. I'm one of them. I witnessed the glazed   3
New York looks through my own glazed pupils, my own white wires
peeping out of my eardrums. I joined the cult a few years ago: the sect of
the little white box worshippers. Every now and again, I go to church —
those huge, luminous Apple stores, pews in the rear, the clerics in
their monastic uniforms all bustling around, or sitting behind the
"Genius Bars," like priests waiting to hear confessions. Others began,
like I did, with a Walkman — and then another kind of clunkier MP3
player. But the sleekness of the iPod won me over. Unlike previous

models, it actually gave me my entire musical collection to rearrange as I saw fit—on the fly, in my pocket. What was once an occasional musical diversion became a compulsive obsession. Now I have my iTunes in my iMac for my iPod in my iWorld. It's Narcissus' heaven: we've finally put the "i" into Me.

And, like all addictive cults, it's spreading. There are now 22 million iPod owners in the United States and Apple is now becoming a mass market company for the first time. Walk through any U.S. airport these days, and you will see person after person gliding through the social ether as if on auto-pilot. Get on a subway, and you're surrounded by a bunch of Stepford commuters, all sealed off from each other, staring into mid-space as if anaesthetized by technology. Don't ask, don't tell, don't over-hear, don't observe. Just tune in and tune out.

It wouldn't be so worrisome if it weren't part of something even bigger. Americans are beginning to narrowcast their own lives. You get your news from your favorite blogs, the ones that won't challenge your own view of the world. You tune into a paid satellite radio service that also aims directly at a small market—for New Age fanatics, or liberal talk, or Christian rock. Television is all cable. Culture is all subculture. Your cell-phones can receive email feeds of your favorite blogger's latest thoughts—seconds after he has posted them—or sports scores for your own team, or stock quotes of just your portfolio. Technology has given us finally a universe entirely for ourselves—where the serendipity of meeting a new stranger, or hearing a piece of music we would never choose for ourselves, or an opinion that might actually force us to change our mind about something are all effectively banished. Atomization by little white boxes and cell-phones. Society without the social. Others who are chosen—not met at random.

Human beings have never lived like this before. Yes, we have always had homes or retreats or places where we went to relax or unwind or shut the world out. But we didn't walk around the world like hermit crabs with our isolation surgically attached. Music in particular was once the preserve of the living room or the concert hall. It was sometimes solitary but it was primarily a shared experience, something that brought people together, gave them the comfort of knowing that others too understood the pleasure of that Brahms symphony or that Beatles album.

But music is as atomized now as living is. And it's also secret. That bloke next to you on the bus could be listening to heavy metal or Gregorian chant. You'll never know. And so, bit by bit, you'll never really know him. And by his very white wires, he is indicating he doesn't really want to know you.

What do we get from this? The awareness of more music, more often. The chance to slip away for a while from everydayness, to give our lives our own sound-track, to still the monotony of the commute, to listen more closely and carefully to music that can lift you up and keep you going. We become masters of our own interests, more connected to people like us over the Internet, more instantly in touch with anything we want or need or think we want and think we need. Ever tried a stairmaster in silence? And why not listen to a Haydn trio while in line at Tesco?

But what are we missing? That hilarious shard of an overheard conversation that stays with you all day; the child whose chatter on the sidewalk takes you back to your own early memories; birdsong; weather; accents; the laughter of others; and those thoughts that come not by filling your head with selected diversion, but by allowing your mind to wander aimlessly through the regular background noise of human and mechanical life. External stimulation can crowd out the interior mind. Even the boredom that we flee has its uses. We are forced to find our own means to overcome it. And so we enrich our life from within, rather than from the static of white wires.

It's hard to give up, though, isn't it? Not so long ago, I was on a trip and realized I had left my iPod behind. Panic. But then something else. I noticed the rhthyms of others again, the sound of the airplane, the opinions of the cabby, the small social cues that had been obscured before. I noticed how others related to each other. And I felt just a little bit connected again. And a little more aware. Try it. There's a world out there. And it has a soundtrack all its own.

THINKING CRITICALLY ABOUT THE TEXT

Sulllivan's title asks whether iPod world represents the end of society. Do you think Sullivan answers his own question? If so, how and where in the text does he do so? If not, why might Sullivan have left the question for us to answer? Explain.

QUESTIONS ON SUBJECT

1. What is Sullivan's thesis in this essay? (Glossary: *Thesis*)

2. What does Sullivan see as the benefits of iPod world? What does he see as the drawbacks?

3. What does Sullivan mean when he writes in paragraph 5, "Culture is all subculture"?

4. What suggestion does Sullivan make at the conclusion of his essay? Is his suggestion an appropriate conclusion for his essay? (Glossary: *Beginnings/Endings*)

QUESTIONS ON STRATEGY

1. What particular features of the iPod lead to the effects Sullivan points out?

2. In paragraph 3, Sullivan equates iPod world to a cult or religion. How does his analogy work? (Glossary: *Analogy*)

3. Sullivan writes in paragraph 6: "Human beings have never lived like this before." How does he use comparison and contrast to help make his point? (Glossary: *Comparison and Contrast*)

4. Cite several examples where Sullivan uses irony in his essay. (Glossary: *Irony*) To what effect does he use this rhetorical device?

5. In his final paragraph Sullivan gives us a brief example of cause and effect at work. What happens when he forgets to take his iPod on a trip?

QUESTIONS ON DICTION AND VOCABULARY

1. Reread paragraph 7. If you didn't already know that Sullivan was an Englishman, would you be able to tell from his diction in this paragraph? Explain.

2. Sullivan uses the words *atomization* (paragraph 5) and *atomized* (7). What does he mean by their use and why do these words work so well for him?

3. How would you characterize Sullivan's style in this essay? Is it formal or informal, chatty or preachy, journalistic or academic, or something else? Support your answer with examples from the text. (Glossary: *Style*)

CLASSROOM ACTIVITY USING CAUSE AND EFFECT

In preparation for a classroom discussion, use your iPod or MP3 player for a morning as you go about your daily campus activities. In the afternoon, do not use the device at all. Make a brief list of the effects of both using and not using the device as a prompt for your later classroom discussion.

WRITING SUGGESTIONS

1. Study the photo on page 433. It is one of a series of poster advertisements for the iPod on which someone has written an interpretation of the meaning of the "i" in "iPod." Write an argument for or against the idea expressed in the graffito: "The 'i' stands for ISOLATION." Feel free to use the ideas and statements that Andrew Sullivan uses in his essay as prompts, quotations, and evidence in your own work, but do not simply parrot what Sullivan has to say. Reach out in new and creative ways to express the causal relationship between the iPod and isolation.

2. Every time a new technological advance has been made that is widely accepted—telephone, radio, television, video, DVDs, cell phones, and similar devices—there are those who decry the innovation as the end of society as we know it. Write an essay in which you argue either that the iPod is just such a device, or that it is different from the others in significant ways. Be sure to include clear explanations that are based in cause and effect analysis.

3. An underlying concern, and perhaps a theme, in Sullivan's essay is that music plays a vital role in our sense of well-being. Each person with an iPod plays, in effect, a personally programmed and designed soundtrack for his or her life. Write an essay in which you examine music as a cause in your life and the way it affects you.

The Real Computer Virus

Carl M. Cannon

Carl M. Cannon was born in San Francisco and majored in journalism at the University of Colorado. For twenty years he worked on a number of newspapers covering local and state politics, education, crime, and race relations. His reporting was instrumental in securing the freedom of a man in Georgia and a man in California who had both been wrongly convicted of murder. In 1989 Cannon's reporting on the Loma Prieta *earthquake for the* San Jose Mercury *won him a Pulitzer Prize. Since 1998, Cannon has been a staff writer for the prestigious* National Journal *where he is now the White House correspondent. Cannon's books include* Boy Genius *(2003), a biography of George W. Bush's advisor Karl Rove, which he wrote with Lou Dubose and Jan Reid; and* The Pursuit of Happiness in Times of War *(2003), which examines the meaning and history of Jefferson's influential and quintessentially American phrase.*

In the following excerpt from "The Real Computer Virus," which first appeared in American Journalism Review *in April 2001, Cannon writes about the problems of obtaining accurate information on the Internet and correcting the misinformation frequently found and spread there.*

PREPARING TO READ

How do you go about fact-checking information from the Internet? Do you check to see who writes or sponsors the Web sites you visit? Do you use more than one or two sources for the information you need? Have you ever had reason to doubt the accuracy of information you have actually used in an assignment?

The Internet is an invaluable information-gathering tool for journal- 1
ists. It also has an unmatched capacity for distributing misinformation, which all too often winds up in the mainstream media.

To commemorate Independence Day last year, *Boston Globe* colum- 2
nist Jeff Jacoby came up with an idea that seemed pretty straightforward. Just explain to his readers what happened to the brave men who signed the Declaration of Independence.

This column caused big trouble for Jacoby when it was discovered 3
that he had lifted the idea and some of its language from a ubiquitous e-mail making the rounds. It touched a particular nerve at the *Globe*, which had recently forced two well-regarded columnists to resign for making up quotes and characters. Jacoby was suspended for four months without pay, generating a fair amount of controversy, much of it because he was the primary conservative voice at an identifiably liberal paper.

But there was a more fundamental issue at play than Jacoby's   4
failure to attribute the information in the column: Much of what the
e-mail contained was factually incorrect. To his credit, Jacoby recognized this flaw and tried, with some success, to correct it. Ann Landers,
however, didn't. She got the same e-mail and simply ran it verbatim in
her column.

Passing along what she described as a "perfect" Independence Day   5
column sent to her from "Ellen" in New Jersey, Ann Landers' epistle
began this way:

Have you ever wondered what happened to the 56 men who signed the   6
Declaration of Independence?

Five signers were captured by the British as traitors and tortured before   7
they died. Twelve had their homes ransacked and burned. Two lost their sons
who served in the Revolutionary Army. . . . Nine of the 56 fought and died
from wounds or hardships of the Revolutionary War. They pledged their lives,
their fortunes and their sacred honor.

Landers' column—like Ellen's e-mail—goes on from that point to   8
list names and explain the purported fates of many of the men. But this
was not the "perfect" column Landers thought it was, for the simple
reason that much of the information in it is simply false—as any Revolutionary War scholar would know readily.

I know because I interviewed some of them. R. J. Rockefeller, direc-   9
tor of reference services at the Maryland State Archives, reveals that
none of the signers was tortured to death by the British. E. Brooke
Harlowe, a political scientist at the College of St. Catherine in St. Paul,
Minnesota, reports that two of the 56 were wounded in battle, rather
than nine being killed. Brown University historian Gordon S. Wood
points out that although the e-mail claims that for signer Thomas
McKean "poverty was his reward," McKean actually ended up being
governor of Pennsylvania and lived in material comfort until age 83.

And so on. What Landers was passing along was a collection of   10
myths and partial truths that had been circulating since at least 1995,
and which has made its way into print in newspaper op-eds and letters-
to-the-editor pages and onto the radio airwaves many times before.
Mark Twain supposedly said, in a less technologically challenging time,
that a lie can make it halfway 'round the world before the truth gets its
boots on. The Internet gives untruth a head start it surely never needed.
And what a head start: If an e-mailer sends a message to 10 people and
each person who receives it passes it on to 10 more, by the ninth transmission this missive could reach a billion people.

This is the real computer virus: misinformation. Despite years of   11
warnings, this malady keeps creeping its way into the newsprint and
onto the airwaves of mainstream news outlets.

One of the things that makes the Internet so appealing is that any-   12
one can pull things off of it. The other side of the coin is that anyone

can put anything on it. This poses a particular challenge for reporters who are taught in journalism school to give more weight to the written word (get the official records!) than to something they hearsay, word-of-mouth at the corner barber shop. But the Web has both official documents and idle gossip, and reporters using it as a research tool—or even a tip sheet—do not always know the difference.

"Journalists should be really skeptical of everything they read   13
online," says Sreenath Sreenivasan, a professor at the Columbia University Graduate School of Journalism. "They should be very aware of where they are on the Web, just the way they would be if they were on the street."

They aren't always.   14

In November 1998, the *New York Times* pulled off the Web—and   15
published—a series of riotously funny Chinese translations of actual Hollywood hits. *The Crying Game* became "Oh No! My Girlfriend Has a Penis!" *My Best Friend's Wedding* became "Help! My Pretend Boyfriend Is Gay." *Batman and Robin* was "Come to My Cave and Wear this Rubber Codpiece, Cute Boy."

If those seemed, in the old newsroom phrase, too good to check,   16
it's because they were. They came from an irreverent Web site called TopFive.com, which bills itself as offering "dangerously original humor."

But even after the *Times* issued a red-faced correction, the "transla-   17
tions" kept showing up. On January 5, 1999, Peter Jennings read the spoof of the title of the movie *Babe* ("The Happy Dumpling-To-Be Who Talks and Solves Agricultural Problems") as if it were factual. Jennings issued a correction 13 days later for his *World News Tonight* gaffe, but that didn't stop things. On April 16, 1999, some of the bogus translations showed up on CNN's *Showbiz Today*. On June 10, a *Los Angeles Times* staff writer threw one of the TopFive.com titles into his sports column. In Hong Kong, he claimed, the title *Field of Dreams* was "Imaginary Dead Ballplayers in a Cornfield."

"What journalists need to do is learn to distinguish between the   18
crap on the Web and the good stuff," says Yale University researcher and lecturer Fred Shapiro. "It's a crucial skill and one that some journalists need to be taught."

Even before President Clinton stirred up controversy with a slew of   19
late-term pardons and commutations, I researched and wrote a 4,000-word article on the historical and legal underpinnings of a U.S. president's power to grant pardons, commutations, and clemency orders. One pertinent constitutional question was whether there are any real restrictions on the presidential pardon authority.

Logging onto Lexis-Nexis, I found several relevant, in-depth law   20
review articles. Some of them cited Internet links to the original cases being cited. In fact these were highlighted "hyperlinks," meaning that with a single click of my mouse I was able to read the controlling

Supreme Court cases dating back to Reconstruction. Within seconds of clicking on those Supreme Court links, I was gazing at the actual words of Salmon P. Chase, the chief justice appointed by Abraham Lincoln. Justice Chase answered my question rather unequivocally: "To the executive alone is entrusted the power of pardon," he wrote with simple eloquence, "and it is granted without limit."

This is not an isolated example. I cover the White House for 21 *National Journal* and, like many of my colleagues, I have developed an utter reliance on the Internet. I do research and interviews online, find phone numbers, check facts and spellings, and research the clips. I can read court cases online, check presidential transcripts, find the true source of quotes, and delve into history.

Some days this is a tool that feels like a magic wand. The riches of 22 the Web are as vast as the journalist's imagination.

The point of these examples is that the Internet has rapidly become 23 such a valuable research tool that it's hard to remember how we did our jobs without it. Need that killer Shakespeare reference to truth-telling from *As You Like It* to spice up that Clinton legacy piece? Log on and find it. Fact-checking the Bible verses slung around by the candidates during the 2000 presidential election? The Bible is not only on the Web but is searchable with a couple of keystrokes. Attorney General John Ashcroft's Senate voting record is there, too, along with his controversial interview with *Southern Partisan* magazine.

Yet in recent months I have found myself quietly checking the 24 validity of almost everything I find in cyberspace and whenever possible doing it the old-fashioned way: consulting reference books in libraries, calling professors or original sources on the phone, double-checking everything. I don't trust the information on the Net very much anymore. It turns out the same technology that gives reporters access to the intellectual richness of the ages also makes misinformation ubiquitous. It shouldn't come as a surprise, but a tool this powerful must be handled with care.

These problems are only going to get worse unless Net users — and 25 journalists — get a whole lot more careful. According to the Nielsen/ NetRatings released on February 15, 168 million Americans logged onto the Web in the first month of the new millennium.

Seven years ago, *American Journalism Review* warned that an over- 26 reliance on Lexis-Nexis was leading to a "misinformation explosion." Since that time, the number of journalists using the data retrieval service has increased exponentially; at many news organizations, libraries have been phased out and reporters do their own searches. This has led, predictably, to an entire subgenre of phony quotes and statistics that won't die.

Sometimes the proliferation of errors carries serious implica- 27 tions. A couple of years ago, Diane Sawyer concluded a *PrimeTime Live* interview with Ellen DeGeneres the night her lesbian television character "came out" by reciting what Sawyer called "a government statistic": gay teenagers are "three times as likely to attempt suicide" as straight teenagers.

This factoid, which Sawyer said was provided to her by DeGeneres, is a crock.

28

Sleuthing by a diligent reporter named Delia M. Rios of Newhouse News Service revealed that this figure is not a government statistic, but rather the opinion of a single San Francisco social worker. In fact, a high-level interagency panel made up of physicians and researchers from the U.S. Department of Health and Human Services, the Centers for Disease Control, the National Institute of Mental Health, and other organizations concluded that there is no evidence that "sexual orientation and suicidality are linked in some direct or indirect manner."

29

Yet, the bogus stat is still routinely cited by certain gay-rights activists, and thanks to Internet-assisted databases, has made its way into the *New York Times*, the *Chicago Tribune*, the *Los Angeles Times* — and onto prime time network television.

30

Joyce Hunter, onetime president of the National Lesbian and Gay Health Association, insists that the available evidence suggests that both gay and straight teens are, instead, emotionally resilient people who "go on to develop a positive sense of self and who go on with their lives." Other clinicians fear that this misinformation could turn into a self-fulfilling prophecy. Peter Muehrer of the National Institutes of Health says he worries that a public hysteria over gay-teen suicide could contribute to "suicide contagion," in which troubled gay teens come to see suicide as a practical, almost normal, way out of their identity struggles.

31

Junk science on the Web — or junk history — has a way of oozing into the mainstream media, often because it proves irresistible to disc jockeys and radio talk-show hosts. The same is true of conspiracy theories and faulty understanding of the law, particularly when the incendiary subject of race relations is involved.

32

An e-mail marked "URGENT! URGENT! URGENT!" flew like the wind through the African American community for more than two years. It warned that blacks' "right to vote" will expire in 2007. The impetus for the e-mail was the impending expiration of the Voting Rights Act, which has since been renewed and, in any event, no longer has anything to do with guaranteeing anyone the right to vote.

33

Nonetheless, the preposterous claim was reiterated by callers to African American radio talk shows. Eventually, it prompted an official rebuttal by the Justice Department and a public disavowal by the Congressional Black Caucus. "The Web has good, useful information," observes David Bositis, senior political analyst for the Joint Center for Political and Economic Studies. "But it also has a lot of garbage."

34

This particular cyberrumor was eventually traced to a naive but   35
well-intentioned college student from Chicago, who toured the South
on a promotional trip sponsored by the NAACP. The mistaken notion
that blacks' right to vote depends on the whims of Congress was given
wide circulation in a guest column in *USA Today* by Camille O. Cosby,
wife of entertainer Bill Cosby.

"Congress once again will decide whether African Americans will   36
be allowed to vote," she wrote, echoing the e-mail. "No other Americans are subjected to this oppressive nonsense."

Black leaders went to great lengths to dispel this hoax, but it ener-   37
gized black voters. The ensuing higher-than-normal black turnout in
the 1998 midterm elections helped Democrats at the polls, led to
House Speaker Newt Gingrich's demise, and may have saved Bill Clinton's job. Could the e-mail hoax have played a role?

Other hoaxes are not so accidental. Last year, as the presidential   38
campaign began heating up, I received an e-mail from a fellow journalist alerting me to an anti–Al Gore Web site she thought contained valuable information. It included a litany of silly statements attributed to
Gore. Some of them were accurate, but several of them I recognized as
being utterances of former Vice President Dan Quayle. Others were
statements never said by either Gore or Quayle.

On October 3, 1999, when liberal movie star Warren Beatty spoke   39
to Americans for Democratic Action about his political views, he said
that he wasn't the only one who worried that corporations were a
threat to democracy. Beatty said that Abraham Lincoln himself had
warned that corporations are "more despotic than monarchy," adding
that Lincoln also said "the money power preys upon the nation in
times of peace, and it conspires against it in times of adversity." Beatty's
populist version of Lincoln hardly squares with his career as a corporate
attorney—he represented Illinois Central Railroad before he ran for
public office—but that didn't faze modern journalists. "That Lincoln
stuff just amazed me," gushed *Newsweek's* Jonathan Alter on *Rivera Live*.
Alter wrote that Beatty's "harshest attacks . . . were actually quotes
from a speech by Abraham Lincoln."

Actually, they weren't. Lincoln's official biographer once called the   40
quote "a bold, unblushing forgery." And in a piece for History News
Service, an online site that often debunks faulty history, Lincoln
scholar Matthew Pinsker said this particular fake Lincoln citation has
been around since 1896. In his speech at the 1992 Republican National
Convention, Ronald Reagan attributed phony conservative sentiments
to Honest Abe, including, "You cannot help the weak by punishing the
strong," and "You cannot help the poor by destroying the rich."

This example underscores a couple of important caveats about the   41
Web. First, bogus quotes were around a long time before the Internet.

Moreover, the Net itself is often a useful tool for those trying to correct canards.

A postscript: Three years ago, while discussing with reporters the pitfalls of the Internet, Hillary Rodham Clinton employed the line often attributed to Twain—and cited earlier in this piece—about a lie making its way halfway 'round the world before the truth could get its boots on. "Well, today," she added, "the lie can be twice around the world before the truth gets out of bed to find its boots." While fact-checking this article, I had reason to call Fred Shapiro at Yale. Perhaps because Mrs. Clinton never mentioned Twain—she attributed it to an "old saying"—my interest was piqued, and I asked Shapiro if he'd ever heard the aphorism. "I have just been intensively researching Twain quotes, and didn't come across this one," he replied. "I would assume that Twain did not say it." 42

Uh-oh. That sent me back into research mode. What I found is that the "Twain" quote has been around. According to a 1996 article by James Bennet of the *New York Times*, Mrs. Clinton (and Al Gore as well) used the line, with attribution to Twain. Other politicians have credited it to Twain as well. Clintonite Paul Begala, writing last year in the *Orlando Sentinel*, used it, giving Twain full credit. So did Republican stalwart Haley Barbour in a *Roll Call* op-ed. In a 1999 column in the *Chattanooga Times*, a writer named L. M. Boyd gave credit for the quote to "the sage Israel Zangwill," adding that famed CBS newsman Edward R. Murrow used it all the time. 43

On the Internet, the responses were even more varied. Several Web sites credited Twain while others attributed the quote to Will Rogers; Reagan-era Interior Secretary James Watt; Winston Churchill; another former British prime minister, James Callaghan; and, in one case, merely to "a French proverb." 44

Possibly all of these sources uttered it at one time or another. Callaghan seems to have done so on November 1, 1976, in an address to the House of Commons. But he attributed the line to the man who is probably its rightful author: a Baptist preacher from England named Charles Haddon Spurgeon, a contemporary of Twain who, according to *Benham's Book of Quotations*, wrote this line: "A lie travels 'round the world, while Truth is putting on her boots." 45

Amen. 46

THINKING CRITICALLY ABOUT THE TEXT

In paragraph 12, Cannon states, "One of the things that makes the Internet so appealing is that anyone can pull things off of it. The other side of the coin is that anyone can put anything on it." Do you agree? Why or why not?

QUESTIONS ON SUBJECT

1. Cannon writes that one cause of journalists' errors is that they don't have much time to check their sources for accuracy. How do you respond? Do you accept that as a proper response?

2. What false understanding of the law in a cyberrumor led to a great deal of anxiety among African Americans?

3. What are the causes of errors in the information found on the Internet, according to Cannon?

4. If, as Cannon argues, the Web is a terrible source for accurate information, what can be done about the increasing numbers of people who have come to rely on it?

5. Have Cannon's ideas about the accuracy of information retrieved from the Web altered your own research methods? Why, or why not?

QUESTIONS ON STRATEGY

1. What is Cannon arguing for in this essay? (Glossary: *Argument*) What is his thesis? (Glossary: *Thesis*)

2. What evidence does Cannon cite to support the fact that misinformation on the Internet can be downright dangerous? (Glossary: *Evidence; Illustration*)

3. How does Cannon use cause and effect analysis in his essay? Cite several examples.

4. Cannon begins with the story of Jeff Jacoby and the *Boston Globe*. Why is this a particularly good example for the beginning of his article? (Glossary: *Beginnings/Endings*)

5. Cannon ends with a postscript about the quotation falsely attributed to Mark Twain: "A lie can make it halfway around the world before the truth can get its boots on." Why is this an apt way of ending his essay? (Glossary: *Beginnings/Endings*)

QUESTIONS ON DICTION AND VOCABULARY

1. How appropriate is "The Real Computer Virus" as a title? (Glossary: *Title*) Is the comparison of misinformation to a computer virus appropriate? (Glossary: *Analogy*) Why or why not?

2. What is Cannon's tone in this essay? (Glossary: *Tone*) What evidence do you find in his diction for your assessment?

3. Cannon labels paragraphs 42–46 "A postscript." Why is that label appropriate?

CLASSROOM ACTIVITY USING CAUSE AND EFFECT ANALYSIS

In preparation for writing an essay of cause and effect analysis, list two effects on society and two effects on personal behavior for one of the following items: television talk shows, iPods, online shopping, all-sports channels, reality television programs, television advertising, fast food, or an item of your choosing. For example, a cell phone could be said to have the following effects:

SOCIETY

Enhanced highway safety in case of accidents
Expansion of the economy

PERSONAL BEHAVIOR

Higher personal phone bills
Risks to driving safety (where cell phone use is allowed)

Be prepared to discuss your answers with the class.

WRITING SUGGESTIONS

1. "According to the Nielsen/NetRatings released on February 15, 168 million Americans logged onto the Web in the first month of the new millennium" (paragraph 25). Why does Cannon cite this figure? (Glossary: *Evidence*) What does Cannon mean when he says "These problems are only going to get worse unless Net users—and journalists—get a whole lot more careful" (25). Write an essay in which you discuss possible effects of misinformation on an increasingly Web-savvy and Web-dependent public. How do incidents of incorrect reporting, such as those Cannon discusses, affect public trust of the media? What skills will people need to better judge what they read both online and off? What measures could be implemented to ensure that information is accurate and reliable? What would the other effects of such measures be?

2. Cannon discusses how the Internet, electronic databases, and e-mail can be used to spread misinformation and disinformation. What do these two terms mean? (Glossary: *Definition*) What examples does Cannon cite as evidence of each? (Glossary: *Evidence; Illustration*) Write an essay in which you explore the differences between misinformation and disinformation. (Glossary: *Comparison and Contrast*) In your opinion, which poses the greater threat? Why?

The Great Kern County Mouse War

Kennedy P. Maize

An environmental journalist, Kennedy P. Maize was born in Pittsburgh, Pennsylvania, in 1944. A 1966 graduate of Penn State University, Maize is a freelance writer whose articles on environmental and energy issues have appeared in Environmental Action, *the* New Republic, Analog, *and* Harper's. *In the early 1990s, Maize's interests in corporate structures and how they interact with environmental concerns led him to start his own newsletter, the* Electricity Daily. *Maize lives in Knoxville, Maryland, where he also maintains a small sheep farm.*

A letter to the editor of the local newspaper about the misguided practice of shooting vultures led Maize to research the events chronicled in the following essay. The essay, which appeared in Audubon *magazine in 1977, explores the war against the rodents of Kern County, California, in the 1920s. Maize's story serves as a lesson for today's readers about just what can happen when humans interfere with the balance of nature.*

PREPARING TO READ

What sorts of animal pests would you love to get rid of? The cockroaches overrunning your apartment, the skunks that spray your dog, the mosquitoes that make a misery of early summer, the feral cats or raccoons raiding neighborhood garbage cans? How might you go about eliminating them? How would your life be improved as a result? What other consequences might occur?

O nce upon a time, some 75 years ago, the good people of Kern County, California, had an idea. They thought they were very smart. They would rid themselves of all the evil predators that killed their domestic animals, frightened their children, and made life unpleasant. 1

So in the early years of this century, the good citizens of Kern County oiled their shotguns, cleaned their traps, and brewed batches of strychnine. For 20 years they killed the evil predators—the skunk, the fox, the badger, the weasel, the snake, the owl, the hawk. Killed them all, every one they could find. The good folk of Kern County were very pleased. 2

In 1924 the good sheepmen of Kern County concocted a final solution to the "coyote problem." They hired a U.S. Biological Survey team (then part of the Department of Agriculture) to exterminate the entire coyote population. Soon there were no more coyotes in Kern County. 3

The good folk of Kern County were filled with satisfaction by what they had accomplished. They supposed they had created a pleasant 4

446

paradise where their chickens would have no natural enemies, their children would never be frightened by talon or fang, and their dogs would never return stinking of skunk. Providence, they were sure, would bless their work with healthy animals, happy children, and bountiful harvests.

Most of the good people of Kern County were either farmers or townsmen in Taft, Tupman, McKittrick, Ford City, and other small villages. There was one city, Bakersfield, a market center with a population of under 10,000 people. Most of the good people of Kern County rarely got to Bakersfield. Despite oil derricks that dotted the landscape, Kern County in the 1920s was rural, agricultural. 5

Farming in Kern County was risky. Every year farmers planted grain in the fertile 25,000 acres of the dry bed of Buena Vista Lake. Three years out of every four the lake bed flooded in the fall, destroying the crop. But the fourth year—what a harvest for the good people of Kern County. 6

Such a year was 1926. There was kafir corn and barley in such bounty that all California took notice of Kern County's good fortune. The good merchants of Kern County rubbed their hands together as they thought about the dresses and cars and fencing and paint and other things the good farmers would buy with their grain receipts. So the good farmers reaped their grain, leaving behind 25,000 acres of stubble and scattered seed. The farmers took their grain to market and felt secure in their good fortune. 7

By October the good people of Kern County had begun to notice a minor annoyance. A farmer came to town one Saturday to buy supplies and a new shotgun, and he told the other farmers and the merchants about his little problem: "I killed nearly 500 mice in my barn last evening," he said. "You'd better sell me some poison, George." 8

Just as the storekeeper was reaching for the rat poison, his wife was telling a neighbor, "I just don't know about this cat of mine. She's getting so lazy. Seems like everywhere I look there's a mouse." 9

And there were mice. Everywhere the good people of Kern County looked, there were mice. The mice had bred in the Buena Vista Lake, unmolested by predators and well fed on residue from the harvest, until there were many millions of them. So many, in fact, that the food supply began to run out. Most were still in the dry lake bed, which looked as if it had just been cultivated, the result of mice burrowing in the ground. Mice were feeding on the grain residue, and continuing to breed. 10

A few mice, maybe a hundred thousand or so, had ventured out of the lake bed by November. The foraging vanguard increased in December. They were invading barns, granaries, and houses looking for food. In some places near the lake the mice were ankle-deep. People killed them by the thousands. "The way we're slaughtering mice," one farmer said, "they'll soon be as scarce as coyotes. Now, if you'll excuse me, I have to shoot some owls I found in my silo." 11

If the farmer was wrong about the effect of killing thousands of 12
mice, he can be excused his error. So far the good citizens of Kern
County had fought only skirmishes in what would quickly become the
Great Kern County Mouse War. But the good people of Kern County
thought they had taken heroic measures and that they had won. After
all, hadn't the West Side Businessmen's Club in Taft donated $50 for
poisoned wheat after the county's deputy horticultural commissioner,
C. H. Bowen, described the problem? Taft Mayor Clarence Williams
said he would hand out the poison to the good farmers. That ought to
do the trick.

The effort seemed to work. By Christmas of 1926 Commissioner 13
Bowen, whom the press was calling "General" for his leadership of the
war against the mice, told reporters, "By the first of the week I expect
our work to be finished." *The Los Angeles Times* of December 29th
reported, "Field mouse infestations at Taft and Tupman have been
brought under control through the use of poisoned grain, the horticultural commissioner's office announced today."

But Kern County didn't understand the dimensions of its mouse 14
problem. All the few hundred pounds of poisoned grain had accomplished was to delay hordes of mice that were marching out of the lake
toward new food supplies. A cold snap at Christmas probably did as
much to cause the delay as did the poisoned grain.

The new year of 1927 opened cold and clear, and the good people of 15
Kern County faced the future with confidence. The mice seemed under
control, and there would be prosperity ahead if they continued their
eternal vigilance against the hawks, owls, coyotes, and other varmints.

Those good people who subscribed to the *Los Angeles Times* may 16
have noticed a small feature article on New Year's Day. A park naturalist
pointed out that the hated coyote is a very good mouser. But, of course,
the article didn't mean much to the good people of Kern County. There
were no coyotes in Kern County.

The cold snap broke on January 6th, and the mice emerged from 17
the lake bed in a squirming, furry wave, driven by starvation. The mice
had consumed every edible item in the lake bed. Scrambling up the
barren, 100-foot Buena Vista Hills, the mice headed for Ford City,
McKittrick, and Taft. Millions of mice were on the march toward food.
U.S. Highway 399, which ran along the lake bed, became slippery with
squashed mice, and cars slid into the ditches. Warning signs reading
"Slow: slippery conditions" were posted.

Superintendent Bob Maguire of the Honolulu Oil Company put 18
men from the derricks on mouse detail. They dug trenches and spread
poisoned barley. Maguire's mouse-control crew killed 50,000 mice in
one day on one small piece of company property.

By January 16th, the U.S. Biological Survey was calling the affair in 19
Kern County the greatest rodent infestation in U.S. history. The only

other comparable incident was a mouse migration in 1908 in Nevada. But the Biological Survey said the Nevada episode was minuscule compared with the problem in Kern County. Observers reported a "moving landscape" as mice poured over the earth in ankle-deep waves.

One January morning during the mouse invasion, a teacher at 20 Conley School near the lake opened her desk for the day's lesson plan. A dozen mice leaped out, and she leaped out the school door, shrieking. Mice were in every wastebasket. Mice occupied the principal's office. Mice darted from classroom to classroom. Mice were everywhere.

On January 15th, a headline appeared in the *Los Angeles Times:* 21 "Army of Field Mice Kill and Eat Sheep at Taft." The article reported, "A skirmishing force of the second army of field mice reported to be invading Taft attacked, killed, and ate a sheep at the San Emidio Ranch." The unlucky ewe was kept in a small pen at the head of a canyon and was unable to escape. The article concluded dryly, "The mice have become a distinct annoyance to golfers on the Petroleum Club links on the Maricopa Road."

By January 19th, the mouse war was the *Times'* lead story on the 22 front page. The headlines said:

Pied Pipers
Lure Mice

Poison Stemming
Vast Hegira

Thousands of Rodents Prey
on Own Appetites During
Kern County Trek

"Gen." Bowen Thinks Peril
to Centers of Population
Has Been Overcome

The story was a full description of what was occurring in Kern 23 County, telling of "roads carpeted with mice" and concluding with the apt observation, "The plague has been aggravated by the fact that for many years past an unceasing warfare has been waged on the natural enemies of the invaders, such as coyotes, hawks, wildcats, and other predatory beasts and birds." The reference to the Pied Piper was a piece of a headline writer's fancy.

Folks around the country offered various ways to redress the natu- 24 ral balance. The northern California town of Merced offered hundreds of hungry cats to the good citizens of Kern County. But cats, it turned out, weren't much of a solution. There were just too many mice. A cat, after killing and eating a dozen or so mice, becomes sated and bored.

Lewis Gingery of Rushville, Missouri, told the good folks of Kern County that a couple of hundred skunks could take care of the problem. He was surprised that local skunks hadn't prevented the population increase in the first place.   25

But the good citizens of Kern County had killed all the skunks, and they still didn't understand what they had done. Mice surging up from the lake bed attracted flocks of hawks, owls, ravens, crows, vultures, and even a couple thousand seagulls which flew in from the coast. As the birds swooped down on the mice, the good people of Kern County shot-gunned them. They hung the carcasses on fenceposts to deter other feathered predators.   26

The good citizens of Kern County were losing the war against the invaders. The mice had multiplied freely over the years. The bumper crop of food in 1926 had produced a bumper crop of mice. The population spurted until the food ran out. Then tens of millions of mice found they had to migrate or starve. The mice moved inexorably. By mid-January they occupied a sector twelve by eight miles.   27

Then the war escalated. On January 19th, it was announced that the chief poison specialist and exterminator for the U.S. Biological Survey — the man who had conquered the 1908 Nevada migration — was being sent from Washington, D.C. The headline writer for the *Times* had been prescient. Stanley E. Piper was the exterminator's reassuring name.   28

Piper arrived in Kern County on Saturday, January 22nd, to examine the area and map his battle plan. On Monday he announced his intentions. Working with a full-time crew of 25 men, Piper would stage a counterattack at Buena Vista Lake.   29

Federal forces set up camp on a high spot in the middle of the dry lake, a place called Pelican Island. The crew then attempted to determine the size of the enemy forces. They dug up an acre of lake bottom and counted the mouse burrows. They counted 4,000 burrows and were stunned. They were facing an army of 100 million mice.   30

Piper quickly hauled in 40 tons of chopped alfalfa, generously laced with strychnine. Piper asked the oil companies to work harder at controlling the spread of the mice outward, and he concentrated on the lake bed.   31

By the end of February, Piper had won. But it had been a costly war. The good farmers of Kern County had lost more than a half-million dollars in damaged crops, buildings, and fences. The good townsfolk had lost a similar amount in property damage and unrealized business revenues. Piper's efforts cost $5,000 for grain and supplies, paid for by the good citizens of Kern County. The great Kern County Mouse War lasted over three months, and mouse deaths amounted to unknown millions. The sweet prosperity of 1926 had turned sour.   32

If one pair of adult mice produces offspring, who in turn produce offspring, who in turn produce offspring, and so on for one year, the result will be over one million mice—unless there are predators. It is a lesson that the good people of Kern County should have learned well. It is a lesson that we all should learn well.

Build a better mousetrap, the old saying has it, and the world will beat a path to your door. The Great Kern County Mouse War proves that no one builds better mousetraps than nature. Let us beat a path to her door.

33

34

THINKING CRITICALLY ABOUT THE TEXT

How could the people of Kern County have dealt with the problem of local predators in other ways than systematically killing them off?

QUESTIONS ON SUBJECT

1. Why was it during a year of bountiful harvest that the mouse population exploded? Why were the people of Kern County initially unable to control the explosion?

2. What connection between causes and effects did the people of Kern County fail to make?

3. Why were cats not an effective solution to the mouse problem? How was the mouse war eventually won?

4. What conflicting roles did the U.S. Biological Survey play in the Mouse War?

QUESTIONS ON STRATEGY

1. What is Maize's thesis? Where in the article is it located? How does its location strengthen the impact of the essay?

2. How does Maize inject humor into his factual account? Point out some examples. Considering that the subject is a serious one, do you think that humor is appropriate? Why or why not?

3. Four times Maize cites the *Los Angeles Times* (paragraphs 13, 16, 21, 22). What are his purposes in doing so?

4. Except for the last two brief paragraphs, "The Great Kern County Mouse War" is a single extended illustration of Maize's thesis, written in the form of a historical narrative that reveals a causal chain. (Glossary: *Narration*) Is one long example sufficient to prove a point? How does he succeed or fail to succeed in turning a story into an argument? (Glossary: *Argumentation; Illustration*)

QUESTIONS ON DICTION AND VOCABULARY

1. Maize uses the adjective "good" two dozen times to describe the people of Kern County. What is his purpose? Is he being ironic? (Glossary: *Irony*)

2. What is the effect of the repetition that Maize employs in the last four sentences of paragraph 20?

3. Maize begins his essay with the expression "Once upon a time." What effect does that expression have on you as you start to read? (Glossary: *Beginnings/Endings*)

CLASSROOM ACTIVITY USING CAUSE AND EFFECT ANALYSIS

Determining causes and effects requires careful thought. Establishing a causal chain of events is no less demanding, but it can also bring clarity and understanding to many complex issues. Consider the following example involving avian influenza, or bird flu:

ULTIMATE CAUSE	Viruses carried by birds
IMMEDIATE CAUSE	Contact with infected birds, or surfaces that are infected
EFFECT	Influenza
EFFECT	Illness, possible death, possible pandemic

Develop a causal chain for each of the following cause and effect pairs. Then mix two of the pairs (for example, develop a causal chain for vacation/anxiety). Be prepared to discuss your answers with the class.

terror alert/fear
vacation/relaxation
making a speech/anxiety
party/fun

WRITING SUGGESTIONS

1. Many other attempts to kill "destructive" animals—not just predators, but also creatures that destroy crops or become household pests—have gone awry. Many people are familiar, for example, with the story of how the insecticide DDT was first hailed but finally banned because it was extremely harmful to many forms of life, including humans. Working with classmates and using library resources, compile a list of instances in which human efforts to eliminate a pest have precipitated a dangerous environmental imbalance. Using Maize's essay as a model, choose, research, and write the story of one of these events.

2. Some environmental crises have been precipitated not by human attempts to destroy pests, but by the introduction, either intentional or inadvertent, of a new species to a particular area. Think, for example, of the huge flocks of starlings that descend from time to time on unsuspecting midwestern towns or of the beautiful purple loosestrife that is taking over the fields of New England. What is being done to combat harmful nonnative species? Following the procedures suggested in the previous assignment, write the story of one introduced species.

WRITING SUGGESTIONS FOR CAUSE AND EFFECT ANALYSIS

1. Write an essay in which you analyze the most significant reasons why you went to college. You may wish to discuss your family background, your high school experience, people and events that influenced your decision, and your goals in college as well as in later life.

2. It is interesting to think of ourselves in terms of the influences that have caused us to be who we are. Write an essay in which you discuss two or three of what you consider the most important influences on your life. Following are some areas you may wish to consider in planning and writing your paper.

    a. a parent
    b. a book or movie
    c. a member of the clergy
    d. a teacher
    e. a friend
    f. a hero
    g. a youth organization
    h. a coach
    i. your neighborhood
    j. your ethnic background

3. Decisions often involve cause and effect relationships; that is, a person usually weighs the possible results of an action before deciding to act. Write an essay in which you consider the possible effects that would result from one decision or another in one of the following controversies.

    a. taxing cars on the basis of fuel consumption
    b. reinstituting the military draft
    c. legalizing marijuana
    d. mandatory licensing of handguns
    e. raising the mandatory fuel efficiency rating of cars
    f. cloning humans
    g. abolishing grades for college courses
    h. raising the minimum wage
    i. mandatory community service (one year) for all eighteen-year-olds
    j. banning the use of pesticides on produce
    k. requiring an ethics course in college

4. Write an essay about a recent achievement of yours or about an important achievement in your community. Explain the causes of this success. Look at all of the underlying elements involved in the accomplishment, and explain how you selected the one main cause or the causal chain that led to the achievement. To do this, you will probably want to use the rhetorical strategy of comparison and contrast. You might also use exemplification and process analysis to explain the connection between your cause and its effect.

CHAPTER 12

Argumentation

WHAT IS ARGUMENTATION?

The word *argument* probably brings to mind verbal disagreements we have all witnessed, if not participated in directly. Occasionally, such disputes are satisfying; you can take pleasure in knowing that you have converted someone to your point of view. More often, though, arguments like these are inconclusive and result only in anger over your opponent's stubbornness or in the frustration of realizing that you have failed to make your position understood. Such dissatisfaction is inevitable because verbal arguments usually arise spontaneously and cannot be thoughtfully planned or researched. Indeed, often it is not until later, in retrospect, that the convincing piece of evidence or the forcefully phrased assertion comes to mind.

Written arguments have much in common with verbal ones: They attempt to convince readers to agree with a particular point of view, to make a particular decision, or to pursue a particular course of action; they involve the presentation of well-chosen evidence and the artful control of language. However, writers of argument have no one around to dispute their words directly, so they must imagine their probable audience to predict the sorts of objections that may be raised. This requires that written arguments be carefully planned. The writer must settle in advance on a specific thesis or proposition rather than grope toward one, as in a verbal argument. There is a greater need for organization, for choosing the most effective types of evidence from all that is available, for determining the strategies of rhetoric, language, and style that will best suit the argument's subject, purpose, thesis, and effect on the intended audience.

Most strong arguments are constructed around an effective thesis statement. Take, for example, the following opening to the essay "The Case for Short Words" by Richard Lederer (page 480).

Thesis statement

When you speak and write, there is no law that says you have to use big words. Short words are as good as long ones, and short, old words—like *sun* and *grass* and *home*—are best of all. A lot of small words, more than you might think, can meet your needs with a strength, grace, and charm that large words do not have.

Several examples support the thesis.

Big words can make the way dark for those who read what you write and hear what you say. Small words cast their clear light on big things—night and day, love and hate, war and peace, and life and death. Big words at times seem strange to the eye and the ear and the mind and the heart. Small words are the ones we seem to have known from the time we were born, like the hearth fire that warms the home.

Note how Lederer uses examples to support his thesis statement. When you read the whole essay, you will want to check whether Lederer's argument is well reasoned and carefully organized. You will also want to check that his argument is logical and persuasive. A strong argument will have all of these qualities.

Persuasive and Logical Argument

Most people who specialize in the study of argument identify two essential categories: persuasion and logic.

Persuasive argument relies primarily on appeals to emotion, to the subconscious, even to bias and prejudice. These appeals involve diction, slanting, figurative language, analogy, rhythmic patterns of speech, and a tone that encourages a positive, active response. Examples of persuasive argument are found in the exaggerated claims of advertisers and in the speech making of politicians and social activists.

Logical argument, on the other hand, appeals primarily to the mind—to the audience's intellectual faculties, understanding, and knowledge. Such appeals depend on the reasoned movement from assertion to evidence to conclusion and on an almost mathematical system of proof and counterproof. Logical argument, unlike persuasion, does not normally impel its audience to action. Logical argument is commonly found in scientific or philosophical articles, in legal decisions, and in technical proposals.

Most arguments, however, are neither purely persuasive nor purely logical in nature. A well-written newspaper editorial that supports a controversial piece of legislation or that proposes a solution to a local problem, for example, will rest on a logical arrangement of assertions and evidence but will employ striking diction and other persuasive patterns of language to make it more effective. Thus the kinds of appeals a writer emphasizes depend on the nature of the topic, the thesis or proposition of the argument, the various kinds of support (e.g., evidence, opinions, examples, facts, statistics) offered, and a thoughtful consideration of the audience. Knowing the differences between persuasive and logical arguments is, then, essential in learning both to read and to write arguments.

Some additional types of arguments that are helpful in expanding your understanding of this strategy are described below.

Informational, or Exploratory, Argument

It is often useful to provide a comprehensive review of the various facets of an issue. This is done to inform an audience, especially one that may not understand why the issue is controversial in the first place, and to help that audience take a position. An example of this kind of argument is Jane E. Brody's "Gene-Altered Foods: A Case against Panic" (page 542). The writer of this type of argument does not take a position but aims, instead, to render the positions taken by the various sides in accurate and clear language. Your instructors may occasionally call for this kind of argumentative writing as a way of teaching you to explore the complexity of a particular issue.

Focused Argument

This kind of argument has only one objective: to change the audience's mind about a controversial issue. Michael Noer, in "Don't Marry Career Women" (page 509), focuses on his concern that women, careers, and marriage do not mix well. Being comprehensive or taking the broad view is not the objective here. If opposing viewpoints are considered, it is usually to show their inadequacies and thereby to strengthen the writer's own position. This is the kind that we usually think of as the traditional argument.

Action-Oriented Argument

This type of argument is highly persuasive and attempts to accomplish a specific task. This is the loud car salesman on your television, the over-the-top subscription solicitation in your mail, the vote-for-me-because-I-am-the-only-candidate-who-can-lower-your-taxes type of argument.

The language is emotionally charged, and buzzwords designed to arouse the emotions of the audience may even be used, along with such propaganda devices as glittering generalities (broad, sweeping statements) and bandwagonism ("Everyone else is voting for me—don't be left out").

Quiet, or Subtle, Argument

Some arguments do not immediately appear to the audience to be arguments at all. They set out to be informative and objective, but when closely examined, they reveal that the author has consciously, or perhaps subconsciously, shaped and slanted the evidence in such a manner as to favor a particular position. Such shaping may be the result of choices in diction that bend the audience to the writer's perspective, or they may be the result of decisions not to include certain types of evidence while admitting others. Such arguments can, of course, be quite convincing, as there are always those who distrust obvious efforts to convince them, preferring to make their own decisions on the issues. Kennedy P. Maize's cause and effect essay, "The Great Kern County Mouse War" (page 446), contains a powerful argument against upsetting the balance of nature.

Reconciliation Argument

Increasingly popular today is a form of argument in which the writer attempts to explore all facets of an issue to find common ground or areas of agreement. Of course, one way of viewing that common ground is to see it as a new argumentative thrust, a new assertion, about which there may yet be more debate. The object, nevertheless, is to lessen stridency and the hardening of positions and to mediate opposing views into a rational and, where appropriate, even practical outcome. Martin Luther King Jr.'s speech "I Have a Dream" (page 486) is perhaps the greatest example of a reconciliation argument of the past century.

USING ARGUMENTATION AS A WRITING STRATEGY

True arguments are limited to assertions about which there is a legitimate and recognized difference of opinion. It is unlikely that anyone will ever need to convince a reader that falling in love is a rare and intense experience, that crime rates should be reduced, or that computers are changing the world. Not everyone would agree, however, that women experience love more intensely than men, that the death penalty reduces the incidence of crime, or that computers are changing the world for the worse; these assertions are arguable and admit differing perspectives. Similarly, a leading heart specialist might argue in a popular magazine that too many doctors are advising patients to have pacemakers implanted when they are not necessary; the editorial writer for a small-town newspaper could urge that a local agency supplying food to poor families be given a larger percentage of the town's budget; and in a lengthy and complex book, a foreign policy specialist might attempt to prove that the current administration exhibits no consistent policy in its relationship with other countries and that the State Department is in need of overhauling. No matter what forum it uses and no matter what its structure, an argument has as its chief purpose the detailed setting forth of a particular point of view and the rebuttal of any opposing views.

The Classical Appeals

Classical thinkers believed that there are three key components in all rhetorical situations or attempts to communicate: the *speaker* (and for us the *writer*) who comments about a *subject* to an *audience*. For purposes of discussion we can isolate each of these three entities, but in actual rhetorical situations they are inseparable, each inextricably tied to and influencing the other two. The ancients also recognized the importance of qualities attached to each of these components that are especially significant in the case of argumentation: *ethos*, which is related to the speaker; *logos,* which is related to the subject; and *pathos*, which is related to the audience. Let's look a little closer at each of these.

Ethos (Greek for "character") has to do with the authority, the credibility, and, to a certain extent, the morals of the speaker or writer. In other words, *ethos* is the speaker's character as perceived by the audience, often based on shared values. Aristotle and Cicero, classical rhetoricians, believed that it was important for the speaker to be credible and to argue for a worthwhile cause. Putting one's argumentative skills in the service of a questionable cause was simply not acceptable. But how did one establish credibility? Sometimes it was gained through achievements outside the rhetorical arena. That is, the speaker had experience with an issue, had argued the subject before, and had been judged to be sincere and honest.

In the case of your own writing, establishing such credentials is not always possible, so you will need to be more concerned than usual with presenting your argument reasonably, sincerely, and in language untainted by excessive emotionalism. Finally, it is well worth remembering that you should always show respect for your audience in your writing.

Logos (Greek for "word"), related as it is to the subject, is the effective presentation of the argument itself. It refers to the speaker's grasp of the subject — his or her knowledge. Is the thesis or claim a worthwhile one?

Is it logical, consistent, and well buttressed by supporting evidence? Is the evidence itself factual, reliable, and convincing? Finally, is the argument so thoughtfully organized and so clearly presented that it has an impact on the audience and could change opinions? Indeed, this aspect of argumentation is the most difficult to accomplish but is, at the same time, the most rewarding.

Pathos (Greek for "emotion") has the most to do with the audience. The essential question is, How does the speaker or writer present an argument or a persuasive essay to maximize its appeal for a given audience? One way, of course, is to appeal to the audience's emotions through the artful and strategic use of well-crafted language. Certain buzzwords, slanted diction, or emotionally loaded language may become either rallying cries or causes of resentment in an argument.

Considering Audience

It is worth remembering at this point that you can never be certain who your audience is; readers range along a spectrum from extremely friendly and sympathetic to extremely hostile and resistant, with a myriad of possibilities in between. The friendly audience will welcome new information and support the writer's position; the hostile audience will look for just the opposite: flaws in logic and examples of dishonest manipulation. With many arguments, there is the potential for a considerable audience of interested parties who are uncommitted. If the targeted audience is judged to be friendly, then the writer needs to be logical, but should feel free to use emotional appeals. If the audience is thought to be hostile, the *logos* must be the writer's immediate concern, and the language should be straightforward and objective. The greatest caution, subtlety, and critical thinking must be applied to the attempt to win over an uncommitted audience.

Argumentation and Other Rhetorical Strategies

In general, writers of argument are interested in explaining aspects of a subject as well as in advocating a particular view. Consequently, they frequently use the other rhetorical strategies in a supportive role. In your efforts to argue convincingly, you may find it necessary to define, to compare and contrast, to analyze causes and effects, to classify, to describe, and to narrate. (For more information on the use of other strategies in argumentation, see the Use Other Rhetorical Strategies heading on page 471.) Nevertheless, it is the writer's attempt to convince, not explain, that is of primary importance in an argumentative essay. In this respect, it is helpful to know that there are two basic patterns of thinking and of presenting our thoughts that are followed in argumentation: *induction* and *deduction*.

Inductive and Deductive Reasoning

Inductive reasoning moves from a set of specific examples to a general statement or principle. As long as the evidence is accurate, pertinent, complete, and sufficient to represent the assertion, the conclusion of an inductive argument can be regarded as valid; if, however, you can spot inaccuracies in the evidence or can point to contrary evidence, you have good reason to doubt the assertion as it stands. Inductive reasoning is the most common of argumentative structures.

Deductive reasoning, more formal and complex than inductive reasoning, moves from an overall premise, rule, or generalization to a more specific conclusion. Deductive logic follows the pattern of the *syllogism*, a simple three-part argument consisting of a major premise, a minor premise, and a conclusion. For example, notice how the following syllogism works.

a. All humans are mortal. *(Major premise)*
b. Catalina is a human. *(Minor premise)*
c. Catalina is mortal. *(Conclusion)*

The conclusion here is true because both premises are true and the logic of the syllogism is valid.

Obviously, a syllogism will fail to work if either of the premises is untrue.

a. All living creatures are mammals. *(Major premise)*
b. A lobster is a living creature. *(Minor premise)*
c. A lobster is a mammal. *(Conclusion)*

The problem is immediately apparent. The major premise is obviously false: There are many living creatures that are not mammals, and a lobster happens to be one of them. Consequently, the conclusion is invalid.

Syllogisms, however, can fail in other ways, even if both premises are objectively true. Such failures occur most often when the arguer jumps to a conclusion without taking obvious exceptions into account.

a. All college students read books. *(Major premise)*
b. Larry reads books. *(Minor premise)*
c. Larry is a college student. *(Conclusion)*

Both the premises in this syllogism are true, but the syllogism is still invalid because it does not take into account that other people besides college students read books. The problem is in the way the major premise has been interpreted: If the minor premise were instead "Larry is a college student," then the valid conclusion "Larry reads books" would logically follow.

It is fairly easy to see the problems in a deductive argument when its premises and conclusion are rendered in the form of a syllogism. It is often more difficult to see errors in logic when the argument is presented discursively, or within the context of a long essay. If you can reduce the argument to its syllogistic form, however, you will have much less difficulty testing its validity. Similarly, if you can isolate and examine out of context the evidence provided to support an inductive assertion, you can more readily evaluate the written inductive argument.

Consider the following excerpt from "The Draft: Why the Country Needs It," an article by James Fallows that first appeared in the *Atlantic* in 1980.

The Vietnam draft was unfair racially, economically, educationally. By every one of those measures, the volunteer Army is less representative still. Libertarians argue that military service should be a matter of choice, but the plain fact is that service in the volunteer force is too frequently dictated by economics. Army enlisted ranks E1 through E4, the privates and corporals, the cannon fodder, the ones who will fight and die, are 36 percent black now. By the Army's own projections, they will be 42 percent black in three years. When other "minorities" are taken into account, we will have, for the first time, an army whose fighting members are mainly "non-majority," or more bluntly, a black and brown army defending a mainly white nation. The military has been an avenue of opportunity of many young blacks. They may well be first-class fighting men. They do not represent the nation.

Such a selective sharing of the burden has destructive spiritual effects in a nation based on the democratic creed. But its practical implications can be quite as grave. The effect of a fair, representative draft is to hold the public hostage to the consequences of its decisions, much as the children's presence in the public schools focuses parents' attention on the quality of the schools. If the citizens are willing to countenance a decision that means that someone's child may die, they may contemplate more deeply if there is the possibility that the child will be theirs. Indeed, I would like to extend this principle even further. Young men of nineteen are rightly suspicious of the congressmen and columnists who urge them to the fore. I wish there were a practical way to resurrect provisions of the amended Selective Service Act of 1940, which raised the draft age to forty-four. Such a gesture might symbolize the desire to offset the historic injustice of the Vietnam draft, as well as suggest the possibility that, when a bellicose columnist recommends dispatching the American forces to Pakistan, he might also realize that he could end up as a gunner in a tank.

Here Fallows presents an inductive argument against the volunteer army and in favor of reinstating a draft. His argument can be summarized as follows:

Assertion: The volunteer army is racially and economically unfair.

Evidence: He points to the disproportionate percentage of blacks in the army, as well as to projections indicating that, within three years of the article's publication, more than half of the army's fighting members will be nonwhite.

Conclusion: "Such a selective sharing of the burden has destructive spiritual effects in a nation based on the democratic creed." Not until there is a fair, representative draft will the powerful majority be held accountable for any decision to go to war.

Fallows's inductive scheme here is, in fact, very effective. The evidence is convincing, and the conclusion is strong. But his argument also depends on a more complicated deductive syllogism.

a. The democratic ideal requires equal representation in the responsibilities of citizenship. *(Major premise)*

b. Military service is a responsibility of citizenship. *(Minor premise)*

c. The democratic ideal requires equal representation in military service. *(Conclusion)*

To attack Fallows's argument, it would be necessary to deny one of his premises.

Fallows also employs a number of other persuasive techniques, including an analogy: "The effect of a fair, representative draft is to hold the public hostage to the consequences of its decisions, much as the children's presence in the public schools focuses parents' attention on the quality of the schools." The use of such an analogy proves nothing, but it can force readers to reconsider their viewpoint and can make them more open-minded. The same is true of Fallows's almost entirely unserious suggestion about raising the draft age to forty-four. Like most writers, Fallows uses persuasive arguments to complement his more important logical ones.

Using Argumentation across the Disciplines

When writing essays in the academic disciplines, you will have many opportunities to use the strategy of argumentation to both organize and strengthen the presentation of your ideas. To determine whether or not argumentation is the right strategy for you in a particular paper, use the four-step method first described in "Determining Your Strategy" (pages 24–25). Consider the following examples, which illustrate how this four-step method works for typical college papers:

Ethics

MAIN IDEA: Suicide is an end-of-life option.

QUESTION: Should a person be allowed to end his or her life when no longer able to maintain an acceptable quality of life?

STRATEGY: Argumentation. The question "Should a person be allowed" triggers a pro/con argument. The writer argues for or against laws that allow physician-assisted suicide, for example.

SUPPORTING STRATEGY: Definition should be used to clarify what is meant by the expression "quality of life." Cause and effect analysis should be used to determine, for example, at what point a person has lost a desirable "quality of life."

Environmental Studies

MAIN IDEA: The burning of fossil fuels is creating greenhouse gas emissions that are, in turn, causing global warming.

QUESTION: What can we do to reduce emissions from the burning of fossil fuels?

STRATEGY: Argumentation. The question "What can we do" suggests an answer in the form of an argument. The writer might want to argue for higher taxes on the burning of fossil fuels, or for the installation of smokestack scrubbers.

SUPPORTING STRATEGY: Cause and effect analysis will be necessary to show how the burning of fossil fuels increases greenhouse emissions and how higher taxes and smokestack scrubbers will work to reduce harmful gases.

Biology

MAIN IDEA: The use of animals in biomedical research is crucial.

QUESTION: Should there be a ban on the use of animals in biomedical research?

STRATEGY: Argumentation. The word *should* signals a pro/con debate: Animals should/should not be used in biomedical research.

SUPPORTING STRATEGY: Comparison and contrast might be used to help make the case that alternatives to the use of animals arebetter/worse than using animals.

SAMPLE STUDENT ESSAY USING ARGUMENTATION AS A WRITING STRATEGY

Mark Jackson wrote the following essay while a student at the University of Cincinnati. Jackson's essay explores a number of arguments made in favor of a liberal arts education. In the course of the essay, Jackson rejects some of these arguments, such as the idea that a liberal arts education makes students well-rounded. He does, however, support the argument that a liberal arts education fosters critical thinking skills, and he comes to the conclusion that the ideal education would balance practical or vocational training and a grounding in the liberal arts.

Title hints at writer's position.

The Liberal Arts:

A Practical View

Mark Jackson

Writer identifies central problem: liberal arts inadequately explained.

Many students question the reasoning behind a liberal arts education. But even though they may have been forced to swallow liberal arts propaganda since junior high, students seldom receive a good explanation for why they should strive to be "well-rounded." They are told that they should value the accumulation of knowledge for its own sake, yet this argument does not convince those, like myself, who believe that knowledge must have some practical value or material benefit to be worth seeking. 1

First argument for liberal arts education

In "What Is an Idea?" Wayne Booth and Marshall Gregory argue convincingly that "a liberal education is an education in ideas — not merely memorizing them, but learning to move among them, balancing one against the other, negotiating relationships, accommodating new arguments, and returning for a closer look" (17). These writers propose that a liberal arts education is valuable to students because it helps to develop their analytical-thinking skills and writing skills. This is, perhaps, one of the best arguments for taking a broad range of classes in many different subjects. 2

Another, less convincing argument

Other, more radical arguments in favor of the liberal arts are less appealing. Lewis Thomas, a prominent scientist and physician, believes that classical Greek should form the backbone of a college student's education. This suggestion seems extreme. It is more reasonable to concentrate on the English language, since many students do not have a firm grasp of basic reading and writing skills. Freshman English and other English courses serve as a better foundation for higher education than classical Greek could. 3

The opposition to a liberal arts curriculum grows out of the   4
values that college-bound students learn from their parents and
peers: They place an immeasurable value on success and disregard
anything that is not pertinent to material achievements. Students
often have trouble seeing what practical value studying a
particular discipline can have for them. Teenagers who are headed
for the world of nine-to-five employment tend to ignore certain
studies in their haste to succeed.

*Writer links
personal experience
to his attitude
toward liberal arts.*

My parents started discussing the possibility of college   5
with me when I was in the sixth grade. They didn't think that it
was important for me to go to college to become a more fulfilled
human being. My mom and dad wanted me to go to college so
that I might not have to live from paycheck to paycheck as they
do. Their reason for wanting me to go to college has become my
primary motivation for pursuing a college degree.

*Writer narrates
personal experience
to illustrate
inadequacy of
arguments put
forth by high-
school counselor.*

I remember getting into an argument with my high school   6
counselor because I didn't want to take a third year of Spanish.
I was an A student in Spanish II, but I hated every minute of the
class. My counselor noticed that I didn't sign up for Spanish III,
so he called me into his office to hassle me. I told him that
I took two years of a foreign language so that I would be
accepted to college, but that I did not want to take a third
year. Mr. Gallivan told me that I needed a third year of a foreign
language to be a "well-rounded" student. My immediate response
was "So what?!" I hated foreign languages, and no counselor
was going to make me take something that I didn't want or need.
I felt Spanish was a waste of time.

I frequently asked my high school counselor why I needed   7
to take subjects like foreign languages and art. He never really
gave me an answer (except for the lame idea about being
"well-rounded"). Instead, Mr. Gallivan always directed my
attention to a sign on the wall of his office which read, "THERE'S
NO REASON FOR IT. IT'S JUST OUR POLICY!" I never found that
a satisfactory explanation.

*Writer cites author-
ity to explain value
of humanities for
career-minded
people.*

Norman Cousins, however, does offer a more reasonable   8
explanation for the necessity of a liberal education. In his essay
"How to Make People Smaller Than They Are," Cousins points out
how valuable the humanities are for career-minded people. He
says, "The irony of the emphasis being placed on careers is that
nothing is more valuable for anyone who has had a professional
or vocational education than to be able to deal with abstractions
or complexities, or to feel comfortable with subtleties of thought

or language, or to think sequentially" (15). Cousins reminds us that technical or vocational knowledge alone will not make one successful in a chosen profession: Unique problems and situations may arise daily in the context of one's job, so an employee must be able to think creatively and deal with events that no textbook ever discussed. The workers who get the promotions and advance to high positions are the ones who can "think on their feet" when they are faced with a complex problem.

Writer points to value of communication skills learned through liberal arts.

Cousins also suggests that the liberal arts teach students communication skills that are critical for success. A shy, introverted person who was a straight A student in college would not make a very good public relations consultant, no matter how keen his or her intellectual abilities. Employees who cannot adequately articulate their ideas to a client or an employer will soon find themselves unemployed, even if they have brilliant ideas. Social integration into a particular work environment would be difficult without good communication skills and a wide range of interests and general knowledge. The broader a person's interests, the more compatible he or she will be with other workers.

9

Thesis: writer calls for balance of liberal arts courses and professional courses.

Though it is obvious that liberal arts courses do have considerable practical value, a college education would not be complete without some job training. The liberal arts should be given equal billing in the college curriculum, but by no means should they become the focal point of higher education. If specialization is outlawed in our institutions of higher learning, then college students might lose their competitive edge. Maxim Gorky has written that "any kind of knowledge is useful" (22), and, of course, most knowledge is useful; but it would be insane to structure the college curriculum around an overview of all disciplines instead of allowing a student to master one subject or profession. Universities must seek to maintain an equilibrium between liberal and specialized education. A liberal arts degree without specialization or intended future specialization (such as a master's degree in a specific field) is useless unless one wants to be a professional game show contestant.

10

Plan of action for college students

Students who want to make the most of their college years should pursue a major course of study while choosing electives or a few minor courses of study from the liberal arts. In this way, scholars can become experts in a profession and

11

still have a broad enough background to ensure versatility, both within and outside the field. In a university's quest to produce "well-rounded" students, specialization must not come to be viewed as an evil practice.

Writer calls for education to better articulate the value of the liberal arts.

      If educators really want to increase the number of liberal   12 arts courses that each student takes, they must first increase the popularity of such studies. It is futile to try to get students to learn something just for the sake of knowing it. They must be given examples, such as those already mentioned, of how a liberal education will further their own interests. Instead of telling students that they need to be "well-rounded" and feeding them meaningless propaganda, counselors and professors should point out the practical value and applications of a broad education in the liberal arts. It is difficult to persuade some college students that becoming a better person is an important goal of higher education. Many students want a college education so that they can make more money and have more power. This is the perceived value of a higher education in their world.

Works Cited

Booth, Wayne, and Marshall Gregory. "What Is an Idea?" *The Harper and Row Reader.* 2nd ed. New York: Harper, 1988. Print.

Cousins, Norman. "How to Make People Smaller Than They Are." *The Saturday Review* Dec. 1978: 15. Print.

Gorky, Maxim. "How I Studied." *On Literature.* Trans. Julius Katzer. Seattle: U of Washington P, 1973. 9-22. Print.

Thomas, Lewis. "Debating the Unknowable." *Atlantic Monthly* July 1981: 49-52. Print.

Analyzing Mark Jackson's Essay of Argumentation: Questions for Discussion

1. Why did Jackson refuse to take Spanish III? How does his personal experience with Spanish and with his guidance counselor relate to his argument?
2. What is Jackson's thesis? Where and how does he present it?
3. Jackson employs several arguments in favor of liberal arts education. How does he classify them? What does he accomplish by including a variety of rationales regarding the validity of a "well-rounded" education?

SUGGESTIONS FOR USING ARGUMENTATION AS A WRITING STRATEGY

As you plan, write, and revise your essay of argumentation, be mindful of the five-step writing process described in Chapter 2 (see pages 14–31). Pay particular attention to the basic requirements and essential ingredients of this writing strategy.

Planning Your Essay of Argumentation

Writing an argument can be very rewarding. By its nature, an argument must be carefully reasoned and thoughtfully structured to have maximum effect. In other words, the *logos* of the argument must be carefully tended. Allow yourself, therefore, enough time to think about your thesis, to gather the evidence you need, and to draft, revise, edit, and proofread your essay. Sloppy thinking, confused expression, and poor organization will be immediately evident to your reader and will make for weaker arguments.

For example, you might be given an assignment in your history class to write a paper explaining what you think was the main cause of the Civil War. How would you approach this topic? First, it would help to assemble a number of possible interpretations of the causes of the Civil War and to examine them closely. Once you have determined what you consider to be the main cause, you will need to develop points that support your position. Then you will need to explain why you did not choose other possibilities, and you will have to assemble reasons that refute them. For instance, you might write an opening similar to this example.

The Fugitive Slave Act Forced the North to Go to War

While the start of the Civil War can be attributed to many factors — states' rights, slavery, a clash between antithetical economic systems, and westward expansion — the final straw for the North was the Fugitive Slave Act. This act, more than any other single element of disagreement between the North and the South, forced the North into a position where the only option was to fight.

Certainly, slavery and the clash over open lands in the West contributed to the growing tensions between the two sides, as did the economically incompatible systems of production — plantation and manufacture — but the Fugitive Slave Act required the North either to actively support slavery or to run the risk of becoming a criminal in defiance of it. The North chose not to support the Fugitive Slave Act and was openly angered by the idea that it should be required to do so by law. This anger and open defiance led directly to the Civil War.

In these opening paragraphs, the author states the main argument for the cause of the Civil War and sets up, in addition, the possible alternatives to this view. The points outlined in the introduction would lead, one by one, to a logical argument asserting that the Fugitive Slave Act was responsible for the onset of the Civil War and refuting the other interpretations.

This introduction is mainly a logical argument. As was mentioned before, writers often use persuasive, or emotional, arguments along with logical ones. Persuasive arguments focus on issues that appeal to people's subconscious or emotional nature, along with their logical powers and intellectual understanding. Such arguments rely on powerful and charged language, and they appeal to the emotions. Persuasive arguments can be especially effective but should not be used without a strong logical backing. Indeed, this is the only way to use emotional persuasion ethically. Emotional persuasion, when not in support of a logical point, can be dangerous in that it can make an illogical point sound appealing to a listener or reader.

Determine Your Thesis or Proposition. Begin by determining a topic that interests you and about which there is some significant difference of opinion or about which you have a number of questions. Find out what's in the news, what people are talking about, what authors and instructors are emphasizing as important intellectual arguments. As you pursue your research, consider what assertion you can make about the topic you chose. The more specific this thesis or proposition, the more directed your research can become and the more focused your ultimate argument will be. While researching your topic, however, be aware that the information may point you in new directions. Don't hesitate at any point to modify or even reject an initial or preliminary thesis as continued research warrants.

A thesis can be placed anywhere in an argument, but it is probably best while learning to write arguments to place the statement of your controlling idea somewhere near the beginning of your composition. Explain the importance of the thesis, and make clear to your reader that you share a common concern or interest in this issue. You may wish to state your central assertion directly in your first or second paragraph so that there is no possibility for your reader to be confused about your position. You may also wish to lead off with a particularly striking piece of evidence to capture your reader's interest.

Consider Your Audience. It is well worth remembering that in no other type of writing is the question of audience more important than in argumentation. Here again, the *ethos* and *pathos* aspects of argumentation come into play. The tone you establish, the type of diction you choose, the kinds of evidence you select to buttress your assertions, and indeed the organizational pattern you design and follow will all influence your audience's perception of your trustworthiness and believability. If you make good judgments about the nature of your audience, respect its knowledge of the subject, and correctly envision whether it is likely to be hostile, neutral, complacent, or receptive, you will be able to tailor the various aspects of your argument appropriately.

Gather Supporting Evidence. For each point of your argument, be sure to provide appropriate and sufficient supporting evidence: verifiable facts and statistics, illustrative examples and narratives, or quotations from authorities. Don't overwhelm your reader with evidence, but don't skimp either; it is important to demonstrate your command of the topic and your control of the thesis by choosing carefully from all the evidence at your disposal. If there are strong arguments on both sides of the issue, you will need to take this into account while making your choices. (See the Consider Refutations to Your Argument section below.)

Organizing and Writing Your Essay of Argumentation

Choose an Organizational Pattern. Once you think that you have sufficient evidence to make your assertion convincing, consider how best to organize your argument. To some extent, your organization will depend on your method of reasoning: inductive, deductive, or a combination of the two. For example, is it necessary to establish a major premise before moving on to discuss a minor premise? Should most of your evidence precede or follow your direct statement of an assertion? Will induction work better with the particular audience you have targeted? As you present your primary points, you may find it effective to move from those that are least important to those that are most important or from those that are least familiar to those that are most familiar. A scratch outline can help, but it is often the case that a writer's most crucial revisions in an argument involve rearranging its components into a sharper, more coherent order. It is often difficult to tell what that order should be until the revision stage of the writing process.

Consider Refutations to Your Argument. As you proceed with your argument, you may wish to take into account well-known and significant opposing arguments. To ignore them would be to suggest to your readers any one of the following: You don't know about them, you know about them and are obviously and unfairly weighting the argument in your favor, or you know about them and have no reasonable answers to them. Grant the validity of the opposing argument or refute it, but respect your reader's intelligence by addressing the problems. Your readers will in turn respect you for doing so.

To avoid weakening your thesis, you must be very clear in your thinking and presentation. It must remain apparent to your readers why your argument is superior to the opposing points of view. If you feel that you cannot introduce opposing arguments because they will weaken rather than strengthen your thesis, you should probably reassess your thesis and the supporting evidence.

Use Other Rhetorical Strategies. Although argument is one of the most powerful single rhetorical strategies, it is almost always strengthened by incorporating other strategies. In every professional selection in this chapter, you will find a number of rhetorical strategies at work.

Combining strategies is probably not something you want to think about when you first try to write an argument. Instead, let the strategies develop naturally as you organize, draft, and revise your essay. As you develop your argument essay, use the following chart as a reminder of what the eight strategies covered previously can do for you.

Strategies for Development

Narration	Telling a story or giving an account of an event
Description	Presenting a picture in words
Illustration	Using examples to illustrate a point or idea
Process Analysis	Explaining how something is done or happens
Comparison and Contrast	Demonstrating likenesses and differences
Division and Classification	Dividing a subject into its parts and placing them in appropriate categories
Definition	Explaining what something is or means
Cause and Effect Analysis	Explaining the causes of an event or the effects of an action

As you draft your essay, look for places where you can use the above strategies to strengthen your argument. For example, do you need a more convincing example, a term defined, a process explained, or the likely effects of an action detailed?

Conclude Forcefully. In the conclusion of your essay, be sure to restate your position in different language, at least briefly. Besides persuading your reader to accept your point of view, you may also want to encourage some specific course of action. Above all, your conclusion should not introduce new information that may surprise your reader; it should seem to follow naturally, almost seamlessly, from the series of points that have been carefully established in the body of the essay. Don't overstate your case, but at the same time don't qualify your conclusion with the use of too many words or phrases like *I think*, *in my opinion*, *maybe*, *sometimes*, and *probably*. Rather than making you seem rational and sensible, these words can often make you sound indecisive and muddled.

Revising and Editing Your Essay of Argumentation

Avoid Faulty Reasoning.　Have someone read your argument, checking sentences for errors in judgment and reasoning. Sometimes others can see easily what you can't because you are so intimately tied to your assertion. Review the following list of errors in reasoning, making sure that you have not committed any of them.

> *Oversimplification*—a foolishly simple solution to what is clearly a complex problem. *The reason we have a balance-of-trade deficit is that foreigners make better products than we do.*
>
> *Hasty generalization*—in inductive reasoning, a generalization that is based on too little evidence or on evidence that is not representative. *It was the best movie I saw this year, and so it should get an Academy Award.*
>
> *Post hoc, ergo propter hoc* ("after this, therefore because of this")— confusing chance or coincidence with causation. The fact that one event comes after another does not necessarily mean that the first event caused the second. *Every time I wear my orange Syracuse sweater to a game, we win.*
>
> *Begging the question*—assuming in a premise something that needs to be proven. *Parking fines work because they keep people from parking illegally.*
>
> *False analogy*—making a misleading analogy between logically connected ideas. *Of course he'll make a fine coach. He was an all-star basketball player.*
>
> *Either/or thinking*—seeing only two alternatives when there may in fact be other possibilities. *Either you love your job or you hate it.*
>
> *Non sequitur* ("it does not follow")—an inference or conclusion that is not clearly related to the established premises or evidence. *She is very sincere; she must know what she is talking about.*
>
> *Name-Calling*—linking a person to a negative idea or symbol. The hope is that by invoking the name the user will elicit a negative reaction without the necessary evidence. *Senator Jones is a bleeding heart.*

Share Your Drafts with Others.　Try sharing the drafts of your essay with other students in your writing class to make sure that your argument works, that it makes its point. Ask them if there are any parts that they do not understand. Have them restate your thesis in their own words. Ask them if you have overlooked any opposing arguments that you should consider and if you have provided enough evidence for your side of the argument to be convincing. If their answers differ from what you intended, have them point to the troublesome parts of your essay and discuss what you can do to improve your argument. If you find their suggestions valid, revise your text accordingly. To maximize the effectiveness of conferences with your peers, utilize the guidelines presented on pages 27–28. Feedback from these conferences often provides one or more places where you can start revising.

Question Your Own Work While Revising and Editing. Revision is best done by asking yourself key questions about what you have written. Begin by reading, preferably aloud, what you have written. Reading aloud forces you to pay attention to every single word, and you are more likely to catch lapses in the logical flow of thought. After you have read your paper through, answer the following questions for revising and editing, and make the necessary changes.

Questions for Revising and Editing: Argumentation

1. Is my thesis or proposition focused? Do I state my thesis well?
2. Assess the different kinds of arguments. Am I using the right technique to argue my thesis? Does my strategy fit my subject matter and audience?
3. Does my presentation include enough evidence to support my thesis? Do I acknowledge opposing points of view in a way that strengthens, rather than weakens, my argument?
4. Have I chosen an appropriate organizational pattern that makes it easy to support my thesis?
5. Have I avoided faulty reasoning within my essay? Have I had a friend read the essay to help me find problems in my logic?
6. Is my conclusion forceful and effective?
7. Have I thought about or attempted to combine rhetorical strategies to strengthen my argument? If so, is the combination of strategies effective? If not, what strategy or strategies would help my argument?
8. Have I used a variety of sentences to enliven my writing?
9. Have I avoided errors in grammar, punctuation, and mechanics?

The Declaration of Independence

Thomas Jefferson

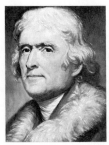 *President, governor, statesman, diplomat, lawyer, architect, philosopher, thinker, and writer, Thomas Jefferson (1743– 1826) is one of the most important figures in U.S. history. He was born in Albemarle County, Virginia, and attended the College of William and Mary. After being admitted to law practice in 1767, he began a long and illustrious career of public service to the colonies and, later, the new republic.*

Jefferson drafted the Declaration of Independence in 1776. Although it was revised by Benjamin Franklin and his colleagues in the Continental Congress, in its sound logic and forceful, direct style the document retains the unmistakable qualities of Jefferson's prose.

PREPARING TO READ

What, for you, is the meaning of democracy? Where do your ideas about democracy come from?

When in the course of human events, it becomes necessary for one people to dissolve the political bonds which have connected them with another, and to assume among the Powers of the earth, the separate and equal station to which the Laws of Nature and of Nature's God entitle them, a decent respect to the opinions of mankind requires that they should declare the causes which impel them to the separation.

We hold these truths to be self-evident, that all men are created equal, that they are endowed by their Creator with certain unalienable Rights, that among these are Life, Liberty and the pursuit of Happiness. That to secure these rights, Governments are instituted among Men deriving their just powers from the consent of the governed. That whenever any Form of Government becomes destructive of these ends, it is the Right of the People to alter or to abolish it, and to institute new Government, laying its foundation on such principles and organizing its powers in such form, as to them shall seem most likely to effect their Safety and Happiness. Prudence, indeed, will dictate that Governments long established should not be changed for light and transient causes; and accordingly all experience hath shown, that mankind are more disposed to suffer, while evils are sufferable, than to right themselves by abolishing the forms to which they are accustomed. But when a long train of abuses and usurpations pursuing invariably the same Object evinces a design to reduce them under absolute Despotism, it is their right, it is their duty, to throw off such government, and to provide new Guards for their future security. Such has been the patient sufferance of these Colonies; and such is now the necessity which constrains them to alter their former Systems of Government. The history of the present King of Great Britain is a history of repeated injuries and usurpations, all having in direct object the establishment of an absolute Tyranny over these States. To prove this, let Facts be submitted to a candid world.

He has refused his Assent to Laws, the most wholesome and necessary for the public good. 3

He has forbidden his Governors to pass Laws of immediate and pressing importance, unless suspended in their operation till his Assent should be obtained; and when so suspended, he has utterly neglected to attend to them. 4

He has refused to pass other Laws for the accommodation of large districts of people, unless those people would relinquish the right of Representation in the Legislature, a right inestimable to them and formidable to tyrants only. 5

He has called together legislative bodies at places unusual, uncomfortable, and distant from the depository of their Public Records, for the sole purpose of fatiguing them into compliance with his measures. 6

He has dissolved Representative Houses repeatedly, for opposing with manly firmness his invasions on the rights of the people. 7

He has refused for a long time, after such dissolutions, to cause others to be elected; whereby the Legislative Powers, incapable of Annihilation, have returned to the People at large for their exercise; the State remaining in the mean time exposed to all the dangers of invasion from without, and convulsions within. 8

He has endeavoured to prevent the population of these States; for that purpose obstructing the Laws of Naturalization of Foreigners; refusing to pass others to encourage their migration hither, and raising the conditions of new Appropriations of Lands. 9

He has obstructed the Administration of Justice, by refusing his Assent to Laws for establishing Judiciary Powers. 10

He has made Judges dependent on his Will alone, for the tenure of their offices, and the amount and payment of their salaries. 11

He has erected a multitude of New Offices, and sent hither swarms of Officers to harass our People, and eat out their substance. 12

He has kept among us, in time of peace, Standing Armies without the Consent of our Legislature. 13

He has affected to render the Military independent of and superior to the Civil Power. 14

He has combined with others to subject us to jurisdictions foreign to our constitution, and unacknowledged by our laws; giving his Assent to their acts of pretended Legislation: 15

For quartering large bodies of armed troops among us: 16

For protecting them, by a mock Trial, from Punishment for any Murders which they should commit on the Inhabitants of these States: 17

For cutting off our Trade with all parts of the world: 18

For imposing Taxes on us without our Consent: 19

For depriving us in many cases, of the benefits of Trial by Jury: 20

For transporting us beyond Seas to be tried for pretended offenses: 21

For abolishing the free System of English Laws in a Neighbouring 22
Province, establishing therein an Arbitrary government, and enlarging
its boundaries so as to render it at once an example and fit instrument
for introducing the same absolute rule into these Colonies:

For taking away our Charters, abolishing our most valuable Laws, 23
and altering fundamentally the Forms of our Governments:

For suspending our own Legislatures, and declaring themselves 24
invested with Power to legislate for us in all cases whatsoever.

He has abdicated Government here, by declaring us out of his Pro- 25
tection and waging War against us.

He has plundered our seas, ravaged our Coasts, burnt our towns 26
and destroyed the Lives of our people.

He is at this time transporting large Armies of foreign Mercenaries 27
to compleat works of death, desolation and tyranny already begun
with circumstances of Cruelty & perfidy scarcely paralleled in the most
barbarous ages, and totally unworthy the Head of a civilized nation.

He has constrained our fellow Citizens taken Captive on the high 28
Seas to bear Arms against their Country, to become the executioners of
their friends and Brethren, or to fall themselves by their Hands.

He has excited domestic insurrections amongst us, and has endeav- 29
oured to bring on the inhabitants of our frontiers, the merciless Indian
Savages, whose known rule of warfare is an undistinguished destruction of all ages, sexes and conditions.

In every stage of these Oppressions We Have Petitioned for Redress in 30
the most humble terms: Our repeated petitions have been answered only
by repeated injury. A Prince, whose character is thus marked by every act
which may define a Tyrant, is unfit to be the ruler of a free People.

Nor have We been wanting in attention to our British brethren. We 31
have warned them from time to time of attempts by their legislature to
extend an unwarrantable jurisdiction over us. We have reminded them
of the circumstances of our emigration and settlement here. We have
appealed to their native justice and magnanimity and we have conjured
them by the ties of our common kindred to disavow these usurpations,
which would inevitably interrupt our connections and correspondence.
They too have been deaf to the voice of justice and of consanguinity. We
must, therefore acquiesce in the necessity, which denounces our Separation, and hold them, as we hold the rest of mankind, Enemies in War, in
Peace Friends.

We, therefore, the Representatives of the United States of America, 32
in General Congress, Assembled, appealing to the Supreme Judge of
the world for the rectitude of our intentions, do, in the Name, and by

Authority of the good People of these Colonies, solemnly publish and declare, That these United Colonies are, and of Right ought to be Free and Independent States; that they are Absolved from all Allegiance to the British Crown, and that all political connection between them and the State of Great Britain, is and ought to be totally dissolved; and that as Free and Independent States, they have full power to levy War, conclude Peace, contract Alliances, establish Commerce, and to do all other Acts and Things which Independent States may of right do. And for the support of this Declaration, with a firm reliance on the protection of Divine Providence, we mutually pledge to each other our lives, our Fortunes and our sacred Honor.

THINKING CRITICALLY ABOUT THE TEXT

Why do you think the Declaration of Independence is still such a powerful and important document more than two hundred years after it was written? Do any parts of it seem more memorable than others? Did any part surprise you in this reading?

QUESTIONS ON SUBJECT

1. Where, according to Jefferson, do rulers get their authority? What does Jefferson believe is the purpose of government?

2. What argument does the Declaration of Independence make for over-throwing any unacceptable government? What assumptions underlie this argument?

3. In paragraphs 3 through 29, Jefferson lists the many ways King George has wronged the colonists. Which of these "injuries and usurpations" (paragraph 2) do you feel are just cause for the colonists to declare their independence?

4. According to the Declaration of Independence, how did the colonists try to persuade the English king to rule more justly?

5. What are the specific declarations that Jefferson makes in his final paragraph?

QUESTIONS ON STRATEGY

1. The Declaration of Independence is a deductive argument; it is therefore possible to present it in the form of a syllogism. What is the major premise, the minor premise, and the conclusion of Jefferson's argument? (Glossary: *Syllogism*)

2. In paragraph 2, Jefferson presents certain "self-evident" truths. What are these truths, and how are they related to the intent of his argument?

3. The list of charges against the king is given as evidence in support of Jefferson's minor premise. Does he offer any evidence in support of his major premise? Why or why not? (Glossary: *Evidence*)

4. What organizational pattern do you see in the list of grievances in paragraphs 3 through 29? (Glossary: *Organization*). Describe the cumulative effect of this list on you as a reader.

5. Explain how Jefferson uses cause and effect thinking to justify the colonists' argument in declaring their independence. (Glossary: *Cause and Effect Analysis*)

QUESTIONS ON DICTION AND VOCABULARY

1. Who is Jefferson's audience, and in what tone does he address this audience? Discuss why this tone is or isn't appropriate for this document. (Glossary: *Audience*)

2. Is the language of the Declaration of Independence coolly reasonable or emotional, or does it change from one to the other? Give examples to support your answer.

3. Paraphrase the following excerpt, and comment on Jefferson's diction and syntax: "They too have been deaf to the voice of justice and of consanguinity. We must, therefore acquiesce in the necessity, which denounces our Separation, and hold them, as we hold the rest of mankind, Enemies in War, in Peace Friends" (paragraph 31). Describe the author's tone in these two sentences. (Glossary: *Diction; Tone*)

CLASSROOM ACTIVITY USING ARGUMENTATION

Use the following test, developed by William V. Haney, to determine your ability to analyze accurately evidence that is presented to you. After completing Haney's test, discuss your answers with other members of your class, and then compare them to the correct answers printed at the end of the test.

THE UNCRITICAL INFERENCE TEST

Directions

1. You will read a brief story. Assume that all of the information presented in the story is definitely accurate and true. Read the story carefully. You may refer back to the story whenever you wish.

2. You will then read statements about the story. Answer them in numerical order. *Do not go back* to fill in answers or to change answers. This will only distort your test score.

3. After you read each statement carefully, determine whether the statement is:
   a. "T"—meaning: On the basis of the information presented in the story the statement is *definitely true.*
   b. "F"—meaning: On the basis of the information presented in the story the statement is *definitely false.*
   c. "?"—The statement *may* be true (or false) but on the basis of the information presented in the story you cannot be definitely certain. (If any part of the statement is doubtful, mark the statement "?".)

4. Indicate your answer by circling either "T" or "F" or "?" opposite the statement.

The Story

Babe Smith has been killed. Police have rounded up six suspects, all of whom are known gangsters. All of them are known to have been near the scene of the killing at the approximate time that it occurred. All had substantial motives for wanting Smith killed. However, one of these suspected gangsters, Slinky Sam, has positively been cleared of guilt.

Statements about the Story

1. Slinky Sam is known to have been near the scene of the killing of Babe Smith.   T   F   ?

2. All six of the rounded-up gangsters were known to have been near the scene of the murder.   T   F   ?

3. Only Slinky Sam has been cleared of guilt.   T   F   ?

4. All six of the rounded-up suspects were near the scene of Smith's killing at the approximate time that it took place.   T   F   ?

5. The police do not know who killed Smith.   T   F   ?

6. All six suspects are known to have been near the scene of the foul deed.   T   F   ?

7. Smith's murderer did not confess of his own free will.   T   F   ?

8. Slinky Sam was not cleared of guilt.   T   F   ?

9. It is known that the six suspects were in the vicinity of the cold-blooded assassination.   T   F   ?

¿˙6 ɟ˙8 ¿˙ㄥ ¿˙9 ¿˙ϛ ⊥˙ㄣ ¿˙Ɛ ¿˙ᄅ ⊥˙Ɩ

WRITING SUGGESTIONS

1. To some people, the Declaration of Independence still accurately reflects America's political philosophy and way of life; to others, it does not. What is your position on this issue? Discuss your analysis of the Declaration of Independence's contemporary relevance, and try to persuade others to your position.

2. How does a monarchy differ from American democracy? Write an essay in which you compare and contrast a particular monarchy and the presidency. How are they similar? You might also consider comparing the presidency with the British monarchy of 1776.

The Case for Short Words

Richard Lederer

Born in 1938, Richard Lederer has been a lifelong student of language. He holds degrees from Haverford College, Harvard University, and the University of New Hampshire. For twenty-seven years he taught English at St. Paul's School in Concord, New Hampshire. Anyone who has read one of his more than thirty books will understand why he has been referred to as "Conan the Grammarian" and "America's wittiest verbalist." Lederer loves language and enjoys writing about its richness and usage by Americans. His books include Anguished English *(1987),* Crazy English *(1989),* Adventures of a Verbivore *(1994),* Nothing Risque, Nothing Gained *(1995),* A Man of My Words: Reflections on the English Language *(2003), and* Word Wizard: Super Bloopers, Rich Reflections, and Other Acts of Word Magic *(2006). In addition to writing books, Lederer pens a weekly syndicated column called "Looking at Language" for newspapers and magazines throughout the country. He is the "Grammar Grappler" for* Writer's Digest, *the language commentator for National Public Radio, and the cohost of* A Way with Words, *a weekly radio program out of San Diego, California.*

In the following selection, a chapter from The Miracle of Language *(1990), Lederer sings the praises of short words and reminds us that well-chosen monosyllabic words can be a writer's best friends because they are functional and often pack a powerful punch. Note the clever way in which he uses short words throughout the essay itself to support his argument.*

PREPARING TO READ

Find a paragraph you like in a book that you enjoyed reading. What is it that appeals to you? What did the author do to make the writing so appealing? Do you like the vocabulary, the flow of the words, the imagery it presents, or something else?

W hen you speak and write, there is no law that says you have to use big words. Short words are as good as long ones, and short, old words—like *sun* and *grass* and *home*—are best of all. A lot of small words, more than you might think, can meet your needs with a strength, grace, and charm that large words do not have. 1

Big words can make the way dark for those who read what you write and hear what you say. Small words cast their clear light on big things—night and day, love and hate, war and peace, and life and death. Big words at times seem strange to the eye and the ear and the mind and the heart. Small words are the ones we seem to have known from the time we were born, like the hearth fire that warms the home. 2

Short words are bright like sparks that glow in the night, prompt   3
like the dawn that greets the day, sharp like the blade of a knife, hot like
salt tears that scald the cheek, quick like moths that flit from flame to
flame, and terse like the dart and sting of a bee.

Here is a sound rule: Use small, old words where you can. If a long   4
word says just what you want to say, do not fear to use it. But know that
our tongue is rich in crisp, brisk, swift, short words. Make them the
spine and the heart of what you speak and write. Short words are like
fast friends. They will not let you down.

The title of this chapter and the four paragraphs that you have just   5
read are wrought entirely of words of one syllable. In setting myself this
task, I did not feel especially cabined, cribbed, or confined. In fact, the
structure helped me to focus on the power of the message I was trying
to put across.

One study shows that twenty words account for twenty-five per-   6
cent of all spoken English words, and all twenty are monosyllabic. In
order of frequency they are: I, *you, the, a, to, is, it, that, of, and, in, what,*
he, this, have, do, she, not, on, and *they.* Other studies indicate that the
fifty most common words in written English are each made of a single
syllable.

For centuries our finest poets and orators have recognized and   7
employed the power of small words to make a straight point between
two minds. A great many of our proverbs punch home their points
with pithy monosyllables: "Where there's a will, there's a way,"
"A stitch in time saves nine," "Spare the rod and spoil the child,"
"A bird in the hand is worth two in the bush."

Nobody used the short word more skillfully than William Shake-   8
speare, whose dying King Lear laments:

> And my poor fool is hang'd! No, no, no life!
> Why should a dog, a horse, a rat have life,
> And thou no breath at all? . . .
> Do you see this? Look on her; look, her lips.
> Look there, look there!

Shakespeare's contemporaries made the King James Bible a center-   9
piece of short words — "And God said, Let there be light: and there was
light. And God saw the light, that it was good." The descendants of such
mighty lines live on in the twentieth century. When asked to explain
his policy to Parliament, Winston Churchill responded with these ringing monosyllables: "I will say: it is to wage war, by sea, land, and air,
with all our might and with all the strength that God can give us." In
his "Death of the Hired Man" Robert Frost observes that "Home is the
place where, when you have to go there,/They have to take you in."

And William H. Johnson uses ten two-letter words to explain his secret of success: "If it is to be,/It is up to me."

You don't have to be a great author, statesman, or philosopher to tap the energy and eloquence of small words. Each winter I ask my ninth graders at St. Paul's School to write a composition composed entirely of one-syllable words. My students greet my request with obligatory moans and groans, but, when they return to class with their essays, most feel that, with the pressure to produce high-sounding polysyllables relieved, they have created some of their most powerful and luminous prose. Here are submissions from two of my ninth graders:

> What can you say to a boy who has left home? You can say that he has done wrong, but he does not care. He has left home so that he will not have to deal with what you say. He wants to go as far as he can. He will do what he wants to do.
>
> This boy does not want to be forced to go to church, to comb his hair, or to be on time. A good time for this boy does not lie in your reach, for what you have he does not want. He dreams of ripped jeans, shorts with no starch, and old socks.
>
> So now this boy is on a bus to a place he dreams of, a place with no rules. This boy now walks a strange street, his long hair blown back by the wind. He wears no coat or tie, just jeans and an old shirt. He hates your world, and he has left it.
>
> — CHARLES SHAFFER

> For a long time we cruised by the coast and at last came to a wide bay past the curve of a hill, at the end of which lay a small town. Our long boat ride at an end, we all stretched and stood up to watch as the boat nosed its way in.
>
> The town climbed up the hill that rose from the shore, a space in front of it left bare for the port. Each house was a clean white with sky blue or grey trim; in front of each one was a small yard, edged by a white stone wall strewn with green vines.
>
> As the town basked in the heat of noon, not a thing stirred in the streets or by the shore. The sun beat down on the sea, the land, and the back of our necks, so that, in spite of the breeze that made the vines sway, we all wished we could hide from the glare in a cool, white house. But, as there was no one to help dock the boat, we had to stand and wait.
>
> At last the head of the crew leaped from the side and strode to a large house on the right. He shoved the door wide, poked his head through the gloom, and roared with a fierce voice. Five or six men came out, and soon the port was loud with the clank of chains and creak of planks as the men caught ropes thrown by the crew, pulled them taut, and tied them to posts. Then they set up a rough plank so we could cross from the deck to the shore. We all made for the large house while the crew watched, glad to be rid of us.
>
> — CELIA WREN

10

You too can tap into the vitality and vigor of compact expression. 11
Take a suggestion from the highway department. At the boundaries of
your speech and prose place a sign that reads "Caution: Small Words
at Work."

THINKING CRITICALLY ABOUT THE TEXT

Reread a piece of writing you turned in earlier this year for any class. Analyze
your choice of words, and describe your writing vocabulary. Did you follow
Lederer's admonition to use short words whenever they are appropriate, or did
you tend to use longer, more important-sounding words? Is Lederer's essay
likely to change the way you write papers in the future? Why or why not?

QUESTIONS ON SUBJECT

1. What rule does Lederer present for writing? What does he do to demonstrate the feasibility of this rule?

2. Lederer states that the twenty words that account for a quarter of all spoken English words are monosyllabic. So are the fifty most common written words. Why, then, do you think Lederer felt it was necessary to argue
   that people should use them? Who is his audience? (Glossary: *Audience*)

3. How do his students react to the assignment he gives them requiring
   short words? How do their essays turn out? What does the assignment
   teach them?

4. In paragraph 10, Lederer refers to the relief his students feel when released
   from "the pressure to produce high-sounding polysyllables." Where does
   this pressure come from? How does it relate to the central purpose of his
   essay?

5. Do you think Lederer's argument will change the way you write? Explain.

QUESTIONS ON STRATEGY

1. As you read Lederer's essay for the first time, were you surprised by his
   announcement in paragraph 5 that the preceding four paragraphs contained only single-syllable words? If not, when were you first aware of
   what he was doing? What does Lederer's strategy tell you about small
   words?

2. Lederer starts using multisyllabic words when discussing the process of
   writing with single-syllable words. Why do you think he abandons his
   single-syllable presentation? Does it diminish the strength of his argument? Explain.

3. Lederer provides two long examples of writing by his own students.
   What does he accomplish by using these examples along with ones from
   famous authors? (Glossary: *Illustration*)

4. Lederer illustrates his argument with examples from several prominent
   authors as well as from students. (Glossary: *Illustration*) Which of these
   examples did you find the most effective? Why? Provide an example

from your own reading that you think is effective in illustrating Lederer's argument.

5. How does Lederer's final paragraph serve to close the essay effectively? (Glossary: *Beginnings/Endings*)

QUESTIONS ON DICTION AND VOCABULARY

1. Lederer uses similes to help the reader form associations and images with short words. (Glossary: *Figures of Speech*) What are some of these similes? Do you find the similes effective in the context of Lederer's argument? Explain.

2. In paragraph 9, Lederer uses such terms as *mighty* and *ringing monosyllables* to describe the passages he gives as examples. Do you think such descriptions are appropriate? Why do you think he includes them?

3. Carefully analyze the two student essays that Lederer presents. In particular, circle all the main verbs that each student uses. (Glossary: *Verb*) What, if anything, do these verbs have in common? What conclusions can you draw about verbs and strong, powerful writing?

CLASSROOM ACTIVITY USING ARGUMENTATION

One strategy in developing a strong argument that most people find convincing is illustration. As Lederer demonstrates, an array of examples, both brief and extended, has a remarkable ability to convince readers of the truth of a proposition. While it is possible to argue a case with one specific example that is both appropriate and representative, most writers find that a varied set of examples often makes a more convincing case. Therefore, it is important to identify your examples before starting to write.

As an exercise in argumentation, choose one of the following position statements:

a. More parking spaces should be provided on campus for students.

b. Children's television programs are marked by a high incidence of violence.

c. Capital punishment is a relatively ineffective deterrent to crime.

d. More computer stations should be provided on campus for students.

e. In-state residency requirements for tuition are unfair at my school.

Make a list of the examples — types of information and evidence — you would need to write an argumentative essay on the topic you choose. Indicate where and how you might obtain this information. Finally, share your list of examples with other students in your class who chose the same topic.

WRITING SUGGESTIONS

1. People tend to avoid single-syllable words because they are afraid they will look inadequate and that their writing will lack sophistication. Are

there situations in which demonstrating command of a large vocabulary is desirable? If you answer yes, present one situation, and argue that the overuse of short words in that situation is potentially detrimental. If you answer no, defend your reasoning. How can the use of short words convey the necessary style and sophistication in all situations?

2. Advertising is an industry that depends on efficient, high-impact words. Choose ten advertising slogans and three jingles that you find effective. For example, "Just Do It" and "Think Different" are two prominent slogans. Analyze the ratio of short to long words in the slogans and jingles, and write an essay in which you present your findings. What is the percentage of short words? Argue that the percentage supports or contradicts Lederer's contention that short words are often best for high-impact communicating.

I Have a Dream

Martin Luther King Jr.

Civil rights leader Martin Luther King Jr. (1929–1968) was the son of a Baptist minister in Atlanta, Georgia. Ordained at the age of eighteen, King went on to earn academic degrees from Morehouse College, Crozer Theological Seminary, Boston University, and Chicago Theological Seminary. He came to prominence in 1955 in Montgomery, Alabama, when he led a successful boycott against the city's segregated bus system. The first president of the Southern Christian Leadership Conference, King became the leading spokesman for the civil rights movement during the 1950s and 1960s, espousing a consistent philosophy of nonviolent resistance to racial injustice. He also championed women's rights and protested the Vietnam War. Named Time *magazine's Man of the Year in 1963, King was awarded the Nobel Peace Prize in 1964. King was assassinated in April 1968 after speaking at a rally in Memphis, Tennessee.*

"I Have a Dream," the keynote address for the March on Washington in 1963, has become one of the most renowned and recognized speeches of the past century. Delivered from the steps of the Lincoln Memorial to commemorate the centennial of the Emancipation Proclamation, King's speech resonates with hope even as it condemns racial oppression.

PREPARING TO READ

Most Americans have seen film clips of King delivering the "I Have a Dream" speech. What do you know of the speech? What do you know of the events and conditions under which King presented it?

Five score years ago, a great American, in whose symbolic shadow we stand, signed the Emancipation Proclamation. This momentous decree came as a great beacon light of hope to millions of Negro slaves who had been seared in the flames of withering injustice. It came as a joyous daybreak to end the long night of captivity. 1

But one hundred years later, we must face the tragic fact that the Negro is still not free. One hundred years later, the life of the Negro is still sadly crippled by the manacles of segregation and the chains of discrimination. One hundred years later, the Negro lives on a lonely island of poverty in the midst of a vast ocean of material prosperity. One hundred years later, the Negro is still languishing in the corners of American society and finds himself an exile in his own land. So we have come here today to dramatize an appalling condition. 2

In a sense we have come to our nation's Capitol to cash a check. When the architects of our republic wrote the magnificent words of the Constitution and the Declaration of Independence, they were signing a 3

486

promissory note to which every American was to fall heir. This note was a promise that all men would be guaranteed the unalienable rights of life, liberty, and the pursuit of happiness.

It is obvious today that America has defaulted on this promissory note insofar as her citizens of color are concerned. Instead of honoring this sacred obligation, America has given the Negro people a bad check; a check which has come back marked "insufficient funds." But we refuse to believe that the bank of justice is bankrupt. We refuse to believe that there are insufficient funds in the great vaults of opportunity of this nation. So we have come to cash this check—a check that will give us upon demand the riches of freedom and the security of justice. We have also come to this hallowed spot to remind America of the fierce urgency of *now*. This is no time to engage in the luxury of cooling off or to take the tranquilizing drug of gradualism. *Now* is the time to make real the promises of Democracy. *Now* is the time to rise from the dark and desolate valley of segregation to the sunlit path of racial justice. *Now* is the time to open the doors of opportunity to all of God's children. *Now* is the time to lift our nation from the quicksands of racial injustice to the solid rock of brotherhood.

It would be fatal for the nation to overlook the urgency of the moment and to underestimate the determination of the Negro. This sweltering summer of the Negro's legitimate discontent will not pass until there is an invigorating autumn of freedom and equality. 1963 is not an end, but a beginning. Those who hope that the Negro needed to blow off steam and will now be content will have a rude awakening if the nation returns to business as usual. There will be neither rest nor tranquility in America until the Negro is granted his citizenship rights. The whirlwinds of revolt will continue to shake the foundations of our nation until the bright day of justice emerges.

But there is something I must say to my people who stand on the warm threshold which leads into the palace of justice. In the process of gaining our rightful place we must not be guilty of wrongful deeds. Let us not seek to satisfy our thirst for freedom by drinking from the cup of bitterness and hatred. We must forever conduct our struggle on the high plane of dignity and discipline. We must not allow our creative protest to degenerate into physical violence. Again and again we must rise to the majestic heights of meeting physical force with soul force. The marvelous new militancy which has engulfed the Negro community must not lead us to a distrust of all white people, for many of our white brothers, as evidenced by their presence here today, have come to realize that their destiny is tied up with our destiny and their freedom is inextricably bound to our freedom. We cannot walk alone.

And as we walk, we must make the pledge that we shall march ahead. We cannot turn back. There are those who are asking the devotees of civil rights, "When will you be satisfied?" We can never be satisfied as

long as the Negro is the victim of the unspeakable horrors of police brutality. We can never be satisfied as long as our bodies, heavy with the
fatigue of travel, cannot gain lodging in the motels of the highways and
the hotels of the cities. We cannot be satisfied as long as the Negro's
basic mobility is from a smaller ghetto to a larger one. We can never be
satisfied as long as a Negro in Mississippi cannot vote and a Negro in
New York believes he has nothing for which to vote. No, no, we are not
satisfied, and we will not be satisfied until justice rolls down like waters
and righteousness like a mighty stream.

    I am not unmindful that some of you have come here out of great
trials and tribulations. Some of you have come fresh from narrow jail
cells. Some of you have come from areas where your quest for freedom
left you battered by the storms of persecution and staggered by the winds
of police brutality. You have been the veterans of creative suffering. Continue to work with the faith that unearned suffering is redemptive.   8

    Go back to Mississippi, go back to Alabama, go back to South
Carolina, go back to Georgia, go back to Louisiana, go back to the slums
and ghettoes of our northern cities, knowing that somehow this situation can and will be changed. Let us not wallow in the valley of despair.   9

    I say to you today, my friends, that in spite of the difficulties and
frustrations of the moment I still have a dream. It is a dream deeply
rooted in the American dream.   10

    I have a dream that one day this nation will rise up and live out the
true meaning of its creed: "We hold these truths to be self-evident; that
all men are created equal."   11

    I have a dream that one day on the red hills of Georgia the sons of
former slaves and the sons of former slaveowners will be able to sit
down together at the table of brotherhood.   12

    I have a dream that the state of Mississippi, a desert state sweltering
with the heat of injustice and oppression, will be transformed into an
oasis of freedom and justice.   13

    I have a dream that my four little children will one day live in a
nation where they will not be judged by the color of their skin but by
the content of their character.   14

    I have a dream today.   15

    I have a dream that the state of Alabama, whose governor's lips are
presently dripping with the words of interposition and nullification,
will be transformed into a situation where little black boys and black
girls will be able to join hands with little white boys and white girls and
walk together as sisters and brothers.   16

    I have a dream today.   17

    I have a dream that one day every valley shall be exalted, every hill
and mountain shall be made low, the rough places will be made plain,
and the crooked places will be made straight, and the glory of the Lord
shall be revealed, and all flesh shall see it together.   18

This is our hope. This is the faith with which I return to the South.   19
With this faith we will be able to hew out of the mountain of despair a
stone of hope. With this faith we will be able to transform the jangling
discords of our nation into a beautiful symphony of brotherhood. With
this faith we will be able to work together, to pray together, to struggle
together, to go to jail together, to stand up for freedom together, knowing that we will be free one day.

This will be the day when all of God's children will be able to sing   20
with new meaning.

> My country, 'tis of thee
> Sweet land of liberty,
>   Of thee I sing:
> Land where my fathers died,
> Land of the pilgrims' pride,
> From every mountainside
>   Let freedom ring.

And if America is to be a great nation this must become true. So let   21
freedom ring from the prodigious hilltops of New Hampshire. Let freedom ring from the mighty mountains of New York. Let freedom ring
from the heightening Alleghenies of Pennsylvania!

Let freedom ring from the snowcapped Rockies of Colorado!   22
Let freedom ring from the curvaceous peaks of California!   23
But not only that; let freedom ring from Stone Mountain of Georgia!   24
Let freedom ring from Lookout Mountain of Tennessee!   25
Let freedom ring from every hill and molehill of Mississippi. From   26
every mountainside, let freedom ring.

When we let freedom ring, when we let it ring from every village   27
and every hamlet, from every state and every city, we will be able to
speed up that day when all of God's children, black men and white
men, Jews and Gentiles, Protestants and Catholics, will be able to join
hands and sing in the words of the old Negro spiritual, "Free at last! free
at last! thank God almighty, we are free at last!"

THINKING CRITICALLY ABOUT THE TEXT

King portrayed an America in 1963 in which there was still systematic oppression of African Americans. What is oppression? Have you ever felt yourself—
or have you known others—to be oppressed or part of a group that is
oppressed? Who are the oppressors? How can oppression be overcome?

QUESTIONS ON SUBJECT

1. Why does King say that the Constitution and the Declaration of Independence act as a "promissory note" (paragraph 3) to the American
   people? In what way has America "defaulted" (4) on its promise?

2. What does King mean when he says that in gaining a rightful place in society "we must not be guilty of wrongful deeds" (paragraph 6)? Why is the issue so important to him?

3. When *will* King be satisfied in his quest for civil rights?

4. What, in a nutshell, is King's dream? What vision does he have for the future?

5. How do you personally respond to the argument King puts forth?

QUESTIONS ON STRATEGY

1. King delivered his address to two audiences: the huge audience that listened to him in person, and another, even larger audience. (Glossary: *Audience*) What is that larger audience? What did King do in his speech to catch its attention and to deliver his point?

2. Explain King's choice of a title. (Glossary: *Title*) Why is the title particularly appropriate given the context in which the speech was delivered? What other titles might he have used?

3. Examine the speech, and determine how King organized his presentation. (Glossary: *Organization*) What are the main sections of the speech and what is the purpose of each? How does the organization serve King's overall purpose? (Glossary: *Purpose*)

4. Review King's opening paragraph. What happened "Five score years ago" and what purpose does King have in invoking its memory? (Glossary: *Beginnings/Endings*)

5. In his final paragraph, King claims that by freeing the Negro we will all be free. What exactly does he mean? Is King simply being hyperbolic or does his claim embody an undeniable truth? Explain.

QUESTIONS ON DICTION AND VOCABULARY

1. King uses parallel constructions and repetition throughout his speech. Identify the phrases and words that he emphasizes. Explain what these techniques add to the persuasiveness of his argument.

2. King makes liberal use of metaphor—and metaphorical imagery—in his speech. (Glossary: *Figures of Speech*) Choose a few examples, and examine what they add to the speech. How do they help King engage his listeners' feelings of injustice and give them hope for a better future?

3. Comment on King's diction. Choose a half dozen words as evidence that his diction is well-chosen and rich.

CLASSROOM ACTIVITY USING ARGUMENTATION

As Martin Luther King Jr.'s speech well demonstrates, the effectiveness of a writer's argument depends in large part on the writer's awareness of audience. For example, if a writer wished to argue for the use of more technology to solve our pressing environmental problems, that argument to a group of environmentalists would need to convince them that the technology would not cause as many environmental problems as it solves, while an argument designed for a group of industrialists might argue that the economic opportunity in developing new technologies is as important as the environmental benefits.

Consider the following proposition:

The university mascot should be changed to reflect the image of our school today.

How would you argue this proposition to the following audiences?

a. the student body
b. the faculty
c. the alumni
d. the administration

As a class, discuss how the consideration of audience impacts the purpose and content of an argument.

WRITING SUGGESTIONS

1. King's language is powerful and his imagery is vivid, but the effectiveness of any speech depends partially upon its delivery. If read in monotone, King's use of repetition and parallel language would sound almost redundant rather than inspiring. Keeping presentation in mind, write a short speech that argues a point of view about which you feel strongly. Use King's speech as a model, and incorporate imagery, repetition, and metaphor to communicate your point. Read your speech aloud to a friend to see how it flows and how effective your use of language is. Refine your presentation—both your text and how you deliver it—and then present your speech to your class.

2. King uses a variety of metaphors in his speech, but a single encompassing metaphor can be useful to establish the tone and purpose of an essay. Write a description based on a metaphor that conveys an overall impression from the beginning. Try to avoid clichés ("My dorm is a beehive," "My life is an empty glass"), but make your metaphor readily understandable. For example, you could say, "A police siren is a lullaby in my neighborhood," or "My town is a car that has gone 15,000 miles since its last oil change." Carry the metaphor through the entire description.

What Does It Mean to Love One's Country?

Michael Parenti

One of the most articulate, fervent, and prolific political writers in America, Michael Parenti is a professor of political science who has taught at a number of colleges and universities both here and abroad. He was born in New York in 1933 and earned his B.A. from City University of New York in 1955, his M.A. from Brown University in 1957, and his Ph.D. from Yale University in 1962. As the author of over 275 articles and twenty books, among them The Sword and the Dollar *(1989),* America Besieged *(1998),* Democracy for the Few *(7th ed., 2002),* The Assassination of Julius Caesar: A People's History of Ancient Rome *(2003), and* The Culture Struggle *(2006), he is in high demand as a lecturer before college audiences and community and labor groups, at scholarly conferences, and as a radio and television guest. His writings have been translated into Arabic, Bangla, Chinese, Dutch, French, German, Greek, Italian, Korean, Persian, Polish, Portuguese, Russian, Serbian, Spanish, Swedish, and Turkish.*

In the following essay, first published in Peace Review *in December 2003, Parenti argues against what he labels "superpatriotism," or "the tendency to place nationalistic pride and supremacy above every other public and ethical consideration. . . ."*

PREPARING TO READ

If you are someone who says you love this country, what do you actually mean? Are you at all critical of our national leaders and their policies regardless of which political party is in office, or are you accepting of their leadership and the direction they are taking this country?

A s a guest on radio talk shows, I have criticized aspects of U.S. for- 1
eign policy. On one such occasion, an irate listener called to ask me, "Don't you love your country?" Here was someone who saw fit to question my patriotism because I questioned the policies of U.S. leaders. The caller was manifesting a common symptom of what might be called "superpatriotism," the tendency to place nationalistic pride and supremacy above every other public and ethical consideration, and the readiness to follow national leaders uncritically in their dealings with other countries, especially confrontations involving the use of U.S. military force and violence.

Whether or not this superpatriotism is the last refuge of scoundrels, 2
as Dr. Johnson might say, it is a highly emotive force used by political leaders and ordinary citizens to discourage critical public discourse and muffle democratic protest. It is time the superpatriots explained what

their brand of patriotism is all about. What, for instance, do they mean when they say they love their country? Do they love every street and lane, every hill and vale? There are many and varied beautiful natural sites within the United States that one might love. Yet most Americans have had direct exposure only to relatively few parts of their nation's vast expanse.

And what of all the natural beauty in other countries, the geo- 3 graphical and geological wonders found throughout the world? Would I be less a patriot if I am forced to conclude that there are parts of Ireland and New Zealand that are just as beautiful — if not more so — than the wondrous sights of the Pacific Northwest region? Would I be considered wanting in love for my country if I felt Paris to be more captivating than San Francisco, or the Piazza Navona in Rome more charming than the Rockefeller Center in New York?

If we love our country, do we love even the ugly parts of it? Do we 4 celebrate and take pride in the urban and suburban blight, the crime-ridden drug-infested neighborhoods, the hungry homeless huddled in urine-stained doorways, the many beggars on the streets of certain cities, the shanty towns and encampments under the freeways, the enormous gap between the obscenely rich and the desperately poor, the breath-choking fumes from congested traffic, the toxic dumps and strip-mined wastelands, the widespread contamination of ground water, the rivers and bays turned into open sewers, the looted and eroded forests, and other such dispiriting things?

Perhaps love of country means loving the American "people." But 5 the people of this nation are a vast aggregate of widely diverse ethnic, religious, and class groups. And even the most gregarious among us know only a tiny portion of the total population. In any case, the more bigoted superpatriots feel no love at all for certain ethnic elements among us and for the many others whose lifestyles or beliefs they detest.

It might be that we can "love" whole peoples in the abstract because 6 we feel some common attachment for being all one nationality, that is, all Americans. But what is so particularly lovable about Americans? We may say we love Americans because they are a particularly nice people, so human, decent, and friendly. But then it is their "humanity" we are appreciating, not their Americanness as such. In any case, quite a few Americans are not particularly nice people, not so decent and friendly. Among the Americans I am not too enamored of are ruthless profiteers, corporate swindlers, corrupt and self-serving leaders, bigots, sexists, violent criminals, and rabid superpatriots.

Perhaps our superpatriots love America for its history? One would 7 doubt it, since there is so much about our country's history and culture that is unknown to them: the struggle for free speech that has continued from the eighteenth century to this day; the fierce and bloody fights for the right to collective bargaining and decent wages and work

conditions; the historic struggles for extending the franchise to all citizens, including women and those without property, for the abolition of
slavery, for civil rights, and for an end to racial segregation and hate
crimes; for free public education, public health, environmental and consumer protections, and occupational safety; for a progressive income
tax, an end to wars of aggression, and a host of other vital peace and
justice issues.

Here certainly is a history that can make one feel proud of one's   8
country and love the valiant people who have battled for political and
economic democracy. The odd thing about most superpatriots is how
ignorant they are of most of this history, especially since so little of it is
taught in the schools. Too bad. It would add more substance to their
love of country.

Also largely untaught is the terrible side of our history. If we must   9
love our country, we need to settle the question: what is there to love
about the extermination of Native American nations which extended
over four centuries and the theft of millions of acres of their lands; the
brutal systematic enslavement of African peoples; the stealing of half of
Mexico; the grabbing of Hawaii, Guam, Puerto Rico, Cuba, and the
Philippines; and the wars of aggression against Mexico, Central America, Canada, Spain, the Philippines, Vietnam, Nicaragua, Grenada,
Panama, Iraq, Yugoslavia, and others?

Should we love our country for its culture? Certainly there is   10
American music and jazz and baseball and all those other nice things
that Ken Burns documents. We have had no Shakespeare or Dante, but
we can be proud of our playwrights and poets, and our art and opera,
our museums and symphony orchestras, our libraries and universities.
Yet, as far as I can tell, the superpatriots evince relatively little interest
in these things. If anything, such arts sometimes come under fire or are
subjected to budget cutbacks by the superpatriots, who prefer to invest
treasure in a humongous military budget. The superpatriots take no
particular pride in Athens; they are too busy building Sparta.

Nor can we who prefer Athens be all that enamored with certain   11
aspects of our culture, such as the mind abuse and wasteland of most
television offerings, the awful movies with their gratuitous violence
and desperate contrivances, the omnipresent and dispiriting commer-
cialism, the boundless corporate greed, the ecological desecration, the
racism of the courts and prisons, the glorification of militarism, and
the economic injustice. All these things are a part of our society and
culture, and they are nothing to cause me to puff myself up and to strut
about with national pride as do the superpatriots.

Many superpatriots say they love America because of its freedom.   12
Supposedly, we can say what we like. Here again, the claim should be
greeted skeptically or at least carefully qualified. We are not as free as
we think. To be too outspoken and too out of step in one's political
opinions is often to put one's career in jeopardy—even in a profession
like teaching which professes a dedication to academic freedom. The
journalists who work for big media conglomerates, and who claim to
be untrammeled in their reportage, overlook the fact that they are free
to say what they like because their bosses like what they say. On those
rare occasions they move a bit beyond the dominant paradigm, they
usually feel the tug of the leash.

The major media in the United States (as well as in the other "West- 13
ern democracies") are owned by giant corporations and influenced by
rich corporate advertisers who seldom, if ever, tolerate any questioning
of the existing private profit system or the doings of a U.S. national
security state that is dedicated to making the world safe for inequality.
The assumptions behind U.S. foreign policy go unexamined and
largely uncriticized in news analysis and commentary. Those who have
critical views regarding capitalism, class power, and U.S. imperialism do
not get an opportunity to reach any mass audience in the United
States. Indeed, the very idea of "U.S. imperialism" would sound strange
to most Americans—but not to millions of people in Latin America,
Africa, the Middle East, and elsewhere.

Our superpatriots love "America" not for its geographical and eco- 14
logical wonders, nor out of any personal attachment to its vast and varied population, nor because of a deep and revealing grasp of its history
and culture. What then? Many of them seem to love this country
because they believe it is "a land of opportunity." As in no other country here we can become rich and successful if we have the right stuff, or
so it is said. But success for one comes by beating out others for the
prize. Individual success is predicated on failure for other individuals.
Room at the top is limited to only a relatively select few, mostly those
who from birth have been supremely advantaged in family income and
social standing.

America has not been a land of opportunity or a success story for 15
the Native Americans (except for a few present-day casino owners),
who have had their lands stolen and their populations sadly reduced
by death and disease; nor for the slaves of yore, and the sharecrop-
pers and indentured servants; nor for the factory workers who toiled
14-hour days in earlier times, who today still face life-threatening occupational hazards, and who see their jobs being exported to Third World
sweatshops; nor for the farm workers who put in long hours at stoop
labor for barely U.S.$10,000 a year, and the millions of others who
are paid poverty-level wages, or who work at joyless dead-end jobs
while struggling to keep their heads above water, or who managed to
attain an education only to find themselves in hopeless debt from student loans.

Even if this economy does reward those who sally forth with an 16
exceptionally competitive capacity and a directed quotidian energy
that allows them to excel over others, what of the rest of us? Is the quality of life to be measured by a society's sound ecology, its human
services, arts, education, and social sensibilities? Or by the ability of
particularly tireless go-getters and ruthless financial buccaneers to
make a killing in the marketplace regardless of the costs to others and
to the environment?

As for the economic freedom of the "free market," it is "free" and works best for those who have a lot of money to begin with. The concentration of wealth and power, which is the essence of the capital accumulation process, does not give many of us the opportunity to become rich but rather causes us to become economically dependent, threatened by unemployment, inflation, and want—and obliged to work harder and harder to stay afloat. 17

And even if it were easy to become a multi-millionaire, what is so great about that? Why should one's ability to make large sums of money be reason to love one's country? What is so admirable about a patriotism that is based on the cash nexus? In any case, there are those of us who do not wish to spend our lives trying to get rich and advantaging ourselves—often at the expense of others—but who want to do work that benefits others and enhances the quality of life for the entire society. Why should we feel patriotic about the rat race? 18

For many superpatriots "America" is less a complex and abounding historical, cultural, and social reality than it is a simplified ideological abstraction, an emotive symbol represented by other, abstract content-less symbols like the flag, which become the objects of uncritical adulation. For the superpatriot, those who cannot share in this uncritical adulation ought to go live in some other country. 19

Sooner or later, let us hope, Americans will rediscover—as they have in the past—that they cannot live on flag waving alone. They will begin to drift off into reality. They will confront the economic irrationalities and global aggrandizement of a system that provides them with endless circuses and extravaganzas of superpatriotism, while denying them the bread of prosperity and their birthright as democratic citizens, their right to live in peace with justice. 20

THINKING CRITICALLY ABOUT THE TEXT

If America is as bad as Parenti describes it, why is it considered by many who emigrate to our shores a beacon of freedom and opportunity? Do they know what they want, or are they misleading themselves?

QUESTIONS ON SUBJECT

1. Who are the people Parenti labels "superpatriots"? How does he describe them?

2. Why does Parenti find superpatriots so problematic? What are their shortcomings as far as he is concerned?

3. What parts of our country's history does Parenti find admirable? Why does he believe that this history should make us proud of our country?

4. In paragraph 9, Parenti describes the "terrible side of our history," which he claims is "largely untaught." What are the highlights of that history, and why do you think it is largely untaught?

5. What is Parenti's hope for superpatriots?

QUESTIONS ON STRATEGY

1. What is Parenti's thesis? (Glossary: *Thesis*) Where in the essay does he offer his thesis?

2. How do paragraphs 9–13 function within the context of Parenti's overall argument?

3. Who is Parenti's audience, and what does he want them to do as a result of reading his essay? (Glossary: *Audience; Purpose*)

4. How does Parenti employ other rhetorical strategies to develop his argument? (Glossary: *Definition; Illustration*)

5. What evidence does Parenti offer for his claim in paragraph 14 that "Individual success is predicated on failure for other individuals"?

QUESTIONS ON DICTION AND VOCABULARY

1. Does Parenti imply in the first sentence of his second paragraph that superpatriots are scoundrels? If so, is this name-calling? What evidence does he offer for this claim? (Glossary: *Logical Fallacies*)

2. In a quotation from *KPFA-Pacifica* that appears on his personal Web page, Parenti has been described as a "right-on mix of scholar and street." The inference we make from this statement is that he thinks and speaks with the nuances of a scholar as well as the boldness of a streetwise person. What evidence, if any, can you find in his diction to support this claim?

3. What is Parenti's tone in this essay? Is it reasonable, calculating, conciliatory, angry, desperate, frustrated, optimistic, or something other than these descriptions?

CLASSROOM ACTIVITY USING ARGUMENTATION

An excellent way to gain some experience in formulating an argumentative position on an issue, and perhaps to establish a thesis, is to engage in a debate with someone else who is on the other side of the question. When one listens to arguments and thinks of refutations and counterarguments, there's a chance for a rehearsal and revision of one's position before it gets into written form. For example, use Parenti's argument about "superpatriotism" as the subject for a class debate. Divide the class into pro and con sides. Each side should elect a spokesperson to present its arguments before the class. Finally, have the class make some estimate of the success of each side in 1) articulating its position, 2) presenting ideas and evidence to support that position, and 3) convincing the audience of its position. The exercise should give each student a good idea of the kind of work that's involved in preparing a written argument.

WRITING SUGGESTIONS

1. Michael Parenti writes the following in paragraph 12: "We are not as free as we think." What does he mean? Write an argument in which you support or take issue with his statement. Think about the kinds of evidence that you use to support your position and how you will refute those who support the opposing view.

2. Parenti puts forth the following question in paragraph 16: "Is the quality of life to be measured by a society's sound ecology, its human services, arts, education, and social responsibility? Or by the ability of particularly tireless go-getters and ruthless financial buccaneers to make a killing in the marketplace regardless of the costs to others and to the environment?" Think about how you might answer Parenti's question, and build an argument against the opposing viewpoint or in favor of some accommodation between what Parenti sees as these two diametrically opposing forces in our country. If you see the question as embodying a classic example of the either/or logical fallacy, argue accordingly.

3. How would you define *patriotism*? In this context consider the photograph on page 494. What are your impressions of this veteran? How do you think Parenti would react to this picture? For you, is this a picture of a superpatriot or simply a man who loves his country? In an essay, explore the meaning and value of patriotism for each of us individually and collectively as a society.

My Father Was an Anonymous Sperm Donor

Katrina Clark

When she wrote the following essay, Katrina Clark was eighteen years old and a student in the undergraduate hearing program at Gallaudet University in Washington, D.C. For most of her life Clark had known only half of her parentage because she was conceived by artificial insemination with the sperm of an anonymous donor. In the decades preceding her conception, the identities of sperm donors were not revealed, so Clark is among the first generation of children so conceived who have been able to learn the identities of their biological fathers. In her essay, Clark tells us how she went about locating her biological father and the relationship she has had with him since. In the process we learn more about her thoughts, emotions, and developing identity than we could from any customary biography of her. She writes, "My search for my father has been unusually successful; most offspring will look for many, many years before they succeed, if they ever do." Clark's argument is that the practice of using anonymous donors is basically wrong and that children conceived in this manner will have a lot of questions as adults: "We're all going to grow into adults and form opinions about the decision to bring us into the world in a way that deprives us of the basic right to know where we came from, what our history is and who both parents are."

Clark's essay first appeared in the Washington Post *on December 17, 2006.*

PREPARING TO READ

Think about the information you have about the circumstances of your conception, birth, and nurturing. What kinds of information would you like to have that you do not possess? What positive or negative differences in your life do you think having such information would make?

I really wasn't expecting anything the day, earlier this year, when I sent an e-mail to a man whose name I had found on the Internet. I was looking for my father, and in some ways this man fit the bill. But I never thought I'd hit pay dirt on my first try. Then I got a reply—with a picture attached.

From my computer screen, my own face seemed to stare back at me. And just like that, after 17 years, the missing piece of the puzzle snapped into place.

The puzzle of who I am.

I'm 18, and for most of my life, I haven't known half my origins. I didn't know where my nose or jaw came from, or my interest in foreign cultures. I obviously got my teeth and my penchant for corny jokes from my mother, along with my feminist perspective. But a whole other part of me was a mystery.

That part came from my father. The only thing was, I had never met him, never heard any stories about him, never seen a picture of him. I didn't know his name. My mother never talked about him—because she didn't have a clue who he was. 5

When she was 32, my mother—single, and worried that she might never marry and have a family—allowed a doctor wearing rubber gloves to inject a syringe of sperm from an unknown man into her uterus so that she could have a baby. I am the result: a donor-conceived child. 6

And for a while, I was pretty angry about it. 7

I was angry at the idea that where donor conception is concerned, everyone focuses on the "parents"—the adults who can make choices about their own lives. The recipient gets sympathy for wanting to have a child. The donor gets a guarantee of anonymity and absolution from any responsibility for the offspring of his "donation." As long as these adults are happy, then donor conception is a success, right? 8

Not so. The children born of these transactions are people, too. Those of us in the first documented generation of donor babies—conceived in the late 1980s and early '90s, when sperm banks became more common and donor insemination began to flourish—are coming of age, and we have something to say. 9

I'm here to tell you that emotionally, many of us are not keeping up. We didn't ask to be born into this situation, with its limitations and confusion. It's hypocritical of parents and medical professionals to assume that biological roots won't matter to the "products" of the cryobanks' service, when the longing for a biological relationship is what brings customers to the banks in the first place. 10

We offspring are recognizing the right that was stripped from us at birth—the right to know who both our parents are. 11

And we're ready to reclaim it. 12

Growing up, it didn't matter that I don't have a dad—or at least that is what I told myself. Just sometimes, when I was small, I would daydream about a tall, lean man picking me up and swinging me around in the front yard, a manly man melting at a touch from his little girl. I wouldn't have minded if he weren't around all the time, as long as I could have the sweet moments of reuniting with his strong arms and hearty laugh. My daydreams always ended abruptly; I knew I would never have a dad. As a coping mechanism, I used to think that he was dead. That made it easier. 13

I've never been angry at my mother—all my life she has been my hero, my everything. She sacrificed so much as a single mother, living on food stamps, trying to make ends meet. I know that many people considered her a pioneer, a trailblazer for a new offshoot of the women's movement. She explained to me when I was quite young why 14 it was that I didn't have a "dad," just a "biological father." I used to love to repeat that word—biological—because it made me feel smart, even though I didn't understand its implications.

Then when I was 9, the mother of one of my classmates ran for 15 political office. I remember seeing a television ad for her, and her family appeared at the end—the complete nuclear household in the back yard, the kids playing on a swing suspended from a tree and eating their father's barbeque. I looked back at my lonely, tired mother, who sat there with a weak smile on her face.

In the middle of the fifth grade, I met a new friend, and we had a 16 lot in common: We both had single mothers. Her mother had suffered through two divorces. My friend didn't have much to say about her dad, mainly because she knew so little about him. But at least she got to visit him and his new family. And I was jealous. Later, in the eighth grade, another friend's father had an affair and her parents divorced. She was in so much pain, and I tried to empathize for the loss of her dad. But I was jealous of her, too, for all the attention she was getting. No one had ever offered me support or sympathy like that.

Around this time, my mother and I moved in with a friend 17 and—along with several other teenagers, one infant and some other adults—lived with her for nearly a year. I went through a teenage anger stage; I would stay in my room, listening to Avril Lavigne and to Eminem's lyrics of broken homes and broken people. I felt broken, too. All the other teenagers in the house had problems with their dads. I would sit with them through tears during various rough times, and then I'd go back to my room and listen to some more Eminem. I was angry, too, and angry that I had nowhere to direct my anger.

When my mother eventually got married, I didn't get along with 18 her husband. For so long, it had been just the two of us, my mom and I, and now I felt like the odd girl out. When she and I quarreled, this new man in our lives took to interjecting his opinion, and I didn't like that. One day, I lost my composure and screamed that he had no authority over me, that he wasn't my father—because I didn't have one.

That was when the emptiness came over me. I realized that I am, in 19 a sense, a freak. I really, truly would never have a dad. I finally understood what it meant to be donor-conceived, and I hated it.

It might have gone on this way indefinitely, but about a year ago 20 I happened to see a television show about a woman who had died of a heart attack. A genetic disease had caused her heart to deteriorate, but she didn't know about her predisposition because she had been adopted as a baby and didn't know her biological families' medical histories. It hit me that I didn't know mine, either. Or half of it, at least.

So I began to research Fairfax Cryobank, the Northern Virginia 21 sperm bank where my mother had been inseminated. I knew that sperm donors are screened and tested thoroughly, but I was still concerned. The bank had been established in 1986, a mere two years before my conception. Many maladies have come to light since then.

I e-mailed the bank five times over the course of a year, requesting medical information about my donor, but no one responded. Then one Friday last spring, I started surfing the Web. Eventually I came upon an archive of "Oprah" shows. One was a show about artificial insemination using anonymous donors. A girl perched on Oprah's couch. Next to her sat her "donor," the man who was her biological father. 22

I froze. Why hadn't I thought of that? If I wanted medical information and a sense of roots, who better to seek out than the man responsible for them? 23

I set out to find my own donor. From the limited information my mother had been given—his blood type, race, ethnicity, eye and hair color and hair texture; his height, weight and body build; his years of college and course of study—I concluded that he had probably graduated from a four-year university in Northern Virginia or the District within a span of three years. Now all I had to do was search through the records and yearbooks of all the possible universities and make some awkward phone calls. I figured if I worked intensely enough, my search would take a minimum of 10 years. But I was ready and willing. 24

A few days later, searching for an online message board for donor-conceived people, I came across a donor and offspring registry. Scanning past some entries for more recent donors, I spotted a donation date closer to what I was looking for. I e-mailed the man who had posted the entry. A few days later he sent a warm response and attached a picture of himself. I read through his pleasant words and scrolled down to look at the photo. My breath stopped. I called for my mother, who rushed in, thinking something was terribly wrong. "I think I've found my biological father," I gasped between sobs. "Look at the picture. . . . That's my face." 25

After a few weeks of e-mailing, this stranger and I took DNA tests. When the results arrived, I tore open the envelope, feeling like a character in a soap opera. Most of the scientific language went over my head, but I understood one fact more clearly than I have ever understood anything in my life: There was, the letter said, a 99.9902 percent chance that this man was my father. After 17 years, I let out a long sigh. 26

I had found the man who had given me blue eyes and blond hair. And it had taken me only a month. 27

My life has changed since then. Once the initial disbelief that I had found my father wore off, my thoughts turned to all the other donor-conceived kids out there who have been or will be holding their breath much longer than I. My search for my father had been unusually successful; most offspring will look for many, many years before they succeed, if they ever do. 28

My heart went out to those others, especially after I participated in a couple of online groups. When I read some of the mothers' thoughts 29 about their choice for conception, it made me feel degraded to nothing more than a vial of frozen sperm. It seemed to me that most of the mothers and donors give little thought to the feelings of the children who would result from their actions. It's not so much that they're cold-hearted as that they don't consider what the children might think once they grow up.

Those of us created with donated sperm won't stay bubbly babies forever. We're all going to grow into adults and form opinions about the decision to bring us into the world in a way that deprives us of the basic right to know where we came from, what our history is and who both our parents are.

Some countries, such as Australia and the United Kingdom, are beginning to move away from the practice of paying donors and granting them anonymity, and making it somewhat easier for offspring to find their biological fathers. I understand anonymity's appeal for so many donors: Even if their offspring were to find them one day—which is becoming more and more probable—they have no legal, social, financial or moral obligation to their children.

But perhaps if donors were not paid and anonymity were no longer guaranteed, those still willing to participate would seriously consider the repercussions of their actions. They would have to be prepared to someday meet the people whom they helped create, to answer questions and to deal with a range of erratic emotions from their offspring. I believe I've let go of any resentment about the way I was conceived. I'm playing the cards I've been dealt and trying to make the best of things. But not all donor-conceived people share this mindset.

As relief about my own situation has come to me, I've talked freely and regularly about being donor-conceived, in public and in private. In the beginning, I also talked about it a lot with my biological father. After a bit, though, I noticed that his enthusiasm for our developing relationship seemed to be waning. When I told him of my suspicion, he confirmed that he was tired of "this whole sperm-donor thing." The irony stings me more each time I think of him saying that. The very thing that brought us together was pushing us in opposite directions.

Even though I've only recently come into contact with him, I wouldn't be able to just suck it up if he stopped communicating with me. There's still so much I want to know. I want to know him. I want to know his family. I'm certain he has no idea how big a role he has played in my life despite his absence—or because of his absence. If I can't be too attached to him as my father, I'll still always be attached to the feeling I now have of *having* a father.

I feel more whole now than I ever have. I love our conversations, even the most trivial ones. I don't love him, and I don't know if I ever will, but I care about him a lot.

Now that he knows I exist, I'm okay if he doesn't care for me in the 36 same way. But I hope he at least thinks of me sometimes.

THINKING CRITICALLY ABOUT THE TEXT

How do you regard Katrina's statement that her mother was "[her] every-thing" and that her mother "sacrificed so much as a single mother" (para-graph 14)? Does her mother bear some responsibility for Clark's sense of emptiness? Why or why not? Can Clark's mother be regarded as a victim?

QUESTIONS ON SUBJECT

1. Explain how Clark discovered who her biological father is. What sur-prised her about the process?

2. In paragraph 33, Clark says that it is ironic that her donor confirmed that he was tired of "this whole sperm-donor thing." What is the irony involved in that statement for her? (Glossary: *Irony*)

3. Clark says that donor offspring are "recognizing the right that was stripped from [them] at birth" (paragraph 11). What is the right to which she refers?

4. Do you believe Clark when she writes in paragraph 32 that she has "let go of any resentment about the way [she] was conceived"? Why or why not?

5. Why does Clark think that paying donors to preserve their anonymity is not a good idea?

QUESTIONS ON STRATEGY

1. What is Clark's basic argument?

2. Does Clark argue inductively, deductively, or does she use some combi-nation of both techniques? Explain. (Glossary: *Deduction*; *Induction*)

3. Why is it important for her personally and for the essay she wrote that both she and the man she suspected of being her donor took DNA tests? (Glossary: *Evidence*)

4. How effective is the beginning of Clark's essay? (Glossary: *Beginnings/ Endings*)

5. Clark uses some one- or two-sentence paragraphs in her essay. Are they successful in furthering her argument? Explain.

QUESTIONS ON DICTION AND VOCABULARY

1. Clark refers to herself as a "freak" in paragraph 19. Do you think her use of that word is appropriate in the context of her essay? Explain.

2. Clark experienced a variety of emotions at various times in her life. What tone does she exhibit in her writing? (Glossary: *Tone*)

3. *Donor* and *donor-conceived* are two special terms Clark uses in this essay. What other special terms and expressions, if any, does she find it helpful to use in discussing her subject?

CLASSROOM ACTIVITY USING ARGUMENTATION

Several days after Clark's essay appeared in the *Washington Post* she was interviewed on National Public Radio. The recording of that interview is available on NPR's Web site: npr.org. As a class, listen to that interview, make notes on it, and discuss the additional information it provides both in content and delivery. For example, Clark says in the interview that it is not now the practice in England to guarantee anonymity and as result donors are not as available as they once were—information she does not include in her essay and that appears to cause her concern.

WRITING SUGGESTIONS

1. Imagine yourself to be either an actual or potential anonymous sperm donor. Write a response to Clark's argument. Provide a context for your argument by offering a summary of her position as you understand it, and then proceed to argue with her main point that donors should not be anonymous nor be paid as a consideration for their anonymity. Consider the concessions that you make, if any, to her argument as you present the opposing view that donors should remain anonymous and be paid for that anonymity as one way of guaranteeing it.

2. Imagine yourself a woman who is considering using the services of a sperm bank. Knowing what you now know from reading Clark's essay, write an argument in favor of or against using sperm from an anonymous donor to conceive a child. Would you want your child to someday know who his or her father is, or would you wish that information to remain anonymous? Consider the risks and benefits in both cases before determining your position.

When World War II began, American women entered the workforce in larger numbers than ever, taking the places of men who had gone off to serve in the armed forces. Most of the jobs held by these women were manual or clerical in nature, not what we would today call careers. After the war ended and the modern women's movement began in the 1960s, women were encouraged to take their rightful places alongside men economically and educationally. They pursued careers in business, law, health sciences, finance, engineering, research, and corporate management, and they worked long hours, traveled, were away from home for days or weeks, and discussed work-related issues over lunch or dinner with their associates much the same way men had been doing for as long as anyone could remember. The world was clearly different for these women than it had been for their mothers and grandmothers. Those who were married and had families were challenged as they had never been before. They wanted to hold down responsible positions but still carry on the traditional duties of wives and mothers. As the popular expression has it, "They wanted it all."

Women in career positions know that changes have occurred in all aspects of their lives and that they have demanded a lot of themselves—demands that are often very difficult to manage—and the sociological studies that have appeared in the past twenty-five years have documented those changes. Stresses have been put on marriages, and divorces have increased in the general society and especially in two-career marriages. Greater earning power has meant that women are not forced by economics to remain in unhappy marriages. Men are sometimes resentful if their spouses earn more than they do. Many women have become dissatisfied with mates who have not exhibited the same ambition and energy they have or who are not willing to adjust to a new set of dynamics, and they have sought new arrangements. Men may be disturbed by untidy homes but still take the attitude that household chores are their wives' responsibility. Both men and women have had to work on tighter schedules to raise their children and complete ever-present and nagging household chores.

Whether two-career couples will continue to struggle with this transition from the "traditional" family situation where the husband works and the wife takes care of the home and children or will be able to accommodate each other and work successfully toward a new definition of marriage and family remains for sociologists to research and analyze. The next few decades will tell us a lot.

On August 22, 2006, the following pair of arguments by Michael Noer and Elizabeth Corcoran was published online by Forbes.com, resulting in an outpouring of e-mail, most of it protesting the argument that Noer put forth but also criticizing Corcoran for what appeared to readers as a less-than-vigorous defense of career women. Noer boldly came out and advised men that if they married career women they were asking for trouble, and he peppered his article with one academic journal finding after another supporting his argument. Corcoran's defense was rapidly prepared and took both a softer and a more personal approach, discussing her own experiences as a career woman and describing how she and her husband have made creative adaptations in their lives and family arrangements to accommodate the two-career marriage they enjoy. In concluding her argument Corcoran writes, "The essence of a good marriage, it seems to me, is that both people have to learn to change and keep on adapting."

PREPARING TO READ

If you are looking forward to marrying, what concerns do you have about the arrangements that you'll be able to make to ensure that you and your spouse will have the income you both desire while maintaining a relatively stress-free and happy marriage? If you are already married, what stresses have you dealt with that grow from your work and career arrangements? How have you managed to keep things on track and moving forward so that both you and your spouse are supportive of each other's efforts?

Don't Marry Career Women

Michael Noer

Michael Noer is a business writer and the founding editor of Forbes.com, *where he currently serves as executive news editor. He was born in 1969 and graduated cum laude from Rice University in 1992 before becoming, in 1993, a Thomas J. Watson Fellow. In that capacity he traveled for fifteen months in Europe and the Middle East studying the history of Santa Claus. In 1999–2000 Noer worked as business editor of* Wired. *When he returned to* Forbes.com, *he helped create the* Forbes Fictional 15, *a collection of satirical biographies of fictional characters — Santa Claus, Richie Rich, Jay Gatsby, Scrooge McDuck, Auric Goldfinger, C. Montgomery Burns, and others — who were known to be rich in their own worlds. Noer has also written special reports on communicating, money, work, and the greatest athletic achievements of all time.*

Noer published "Don't Marry Career Women" for Forbes.com *on August 22, 2006.*

Guys: A word of advice. Marry pretty women or ugly ones. Short ones or tall ones. Blondes or brunettes. Just, whatever you do, don't marry a woman with a career.

Why? Because if many social scientists are to be believed, you run a higher risk of having a rocky marriage. While everyone knows that marriage can be stressful, recent studies have found professional women are more likely to get divorced, more likely to cheat, less likely to have children, and, if they do have kids, they are more likely to be unhappy about it. A recent study in *Social Forces*, a research journal, found that women — even those with a "feminist" outlook—are happier when their husband is the primary breadwinner.

Not a happy conclusion, especially given that many men, particularly successful men, are attracted to women with similar goals and aspirations. And why not? After all, your typical career girl is well-educated, ambitious, informed and engaged. All seemingly good things, right? Sure . . . at least until you get married. Then, to put it bluntly, the more successful she is the more likely she is to grow dissatisfied with you. Sound familiar?

Many factors contribute to a stable marriage, including the marital status of your spouse's parents (folks with divorced parents are significantly more likely to get divorced themselves), age at first marriage, race, religious beliefs and socio-economic status. And, of course, many working women are indeed happily and fruitfully married—it's just that they are less likely to be so than non-working women. And that, statistically speaking, is the rub.

To be clear, we're not talking about a high-school dropout minding a cash register. For our purposes, a "career girl" has a university-level (or higher) education, works more than 35 hours a week outside the home and makes more than $30,000 a year.

If a host of studies are to be believed, marrying these women is asking 6 for trouble. If they quit their jobs and stay home with the kids, they will be unhappy (*Journal of Marriage and Family*, 2003). They will be unhappy if they make more money than you do (*Social Forces*, 2006). You will be unhappy if they make more money than you do (*Journal of Marriage and Family*, 2001). You will be more likely to fall ill (*American Journal of Sociology*). Even your house will be dirtier (Institute for Social Research).

Why? Well, despite the fact that the link between work, women and 7 divorce rates is complex and controversial, much of the reasoning is based on a lot of economic theory and a bit of common sense. In classic economics, a marriage is, at least in part, an exercise in labor specialization. Traditionally men have tended to do "market" or paid work outside the home and women have tended to do "non-market" or household work, including raising children. All of the work must get done by somebody, and this pairing, regardless of who is in the home and who is outside the home, accomplishes that goal. Nobel laureate Gary S. Becker argued that when the labor specialization in a marriage decreases — if, for example, both spouses have careers — the overall value of the marriage is lower for both partners because less of the total needed work is getting done, making life harder for both partners and divorce more likely. And, indeed, empirical studies have concluded just that.

In 2004, John H. Johnson examined data from the Survey of 8 Income and Program Participation and concluded that gender has a significant influence on the relationship between work hours and increases in the probability of divorce. Women's work hours consistently increase divorce, whereas increases in men's work hours often have no statistical effect. "I also find that the incidence of divorce is far higher in couples where both spouses are working than in couples where only one spouse is employed," Johnson says. A few other studies, which have focused on employment (as opposed to working hours), have concluded that working outside the home actually increases marital stability, at least when the marriage is a happy one. But even in these studies, wives' employment does correlate positively to divorce rates, when the marriage is of "low marital quality."

The other reason a career can hurt a marriage will be obvious to 9 anyone who has seen their mate run off with a co-worker: When your spouse works outside the home, chances increase they'll meet someone they like more than you. "The work environment provides a host of potential partners," researcher Adrian J. Blow reported in the *Journal of Marital and Family Therapy*, "and individuals frequently find themselves spending a great deal of time with these individuals."

There's more: According to a wide-ranging review of the published 10 literature, highly educated people are more likely to have had extra-marital sex (those with graduate degrees are 1.75 more likely to have cheated than those with high school diplomas). Additionally, individuals who earn more than $30,000 a year are more likely to cheat.

And if the cheating leads to divorce, you're really in trouble. 11 Divorce has been positively correlated with higher rates of alcoholism, clinical depression and suicide. Other studies have associated divorce with increased rates of cancer, stroke, and sexually-transmitted disease. Plus divorce is financially devastating. According to one recent study on "Marriage and Divorce's Impact on Wealth," published in *The Journal of Sociology*, divorced people see their overall net worth drop an average of 77%.

So why not just stay single? Because, academically speaking, a solid 12 marriage has a host of benefits beyond just individual "happiness." There are broader social and health implications as well. According to a 2004 paper entitled "What Do Social Scientists Know About the Benefits of Marriage?" marriage is positively associated with "better outcomes for children under most circumstances," higher earnings for adult men, and "being married and being in a satisfying marriage are positively associated with health and negatively associated with mortality." In other words, a good marriage is associated with a higher income, a longer, healthier life and better-adjusted kids.

A word of caution, though: As with any social scientific study, it's 13 important not to confuse correlation with causation. In other words, just because married folks are healthier than single people, it doesn't mean that marriage is causing the health gains. It could just be that healthier people are more likely to be married.

THINKING CRITICALLY ABOUT THE TEXT

Just because academic studies indicate that women, careers, and marriage do not mix well, is there any reason to believe that a particular marriage will fail? Are there not special circumstances in every marriage that allow for success despite the correlations that Noer points out? Should the statistics be ignored, however?

EXAMINING THE ISSUE

1. What is Noer's thesis? Where does he state it? (Glossary: *Thesis*)

2. Why does Noer say "many men, particularly successful men, are attracted to women with similar goals and aspirations" (paragraph 3)?

3. What is the relationship, according to Noer, between a stable marriage and the marital status of a spouse's parents? What evidence do you see of this in your own experience? (Glossary: *Evidence*)

4. In paragraph 4, Noer writes: "And that, statistically speaking, is the rub." What does he mean?

5. Noer offers no specific citations to the studies to which he refers. Would you like to have those citations? Why do you think he did not include them? Do you have reason to doubt either the quality of the research or his accuracy in reporting it? Explain.

6. Noer writes in paragraph 13 that as far as successful marriages are concerned, one must not "confuse correlation with causation." In other words, as he writes, "It could just be that happier people are more likely to be married." Is it possible that he may be similarly confused in his interpretation of the studies he's referred to earlier in his article? Explain.

Don't Marry a Lazy Man

Elizabeth Corcoran

Elizabeth Corcoran was born in Elmhurst, Illinois, in 1962 and received her bachelor's degree from Georgetown University, where she majored in economics. She has been a staff writer or editor for a number of publications, including Scientific American, *the* Washington Post, *and* Forbes. *In addition, she has written articles for the* New York Times, Science *magazine,* Fortune, *and the* San Francisco Chronicle. *Corcoran has been a featured commentator on the "Forbes on Fox" business news show and is a frequent moderator and speaker at conferences. She has won several awards for her writing and reporting. When asked to comment on her counterpoint argument in response to Michael Noer's "Don't Marry Career Women," she wrote the following:*

> *Forbes.com* published Michael Noer's essay "Don't Marry Career Women" bright and early on August 22. Yikes! Like many, many people, I read the essay online and had a different opinion. Since I had other commitments that day, I had only about an hour to write a response, which left no time to analyze the studies Noer cites or to find alternative "evidence." I gave myself two guidelines: First: keep a light touch. Writing an angry reaction, I thought, would only make his points sound more credible. Second: I didn't want to attack women who opted out of the workplace to raise their family. I wanted to point out the fallacies in Noer's argument—not beat up on someone else. Given that, I boiled Noer's argument down to what seemed to be its core assertions: Married women are more likely to cheat. Your house will be dirty. Men are intimidated by wives who out-earn them. Working spouses don't divide up chores very well. I figured I'd end on an upbeat note by highlighting a positive element of having a working spouse.

Forbes *received hundreds of e-mails in response to this pair of essays. Clearly, these are far from the last words on the subject!*

Girlfriends: A word of advice. Ask your man the following question: When was the last time you learned something useful, either at home or work?

If the last new skill your guy learned was how to tie his shoes in the second grade, dump him. If he can pick up new ideas faster than your puppy, you've got a winner.

I'm not usually a fan of dipstick tests, particularly when it comes to marriage and relationships. But a downright frightening story written by my colleague, Michael Noer, on our Web site today drove me to it. According to the experts cited by Michael, marrying a "career girl" seems to lead to a fate worse than tangling with a hungry cougar.

OK, call me a cougar. I've been working since the day I graduated   4
from college 20-odd years ago. I have two grade-school-aged children.
Work definitely takes up more than 35 hours a week for me. Thank-
fully, I do seem to make more than $30,000. All of which, according to
Michael, should make me a wretched wife.

In spite of those dangerous statistics, my husband and I are about   5
to celebrate our 18th wedding anniversary. You'll see us snuggling at a
mountain-winery concert this month, enjoying the occasion. I don't
think I'm all that unusual—so it seemed like a good time to test
Michael's grim assertions.

The experts cited in his story think that professional women are   6
more likely to get divorced, to cheat and to be grumpy about either having kids or not having them. But rather than rush to blame the woman,
let's not overlook the other key variable: What is the guy doing?

Take, for instance, the claim that professional women are more   7
likely to get divorced, because they're more likely to meet someone in
the workforce who will be "more attractive" than that old squashed-
couch hubby at home.

Women have faced this kind of competition squarely for years. Say   8
you marry your college heartthrob. Ten years later, he's working with
some good-looking gals—nymphets just out of college, or the more
sophisticated types who spent two years building houses in Africa
before they went to Stanford Business School. What do you do? A: Stay
home, whine and eat chocolate B: Take up rock climbing, read interesting books and continue to develop that interesting personality he fell
in love with in the first place.

Note to guys: Start by going to the gym. Then try some new music.   9
Or a book. Or a movie. Keep connected to the rest of the world. You'll
win—and so will your marriage.

There is, of course, the continual dilemma of who does the work   10
around the house. But if both spouses are working, guess what?
They've got enough income to hire someone else to fold laundry, mop
floors, etc.

Money is a problem? Honestly, the times money has been the   11
biggest problem for us have been when we were short of it—not when
one of us is earning more than the other. When we have enough to pay
the bills, have some fun and save a bit, seems like the rules of pre-
school should take over: Play nice, be fair and take turns.

In two-career couples, Michael frets, there's less specialization in the   12
marriage, so supposedly the union becomes less useful to either party.
Look more closely, Mike! Any long-running marriage is packed full of
carefully developed—and charmingly offsetting—areas of expertise.

For us, the list starts with taxes, vacation planning and investment   13
management. My husband likes that stuff, and it leaves me yawning.

Bless him for doing it. Give me the wireless Internet system, the garden or just about any routine home repairs and I'm suddenly the savant. Tear us apart, and we'd both be pitiful idiots trying to learn unfamiliar routines.

Michael is right that longer work hours force two-career couples to try harder to clear out blocks of family time. When we do, though, we get to enjoy a lot more. We understand each other's career jokes and frustrations. We're better sounding boards on what to do next. And at dinner parties, we actually like to be seated at the same table. 14

The essence of a good marriage, it seems to me, is that both people have to learn to change and keep on adapting. Children bring tons of change. Mothers encounter it first during the nine months of pregnancy, starting with changing body dimensions. But fathers have to learn to adapt, too, by learning to help care for children, to take charge of new aspects of a household, to adapt as the mothers change. 15

So guys, if you're game for an exciting life, go ahead and marry a professional gal. 16

THINKING CRITICALLY ABOUT THE TEXT

Corcoran, by her own admission, needed to respond quickly to Noer's argument and did not have an opportunity to examine the research studies he refers to in his article. Are the issues she raises from a personal standpoint, in particular the points she makes based on her own marriage, sufficient to counter the statistical studies Noer uses as his evidence? Do they fail the test of argument or do they offer their own empirical evidence, proof that statistics are not always the final answer?

EXAMINING THE ISSUE

1. What is Corcoran's thesis? (Glossary: *Thesis*)
2. Corcoran begins with the question of when "your man" last "learned something useful." What is the intent of her question? How does it tie into the rest of her argument? How does it relate to Noer's argument?
3. Does Corcoran disprove Noer's argument? Explain.
4. Is Corcoran fair in referring to the good-looking women in the office as "nymphets"?
5. Has Corcoran unfairly stereotyped married men as out of shape and not doing what it takes to, as she says in paragraph 9, "keep connected to the rest of the world"?
6. What concessions, if any, does Corcoran make to Noer's argument?

MAKING CONNECTIONS: WRITING AND DISCUSSION SUGGESTIONS FOR "DOES A HEALTHY CAREER EQUAL AN UNHEALTHY MARRIAGE?"

The following questions are offered to help you start making meaningful connections between the two articles in this argument pairing. These questions can be used for classroom discussion, or you can choose to answer any one of them by writing an essay. If you are writing an essay, be sure to make several references to the articles. With several of the questions, some additional research may be required. To begin your research online, go to bedford stmartins.com/subjectandstrategy and click on Argument Pair: Work and Marriage or browse the thematic directory of annotated links.

1. Research the studies done on any one of the issues raised by Noer and Corcoran, or a related issue that concerns you, in order to build an argument of your own. Some of the issues you might want to consider are the following:
   - marital happiness based on income
   - trends in work specialization within the home
   - marital status of one's spouse's parents
   - rates of divorce in two-career marriages
   - attitudes of men toward spouses whose income is greater than theirs
   - the role of feminist attitudes in marital happiness or success

2. Locate several of the studies that Noer refers to in his article. Is his reporting of the studies you examined accurate? Do they support his findings or are there qualifications to his assessment that you think need to be taken into consideration?

3. Discuss the statement that Corcoran has made about the writing of her counterpoint argument. Do you find it helpful in understanding her argument? Why or why not?

4. Noer has been vilified—and called names that are in some cases unprintable—for publishing his article. Has he been unfair, inaccurate, nasty, insensitive? Can he be accused of waging a war against marriage? Is he simply presenting the truth, however unpalatable, as he finds it? Write your own counterargument to Noer's article. Where, if anywhere, has he failed to understand the situation? Is it enough to gather a group of studies and to draw generalizations from them? If not, what do you think is needed? Has he himself in some way confused correlation with causation?

5. Not surprisingly, most people fall in love and marry without the aid of sociological studies, so of what usefulness are the arguments Noer and Corcoran put forward? If you are unmarried, can you know for certain before you marry what issues and adjustments you'll have to make along the way? If you think the studies referred to and the issues raised are important ones, discuss why you think so.

Since Great Britain gained control over what is now the United States, English has been the dominant language in our country. Despite the multitude of cultures and ethnicities that comprise the United States, English has been a common thread linking them together. It may be somewhat surprising, then, that there is no official U.S. language. Now, even as English literacy becomes a necessity for people in many parts of the world, some people in the United States believe its primacy is being threatened here at home. Much of the current controversy focuses on Hispanic communities with large Spanish-speaking populations who may feel little or no pressure to learn English. Yet in order for everyone to participate in our society, some way must be found to bridge the communication gap.

Recent government efforts in this regard have included bilingual programs in schools, bilingual ballots, bilingual emergency notices, and so on. The goal of these measures is to maintain a respect for the heritage and language of the non–English speakers while they learn the English language. The programs have come under fire, however, from those who believe that the U.S. government should conduct itself only in English. If people come here, the argument goes, they should take the responsibility to learn the native language as quickly as possible. And, English-only proponents reason, if immigrants do not or are not willing to learn English, the government should not accommodate them in another language. Moreover, there should be a mandate that the official language of the United States is English and that the government will conduct business in no other language. Many state governments have, in fact, already made such a declaration.

The other side of the argument has two components. One is the belief that it is discriminatory to mandate English because those who do not speak it are then denied basic rights until they learn the language. The second part of this argument is that the current situation is nothing new: There have always been groups of immigrants who were slow to assimilate into American culture, but they all eventually integrated, and the controversy will resolve itself. Furthermore, English is not threatened, and its use does not need to be legislated. Indeed, according to English-only critics, declaring English the official U.S. language could create far more problems than it solves.

The following two selections address the issue from opposite sides. In the first article, Charles Krauthammer argues in favor of making English the official language of the United States. Having grown up in the Canadian province of Quebec, Krauthammer experienced firsthand what he calls "the perils of bilingualism." He believes that because immigration and assimilation patterns in the United States are changing, it is time to make English the official language of the land. Robert D. King in "Should English Be the Law?" comes to the opposite conclusion. In the context of our history and that of countries around the world, he does not believe that English is under siege in the United States. King notes that compared with similar situations in other countries, including the French Canadian separatist crisis to our north, the problems here seem to be trivial. If being American still means anything unique, he concludes, we should be able to enjoy our linguistic diversity rather than be threatened by it.

PREPARING TO READ

It is now possible to go many places in the world and get along pretty well in English, no matter what other languages are spoken in the host country. If you were to emigrate, how hard would you work to learn the predominant language of your chosen country? What advantages would there be in learning that language, even if you could get by in English? How would you feel if the country had a law that forced you to learn its language as quickly as possible? Write down your thoughts about these questions.

In Plain English: Let's Make It Official

Charles Krauthammer

Pulitzer Prize–winning columnist and commentator Charles Krauthammer was born in 1950 in New York City to parents of French citizenship. He grew up in Montreal and graduated from McGill University in 1970. The following year he continued his studies in political science as a Commonwealth Scholar at Balliol College, Oxford. In 1972 he moved to the United States and enrolled in Harvard Medical School, earning his M.D. in psychiatry in 1975. In 1978 he joined Jimmy Carter's administration to direct planning in psychiatric research, and later he served as speechwriter for Vice President Walter Mondale and senior editor at the New Republic. *As a journalist, Krauthammer quickly gained a reputation for his clear prose and sound arguments. He is widely recognized and respected for his political and social columns, which appear regularly in the* Washington Post, Time, *the* New Republic, *and* The Weekly Standard. *In 1985 he published* Cutting Edges: Making Sense of the Eighties, *a collection of his essays. One critic commented that "Krauthammer is at his best when he writes not so much about 'hard' politics as about political culture . . . and beyond that about the contemporary social climate in general."*

In the following essay, first published in Time *on June 12, 2006, Krauthammer presents the case for making English the official language of the United States. He strongly believes that America's unprecedented success as a nation can be traced to the unifying force of the English language.*

Growing up (as I did) in the province of Québec, you learn not just the joys but also the perils of bilingualism. A separate national identity, revolving entirely around "Francophonie," became a raging issue that led to social unrest, terrorism, threats of separation and a referendum that came within a hair's breadth of breaking up Canada. 1

Canada, of course, had no choice about bilingualism. It is a country created of two nations at its birth, and has ever since been trying to cope with that inherently divisive fact. The U.S., by contrast blessed with a single common language for two centuries, seems blithely and gratuitously to be ready to import bilingualism with all its attendant divisiveness and antagonisms. 2

One of the major reasons for America's great success as the world's first "universal nation," for its astonishing and unmatched capacity for assimilating immigrants, has been that an automatic part of acculturation was the acquisition of English. And yet during the great immigration debate now raging in Congress, the people's representatives cannot make up their minds whether the current dominance of English should be declared a national asset, worthy of enshrinement in law. 3

519

The Senate could not bring itself to declare English the country's "official language." The best it could do was pass an amendment to the immigration bill tepidly declaring English the "national language." Yet even that was too much for Senate Democratic leader Harry Reid, who called that resolution "racist." 4

Less hyperbolic opponents point out that granting special official status to English is simply unnecessary: America has been accepting foreign-language-speaking immigrants forever — Brooklyn is so polyglot it is a veritable Babel — and yet we've done just fine. What's the great worry about Spanish? 5

The worry is this. Polyglot is fine. When immigrants, like those in Brooklyn, are members of a myriad of linguistic communities, each tiny and discrete, there is no threat to the common culture. No immigrant presumes to make the demand that the state grant special status to his language. He may speak it in the street and proudly teach it to his children, but he knows that his future and certainly theirs lie inevitably in learning English as the gateway to American life. 6

But all of that changes when you have an enormous, linguistically monoclonal immigration as we do today from Latin America. Then you get not Brooklyn's successful Babel but Canada's restive Québec. Monoclonal immigration is new for the U.S., and it changes things radically. If at the turn of the 20th century, Ellis Island had greeted teeming masses speaking not 50 languages but just, say, German, America might not have enjoyed the same success at assimilation and national unity that it has. 7

Today's monoclonal linguistic culture is far from hypothetical. Growing rapidly through immigration, it creates large communities — in some places already majorities — so overwhelmingly Spanish speaking that, in time, they may quite naturally demand the rights and official recognition for Spanish that French has in French-speaking Québec. 8

That would not be the end of the world — Canada is a decent place — but the beginning of a new one for the U.S., a world far more complicated and fraught with division. History has blessed us with all the freedom and advantages of multiculturalism. But it has also blessed us, because of the accident of our origins, with a linguistic unity that brings a critically needed cohesion to a nation as diverse, multiracial and multiethnic as America. Why gratuitously throw away that priceless asset? How mindless to call the desire to retain it "racist." 9

I speak three languages. My late father spoke nine. When he became a naturalized American in midcentury, it never occurred to him to demand of his new and beneficent land that whenever its government had business with him — tax forms, court proceedings, ballot boxes — that it should be required to communicate in French, his best language, rather than English, his last and relatively weakest. 10

English is the U.S.'s national and common language. But that may change over time unless we change our assimilation norms. Making 11

English the official language is the first step toward establishing those norms. "Official" means the language of the government and its institutions. "Official" makes clear our expectations of acculturation. "Official" means that every citizen, upon entering America's most sacred political space, the voting booth, should minimally be able to identify the words President and Vice President and county commissioner and judge. The immigrant, of course, has the right to speak whatever he wants. But he must understand that when he comes to the U.S., swears allegiance and accepts its bounty, he undertakes to join its civic culture. In English.

THINKING CRITICALLY ABOUT THE TEXT

Krauthammer grew up in Montreal in the heart of the province of Quebec. What did his experiences there teach him about the differences between the province of Quebec and the United States? In what ways do these differences help you understand why Krauthammer strongly believes that America needs to make English its official language?

EXAMINING THE ISSUE

1. According to Krauthammer, what has been one of the most important reasons for America's success as a nation?

2. How does Krauthammer counter those people who believe that "granting special official status to English is simply unnecessary"?

3. What is "monoclonal immigration"? In what ways does monoclonal immigration affect assimilation and national unity? Explain.

4. How does Krauthammer answer the question, "What's the great worry about Spanish"? What do you see as his greatest fear?

5. Why does Krauthammer believe that "linguistic unity" is so important for the United States at this point in its history? Do you agree with his assessment of the situation? Explain why or why not.

6. What, for Krauthammer, is the difference between "declaring English the 'national language'" and making English the "official language"? What does he believe the label "official" will mean for future generations?

Should English Be the Law?

Robert D. King

Scholar and teacher, Robert D. King was born in Mississippi in 1936. He graduated from the Georgia Institute of Technology in 1959 with a degree in mathematics. After a brief stint at IBM, King went to the University of Wisconsin, receiving a Ph.D. in German linguistics in 1965. He was hired by the University of Texas at Austin to teach German that same year and has spent more than four decades there teaching linguistics and Asian studies in addition to German. He also served as the dean of the College of Liberal Arts from 1979 until 1989 and currently holds the Audre and Bernard Rapoport Regents Chair of Liberal Arts. In 1969 he published Historical Linguistics and Generative Grammar, *a comprehensive look at historical linguistics through the lens of Noam Chomsky's theory of generative grammar. Indian studies captured King's attention in the 1990s, and he wrote* Nehru and the Language of Politics of India *(1996).*

The language of politics of the United States has become a hot topic in recent years as well. In the following selection, first published in the April 1997 issue of the Atlantic, *King provides historical background and perspective on the English-only debate. He believes we should "relax and luxuriate in our linguistic richness and our traditional tolerance of language differences."*

We have known race riots, draft riots, labor violence, secession, anti-war protests, and a whiskey rebellion, but one kind of trouble we've never had: a language riot. Language riot? It sounds like a joke. The very idea of language as a political force—as something that might threaten to split a country wide apart—is alien to our way of thinking and to our cultural traditions. 1

This may be changing. On August 1 of last year [1996] the U.S. House of Representatives approved a bill that would make English the official language of the United States. The vote was 259 to 169, with 223 Republicans and thirty-six Democrats voting in favor and eight Republicans, 160 Democrats, and one independent voting against. The debate was intense, acrid, and partisan. On March 25 of last year the Supreme Court agreed to review a case involving an Arizona law that would require public employees to conduct government business only in English. Arizona is one of several states that have passed "Official English" or "English Only" laws. The appeal to the Supreme Court followed a 6-to-5 ruling, in October of 1995, by a federal appeals court striking down the Arizona law. These events suggest how divisive a public issue language could become in America—even if it has until now scarcely been taken seriously. 2

Traditionally, the American way has been to make English the national language—but to do so quietly, locally, without fuss. The Constitution is silent on language: the Founding Fathers had no need to legislate that English be the official language of the country. It has always been taken for granted that English *is* the national language, and that one must learn English in order to make it in America.

To say that language has never been a major force in American history or politics, however, is not to say that politicians have always resisted linguistic jingoism. In 1753 Benjamin Franklin voiced his concern that German immigrants were not learning English: "Those [Germans] who come hither are generally the most ignorant Stupid Sort of their own Nation. . . . they will soon so out number us, that all the advantages we have will not, in My Opinion, be able to preserve our language, and even our government will become precarious." Theodore Roosevelt articulated the unspoken American linguistic-melting-pot theory when he boomed, "We have room for but one language here, and that is the English language, for we intended to see that the crucible turns our people out as Americans, of American nationality, and not as dwellers in a polyglot boarding house." And: "We must have but one flag. We must also have but one language. That must be the language of the Declaration of Independence, of Washington's Farewell address, of Lincoln's Gettysburg speech and Second Inaugural."

OFFICIAL ENGLISH

TR's linguistic tub-thumping long typified the tradition of American politics. That tradition began to change in the wake of the anything-goes attitudes and the celebration of cultural differences arising in the 1960s. A 1975 amendment to the Voting Rights Act of 1965 mandated the "bilingual ballot" under certain circumstances, notably when the voters of selected language groups reached five percent or more in a voting district. Bilingual education became a byword of educational thinking during the 1960s. By the 1970s linguists had demonstrated convincingly—at least to other academics—that black English (today called African-American vernacular English or Ebonics) was not "bad" English but a different kind of authentic English with its own rules. Predictably, there have been scattered demands that black English be included in bilingual-education programs.

It was against this background that the movement to make English the official language of the country arose. In 1981 Senator S. I. Hayakawa, long a leading critic of bilingual education and bilingual ballots, introduced in the U.S. Senate a constitutional amendment that not only would have made English the official language but would have prohibited federal and state laws and regulations requiring the use of other languages. His English Language Amendment died in the Ninety-seventh Congress.

In 1983 the organization called U.S. English was founded by Hayakawa and John Tanton, a Michigan ophthalmologist. The primary purpose of the organization was to promote English as the official language of the United States. (The best background readings on America's "neolinguisticism" are the books *Hold Your Tongue,* by James Crawford, and *Language Loyalties,* edited by Crawford, both published in 1992.) Official English initiatives were passed by California in 1986, by Arkansas, Mississippi, North Carolina, North Dakota, and South Carolina in 1987, by Colorado, Florida, and Arizona in 1988, and by Alabama in 1990. The majorities voting for these initiatives were generally not insubstantial: California's, for example, passed by 73 percent.

It was probably inevitable that the Official English (or English Only—the two names are used almost interchangeably) movement would acquire a conservative, almost reactionary undertone in the 1990s. Official English is politically very incorrect. But its cofounder John Tanton brought with him strong liberal credentials. He had been active in the Sierra Club and Planned Parenthood, and in the 1970s served as the national president of Zero Population Growth. Early advisers of U.S. English resist ideological pigeonholing: they included Walter Annenberg, Jacques Barzun, Bruno Bettelheim, Alistair Cooke, Denton Cooley, Walter Cronkite, Angier Biddle Duke, George Gilder, Sidney Hook, Norman Podhoretz, Arnold Schwarzenegger, and Karl Shapiro. In 1987 U.S. English installed as its president Linda Chávez, a Hispanic who had been prominent in the Reagan Administration. A year later she resigned her position, citing "repugnant" and "anti-Hispanic" overtones in an internal memorandum written by Tanton. Tanton, too, resigned, and Walter Cronkite, describing the affair as "embarrassing," left the advisory board. One board member, Norman Cousins, defected in 1986, alluding to the "negative symbolic significance" of California's Official English initiative, Proposition 63. The current chairman of the board and CEO of U.S. English is Mauro E. Mujica, who claims that the organization has 650,000 members.

The popular wisdom is that conservatives are pro and liberals con. True, conservatives such as George Will and William F. Buckley Jr. have written columns supporting Official English. But would anyone characterize as conservatives the present and past U.S. English board members Alistair Cooke, Walter Cronkite, and Norman Cousins? One of the strongest opponents of bilingual education is the Mexican-American writer Richard Rodriguez, best known for his eloquent autobiography, *Hunger of Memory* (1982). There is a strain of American liberalism that defines itself in nostalgic devotion to the melting pot.

For several years relevant bills awaited consideration in the U.S. House of Representatives. The Emerson Bill (H.R. 123), passed by the

House last August, specifies English as the official language of government, and requires that the government "preserve and enhance" the official status of English. Exceptions are made for the teaching of foreign languages; for actions necessary for public health, international relations, foreign trade, and the protection of the rights of criminal defendants; and for the use of "terms of art" from languages other than English. It would, for example, stop the Internal Revenue Service from sending out income-tax forms and instructions in languages other than English, but it would not ban the use of foreign languages in census materials or documents dealing with national security. *"E Pluribus Unum"* can still appear on American money. U.S. English supports the bill.

What are the chances that some version of Official English will become federal law? Any language bill will face tough odds in the Senate, because some western senators have opposed English Only measures in the past for various reasons, among them a desire by Republicans not to alienate the growing number of Hispanic Republicans, most of whom are uncomfortable with mandated monolingualism. Texas Governor George W. Bush, too, has forthrightly said that he would oppose any English Only proposals in his state. Several of the Republican candidates for President in 1996 (an interesting exception is Phil Gramm) endorsed versions of Official English, as has Newt Gingrich. While governor of Arkansas, Bill Clinton signed into law an English Only bill. As President, he has described his earlier action as a mistake.

Many issues intersect in the controversy over Official English: immigration (above all), the rights of minorities (Spanish-speaking minorities in particular), the pros and cons of bilingual education, tolerance, how best to educate the children of immigrants, and the place of cultural diversity in school curricula and in American society in general. The question that lies at the root of most of the uneasiness is this: Is America threatened by the preservation of languages other than English? Will America, if it continues on its traditional path of benign linguistic neglect, go the way of Belgium, Canada, and Sri Lanka—three countries among many whose unity is gravely imperiled by language and ethnic conflicts?

LANGUAGE AND NATIONALITY

Language and nationalism were not always so intimately intertwined. Never in the heyday of rule by sovereign was it a condition of employment that the King be able to speak the language of his subjects. George I spoke no English and spent much of his time away from England, attempting to use the power of his kingship to shore up his German possessions. In the Middle Ages nationalism was not even part of the picture: one owed loyalty to a lord, a prince, a ruler, a family, a tribe, a church, a piece of land, but not to a nation and least of all to a nation as a language unit. The capital city of the Austrian Hapsburg empire was Vienna, its ruler a monarch with effective control of peoples of the most varied and incompatible ethnicities, and languages, throughout Central and Eastern Europe. The official language, and the lingua franca as well, was German. While it stood — and it stood for hundreds of years — the empire was an anachronistic relic of what for most of human history had been the normal relationship between country and language: none.

The marriage of language and nationalism goes back at least to Romanticism and specifically to Rousseau, who argued in his *Essay on the Origin of Languages* that language must develop before politics is possible and that language originally distinguished nations from one another. A little-remembered aim of the French Revolution — itself the legacy of Rousseau — was to impose a national language on France, where regional languages such as Provençal, Breton, and Basque were still strong competitors against standard French, the French of the Ile de France. As late as 1789, when the Revolution began, half the population of the south of France, which spoke Provençal, did not understand French. A century earlier the playwright Racine said that he had had to resort to Spanish and Italian to make himself understood in the southern French town of Uzès. After the Revolution nationhood itself became aligned with language. 14

In 1846 Jacob Grimm, one of the Brothers Grimm of fairy-tale fame but better known in the linguistic establishment as a forerunner of modern comparative and historical linguists, said that "a nation is the totality of people who speak the same language." After midcentury, language was invoked more than any other single criterion to define nationality. Language as a political force helped to bring about the unification of Italy and of Germany and the secession of Norway from its union with Sweden in 1905. Arnold Toynbee observed — unhappily — soon after the First World War that "the growing consciousness of Nationality had attached itself neither to traditional frontiers nor to new geographical associations but almost exclusively to mother tongues." 15

The crowning triumph of the new desideratum was the Treaty of Versailles, in 1919, when the allied victors of the First World War began redrawing the map of Central and Eastern Europe according to nationality as best they could. The magic word was "self-determination," and none of Woodrow Wilson's Fourteen Points mentioned the word "language" at all. Self-determination was thought of as being related to "nationality," which today we would be more likely to call "ethnicity"; but language was simpler to identify than nationality or ethnicity. When it came to drawing the boundary lines of various countries — Czechoslovakia, Yugoslavia, Romania, Hungary, Albania, Bulgaria, Poland — it was principally language that guided the draftsman's hand. (The main exceptions were Alsace-Lorraine, South Tyrol, and the 16

German-speaking parts of Bohemia and Moravia.) Almost by default language became the defining characteristic of nationality.

And so it remains today. In much of the world, ethnic unity and cultural identification are routinely defined by language. To be Arab is to speak Arabic. Bengali identity is based on language in spite of the division of Bengali-speakers between Hindu India and Muslim Bangladesh. When eastern Pakistan seceded from greater Pakistan in 1971, it named itself Bangladesh: *desa* means "country"; *bangla* means not the Bengali people or the Bengali territory but the Bengali language.

Scratch most nationalist movements and you find a linguistic grievance. The demands for independence of the Baltic states (Latvia, Lithuania, and Estonia) were intimately bound up with fears for the loss of their respective languages and cultures in a sea of Russianness. In Belgium the war between French and Flemish threatens an already weakly fused country. The present atmosphere of Belgium is dark and anxious, costive; the metaphor of divorce is a staple of private and public discourse. The lines of terrorism in Sri Lanka are drawn between Tamil Hindus and Sinhalese Buddhists—and also between the Tamil and Sinhalese languages. Worship of the French language fortifies the movement for an independent Quebec. Whether a united Canada will survive into the twenty-first century is a question too close to call. Much of the anxiety about language in the United States is probably fueled by the "Quebec problem": unlike Belgium, which is a small European country, or Sri Lanka, which is halfway around the world, Canada is our close neighbor.

Language is a convenient surrogate for nonlinguistic claims that are often awkward to articulate, for they amount to a demand for more political and economic power. Militant Sikhs in India call for a state of their own: Khalistan ("Land of the Pure" in Punjabi). They frequently couch this as a demand for a linguistic state, which has a certain simplicity about it, a clarity of motive—justice, even, because states in India are normally linguistic states. But the Sikh demands blend religion, economics, language, and retribution for sins both punished and unpunished in a country where old sins cast long shadows.

Language is an explosive issue in the countries of the former Soviet Union. The language conflict in Estonia has been especially bitter. Ethnic Russians make up almost a third of Estonia's population, and most of them do not speak or read Estonian, although Russians have lived in Estonia for more than a generation. Estonia has passed legislation requiring knowledge of the Estonian language as a condition of citizenship. Nationalist groups in independent Lithuania sought restrictions on the use of Polish—again, old sins, long shadows.

In 1995 protests erupted in Moldova, formerly the Moldavian Soviet Socialist Republic, over language and the teaching of Moldovan history. Was Moldovan history a part of Romanian history or of Soviet history? Was Moldova's language Romanian? Moldovan—earlier called Moldavian—*is* Romanian, just as American English and British English are both English. But in the days of the Moldavian SSR, Moscow insisted that the two languages were different, and in a piece of linguistic non-sense required Moldavian to be written in the Cyrillic alphabet to strengthen the case that it was not Romanian.

The official language of Yugoslavia was Serbo-Croatian, which was never so much a language as a political accommodation. The Serbian and Croatian languages are mutually intelligible. Serbian is written in the Cyrillic alphabet, is identified with the Eastern Orthodox branch of the Catholic Church, and borrows its high-culture words from the east—from Russian and Old Church Slavic. Croatian is written in the Roman alphabet, is identified with Roman Catholicism and borrows its high-culture words from the west—from German, for example, and Latin. One of the first things the newly autonomous Republic of Serbia did, in 1991, was to pass a law decreeing Serbian in the Cyrillic alphabet the official language of the country. With Croatia divorced from Serbia, the Croatian and Serbian languages are diverging more and more. Serbo-Croatian has now passed into history, a language-museum relic from the brief period when Serbs and Croats called themselves Yugoslavs and pretended to like each other. 22

Slovakia, relieved now of the need to accommodate to Czech cosmopolitan sensibilities, has passed a law making Slovak its official language. (Czech is to Slovak pretty much as Croatian is to Serbian.) Doctors in state hospitals must speak to patients in Slovak, even if another language would aid diagnosis and treatment. Some 600,000 Slovaks—more than 10 percent of the population—are ethnically Hungarian. Even staff meetings in Hungarian-language schools must be in Slovak. (The government dropped a stipulation that church weddings be conducted in Slovak after heavy opposition from the Roman Catholic Church.) Language inspectors are told to weed out "all sins perpetrated on the regular Slovak language." Tensions between Slovaks and Hungarians, who had been getting along, have begun to arise. 23

The twentieth century is ending as it began—with trouble in the Balkans and with nationalist tensions flaring up in other parts of the globe. (Toward the end of his life Bismarck predicted that "some damn fool thing in the Balkans" would ignite the next war.) Language isn't always part of the problem. But it usually is. 24

UNIQUE OTHERNESS

Is there no hope for language tolerance? Some countries manage to maintain their unity in the face of multilingualism. Examples are Finland, with a Swedish minority, and a number of African and Southeast 25

Asian countries. Two others could not be more unlike as countries go: Switzerland and India.

German, French, Italian, and Romansh are the languages of   26
Switzerland. The first three can be and are used for official purposes; all four are designated "national" languages. Switzerland is politically almost hyperstable. It has language problems (Romansh is losing ground), but they are not major, and they are never allowed to threaten national unity.

Contrary to public perception, India gets along pretty well with a   27
host of different languages. The Indian constitution officially recognizes nineteen languages, English among them. Hindi is specified in the constitution as the national language of India, but that is a pious postcolonial fiction: outside the Hindi-speaking northern heartland of India, people don't want to learn it. English functions more nearly than Hindi as India's lingua franca.

From 1947, when India obtained its independence from the   28
British, until the 1960s blood ran in the streets and people died because of language. Hindi absolutists wanted to force Hindi on the entire country, which would have split India between north and south and opened up other fracture lines as well. For as long as possible Jawaharlal Nehru, independent India's first Prime Minister, resisted nationalist demands to redraw the capricious state boundaries of British India according to language. By the time he capitulated, the country had gained a precious decade to prove its viability as a union.

Why is it that India preserves its unity with not just two languages   29
to contend with, as Belgium, Canada, and Sri Lanka have, but nineteen? The answer is that India, like Switzerland, has a strong national identity. The two countries share something big and almost mystical that holds each together in a union transcending language. That something I call "unique otherness."

The Swiss have what the political scientist Karl Deutsch called   30
"learned habits, preferences, symbols, memories, and patterns of landholding": customs, cultural traditions, and political institutions that bind them closer to one another than to people of France, Germany, or Italy living just across the border and speaking the same language. There is Switzerland's traditional neutrality, its system of universal military training (the "citizen army"), its consensual allegiance to a strong Swiss franc—and fondue, yodeling, skiing, and mountains. Set against all this, the fact that Switzerland has four languages doesn't even approach the threshold of becoming a threat.

As for India, what Vincent Smith, in the *Oxford History of India,* calls   31
its "deep underlying fundamental unity" resides in institutions and beliefs such as caste, cow worship, sacred places, and much more. Consider *dharma, karma,* and *maya,* the three root convictions of Hinduism; India's historical epics; Gandhi; *ahimsa* (nonviolence); vegetarianism;

a distinctive cuisine and way of eating; marriage customs; a shared past; and what the Indologist Ainslie Embree calls "Brahmanical ideology." In other words, "We are Indian; we are different."

Belgium and Canada have never managed to forge a stable national identity; Czechoslovakia and Yugoslavia never did either. Unique otherness immunizes countries against linguistic destabilization. Even Switzerland and especially India have problems; in any country with as many different languages as India has, language will never *not* be a problem. However, it is one thing to have a major illness with a bleak prognosis; it is another to have a condition that is irritating and occasionally painful but not life-threatening. 32

History teaches a plain lesson about language and governments: there is almost nothing the government of a free country can do to change language usage and practice significantly, to force its citizens to use certain languages in preference to others, and to discourage people from speaking a language they wish to continue to speak. (The rebirth of Hebrew in Palestine and Israel's successful mandate that Hebrew be spoken and written by Israelis is a unique event in the annals of language history.) Quebec has since the 1970s passed an array of laws giving French a virtual monopoly in the province. One consequence—unintended, one wishes to believe—of these laws is that last year kosher products imported for Passover were kept off the shelves, because the packages were not labeled in French. Wise governments keep their hands off language to the extent that it is politically possible to do so. 33

We like to believe that to pass a law is to change behavior; but passing laws about language, in a free society, almost never changes attitudes or behavior. Gaelic (Irish) is living out a slow, inexorable decline in Ireland despite enormous government support of every possible kind since Ireland gained its independence from Britain. The Welsh language, in contrast, is alive today in Wales in spite of heavy discrimination during its history. Three out of four people in the northern and western counties of Gwynedd and Dyfed speak Welsh. 34

I said earlier that language is a convenient surrogate for other national problems. Official English obviously has a lot to do with concern about immigration, perhaps especially Hispanic immigration. America may be threatened by immigration; I don't know. But America is not threatened by language. 35

The usual arguments made by academics against Official English are commonsensical. Who needs a law when, according to the 1990 census, 94 percent of American residents speak English anyway? (Mauro E. Mujica, the chairman of U.S. English, cites a higher figure: 97 percent.) Not many of today's immigrants will see their first language survive into the second generation. This is in fact the common lament of first-generation immigrants: their children are not learning their language and are losing the culture of their parents. Spanish is hardly a 36 threat to English, in spite of isolated (and easily visible) cases such as Miami, New York City, and pockets of the Southwest and southern California. The everyday language of south Texas is Spanish, and yet south Texas is not about to secede from America.

But empirical, calm arguments don't engage the real issue: language is a symbol, an icon. Nobody who favors a constitutional ban against flag burning will ever be persuaded by the argument that the flag is, after all, just a "piece of cloth." A draft card in the 1960s was never merely a piece of paper. Neither is a marriage license. 37

Language, as one linguist has said, is "not primarily a means of communication but a means of communion." Romanticism exalted language, made it mystical, sublime—a bond of national identity. At the same time, Romanticism created a monster: it made of language a means for destroying a country. 38

America has that unique otherness of which I spoke. In spite of all our racial divisions and economic unfairness, we have the frontier tradition, respect for the individual, and opportunity; we have our love affair with the automobile; we have in our history a civil war that freed the slaves and was fought with valor; and we have sports, hot dogs, hamburgers, and milk shakes—things big and small, noble and petty, important and trifling. "We are Americans; we are different." 39

If I'm wrong, then the great American experiment will fail—not because of language but because it no longer means anything to be an American; because we have forfeited that "willingness of the heart" that F. Scott Fitzgerald wrote was America; because we are not long joined by Lincoln's "mystic chords of memory." 40

We are not even close to the danger point. I suggest that we relax and luxuriate in our linguistic richness and our traditional tolerance of language differences. Language does not threaten American unity. Benign neglect is a good policy for any country when it comes to language, and it's a good policy for America. 41

THINKING CRITICALLY ABOUT THE TEXT

What does King mean by the term "unique otherness"? What do you see as America's "unique otherness"? Do you agree with King's assessment that America's "unique otherness" will help us transcend our language differences? Why, or why not?

EXAMINING THE ISSUE

1. According to King, "it has always been taken for granted that English *is* the national language, and that one must learn English in order to make it in America" (paragraph 3). What has changed in recent years to make the learning of English a political issue?

2. What does King mean when he says, "Official English is politically very incorrect"(paragraph 8)?

3. What, according to King, makes the English-only issue so controversial? What other issues complicate the decision to make English the nation's language?

4. Why do you think King takes time to explain the evolution of the relationship between language and nationality in Europe and the rest of the world? What insights into the English-only issue does this brief history of language and culture give you? Explain.

5. King quotes a linguist as saying that language is "not primarily a means of communication but a means of communion" (paragraph 38). Do you think it is important for Americans to understand this difference? Explain.

6. King concludes that "benign neglect is a good policy for any country when it comes to language, and it's a good policy for America" (paragraph 41). Do you share King's optimistic view?

MAKING CONNECTIONS: WRITING AND DISCUSSION SUGGESTIONS FOR "SHOULD ENGLISH BE THE LAW?"

The following questions are offered to help you start making meaningful connections between the two articles in this argument pairing. If you are writing an essay, be sure to make specific references to at least one of the paired articles. With several of the questions, some additional research may be required. To begin your research online, go to bedfordstmartins.com/subjectandstrategy and click on Argument Pair: English-Only or browse the thematic directory of annotated links.

1. Robert D. King explains that "in much of the world, ethnic unity and cultural identification are routinely defined by language" (paragraph 17). To what extent is this true in the United States? Why is it sometimes difficult for nonnative speakers of English who immigrate to the United States to take ownership of Standard English? What does it mean to you to take ownership of language? Does one need this ownership to succeed? Write an essay in which you explore the meaning of language ownership.

2. The selections by Krauthammer and King address immigrant assimilation from an academic viewpoint, but it is a highly personal subject for those who come here from other countries. After all, they must confront their English-language deficiencies right from the start. When American students study a foreign language at school, however, almost all of the speaking and instruction is in English until they progress far enough to understand instruction and detailed conversations in the other language. Think about your classroom experience in learning a foreign language. What are the most difficult challenges for you in language studies? Are you comfortable expressing yourself in the language? If you absolutely needed to communicate in that language, how well could you do it? How do you respond to people who are just learning English? Do you get impatient with them or assume that they are poorly educated? Write an essay about how well you think you would do if suddenly you had to function in another country with a different language. How would you deal with people who were impatient with your language skills or dismissive of you? How self-conscious do you think you would be? You may find it helpful to review what you wrote in response to the "Preparing to Read" question on page 518 before starting your essay.

3. While it's no secret that English is the common language of the United States, few of us know that our country has been extremely cautious about promoting a government-mandated "official" language. Why do you suppose the federal government has chosen to take a hands-off position on the language issue? If it has not been necessary to mandate English in the past, why do you think that people now feel a need to declare English the "official language" of the United States? Do you think that this need is real? Write an essay in which you articulate your position on the English-only issue.

4. Is the English-only debate a political issue, a social issue, an economic issue, or some combination of the three? In this context, what do you see as the relationship between language and power? Write an essay in which you explore the relationship between language and power as it pertains to the English-only debate.

5. In preparation for writing an essay about assimilating non-English speaking immigrants into American society, consider the following three statements:

   a. At this time, it is highly unlikely that Congress will legislate that English is the official language of the United States.
   b. Immigrants should learn English as quickly as possible after arriving in the United States.
   c. The culture and languages of immigrants should be respected and valued so that bitterness and resentment will not be fostered, even as immigrants are assimilated into American society.

What is the best way to assimilate non–English-speaking immigrants into our society? Write an essay in which you propose how the United States, as a nation, can make the two latter statements a reality without resorting to an English-only solution. How can we effectively deal with the transition for immigrants without provoking any ill will?

ARGUMENT PAIR: IS GENETICALLY ENGINEERED FOOD SAFE?

In 1960 Dr. Seuss, in the character of Sam-I-Am, first asked children the world over, "Do you like green eggs and ham?" The knee-jerk answer to Sam's question about this strange new food was "I will not eat them anywhere. I do not eat green eggs and ham." To get some peace from Sam's constant badgering, the nameless protagonist finally agrees to try them and discovers, "I like green eggs and ham." Today discussion continues about the foods we consume, but the debate has moved beyond the pages of a children's book. The strange new foods are ones that have been genetically modified; unlike green eggs and ham, these new foods are not visibly different. Biotechnology has created a new world of agriculture that—depending upon your point of view—is either the answer to the world's food supply and environmental problems or an environmental holocaust in the making. The truth perhaps lies somewhere between these two positions.

We have selected two writers to give contrasting perspectives on the controversy surrounding genetically modified food in hopes of provoking serious discussion and good argumentative essays about a technology that affects the food we eat and the environment we inhabit. Biologist David Ehrenfeld believes that the so-called biotech miracles in agriculture are based upon shaky science at best. In "A Techno-Pox Upon the Land," he argues that biotech corporations should come under close scrutiny, as they are apt to ignore consumer fears and environmental questions in their quest for profits. Nutrition and diet expert Jane E. Brody tries to reassure readers that there's little cause for panic when it comes to genetically modified foods. In "Gene-Altered Foods: A Case Against Panic," she surveys the current and potential benefits of genetic engineering as well as the real and potential risks.

PREPARING TO READ

How much do you know about the food you eat? Do you know where and how it was grown or raised? Do you look for labels that say "organic" when shopping? What have you heard or read about genetically engineered foods? What questions would you like answers to before making the decision to eat genetically engineered foods?

A Techno-Pox Upon the Land

David Ehrenfeld

 *David Ehrenfeld was born in 1938 in New York City. He received his B.A. in 1959 and M.D. in 1963 from Harvard University and his Ph.D. in 1966 from the University of Florida. Since 1974 he has been a professor of biology at Rutgers University. Ehrenfeld has written extensively on biology, conservation, and biotechnology in scientific journals. His books include* Biological Conservation *(1970),* Conserving Life on Earth *(1972),* The Arrogance of Humanism *(1978),* Beginning Again: People and Nature in the New Millennium *(1993), and* Swimming Lessons: Keeping Afloat in the Age of Technology *(2002).*

The following essay, first published in Harper's *magazine in October 1997, was taken from the lecture "A Cruel and Transient Agriculture" that Ehrenfeld gave at Marist College in Poughkeepsie, New York, in April 1997. Here he takes biotech corporations to task for putting profits ahead of consumer and environmental concerns.*

The modern history of agriculture has two faces. The first, a happy face, is turned toward nonfarmers who live in the developed world. It speaks brightly of technological miracles, such as the "Green Revolution" and, more recently, genetic engineering, that have resulted in the increased production of food for the world's hungry. The second face is turned toward the few remaining farmers who have survived these miracles. It is downcast and silent, like a mourner at a funeral.

The Green Revolution, a fundamental change in agricultural technology, arose in the 1960s and '70s from the assumption that poverty and hunger in poor countries were the result of low agricultural productivity, that subsistence farming as it had occurred for centuries was the basis of a brutish existence. In response to this assumption, plant breeders hit on an elegant method to increase dramatically the yield of the world's most important crops, especially wheat and rice. Put simply, this plan involved redesigning the plants themselves, increasing the size of the plants' reproductive parts—the seed that we eat—and decreasing the size of the vegetative parts—the stems, roots, and leaves that we throw away. From a technical point of view, this worked. Unfortunately, that's not the end of the story. As in other seemingly simple, technical manipulations of nature, there have been undesirable and unintended consequences.

The primary problem is that Green Revolution agribusiness requires vast amounts of energy to grow and sustain these "miracle crops." Oil must be burned to make the large quantities of nitrogen fertilizer on which these plants depend. Farmers also must invest heavily in toxic herbicides, insecticides, and fungicides; in irrigation systems; and in spraying, harvesting, and processing machinery for the weakened, seed-heavy plants. Large sums of money must be borrowed to pay for these "inputs" before the growing season starts in the hope that crop sales will allow farmers to repay the debt later in the season. When that hope is frustrated, the farmer often loses his farm and is driven into a migrant pool of cheap labor for corporate-farming operations or is forced to seek work in the landless, teeming cities.

The Green Revolution is an early instance of the co-opting of human needs by the technoeconomic system. It is not a black-and-white example: some farmers have been able to keep on farming in spite of the high inputs required; others are mixing traditional methods of farming with selected newer technologies. But the latest manifestation of corporate agriculture, genetic engineering, *is* black-and-white. Excluding military spending on fabulously expensive, dysfunctional weapons systems, there is no more dramatic case of people having their needs appropriated for the sake of profit at any cost. Like high-input agriculture, genetic engineering is often justified as a humane technology, one that feeds more people with better food. Nothing could be further from the truth. With very few exceptions, the whole point of genetic engineering is to increase the sales of chemicals and bioengineered products to dependent farmers, and to increase the dependence of farmers on their new handlers, the seed companies and the oil, chemical, and pharmaceutical companies that own them.

Social problems aside, this new agricultural biotechnology is on much shakier scientific ground than the Green Revolution ever was. Genetic engineering is based on the premise that we can take a gene from species A, where it does some desirable thing, and move it into species B, where it will continue to do that same desirable thing. Most genetic engineers know that this is not always true, but the biotech industry as a whole acts as if it were. First, genes are not like tiny machines. The expression of their output can change when they are put in a new genetic and cellular environment. Second, genes usually have multiple effects. Undesirable effects that are suppressed in species A may be expressed when the gene is moved to species B. And third, many of the most important, genetically regulated traits that agricultural researchers deal with are controlled by multiple genes, perhaps on different chromosomes, and these are very resistant to manipulation by transgenic technology.

Because of these scientific limitations, agricultural biotechnology has been largely confined to applications that are basically simple-minded despite their technical complexity. Even here we find problems. The production of herbicide-resistant crop seeds is one example. Green Revolution crops tend to be on the wimpy side when it comes to competing with weeds—hence the heavy use of herbicides in recent decades. But many of the weeds are relatives of the crops, so the herbicides that kill the weeds can kill the crops too, given bad luck with weather and the timing of spraying. Enter the seed/chemical companies with a clever, profitable, unscrupulous idea. Why not introduce the gene for resistance to our own brand of herbicide into our own crop seeds, and then sell the patented seeds and patented herbicide as a package?

Never mind that this encourages farmers to apply recklessly large 7 amounts of weedkiller, and that many herbicides have been associated with human sickness, including lymphoma. Nor that the genes for herbicide resistance can move naturally from the crops to the related weeds via pollen transfer, rendering the herbicide ineffective in a few years. What matters, as an agricultural biotechnologist once remarked to me, is earning enough profit to keep the company happy.

A related agricultural biotechnology is the transfer of bacterial or 8 plant genes that produce a natural insecticide directly into crops such as corn and cotton. An example is Bt (*Bacillus thuringiensis*), which has been widely used as an external dust or spray to kill harmful beetles and moths. In this traditional use, Bt breaks down into harmless components in a day or two, and the surviving pests do not get a chance to evolve resistance to it. But with Bt now produced continuously inside genetically engineered crops, which are planted over hundreds of thousands of acres, the emergence of genetic resistance among the pests becomes almost a certainty.

Monsanto, one of the world's largest manufacturers of agricultural 9 chemicals, has patented cottonseed containing genes for Bt. Advertised as being effective against bollworms without the use of additional insecticides, 1,800,000 acres in five southern states were planted with this transgenic seed in 1996, at a cost to farmers of not only the seed itself but an additional $32-per-acre "technology fee" paid to Monsanto. Heavy bollworm infestation occurred in spite of the special seed, forcing farmers to spray expensive insecticides anyway. Those farmers who wanted to use seeds from the surviving crop to replace the damaged crop found that Monsanto's licensing agreement, like most others in the industry, permitted them only one planting.

Troubles with Monsanto's genetically engineered seed have not been 10 confined to cotton. This past May, Monsanto Canada and its licensee, Limagrain Canada Seeds, recalled 60,000 bags of "Roundup-ready" canola seeds because they mistakenly contained a gene that had not been tested by the government for human consumption. These seeds, engineered to resist Monsanto's most profitable product, the herbicide Roundup, were enough to plant more than 600,000 acres. Two farmers had already planted the seeds when Monsanto discovered its mistake.

There is another shaky scientific premise of agricultural biotech- 11 nology. This concerns the transfer of animal or plant genes from the parent species into microorganisms, so that the valuable products of these genes can then be produced in large commercial batches. The assumption here is that these transgenic products, when administered back to the parent species in large doses, will simply increase whatever desirable effect they normally have. Again, this is simplistic thinking that totally ignores the great complexity of living organisms and the consequences of tampering with them.

In the United States, one of the most widely deployed instances of this sort of biotechnology is the use of recombinant bovine growth hormone (rBGH), which is produced by placing slightly modified cow genes into fermentation tanks containing bacteria, then injected into lactating cows to make them yield more milk. This is done despite our nationwide milk glut and despite the fact that the use of rBGH will probably accelerate the demise of the small dairy farm, since only large farms are able to take on the extra debt for the more expensive feeds, the high-tech feed-management systems, and the added veterinary care that go along with its use.

The side effects of rBGH on cows are also serious. Recombinant BGH–related problems—as stated on the package insert by its manufacturer, Monsanto—include bloat, diarrhea, diseases of the knees and feet, feeding disorders, fevers, reduced blood hemoglobin levels, cystic ovaries, uterine pathology, reduced pregnancy rates, smaller calves, and mastitis—a breast infection that can result, according to the insert, in "visibly abnormal milk." Treatment of mastitis can lead to the presence of antibiotics in milk, probably accelerating the spread of antibiotic resistance among bacteria that cause human disease. Milk from rBGH-treated cows may also contain insulin growth factor, IGF-1, which has been implicated in human breast and gastrointestinal cancers.

Another potential problem is an indirect side effect of the special nutritional requirements of rBGH-treated cows. Because these cows require more protein, their food is supplemented with ground-up animals, a practice that has been associated with bovine spongiform encephalopathy, also known as "mad cow disease." The recent British epidemic of BSE appears to have been associated with an increased incidence of the disease's human analogue, Creutzfeldt-Jakob disease. There seems little reason to increase the risk of this terrible disease for the sake of a biotechnology that we don't need. If cows stay off of hormones and concentrate on eating grass, all of us will be much better off.

Meanwhile the biotechnology juggernaut rolls on, converting humanity's collective agricultural heritage from an enduring, farmer-controlled lifestyle to an energy-dependent, corporate "process." The ultimate co-optation is the patenting of life. The Supreme Court's ruling in the case of *Diamond v. Chakrabarty* in 1980 paved the way for corporations to obtain industrial, or "utility," patents on living organisms, from bacteria to human cells. These patents operate like the patents on mechanical inventions, granting the patent holder a more sweeping and long-lasting control than had been conferred by the older forms of plant patents. The upshot of this is that farmers who save seeds from utility-patented crop plants for replanting on their own farms next year may have committed a federal crime; it also means that farmers breeding utility-patented cattle may have to pay royalties to the corporation holding the patent.

The life patents allowed by the U.S. Patent Office have been remark- 16 ably broad. Agracetus, a subsidiary of Monsanto, was issued patents covering all genetically engineered cotton. The patents are currently being challenged but remain in effect until corporate appeals are exhausted. Companies such as DNA Plant Technology, Calgene, and others are taking out patents that cover many recombinant varieties of vegetable species, from garden peas to the entire genus *Brassica*, which includes broccoli, cabbage, and cauliflower. The German chemical and pharmaceutical giant Hoechst has obtained multiple patents for medical uses of a species of *Coleus*, despite the fact that this medicinal plant has been used since antiquity in Hindu and Ayurvedic medicine to treat cardiovascular, respiratory, digestive, and neurological diseases.

Somehow, in the chaos of technological change, we have lost the 17 distinction between a person and a corporation, inexplicably valuing profit at any cost over basic human needs. In doing so we have forsaken our farmers, the spiritual descendants of those early Hebrew and Greek farmers and pastoralists who first gave us our understanding of social justice, democracy, and the existence of a power greater than our own. No amount of lip service to the goal of feeding the world's hungry or to the glory of a new technology, and no amount of transient increases in the world's grain production, can hide this terrible truth.

THINKING CRITICALLY ABOUT THE TEXT

In his opening paragraph, Ehrenfeld describes the two faces of modern agriculture. One face is happy, the other is "downcast and silent." Ehrenfeld claims that the general public sees only the happy face and hears the good news of "technological miracles" in agriculture. What clues does Ehrenfeld give to explain why the public rarely sees the more somber face? Explain.

EXAMINING THE ISSUE

1. What was the Green Revolution that started in the 1960s and 1970s? On what grounds does Ehrenfeld find fault with this change in agricultural practice?

2. According to Ehrenfeld, what is the real purpose of biotechnology? By the end of his essay has he convinced you that he is right? Why or why not?

3. Ehrenfeld claims that the new agricultural biotechnology is founded on shaky scientific ground. What does he think are the scientific limitations of genetic engineering?

4. What problems does Ehrenfeld find with the production of herbicide-resistant crops or crops that produce their own insecticides? What evidence does he present to support his claims? (Glossary: *Evidence*)

5. Ehrenfeld believes that recombinant bovine growth hormone (rGBH) is an example of yet one more "shaky scientific premise of agricultural biotechnology" (paragraph 11). Explain how rGBH is supposed to work—how the hormone is produced and how it is used. What are the risks associated with the use of rGBH? Do you think the claimed benefits of rGBH use outweigh the potential risks? Explain.

6. What do you think Ehrenfeld means when he says, "In the chaos of technological change, we have lost the distinction between a person and a corporation, inexplicably valuing profit at any cost over basic human needs" (paragraph 17). What is the "terrible truth" he alludes to in his closing sentence? What are the implications if we say "no" to biotechnology and instead support "traditional" agriculture? Explain.

Gene-Altered Foods: A Case Against Panic

Jane E. Brody

Popular syndicated columnist Jane E. Brody was born in Brooklyn, New York, in 1941. She earned her B.S. from Cornell University in 1962 and her M.S. from the University of Wisconsin–Madison in 1963. After a two-year stint as a reporter for the Minneapolis Tribune, *Brody was hired by the* New York Times *to become a full-time science writer. In 1976 her popular column "Personal Health" debuted, and it has remained a mainstay of the* Times *ever since. Readers' questions, health issues in the media, and medical journal studies have provided her with topics over the years. Brody's problem with her own weight fueled her interest in food, nutrition, and diet, resulting in the publication of* Jane Brody's Nutrition Book *(1981) and the companion volume* Jane Brody's Good Food Book *(1985). In 2001 she wrote* The New York Times Guide to Alternative Health *with Denise Frady. When not writing, Brody lectures on health and nutrition and has starred in the PBS series* Good Health from Jane Brody's Kitchen.

In "Gene-Altered Foods: A Case Against Panic," a "Personal Health" column from the December 5, 2000, issue of the New York Times, *Brody seeks to relieve public anxiety about the genetic modification of food.*

Ask American consumers whether they support the use of biotechnology in food and agriculture and nearly 70 percent say they do. But ask the question another way, "Do you approve of genetically engineered (or genetically modified) foods?" and two-thirds say they do not. 1

Yet there is no difference between them. The techniques involved and the products that result are identical. Rather, the words "genetic" and "engineer" seem to provoke alarm among millions of consumers. 2

The situation recalls the introduction of the M.R.I. (for magnetic resonance imaging), which was originally called an N.M.R., for nuclear magnetic resonance. The word nuclear caused such public concern, it threatened to stymie the growth of this valuable medical tool. 3

The idea of genetically modified foods, known as G.M. foods, is particularly frightening to those who know little about how foods are now produced and how modern genetic technology, if properly regulated, could result in significant improvements by reducing environmental hazards, improving the nutritional value of foods, enhancing agricultural productivity and fostering the survival worldwide of small farms and the rural landscape. 4

Without G.M. foods, Dr. Alan McHughen, a biotechnologist at the University of Saskatchewan, told a recent conference on agricultural biotechnology at Cornell, the earth will not be able to feed the ever-growing billions of people who inhabit it.

Still, there are good reasons for concern about a powerful technology that is currently imperfectly regulated and could, if inadequately tested or misapplied, bring on both nutritional and environmental havoc. To render a rational opinion on the subject and make reasoned choices in the marketplace, it is essential to understand what genetic engineering of foods and crops involves and its potential benefits and risks.

GENETICS IN AGRICULTURE

People have been genetically modifying foods and crops for tens of thousands of years. The most commonly used method has involved crossing two parents with different desirable characteristics in an effort to produce offspring that express the best of both of them. That and another approach, inducing mutations, are time-consuming and hit-or-miss and can result in good and bad characteristics.

Genetic engineering, on the other hand, involves the introduction into a plant or animal or micro-organism of a single gene or group of genes that are known quantities, genes that dictate the production of one or more desired elements, for example, the ability to resist the attack of insects, withstand herbicide treatments, or produce foods with higher levels of essential nutrients.

Since all organisms use the same genetic material (DNA), the power of the technique includes the ability to transfer genes between organisms that normally would never interbreed.

Thus, an antifreeze gene from Arctic flounder has been introduced into strawberries to extend their growing season in northern climates. But contrary to what many people think, this does not make the strawberries "fishy" any more than the use of porcine insulin turned people into pigs.

Dr. Steven Kresovich, a plant breeder at Cornell, said, "Genes should be characterized by function, not origin. It's not a flounder gene but a cold tolerance gene that was introduced into strawberries."

As Dr. McHughen points out in his new book, *Pandora's Picnic Basket: The Potential and Hazards of Genetically Modified Foods,* people share about 7,000 genes with a worm called *C. elegans*. The main difference between organisms lies in the total number of genes their cells contain, how the genes are arranged and which ones are turned on or off in different cells at different times.

CURRENT AND POTENTIAL BENEFITS

An insecticidal toxin from a bacterium called *Bacillus thuringiensis* (Bt)   13
has been genetically introduced into two major field crops, corn and
cotton, resulting in increased productivity and decreased use of pesticides, which means less environmental contamination and greater
profits for farmers. For example, by growing Bt cotton, farmers could
reduce spraying for bollworm and budworm from seven times a season
to none. Bt corn also contains much lower levels of fungal toxins,
which are potentially carcinogenic.

The genetic introduction of herbicide tolerance into soybeans is   14
saving farmers about $200 million a year by reducing the number of
applications of herbicide needed to control weed growth, said Leonard
Gianessi, a pesticide analyst at the National Center for Food and Agricultural Policy, a research organization in Washington.

Genetically engineered pharmaceuticals are already widely used,   15
with more than 150 products on the market. Since 1978, genetically
modified bacteria have been producing human insulin, which is used
by 3.3 million people with diabetes.

Future food benefits are likely to accrue directly to the consumer.   16
For example, genetic engineers have developed golden rice, a yellow rice
rich in beta carotene (which the body converts to vitamin A) and iron.

If farmers in developing countries accept this crop and if the mil-   17
lions of people who suffer from nutrient deficiencies will eat it, golden
rice could prevent widespread anemia and blindness in half a million
children a year and the deaths of one million to two million children
who succumb each year to the consequences of vitamin A deficiency.

Future possibilities include peanuts or shrimp lacking proteins that   18
can cause life-threatening food allergies, fruits and vegetables with
longer shelf lives, foods with fewer toxicants and antinutrients, meat
and dairy products and oils with heart-healthier fats, and foods that
deliver vaccines.

REAL AND POTENTIAL RISKS

G.M. foods and crops arrived without adequate mechanisms in place to   19
regulate them. Three agencies are responsible for monitoring their
safety for consumers, farmers, and the environment: the Food and
Drug Administration, the Department of Agriculture, and the Environmental Protection Agency. But the drug agency says its law does not
allow it to require premarket testing of G.M. foods unless they contain
a new substance that is not "generally recognized as safe."

For most products, safety tests are done voluntarily by producers.   20
The recent recall of taco shells containing G.M. corn that had not been
approved for human consumption was done voluntarily by the producer.

The agency is now formulating new guidelines to test G.M. products and to label foods as "G.M.-free" but says it lacks a legal basis to require labeling of G.M. foods.

"In the current environment, such a label would be almost a kiss of death on a product," said Dr. Michael Jacobson, director of the Center for Science in the Public Interest, a nonprofit consumer group. "But it may be that the public is simply not going to have confidence in transgenic ingredients if their presence is kept secret."

21

The introduction of possible food allergens through genetic engineering is a major concern. If the most common sources of food allergens—peanuts, shellfish, celery, nuts, milk, or eggs—had to pass through an approval process today, they would never make it to market.

22

But consumers could be taken unaware if an otherwise safe food was genetically endowed with an allergen, as almost happened with an allergenic protein from Brazil nuts. Even if known allergenic proteins are avoided in G.M. foods, it is hard to predict allergenicity of new proteins.

23

A potentially serious environmental risk involves the "escape" of G.M. genes from crops into the environment, where they may harm innocent organisms or contaminate crops that are meant to be G.M.-free.

24

Dr. Jacobson concluded, "Now is the time, while agricultural biotechnology is still young, for Congress and regulatory agencies to create the framework that will maximize the safe use of these products, bolster public confidence in them and allow all of humankind to benefit from their enormous potential." Two Congressional bills now under discussion can do much to assure safer use of agricultural biotechnology, he said.

25

THINKING CRITICALLY ABOUT THE TEXT

Brody provides readers with a reasonably objective overview of the current and potential benefits as well as the real and potential risks of genetically modified foods. Do you agree with her assessment that there is no cause for panic at present? Explain.

EXAMINING THE ISSUE

1. Why do you suppose two-thirds of American consumers are alarmed by the words "genetically engineered" but not by the word "biotechnology"? Do these words frighten you?

2. What does Brody see as the advantages and disadvantages of genetic technology? Why does Brody take the time to explain what genetic engineering involves? Does her explanation reduce any anxiety you may have had about this technology?

3. Brody is quick to qualify her praise of genetic technology with the phrase "if properly regulated" (paragraph 4). Why is proper regulation so important?

4. Michael Jacobson points to the product-labeling dilemma facing producers of genetically modified foods. He says that "in the current environment, such a label would be almost a kiss of death on a product. But it may be that the public is simply not going to have confidence in transgenic ingredients if their presence is kept secret" (paragraph 21). How can we move beyond this impasse so as to enjoy the benefits of this technology while keeping the risks in check?

MAKING CONNECTIONS: WRITING AND DISCUSSION SUGGESTIONS FOR "IS GENETICALLY ENGINEERED FOOD SAFE?"

The following questions are offered to help you start making meaningful connections between the articles in this argument pairing. These questions can be used for class discussion, or you can choose to answer any one of them by writing an essay. If you write an essay, be sure to make specific references to both of the articles. With several of the questions, some additional research may be required. To begin your research online, go to bedfordstmartins.com/subjectandstrategy and click on Argument Pair: Genetically Engineered Food or browse the thematic directory of annotated links.

1. In discussing "Roundup ready" plant varieties, Ehrenfeld states that "genes for herbicide resistance can move naturally from the crops to the related weeds via pollen transfer, rendering the herbicide ineffective in a few years" (paragraph 7). Given the possibility that desirable genes in crops could one day be expressed in undesirable weeds, should we even bother with genetic modification? Why or why not? Do the potential risks outweigh the potential benefits? Do you think scientists can solve the problem Ehrenfeld describes? Explain. Write an essay in which you argue for or against the continued development of genetically modified crops.

2. More and more people want to know what the foods they consume contain, including how much fat, carbohydrates, sodium, and cholesterol and whether the product is "organic." As Brody explains, however, the Food and Drug Administration (FDA) "lacks a legal basis to require labeling of G.M. foods" (paragraph 20). Should government require food manufacturers to label genetically modified ingredients? Do you agree with Michael Jacobson that "the public is simply not going to have confidence in transgenic ingredients if their presence is kept secret" (21)? Explain. If "people have been genetically modifying foods and crops for tens of thousands of years" (7), is it even possible to determine what to label as genetically modified? Why or why not? Write a letter to Congress in which you argue for or against granting the FDA power to label genetically modified foods. Be mindful of your audience. (Glossary: *Audience*) Before you write, refer to your Preparing to Read response for this cluster.

3. Poet and environmentalist Wendell Berry has said that "it is impossible to care more or differently for each other than we care for the land." What do you think he means? As stewards of the Earth, what responsibilities do we have toward the land? Toward each other? How can humans work in partnership with the land? Using your own experience, observations, and ideas from the readings, write an argumentative essay that answers these questions.

WRITING SUGGESTIONS FOR ARGUMENTATION

1. Think of a product that you like and want to use even though it has an annoying feature. Write a letter of complaint in which you attempt to persuade the manufacturer to improve the product. Your letter should include the following points:

    a. A statement concerning the nature of the problem
    b. Evidence supporting or explaining your complaint
    c. Suggestions for improving the product

2. Select one of the position statements that follow, and write an argumentative essay in which you defend that statement.

    a. Living in a dormitory is (*or* is not) as desirable as living off-campus.
    b. Student government shows (*or* does not show) that the democratic process is effective.
    c. America should (*or* should not) be a refuge for the oppressed.
    d. School spirit is (*or* is not) as important as it ever was.
    e. Interest in religion is (*or* is not) increasing in the United States.
    f. We have (*or* have not) brought air pollution under control in the United States.
    g. The need to develop alternative energy sources is (*or* is not) serious.
    h. America's great cities are (*or* are not) thriving.
    i. Fraternities and sororities do (*or* do not) build character.
    j. We have (*or* have not) found effective means to dispose of nuclear or chemical wastes.
    k. Fair play is (*or* is not) a thing of the past.
    l. Human life is (*or* is not) valued in a technological society.
    m. The consumer does (*or* does not) need to be protected.
    n. The family farm in America is (*or* is not) in danger of extinction.
    o. Grades do (*or* do not) encourage learning.
    p. America is (*or* is not) a violent society.
    q. Television is (*or* is not) a positive cultural force in America.
    r. America should (*or* should not) feel a commitment to the starving peoples of the world.
    s. The federal government should (*or* should not) regulate all utilities.
    t. Money is (*or* is not) the path to happiness.
    u. Animals do (*or* do not) have rights.
    v. Competition is (*or* is not) killing us.
    w. America is (*or* is not) becoming a society with deteriorating values.

3. Think of something on your campus or in your community that you would like to see changed. Write a persuasive argument that explains what is wrong and how you think it ought to be changed. Make sure you incorporate other writing strategies into your essay—for example, description, narration, or illustration — to increase the effectiveness of your persuasive argument. (Glossary: *Description; Illustration; Narration*)

4. Read some articles in the editorial section of today's paper, and pick one with which you agree or disagree. Write a letter to the editor that

presents your point of view. Use a logical argument to support or refute the editorial's assertions. Depending on the editorial, you might choose to use different rhetorical strategies to reach your audience. (Glossary: *Audience*) You might use cause and effect, for example, to show the correct (or incorrect) connections made by the editorial. (Glossary: *Cause and Effect Analysis*)

5. Working with a partner, choose a controversial topic like the legalization of medical marijuana or any of the topics in writing suggestion 2. Each partner should argue one side of the issue. Decide who is going to write on which side of the issue, and keep in mind that there are often more than two sides to an issue. Then each of you should write an essay trying to convince your partner that your position is the most logical and correct.

CHAPTER **13**

Combining Strategies

Each of the chapters of *Subject & Strategy* emphasizes a particular writing strategy: narration, description, illustration, process analysis, and so forth. The essays and selections within each of these chapters use the given strategy as the dominant method of development. It is important to remember, however, that the dominant strategy is rarely the only one used to develop a piece of writing. To fully explore their topics, writers find it helpful and necessary to use other strategies in combination with the dominant strategy. Very seldom does an essay use one strategy exclusively. To highlight and reinforce this point, we focus on the use of multiple strategies in the Questions on Strategy section following each professional selection.

While some essays are developed *primarily* through the use of a single mode, it is more the norm in good writing that writers take advantage of the options open to them, using multiple strategies in artful combinations to achieve memorable results. It is to this end that we have gathered the essays in this Combining Strategies chapter and ask additional questions about the authors' use of multiple strategies. These essays illustrate the ways that writers use a number of strategies to support the dominant strategy. You will encounter such combinations of strategies in the reading and writing you do in other college courses. Beyond the classroom, you might write a business proposal using both description and cause and effect to make an argument for a new marketing plan. Or you might use narration, description, and illustration to write a news story for a company newsletter or a letter to the editor of your local newspaper.

WHAT DOES IT MEAN TO COMBINE STRATEGIES?

The following essay by Sydney Harris reveals how several strategies can be used effectively, even in a brief piece of writing. Although primarily a work of definition, notice how "A Jerk" also uses illustration and personal narrative to engage the reader and achieve Harris's purpose.

A JERK

I don't know whether history repeats itself, but biography certainly does. The other day, Michael came in and asked me what a "jerk" was—the same question Carolyn put to me a dozen years ago.

At that time, I fluffed her off with some inane answer, such as "A jerk isn't a very nice person," but both of us knew it was an unsatisfactory reply. When she went to bed, I began trying to work up a suitable definition.

It is a marvelously apt word, of course. Until it was coined, not more than 25 years ago, there was really no single word in English to describe the kind of person who is a jerk—"boob" and "simp" were too old hat, and besides they really didn't fit, for they could be lovable, and a jerk never is.

Thinking it over, I decided that a jerk is basically a person without insight. He is not necessarily a fool or a dope, because some extremely clever persons can be jerks. In fact, it has little to do with intelligence as we commonly think of it; it is, rather, a kind of subtle but persuasive aroma emanating from the inner part of the personality.

I know a college president who can be described only as a jerk. He is not an unintelligent man, nor unlearned, nor even unschooled in the social amenities. Yet he is a jerk *cum laude,* because of a fatal flaw in his nature—he is totally incapable of looking into the mirror of his soul and shuddering at what he sees there.

A jerk, then, is a man (or woman) who is utterly unable to see himself as he appears to others. He has no grace, he is tactless without meaning to be, he is a bore even to his best friends, he is an egotist without charm. All of us are egotists to some extent, but most of us—unlike the jerk—are perfectly and horribly aware of it when we make asses of ourselves. The jerk never knows.

WHY DO WRITERS COMBINE STRATEGIES?

Essays that employ thoughtful combinations of rhetorical strategies have some obvious advantages for the writer and the reader. By reading the work of professional writers, you can learn how multiple strategies can be used to your advantage—how a paragraph of narration, a vivid description, a clarifying instance of comparison and contrast, or a helpful definition can vary the interest level or terrain of an essay. More important, they answer a reader's need to know and to understand your purpose and thesis.

For example, let's suppose you wanted to write an essay on the slang you hear on campus. You might find it helpful to use a variety of strategies.

- *Definition*—to explain what slang is
- *Illustration*—to give examples of slang
- *Comparison and contrast*—to differentiate slang from other types of speech, such as idioms or technical language
- *Division and classification*—to categorize different types of slang or different topics that slang terms are used for, such as courses, students, food, grades

Or let's say you wanted to write a paper on the Japanese Americans who were sent to internment camps during World War II while the United States was at war with Japan. The following strategies would be available to you.

- *Illustration*—to illustrate several particular cases of families that were sent to internment camps
- *Narration*—to tell the stories of former camp residents, including their first reaction to their internment and their actual experiences in the camps
- *Cause and effect*—to examine the reasons why the United States government interned Japanese Americans and the long-term effects of this policy

When you rely on a single mode or approach to an essay, you may limit yourself and lose the opportunity to come at your subject from a number of different angles, all of which complete the picture and any one of which might be the most insightful or engaging and, therefore, the most memorable for the reader. This is particularly the case with essays that attempt to persuade or argue. The task of changing readers' beliefs and thoughts is so difficult that writers look for any combination of strategies that will make their arguments more convincing.

SAMPLE STUDENT ESSAY USING A COMBINATION OF STRATEGIES

While a senior at the University of Vermont, English major Tara E. Ketch took a course in children's literature and was asked to write a term paper on some aspect of the literature she was studying. She knew that she would soon be looking for a teaching position and realized that any teaching job she accepted would bring her face-to-face with the difficult task of selecting appropriate reading materials. Ketch understood, as well, that she would have to confront criticism of her choices, so she decided to delve a little deeper into the subject of censorship, particularly of children's and adolescent literature. She was interested in learning more about why people want to censor certain books so that she could consider an appropriate response to their efforts. In a way, she wanted to begin to develop her own teaching philosophy with respect to text selection. Her essay naturally incorporated several rhetorical modes working in combination. As you read Ketch's essay, notice how naturally she has used the supporting strategies of definition, cause and effect, and illustration to enhance the dominant strategy of argumentation.

Kids, You Can't Read
That Book!

Tara E. Ketch

Definition of censorship and censors' activities

Censorship is the restriction or suppression of speech or writing that is thought to have a negative influence. In the case of children's and adolescent literature the censors are very often school officials, parents, or adults in the community who wish to monitor and influence what children are reading. For whatever

Cause and effect: Pressure is put on school boards, and questions are raised.

reason, they are saying, "Kids, you can't read that book; it is not fit for your eyes." To ensure that these books do not end up in the schools, pressure groups influence school boards not to purchase them or to restrict their use if they have already been purchased.

Argumentation: Who will decide on censorship issues?

Such actions present serious questions for educators. Who will decide what materials are fit for American schoolchildren?

The federal government has set limits on censorship and encouraged local communities to make educational decisions. In the 1968 case of *Emerson v. Arkansas,* the Supreme Court stated,

Illustration: Supreme Court decisions

"Public education in our nation is committed to the control of state and local authorities. Courts do not and cannot intervene in the resolution of conflicts which arise in the daily operation of school systems and which do not directly and sharply implicate basic constitutional values" (Reichman 3). In 1982, the Supreme Court ruled that "local school boards may not remove books from

Cause and effect: Result of Supreme Court decisions

school library shelves simply because they dislike the ideas contained in those books and seek by their removal to prescribe

1

2

what shall be orthodox in politics, nationalism, religion, or other matters of opinion" (Reichman 3). These two rulings contradict each other. The outcome is that children's books continue to be banned in school systems for many reasons.

One important reason books are banned is family values. 3
The censor may attack a book because it goes against his or her personal values. For example, it may contain "offensive" language. Most problems with books seem to come out of the author's use of language. This is especially true of adolescent literature. In a list of the most frequently banned books in the 1990s, J. D. Salinger's *Catcher in the Rye* took the number three slot because of objections to its language. A parent found words such as *hell, Chrissakes, bastard, damn,* and *crap* to be

unacceptable (Foerstel 147). The fear was that such language was being condoned by the school when such a book was taught. In a debate about Katherine Paterson's *Bridge to Terabithia,* a woman protested the use of the words *snotty* and *shut up* along with *Lord* and *damn.* She said, "Freedom of speech was not intended to guarantee schools the right to intrude on traditional family values without warning and regardless of the availability

of non-offensive alternatives" (Reichman 38). The school board in this case decided that the book had a value that transcended the use of the few offensive words. That a book has redeeming value is the primary argument against such censorship. If we ignore all books that contain profanity, we are missing out on a lot of valuable literature.

Other people hold dear the value that children should not 4
be exposed to anything depressing or violent. Not surprisingly, several communities have tried to get certain fairy tales banned because they are violent in nature. *Jack and the Beanstalk* and *Little Red Riding Hood* came under attack for this reason. In both

cases the books were kept in the school system (Burress 283–91). The argument against their removal involved the fact that the violence was tied to fantasy. It was not in the child's everyday realm and therefore not threatening. Judy Blume's *Blubber* has

been questioned for its portrayal of unhappy child characters. Some parents refuse to recognize the fact that not all children have a happy and carefree existence. Judy Blume has her own ideas about childhood that she uses as an attack against such

censorship. She argues, "Children have little control over their lives, and this causes both anger and unhappiness. Childhood can be a terrible time of life. No kid wants to stay a kid. . . . The fantasy of childhood is to be an adult" (West 12). *Bridge to Terabithia* has also been seen as a harsh portrayal of life because it deals with the death of a child. Some parents want to shelter their children from the reality of death. Others find that a book such as *Bridge to Terabithia* is a natural way for children to be exposed to that sensitive topic.

Illustration: Death of a child character

Another family value that comes into play in censorship is the idea that children should be protected from sexuality. Maurice Sendak's *In the Night Kitchen* shows a naked little boy, and although there is no sexual connotation, many people were incensed by the book. In New York, in 1990, parents tried to have the book removed from an elementary school. In Maine, a parent wanted the book removed because she felt it encouraged child molestation (Foerstel 201). Many of Judy Blume's books have also come under fire for their portrayal of sexual themes in adolescence. *Are You There, God? It's Me, Margaret* has been blacklisted for its frank discussion of menstruation and adolescent development. *Forever* is even worse to some because it mentions intercourse and abortion. As topics of discussion, these subjects are alien to many adults who grew up in environments where sex was not talked about; therefore, they try to perpetuate the cycle of silence by keeping these kinds of books from children. They may also worry that these books will encourage sexual activity. This fear extends to textbooks that educate children and adolescents about their bodies and sexual reproduction. Many try to ban gay and lesbian literature because they feel that homosexuality is obscene and that books about these subjects might encourage homosexual behavior and lifestyles. *All-American Boys* was donated to a California high school, but when administrators realized that it discussed homosexuality, the book was seized and then "lost" (Reichman 43). Alyson Wonderland Publications has also published two children's books to explain the gay lifestyle to children: Michael Willhoite's *Daddy's Roommate* and Leslea Newman's *Heather Has Two Mommies*. These, not surprisingly, have met with a lot of opposition.

5

Cause and effect: Third reason why children's and adolescents' books are banned

Illustration: Sexuality as topic

Cause and effect: Explanation of reasons for banning books with sexual topics

Illustration: Books that discuss gay and lesbian themes

Often there are religious concerns as well. Religion is in many cases the foundation for people's moral beliefs. Censorship of books because of their language, violence, and sexuality happens as much in the name of religion as family values. Religion is also used as an issue in censorship for other reasons. Some people want the Bible when used as literature banned from

6

Cause and effect: Fourth reason why children's and adolescents' books are banned

Illustration: Books banned for religious reasons

classrooms. Not only does teaching the Bible as literature present a problem for parents who want the Bible focused on as sacred material, but it is equally offensive to people who feel that religious documents should be kept out of the classroom (Burress 219). Sometimes religious considerations take the form of censorship of books that in any way involve the occult. The picture book *Witches, Pumpkins, and Grinning Ghosts* was considered inappropriate because it "interests little minds into accepting the Devil with all his evil works" (Reichman 51). Ironically, "witches" sought the banning of *Hansel and Gretel* because it portrayed their religion in a negative light (Reichman 50). Greek and Roman mythology has also been attacked by religious groups because it discusses gods other than the Christian one. Christians also fought to ban books on evolution that called into question their religious beliefs.

Cause and effect: Fifth reason why children's and adolescents' books are banned

Illustration: Books banned for racial reasons

Yet another reason for the censorship of children's books is concern over racism and sexism. Minority groups have often made efforts to combat stereotypes and racial prejudices through censorship. The idea is that if children are exposed to sexism and racism in books, they will learn it. Mark Twain's *The Adventures of Huckleberry Finn* is a good example of a text that has been banned because of its racist language. The use of the term *nigger* has offended many African Americans. The problem with this criticism is that the novel was not examined for its intention, which was to question the racist attitude of the South. Twain was not a racist. Nevertheless, *Huckleberry Finn* has become one of the most frequently banned books in the United States. Women have also tried to censor nursery rhymes and children's stories that reinforce negative images of women. Some have argued in opposition that to remove all books that are sexist and racist would be to remove a piece of our history that we can learn from.

Central question is raised: Should we censor children's books? Answers are given.

With this brief background and a review of some of the reasons used to ban children's books, how might the question "Should we censor children's books?" be answered? On the one hand, we should realize that there are age-appropriate themes for children. For example, elementary school children should not be exposed to the ideas of rape and abortion that occur in some young adult novels. Young adults should not be exposed to extremely violent novels like Anthony Burgess's *A Clockwork Orange*, which they may not understand at such a young age. Does this mean these books should be removed from school

Argumentation: The writer provides various criteria for making decisions about what is appropriate reading for children. Discussion of these criteria generally follows the writer's sequencing of the reasons why people attempt to censor children's and adolescents' books.

libraries? Perhaps not. Libraries should be resources for children to broaden their horizons. If a child independently seeks out a controversial novel, the child should not be stopped from doing so. Exposure to a rich diversity of works is always advisable. A good way to decide if a book should be taught is if its message speaks to the children. What if this message is couched in profanity? If it is in a character representation, kids can understand the context without feeling compelled to emulate the behavior. If children are constantly exposed to books that throw reality in their faces in a violent way, then their attitudes will reflect it. So, it is the job of educators to present different types of materials to balance the children's exposure.

As far as sexuality goes, it's fine for libraries to include children's books that focus on this subject if the objective is to educate or make transitions easier for the child. Religion, however, should not be focused on in the classroom because it causes too much conflict for different groups. This does not mean that religious works should be banned from school libraries. Children should have access to different religious materials to explore world religions and various belief systems. Lastly, if sexism and racism appear in books, those books should not automatically be banned. They can be useful tools for increasing understanding in our society. 9

Argumentation: Concluding statement calls for understanding and sensitivity in dealing with censorship and book selection for children and adolescents.

The efforts to censor what our children are reading can turn into potentially explosive situations and cause a great deal of misunderstanding and hurt feelings within our schools and communities. If we can gain an understanding of the major reasons why people have sought to censor what our kids are reading, we will be better prepared to respond to those efforts in a sensitive and reasonable manner. More importantly, we will be able to provide the best educational opportunity for our children through a sensible approach, one that neither overly restricts the range of their reading nor allows them to read any and all books no matter how inappropriate they might be for them. 10

Works Cited

Burress, Lee. *Battle of the Books: Literary Censorship in the Public Schools, 1950-1985.* New York: Scarecrow, 1989. Print.

Foerstel, Herbert. *Banned in the U.S.A.: A Reference Guide to Book Censorship in Schools and Public Libraries.* London: Greenwood, 1994. Print.

Reichman, Henry. *Censorship and Selection: Issues and Answers to Schools.* Chicago: American Library Association, 1993. Print.

West, Mark. *Trust Your Children: Voices against Censorship in Children's Literature*. London: Neal-Schuman, 1988. Print.

Analyzing Tara E. Ketch's Essay of Combining Strategies: Questions for Discussion

1. What is Ketch's thesis?
2. How do the two rulings of the U.S. Supreme Court on educational decisions within communities conflict?
3. What reasons does Ketch give for the banning of children's and adolescents' books in schools?
4. How does Ketch answer the question "Should we censor children's books?" Do you agree with her?

SUGGESTIONS FOR USING A COMBINATION OF STRATEGIES IN AN ESSAY

As you plan, write, and revise your essay using a combination of strategies, be mindful of the five-step writing process described in Chapter 2 (see pages 14–31). Pay particular attention to the basic requirements and essential ingredients of this writing strategy.

Planning Your Essay of Combined Strategies

Planning is an essential part of writing a good essay using a combination of strategies. You can save yourself a great deal of trouble by taking the time to think about the key building blocks of your essay before you actually begin to write. Before you can start combining strategies in your writing, it's essential that you have a firm understanding of the purposes and workings of each strategy. Once you become familiar with how the strategies work, you should be able to recognize ways to use and combine them in your writing. Sometimes you will find yourself using a particular strategy almost intuitively. When you encounter a difficult or abstract term or concept — *liberal,* for example — you will define it almost as a matter of course. If you become perplexed because you are having trouble getting your readers to appreciate the severity of a problem, a quick review of the strategies will remind you that you could use description and illustration. Knowledge of the individual strategies is crucial because there are no formulas or prescriptions for combining strategies. The more you write and the more aware you are of the options available to you, the more skillful you will become at thinking critically about your topic, developing your ideas, and conveying your thoughts to your readers.

Determine Your Purpose.   Your purpose in writing is defined as what you are trying to achieve. The most common purposes in nonfiction writing are (1) to express your thoughts and feelings about a life experience, (2) to inform your readers by explaining something about the world around them, and (3) to persuade readers to some belief or action. Your purpose will determine the dominant strategy you use in your essay. If your major purpose is to tell a story of a river-rafting trip, you will use narration. If you wish to re-create the experience of a famous landmark for the first time, you may find description helpful. If you wish to inform your readers, you may find definition, cause and effect, process analysis, comparison and contrast, or division and classification to be best suited to your needs. If you wish to convince your readers of a certain belief or course of action, argumentation is an obvious choice.

Formulate a Thesis Statement.   Regardless of the purpose you have set for yourself in writing an essay, it is essential that you commit to a thesis statement, usually a one- or two-sentence statement giving the main point of your essay.

> Party primaries are an indispensable part of the American political process.

> Antibiotics are not nearly as effective as they once were in combating infections among humans.

A question is not a thesis statement. If you find yourself writing a thesis statement that asks a question, answer the question first and then turn your answer into a thesis statement. A thesis statement can be presented anywhere in an essay, but usually it is presented at the beginning of a composition, sometimes after a few introductory sentences that set a context for it.

Organizing Your Essay of Combined Strategies

Determine Your Dominant Strategy.   Depending on your purpose for writing, your thesis statement, and the kinds of information you have gathered in preparing to write your essay, you may use any of the following strategies as the dominant strategy for your essay: narration, description, illustration, process analysis, comparison and contrast, division and classification, definition, cause and effect analysis, and argumentation. Indeed, *Subject & Strategy* is aimed at helping you understand these strategies and effectively implement them in developing your essays.

Determine Your Supporting Strategies.   The questions listed below—
organized by rhetorical strategy—will help you decide which strategies
will be most helpful to you in the service of the dominant strategy you
have chosen for your essay and in achieving your overall purpose.

- *Narration.* Are you trying to report or recount an anecdote, an experience, or an event? Does any part of your essay include the telling
  of a story (something that happened to you or to a person you
  include in your essay)?
- *Description.* Does a person, place, or object play a prominent role in
  your essay? Would the tone, pacing, or overall purpose of your
  essay benefit from sensory details?
- *Illustration.* Are there examples—facts, statistics, cases in point,
  personal experiences, interview quotations—that you could add to
  help you achieve the purpose of your essay?
- *Process analysis.* Would any part of your essay be clearer if you
  included concrete directions about a certain process? Are there
  processes that readers would like to understand better? Are you
  evaluating any processes?
- *Comparison and contrast.* Does your essay contain two or more
  related subjects? Are you evaluating or analyzing two or more people, places, processes, events, or things? Do you need to establish
  the similarities and differences between two or more elements?
- *Division and classification.* Are you trying to explain a broad and
  complicated subject? Would it benefit your essay to reduce this
  subject to more manageable parts to focus your discussion?
- *Definition.* Who is your audience? Does your essay focus on any
  abstract, specialized, or new terms that need further explanation so
  readers understand your point? Does any important word in your
  essay have many meanings and need to be clarified?
- *Cause and effect analysis.* Are you examining past events or their
  outcomes? Is your purpose to inform, speculate, or argue about
  why an identifiable fact happens the way it does?
- *Argumentation.* Are you trying to explain aspects of a particular subject, and are you trying to advocate a specific opinion on this subject or issue in your essay?

Revising and Editing Your Essay
of Combined Strategies

Listen to What Your Classmates Have to Say.   The importance of
student peer conferences cannot be stressed enough, particularly as you

revise and edit your essay. Often others in your class will readily see that the basis for your classification needs adjustment or that there are inconsistencies in your division categories that can easily be corrected—problems that you can't see yourself because you are too close to your essay. Or perhaps you need more and better transitions to link the discussions of your categories; or you may need more examples. So take advantage of suggestions when you know them to be valid, and make revisions accordingly.

Question Your Own Work While Revising and Editing.   Revision is best done by asking yourself key questions about what you have written. Begin by reading, preferably aloud, what you have written. Reading aloud forces you to pay attention to every single word, and you are more likely to catch lapses in the logical flow of thought. After you have read your paper through, answer the following questions for revising and editing and make the necessary changes.

Questions for Revising and Editing: Combining Strategies

1. Do I have a purpose for my essay?
2. Is my thesis statement clear?
3. Does my dominant strategy reflect my purpose and my thesis statement?
4. Do my subordinate strategies effectively support the dominant strategy of my essay?
5. Are my subordinate strategies woven into my essay in a natural manner?
6. Have I revised and edited my essay to avoid wordiness?
7. Have I avoided errors in grammar, punctuation, and mechanics?

On Dumpster Diving

Lars Eighner

Born in Texas in 1948, Lars Eighner attended the University of Texas–Austin. After graduation, he wrote essays and fiction, and several of his articles were published in magazines like Threepenny Review, *the* Guide, *and* Inches. *A volume of short stories,* Bayou Boy and Other Stories, *was published in 1985. Eighner became homeless in 1988 when he left his job as an attendant at a mental hospital. The following piece, which appeared in the* Utne Reader, *is an abridged version of an essay that first appeared in* Threepenny Review. *The piece eventually became part of Eighner's startling account of the three years he spent as a homeless person,* Travels with Lizbeth *(1993). His publications include the novels* Pawn to Queen Four *(1995) and* Whispered in the Dark *(1996) and the nonfiction book* Gay Cosmos *(1995).*

Eighner uses a number of rhetorical strategies in "On Dumpster Diving," but pay particular attention to how his delineation of the "stages that a person goes through in learning to scavenge" contributes to the success of the essay as a whole.

PREPARING TO READ

Are you a pack rat, or do you get rid of what is not immediately useful to you? Outside of the usual kitchen garbage and empty toothpaste tubes, how do you make the decision to throw something away?

I began Dumpster diving about a year before I became homeless. 1

I prefer the term *scavenging.* I have heard people, evidently meaning to be polite, use the word *foraging,* but I prefer to reserve that word for gathering nuts and berries and such, which I also do, according to the season and opportunity. 2

I like the frankness of the word *scavenging.* I live from the refuse of others. I am a scavenger. I think it a sound and honorable niche, although if I could I would naturally prefer to live the comfortable consumer life, perhaps—and only perhaps—as a slightly less wasteful consumer owing to what I have learned as a scavenger. 3

Except for jeans, all my clothes come from Dumpsters. Boom boxes, candles, bedding, toilet paper, medicine, books, a typewriter, a virgin male love doll, coins sometimes amounting to many dollars: all came from Dumpsters. And, yes, I eat from Dumpsters, too. 4

There is a predictable series of stages that a person goes through in learning to scavenge. At first the new scavenger is filled with disgust and self-loathing. He is ashamed of being seen. 5

This stage passes with experience. The scavenger finds a pair of running shoes that fit and look and smell brand-new. He finds a pocket calculator in perfect working order. He finds pristine ice cream, still frozen, more than he can eat or keep. He begins to understand: people do throw away perfectly good stuff, a lot of perfectly good stuff. 6

At this stage he may become lost and never recover: All the Dumpster divers I have known come to the point of trying to acquire everything they touch. Why not take it, they reason, it is all free. This is, of course, hopeless, and most divers come to realize that they must restrict themselves to items of relatively immediate utility. 7

The finding of objects is becoming something of an urban art. Even respectable, employed people will sometimes find something tempting sticking out of a Dumpster or standing beside one. Quite a number of people, not all of them of the bohemian type, are willing to brag that they found this or that piece in the trash. 8

But eating from Dumpsters is the thing that separates the dilettanti from the professionals. Eating safely involves three principles: using the senses and common sense to evaluate the condition of the found materials; knowing the Dumpsters of a given area and checking them regularly; and seeking always to answer the question "Why was this discarded?" 9

Yet perfectly good food can be found in Dumpsters. Canned goods, for example, turn up fairly often in the Dumpsters I frequent. I also have few qualms about dry foods such as crackers, cookies, cereal, chips, and pasta if they are free of visible contaminants and still dry and crisp. Raw fruits and vegetables with intact skins seem perfectly safe to me, excluding, of course, the obviously rotten. Many are discarded for minor imperfections that can be pared away. 10

A typical discard is a half jar of peanut butter — though nonorganic peanut butter does not require refrigeration and is unlikely to spoil in any reasonable time. One of my favorite finds is yogurt — often discarded, still sealed, when the expiration date has passed — because it will keep for several days, even in warm weather. 11

No matter how careful I am I still get dysentery at least once a month, oftener in warm weather. I do not want to paint too romantic a picture. Dumpster diving has serious drawbacks as a way of life. 12

I find from the experience of scavenging two rather deep lessons. The first is to take what I can use and let the rest go. I have come to think that there is no value in the abstract. A thing I cannot use or make useful, perhaps by trading, has no value, however fine or rare it may be. 13

The second lesson is the transience of material being. I do not suppose that ideas are immortal, but certainly they are longer-lived than material objects. 14

The things I find in Dumpsters, the love letters and rag dolls of so many lives, remind me of this lesson. Now I hardly pick up a thing without envisioning the time I will cast it away. This, I think, is a 15

healthy state of mind. Almost everything I have now has already been cast out at least once, proving that what I own is valueless to someone.

I find that my desire to grab for the gaudy bauble has been largely   16
sated. I think this is an attitude I share with the very wealthy — we both know there is plenty more where whatever we have came from. Between us are the rat-race millions who have confounded their selves with the objects they grasp and who nightly scavenge the cable channels for they know not what.

I am sorry for them.   17

THINKING CRITICALLY ABOUT THE TEXT

In paragraph 15, Eighner writes, "I hardly pick up a thing without envisioning the time I will cast it away. This, I think, is a healthy state of mind." React to this statement. Do you think such an attitude is healthy or defeatist? If many people thought this way, what impact would it have on our consumer society?

QUESTIONS ON SUBJECT

1. What stages do beginning Dumpster divers go through before they become what Eighner terms "professionals" (paragraph 9)? What

examples does Eighner use to illustrate the passage through these stages? (Glossary: *Illustration*)

2. What three principles does one need to follow in order to eat safely from Dumpsters? What foods are best to eat from Dumpsters? What are the risks?

3. What two lessons has Eighner learned from his Dumpster diving experiences? Why are they significant to him?

4. Dumpster diving has had a profound effect on Eighner and the way he lives. How do his explanations of choices he makes, such as deciding which items to keep, enhance his presentation of the practical art of Dumpster diving?

5. How do you respond to Eighner's Dumpster diving practices? Are you shocked? Bemused? Accepting? Challenged?

QUESTIONS ON STRATEGY

1. Eighner's essay deals with both the immediate, physical aspects of Dumpster diving, such as what can be found in a typical Dumpster and the physical price one pays for eating out of them, and the larger, abstract issues that Dumpster diving raises, such as materialism and the transience of material objects. (Glossary: *Concrete/Abstract*) Why does he describe the concrete things before he discusses the abstract issues raised by their presence in Dumpsters? What does he achieve by using both types of elements?

2. Eighner's account of Dumpster diving focuses primarily on the odd appeal and interest inherent in the activity. Paragraph 12 is his one disclaimer, in which he states, "I do not want to paint too romantic a picture." Why does Eighner include this disclaimer? How does it add to the effectiveness of his piece? Why do you think it is so brief and abrupt?

3. Eighner uses many rhetorical techniques in his essay, but its core is a fairly complete process analysis of how to Dumpster dive. (Glossary: *Process Analysis*) Summarize this process analysis. Why do you think Eighner did not title the essay "How to Dumpster Dive"?

4. Discuss how Eighner uses illustration to bring the world of Dumpster diving to life. (Glossary: *Illustration*) What characterizes the examples he uses?

5. Writers often use process analysis in conjunction with other strategies, especially argument, to try to improve the way a process is carried out. (Glossary: *Argument; Process Analysis*) In this essay, Eighner uses a full process analysis to lay out his views on American values and materialism. How is this an effective way to combine strategies? Think of other arguments that could be strengthened if they included elements of process analysis.

QUESTIONS ON DICTION AND VOCABULARY

1. Eighner says he prefers the word *scavenging* to *Dumpster diving* or *foraging*. What do those three terms mean to him? Why do you think he finds the

discussion of the terms important enough to discuss at the beginning of his essay? (Glossary: *Diction*)

2. According to Eighner, "eating from Dumpsters is the thing that separates the dilettanti from the professionals" (paragraph 9). What do the words *dilettante* and *professional* connote to you? (Glossary: *Connotation/Denotation*) Why does Eighner choose to use them instead of the more straight-forward *casual* and *serious*?

3. Eighner says, "The finding of objects is becoming something of an urban art" (paragraph 8). What does this sentence mean to you? Based on the essay, do you find his use of the word *art* appropriate when discussing any aspect of Dumpster diving? Why or why not?

CLASSROOM ACTIVITY FOR COMBINING STRATEGIES

As a class, discuss the strategies that Eighner uses in his essay: narration, cause and effect, illustration, and definition, for example. Where in the essay has he used each strategy and to what end? Has he used any other strategies not mentioned above? Explain.

WRITING SUGGESTIONS

1. Write a process analysis in which you relate how you acquire a consumer item of some importance or expense to you. (Glossary: *Process Analysis*) Do you compare brands, store prices, and so on? (Glossary: *Comparison and Contrast*) What are your priorities—must the item be stylish or durable, offer good overall value, give high performance? How do you decide to spend your money? In other words, what determines which items are worth the sacrifice?

2. In paragraph 3 Eighner states that he "live[s] from the refuse of others." How does his confession affect you? Do you think that we have become a throwaway society? If so, how? How do Eighner's accounts of homeless-ness and Dumpster diving make you feel about your own consumerism and trash habits? Write an essay in which you examine the things you throw away in a single day. What items did you get rid of? Why? Could those items be used by someone else? Have you ever felt guilty about throwing something away? If so, what was it and why?

3. One person's treasure is another person's trash. That is especially true around college campuses, when students who are moving often throw away their large—but frequently still useful—personal possessions. In the photograph on page 564 by Christopher S. Johnson, taken in Cambridge, Massachusetts, the college Dumpsters have obviously become focal points of interest for others in the community. Perhaps this could be termed the purest form of recycling, and it underscores the transient nature of our material possessions. Choose a theme derived from the photograph and Eighner's essay—for example, the treasure/trash statement above or the transience of material goods—and write an essay developed by using at least three different strategies in combination.

The Obligation to Endure

Rachel Carson

Rachel Carson (1907–1964) was born in Springdale, Penn-sylvania. A zoologist and accomplished writer, she wrote much about the marine world and taught at Johns Hopkins and the University of Maryland. Her delightfully warm and sensitive interpretations of scientific data in Under the Sea *(1941),* The Sea Around Us *(1951), and* The Edge of the Sea *(1955) made these books very popular.* The Sea Around Us *won Carson the National Book Award. But it was* Silent Spring *(1962), her study of herbicides and insecticides, that made Carson a controversial figure. Carson's allegations prompted President John F. Kennedy to appoint a commission to study the problem of indiscriminate use of pesticides. Though some have denounced her as an alarmist, she is nevertheless recognized as having been a pow-erful force in the ecology movement.*

In "The Obligation to Endure," the second chapter of Silent Spring, *Carson argues for a more responsible use of pesticides.*

PREPARING TO READ

Think about the nature of the interaction between humans and the world in which they live. How would you characterize that interaction? Have humans had too much power over their surroundings? Not enough? Or just the right amount, in your estimation?

The history of life on earth has been a history of interaction between living things and their surroundings. To a large extent, the physical form and the habits of the earth's vegetation and its animal life have been molded by the environment. Considering the whole span of earthly time, the opposite effect, in which life actually modifies its sur-roundings, has been relatively slight. Only within the moment of time represented by the present century has one species—man—acquired significant power to alter the nature of his world.

During the past quarter century this power has not only increased to one of disturbing magnitude but it has changed in character. The most alarming of all man's assaults upon the environment is the con-tamination of air, earth, rivers, and sea with dangerous and even lethal materials. This pollution is for the most part irrecoverable; the chain of evil it initiates not only in the world that must support life but in living tissues is for the most part irreversible. In this now universal contami-nation of the environment, chemicals are the sinister and little recog-nized partners of radiation in changing the very nature of the world— the very nature of its life. Strontium 90, released through nuclear explosions into the air, comes to earth in rain or drifts down as fallout, lodges in soil, enters the grass or corn or wheat grown there, and in time takes up its abode in the bones of a human being, there to remain until his death. Similarly, chemicals sprayed on croplands or forests or garden lie long in soil, entering into living organisms, passing from one to another in a chain of poisoning and death. Or they pass mysteriously by underground streams until they emerge and through the alchemy of air and sunlight, combine into new forms that kill vegetation, sicken cattle, and work unknown harm on those who drink from once pure wells. As Albert Schweitzer has said, "Man can hardly even recognize the devils of his own creation."

It took hundreds of millions of years to produce the life that now   3
inhabits the earth—eons of time in which that developing and evolving and diversifying life reached a state of adjustment and balance with its surroundings. The environment, rigorously shaping and directing the life it supported, contained elements that were hostile as well as supporting. Certain rocks gave out dangerous radiation; even within the light of the sun, from which all life draws its energy, there were short-wave radiations with power to injure. Given time—time not in years but in millennia—life adjusts, and a balance has been reached. For time is the essential ingredient; but in the modern world there is no time.

The rapidity of change and the speed with which new situations   4
are created follow the impetuous and heedless pace of man rather than the deliberate pace of nature. Radiation is no longer merely the background radiation of rocks, the bombardment of cosmic rays, the ultraviolet of the sun that have existed before there was any life on earth; radiation is now the unnatural creation of man's tampering with the atom. The chemicals to which life is asked to make its adjustment are no longer merely the calcium and silica and copper and all the rest of the minerals washed out of the rocks and carried in rivers to the sea; they are the synthetic creations of man's inventive mind, brewed in his laboratories, and having no counterparts in nature.

To adjust to these chemicals would require time on the scale that is   5
nature's; it would require not merely the years of a man's life but the life of generations. And even this, were it by some miracle possible, would be futile, for the new chemicals come from our laboratories in an endless stream; almost five hundred annually find their way into actual use in the United States alone. The figure is staggering and its implications are not easily grasped—500 new chemicals to which the bodies of men and animals are required somehow to adapt each year, chemicals totally outside the limits of biologic experience.

Among them are many that are used in man's war against nature.   6
Since the mid-1940's over 200 basic chemicals have been created for use in killing insects, weeds, rodents, and other organisms described in

the modern vernacular as "pests"; and they are sold under several thousand different brand names.

These sprays, dusts, and aerosols are now applied almost universally to farms, gardens, forests, and homes—nonselective chemicals that have the power to kill every insect, the "good" and the "bad," to still the song of birds and the leaping of fish in the streams, to coat the leaves with a deadly film, and to linger on in soil—all this though the intended target may be only a few weeds or insects. Can anyone believe it is possible to lay down such a barrage of poisons on the surface of the earth without making it unfit for all life? They should not be called "insecticides," but "biocides."

The whole process of spraying seems caught up in an endless spiral. Since DDT was released for civilian use, a process of escalation has been going on in which ever more toxic materials must be found. This has happened because insects, in a triumphant vindication of Darwin's principle of the survival of the fittest, have evolved super races immune to the particular insecticide used, hence a deadlier one has always to be developed—and then a deadlier one than that. It has happened also because destructive insects often undergo a "flareback," or resurgence, after spraying, in numbers greater than before. Thus the chemical war is never won, and all life is caught in its violent crossfire.

Along with the possibility of the extinction of mankind by nuclear war, the central problem of our age has therefore become the contamination of man's total environment with such substances of incredible potential for harm—substances that accumulate in the tissues of plants and animals and even penetrate the germ cells to shatter or alter the very material of heredity upon which the shape of the future depends.

Some would-be architects of our future look toward a time when it will be possible to alter the human germ plasm by design. But we may easily be doing so now by inadvertence, for many chemicals, like radiation, bring about gene mutations. It is ironic to think that man might determine his own future by something so seemingly trivial as the choice of an insect spray.

All this has been risked—for what? Future historians may well be amazed by our distorted sense of proportion. How could intelligent beings seek to control a few unwanted species by a method that contaminated the entire environment and brought the threat of disease and death even to their own kind? Yet this is precisely what we have done. We have done it, moreover, for reasons that collapse the moment we examine them. We are told that the enormous and expanding use of pesticides is necessary to maintain farm production. Yet is our real problem not one of *overproduction*? Our farms, despite measures to remove acreages from production and to pay farmers *not* to produce, have yielded such a staggering excess of crops that the American

7

8

9

10

11

taxpayer in 1962 is paying out more than one billion dollars a year as the total carrying cost of the surplus-food storage program. And is the situation helped when one branch of the Agriculture Department tries to reduce production while another states, as it did in 1958, "It is believed generally that reduction of crop acreages under provisions of the Soil Bank will stimulate interest in use of chemicals to obtain maximum production on the land retained in crops"?

All this is not to say there is no insect problem and no need of control. I am saying, rather, that control must be geared to realities, not to mythical situations, and that the methods employed must be such that they do not destroy us along with the insects. 12

The problem whose attempted solution has brought such a train of disaster in its wake is an accompaniment of our modern way of life Long before the age of man, insects inhabited the earth — a group of extraordinarily varied and adaptable beings. Over the course of time since man's advent, a small percentage of the more than half a million species of insects have come into conflict with human welfare in two principal ways: as competitors for the food supply and as carriers of human disease. 13

Disease-carrying insects become important where human beings are crowded together, especially under conditions where sanitation is poor, as in time of natural disaster or war or in situations of extreme poverty and deprivation. Then control of some sort becomes necessary. It is a sobering fact, however, that the method of massive chemical control has had only limited success, and also threatens to worsen the very conditions it is intended to curb. 14

Under primitive agricultural conditions the farmer had few insect problems. These arose with the intensification of agriculture — the devotion of immense acreages to a single crop. Such a system set the stage for explosive increases in specific insect populations. Single-crop farming does not take advantage of the principles by which nature works; it is agriculture as an engineer might conceive it to be. Nature has introduced great variety into the landscape, but man has displayed a passion for simplifying it. Thus he undoes the built-in checks and balances by which nature holds the species within bounds. One important natural check is a limit on the amount of suitable habitat for each species. Obviously then, an insect that lives on wheat can build up its population to much higher levels on a farm devoted to wheat than on one in which wheat is intermingled with other crops to which the insect is not adapted. 15

The same thing happens in other situations. A generation or more ago, the towns of large areas of the United States lined their streets with the noble elm tree. Now the beauty they hopefully created is threatened with complete destruction as disease sweeps through the elms, carried by a beetle that would have only limited chance to build up 16 large populations and to spread from tree to tree if the elms were only occasional trees in a richly diversified planting.

Another factor in the modem insect problem is one that must be viewed against a background of geologic and human history: the spreading of thousands of different kinds of organisms from their native homes to invade new territories. This worldwide migration has been studied and graphically described by the British ecologist Charles Elton in his recent book *The Ecology of Invasions*. During the Cretaceous Period, some hundred million years ago, flooding seas cut many land bridges between continents and living things found themselves confined in what Elton calls "colossal separate nature reserves." There, isolated from others of their kind, they developed many new species. When some of the land masses were joined again, about 15 million years ago, these species began to move out into new territories—a movement that is not only still in progress but is now receiving considerable assistance from man.

The importation of plants is the primary agent in the modern spread of species, for animals have almost invariably gone along with the plants, quarantine being a comparatively recent and not completely effective innovation. The United States Office of Plant Introduction alone has introduced almost 200,000 species and varieties of plants from all over the world. Nearly half of the 180 or so major insect enemies of plants in the United States are accidental imports from abroad, and most of them have come as hitchhikers on plants.

In new territory, out of reach of the restraining hand of the natural enemies that kept down its numbers in its native land, an invading plant or animal is able to become enormously abundant. Thus it is no accident that our most troublesome insects are introduced species.

These invasions, both the naturally occurring and those dependent on human assistance, are likely to continue indefinitely. Quarantine and massive chemical campaigns are only extremely expensive ways of buying time. We are faced, according to Dr. Elton, "with a life-and-death need not just to find new technological means of suppressing this plant or that animal"; instead we need the basic knowledge of animal populations and their relations to their surroundings that will "promote an even balance and damp down the explosive power of outbreaks and new invasions."

Much of the necessary knowledge is now available but we do not use it. We train ecologists in our universities and even employ them in our governmental agencies but we seldom take their advice. We allow the chemical death rain to fall as though there were no alternative, whereas in fact there are many, and our ingenuity could soon discover many more if given opportunity.

Have we fallen into a mesmerized state that makes us accept as inevitable that which is inferior or detrimental, as though having lost the will or the vision to demand that which is good? Such thinking, in the words of the ecologist Paul Shepard, "idealizes life with only its head out of water, inches above the limits of toleration of the corruption of its own environment. . . . Why should we tolerate a diet of weak poisons, a home in insipid surroundings, a circle of acquaintances who are not quite our enemies, the noise of motors with just enough relief to prevent insanity? Who would want to live in a world which is just not quite fatal?"

Yet such a world is pressed upon us. The crusade to create a chemi-   23
cally sterile, insect-free world seems to have engendered a fanatic zeal on the part of many specialists and most of the so-called control agencies. On every hand there is evidence that those engaged in spraying operations exercise a ruthless power. "The regulatory entomologists . . . function as prosecutor, judge and jury, tax assessor and collector and sheriff to enforce their own orders," said Connecticut entomologist Neely Turner. The most flagrant abuses go unchecked in both state and federal agencies.

It is not my contention that chemical insecticides must never be   24
used. I do contend that we have put poisonous and biologically potent chemicals indiscriminately into the hands of persons largely or wholly ignorant of their potentials for harm. We have subjected enormous numbers of people to contact with these poisons, without their consent and often without their knowledge. If the Bill of Rights contains no guarantee that a citizen shall be secure against lethal poisons distributed either by private individuals or by public officials, it is surely only because our forefathers, despite their considerable wisdom and foresight, could conceive of no such problem.

I contend, furthermore, that we have allowed these chemicals to be   25
used with little or no advance investigation of their effect on soil, water, wildlife, and man himself. Future generations are unlikely to condone our lack of prudent concern for the integrity of the natural world that supports all life.

There is still very limited awareness of the nature of the threat. This   26
is an era of specialists, each of whom sees his own problem and is unaware of or intolerant of the larger frame into which it fits. It is also an era dominated by industry, in which the right to make a dollar at whatever cost is seldom challenged. When the public protests, confronted with some obvious evidence of damaging results of pesticide applications, it is fed little tranquilizing pills of half truth. We urgently need an end to these false assurances, to the sugar coating of unpalatable facts. It is the public that is being asked to assume the risks that the insect controllers calculate. The public must decide whether it wishes to continue on the present road, and it can do so only when in full possession of the facts. In the words of Jean Rostand, "The obligation to endure gives us the right to know."

THINKING CRITICALLY ABOUT THE TEXT

In what ways, if any, have your ideas about the interaction of humans and their environment changed as a result of reading Carson's essay? Are you more inclined now to see humans as vulnerable to their environment or the environment as vulnerable to humans? Explain.

QUESTIONS ON SUBJECT

1. Humans in the twentieth and twenty-first centuries have acquired the power to modify their environment. Why does Carson find this power so disturbing?

2. According to Carson, what is the "chain of evil" (paragraph 2) that pollution initiates?

3. Why are "the pace of nature" and the "pace of man" in conflict (paragraph 4)? What problems are created by this conflict?

4. What is the "flareback" that Carson refers to in paragraph 8? How does it add to the problems associated with the spraying of chemicals?

5. Carson devotes much of her essay to a critical examination of the use of insecticides to control the insect population. What are her attitudes toward chemical insecticides and insect control?

QUESTIONS ON STRATEGY

1. What is the significance of the title that Carson has given her essay? From what does she derive her title? (Glossary: *Title*)

2. What types of evidence does Carson use to support her argument? Are you convinced by her evidence? Why or why not? (Glossary: *Evidence*)

3. A useful strategy in argumentation is to anticipate and refute an opponent's arguments. Where in her essay does Carson employ this strategy and how effective is her use of it?

4. Find examples of illustration and process analysis that Carson uses to develop her argument. What other strategies of development does she employ in her essay? (Glossary: *Illustration, Process Analysis*)

QUESTIONS ON DICTION AND VOCABULARY

1. Carson's essay in large part examines "man's war against nature." Identify the words and phrases that Carson uses to develop and sustain the image of warfare. How appropriate, in your opinion, is this dominant image?

2. What is the connotative value of the italicized words or phrases in each of the following lines from the essay? (Glossary: *Connotation/Denotation*)

   a. considering the whole span of *earthly time* (paragraph 1)

   b. the *chain of evil* it initiates (2)

   c. chemicals are the *sinister* and little recognized *partners* of radiation (2)

   d. through the *alchemy* of air and sunlight (2)

   e. man has displayed a *passion* for simplifying it (15)

   f. most of them have come as *hitchhikers* on plants (18)

   g. we allow the *chemical death rain* to fall (21)

   h. it is surely only because our *forefathers* (24)

   i. it is fed little *tranquilizing pills of half truth* (26)

   j. *sugar coating* of unpalatable facts (26)

3. Why does Carson believe that chemicals designed to kill insects should not be called "insecticides" but "biocides"?

CLASSROOM ACTIVITY FOR COMBINING STRATEGIES

Choose from your local newspaper an editorial dealing with a controversial environmental problem. Outline the issues involved. Now assume that you have been given equal space in the newspaper in which to present the opposing viewpoint. Make some notes for an argument in rebuttal and for how you might employ various strategies of development—say, narration, process analysis, comparison and contrast, and illustration—in support of your main argument.

WRITING SUGGESTIONS

1. In 1962, Rachel Carson charged that "we have put poisonous and biologically potent chemicals indiscriminately into the hands of persons largely or wholly ignorant of their potential for harm." The validity of her charge is everywhere evident today. Write an essay about chemical abuse using specific examples that have been brought to our attention in recent years.

2. Argue for or against the following proposition: We should ban the use of herbicides and insecticides. Be sure to employ as many different strategies as you can in developing your essay and in bolstering your position.

3. With the aid of Internet research, argue that our federal regulatory agencies have or have not done enough since Carson's *Silent Spring* was published nearly fifty years ago to minimize our blind dependence on harmful herbicides and insecticides.

On Being a Cripple

Nancy Mairs

 *Nancy Mairs, a poet and writer, was born in Long Beach, California, in 1943. She attended Wheaton College in Massachusetts, where she earned a B.A. in English in 1964. From 1964 until 1972, Mairs took a number of teaching and writing jobs around Boston, and it was during this period that she learned she had multiple sclerosis and experienced major depression. In 1972, Mairs decided to pursue a career in writing and entered the creative writing program at the University of Arizona, where she earned an M.F.A. in poetry (1975) and then a Ph.D. in English (1984). In works like* Plaintext *(1986),* Carnal Acts *(1990),* Waist High in the World *(1997), and* A Troubled Guest *(2001), which consist mostly of autobiographical essays, Mairs has refused to deny or cover up the specificities of her life as a woman. In fact, Mairs has often used the most intimate details of her inner life as the essential material of her art. Through her writing, Mairs has called into question what can and cannot be revealed about one's life in writing for a public audience.*

"On Being a Cripple" is an essay from her critically acclaimed Plaintext. *In this essay, she writes poignantly about living with MS and about the strategies she has developed to cope with it. But, more important, she has written of the ways in which "being a cripple" has intensified and even enhanced her artistic vision.*

PREPARING TO READ

The word *cripple* carries powerful connotations. What visual and emotional responses does it arouse in you? Do you object to the word? Why or why not?

> To escape is nothing. Not to escape is nothing.
>
> —LOUISE BOGAN

The other day I was thinking of writing an essay on being a cripple. I was thinking hard in one of the stalls of the women's room in my office building, as I was shoving my shirt into my jeans and tugging up my zipper. Preoccupied, I flushed, picked up my book bag, took my cane down from the hook, and unlatched the door. So many movements unbalanced me, and as I pulled the door open I fell over backward, landing fully clothed on the toilet seat with my legs splayed in front of me: the old beetle-on-its-back routine. Saturday afternoon, the building deserted, I was free to laugh aloud as I wriggled back to my feet, my voice bouncing off the yellowish tiles from all directions. Had anyone been there with me, I'd have been still and faint and hot with chagrin. I decided that it was high time to write the essay.

1

First, the matter of semantics. I am a cripple. I choose this word to name me. I choose from among several possibilities, the most common of which are "handicapped" and "disabled." I made the choice a number of years ago, without thinking, unaware of my motives for doing so. Even now, I'm not sure what those motives are, but I recognize that they are complex and not entirely flattering. People—crippled or not—wince at the word "cripple," as they do not at "handicapped" or "disabled." Perhaps I want them to wince. I want them to see me as a tough customer, one to whom the fates/gods/viruses have not been kind, but who can face the brutal truth of her existence squarely. As a cripple, I swagger.

But, to be fair to myself, a certain amount of honesty underlies my choice. "Cripple" seems to me a clean word, straightforward and precise. It has an honorable history, having made its first appearance in the Lindisfarne Gospel in the tenth century. As a lover of words, I like the accuracy with which it describes my condition: I have lost the full use of my limbs. "Disabled," by contrast, suggests an incapacity, physical or mental. And I certainly don't like "handicapped," which implies that I have deliberately been put at a disadvantage, by whom I can't imagine (my God is not a Handicapper General), in order to equalize chances in the great race of life. These words seem to me to be moving away from my condition, to be widening the gap between word and reality. Most remote is the recently coined euphemism "differently abled," which partakes of the same semantic hopefulness that transformed countries from "undeveloped" to "underdeveloped," then to "less developed," and finally to "developing" nations. People have continued to starve in those countries during the shift. Some realities do not obey the dictates of language.

Mine is one of them. Whatever you call me, I remain crippled. But I don't care what you call me, so long as it isn't "differently abled," which strikes me as pure verbal garbage designed, by its ability to describe anyone, to describe no one. I subscribe to George Orwell's thesis that "the slovenliness of our language makes it easier for us to have foolish thoughts." And I refuse to participate in the degeneration of the language to the extent that I deny that I have lost anything in the course of this calamitous disease; I refuse to pretend that the only differences between you and me are the various ordinary ones that distinguish any one person from another. But call me "disabled" or "handicapped" if you like. I have long since grown accustomed to them; and if they are vague, at least they hint at the truth. Moreover, I use them myself. Society is no readier to accept crippledness than to accept death, war, sex, sweat, or wrinkles. I would never refer to another person as a cripple. It is the word I use to name only myself.

I haven't always been crippled, a fact for which I am soundly grateful. To be whole of limb is, I know from experience, infinitely more pleasant and useful than to be crippled; and if that knowledge leaves me open to bitterness at my loss, the physical soundness I once enjoyed (though I did not enjoy it half enough) is well worth the occasional stab of regret. Though never any good at sports, I was a normally active child and young adult. I climbed trees, played hopscotch, jumped rope, skated, swam, rode my bicycle, sailed. I despised team sports, spending some of the wretchedest afternoons of my life sweaty and humiliated, behind a field-hockey stick and under a basketball hoop. I tramped alone for miles along the bridle paths that webbed the woods behind the house I grew up in. I swayed through countless dim hours in the arms of one man or another under the scattered shot of light from mirrored balls, and gyrated through countless more as Tab Hunter and Johnny Mathis gave way to the Rolling Stones, Creedence Clearwater Revival, Cream. I walked down the aisle. I pushed baby carriages, changed tires in the rain, marched for peace.

When I was twenty-eight I started to trip and drop things. What at 6 first seemed my natural clumsiness soon became too pronounced to shrug off. I consulted a neurologist, who told me that I had a brain tumor. A battery of tests, increasingly disagreeable, revealed no tumor. About a year and a half later I developed a blurred spot in one eye. I had, at last, the episodes "disseminated in space and time" requisite for a diagnosis: multiple sclerosis. I have never been sorry for the doctor's initial misdiagnosis, however. For almost a week, until the negative results of the tests were in, I thought that I was going to die right away. Every day for the past nearly ten years, then, has been a kind of gift. I accept all gifts.

Multiple sclerosis is a chronic degenerative disease of the central 7 nervous system, in which the myelin that sheathes the nerves is somehow eaten away and scar tissue forms in its place, interrupting the nerves' signals. During its course, which is unpredictable and uncontrollable, one may lose vision, hearing, speech, the ability to walk, control of bladder and/or bowels, strength in any or all extremities, sensitivity to touch, vibration, and/or pain, potency, coordination of movements—the list of possibilities is lengthy and yes, horrifying. One may also lose one's sense of humor. That's the easiest to lose and the hardest to survive without.

In the past ten years, I have sustained some of these losses. Charac- 8 teristic of MS are sudden attacks, called exacerbations, followed by remissions, and these I have not had. Instead, my disease has been slowly progressive. My left leg is now so weak that I walk with the aid of a brace and a cane; and for distances I use an Amigo, a variation on the electric wheelchair that looks rather like an electrified kiddie car. I no longer have much use of my left hand. Now my right side is weakening as well. I still have the blurred spot in my right eye. Overall, though, I've been lucky so far. My world has, of necessity, been circumscribed by my losses, but the terrain left me has been ample enough for me to continue many of the activities that absorb me: writing, teaching, raising children and cats and plants and snakes, reading, speaking publicly about MS and depression, even playing bridge with people patient and honorable enough to let me scatter cards every which way without sneaking a peek.

Lest I begin to sound like Pollyanna, however, let me say that I don't like having MS. I hate it. My life holds realities—harsh ones, some of them—that no right-minded human being ought to accept without grumbling. One of them is fatigue. I know of no one with MS who does not complain of bone-weariness; in a disease that presents an astonishing variety of symptoms, fatigue seems to be a common factor. I wake up in the morning feeling the way most people do at the end of a bad day, and I take it from there. As a result, I spend a lot of time *in extremis* and, impatient with limitation, I tend to ignore my fatigue until my body breaks down in some way and forces rest. Then I miss picnics, dinner parties, poetry readings, the brief visits of old friends from out of town. The offspring of a puritanical tradition of exceptional venerability, I cannot view these lapses without shame. My life often seems a series of small failures to do as I ought.

I lead, on the whole, an ordinary life, probably rather like the one I would have led had I not had MS. I am lucky that my predilections were already solitary, sedentary, and bookish—unlike the world-famous French cellist I have read about, or the young woman I talked with one long afternoon who wanted only to be a jockey. I had just begun graduate school when I found out something was wrong with me, and I have remained, interminably, a graduate student. Perhaps I would not have if I'd thought I had the stamina to return to a full-time job as a technical editor; but I've enjoyed my studies.

In addition to studying, I teach writing courses. I also teach medical students how to give neurological examinations. I pick up freelance editing jobs here and there. I have raised a foster son and sent him into the world, where he has made me two grandbabies, and I am still escorting my daughter and son through adolescence. I go to Mass every Saturday. I am a superb, if messy, cook. I am also an enthusiastic laundress, capable of sorting a hamper full of clothes into five subtly differentiated piles, but a terrible housekeeper. I can do italic writing and, in an emergency, bathe an oil-soaked cat. I play a fiendish game of Scrabble. When I have the time and the money, I like to sit on my front steps with my husband, drinking Amaretto and smoking a cigar, as we imagine our counterparts in Leningrad and make sure that the sun gets down once more behind the sharp childish scrawl of the Tucson Mountains.

This lively plenty has its bleak complement, of course, in all the things I can no longer do. I will never run again, except in dreams, and one day I may have to write that I will never walk again. I like to go camping, but I can't follow George and the children along the trails

9

10

11

12

that wander out of a campsite through the desert or into the mountains. In fact, even on the level I've learned never to check the weather or try to hold a coherent conversation: I need all my attention for my wayward feet. Of late, I have begun to catch myself wondering how people can propel themselves without canes. With only one usable hand, I have to select my clothing with care not so much for style as for ease of ingress and egress, and even so, dressing can be laborious. I can no longer do fine stitchery, pick up babies, play the piano, braid my hair. I am immobilized by acute attacks of depression, which may or may not be physiologically related to MS but are certainly its logical concomitant.

These two elements, the plenty and the privation, are never pure, 13 nor are the delight and wretchedness that accompany them. Almost every pickle that I get into as a result of my weakness and clumsiness— and I get into plenty—is funny as well as maddening and sometimes painful. I recall one May afternoon when a friend and I were going out for a drink after finishing up at school. As we were climbing into opposite sides of my car, chatting, I tripped and fell, flat and hard, onto the asphalt parking lot, my abrupt departure interrupting him in mid-sentence. "Where'd you go?" he called as he came around the back of the car to find me hauling myself up by the door frame. "Are you all right?" Yes, I told him, I was fine, just a bit rattly, and we drove off to find a shady patio and some beer. When I got home an hour or so later, my daughter greeted me with "What have you done to yourself?" I looked down. One elbow of my white turtleneck with the green froggies, one knee of my white trousers, one white kneesock were blood-soaked. We peeled off the clothes and inspected the damage, which was nasty enough but not alarming. That part wasn't funny: The abrasions took a long time to heal, and one got a little infected. Even so, when I think of my friend talking earnestly, suddenly, to the hot thin air while I dropped from his view as though through a trap door, I find the image as silly as something from a Marx Brothers movie.

I may find it easier than other cripples to amuse myself because I 14 live propped by the acceptance and the assistance and, sometimes, the amusement of those around me. Grocery clerks tear my checks out of my checkbook for me, and sales clerks find chairs to put into dressing rooms when I want to try on clothes. The people I work with make sure I teach at times when I am least likely to be fatigued, in places I can get to, with the materials I need. My students, with one anonymous exception (in an end-of-the-semester evaluation) have been unperturbed by my disability. Some even like it. One was immensely cheered by the information that I paint my own fingernails; she decided, she told me, that if I could go to such trouble over fine details, she could keep on writing essays. I suppose I became some sort of bright-fingered muse. She wrote good essays, too.

The most important struts in the framework of my existence, of   15
course, are my husband and children. Dismayingly few marriages survive the MS test, and why should they? Most twenty-two- and nine-
teen-year-olds, like George and me, can vow in clear conscience, after a
childhood of chickenpox and summer colds, to keep one another in
sickness and in health so long as they both shall live. Not many are
equipped for catastrophe: the dismay, the depression, the extra work,
the boredom that a degenerative disease can insinuate into a relationship. And our society, with its emphasis on fun and its association of
fun with physical performance, offers little encouragement for a whole
spouse to stay with a crippled partner. Children experience similar
stresses when faced with a crippled parent, and they are more helpless,
since parents and children can't usually get divorced. They hate, of
course, to be different from their peers, and the child whose mother is
tacking down the aisle of a school auditorium packed with proud parents like a Cape Cod dinghy in a stiff breeze jolly well stands out in a
crowd. Deprived of legal divorce, the child can at least deny the
mother's disability, even her existence, forgetting to tell her about
recitals and PTA meetings, refusing to accompany her to stores or
church or the movies, never inviting friends to the house. Many do.

But I've been limping along for ten years now, and so far George   16
and the children are still at my left elbow, holding tight. Anne and
Matthew vacuum floors and dust furniture and haul trash and rake up
dog droppings and button my cuffs and bake lasagne and Toll House
cookies with just enough grumbling so I know that they don't have
brain fever. And far from hiding me, they're forever dragging me by
racks of fancy clothes or through teeming school corridors, or welcom-
ing gaggles of friends while I'm wandering through the house in Anne's
filmy pink babydoll pajamas. George generally calls before he brings
someone home, but he does just as many dumb thankless chores as the
children. And they all yell at me, laugh at some of my jokes, write me
funny letters when we're apart—in short, treat me as an ordinary
human being for whom they have some use. I think they like me.
Unless they're faking. . . .

Faking. There's the rub. Tugging at the fringes of my consciousness   17
always is the terror that people are kind to me only because I'm a cripple. My mother almost shattered me once, with that instinct mothers
have—blind, I think, in this case, but unerring nonetheless—for striking blows along the fault-lines of their children's hearts, by telling me,
in an attack on my selfishness, "We all have to make allowances for
you, of course, because of the way you are." From the distance of a couple of years, I have to admit that I haven't any idea just what she
meant, and I'm not sure that she knew either. She was awfully angry.
But at the time, as the words thudded home, I felt my worst fear, suddenly realized. I could bear being called selfish: I am. But I couldn't bear

the corroboration that those around me were doing in fact what I'd always suspected them of doing, professing fondness while silently putting up with me because of the way I am. A cripple. I've been a little cracked ever since.

Along with this fear that people are secretly accepting shoddy goods comes a relentless pressure to please — to prove myself worth the burdens I impose, I guess, or to build a substantial account of goodwill against which I may write drafts in times of need. Part of the pressure arises from social expectations. In our society, anyone who deviates from the norm had better find some way to compensate. Like fat people, who are expected to be jolly, cripples must bear their lot meekly and cheerfully. A grumpy cripple isn't playing by the rules. And much of the pressure is self-generated. Early on I vowed that, if I had to have MS, by God I was going to do it well. This is a class act, ladies and gentlemen. No tears, no recriminations, no faintheartedness. 18

One way and another, then, I wind up feeling like Tiny Tim, peering over the edge of the table at the Christmas goose, waving my crutch, piping down God's blessing on us all. Only sometimes I don't want to play Tiny Tim. I'd rather be Caliban, a most scurvy monster. Fortunately, at home no one much cares whether I'm a good cripple or a bad cripple as long as I make vichyssoise with fair regularity. One evening several years ago, Anne was reading at the dining-room table while I cooked dinner. As I opened a can of tomatoes, the can slipped in my left hand and juice spattered me and the counter with bloody spots. Fatigued and infuriated, I bellowed, "I'm so sick of being crippled!" Anne glanced at me over the top of her book. "There now," she said, "do you feel better?" "Yes," I said, "yes, I do." She went back to her reading. I felt better. That's about all the attention my scurviness ever gets. 19

Because I hate being crippled, I sometimes hate myself for being a cripple. Over the years I have come to expect — even accept — attacks of violent self-loathing. Luckily, in general our society no longer connects deformity and disease directly with evil (though a charismatic once told me that I have MS because a devil is in me) and so I'm allowed to move largely at will, even among small children. But I'm not sure that this revision of attitude has been particularly helpful. Physical imperfection, even freed of moral disapprobation, still defies and violates the ideal, especially for women, whose confinement in their bodies as objects of desire is far from over. Each age, of course, has its ideal, and I doubt that ours is any better or worse than any other. Today's ideal woman, who lives on the glossy pages of dozens of magazines, seems to be between the ages of eighteen and twenty-five; her hair has body, her teeth flash white, her breath smells minty, her underarms are dry; she has a career but is still a fabulous cook, especially of meals that take less than twenty minutes to prepare; she does not ordinarily 20 appear to have a husband or children; she is trim and deeply tanned; she jogs, swims, plays tennis, rides a bicycle, sails, but does not bowl; she travels widely, even to out-of-the-way places like Finland and Samoa, always in the company of the ideal man, who possesses a nearly identical set of characteristics. There are a few exceptions. Though usually white and often blonde, she may be black, Hispanic, Asian, or Native American, so long as she is unusually sleek. She may be old, provided she is selling a laxative or is Lauren Bacall. If she is selling a detergent, she may be married and have a flock of strikingly messy children. But she is never a cripple.

Like many women I know, I have always had an uneasy relationship 21 with my body. I was not a popular child, largely, I think now, because I was peculiar: intelligent, intense, moody, shy, given to unexpected actions and inexplicable notions and emotions. But as I entered adolescence, I believed myself unpopular because I was homely: my breasts too flat, my mouth too wide, my hips too narrow, my clothing never quite right in fit or style. I was not, in fact, particularly ugly, old photographs inform me, though I was well off the ideal; but I carried this sense of self-alienation with me into adulthood, where it regenerated in response to the depredations of MS. Even with my brace I walk with a limp so pronounced that, seeing myself on the videotape of a television program on the disabled, I couldn't believe that anything but an inchworm could make progress humping along like that. My shoulders droop and my pelvis thrusts forward as I try to balance myself upright, throwing my frame into a bony S. As a result of contractures, one shoulder is higher than the other and I carry one arm bent in front of me, the fingers curled into a claw. My left arm and leg have wasted into pipe-stems, and I try always to keep them covered. When I think about how my body must look to others, especially to men, to whom I have been trained to display myself, I feel ludicrous, even loathsome.

At my age, however, I don't spend much time thinking about my 22 appearance. The burning egocentricity of adolescence, which assures one that all the world is looking all the time, has passed, thank God, and I'm generally too caught up in what I'm doing to step back, as I used to, and watch myself as though upon a stage. I'm also too old to believe in the accuracy of self-image. I know that I'm not a hideous crone, that in fact, when I'm rested, well dressed, and well made up, I look fine. The self-loathing I feel is neither physically nor intellectually substantial. What I hate is not me but a disease.

I am not a disease. 23

And a disease is not—at least not singlehandedly—going to deter- 24 mine who I am, though at first it seemed to be going to. Adjusting to a chronic incurable illness, I have moved through a process similar to that outlined by Elizabeth Kübler-Ross in *On Death and Dying*. The major difference—and it is far more significant than most people recognize—is that I can't be sure of the outcome, as the terminally ill cancer patient can. Research studies indicate that, with proper medical care, I may achieve a "normal" life span. And in our society, with its vision of death as the ultimate evil, worse even than decrepitude, the response to such news is, "Oh well, at least you're not going to *die*." Are there worse things than dying? I think that there may be.

I think of two women I know, both with MS, both enough older 25 than I to have served as models. One took to her bed several years ago and has been there ever since. Although she can sit in a high-backed wheelchair, because she is incontinent she refuses to go out at all, even though incontinence pants, which are readily available at any pharmacy, could protect her from embarrassment. Instead, she stays at home and insists that her husband, a small quiet man, a retired civil servant, stay there with her except for a quick weekly foray to the supermarket. The other woman, whose illness was diagnosed when she was eighteen, a nursing student engaged to a young doctor, finished her training, married her doctor, accompanied him to Germany when he was in the service, bore three sons and a daughter, now grown and gone. When she can, she travels with her husband; she plays bridge, embroiders, swims regularly; she works, like me, as a symptomatic-patient instructor of medical students in neurology. Guess which woman I hope to be.

At the beginning, I thought about having MS almost incessantly. 26 And because of the unpredictable course of the disease, my thoughts were always terrified. Each night I'd get into bed wondering whether I'd get out again the next morning, whether I'd be able to see, to speak, to hold a pen between my fingers. Knowing that the day might come when I'd be physically incapable of killing myself, I thought perhaps I ought to do so right away, while I still had the strength. Gradually I came to understand that the Nancy who might one day lie inert under a bedsheet, arms and legs paralyzed, unable to feed or bathe herself, unable to reach out for a gun, a bottle of pills, was not the Nancy I was at present, and that I could not presume to make decisions for that future Nancy, who might well not want in the least to die. Now the only provision I've made for the future Nancy is that when the time comes—and it is likely to come in the form of pneumonia, friend to the weak and the old—I am not to be treated with machines and medications. If she is unable to communicate by then, I hope she will be satisfied with these terms.

Thinking all the time about having MS grew tiresome and intru- 27 sive, especially in the large and tragic mode in which I was accustomed to considering my plight. Months and even years went by without catastrophe (at least without one related to MS), and really I was awfully busy, what with George and children and snakes and students and poems, and I hadn't the time, let alone the inclination, to devote myself to being a disease. Too, the richer my life became, the funnier it seemed, as though there were some connection between largesse and laughter, and so my tragic stance began to waver until, even with the aid of a brace and cane, I couldn't hold it for very long at a time.

After several years I was satisfied with my adjustment. I had suffered 28 my grief and fury and terror, I thought, but now I was at ease with my lot. Then one summer day I set out with George and the children across the desert for a vacation in California. Part way to Yuma I became aware that my right leg felt funny. "I think I've had an exacerbation," I told George. "What shall we do?" he asked. "I think we'd better get the hell to California," I said, "because I don't know whether I'll ever make it again." So we went on to San Diego and then to Orange, and up the Pacific Coast Highway to Santa Cruz, across to Yosemite, down to Sequoia and Joshua Tree, and so back over the desert to home. It was a fine two-week trip, filled with friends and fair weather, and I wouldn't have missed it for the world, though I did in fact make it back to California two years later. Nor would there have been any point in missing it, since in MS, once the symptoms have appeared, the neurological damage has been done, and there's no way to predict or prevent that damage.

The incident spoiled my self-satisfaction, however. It renewed my 29 grief and fury and terror, and I learned that one never finishes adjusting to MS. I don't know now why I thought one would. One does not, after all, finish adjusting to life, and MS is simply a fact of my life—not my favorite fact, of course—but as ordinary as my nose and my tropical fish and my yellow Mazda station wagon. It may at any time get worse, but no amount of worry or anticipation can prepare me for a new loss. My life is a lesson in losses. I learn one at a time.

And I had best be patient in the learning, since I'll have to do it like 30 it or not. As any rock fan knows, you can't always get what you want. Particularly when you have MS. You can't, for example, get cured. In recent years researchers and the organizations that fund research have started to pay MS some attention even though it isn't fatal; perhaps they have begun to see that life is something other than a quantitative phenomenon, that one may be very much alive for a very long time in a life that isn't worth living. The researchers have made some progress toward understanding the mechanism of the disease: It may well be an autoimmune reaction triggered by a slow-acting virus. But they are nowhere near its prevention, control, or cure. And most of us want to be cured. Some, unable to accept incurability, grasp at one treatment after another, no matter how bizarre: megavitamin therapy, gluten-free diet, injections of cobra venom, hypothermal suits, lymphocytopharesis, hyperbaric chambers. Many treatments are probably harmless enough, but none are curative.

The absence of a cure often makes MS patients bitter toward their 31 doctors. Doctors are, after all, the priests of modern society, the new shamans, whose business is to heal, and many an MS patient roves from one to another, searching for the "good" doctor who will make him well. Doctors too think of themselves as healers, and for this reason many have trouble dealing with MS patients, whose disease in its intransigence defeats their aims and mocks their skills. Too few doctors, it is true, treat their patients as whole human beings, but the reverse is also true. I have always tried to be gentle with my doctors, who often have more at stake in terms of ego than I do. I may be frustrated, maddened, depressed by the incurability of my disease, but I am not diminished by it, and they are. When I push myself up from my seat in the waiting room and stumble toward them, I incarnate the limitation of their powers. The least I can do is refuse to press on their tenderest spots.

This gentleness is part of the reason that I'm not sorry to be a cripple. I didn't have it before. Perhaps I'd have developed it anyway— how could I know such a thing?—and I wish I had more of it, but I'm glad of what I have. It has opened and enriched my life enormously, this sense that my frailty and need must be mirrored in others, that in searching for and shaping a stable core in a life wrenched by change and loss, change and loss, I must recognize the same process, under individual conditions, in the lives around me. I do not deprecate such knowledge, however I've come by it. 32

All the same, if a cure were found, would I take it? In a minute. I may be a cripple, but I'm only occasionally a loony and never a saint. Anyway, in my brand of theology God doesn't give bonus points for a limp. I'd take a cure; I just don't need one. A friend who also has MS startled me once by asking, "Do you ever say to yourself, 'Why me, Lord?'" "No, Michael, I don't," I told him, "because whenever I try, the only response I can think of is 'Why not?'" If I could make a cosmic deal, who would I put in my place? What in my life would I give up in exchange for sound limbs and a thrilling rush of energy? No one. Nothing. I might as well do the job myself. Now that I'm getting the hang of it. 33

THINKING CRITICALLY ABOUT THE TEXT

According to the old saying, every cloud has a silver lining. Mairs weighs both the positive and negative sides of dealing with a difficult illness. Why and how does adversity bring out the good in people? Consider her responses as well as your own.

QUESTIONS ON SUBJECT

1. Why does Mairs choose to identify herself by the term *cripple*? What objections does she have to terms more generally accepted in American culture today (i.e., *disabled, handicapped*)? How do you think she would respond to the more current phrase, *physically challenged*?

2. Mairs says she had been planning to write this essay for some time. What incident finally prompted her to do it? What is noteworthy about her response to this incident?

3. In paragraph 5, review the normal activities Mairs engaged in as a child and young adult. Why do you think she chooses to list these particular activities?

4. As Mairs sees it, what is the relationship that exists between doctors and people with multiple sclerosis?

5. Does Mairs feel diminished by her affliction? Why, or why not? Do you think she's being honest in her assessment?

QUESTIONS ON STRATEGY

1. For what purpose does Mairs introduce her essay with the quote from Louise Bogan? (Glossary: *Purpose*) How does this quote bear on her topic?

2. Although this long essay covers many years and numerous ideas, it flows seamlessly for the reader. In large measure, this unity is brought about by the use of careful transitions from paragraph to paragraph. (Glossary: *Transitions; Unity*) Find several examples of transitions that move the piece forward effectively even though the paragraphs they connect are quite different in form or content.

3. Mairs says that an MS sufferer may lose many things in life, including a sense of humor, "the easiest to lose and the hardest to survive without" (paragraph 7). What are some of the many ways she shows that she has not lost hers? Is humor appropriate in a piece of writing about such a dire topic?

4. Mairs does not recount her struggles with MS as a strict narrative in chronological order. (Glossary: *Narration*) Why do you think she chooses to structure her essay largely on the contrast between past and present? (Glossary: *Comparison and Contrast*)

5. Throughout this essay, Mairs uses brief narrative vignettes, such as her dropping a can of tomatoes or her family trip to California, to illustrate her points about living with multiple sclerosis. (Glossary: *Illustration; Narration*) Explain how these two strategies together support Mairs's purpose.

QUESTIONS ON DICTION AND VOCABULARY

1. What does Mairs mean when she says, at the end of paragraph 3, "Some realities do not obey the dictates of language"? By what example does she illustrate this assertion? (Glossary: *Illustration*)

2. Why does Mairs describe herself as a "bright-fingered muse" at the end of paragraph 14? Beyond the incident she describes here, what is the significance of the phrase? In what ways do you think this phrase reflects the way Mairs views herself?

3. What is Mairs's tone in this essay? How does she establish her tone? (Glossary: *Tone*)

CLASSROOM ACTIVITY FOR COMBINING STRATEGIES

Mairs's extended definition makes a point about how events in life often lead to choices and varying results—for example, her description in paragraph 25 of two different women with multiple sclerosis. As a class, discuss how Mairs uses cause and effect to support her extended definition and her main point.

WRITING SUGGESTIONS

1. Mairs says, "I lead, on the whole, an ordinary life" (paragraph 10). Many of her readers could be excused for considering it quite extraordinary. What is an ordinary life? How much of what one considers ordinary depends on one's perspective? Write an essay in which you define an ordinary life, including examples of how you follow and fail to follow your own definition. (Glossary: *Definition*)

2. Interview a student or faculty member at your college or university who would meet Mairs's definition of a "cripple." How does this person's experience of academic life compare with hers? With what particular difficulties and successes has your interviewee been faced? Write an essay illustrating the life led in an academic institution by the person you interviewed. (Glossary: *Illustration*)

3. Many laws have been enacted at both the national and the state levels to provide equal access and opportunities for people with disabilities. Acquaint yourself with the major laws in your area, with the effects of these laws, and with the cost of implementing them. Do the research in your college library and on the Internet. How much responsibility—in terms of money, time, and adaptive technology—should a society assume for people who need special accommodations? Write an essay in which you examine the role you feel society should play in the lives of the disabled.

Shooting an Elephant

George Orwell

 *George Orwell (1903–1950) was capable of capturing the reader's imagination as few writers have ever done. Born in Bengal, India, but raised and educated in England, he chose to work as a civil servant in the British colonies after his schooling and was sent to Burma at nineteen as an assistant superintendent of police. Disillusioned by his firsthand experiences of public life under British colonial rule, he resigned in 1929 and returned to England to begin a career in writing. He captured the exotic mystery of life in the colonies, along with its many injustices and ironies, in such works as* Down and Out in Paris and London *(1933) and* The Road to Wigan Pier *(1937). His most famous books are, of course,* Animal Farm *(1945), a satire on the Russian Revolution, and* 1984 *(1949), a chilling novel set in an imagined totalitarian state of the future. Orwell maintained a lifelong interest in international social and political issues.*

"Shooting an Elephant" was published in the British magazine New Writing *in 1936. Adolf Hitler, Benito Mussolini, and Joseph Stalin were in power, building the "younger empires" that Orwell refers to in the second paragraph, and the old British Empire was soon to decline, as Orwell predicted. In this essay, Orwell tells of a time when, in a position of authority, he found himself compelled to act against his convictions.*

PREPARING TO READ

Have you ever acted against your better judgment to save face with your friends or relatives? What motivated you to take the action that you did, and what did you learn from the experience?

I n Moulmein, in Lower Burma, I was hated by large numbers of people—the only time in my life that I have been important enough for this to happen to me. I was subdivisional police officer of the town, and in an aimless, petty kind of way anti-European feeling was very bitter. No one had the guts to raise a riot, but if a European woman went through the bazaars alone somebody would probably spit betel juice[1] over her dress. As a police officer I was an obvious target and was baited whenever it seemed safe to do so. When a nimble Burman tripped me up on the football field and the referee (another Burman) looked the other way, the crowd yelled with hideous laughter. This happened more than once. In the end the sneering yellow faces of young men that met me everywhere, the insults hooted after me when I was at a

1

---

1. The juice of an Asiatic plant whose leaves are chewed to induce narcotic effects. (Ed.)

safe distance, got badly on my nerves. The young Buddhist priests were the worst of all. There were several thousands of them in the town and none of them seemed to have anything to do except stand on street corners and jeer at Europeans.

All this was perplexing and upsetting. For at that time I had already made up my mind that imperialism was an evil thing and the sooner I chucked up my job and got out of it the better. Theoretically—and secretly, of course—I was all for the Burmese and all against the oppressors, the British. As for the job I was doing, I hated it more bitterly than I can perhaps make clear. In a job like that you see the dirty work of Empire at close quarters. The wretched prisoners huddling in the stinking cages of the lockups, the grey, cowed faces of the long-term convicts, the scarred buttocks of the men who had been flogged with bamboos— all these oppressed me with an intolerable sense of guilt. But I could get nothing into perspective. I was young and ill-educated and I had had to think out my problems in the utter silence that is imposed on every Englishman in the East. I did not even know that the British Empire is dying, still less did I know that it is a great deal better than the younger empires that are going to supplant it. All I knew was that I was stuck between my hatred of the empire I served and my rage against the evil-spirited little beasts who tried to make my job impossible. With one part of my mind I thought of the British Raj[2] as an unbreakable tyranny, as something clamped down, in *saecula saeculorum*,[3] upon the will of prostrate peoples; with another part I thought that the greatest joy in the world would be to drive a bayonet into a Buddhist priest's guts. Feelings like these are the normal byproducts of imperialism; ask any Anglo-Indian official, if you can catch him off duty.

One day something happened which in a roundabout way was enlightening. It was a tiny incident in itself, but it gave me a better glimpse than I had had before of the real nature of imperialism—the real motives for which despotic governments act. Early one morning the subinspector at a police station the other end of town rang me up on the phone and said that an elephant was ravaging the bazaar. Would I please come and do something about it? I did not know what I could do, but I wanted to see what was happening and I got on to a pony and started out. I took my rifle, an old .44 Winchester and much too small to kill an elephant, but I thought the noise might be useful *in terrorem*. Various Burmans stopped me on the way and told me about the elephant's doings. It was not, of course, a wild elephant, but a tame one which had gone "must."[4] It had been chained up, as tame elephants always are

---

2. British rule, especially in India. (Ed.)
3. From time immemorial. (Ed.)
4. That is, gone into an uncontrollable frenzy. (Ed.)

when their attack of "must" is due, but on the previous night it had broken its chain and escaped. Its mahout,[5] the only person who could manage it when it was in that state, had set out in pursuit, but had taken the wrong direction and was now twelve hours' journey away, and in the morning the elephant had suddenly reappeared in the town. The Burmese population had no weapons and were quite helpless against it. It had already destroyed somebody's bamboo hut, killed a cow and raided some fruit stalls and devoured the stock; also it had met the municipal rubbish van and, when the driver jumped out and took to his heels, had turned the van over and inflicted violences upon it.

The Burmese subinspector and some Indian constables were wait- 4
ing for me in the quarter where the elephant had been seen. It was a very poor quarter, a labyrinth of squalid bamboo huts, thatched with palmleaf, winding all over a steep hillside. I remember that it was a cloudy, stuffy morning at the beginning of the rains. We began questioning the people as to where the elephant had gone and, as usual, failed to get any definite information. That is invariably the case in the East; a story always sounds clear enough at a distance, but the nearer you get to the scene of events the vaguer it becomes. Some of the people said that the elephant had gone in one direction, some said that he had gone in another, some professed not even to have heard of any elephant. I had almost made up my mind that the whole story was a pack of lies, when we heard yells a little distance away. There was a loud, scandalized cry of "Go away, child! Go away this instant!" and an old woman with a switch in her hand came round the corner of a hut, violently shooing away a crowd of naked children. Some more women followed, clicking their tongues and exclaiming; evidently there was something that the children ought not to have seen. I rounded the hut and saw a man's dead body sprawling in the mud. He was an Indian, a black Dravidian coolie,[6] almost naked, and he could not have been dead many minutes. The people said that the elephant had come suddenly upon him round the corner of the hut, caught him with its trunk, put its foot on his back and ground him into the earth. This was the rainy season and the ground was soft, and his face had scored a trench a foot deep and a couple of yards long. He was lying on his belly with arms crucified and head sharply twisted to one side. His face was coated with mud, the eyes wide open, the teeth bared and grinning with an expression of unendurable agony. (Never tell me, by the way, that the dead look peaceful. Most of the corpses I have seen looked devilish.) The friction of the great beast's foot had stripped the skin from his back as neatly as one skins a rabbit. As soon as I saw the dead man I

5. The keeper and driver of an elephant. (Ed.)
6. An unskilled laborer. (Ed.)

sent an orderly to a friend's house nearby to borrow an elephant rifle. I had already sent back the pony, not wanting it to go mad with fright and throw me if it smelled the elephant.

The orderly came back in a few minutes with a rifle and five car- 5 tridges, and meanwhile some Burmans had arrived and told us that the elephant was in the paddy fields below, only a few hundred yards away. As I started forward practically the whole population of the quarter flocked out of the houses and followed me. They had seen the rifle and were all shouting excitedly that I was going to shoot the elephant. They had not shown much interest in the elephant when he was merely ravaging their homes, but it was different now that he was going to be shot. It was a bit of fun to them, as it would be to an English crowd; besides they wanted the meat. It made me vaguely uneasy. I had no intention of shooting the elephant—I had merely sent for the rifle to defend myself if necessary—and it is always unnerving to have a crowd following you. I marched down the hill, looking and feeling a fool, with the rifle over my shoulder and an ever-growing army of people jostling at my heels. At the bottom, when you got away from the huts, there was a metalled road[7] and beyond that a miry waste of paddy fields a thousand yards across, not yet ploughed but soggy from the first rains and dotted with coarse grass. The elephant was standing eight yards from the road, his left side towards us. He took not the slightest notice of the crowd's approach. He was tearing up bunches of grass, beating them against his knees to clean them and stuffing them into his mouth.

I had halted on the road. As soon as I saw the elephant I knew with 6 perfect certainty that I ought not to shoot him. It is a serious matter to shoot a working elephant—it is comparable to destroying a huge and costly piece of machinery—and obviously one ought not to do it if it can possibly be avoided. And at that distance, peacefully eating, the elephant looked no more dangerous than a cow. I thought then and I think now that his attack of "must" was already passing off; in which case he would merely wander harmlessly about until the mahout came back and caught him. Moreover, I did not in the least want to shoot him. I decided that I would watch him for a little while to make sure that he did not turn savage again, and then go home.

But at that moment, I glanced round at the crowd that had fol- 7 lowed me. It was an immense crowd, two thousand at the least and growing every minute. It blocked the road for a long distance on either side. I looked at the sea of yellow faces above the garish clothes—faces all happy and excited over this bit of fun, all certain that the elephant was going to be shot. They were watching me as they would watch a

---

7. A road made of broken or crushed stone. (Ed.)

conjuror about to perform a trick. They did not like me, but with the magical rifle in my hands I was momentarily worth watching. And suddenly I realized that I should have to shoot the elephant after all. The people expected it of me and I had got to do it; I could feel their two thousand wills pressing me forward, irresistibly. And it was at this moment, as I stood there with the rifle in my hands, that I first grasped the hollowness, the futility of the white man's dominion in the East. Here was I, the white man with his gun, standing in front of the unarmed native crowd—seemingly the leading actor of the piece; but in reality I was only an absurd puppet pushed to and fro by the will of those yellow faces behind. I perceived in this moment that when the white man turns tyrant it is his own freedom that he destroys. He becomes a sort of hollow, posing dummy, the conventionalized figure of a sahib.[8] For it is the condition of his rule that he shall spend his life in trying to impress the "natives," and so in every crisis he has got to do what the "natives" expect of him. He wears a mask, and his face grows to fit it. I had got to shoot the elephant. I had committed myself to doing it when I sent for the rifle. A sahib has got to act like a sahib; he has got to appear resolute, to know his own mind and do definite things. To come all that way, rifle in hand, with two thousand people marching at my heels, and then to trail feebly away, having done nothing—no, that was impossible. The crowd would laugh at me. And my whole life, every white man's life in the East, was one long struggle not to be laughed at.

But I did not want to shoot the elephant. I watched him beating his bunch of grass against his knees, with that preoccupied grandmotherly air that elephants have. It seemed to me that it would be murder to shoot him. At that age I was not squeamish about killing animals, but I had never shot an elephant and never wanted to. (Somehow it always seems worse to kill a *large* animal.) Besides, there was the beast's owner to be considered. Alive, the elephant was worth at least a hundred pounds; dead, he would only be worth the value of his tusks, five pounds, possibly. But I had got to act quickly. I turned to some experienced-looking Burmans who had been there when we arrived, and asked them how the elephant had been behaving. They all said the same thing: He took no notice of you if you left him alone, but he might charge if you went too close to him. 8

It was perfectly clear to me what I ought to do. I ought to walk up to within, say, twenty-five yards of the elephant and test his behavior. If he charged, I could shoot; if he took no notice of me, it would be safe to leave him until the mahout came back. But also I knew that I was going to do no such thing. I was a poor shot with a rifle and the ground 9

---

8. A title of respect when addressing Europeans in colonial India. (Ed.)

was soft mud into which one would sink at every step. If the elephant charged and I missed him, I should have about as much chance as a toad under a steamroller. But even then I was not thinking particularly of my own skin, only of the watchful yellow faces behind. For at that moment, with the crowd watching me, I was not afraid in the ordinary sense, as I would have been if I had been alone. A white man mustn't be frightened in front of "natives"; and so, in general, he isn't frightened. The sole thought in my mind was that if anything went wrong those two thousand Burmans would see me pursued, caught, trampled on, and reduced to a grinning corpse like that Indian up the hill. And if that happened it was quite probable that some of them would laugh. That would never do. There was only one alternative. I shoved the cartridges into the magazine and lay down on the road to get a better aim.

The crowd grew very still, and a deep, low, happy sigh, as of people   10
who see the theater curtain go up at last, breathed from innumerable throats. They were going to have their bit of fun after all. The rifle was a beautiful German thing with cross-hair sights. I did not then know that in shooting an elephant one would shoot to cut an imaginary bar running from ear-hole to ear-hole. I ought, therefore, as the elephant was sideways on, to have aimed straight at his ear-hole; actually I aimed several inches in front of this, thinking the brain would be further forward.

When I pulled the trigger I did not hear the bang or feel the kick—   11
one never does when a shot goes home—but I heard the devilish roar of glee that went up from the crowd. In that instant, in too short a time, one would have thought, even for the bullet to get there, a mysterious, terrible change had come over the elephant. He neither stirred nor fell, but every line of his body had altered. He looked suddenly stricken, shrunken, immensely old, as though the frightful impact of the bullet had paralyzed him without knocking him down. At last, after what seemed a long time—it might have been five seconds, I dare say—he sagged flabbily to his knees. His mouth slobbered. An enormous senility seemed to have settled upon him. One could have imagined him thousands of years old. I fired again into the same spot. At the second shot he did not collapse but climbed with desperate slowness to his feet and stood weakly upright, with legs sagging and head drooping. I fired a third time. That was the shot that did for him. You could see the agony of it jolt his whole body and knock the last remnant of strength from his legs. But in falling he seemed for a moment to rise, for as his hind legs collapsed beneath him he seemed to tower upward like a huge rock toppling, his trunk reaching skywards like a tree. He trumpeted, for the first and only time. And then down he came, his belly towards me, with a crash that seemed to shake the ground even where I lay.

I got up. The Burmans were already racing past me across the mud.   12
It was obvious that the elephant would never rise again, but he was not

dead. He was breathing very rhythmically with long rattling gasps, his great mound of a side painfully rising and falling. His mouth was wide open. I could see far down into caverns of pale pink throat. I waited a long time for him to die, but his breathing did not weaken. Finally I fired my two remaining shots into the spot where I thought his heart must be. The thick blood welled out of him like red velvet, but still he did not die. His body did not even jerk when the shots hit him, the tortured breathing continued without a pause. He was dying, very slowly and in great agony, but in some world remote from me where not even a bullet could damage him further. I felt I had got to put an end to that dreadful noise. It seemed dreadful to see the great beast lying there, powerless to move and yet powerless to die, and not even to be able to finish him. I sent back for my small rifle and poured shot after shot into his heart and down his throat. They seemed to make no impression. The tortured gasps continued as steadily as the ticking of a clock.

In the end I could not stand it any longer and went away. I heard later that it took him half an hour to die. Burmans were bringing dahs[9] and baskets even before I left, and I was told they had stripped his body almost to the bones by the afternoon.   13

Afterwards, of course, there were endless discussions about the shooting of the elephant. The owner was furious, but he was only an Indian and could do nothing. Besides, legally I had done the right thing, for a mad elephant has to be killed, like a mad dog, if its owner fails to control it. Among the Europeans opinion was divided. The older men said I was right, the younger men said it was a damn shame to shoot an elephant for killing a coolie, because the elephant was worth more than any damn Coringhee coolie. And afterwards I was very glad that the coolie had been killed; it put me legally in the right and it gave me sufficient pretext for shooting the elephant. I often wondered whether any of the others grasped that I had done it solely to avoid looking a fool.   14

THINKING CRITICALLY ABOUT THE TEXT

Even though Orwell does not want to shoot the elephant, he does. How does he rationalize his behavior? On what grounds was Orwell legally in the right? What alternatives did he have? What do you think Orwell learned from this incident?

QUESTIONS ON SUBJECT

1. What do you suppose would have happened had Orwell not sent for an elephant rifle?

---

9. Heavy knives. (Ed.)

2. What is imperialism, and what discovery about imperialism does Orwell make during the course of the event he narrates?

3. What does Orwell mean when he says, "I was very glad that the coolie had been killed" (paragraph 14)?

4. What is the point of Orwell's final paragraph? How does that paragraph affect your response to the whole essay?

5. Orwell wrote "Shooting an Elephant" some years after the event occurred. What does his account of the event gain with the passage of time? Explain.

QUESTIONS ON STRATEGY

1. Why do you think Orwell is so meticulous in establishing the setting for his essay in paragraphs 1 and 2?

2. What do you think was Orwell's purpose in telling this story? (Glossary: *Purpose*) Cite evidence from the text that indicates to you that purpose. Does he accomplish his purpose?

3. Orwell is quick to capitalize on the ironies of the circumstances surrounding the events he narrates. (Glossary: *Irony*) Identify any circumstances you found ironic, and explain what this irony contributes to Orwell's overall purpose.

4. What part of the essay struck you most strongly? The shooting itself? Orwell's feelings? The descriptions of the Burmans and their behavior? What is it about Orwell's prose that enhances the impact of that passage for you? Explain.

5. "Shooting an Elephant" is, first of all, a narrative; Orwell has a story to tell. (Glossary: *Narration*) But Orwell uses other strategies in support of narration to help develop and give meaning to his story. Identify passages in which Orwell uses description, illustration, and cause and effect analysis, and explain how each enhances the incident he narrates. (Glossary: *Cause and Effect Analysis; Description; Illustration*)

QUESTIONS ON DICTION AND VOCABULARY

1. A British citizen, Orwell uses British English. Cite several examples of this British diction. How might an American say the same thing?

2. Identify several of the metaphors and similes that Orwell uses, and explain what each adds to his descriptions in this essay. (Glossary: *Figures of Speech*)

3. As a writer, Orwell always advocated using strong action verbs because they are vivid and eliminate unnecessary modification. (Glossary: *Verb*) For example, in paragraph 1 he uses the verb *jeer* instead of the verb *yell* plus the adverb *derisively*. Identify other strong verbs that you found particularly striking. What do these strong verbs add to Orwell's prose style?

CLASSROOM ACTIVITY FOR COMBINING STRATEGIES

Orwell's argument is couched in a very moving and affecting narrative replete with powerful descriptions. Think about how you might use narration to enhance an argument you have already written or are planning to write. How might your case, in effect, be made by telling a story—by showing rather than telling? Think about whether it would be more effective in your case to present your argument in one long narrative or to use several episodes to make your point. Discuss your approach with other members of your class to get their responses to your plans.

WRITING SUGGESTIONS

1. Write an essay recounting a situation in which you felt compelled to act against your convictions. (Glossary: *Narration*) Before you start writing, you may find it helpful to consider one or more of the following questions and to review your Preparing to Read response for this essay. How can you justify your action? How much freedom of choice did you actually have, and what were the limits on your freedom? On what basis can you refuse to subordinate your convictions to others' or to society's?

2. Consider situations in which you have been a leader, like Orwell, or a follower. As a leader, what was your attitude toward your followers? As a follower, what did you feel toward your leader? Using Orwell's essay and your own experiences, what conclusions can you draw about leaders and followers? Write an essay in which you explore the relationship between leaders and followers.

A Modest Proposal

Jonathan Swift

One of the world's great satirists, Jonathan Swift was born in 1667 to English parents in Dublin, Ireland, and was educated at Trinity College. When his early efforts at a literary career in England met no success, he returned to Ireland in 1694 and was ordained an Anglican clergyman. From 1713 until his death in 1745, he was dean of Dublin's St. Patricks's Cathedral. A prolific chronicler of human folly, Swift is best known as the author of Gulliver's Travels *and of the work included here, "A Modest Proposal."*

In the 1720s Ireland had suffered several famines, but the English gentry, who owned most of the land, did nothing to alleviate the suffering of tenant farmers and their families; nor would the English government intervene. A number of pamphlets were circulated proposing solutions to the Irish problem.

"A Modest Proposal," published anonymously in 1729, was Swift's ironic contribution to the discussion.

PREPARING TO READ

Satire is a literary and dramatic art form wherein the shortcomings, foibles, abuses, and idiocies of both people and institutions are accented and held up for ridicule in order to shame their perpetrators into reforming themselves. Perhaps the very easiest way to see satire around us today is in the work of our political cartoonists. Think of individuals and institutions both here and abroad who today might make good subjects for satire.

FOR PREVENTING THE CHILDREN OF POOR PEOPLE IN IRELAND
FROM BEING A BURDEN TO THEIR PARENTS OR COUNTRY,
AND FOR MAKING THEM BENEFICIAL TO THE PUBLIC

I t is a melancholy object to those who walk through this great town[1] or travel in the country, when they see the streets, the roads, and cabin doors, crowded with beggars of the female sex, followed by three, four, or six children, all in rags and importuning every passenger for an alms. These mothers, instead of being able to work for their honest livelihood, are forced to employ all their time in strolling to beg sustenance for their helpless infants, who, as they grow up, either turn

1

---

1. Dublin. (Ed.)

thieves for want of work, or leave their dear native country to fight for the Pretender in Spain, or sell themselves to the Barbadoes.[2]

I think it is agreed by all parties that this prodigious number of children in the arms, or on the backs, or at the heels of their mothers, and frequently of their fathers, is in the present deplorable state of the kingdom a very great additional grievance; and therefore whoever could find out a fair, cheap, and easy method of making these children sound, useful members of the commonwealth would deserve so well of the public as to have his statue set up for a preserver of the nation.

But my intention is very far from being confined to provide only for the children of professed beggars; it is of a much greater extent, and shall take in the whole number of infants at a certain age who are born of parents in effect as little able to support them as those who demand our charity in the streets.

As to my own part, having turned my thoughts for many years upon this important subject, and maturely weighed the several schemes of other projectors,[3] I have always found them grossly mistaken in their computation. It is true, a child just dropped from its dam may be supported by her milk for a solar year, with little other nourishment; at most not above the value of two shillings, which the mother may certainly get, or the value in scraps, by her lawful occupation of begging; and it is exactly at one year old that I propose to provide for them in such a manner as instead of being a charge upon their parents or the parish, or wanting food and raiment for the rest of their lives, they shall on the contrary contribute to the feeding, and partly to the clothing, of many thousands.

There is likewise another great advantage in my scheme, that it will prevent those voluntary abortions, and that horrid practice of women murdering their bastard children, alas, too frequent among us, sacrificing the poor innocent babes, I doubt, more to avoid the expense than the shame, which would move tears and pity in the most savage and inhuman breast.

The number of souls in this kingdom[4] being usually reckoned one million and a half, of these I calculate there may be about two hundred thousand couples whose wives are breeders; from which number I subtract thirty thousand couples who are able to maintain their own children, although I apprehend there cannot be so many under the present

2. Many Irish Catholics were loyal to James Stuart, a claimant (or "pretender") to the English crown, and followed him into exile. Others, stricken by poverty, sold themselves into virtual slavery in order to escape to British colonies (like Barbadoes) in the New World. (Ed.)

3. Proposers of solutions. (Ed.)

4. Ireland. (Ed.)

distresses of the kingdom; but this being granted, there will remain an hundred and seventy thousand breeders. I again subtract fifty thousand for those women who miscarry, or whose children die by accident or disease within the year. There only remain an hundred and twenty thousand children of poor parents annually born. The question therefore is, how this number shall be reared and provided for, which, as I have already said, under the present situation of affairs, is utterly impossible by all the methods hitherto proposed. For we can neither employ them in handicraft or agriculture; we neither build houses (I mean in the country) nor cultivate land. They can very seldom pick up a livelihood by stealing till they arrive at six years old, except where they are of towardly parts;[5] although I confess they learn the rudiments much earlier, during which time they can however be looked upon only as probationers, as I have been informed by a principal gentleman in the county of Cavan, who protested to me that he never knew above one or two instances under the age of six, even in a part of the kingdom so renowned for the quickest proficiency in that art.

7   I am assured by our merchants that a boy or a girl before twelve years old is no salable commodity; and even when they come to this age they will not yield above three pounds, or three pounds and half a crown at most on the Exchange; which cannot turn to account either to the parents or the kingdom, the charge of nutriment and rags having been at least four times that value.

8   I shall now therefore humbly propose my own thoughts, which I hope will not be liable to the least objection.

9   I have been assured by a very knowing American of my acquaintance in London, that a young healthy child well nursed is at a year old a most delicious, nourishing, and wholesome food, whether stewed, roasted, baked, or boiled; and I make no doubt that it will equally serve in a fricassee or a ragout.[6]

10   I do therefore humbly offer it to public consideration that of the hundred and twenty thousand children, already computed, twenty thousand may be reserved for breed, whereof only one fourth part to be males, which is more than we allow to sheep, black cattle, or swine; and my reason is that these children are seldom the fruits of marriage, a circumstance not much regarded by our savages, therefore one male will be sufficient to serve four females. That the remaining hundred thousand may at a year old be offered in sale to the persons of quality and fortune through the kingdom, always advising the mother to let them suck plentifully in the last month, so as to render them plump and fat for a good table. A child will make two dishes at an entertainment for

---

5. Or "advanced for their age." (Ed.)
6. Types of stews. (Ed.)

friends; and when the family dines alone, the fore or hind quarter will make a reasonable dish, and seasoned with a little pepper or salt will be very good boiled on the fourth day, especially in winter.

I have reckoned upon a medium that a child just born will weigh twelve pounds, and in a solar year if tolerably nursed increaseth to twenty-eight pounds.

I grant this food will be somewhat dear, and therefore very proper for landlords, who, as they have already devoured most of the parents, seem to have the best title to the children.

Infant's flesh will be in season throughout the year, but more plentiful in March, and a little before and after. For we are told by a grave author, an eminent French physician,[7] that fish being a prolific diet, there are more children born in Roman Catholic countries about nine months after Lent than at any other season; therefore, reckoning a year after Lent, the markets will be more glutted than usual, because the number of popish infants is at least three to one in this kingdom; and therefore it will have one other collateral advantage, by lessening the number of papists among us.

I have already computed the charge of nursing a beggar's child (in which list I reckon all cottagers, laborers, and four fifths of the farmers) to be about two shillings per annum, rags included; and I believe no gentleman would repine to give ten shillings for the carcass of a good fat child, which, as I have said, will make four dishes of excellent nutritive meat, when he hath only some particular friend or his own family to dine with him. Thus the squire will learn to be a good landlord, and grow popular among the tenants; the mother will have eight shillings net profit, and be fit for work till she produces another child.

Those who are more thrifty (as I must confess the times require) may flay the carcass; the skin of which artificially[8] dressed will make admirable gloves for ladies, and summer boots for fine gentlemen.

As to our city of Dublin, shambles[9] may be appointed for this purpose in the most convenient parts of it, and butchers we may be assured will not be wanting; although I rather recommend buying the children alive, and dressing them hot from the knife as we do roasting pigs.

A very worthy person, a true lover of his country, and whose virtues I highly esteem, was lately pleased in discoursing on this matter to offer a refinement upon my scheme. He said that many gentlemen of this kingdom, having of late destroyed their deer, he conceived that the want of venison might be well supplied by the bodies of young lads and

---

7. François Rabelais (c. 1494–1553), a French satirist—not at all "grave"— whom Swift admired for his broad humor and sharp wit. (Ed.)

8. Skillfully, artfully. (Ed.)

9. Slaughterhouses. (Ed.)

maidens, not exceeding fourteen years of age nor under twelve, so great a number of both sexes in every county being now ready to starve for want of work and service; and these to be disposed of by their parents, if alive, or otherwise by their nearest relations. But with due deference to so excellent a friend and so deserving a patriot, I cannot be altogether in his sentiments; for as to the males, my American acquaintance assured me from frequent experience that their flesh was generally tough and lean, like that of our schoolboys, by continual exercise, and their taste disagreeable; and to fatten them would not answer the charge. Then as to the females, it would, I think with humble submission, be a loss to the public, because they soon would become breeders themselves: and besides, it is not improbable that some scrupulous people might be apt to censure such a practice (although indeed very unjustly) as a little bordering upon cruelty; which, I confess, hath always been with me the strongest objection against any project, how well soever intended.

But in order to justify my friend, he confessed that this expedient was put into his head by the famous Psalmanazar,[10] a native of the island Formosa, who came from thence to London above twenty years ago, and in conversation told my friend that in his country when any young person happened to be put to death, the executioner sold the carcass to persons of quality as a prime dainty; and that in his time the body of a plump girl of fifteen, who was crucified for an attempt to poison the emperor, was sold to his Imperial Majesty's prime minister of state, and other great mandarins of the court, in joints from the gibbet, at four hundred crowns. Neither indeed can I deny that if the same use were made of several plump young girls in this town, who without one single groat to their fortunes cannot stir abroad without a chair, and appear at the playhouse and assemblies in foreign fineries which they never will pay for, the kingdom would not be the worse. 18

Some persons of a desponding spirit are in great concern about that vast number of poor people who are aged, diseased, or maimed, and I have been desired to employ my thoughts what course may be taken to ease the nation of so grievous an encumbrance. But I am not in the least pain upon that matter, because it is very well known that they are every day dying and rotting by cold and famine, and filth and vermin, as fast as can be reasonably expected. And as to the younger laborers, they are now in almost as hopeful a condition. They cannot get work, and consequently pine away for want of nourishment to a degree that if at any time they are accidentally hired to common labor, they have not strength to perform it; and thus the country and themselves are happily delivered from the evils to come. 19

---

10. George Psalmanazar (c. 1679–1763), a French imposter who fooled London society with his tales of human sacrifice and cannibalism on Formosa. (Ed.)

I have too long digressed, and therefore shall return to my subject. I think the advantages by the proposal which I have made are obvious and many, as well as of the highest importance.   20

For first, as I have already observed, it would greatly lessen the number of Papists, with whom we are yearly overrun, being the principal breeders of the nation as well as our most dangerous enemies; and who stay at home on purpose to deliver the kingdom to the Pretender, hoping to take their advantage by the absence of so many good Protestants, who have chosen rather to leave their country than stay at home and pay tithes against their conscience to an Episcopal curate.   21

Secondly, the poorer tenants will have something valuable of their own, which by law may be made liable to distress,[11] and help to pay their landlord's rent, their corn and cattle being already seized and money a thing unknown.   22

Thirdly, whereas the maintenance of an hundred thousand children, from two years old and upwards, cannot be computed at less than ten shillings a piece per annum, the nation's stock will be thereby increased fifty thousand pounds per annum, besides the profit of a new dish introduced to the tables of all gentlemen of fortune in the kingdom who have any refinement in taste. And the money will circulate among ourselves, the goods being entirely of our own growth and manufacture.   23

Fourthly, the constant breeders, besides the gain of eight shillings sterling per annum by the sale of their children, will be rid of the charge of maintaining them after the first year.   24

Fifthly, this food would likewise bring great custom to taverns, where the vintners will certainly be so prudent as to procure the best receipts for dressing it to perfection, and consequently have their houses frequented by all the fine gentlemen, who justly value themselves upon their knowledge in good eating; and a skillful cook, who understands how to oblige his guests, will contrive to make it as expensive as they please.   25

Sixthly, this would be a great inducement to marriage, which all wise nations have either encouraged by rewards or enforced by laws and penalties. It would increase the care and tenderness of mothers toward their children, when they were sure of a settlement for life to the poor babes, provided in some sort by the public, to their annual profit instead of expense. We should see an honest emulation among the married women, which of them could bring the fattest child to the market. Men would become as fond of their wives during the time of their pregnancy as they are now of their mares in foal, their cows in calf, or sows when they are ready to farrow; nor offer to beat or kick them (as is too frequent a practice) for fear of a miscarriage.   26

---

11. Subject to seizure by creditors. (Ed.)

Many other advantages might be enumerated. For instance, the addi- 27
tion of some thousand carcasses in our exportation of barreled beef, the
propagation of swine's flesh, and improvement in the art of making good
bacon, so much wanted among us by the great destruction of pigs, too frequent at our tables, which are no way comparable in taste or magnifi-
cence to a well-grown, fat, yearling child, which roasted whole will make
a considerable figure at a lord mayor's feast or any other public entertainment. But this and many others I omit, being studious of brevity.

Supposing that one thousand families in this city would be con- 28
stant customers for infants' flesh, besides others who might have it at
merry meetings, particularly weddings and christenings, I compute
that Dublin would take off annually about twenty thousand carcasses,
and the rest of the kingdom (where probably they will be sold somewhat cheaper) the remaining eighty thousand.

I can think of no one objection that will possibly be raised against 29
this proposal, unless it should be urged that the number of people will
be thereby much lessened in the kingdom. This I freely own, and it was
indeed one principal design in offering it to the world. I desire the
reader will observe, that I calculate my remedy for this one individual
kingdom of Ireland and for no other that ever was, is, or I think ever
can be upon earth. Therefore let no man talk to me of other expedients:
of taxing our absentees at five shillings a pound: of using neither
clothes nor household furniture except what is of our own growth and
manufacture: of utterly rejecting the materials and instruments that
promote foreign luxury: of curing the expensiveness of pride, vanity,
idleness, and gaming in our women: of introducing a vein of parsimony, prudence, and temperance: of learning to love our country, in
the want of which we differ even from Laplanders and the inhabitants
of Topinamhoo:[12] of quitting our animosities and factions, nor acting
any longer like the Jews, who were murdering one another at the very
moment their city was taken:[13] of being a little cautious not to sell our
country and conscience for nothing: of teaching landlords to have at
least one degree of mercy toward their tenants: lastly, of putting a spirit
of honesty, industry, and skill into our shopkeepers; who, if a resolution could now be taken to buy only our native goods, would immediately unite to cheat and exact upon us in the price, the measure, and
the goodness, nor could ever yet be brought to make one fair proposal
of just dealing, though often and earnestly invited to it.

---

12. In other words, even from Laplanders who love their icy tundra and primitive Brazilian tribes who love their jungle. (Ed.)
13. Swift refers to the Roman siege of Jerusalem in A.D. 70; the inhabitants lost
the city because they dissolved into violent factions. (Ed.)

Therefore I repeat, let no man talk to me of these and the like expedients, till he hath at least some glimpse of hope that there will ever be some hearty and sincere attempt to put them in practice. 30

But as to myself, having been wearied out for many years with offering vain, idle, visionary thoughts, and at length utterly despairing of success, I fortunately fell upon this proposal, which, as it is wholly new, so it hath something solid and real, of no expense and little trouble, full in our own power, and whereby we can incur no danger in disobliging England. For this kind of commodity will not bear exportation, the flesh being of too tender a consistence to admit a long continuance in salt, although perhaps I could name a country which would be glad to eat up our whole nation without it. 31

After all, I am not so violently bent upon my own opinion as to reject any offer proposed by wise men, which shall be found equally innocent, cheap, easy, and effectual. But before something of that kind shall be advanced in contradiction to my scheme, and offering a better, I desire the author or authors will be pleased maturely to consider two points. First, as things now stand, how they will be able to find food and raiment for an hundred thousand useless mouths and backs. And secondly, there being a round million of creatures in human figure throughout this kingdom, whose sole subsistence put into a common stock would leave them in debt two millions of pounds sterling, adding those who are beggars by profession to the bulk of farmers, cottagers, and laborers, with their wives and children who are beggars in effect; I desire those politicians who dislike my overture, and may perhaps be so bold to attempt an answer, that they will first ask the parents of these mortals whether they would not at this day think it a great happiness to have been sold for food at a year old in the manner I prescribe, and thereby have avoided such a perpetual scene of misfortunes as they have since gone through by the oppression of landlords, the impossibility of paying rent without money or trade, the want of common sustenance, with neither house nor clothes to cover them from the inclemencies of the weather, and the most inevitable prospect of entailing the like or greater miseries upon their breed forever. 32

I profess, in the sincerity of my heart, that I have not the least personal interest in endeavoring to promote this necessary work, having no other motive than the public good of my country, by advancing our trade, providing for infants, relieving the poor, and giving some pleasure to the rich. I have no children by which I can propose to get a single penny; the youngest being nine years old, and my wife past childbearing. 33

THINKING CRITICALLY ABOUT THE TEXT

Satire often has a "stealth quality" about it; that is, the audience for it often does not realize at first that the author of the satire is not being serious. At some point in the satire the audience usually catches on and then begins to see the larger issue at the center of the satire. At what point in your reading did you begin to catch on to Swift's technique and larger, more important, message?

QUESTIONS ON SUBJECT

1. What problem is being addressed in this essay? Describe the specific solution being proposed. What are the proposal's "advantages" (paragraph 20)?

2. What "other expedients" (29) are dismissed as "vain, idle, visionary thoughts" (31)? What do paragraphs 29 through 31 tell you about Swift's purpose? (Glossary: *Purpose*)

3. Describe the "author" of the proposal. Why does Swift choose such a character to present this plan? When can you detect Swift's own voice coming through?

4. What is the meaning and the significance of the title? (Glossary: *Title*)

5. In paragraph 2 Swift talks of making Ireland's "children sound, useful members of the commonwealth." In what way is this statement ironic? Cite several other examples of Swift's irony. (Glossary: *Irony*)

QUESTIONS ON STRATEGY

1. Toward what belief and/or action is Swift attempting to persuade his readers? How does he go about doing so? For example, did you feel a sense of outrage at any point in the essay? Did you feel that the essay was humorous at any point? If so, where and why?

2. What is the effect of the first paragraph of the essay? How does it serve to introduce the proposal? (Glossary: *Beginnings*)

3. What strategies does Swift use in this essay to make his proposer sound like an authority? Explain how this sense of authority relates to Swift's real purpose.

4. In what ways can the argument presented in this essay be seen as logical? What is the effect, for example, of the complicated calculations in paragraph 6?

5. What strategies, in addition to argumentation, does Swift use to develop his satire? Cite examples to support your answer. (Glossary: *Argumentation*)

QUESTIONS ON DICTION AND VOCABULARY

1. It is not easy to summarize Swift's tone in a single word, but how would you describe the overall tone he establishes? Point to specific passages in the essay where you find his language particularly effective.

2. What is Swift's intent in using the term *modest*? (Glossary: *Purpose*)

3. In paragraph 6 Swift refers to women as "breeders." In terms of his proposal, why is the diction appropriate? (Glossary: *Appropriateness*) Cite other examples of such diction used to describe the poor people of Ireland.

CLASSROOM ACTIVITY FOR COMBINING STRATEGIES

Imagine that you will write a satire based on the model of Swift's "A Modest Proposal." Think in terms of attacking the foolish thinking or absurdity of a situation you find on the national, state, or local level and how your satire will get people to think about that issue in productive ways. What additional strategies might you employ to accomplish your satire? Discuss your possible approaches to this assignment with other members of your class.

WRITING SUGGESTIONS

1. Write a modest proposal of your own to solve a difficult social or political problem of the present day or, on a smaller scale, a problem you see facing your school or community.

2. What is the most effective way to bring about social change and to influence societal attitudes? Would Swift's methods work today, or would they have to be significantly modified? Concentrating on the sorts of changes you have witnessed over the last ten years, write an essay in which you describe how best to influence public opinion.

WRITING SUGGESTIONS FOR COMBINING STRATEGIES

1. Select a piece you have written for this class in which you used one primary writing strategy, and rewrite it using another. For example, choose a description you wrote in response to an exercise at the end of Chapter 4, and redraft it as a process analysis. Remember that the choice of a writing strategy influences the writer's "voice"—a descriptive piece might be lyrical, while a process analysis might be straightforward. How does your voice change along with the strategy? Does your assumed audience change as well? (Glossary: *Audience*)

    If time allows, try this exercise with someone else in your class. Exchange a piece of writing with another student, and rewrite it using a different strategy. Discuss the choices you each made.

2. Select an essay you have written this semester, either for this class or another class. What was the primary writing strategy you used? Build upon this essay by integrating another strategy. For example, if you wrote an argument paper for a political science class, you might try using narrative to give some historical background to the paper. (Glossary: *Argumentation; Narration*) For a paper in the natural sciences, you could use subjective description to open the paper up to nonscientists. (Glossary: *Objective/Subjective*) How does this new strategy affect the balance of your paper? Does the new strategy require you to change anything else about your paper?

3. The choice of a writing strategy reflects an author's voice—the persona he or she assumes in relation to the reader. Read back through any personal writing you've done this semester—a journal, letters to friends, e-mail. Can you identify the strategies you use outside of "formal" academic writing, as part of your natural writing voice? Write a few pages analyzing these strategies and your writing "voice," using one of the rhetorical strategies studied this term. For example, you could compare and contrast your e-mail postings to your letters home. (Glossary: *Comparison and Contrast*) Or you could do a cause and effect analysis of how being at college has changed the tone or style of your journal writing. (Glossary: *Cause and Effect Analysis*)

CHAPTER 14

Editing for Grammar, Punctuation, and Sentence Style

Once you have revised your essay and you are confident that you have said what you wanted to say, you are ready to begin editing your essay. It's at the editing stage of the writing process that you identify and correct errors in grammar, punctuation, and sentence style. You don't want a series of small errors to detract from your paper. More importantly, such errors can cause readers to have second thoughts about the content of your essay.

This chapter addresses twelve common writing problems that instructors from around the country told us trouble their students most. For more guidance with these or other editing concerns, be sure to refer to a writer's handbook or ask your instructor for help. To practice identifying and correcting these and other writing problems, go to <bedfordstmartins.com/subjectandstrategy> and click on "Exercise Central."

1. RUN-ONS: FUSED SENTENCES AND COMMA SPLICES

Writers can become so absorbed in getting their ideas down on paper that they sometimes combine two independent clauses (complete sentences that can stand alone when punctuated with a period) incorrectly, creating a *run-on sentence*. A run-on sentence fails to show where one thought ends and another begins, and it can confuse readers. There are two types of run-on sentences: the fused sentence and the comma splice.

A *fused sentence* occurs when a writer joins two main clauses with no punctuation and no coordinating conjunction.

FUSED SENTENCE   The delegates at the state political convention could not decide on a leader they were beginning to show their frustration.

A *comma splice* occurs when a writer uses only a comma to join two or more main clauses.

COMMA SPLICE   The delegates at the state political convention could not decide on a leader, they were beginning to show their frustration.

There are five ways to fix run-on sentences.

1. Create two separate sentences with a period.

EDITED   The delegates at the state political convention could not decide on a leader ~~they~~ . They were beginning to show their frustration.

2. Use a comma and a coordinating conjunction to join the two sentences.

EDITED   The delegates at the state political convention could not decide on a leader , and they were beginning to show their frustration.

3. Use a semicolon to separate the two sentences.

EDITED   The delegates at the state political convention could not decide on a leader ; they were beginning to show their frustration.

4. Use a semicolon followed by a transitional word or expression and a comma to join the two sentences.

EDITED   The delegates at the state political convention could not decide on a leader ; consequently, they were beginning to show their frustration.

5. Subordinate one sentence to the other, using a subordinate conjunction or a relative pronoun.

EDITED   The ^{When the} delegates at the state political convention could not decide on a leader, they were beginning to show their frustration.

EDITED   The delegates at the state political convention ^{, who were beginning to show their frustration,} could not decide on a leader. they were beginning to show their frustration.

2. SENTENCE FRAGMENTS

A *sentence fragment* is a part of a sentence presented as if it were a complete sentence. Even if a word group begins with a capital letter and ends with a period, question mark, or exclamation point, it is not a sentence unless it has a subject (the person, place, or thing the sentence is about) and a verb (a word that tells what the subject does) and expresses a complete thought.

> SENTENCE FRAGMENT   My music group decided to study the early works of Mozart. *The child prodigy from Austria.*

Word groups that do not express complete thoughts are often freestanding subordinate clauses beginning with a subordinating conjunction such as *although, because, since, so, that,* or *unless.*

> SENTENCE FRAGMENT   The company president met with the management team every week. *So that problems were rarely ignored.*

You can correct sentence fragments in one of two ways.

1. Integrate the fragment into a nearby sentence.

EDITED   My music group decided to study the early works of Mozart^{, the}/ The child prodigy from Austria.

EDITED   The company president met with the management team every week^{, so}/ So that problems were rarely ignored.

2. Develop the fragment itself into a complete sentence by adding a subject or a verb.

EDITED   My music group decided to study the early works of Mozart. The
                child prodigy was from Austria.

EDITED   The company president met with the management team every
                week. ~~So that problems~~ Problems were rarely ignored.

Sentence fragments are not always wrong. In fact, if not overused, a deliberate sentence fragment can add emphasis. In narratives, deliberate sentence fragments are most commonly used in dialogue and in descriptive passages that set a mood or tone. In the following passage taken from "Not Close Enough for Comfort" (pages 93–95), David P. Bardeen uses fragments to set the stage for the unsettling luncheon meeting he had with his brother Will:

I asked him about his recent trip. He asked me about work. Short questions. One-word answers. Then an awkward pause.

3. COMMA FAULTS

Commas help communicate meaning by eliminating possible misreadings. Consider this sentence:

After visiting William Alan Lee went to French class.

Depending upon where you put the comma, it could be Lee, Alan Lee, or William Alan Lee who goes to French class.

EDITED   After visiting William Alan, Lee went to French class.

EDITED   After visiting William, Alan Lee went to French class.

EDITED   After visiting, William Alan Lee went to French class.

The comma, of all the marks of punctuation, has the greatest variety of uses, which, in turn, can lead to using the comma incorrectly. Remember, in every case the comma functions in one of two basic ways—to *separate* or to *enclose* elements in a sentence. By learning a few basic rules for comma use, you will be able to identify and correct common comma faults.

1. Use a comma to separate two independent clauses joined by a coordinating conjunction.

| INCORRECT | Tolstoy wrote many popular short stories but he is perhaps best known for his novels. |
| EDITED | Tolstoy wrote many popular short stories, but he is perhaps best known for his novels. |

2. Use a comma to separate an introductory phrase or clause from the main clause of a sentence.

INCORRECT	In his book *Life on the Mississippi* Mark Twain describes his days as a riverboat pilot.
EDITED	In his book *Life on the Mississippi*, Mark Twain describes his days as a riverboat pilot.
INCORRECT	When the former Soviet Union collapsed residents of Moscow had to struggle just to survive.
EDITED	When the former Soviet Union collapsed, residents of Moscow had to struggle just to survive.

3. Use commas to enclose nonrestrictive elements.   When an adjective phrase or clause adds information that is essential to the meaning of a sentence, it is said to be *restrictive* and should not be set off with commas.

> The woman wearing the beige linen suit works with Homeland Security.

The adjective phrase *wearing the beige linen suit* is essential and thus should not be set off with commas; without this information, we have no way of identifying which woman works with Homeland Security.

When an adjective phrase or clause does not add information that is essential to the meaning of the sentence, it is said to be *nonrestrictive* and should be enclosed with commas.

| INCORRECT | Utopian literature which was popular during the late nineteenth century seems to emerge at times of economic and political unrest. |
| EDITED | Utopian literature, which was popular during the late nineteenth century, seems to emerge at times of economic and political unrest. |

4. Use commas to separate items in a series.

INCORRECT The three staples of the diet in Thailand are rice fish and fruit.

EDITED The three staples of the diet in Thailand are rice, fish, and fruit.

4. SUBJECT-VERB AGREEMENT

Subjects and verbs must agree in number—that is, a singular subject (one person, place, or thing) must take a singular verb, and a plural subject (more than one person, place, or thing) must take a plural verb. While most native speakers of English use proper subject-verb agreement in their writing without thinking about it, there are some sentence constructions that can be troublesome.

Intervening Prepositional Phrases

When the relationship between the subject and the verb in a sentence is not clear, the culprit is usually an intervening prepositional phrase (a phrase that begins with a preposition such as *on, of, in, at,* or *between*). To make sure the subject agrees with its verb in a sentence with an intervening prepositional phrase, mentally cross out the phrase (*of the term* in the following example) to isolate the subject and the verb and determine if they agree.

INCORRECT The first one hundred days of the term is the president's honeymoon period.

EDITED The first one hundred days of the term ~~is~~ *are* the president's honeymoon period.

Compound Subjects

Writers often have difficulty with subject-verb agreement in sentences with compound subjects (two or more subjects joined together with the word *and*). As a general rule, compound subjects take plural verbs.

INCORRECT My iPod, computer, and television was stolen.

EDITED My iPod, computer, and television ~~was~~ *were* stolen.

However, in sentences with subjects joined by *either . . . or, neither . . . nor,* or *not only . . . but also,* the verb must agree with the subject closest to it.

> INCORRECT   Neither the students nor the professor are satisfied with the lab equipment.
>
> EDITED   Neither the students nor the professor ~~are~~ ^is^ satisfied with the lab equipment.

5. UNCLEAR PRONOUN REFERENCES

The noun to which a pronoun refers is called its *antecedent* or *referent.* Be sure to place a pronoun as close to its antecedent as possible so that the relationship between them is clear. The more words that intervene between the antecedent and the pronoun, the more chance there is for confusion. When the relationship between a pronoun and its antecedent is unclear, the sentence becomes inaccurate or ambiguous. While editing your writing, look for and correct ambiguous, vague, or implied pronoun references.

Ambiguous References

Make sure all your pronouns clearly refer to specific antecedents. If a pronoun can refer to more than one antecedent, the sentence is ambiguous.

> AMBIGUOUS   Adler sought to convince the reader to mark up *his* book.

In this sentence, the antecedent of the pronoun *his* could be either *Adler* or *reader.* Does Adler want his particular book marked up, or does he want the reader to mark up his or her own book? To make an ambiguous antecedent clear, either repeat the correct antecedent or rewrite the sentence.

> EDITED   Adler sought to convince the reader to mark up ~~his~~ ^Adler's^ book.
>
> EDITED   Adler sought to convince the reader to mark up ~~his~~ ^his or her^ book.

Vague References

Whenever you use *it, they, you, this, that,* or *which* to refer to a general idea in a preceding clause or sentence, be sure that the connection between the pronoun and the general idea is clear, When these pronouns lack a specific antecedent, you give readers an impression of vagueness and carelessness. To correct the problem, either substitute a noun for the pronoun or provide an antecedent to which the pronoun can clearly refer.

> VAGUE The tornadoes damaged many of the homes in the area, but it has not yet been determined.
>
> EDITED The tornadoes damaged many of the homes in the area, but <ins>the extent of the damage</ins> ~~it~~ has not yet been determined.
>
> VAGUE In the book, they wrote that Samantha had an addictive personality.
>
> EDITED In the book, ~~they wrote that~~ Samantha had an addictive personality.

Whenever the connection between the general idea and the pronoun is simple and clear, no confusion results. Consider the following example:

> The stock market rose for a third consecutive week, and *this* lifted most investors' spirits.

Implied References

Make every pronoun refer to a stated, not an implied, antecedent. Every time you use a pronoun in a sentence, you should be able to identify its noun equivalent. If you cannot, use a noun instead.

> IMPLIED After all of the editing and formatting, it was finished.
>
> EDITED After all of the editing and formatting, <ins>the research report</ins> ~~it~~ was finished.

Sometimes a modifier or possessive that implies a noun is mistaken for an antecedent.

> IMPLIED In G. Anthony Gorry's "Steal This MP3 File: What Is Theft?" he shows how technology might be shaping the attitudes of today's youth.
>
> EDITED In ~~G. Anthony Gorry's~~ "Steal This MP3 File: What Is Theft?" <ins>G. Anthony Gorry</ins> ~~he~~ shows how technology might be shaping the attitudes of today's youth.

6. PRONOUN-ANTECEDENT AGREEMENT

Personal pronouns must agree with their antecedents in *person, number,* and *gender.*

Agreement in Person

There are three types of personal pronouns: first person (*I* and *we*), second person (*you*), and third person (*he, she, it,* and *they*). To agree in person, first-person pronouns must refer to first-person antecedents, second-person pronouns to second-person antecedents, and third-person pronouns to third-person antecedents.

INCORRECT   A scientist should consider all the data carefully before you draw a conclusion.

EDITED   A scientist should consider all the data carefully before *he or she draws* ~~you draw~~ a conclusion.

Agreement in Number

To agree in number, a singular pronoun must refer to a singular antecedent, and a plural pronoun must refer to a plural antecedent. When two or more antecedents are joined by the word *and,* the pronoun must be plural.

INCORRECT   Karen, Rachel, and Sofia took her electives in history.

EDITED   Karen, Rachel, and Sofia took *their* ~~her~~ electives in history.

When the subject of a sentence is an indefinite pronoun such as *everyone, each, everybody, anyone, anybody, everything, either, one, neither, someone,* or *something,* use a singular pronoun to refer to it, or recast the sentence to eliminate the agreement problem.

INCORRECT   Each of the women submitted their résumé.

EDITED   Each of the women submitted *her* ~~their~~ résumé.

EDITED   *Both* ~~Each~~ of the women submitted their *résumés* ~~résumé~~.

If a collective noun (army, community, team, herd, committee, association) is understood as a unit, it takes a singular pronoun; if it is understood in terms of its individual members, it takes a plural pronoun.

AS A UNIT   The class presented its annual spring musical.

AS INDIVIDUAL MEMBERS   The class agreed to pay for their own art supplies.

Agreement in Gender

Traditionally, a masculine, singular pronoun has been used for indefinite antecedents (such as *anyone, someone,* and *everyone*) and to refer to generic antecedents (such as *employee, student, athlete, secretary, doctor,* and *computer specialist*). But *anyone* can be female or male, and women are employees (or students, athletes, secretaries, doctors, and computer specialists), too. The use of masculine pronouns to refer to both females and males is considered sexist; that is, such usage leaves out women as a segment of society or diminishes their presence. Instead, use *he or she, his or her.* Or in an extended piece of writing, alternate in a balanced way the use of *he* and *she* throughout. Sometimes the best solution is to rewrite the sentence to put it in the plural or to avoid the problem altogether.

SEXIST If any student wants to attend the opening performance
of *King Lear,* he will have to purchase a ticket by Wednesday.

EDITED If any student wants to attend the opening performance of *King*
Lear, ~~he~~ [he or she] will have to purchase a ticket by Wednesday.

EDITED If any ~~student~~ [students] wants ~~to~~ attend the opening performance of *King*
Lear, ~~he~~ [they] will have to purchase ~~a ticket~~ [tickets] by Wednesday.

EDITED ~~If any student wants to attend~~ [All tickets for] the opening performance of *King*
Lear, ~~he will have to purchase a ticket~~ [must be purchased] by Wednesday.

7. DANGLING AND MISPLACED MODIFIERS

A *modifier* is a word or group of words that describes or gives additional information about other words in a sentence. The words, phrases, and clauses that function as modifiers in a sentence can usually be moved around freely, so place them carefully to avoid unintentionally confusing—or amusing—your reader. As a rule, place modifiers as close as possible to the words you want to modify. Two common problems arise with modifiers: the misplaced modifier and the dangling modifier.

Misplaced Modifiers

A *misplaced modifier* unintentionally modifies the wrong word in a sentence because it is placed incorrectly.

MISPLACED The waiter brought a steak to the man covered with onions.

EDITED The waiter brought a steak [covered with onions] to the man ~~covered with onions~~.

Dangling Modifiers

A *dangling modifier* usually appears at the beginning of a sentence and does not logically relate to the main clause of the sentence. The dangling modifier wants to modify a word—often an unstated subject—that does not appear in the sentence. To eliminate a dangling modifier, give the dangling phrase a subject.

DANGLING Staring into the distance, large rain clouds form.

EDITED Staring into the distance, ^Jon saw^ large rain clouds form.

DANGLING Walking on the ceiling, he noticed a beautiful luna moth.

EDITED ~~Walking on the ceiling, he~~ ^He^ noticed a beautiful luna moth ^walking on the ceiling^.

8. FAULTY PARALLELISM

Parallelism is the repetition of word order or grammatical form either within a single sentence or in several sentences that develop the same central idea. As a rhetorical device, parallel structure can aid coherence and add emphasis. Franklin Roosevelt's famous Depression-era statement "I see one-third of a nation *ill-housed, ill-clad,* and *ill-nourished*" illustrates effective parallelism. Use parallel grammatical structures to emphasize the similarities and differences between the items being compared. Look for opportunities to use parallel constructions with paired items or items in a series, paired items using correlative conjunctions, and comparisons using *than* or *as*.

Paired Items or Items in a Series

Parallel structures can be used to balance a word with a word, a phrase with a phrase, or a clause with a clause whenever you use paired items or items in a series—as in the Roosevelt example above.

1. Balance a word with a word.

FAULTY Like the hunter, the photographer has to understand the animal's patterns, characteristics, and where it lives.

EDITED Like the hunter, the photographer has to understand the animal's patterns, characteristics, and ^habitat^ ~~where it lives~~.

2. Balance a phrase with a phrase.

FAULTY The hunter carries a handgun and two rifles, different kinds of ammunition, and a variety of sights and telescopes to increase his chances of success.

EDITED   The hunter carries ~~a handgun and two rifles~~ *several types of guns*, different kinds of ammunition, and a variety of sights and telescopes to increase his chances of success.

3. Balance a clause with a clause

FAULTY   Shooting is highly aggressive, photography is passive; shooting eliminates forever, photography preserves.

EDITED   Shooting is ~~highly~~ aggressive, photography is passive; shooting eliminates ~~forever~~, photography preserves.

Paired Items Using Correlative Conjunctions

When linking paired items with a correlative conjunction (*either/or, neither/nor, not only/but also, both/and, whether/or*) in a sentence, make sure that the elements being connected are parallel in form. Delete any unnecessary or repeated words.

INCORRECT   The lecture was both enjoyable and it was a form of education.

EDITED   The lecture was both enjoyable and ~~it was a form of education~~ *educational*.

Comparisons Using *Than* or *As*

Make sure that the elements of the comparison are parallel in form. Delete any unnecessary or repeated words.

INCORRECT   It would be better to study now than waiting until the night before the exam.

EDITED   It would be better to study now than ~~waiting~~ *to wait* until the night before the exam.

9. WEAK NOUNS AND VERBS

The essence of a sentence is its subject and its verb. The subject—usually a noun or pronoun—identifies who or what the sentence is about, and the verb captures the subject's action or state of being. Sentences often lose their vitality and liveliness when the subject and the verb are lost in weak language or buried.

Weak Nouns

Always opt for specific nouns when you can; they make your writing more visual. While general words like *people, animal,* or *dessert* name groups or classes of objects, qualities, or actions, specific words like *Samantha, camel,* and *pecan pie* appeal to readers more because they name individual objects, qualities, or actions within a group. Think about it—don't you prefer reading about specifics rather than generalities?

WEAK NOUN   The flowers stretched toward the bright light of the sun.

EDITED   The ~~flowers~~ tulips stretched toward the bright light of the sun.

Strong Verbs

Strong verbs energize your writing by giving it a sense of action. Verbs like *gallop, scramble, snicker, tweak, fling, exhaust, smash, tear, smear, wrangle,* and *smash* provide readers with a vivid picture of specific actions. As you reread what you have written, be on the lookout for weak verbs like *is, are, have, deal with, make, give, do, use, get, add, become, go, appear,* and *seem.* When you encounter one of these verbs or others like them, seize the opportunity to substitute a strong action verb for a weak one.

WEAK VERB   Local Boys and Girls Clubs in America assist in the promotion of self-esteem, individual achievement, and teamwork.

EDITED   Local Boys and Girls Clubs in America ~~assist in the promotion of~~ promote self-esteem, individual achievement, and teamwork.

While editing your essay, look for opportunities to replace weak nouns and verbs with strong nouns and action verbs. The more specific and strong you make your nouns and verbs, the more lively, descriptive, and concise your writing will be.

When you have difficulty thinking of strong, specific nouns and verbs, reach for a dictionary or a thesaurus—but only if you are sure you can discern the best word for your purpose. Thesauruses are available free online and in inexpensive paperback editions; most word processing programs include a thesaurus as well.

10. SHIFTS IN VERB TENSE, MOOD, AND VOICE

Shifts in Tense

A verb's tense indicates when an action takes place—sometime in the past, right now, or in the future. Using verb tense correctly helps your readers understand time changes in your writing. Using different verb tenses within a sentence—called a *shift* in tense—without a logical reason confuses readers. Unnecessary shifts in verb tense are especially noticeable in narration and process analysis writing, which are sequence and time oriented. Generally, you should write in the present or past tense and maintain that tense throughout your sentence.

INCORRECT   The painter studied the scene and pulls a fan brush decisively from her cup.

EDITED   The painter studied the scene and ~~pulls~~ pulled a fan brush decisively from her cup.

Shifts in Mood

Verbs in English have three moods: the *indicative,* the *imperative,* and the *subjunctive.* Problems with inconsistency usually occur with the imperative mood.

INCORRECT   In learning a second language, arm yourself with basic vocabulary, and it is also important to practice speaking aloud daily.

EDITED   In learning a second language, arm yourself with basic vocabulary, and ~~it is also important to~~ practice speaking aloud daily.

Shifts in Voice

Shifts in voice—from active voice to passive voice—usually go hand in hand with inconsistencies in the subject of a sentence.

INCORRECT   The archeologists could see the effects of vandalism as the Mayan tomb was entered.

EDITED   The archeologists could see the effects of vandalism as they entered the Mayan tomb ~~was entered~~.

11. WORDINESS

Wordiness occurs in sentences that contain words that do not contribute to the sentence's meaning. Wordiness can be eliminated by (1) using the active voice, (2) avoiding "there is" and "it is," (3) eliminating redundancies, (4) deleting empty words and phrases, and (5) simplifying inflated expressions.

1. Use the active voice rather than the passive voice. The active voice emphasizes the doer of an action rather than the receiver of an action. Not only is the active voice more concise than the passive voice, it is a much more vigorous form of expression.

> PASSIVE   *The inhabitants of Londonderry were overwhelmed* by the burgeoning rodent population.
>
> ACTIVE   *The burgeoning rodent population overwhelmed* the inhabitants of Londonderry.

In the active sentence, *The burgeoning rodent population* is made the subject of the sentence and is moved to the beginning of the sentence—a position of importance—while the verb *overwhelmed* is made an active verb.

2. Avoid "There is" and "It is." "There is" and "It is" are expletives—words or phrases that do not contribute any meaning but are added only to fill out a sentence. They may be necessary with references to time and weather, but they should be avoided in other circumstances.

> WORDY   There were many acts of heroism following the earthquake.
>
> EDITED   ~~There were many~~ ^Many^ acts of heroism ~~following~~ ^followed^ the earthquake.

Notice how the edited sentence eliminates the expletive and reveals a specific subject—*acts*—and an action verb—*followed*.

3. Eliminate redundancies. Unnecessary repetition often creeps into our writing and should be eliminated. For example, how often have you written expressions such as *large in size, completely filled, academic scholar,* or *I thought in my mind?* Edit such expressions by deleting the unnecessary words or using synonyms.

Sometimes our intent is to add emphasis, but the net effect is extra words that contribute little or nothing to a sentence's meaning.

> REDUNDANT   A big huge cloud was advancing on the crowded stadium.
>
> EDITED   A ~~big~~ huge cloud was advancing on the crowded stadium.

REDUNDANT After studying all night, he knew the basic and fundamental principles of geometry.

EDITED After studying all night, he knew the basic ~~and fundamental~~

principles of geometry.

4. Delete empty words and phrases.   Look for words and phrases we use every day that carry no meaning—words that should be eliminated from your writing during the editing process.

EMPTY One commentator believes that America is for all intents and purposes a materialistic society.

EDITED One commentator believes that America is ~~for all intents and~~

~~purposes~~ a materialistic society.

Following are examples of some other words and expressions that most often can be eliminated.

basically	I think/I feel/I believe
essentially	it seems to me
generally	kind of/sort of
very	tend to
surely	quite
truly	extremely
really	severely

5. Simplify inflated expressions.   Sometimes we use expressions we think sound authoritative in hopes of seeming knowledgable. We write *at this point in time* (instead of *now*) or *in the event that* (instead of *if*). However, it is best to write directly and forcefully and to use clear language. Edit inflated or pompous language to its core meaning.

INFLATED The law office hired two people who have a complete knowledge of environmental policy.

EDITED The law office hired two people who ~~have a complete knowledge~~ *are* *experts.* ~~of~~ environmental policy.

INFLATED The president was late on account of the fact that her helicopter would not start.

EDITED The president was late ~~on account of the fact that~~ *because* her

helicopter would not start.

12. SENTENCE VARIETY

While editing your essays, you can add interest and readability to your writing with more sentence variety. You should, however, seek variety in sentence structure not as an end in itself but as a more accurate means of reflecting your thoughts and giving emphasis where emphasis is needed. Look for opportunities to achieve sentence variety by combining short choppy sentences, varying sentence openings, and reducing the number of compound sentences.

Short Choppy Sentences

To make your writing more interesting, use one of the following five methods to combine short choppy sentences into one longer sentence.

1. Use subordinating and coordinating conjunctions to relate and connect ideas. The coordinating conjunctions *and, but, or, nor, for, so,* and *yet* can be used to connect two or more simple sentences. A subordinating conjunction, on the other hand, introduces a subordinate clause and connects it to a main clause. Common subordinating conjunctions include:

after	before	so	when
although	even if	than	where
as	if	that	whereas
as if	in order that	though	wherever
as though	rather than	unless	whether
because	since	until	while

SHORT AND CHOPPY — Short words are as good as long ones. Short old words — like *sun* and *grass* and *home* — are best of all.

COMBINED — Short words are as good as long ones, and short old words—like *sun* and *grass* and *home*—are best of all.

— RICHARD LEDERER,
"The Case for Short Words," page 480

2. Use modifiers effectively. Instead of writing a separate descriptive sentence, combine an adjective modifier to convey a more graphic picture in a single sentence.

SHORT AND CHOPPY   The people who breed German shepherds in Appleton, Wisconsin, are also farmers. And they are wonderful farmers.

COMBINED   The people who breed German shepherds in Appleton,
     wonderful
Wisconsin, are also ‸ farmers. ~~And they are wonderful~~

~~farmers.~~

3. Use a semicolon or colon to link closely related ideas.

SHORT AND CHOPPY   Pollution from carbon emissions remains a serious environmental problem. In some respects it is the most serious problem.

COMBINED   Pollution from carbon emissions remains a serious
     ; in
environmental problem‸ ~~In~~ some respects it is the

most serious problem.

4. Use parallel constructions.   Parallel constructions use repeated word order or repeated grammatical form to highlight and develop a central idea. As a rhetorical device, parallelism can aid coherence and add emphasis.

SHORT AND CHOPPY   The school busing issue is not about comfort. It concerns fairness.

COMBINED   The school busing issue is not about
     but about
comfort‸ ~~It concerns~~ fairness.

Sentence Openings

More than half of all sentences in English begin with the subject of the sentence followed by the verb and any objects. The following sentences all illustrate this basic pattern:

Martha plays the saxophone.

The president vetoed the tax bill before leaving Washington for the holidays.

The upcoming lecture series will formally launch the fund-raising campaign for a new civic center.

If all the sentences in a particular passage in your essay begin this way, the effect on your readers is monotony. With a little practice, you will discover just how flexible the English language is. Consider the different ways in which one sentence can be rewritten so as to vary its beginning and add interest.

ORIGINAL | Candidates debated the issue of military service for women in the auditorium and did not know that a demonstration was going on outside.

VARIED OPENINGS | *Debating the issue of military service for women,* the candidates in the auditorium did not know that a demonstration was going on outside.

In the auditorium, the candidates debated the issue of military service for women, not knowing that a demonstration was going on outside.

As they debated the issue of military service for women, the candidates in the auditorium did not know that a demonstration was going on outside.

Another way of changing the usual subject-verb-object order of sentences is to invert—or reverse—the normal order. Do not, however, sacrifice proper emphasis to gain variety.

Usual Order	Inverted Order
The crowd stormed out.	Out stormed the crowd.
The enemy would never accept that.	That the enemy would never accept.
They could be friendly and civil.	Friendly and civil they could be.

Compound Sentences

Like a series of short, simple sentences, too many compound sentences—two or more sentences joined by coordinating conjunctions—give the impression of haste and thoughtlessness. As you edit your paper, watch for the word *and* used as a coordinating conjunction. If you discover that you have overused *and,* try one of the following four methods to remedy the situation, giving important ideas more emphasis and making it easier for your reader to follow your thought.

1. Change a compound sentence into a simple sentence with a modifier or an appositive.

COMPOUND   Richard Lederer is a linguist, and he is humorous, and he has a weekly radio program about language.

                 ,a humorous

APPOSITIVE   Richard Lederer ~~is a~~ linguist, ~~and he is humorous, and he~~ has a weekly radio program about language.

2. Change a compound sentence into a simple sentence with a compound predicate.

COMPOUND   Martin Luther King Jr. chastises America for not honoring its obligations to people of color, and he dreams of a day when racism will no longer exist.

COMPOUND PREDICATE   Martin Luther King Jr. chastises America for not honoring its obligations to people of color/ and ~~he~~ dreams of a day when racism will no longer exist.

3. Change a compound sentence into a simple sentence with a phrase or phrases.

COMPOUND   Women have a number of options in the military, and the responsibilities are significant.

                 with significant responsibilities .

WITH A PHRASE   Women have a number of options in the military, ~~and the responsibilities are significant.~~

4. Change a compound sentence into a complex sentence.

COMPOUND   Farmers are using new technologies, and agriculture is becoming completely industrialized.

        Because

COMPLEX   Farmers are using new technologies, ~~and~~ agriculture is becoming completely industrialized.

CHAPTER 15

Writing a Researched Essay

A documented paper is not very different from the other writing in your college writing course. You will find yourself drawing heavily on what you learned in Chapter 2 (pages 14–31). First you determine what you want to say, then you decide on a purpose, consider your audience, develop a thesis, collect your evidence, write a first draft, revise and edit, and prepare a final copy. What differentiates the documented paper from other kinds of papers is your use of outside sources and how you acknowledge them.

In this chapter, you will learn some valuable research techniques:

- How to establish a realistic schedule for your research project
- How to locate and use print and Internet sources
- How to evaluate print and Internet sources
- How to develop a working bibliography
- How to conduct research on the Internet using directory and keyword searches
- How to take useful notes
- How to summarize, paraphrase, and quote your sources
- How to integrate your notes into your paper
- How to acknowledge your sources using Modern Language Association (MLA) style in-text citations and a list of works cited
- How to avoid plagiarism

Your library research will involve working with both print and electronic sources. In both cases, however, the process is essentially the same. Your aim is to select the most appropriate sources for your research from the many that are available on your topic.

A research project easily spans several weeks. So as not to lose track of time and find yourself facing an impossible deadline at the last moment, establish a realistic schedule for completing key tasks. By thinking of the research paper as a multi-staged process, you avoid becoming overwhelmed by the size of the whole undertaking.

Your schedule should allow at least a few days to accommodate unforeseen needs and delays. Use the following template, which lists the essential steps in writing a research paper, to plan your own research schedule:

Research Paper Schedule

Task	Completion Date
1. Choose a research topic and pose a worthwhile question.	__ / __ / __
2. Locate print and electronic sources.	__ / __ / __
3. Develop a working bibliography.	__ / __ / __
4. Evaluate your sources.	__ / __ / __
5. Read your sources, taking complete and accurate notes.	__ / __ / __
6. Develop a preliminary thesis and make a working outline.	__ / __ / __
7. Write a draft of your paper, integrating sources you have summarized, paraphrased, and quoted.	__ / __ / __
8. Visit your college writing center for help with your revision.	__ / __ / __
9. Decide on a final thesis and modify your outline.	__ / __ / __
10. Revise your paper and properly cite all borrowed materials.	__ / __ / __
11. Prepare a list of works cited.	__ / __ / __
12. Prepare the final manuscript and proofread.	__ / __ / __
13. Submit research paper.	__ / __ / __

USING PRINT AND ONLINE SOURCES

In most cases, you should use print sources (books, newspapers, journals, magazines, encyclopedias, pamphlets, brochures, and government documents) as your primary tools for research. Print sources, unlike many Internet sources, are often reviewed by experts in the field before they are published, generally overseen by a reputable publishing company or organization, and examined by editors and fact checkers for accuracy and reliability. Unless you are instructed otherwise, you should try to use print sources in your research.

The best place to start any search for print and online sources is your college library's home page (see figure below). Here you will find links to the computerized catalog of book holdings, online reference works, periodical databases, electronic journals, and a list of full-text databases. You'll also find links for subject study guides and for help conducting your research.

To find print sources, search through your library's reference works, electronic catalog, periodical indexes, and other databases to generate a preliminary listing of books, magazine and newspaper articles, public documents and reports, and other sources that may be helpful in exploring your topic. At this early stage, it is better to err on the side of listing too many sources. Then, later on, you will not have to backtrack to find sources you discarded too hastily.

You will find that Internet sources can be informative and valuable additions to your research. The Internet is especially useful in providing recent data, stories, and reports. For example, you might find a just-published article from a university laboratory, or a news story in your local newspaper's online archives. Generally, however, Internet sources should be used alongside print sources and not as a replacement for them. Whereas print sources are generally published under the guidance of a publisher or an organization, practically anyone with access to a computer and an Internet connection can put text and

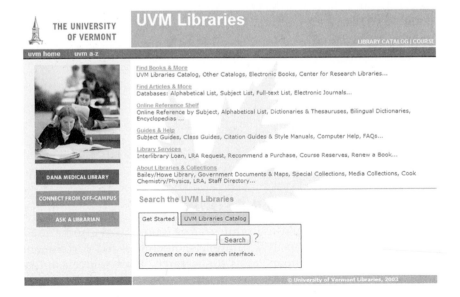

pictures on the Internet; there is often no governing body that checks for content or accuracy. The Internet offers a vast number of useful and carefully maintained resources, but it also contains much unreliable information. It is your responsibility to determine whether a given Internet source should be trusted.

If you do not know how to access the Internet, or if you need more instruction on conducting Internet searches, go to your on-campus computer center for more information, or consult one of the many books written for Internet beginners. You can also access valuable information for searching the Internet at Diana Hacker's *Research and Documentation Online* <www.dianahacker.com.resdoc>.

Evaluate Your Print and Online Sources

You will not have to spend much time in the library to realize that you do not have time to read every print and online source that appears relevant. Given the abundance of print and Internet sources, the key to successful research is identifying those books, articles, Web sites, and other online sources that will help you most. You must evaluate your potential sources to determine which materials you will read, which you will skim, and which you will simply eliminate. Here are some evaluation strategies and questions to assist you in identifying your most promising sources.

STRATEGIES FOR EVALUATING PRINT AND ONLINE SOURCES

Evaluating a Book

- Read the dust jacket or cover copy for insights into the book's coverage and currency as well as the author's expertise.
- Scan the table of contents and identify any promising chapters.
- Read the author's preface, looking for his or her thesis and purpose.
- Check the index for key words or key phrases related to your research topic.
- Read the opening and concluding paragraphs of any promising chapter; if you are unsure about its usefulness, skim the whole chapter.
- Does the author have a discernable bias?

Evaluating an Article

- What do you know about the journal or magazine publishing the article? Scholarly journals (*American Economic Review, Journal of Marriage and the Family, The Wilson Quarterly*) publish articles about original research written by authorities in the field. Research essays always cite their sources in footnotes or bibliographies. Popular news and general interest magazines (*National Geographic, Smithsonian, Time, Ebony*), on the other hand, publish informative, entertaining, and easy-to-read articles written by editorial staff or freelance writers. Popular essays sometimes cite sources but often do not.

- What is the reputation of the journal or magazine? Determine the publisher or sponsor. Is it an academic institution or a commercial enterprise or individual? Does the publisher or publication have a reputation for accuracy and objectivity?
- Who are the readers of this journal or magazine?
- What are the author's credentials?
- Consider the title or headline of the article as well as the opening paragraph or two and the conclusion. Does the source appear to be too general or too technical for your needs and audience?
- For articles in journals, read the abstract (a summary of the main points) if there is one. Examine any photographs, charts, graphs, or other illustrations that accompany the article. Determine how useful they might be for your research purposes.

Evaluating a Web Site

- Consider the type of Web site. Is this site a personal blog or a professional publication? Often the URL, especially the top-level domain name, can give you a clue about the kinds of information provided and the type of organization behind the site. Common suffixes include:

  .com — business/commercial/personal
  .edu — educational institution
  .gov — government sponsored
  .net — various types of networks
  .org — nonprofit organization, but also some commercial/personal

- Be advised that *.org* is not regulated like *.edu* and *.gov,* for example. Most nonprofits use *.org,* but many commercial and personal sites do as well.
- Examine the home page of the site. Does the content appear to be related to your research topic?
- Is there an *About* link on the home page that takes you to background information on the site's sponsor? Is there a mission statement, history, or statement of philosophy? Can you verify whether the site is official — actually sanctioned by the organization or company?
- Identify the author of the site. What are the author's qualifications for writing on this subject?

- Is a print equivalent available? Is the Web version more or less extensive than the print version?
- When was the site last updated? Is the content current enough for your purposes?

You can also find sources on the Internet itself that offer useful guidelines for evaluating electronic sources. One excellent example was created by reference librarians at the Wolfgram Memorial Library of Widener University. Google *Wolfgram evaluate web pages* or visit <www3. widener.edu/Academics/Libraries/Wolfgram_Memorial_Library/Evaluate_ Web_Pages/659/>.

On the basis of your evaluation, select the most promising books, articles, and Web sites to pursue in depth for your research project.

Analyze Your Print and Online Sources

Before beginning to take notes, it is essential that you carefully analyze your sources for their thesis, overall argument, amount and credibility of evidence, bias, and reliability in helping you explore your research topic. Look for the writers' main ideas, key examples, strongest arguments, and conclusions. Read critically, and while it is easy to become absorbed in sources that support your own beliefs, always seek out several sources with opposing viewpoints, if only to test your own position. Look for information about the authors themselves—information that will help you determine their authority and where they position themselves in the broader conversation on the issue. You should also know the reputation and special interests of book publishers and magazines, because you are likely to get different views—conservative, liberal, international, feminist—on the same topic depending on the publication you read. Use the following checklist to assist you in analyzing your print and online sources.

CHECKLIST FOR ANALYZING PRINT AND ONLINE SOURCES

- What is the writer's thesis or claim?
- How does the writer support this thesis? Does the evidence seem reasonable and ample, or is it mainly anecdotal?
- Does the writer consider opposing viewpoints?
- Does the writer have any obvious political or religious biases? Is the writer associated with any special-interest groups such as Planned Parenthood, Greenpeace, Amnesty International, or the National Rifle Association?
- Is the writer an expert on the subject? Do other writers mention this author in their work?

- Is important information documented through footnotes or links so that it can be verified or corroborated in other sources?
- What is the author's purpose — to inform or to argue for a particular position or action?
- Do the writer's thesis and purpose clearly relate to your research topic?
- Does the source reflect current thinking and research in the field?

Develop a Working Bibliography for Your Print and Online Sources

As you discover books, journal and magazine articles, newspaper stories, and Web sites that you think might be helpful, you need to start maintaining a record of important information about each source. This record, called a working bibliography, will enable you to know where sources are located as well as what they are when it comes time to consult them or acknowledge them in your list of works cited or final bibliography (see pages 650–56 and 660). In all likelihood, your working bibliography will contain more sources than you actually consult and include in your list of works cited.

Some people find it easy to make a separate bibliography card, using a 3- by 5-inch index card, for each work that you think you might be helpful to your research. As your collection of cards grows, alphabetize them by the authors' last names. By using a separate card for each book, article, or Web site, you can continually edit your working bibliography, dropping sources that did not prove helpful for one reason or another and adding new ones.

With the computerization of most library resources, you now have the option to copy and paste bibliographic information from the library computer catalog and periodical indexes or from the Internet into a document on your computer that you can edit/add/delete/search throughout the research process. Or you can track your project online with the Bedford Bibliographer <bedfordstmartins.com/bibliographer>. The advantage of the copy/paste option over the index card method is accuracy, especially in punctuation, spelling, and capitalization — details that are essential in accessing Internet sites.

CHECKLIST FOR A WORKING BIBLIOGRAPHY OF PRINT
AND ONLINE SOURCES

For Books

- Library call number
- Names of all authors, editors, and translators
- Title and subtitle

- Publication data:

   Place of publication (city and state)
   Publisher's name
   Date of publication

- Edition (if not first) and volume number (if applicable)
- Medium (*Print* or *Web*)

For Periodical Articles

- Names of all authors
- Name and subtitle of article
- Title of journal, magazine, or newspaper
- Publication data:

   Volume number (when applicable) and issue number
   Date of issue
   Page numbers

- Medium (*Print* or *Web*)

For Internet Sources

- Names of all authors and/or editors
- Title and subtitle of the document
- Title of the longer work to which the document belongs (if applicable)
- Title of the site or discussion list
- Name of company or organization that owns the Web site
- Date of release, online posting, or latest revision
- Format of online source (Web page, .pdf, podcast)
- Date you accessed the site
- Electronic address (URL) or digital object identifier (DOI)

For Other Sources

- Name of author, government agency, organization, company, recording artist, personality, etc.
- Title of the work
- Format (pamphlet, unpublished diary, interview, television broadcast, etc.)
- Publication or production data:

   Name of publisher or producer
   Date of publication, production, or release
   Identifying codes or numbers (if applicable)

ELECTRONIC RESEARCH: KEYWORD SEARCHES AND SUBJECT DIRECTORIES

Using Keyword Searches to Locate Information in the Library and on the Internet

When searching for sources about your topic in an electronic database, in the library's computerized catalog, or on the Internet, you should start with a keyword search. To make the most efficient use of your time, you will want to know how to conduct a keyword search that is likely to yield solid sources and leads for your research project. As obvious or simple as it may sound, the key to a successful keyword search is the quality of the keywords you generate about your topic. You might find it helpful to start a list of potential keywords as you begin your research and add to it as your work proceeds. Often you will discover combinations of keywords that will lead you right to the sources you need.

Databases and library catalogs index sources by author, title, and year of publication, as well as by subject headings assigned by a cataloger who has previewed the source. The key here is to find a keyword that matches one of the subject headings. Once you begin to locate sources that are on your topic, be sure to note the subject headings listed for each source. You can use these subject headings as keywords to lead you to additional book sources or, later, to articles in periodicals using full-text databases like *Info Trac, LexisNexis, Expanded Academic ASAP,* or *JSTOR* to which your library subscribes. The figure on page 637 shows a typical book entry in a computer catalog. Notice the additional subject headings, which can be used as possible keywords.

The keyword search process is somewhat different—more wide open—when you are searching on the Web. It is always a good idea to look for search tips on the help screens or advanced search instructions for the search engine you are using before initiating a keyword search. When you type in a keyword in the "Search" box on a search engine's home page, the search engine electronically scans Web sites looking to match your keyword to titles and texts. On the Web, the quality of the search terms—keywords—is determined by the relevance of the hits on the first page or two that comes up. While it is not uncommon for a search, especially one on the Internet, to yield between 500,000 and 1,000,000 hits, the search engine's algorithm puts the best sources up front. If after scanning the first couple of pages of results you determine that these sites seem off topic, you will need to refine your search terms to either narrow or broaden your search.

COMPUTER CATALOG SCREEN: COMPLETE RECORD FOR A BOOK

Database Name: University of Vermont Libraries
Search Request: Title = apes, language
Search Results: Displaying 1 of 1 entries

◀ Previous   Next ▶

Long View   MARC View

Apes, language, and the human mind / Sue Savage-Rumbaugh, Stuart G....

Main Author: Savage-Rumbaugh, E. Sue, 1946-
Title: Apes, language, and the human mind / Sue Savage-Rumbaugh, Stuart G. Shanker, Talbot J. Taylor.
Published: New York : Oxford University Press, 1998.
Description: x, 244 p. : ill. ; 24 cm.
Subject(s): Bonobo --Psychology.
Kanzi (Bonobo)
Human-animal communication.
Language acquisition.
Neurolinguistics.

Collection: Bailey/Howe Books (3rd Floor)
Call Number: QL737.P96 S254 1998
Number of Items: 1
Status: Not Charged Check Shelf

Refining Keyword Searches on the Web

While some variation in command terms and characters exists among electronic databases and popular search engines on the Internet, the following functions are almost universally accepted. If you have a particular question about refining your keyword search, seek assistance by clicking on "Help" or "Advanced Search."

- Use quotation marks or parentheses to indicate that you are searching for words in exact sequence—e.g., "whooping cough"; (Supreme Court).
- Use AND or a plus sign (+) between words to narrow your search by specifying that all words need to appear in a document—e.g., tobacco AND cancer; Shakespeare + sonnet.
- Use NOT or a minus sign (–) between words to narrow your search by eliminating unwanted words—e.g., monopoly NOT game, cowboys–Dallas.
- Use OR to broaden your search by requiring that only one of the words need appear—e.g., buffalo OR bison.
- Use an asterisk (*) to indicate that you will accept variations of a term—e.g., "food label*" for food labels, food labeling, and so forth.

Using Subject Directories to Define and Develop Your Research Topic

If you are undecided as to exactly what you want to write about, the subject directories on the home pages of search engines make it easy to browse the Web by various subjects and topics for ideas that interest you. Subject directories can also be a big help if you have a topic but are undecided about your exact research question or if you simply want to see if there is enough material to supplement your research work with print sources. Once you choose a subject area in the directory, you can select more specialized subdirectories, eventually arriving at a list of sites closely related to your topic.

The most common question students have at this stage of a Web search is, "How can I tell if I'm looking in the right place?" There is no straight answer; if more than one subject area sounds plausible, you will have to dig more deeply into each of their subdirectories, using logic and the process of elimination to determine which one is likely to produce the best leads for your topic. In most cases, it doesn't take long—usually just one or two clicks—to figure out whether you're searching in the right subject area. If you click on a subject area and none of the topics listed in its subdirectories seems to pertain even remotely to your research topic, try a different subject area. As you browse through various subject directories and subdirectories, keep a running list of keywords associated with your topic that you can use in subsequent keyword searches.

NOTE TAKING

As you read, take notes. You're looking for ideas, facts, opinions, statistics, examples, and evidence that you think will be useful in writing your paper. As you work through the articles, look for recurring themes, and mark the places where the writers are in agreement and where they differ in their views. Try to remember that the effectiveness of your paper is largely determined by the quality—not necessarily the quantity—of your notes. The purpose of a research paper is not to present a collection of quotes that show you've read all the material and can report what others have said about your topic. Your goal is to analyze, evaluate, and synthesize the information you collect—in other words, to enter into the discussion of the issues and thereby take ownership of your topic. You want to view the results of your research from your own perspective and arrive at an informed opinion of your topic.

Now for some practical advice on taking notes: First, be systematic. As a rule, write one note on a card, and use cards of uniform size, preferably 4- by 6-inch cards because they are large enough to accommodate even a long note on a single card and yet small enough to be easily handled and carried. More important, when you get to the planning and writing stage, you will be able to sequence your notes according to the plan you have envisioned for your paper. Furthermore, should you decide to alter your organizational plan, you can easily reorder your cards to reflect those revisions.

Second, try not to take too many notes. One good way to help decide whether to take a note is to ask yourself, "How exactly does this material help prove or disprove my thesis?" You might even try envisioning where in your paper you could use the information. If it does not seem relevant to your thesis, don't bother to take a note.

Once you decide to take a note, you must decide whether to summarize, paraphrase, or quote directly. The approach that you take is largely determined by the content of the passage and the way you envision using it in your paper. All of the examples in the following discussion are taken from articles in *Subject & Strategy*.

Summary

When you *summarize* material from one of your sources, you capture in condensed form the essential idea of a passage, article, or entire chapter. Summaries are particularly useful when you are working with lengthy, detailed arguments or long passages of narrative or descriptive background information where the details are not germane to the overall thrust of your paper. You simply want to capture the essence of the passage while dispensing with the details because you are confident that your readers will readily understand the point being made or do not need to be convinced about the validity of the point. Because you are distilling information, a summary is always shorter than the original; often a chapter or more can be reduced to a paragraph, or several paragraphs to a sentence or two. Remember, in writing a summary you should use your own words.

Consider the following paragraphs in which Richard Lederer compares big words with small words.

> When you speak and write, there is no law that says you have to use big words. Short words are as good as long ones, and short, old words — like *sun* and *grass* and *home* — are best of all. A lot of small words, more than you might think, can meet your needs with a strength, grace, and charm that large words do not have.
>
> Big words can make the way dark for those who read what you write and hear what you say. Small words cast their clear light on big things — night and day, love and hate, war and peace, and life and death. Big words at times seem strange to the eye and the ear and the mind and the heart. Small words are the ones we seem to have known from the time we were born, like the hearth fire that warms the home.
>
> — RICHARD LEDERER,
> "The Case for Short Words," page 480

A student wishing to capture the gist of Lederer's point without repeating his detailed contrast wrote the following summary.

SUMMARY NOTE CARD

Short words

Lederer favors short words for their clarity, familiarity, durability, and overall usefulness.

Lederer, 480

Paraphrase

When you *paraphrase* a source, you restate the information in your own words instead of quoting directly. Unlike a summary, which gives a brief overview of the essential information in the original, a paraphrase seeks to maintain the same level of detail as the original to aid readers in understanding or believing the information presented. A paraphrase presents the original information in approximately the same number of words, but in the paraphraser's own wording. To put it another way, your paraphrase should closely parallel the presentation of ideas in the original but should not use the same words or sentence structure as the original. Even though you are using your own words in a paraphrase, it's important to remember that you are borrowing ideas and therefore must acknowledge the source of these ideas with a citation.

How would you paraphrase the following passage from a speech by Martin Luther King Jr.?

> But one hundred years later [after the Emancipation Proclamation], we must face the tragic fact that the Negro is still not free. One hundred years later, the life of the Negro is still sadly crippled by the manacles of segregation and the chains of discrimination. One hundred years later, the Negro lives on a lonely island of poverty in the midst of a vast ocean of material prosperity. One hundred years later, the Negro is still languishing in the corners of American society and finds himself an exile in his own land.
>
> —Martin Luther King Jr.,
> "I Have a Dream," page 486

The following note card illustrates how one student paraphrased the passage from King's speech.

PARAPHRASE NOTE CARD

Unfulfilled promises

On the one hundredth anniversary of the Emancipation Proclamation, African Americans find themselves still a marginalized people. African Americans do not experience the freedom that other Americans do. In a land of opportunity and plenty, racism and poverty affect the way they live their lives, separating them from mainstream society.

King, 486

In most cases, it is better to summarize or paraphrase materials— which by definition means using your own words—instead of quoting verbatim (word for word). Capturing an idea in your own words ensures that you have thought about and understood what your source is saying.

Direct Quotation

When you directly *quote* a source, you copy the words of your source exactly, putting all quoted material in quotation marks. When you make a quotation note card, carefully check for accuracy, including punctuation and capitalization. Be selective about what you choose to quote; reserve direct quotation for important ideas stated memorably, for especially clear explanations by authorities, and for arguments by proponents of a particular position in their own words.

Consider, for example, Deborah Tannen's powerful contrast between the ways boys and girls communicate:

> The girls in my study tended to talk at length about one topic, but the boys tended to jump from topic to topic. The second-grade girls exchanged stories about people they knew. The second-grade boys teased, told jokes, noticed things in the room, and talked about finding games to play. The sixth-grade girls talked about problems with a mutual friend. The sixth-grade boys talked about 55 different topics, none of which extended over more than a few turns.
>
> —DEBORAH TANNEN,
> "Sex, Lies, and Conversation," page 295

QUOTATION NOTE CARD

Conversation differences

"The girls in my study tended to talk at length about one topic, but the boys tended to jump from topic to topic. The second-grade girls exchanged stories about people they knew. The second-grade boys teased, told jokes, noticed things in the room, and talked about finding games to play. The sixth-grade girls talked about problems with a mutual friend. The sixth-grade boys talked about 55 different topics, none of which extended over more than a few turns."

Tannen, 295

On occasion, you'll find a useful passage with some memorable wording in it. Avoid the temptation to quote the whole passage; instead you can combine summary or paraphrase with direct quotation.

Consider the following paragraph from Rosalind Wiseman's essay on schoolgirls' roles in cliques.

Information about each other is currency in Girl World. The Banker creates chaos everywhere she goes by banking information about girls in her social sphere and dispensing it at strategic intervals for her own benefit. For instance, if a girl has said something negative about another girl, the Banker will casually mention it to someone in conversation because she knows it's going to cause a conflict and strengthen her status as someone "in the know." She can get girls to trust her because when she pumps them for information it doesn't seem like gossip; instead, she does it in an innocent, I'm-trying-to-be-your-friend way.

— ROSALIND WISEMAN,
"The Queen Bee and Her Court," page 320

Note how the student who took the following note was careful to put quotation marks around all words that have been borrowed directly.

QUOTATION AND SUMMARY NOTE CARD

Clique characters

Perhaps the most dangerous character in the clique is the Banker, who "creates chaos everywhere she goes by banking information about girls in her social sphere and dispensing it at strategic intervals for her own benefit. For instance, if a girl has said something negative about another girl, the Banker will casually mention it to someone in conversation because she knows it's going to cause a conflict and strengthen her status as someone 'in the know.'"

Wiseman, 320

Taking Notes on Internet Sources

You can take notes from the Internet just as you would with print sources. You will need to decide whether to summarize, paraphrase, or quote directly the information you wish to borrow. Copy the material into a separate document by using your mouse to highlight the portion of the text you want to save and then using the copy and paste features to add it to your research notes.

INTEGRATING QUOTATIONS INTO YOUR TEXT

Whenever you want to use borrowed material, be it a summary, paraphrase, or quotation, it's best to introduce the material with a *signal phrase*—a phrase that alerts the reader that borrowed information is to follow. A signal phrase usually consists of the author's name and a verb. Well-chosen signal phrases help you integrate quotations, paraphrases, and summaries into the flow of your paper. Besides, signal phrases let your reader know who is speaking and, in the case of summaries and paraphrases, exactly where your ideas end and someone else's begin. Never confuse your reader with a quotation that appears suddenly without introduction in your paper. Unannounced quotations leave your reader wondering how the quoted material relates to the point you are trying to make.

UNANNOUNCED QUOTATION

It's no secret that digital technology is having profound effects on American society, often shaping our very attitudes about the world. We're living at a time when this technology makes it not only possible, but also surprisingly easy for us to copy and share software, music, and video. Is this a good situation? Software and music companies see such copying as theft or a violation of copyright law. "[M]any of my students see matters differently. They freely copy and share music. And they copy and share software, even though such copying is often illegal" (Gorry 390).

In the following revision, the student integrated the quotation into the text not only by means of a signal phrase, but in a number of other ways as well. By giving the name of the writer being quoted, referring to his authority on the subject, noting that the writer is speaking from experience, and using the verb *counters,* the student provides more context so that the reader can better understand how this quotation is positioned within the discussion.

INTEGRATED QUOTATION

It's no secret that digital technology is having profound effects on American society, often shaping our very attitudes about the world. We're living at a time when this technology makes it not only possible, but also surprisingly easy for us to copy and share software, music, and video. Is this a good situation? Software and music companies see such copying as theft or a violation of copyright law. "[M]any of my students see matters differently," counters information technology specialist and Rice University professor G. Anthony Gorry. "They freely copy and share music. And they copy and share software, even though such copying is often illegal" (390).

How well you integrate a quote, paraphrase, or summary into your paper depends partly on varying your signal phrases and, in particular, choosing a verb for the signal phrase that accurately conveys the tone and intent of the writer you are citing. If a writer is arguing, use the verb *argues* (or *asserts, claims,* or *contends*); if the writer is contesting a particular position or fact, use the verb *contests* (or *denies, disputes, refutes,* or *rejects*). In using verbs that are specific to the situation in your paper, you bring your readers into the intellectual debate as well as avoid the monotony of repeating such all-purpose verbs as *says* or *writes.*

You should always try to use a signal phrase that fits the situation in your essay. The following are just a few examples of how you can vary signal phrases to add interest to your paper.

Malcolm X confesses that . . .

As professor of linguistics at Georgetown University Deborah Tannen has observed . . .

Bruce Catton, noted Civil War historian, emphasizes . . .

Rosalind Wiseman rejects the widely held belief that . . .

Robert Ramirez enriches our understanding of . . .

Carolina A. Miranda, a Latina living and working in New York City, explores . . .

Here are other verbs that you might use when constructing signal phrases.

acknowledges	declares	points out
adds	endorses	reasons
admits	grants	reports
believes	implies	responds
compares	insists	suggests
confirms		

A NOTE ON PLAGIARISM

The importance of honesty and accuracy in doing library research can't be stressed enough. Any material borrowed word for word must be placed within quotation marks and be properly cited; any idea, explanation, or argument you have paraphrased or summarized must be documented, and it must be clear where the paraphrased material begins and ends. In short, to use someone else's ideas, whether in their original form or in an altered form, without proper acknowledgment is to be guilty of plagiarism. And plagiarism is plagiarism even if it is accidental. A little attention and effort at the note-taking stage can go a long way toward eliminating the possibility of inadvertent plagiarism. Check all direct quotations against the wording of the original, and double-check your paraphrases to be sure that you have not used the writer's wording or sentence structure. It is easy to forget to put quotation marks around material taken verbatim or to use the same sentence structure and most of the same words—substituting a synonym here and there—and record it as a paraphrase. In working closely with the ideas and words of others, intellectual honesty demands that we distinguish between what we borrow—and therefore acknowledge in a citation—and what is our own.

While writing your paper, be careful whenever you incorporate one of your notes into your paper: Make sure that you put quotation marks around material taken verbatim, and double-check your text against your note card—or, better yet, against the original if you have it on hand—to make sure that your quotation is accurate. When paraphrasing or summarizing, make sure you haven't inadvertently borrowed key words or sentence structures from the original.

To learn more about how you can avoid plagiarism, go to the "Tutorial on Avoiding Plagiarism" at <bedfordstmartins.com/plagiarismtutorial>. There you will find information on the consequences of plagiarism, tutorials explaining what sources to acknowledge, how to keep good notes, how to organize your research, and how to appropriately integrate sources. Exercises are included throughout the tutorial to help you practice skills like integrating sources and recognizing acceptable paraphrases and summaries.

Using Quotation Marks for Language Borrowed Directly

Whenever you use another person's exact words or sentences, you must enclose the borrowed language in quotation marks. Without quotation marks you give your reader the impression that the wording is your own. Even if you cite the source, you are guilty of plagiarism if you fail to use quotation marks. The following example demonstrates both plagiarism and a correct citation for a direct quotation.

ORIGINAL SOURCE

On my father's side, I figured, high cheekbones and almond eyes probably showed evidence of native-Andean blood. The aquiline profiles and curly hair on my mother's side, on the other hand, are common on Mediterranean shores. My best guess: I was mostly European, a bit of native South American and perhaps a dash of Middle Eastern.

—Carolina A. Miranda,
"Diving into the Gene Pool," page 331

PLAGIARISM

On my father's side, I figured, high cheekbones and almond eyes probably showed evidence of native-Andean blood, confesses Carolina A. Miranda. The aquiline profiles and curly hair on my mother's side, on the other hand, are common on Mediterranean shores. My best guess: I was mostly European, a bit of native South American and perhaps a dash of Middle Eastern (331).

CORRECT CITATION OF BORROWED WORDS IN QUOTATION MARKS

"On my father's side, I figured, high cheekbones and almond eyes probably showed evidence of native-Andean blood," confesses Carolina A. Miranda. "The aquiline profiles and curly hair on my mother's side, on the other hand, are common on Mediterranean shores. My best guess: I was mostly European, a bit of native South American and perhaps a dash of Middle Eastern" (331).

Using Your Own Words and Word Order
When Summarizing and Paraphrasing

When summarizing or paraphrasing a source you need to use your own language. Pay particular attention to word choice and word order, especially if you are paraphrasing. Remember, it is not enough simply to use a synonym here or there and think you have paraphrased the source; you *must* restate the idea from the original in your own words, using your own style and sentence structure. In the following example, notice how plagiarism can occur when care is not taken in the wording or sentence structure of a paraphrase. Notice that in the acceptable paraphrase, the student writer uses her own language and sentence structure.

ORIGINAL SOURCE

Stereotypes are a kind of gossip about the world, a gossip that makes us prejudge people before we ever lay eyes on them. Hence it is not surprising that stereotypes have something to do with the dark world of prejudice. Explore most prejudices (note that the word means prejudgment) and you will find a cruel stereotype at the core of each one.

—Robert L. Heilbroner,
"Don't Let Stereotypes Warp Your Judgments," page 254

UNACCEPTABLY CLOSE WORDING

According to Heilbroner, we prejudge other people even before we have seen them when we think in stereotypes. That stereotypes are related to the ugly world of prejudice should not surprise anyone. If you explore the heart of most prejudices, beliefs that literally prejudge, you will discover a mean stereotype lurking (254).

UNACCEPTABLY CLOSE SENTENCE STRUCTURE

Heilbroner believes that stereotypes are images of people, images that enable people to prejudge other people before they have seen them. Therefore, no one should find it surprising that stereotypes are somehow related to the ugly world of prejudice. Examine most prejudices (the word literally means prejudgment) and you will uncover a vicious stereotype at the center of each (254).

ACCEPTABLE PARAPHRASE

Heilbroner believes that there is a link between stereotypes and the hurtful practice of prejudice. Stereotypes make for easy conversation, a kind of shorthand that enables us to find fault with people before ever meeting them. If you were to dissect most human prejudices, you would likely discover an ugly stereotype lurking somewhere inside it (254).

Preventing Plagiarism

Questions to Ask about Direct Quotations

- Do quotation marks clearly indicate the language that I borrowed verbatim?
- Is the language of the quotation accurate, with no missing or misquoted words or phrases?
- Do brackets or ellipsis marks clearly indicate any changes or omissions I have introduced?
- Does a signal phrase naming the author introduce each quotation? Does the verb in the signal phrase help establish a context for each quotation?
- Does a parenthetical page citation follow each quotation?

Questions to Ask about Summaries and Paraphrases

- Is each summary and paraphrase written in my own words and style?
- Does each summary and paraphrase accurately represent the opinion, position, or reasoning of the original writer?
- Does each summary and paraphrase start with a signal phrase so that readers know where my borrowed material begins?
- Does each summary and paraphrase conclude with a parenthetical page citation?

Questions to Ask about Facts and Statistics

- Do I use a signal phrase or some other marker to introduce each fact or statistic that is not common knowledge so that readers know where the borrowed material begins?
- Is each fact or statistic that is not common knowledge clearly documented with a parenthetical page citation?

Finally, as you proofread your final draft, check all your citations one last time. If at any time while you are taking notes or writing your paper you have a question about plagiarism, consult your instructor for clarification and guidance before proceeding.

DOCUMENTING SOURCES

When you summarize, paraphrase, or quote a person's thoughts and ideas, and when you use facts or statistics that are not commonly known or believed, you must properly acknowledge the source of your information. You must document the source of your information when you

- Quote a source word for word
- Refer to information and ideas from another source that you present in your own words as either a paraphrase or a summary
- Cite statistics, tables, charts, or graphs

You do not need to document

- Your own observations, experiences, and ideas
- Factual information available in a number of reference works (known as "common knowledge")
- Proverbs, sayings, and familiar quotations

A reference to the source of your borrowed information is called a *citation*. There are many systems for making citations, and your citations must consistently follow one of these systems. The documentation style recommended by the Modern Language Association (MLA) is commonly used in English and the humanities and is the style used for student papers throughout this book. Another common system is American Psychological Association (APA) style, which is used in the social sciences. In general, your instructor will tell you which system to use. For more information on documentation styles, consult the appropriate manual or handbook. For MLA style, consult the *MLA Handbook for Writers of Research Papers,* 7th ed. (New York: MLA, 2009).

There are two components of documentation in a research paper: the *in-text citation,* placed in the body of your paper, and the *list of works cited,* which provides complete publication data on your sources and is placed at the end of your paper.

In-Text Citations

Most in-text citations, also known as parenthetical citations, consist of only the author's last name and a page reference. Usually, the author's name is given in an introductory or signal phrase at the beginning of the borrowed material, and the page reference is given in parentheses at the end. If the author's name is not given at the beginning, it belongs in the parentheses along with the page reference. The parenthetical reference signals the end of the borrowed material and directs your readers to the list of works cited should they want to pursue a source. You should treat electronic sources as you would print sources; keep in mind that some electronic sources do not use page numbers, or use paragraph numbers instead of page numbers.

Consider the following examples of in-text citations from a student paper that borrows information from essays in *Subject & Strategy*.

IN-TEXT CITATIONS (MLA STYLE)

Many people are surprised to discover that English is not the official language of the United States. Today, even as English literacy becomes a necessity for people in many parts of the world, some people in the United States believe its primacy is being threatened right at home. Much of the current controversy focuses on Hispanic communities with large Spanish-speaking populations who may feel little or no pressure to learn English. Columnist and cultural critic Charles Krauthammer believes

Citation with author's name in the signal phrase

English should be America's official language. He notes that this country has been "blessed . . . with a linguistic unity that brings a critically needed cohesion to a nation as diverse, multiracial and multiethnic as America" and that communities such as these threaten the bond created by a common language (520). There are others, however, who think that "Language does not threaten American unity. Benign neglect is a good policy for any country

Citation with author's name in parentheses

when it comes to language, and it's a good policy for America" (King 531).

Works Cited

King, Robert D. "Should English Be the Law?" *Subject & Strategy*. 11th ed. Eds. Paul Eschholz and Alfred Rosa. Boston: Bedford, 2008. 522-31. Print.

Krauthammer, Charles. "In Plain English: Let's Make It Official." *Subject & Strategy*. 11th ed. Eds. Paul Eschholz and Alfred Rosa. Boston: Bedford, 2008. 519-21. Print.

In the preceding example, page references are to the articles as they appear here in *Subject & Strategy*. For articles and books located in the library, consult the following MLA guidelines for the list of works cited or the appropriate manual or handbook.

LIST OF WORKS CITED

In this section, you will find general guidelines for creating a list of works cited, followed by sample entries designed to cover the citation situations you will encounter most often. Make sure that you follow the formats as they appear on the following pages.

General Guidelines for a List of Works Cited Page

- Begin the list on a fresh page following the last page of text.
- Organize the list alphabetically by the author's last name. If the entry has no author name, alphabetize by the first major word of the title.
- Double-space the list (between and within entries).
- Begin each entry at the left margin. If the entry is longer than one line, indent the second and subsequent lines five spaces or one-half inch.
- Do not number the entries.

Books

BOOK BY ONE AUTHOR

Feel free to use a shortened version of the publisher's name — for example, *Houghton* for Houghton Mifflin, or *Cambridge UP* for Cambridge University Press.

> Kitwana, Bakari. *Why White Kids Love Hip Hop*. New York: Basic, 2005. Print.

BOOK BY TWO OR THREE AUTHORS

List the authors in the order in which they appear on the title page.

> Douglas, Susan, and Meredith Michaels. *The Mammy Myth: The Idealization of Motherhood and How It Has Undermined Women*. New York: Free, 2004. Print.

BOOK BY FOUR OR MORE AUTHORS

List the first author in the same way as for a single-author book, followed by a comma and the abbreviation *et al.* ("and others").

> Beardsley, John, et al. *Gee's Bend: The Women and Their Quilts*. Atlanta: Tinwood, 2002. Print.

TWO OR MORE SOURCES BY THE SAME AUTHOR

List two or more sources by the same author in alphabetical order by the first main word of the title. List the first source by the author's name. After the first source, in place of the author's name substitute three unspaced hyphens followed by a period.

> Twitchell, James B. *Branded Nation: When Culture Goes Pop*. New York: Simon, 2004. Print.
> ---. "The Branding of Higher Ed." *Forbes* 25 Nov. 2002: 50. Print.

---. *Living It Up: America's Love Affair with Luxury.* New York: Columbia UP, 2002. Print.

REVISED EDITION

Grout, Donald J., and Claude V. Palisca. *A History of Western Music.* 6th ed. New York: Norton, 2000. Print.

EDITED BOOK

Du Bois, W. E. B. *The Education of Black People: Ten Critiques, 1906-1960.* Ed. Herbert Aptheker. New York: Monthly Review, 2003. Print.

TRANSLATION

Camus, Albert. *The Stranger.* Trans. Matthew Ward. New York: Knopf, 1988. Print.

ANTHOLOGY

Eschholz, Paul, and Alfred Rosa, eds. *Subject & Strategy.* 11th ed. Boston: Bedford, 2008. Print.

SELECTION FROM AN ANTHOLOGY

Hwang, Caroline. "The Good Daughter." *Models for Writers.* Eds. Alfred Rosa and Paul Eschholz. 9th ed. Boston: Bedford, 2007. Print.

SECTION OR CHAPTER FROM A BOOK

Rufus, Anneli. "Bizarre as I Wanna Be." *Party of One: The Loner's Manifesto.* New York: Marlowe, 2003. Print.

Periodicals

ARTICLE IN A JOURNAL NUMBERED BY ISSUE ALONE

Some journals are numbered by issue and do not have volume numbers. For these journals, the year of publication, in parentheses, follows the issue number.

Yiwu, Liao. "The Survivor." *Paris Review* 185 (2008): 15-22. Print.

ARTICLE IN A JOURNAL NUMBERED BY VOLUME AND ISSUE

Some journals are numbered by both volume and issue. For these journals, follow the volume number with a period and the issue number. Then give the year of publication in parentheses.

Hilmes, Michele. "Where Is PBS's *Oprah*?: Media Studies and the Fear of the Popular." *Journal of Communication* 54.1 (2004): 174-177. Print.

ARTICLE IN A MONTHLY MAGAZINE

Abbreviate all months except May, June, and July.

Kaiser, Charles. "Civil Marriage, Civil Rights." *The Advocate* Mar. 2004: 72. Print.

ARTICLE IN A WEEKLY OR BIWEEKLY MAGAZINE

If an article in a magazine or newspaper is not printed on consecutive pages—for example, an article might begin on page 45, then skip to 48—include only the first page, followed by a plus sign.

Bartlett, Donald L., and James B. Steele. "Why We Pay So Much for Drugs." *Time* 2 Feb. 2004: 45+. Print.

ARTICLE IN A NEWSPAPER

If the newspaper lists an edition, add a comma after the date and specify the edition.

Wheeler, Ginger. "Weighing In on Chubby Kids: Smart Strategies to Curb Obesity." *Chicago Tribune* 9 Mar. 2004, final ed.: C11+. Print.

EDITORIAL (SIGNED/UNSIGNED)

Jackson, Derrick Z. "The Winner: Hypocrisy." Editorial. *Boston Globe* 6 Feb. 2004, 3rd ed.: A19. Print.

"Rescuing Education Reform." Editorial. *New York Times* 2 Mar. 2004, late ed.: A22. Print.

LETTER TO THE EDITOR

Liu, Penny. Letter. *New York Times* 17 Jan. 2004, late ed.: A14. Print.

Internet Sources

Citations for Internet sources follow the same rules as citations for print sources, but several additional pieces of information are required to cite an Internet source: the date of the source's electronic publication or copyright (if available), the medium (*Web*), and the date you accessed the source. Additionally, citations for different types of Internet sources require different types of information, so be sure to review the models that follow. (Note: MLA style discourages the use of Uniform Resource Locators [URLs], which can change frequently. Only include a URL if a reader would be unable to locate your source without one. In this case, enclose the URL in angle brackets after the access date, followed by a period.)

ENTIRE WEB SITE (SCHOLARLY PROJECT, INFORMATION DATABASE, OR PROFESSIONAL WEB SITE)

Include the name of the sponsoring organization, the date of the site's last update, if known, the medium, and the date of your access.

> *BBC: Religion & Ethics.* British Broadcasting Company, 2007. Web.
> 29 June 2007.
>
> *The Victorian Web.* Ed. George P. Landow. Brown U, 19 Apr. 2006. Web.
> 25 Mar. 2007.

SHORT WORK FROM A WEB SITE

> "Designer Babies." *BBC: Religion & Ethics.* British Broadcasting Company,
> 2007. Web. 29 June 2007.
>
> Wojtczak, Helena. "The Women's Social & Political Union." *The Victorian Web.*
> Ed. George P. Landow. Brown U, 19 Apr. 2006. Web. 25 Mar. 2007.

UNITITLED HOME PAGE ON PERSONAL WEB SITE

> Walker, Rob. Home page. N.p., 14 Mar. 2007. Web. 18 Mar. 2007.

ONLINE BOOK

> Whitman, Walt. *Leaves of Grass.* 1900. *Bartleby.com: Great Books Online.* Ed.
> Steven van Leeuwen. Web. 6 Mar. 2007.

SECTION OR CHAPTER FROM AN ONLINE BOOK

> Whitman, Walt. "Crossing Brooklyn Ferry." *Leaves of Grass.* 1900.
> *Bartleby.com: Great Books Online.* Ed. Steven van Leeuwen.
> Web. 6 Feb. 2007.

ARTICLE IN AN ONLINE SCHOLARLY JOURNAL

> Drury, Nevill. "How Can I Teach Peace When the Book Only Covers War?" *The
> Online Journal of Peace and Conflict Resolution* 5.1 (2003): n. pag. Web.
> 18 Sept. 2007.

ARTICLE IN AN ONLINE MAGAZINE

> Dicarlo, Lisa. "Six Degrees of Tiger Woods." *Forbes.com.* Forbes, Mar. 2004.
> Web. 19 Apr. 2007.

ARTICLE IN AN ONLINE NEWSPAPER

> Bhatt, Sanjay. "Got Game? Foundation Promotes Chess as Classroom Learning Tool." *Seattle Times Online*. Seattle Times, 15 Mar. 2004. Web. 18 Apr. 2007.

ARTICLE IN AN ONLINE REFERENCE WORK

> "Chili Pepper." *Encyclopedia Britannica*. Encyclopedia Britannica Premium Service, Web. 11 Dec. 2007.

ARTICLE FROM AN ONLINE DATABSE

Follow the guidelines for citing an article from a print periodical. Complete the citation by providing the name of the database, italicized, followed by the medium and date of access.

> Strimel, Courtney B. "The Politics of Terror: Rereading *Harry Potter*." *Children's Literature in Education* Mar. 2004: 35-53. *Academic Search Premier*. Web. 22 Feb. 2007.

E-MAIL

> Odell, Nathan. "Re: Photo for Alice Walker." E-mail to Paul A. Eschholz. 12 Mar. 2007.

ONLINE POSTING

If the post has no title, include a description, such as *Online posting*.

> Cook, Hardy M. "Falstaff and Other 'Heavy' Costumes." Shaksper: The Global Electronic Shakespeare Conf. 17 Mar. 2004. Web. 1 Apr. 2007.

Other Nonprint Sources

TELEVISION OR RADIO PROGRAM

> "The New Americans." *Independent Lens*. Narr. Don Cheadle. By Gita Saedi, Gordon Quinn, and Steve James. PBS. KLRN, San Antonio, 31 Mar. 2004. Television.

FILM OR VIDEO RECORDING

> *Schindler's List*. Dir. Steven Spielberg. Perf. Liam Neeson, Ralph Fiennes, and Ben Kingsley. 1993. Universal, 2004. DVD.

PERSONAL INTERVIEW
>Kozalek, Mark. Personal interview. 22 Jan. 2008.

LECTURE
>England, Paula. "Gender and Inequality: Trends and Causes." President's
>Distinguished Lecture Series. U. of Vermont. Memorial Lounge,
>Burlington. 22 Mar. 2004. Lecture.

A DOCUMENTED STUDENT ESSAY

Krista Gonnerman's essay grew out of reading *Subject & Strategy*. Her assignment was to write a documented essay on a current topic of debate. She knew from experience that to write a good essay, she would have to choose a topic she cared about. She also knew that she should allow herself time to gather her ideas and to focus her topic. After reading several selections in the Argumentation and Cause and Effect Analysis chapters and closely observing the trends of television advertising, Gonnerman found her topic. She started to see this paper as an opportunity to become more informed, to articulate her position, and to explore her observations.

Gonnerman began by brainstorming about her topic. She listed all the ideas, facts, questions, arguments, refutations, and causes and effects that came to mind as she thought about prescription drug advertisements. She then went to the library to find additional information and located several sources. Once confident that she had enough information, she made a rough outline of an organizational pattern. Keeping this pattern in mind, Gonnerman wrote a first draft. Later she went back and examined it carefully, assessing how it could be improved.

Gonnerman was writing this essay in the second half of the semester, after she had read a number of essays and had learned the importance of good paragraphing, unity, and sound organization. In revising her first draft, Gonnerman found where phrases and even whole sentences could be added to clarify her meaning. She moved some sentences, added transitions, and rewrote her concluding paragraphs to make them more forceful and persuasive. As you read Gonnerman's final draft, notice how she develops each of her paragraphs, how she uses specific information and examples to support her thesis, and how she uses the MLA in-text citation system to acknowledge her sources. Finally, notice how Gonnerman uses her opening paragraph to establish a context for her essay and how she uses her concluding paragraph to bring her essay back full circle.

Gonnerman 1

Writer's last name and page number

Krista Gonnerman

English 001

Professor Smith

May 27, 2003

Writer's name, course information, and date—all double-spaced

Pharmaceutical Advertising

Title centered

Turn on the television, wait for the commercial breaks, and you are guaranteed to see them: direct-to-consumer (DTC) pharmaceutical advertisements. In fact, as Candis McLean reports, "Americans now see an average of nine prescription ads per day on television" (38). Count the number of times you have seen advertisements for these products in the past week: Allegra, an allergy medication; Celebrex, a medication for arthritis pain; Clarinex, another allergy medication; Detrol, a pill to help control overactive bladder; Lamisil, a drug to combat toenail fungus; Lipitor, a medication used to lower cholesterol; Nexium, an acid reflux medication; Procrit, a medication meant to increase red blood cell production; Viagra, a medication for impotence; and Zoloft, an antidepressant. The list of drugs currently promoted on television seems endless and overwhelming. Flashy, celebrity endorsed, emotionally appealing, with snappy tag lines and occasionally catchy tunes, these thirty-second sound bites typically show healthy people enjoying life. And we are left to infer that these people are active, healthy, and happy because they use the advertised product.

In-text citation with author's name given in signal phrase and page number parenthetically

Catalog of examples illustrates her point that pharmaceutical advertisements are everywhere.

According to an NJBIZ survey, the pharmaceutical industry "has tripled drug advertising since 1996 to nearly $2.5 billion a year. . . . Of the print and broadcast ads, 60% were for just 20 medications" (4). McLean echoes this survey, reporting that industry spending is "up 28% from 1999 and 40 times the $55 million spent on mass media ads in 1991" (40); while West notes that in 1998 alone, drug companies spent more than $500 million solely on television advertising (A5). How can we account for this tremendous growth in pharmaceutical advertising, and how should consumers respond to such advertising?

Cites surveys to document increased advertising since mid-1990s

Writer asks questions that will be answered in this research paper.

The most significant and encompassing cause behind this veritable explosion of pharmaceutical advertising on television occurred in 1997 when the Federal Drug Administration (FDA) relaxed the regulations overseeing pharmaceutical advertising on television. Prior to 1997, the FDA regulations addressing prescription drug

Writer presents first cause for explosion in advertising.

advertisements were so strict that few manufacturers bothered to promote their drugs in the media. According to West, those drug manufacturers who sought to advertise on television were restricted to telecasting "a drug's name without stating its purpose. Or stating a drug's purpose without saying its name. Or stating a drug's name and medical purpose only if the patient insert was scrolled on the screen" (A6).

In 1996, the pharmaceutical industry filed a freedom of speech challenge and won, and in August of the following year the FDA's Division of Drug Marketing and Communications issued the revised regulations that are still in effect today. Currently, as West notes, "drug companies can now tell viewers . . . what their drug is used for without reciting or scrolling the entire Patient Insert; a major statement of serious side effects and a phone number or other route of obtaining the rest of the information" is now all that is required of the commercial (A6). No longer hampered by restrictions, the pharmaceutical industry began in 1997 and has continued to focus its advertising budget on television. According to *Editor & Publisher,* "the National Institute for Health Care Management in Washington reports that $1.8 billion was spent on d-t-c pharmaceutical advertising last year [1999], with $1.1 billion on TV" (33).

A second, but debatable, cause may originate in patients' becoming more proactive about their own health care. Both Carol Lewis, writing in *FDA Consumer,* and Dr. Sidney Wolfe, writing in the *New England Journal of Medicine,* note that beginning in the mid-1980s there was an increase in the number of individuals 1) seeking more medical information than they were being given by their doctors and 2) making medical decisions affecting their own health care. Wolfe and Lewis suggest that based on the pharmaceutical industry's awareness of this groundswell, the industry may have begun producing ads aimed at such consumers (Lewis 9; Wolfe 524–26). Although these anecdotal, undocumented conjectures by Lewis and Wolfe appear plausible, there is little to support the suggestion that greater patient involvement led to the dramatic increase in pharmaceutical advertisements on television.

Other causes for the proliferation of pharmaceutical advertisements have been suggested, but these ideas lack merit. For example, it has been suggested that because many individuals do not want to

After her first mention of the Federal Drug Adminis- tration in the previous paragraph, the writer presents the abbrevia- tion FDA in parentheses so she can use only the abbreviation in subsequent references.

Second cause for prolifera- tion of phar- maceutical advertising

Paraphrase of two sources with authors' names in a signal phrase

Writer includes both sources in parenthetical citation at conclusion of the para- phrase.

Other causes of advertising expansion

Gonnerman   3

make the necessary lifestyle changes, such as exercising and eating right — changes that would result in real health benefits — the pharmaceutical industry began running commercials, in part, to encourage individuals to seek out their doctors as a first step toward a healthier life. But the pharmaceutical industry is a for-profit industry, and its DTC commercials look to market products for the primary purpose of enhancing their own bottom lines, not to encourage consumers to embrace healthier lifestyles that will lead to their — potentially — not needing medications.

The July 2001 issue of *Health Care Strategic Management* reported that "The Coalition for Healthcare Communication, a group of advertising agencies and medical publications dependent on drug advertising, said that an analysis of leading published consumer surveys provides strong evidence that [DTC] advertising of prescription drugs is a valued source of health care information" ("Drug Industry Study," 10). In other words, the pharmaceutical industry began running the ads as a way of providing information-hungry patients with reliable knowledge. But as Maryann Napoli sarcastically notes, "Anyone trying to sell you something isn't going to give you the most balanced picture of the product's effectiveness and risks" (3). Or as Dr. Wolfe argues, "The education of patients . . . is too important to be left to the pharmaceutical industry, with its pseudo educational campaigns designed, first and foremost, to promote drugs" (526). Is it too cynical to think that pharmaceutical advertisements take advantage of "lazy" consumers who prefer the quick-fix medical solution to more demanding and sometimes time-consuming lifestyle changes?

The 1997 FDA regulatory revisions on media advertisements provided the pharmaceutical industry the opportunity to inundate television with its products. As consumers, however, it is our responsibility to understand what we are seeing and hearing and not to accept blindly the messages in the industry's thirty-second sound bites. While we can use the information conveyed in the commercials to help us make more informed decisions about our health care or use the information in consultation with our physicians, we must never forget that the commercials are meant to sell products, and if those products improve our health, it is merely a consequence of the industry's primary motive — profit.

Writer uses brackets within a quotation to explain that it is DTC advertising that the source is commenting upon.

Conclusion: Writer answers questions posed earlier.

The heading Works Cited is centered at the top of page.

Writer uses MLA style for her list of works cited. The list begins on a new page. Entries are presented in alphabetical order. The first line of each entry begins at the left margin; subsequent lines are indented five spaces. Double space within entries as well as between entries.

The correct MLA forms for various other kinds of publications are given on pages 650–56.

Works Cited

"Drug Industry Study Finds Direct-to-Consumer Ads Help Customers."
    Health Care Strategic Management July 2001: 10. Print.

Lewis, Carol. "The Impact of Direct-to-Consumer Advertising." *FDA
    Consumer* Mar/Apr. 2003: 9. *MasterFILE Premier*. Web. 20 May
    2003.

Liebeskind, Ken. "Targeted Ads for New Drugs a Shot in the Arm." *Editor
    & Publisher* Nov. 2000: 33. Print.

McLean, Candis. "The Real Drug Pushers." *Report/Newsmagazine* 19 Mar.
    2001: 38-42. *MasterFILE Premier*. Web. 20 May 2003.

Napoli, Maryann. "Those Omnipresent Prescription Drug Ads: What to
    Look Out For." *Healthfacts* June 2001: 3. Print.

"NJBIZ." *Business News New Jersey* 25 Feb. 2002: 3-5. *MasterFILE
    Premier*. Web. 20 May 2003.

West, Diane. "DTC Ponders the Twilight Zone of TV Advertising."
    Pharmaceutical Executive May 1999: A4-A8. *MasterFILE Premier*.
    Web. 20 May 2003.

Wolfe, Sidney M. "Direct-to-Consumer Advertising — Education or
    Emotion Promotion?" *New England Journal of Medicine* 346.7
    (2002): 524-26. *MasterFILE Premier*. Web. 20 May 2003.

Glossary of Rhetorical Terms

Abstract   See *Concrete/Abstract.*

Allusion   An allusion is a passing reference to a familiar person, place, or thing drawn from history, the Bible, mythology, or literature. An allusion is an economical way for a writer to capture the essence of an idea, atmosphere, emotion, or historical era, as in "The scandal was his Watergate," or "He saw himself as a modern Job," or "Everyone there held those truths to be self-evident." An allusion should be familiar to the reader; if it is not, it will add nothing to the meaning.

Analogy   Analogy is a special form of comparison in which the writer explains something unfamiliar by comparing it to something familiar: "A transmission line is simply a pipeline for electricity. In the case of a water pipeline, more water will flow through the pipe as water pressure increases. The same is true of a transmission line for electricity." See also the discussion of analogy on pages 260–61.

Analytical Reading   Reading analytically means reading actively, paying close attention to both the content and the structure of the text. Analytical reading often involves answering several basic questions about the piece of writing under consideration:

1. What does the author want to say? What is his or her main point?

2. Why does the author want to say it? What is his or her purpose?

3. What strategy or strategies does the author use?

4. Why and how does the author's writing strategy suit both the subject and the purpose?

5. What is special about the way the author uses the strategy?

6. How effective is the essay? Why?

For a detailed example of analytical reading, see Chapter 1.

Appropriateness   See *Diction.*

Argument   Argument is one of the four basic types of prose. (Narration, description, and exposition are the other three.) To argue is to attempt to convince the reader to agree with a point of view, to make a given decision, or to pursue a particular course of action. Logical argument is based on reasonable explanations and appeals to the reader's intelligence. See Chapter 12 for further discussion of argumentation. See also *Logical Fallacies; Persuasion.*

Assertion   The thesis or proposition that a writer puts forward in an argument.

Assumption   A belief or principle, stated or implied, that is taken for granted.

Attitude   A writer's attitude reflects his or her opinion of a subject. For example, a writer can think very positively or very negatively about a subject. In most cases, the writer's attitude falls somewhere between these two extremes. See also *Tone.*

Audience   An audience is the intended readership for a piece of writing. For example, the readers of a national weekly newsmagazine come from all walks of life and have diverse opinions, attitudes, and educational experiences. In contrast, the readership for an organic chemistry journal is made up of people whose interests and educational backgrounds are quite similar. The essays in this book are intended for general readers — intelligent people who may lack specific information about the subject being discussed.

Beginnings/Endings   A *beginning* is the sentence, group of sentences, or section that introduces an essay. Good beginnings usually identify the thesis or controlling idea, attempt to interest the reader, and establish a tone. Some effective ways in which writers begin essays include (1) telling an anecdote that illustrates the thesis, (2) providing a controversial statement or opinion that engages the reader's interest, (3) presenting startling statistics or facts, (4) defining a term that is central to the discussion that follows, (5) asking thought-provoking questions, (6) providing a quotation that illustrates the thesis, (7) referring to a current event that helps establish the thesis, or (8) showing the significance of the subject or stressing its importance to the reader.

An *ending* is the sentence or group of sentences that brings an essay to closure. Good endings are purposeful and well planned. Endings satisfy readers when they are the natural outgrowths of the essays themselves and convey a sense of finality or completion. Good essays do not simply stop; they conclude.

Cause and Effect Analysis   Cause and effect analysis is one of the types of exposition. (Process analysis, definition, division and classification, illustration, and comparison and contrast are the others.) Cause and effect analysis answers the question *why?* It explains the reasons for an occurrence or the consequences of an action. See Chapter 11 for a detailed discussion of cause and effect analysis. See also *Exposition.*

Claim   The thesis or proposition put forth in an argument.

Classification   Classification, along with division, is one of the types of exposition. (Process analysis, definition, comparison and contrast, illustration, and cause and effect analysis are the others.) When classifying, the writer arranges and sorts people, places, or things into categories according to their differing characteristics, thus making them more manageable for the writer and more understandable for the reader. See Chapter 9 for a detailed discussion of classification. See also *Division; Exposition.*

Cliché   A cliché is an expression that has become ineffective through overuse. Expressions such as *quick as a flash, dry as dust, jump for joy,* and *slow as molasses* are all clichés. Good writers normally avoid such trite expressions and seek instead to express themselves in fresh and forceful language.

Coherence   Coherence is a quality of good writing that results when all sentences, paragraphs, and longer divisions of an essay are naturally connected. Coherent writing is achieved through (1) a logical sequence of ideas (arranged in chronological order, spatial order, order of importance, or some other appropriate order), (2) the thoughtful repetition of key words and ideas, (3) a pace suitable for your topic and reader, and (4) the use of transitional words and expressions. Coherence should not be confused with unity. (See *Unity.*) See also *Transitions.*

Colloquial Expressions   A colloquial expression is characteristic of or appropriate to spoken language or to writing that seeks its effect. Colloquial expressions are informal, as *chem, gym, come up with, be at loose ends, won't,* and *photo* illustrate. Thus, colloquial expressions are acceptable in formal writing only if they are used purposefully.

Comparison and Contrast   Comparison and contrast is one of the types of exposition. (Process analysis, definition, division and classification, illustration, and cause and effect analysis are the others.) In comparison and contrast, the writer points out the similarities and differences between two or more subjects in the same class or category. The function of any comparison and contrast is to clarify — to reach some conclusion about the items being compared and contrasted. See Chapter 8 for a detailed discussion of comparison and contrast. See also *Exposition.*

Conclusions   See *Beginnings/Endings.*

Concrete/Abstract   A *concrete* word names a specific object, person, place, or action that can be directly perceived by the senses: *car, bread, building, book, Abraham Lincoln, Chicago,* or *hiking.* An *abstract word,* in contrast, refers to general qualities, conditions, ideas, actions, or relationships that cannot be directly perceived by the senses: *bravery, dedication, excellence, anxiety, stress, thinking,* or *hatred.*

Although writers must use both concrete and abstract language, good writers avoid using too many abstract words. Instead, they rely on concrete words to define and illustrate abstractions. Because concrete words affect the senses, they are easily comprehended by the reader.

Connotation/Denotation   Both connotation and denotation refer to the meanings of words. *Denotation* is the dictionary meaning of a word, the literal meaning. *Connotation,* on the other hand, is the implied or suggested meaning of a word. For example, the denotation of *lamb* is "a young sheep." The connotations of lamb are numerous: *gentle, docile, weak, peaceful, blessed, sacrificial, blood, spring, frisky, pure, innocent* and so on. Good writers are sensitive to both the denotations and the connotations of words, and they use these meanings to their advantage in their writing. See also *Slanting.*

Controlling Idea   See *Thesis.*

Deduction   Deduction is the process of reasoning from a stated premise to a necessary conclusion. This form of reasoning moves from the general to the specific. See Chapter 12 for a discussion of deductive reasoning and its relation to argumentative writing. See also *Induction; Syllogism.*

Definition   Definition is one of the types of exposition. (Process analysis, division and classification, comparison and contrast, illustration, and cause and effect analysis are the others.) Definition is a statement of the meaning of a word. A definition may be either brief or extended, part of an essay or an entire essay itself. See Chapter 10 for a detailed discussion of definition. See also *Exposition.*

Denotation   See *Connotation/Denotation.*

Description   Description is one of the four basic types of prose. (Narration, exposition, and argument are the other three.) Description tells how a person, place, or thing is perceived by the five senses. Objective description reports these sensory qualities factually, whereas subjective description gives the writer's interpretation of them. See Chapter 5 for a detailed discussion of description.

Dialogue   Dialogue is conversation that is recorded in a piece of writing. Through dialogue writers reveal important aspects of characters' personalities as well as events in the narrative.

Diction   Diction refers to a writer's choice and use of words. Good diction is precise and appropriate — the words mean exactly what the writer intends, and the words are well suited to the writer's subject, intended audience, and purpose in writing. The word-conscious writer knows that there are differences among *aged*, *old*, and *elderly*; *blue*, *navy*, and *azure*; and *disturbed*, *angry*, and *irritated*. Furthermore, this writer knows in which situation to use each word. See also *Connotation/Denotation*.

Division   Like comparison and contrast, division and classification are separate yet closely related mental operations. Division involves breaking down a single large unit into smaller subunits or breaking down a large group of items into discrete categories. For example, the student body at your college or university can be divided into categories according to different criteria (by class, by home state or country, by sex, and so on).

Dominant Impression   A dominant impression is the single mood, atmosphere, or quality a writer emphasizes in a piece of descriptive writing. The dominant impression is created through the careful selection of details and is, of course, influenced by the writer's subject, audience, and purpose. See also the discussion on pages 114–15 in Chapter 5.

Draft   A draft is a version of a piece of writing at a particular stage in the writing process. The first version produced is usually called the *rough draft* or *first draft* and is a writer's beginning attempt to give overall shape to his or her ideas. Subsequent versions are called *revised drafts*. The copy presented for publication is the *final draft*.

Editing   During the editing stage of the writing process, the writer makes his or her prose conform to the conventions of the language. This includes making final improvements in sentence structure and diction, and proofreading for wordiness and errors in grammar, usage, spelling, and punctuation. After editing, the writer is ready to prepare a final copy.

Emphasis   Emphasis is the placement of important ideas and words within sentences and longer units of writing so that they have the greatest impact. In general, the end has the most impact, and the beginning nearly as much; the middle has the least. See also *Organization*.

Endings   See *Beginnings/Endings*.

Essay   An essay is a relatively short piece of nonfiction in which the writer attempts to make one or more closely related points. A good essay is purposeful, informative, and well organized.

Ethos   A type of argumentative proof having to do with the ethics of the arguer: honesty, trustworthiness, and even morals.

Evaluation   An evaluation of a piece of writing is an assessment of its effectiveness or merit. In evaluating a piece of writing, you should ask the following questions: What is the writer's purpose? Is it a worthwhile purpose? Does the writer achieve the purpose? Is the writer's information sufficient and accurate? What are the strengths of the essay? What are its weaknesses? Depending on the type of writing and the purpose, more specific questions can also be asked. For example, with an argument you could ask: Does the writer follow the principles of logical thinking? Is the writer's evidence convincing?

Evidence   Evidence is the data on which a judgment or argument is based or by which proof or probability is established. Evidence usually takes the form of statistics, facts, names, examples or illustrations, and opinions of authorities.

Examples   Examples illustrate a larger idea or represent something of which they are a part. An example is a basic means of developing or clarifying an idea. Furthermore, examples enable writers to show and not simply tell readers what they mean. The terms *example* and *illustration* are sometimes used interchangeably. See also the discussion of illustration on pages 150–51 in Chapter 6.

Exposition   Exposition is one of the four basic types of prose. (Narration, description, and argument are the other three.) The purpose of exposition is to clarify, explain, and inform. The methods of exposition presented in this text are process analysis, definition, division and classification, comparison and contrast, illustration, and cause and effect analysis. For a detailed discussion of each of these methods of exposition, see the appropriate chapter.

Fact   A piece of information presented as having a verifiable certainty or reality.

Fallacy   See *Logical Fallacies*.

Figures of Speech   Figures of speech are brief, imaginative comparisons that highlight the similarities between things that are basically dissimilar. They make writing vivid and interesting and therefore more memorable. The most common figures of speech are these:

Simile — An implicit comparison introduced by *like* or *as*: "The fighter's hands were *like* stone."

Metaphor — An implied comparison that uses one thing as the equivalent of another: "All the world's a stage."

Personification — A special kind of simile or metaphor in which human traits are assigned to an inanimate object: "The engine coughed and then stopped."

Focus   Focus is the limitation that a writer gives his or her subject. The writer's task is to select a manageable topic given the constraints of time, space, and purpose. For example, within the general subject of sports, a writer could focus on government support of amateur athletes or narrow the focus further to government support of Olympic athletes.

General   See *Specific/General*.

Idiom   An idiom is a word or phrase that is used habitually with a particular meaning in a language. The meaning of an idiom is not always readily apparent to nonnative speakers of that language. For example, *catch cold, hold a job, make up your mind*, and *give them a hand* are all idioms in English.

Illustration   Illustration is a type of exposition. (Definition, division and classification, comparison and contrast, cause and effect analysis, and process analysis are the others.) With illustration the writer uses examples — specific facts, opinions, samples, and anecdotes or stories — to support a generalization and to make it more vivid, understandable, and persuasive. See Chapter 6 for a detailed discussion of illustration. See also *Examples*.

Induction   Induction is the process of reasoning to a conclusion about all members of a class through an examination of only a few members of the class. This form of reasoning moves from the particular to the general. See Chapter 12 for a discussion of inductive reasoning and its relation to argumentative writing. Also see *Deduction*.

Introductions   See *Beginnings/Endings*.

Irony   Irony is the use of words to suggest something different from their literal meaning. For example, when Jonathan Swift proposes in "A Modest Proposal" that Ireland's problems could be solved if the people of Ireland fattened their babies and sold them to the English landlords for food, he meant that almost any other solution would be preferable. A writer can use irony to establish a special relationship with the reader and to add an extra dimension or twist to the meaning of a word or phrase.

Jargon   See *Technical Language*.

Logical Fallacies   A logical fallacy is an error in reasoning that renders an argument invalid. Some of the more common logical fallacies are these:

Oversimplification — The tendency to provide simple solutions to complex problems: "The reason we have inflation today is that OPEC has unreasonably raised the price of oil."

Non sequitur ("it does not follow") — An inference or conclusion that does not follow from established premises or evidence: "It was the best movie I saw this year, and it should get an Academy Award."

Post hoc, ergo propter hoc ("after this, therefore because of this") — Confusing chance or coincidence with causation. Because one event comes after another one, it does not necessarily mean that the first event caused the second: "I won't say I caught a cold at the hockey game, but I certainly didn't have it before I went there."

Begging the question — Assuming in a premise that which needs to be proven: "If American autoworkers built a better product, foreign auto sales would not be so high."

False analogy — Making a misleading analogy between logically unconnected ideas: "He was a brilliant basketball player; therefore, there's no question in my mind that he will be a fine coach."

Either/or thinking — The tendency to see an issue as having only two sides: "Used car salespeople are either honest or crooked."

See also Chapter 12.

Logical Reasoning See *Deduction; Induction.*

Logos A type of argumentative proof having to do with the logical qualities of an argument: data, evidence, and factual information.

Metaphor See *Figures of Speech.*

Narration Narration is one of the four basic types of prose. (Description, exposition, and argument are the other three.) To narrate is to tell a story, to tell what happened. Although narration is most often used in fiction, it is also important in nonfiction, either by itself or in conjunction with other types of prose. See Chapter 4 for a detailed discussion of narration.

Objective/Subjective *Objective* writing is factual and impersonal, whereas subjective writing, sometimes called *impressionistic* writing, relies heavily on personal interpretation. For a discussion of objective description and subjective description, see Chapter 5.

Opinion An opinion is a belief or conclusion not substantiated by positive knowledge or proof. An opinion reveals personal feelings or attitudes or states a position. Opinion should not be confused with argument.

Organization In writing, organization is the thoughtful arrangement and presentation of one's points or ideas. Narration is often organized chronologically. Exposition may be organized from simplest to most complex or from most familiar to least familiar. Argument may be organized from least important to most important. There is no single correct pattern of organization for a given piece of writing, but good writers are careful to discover an order of presentation suitable for their audience and their purpose.

Paradox A paradox is a seemingly contradictory statement that may nonetheless be true. For example, "We little know what we have until we lose it" is a paradoxical statement.

Paragraph The paragraph, the single most important unit of thought in an essay, is a series of closely related sentences. These sentences adequately develop the central or controlling idea of the paragraph. This central or controlling idea, usually stated in a topic sentence, is necessarily related to the purpose of the whole composition. A well-written paragraph has several distinguishing characteristics: a clearly stated or implied topic sentence, adequate development, unity, coherence, and an appropriate organizational strategy.

Parallelism Parallel structure is the repetition of word order or form either within a single sentence or in several sentences that develop the same central idea.

As a rhetorical device, parallelism can aid coherence and add emphasis. Roosevelt's statement, "I see one third of a nation ill-housed, ill-clad, ill-nourished," illustrates effective parallelism.

Pathos A type of argumentative proof having to do with audience: emotional language, connotative diction, and appeals to certain values.

Personification See *Figures of Speech*.

Persuasion Persuasion, or persuasive argument, is an attempt to convince readers to agree with a point of view, to make a given decision, or to pursue a particular course of action. Persuasion appeals heavily to the emotions, whereas logical argument does not. For the distinction between logical argument and persuasive argument, see Chapter 12.

Point of View Point of view refers to the grammatical person of the speaker in an essay. For example, a first-person point of view uses the pronoun *I* and is commonly found in autobiography and the personal essay; a third-person point of view uses the pronouns *he, she,* or *it* and is commonly found in objective writing. See Chapter 4 for a discussion of point of view in narration.

Prewriting Prewriting encompasses all the activities that take place before a writer actually starts a rough draft. During the prewriting stage of the writing process, the writer selects a subject area, focuses on a particular topic, collects information and makes notes, brainstorms for ideas, discovers connections between pieces of information, determines a thesis and purpose, rehearses portions of the writing in his or her mind or on paper, and makes a scratch outline. For some suggestions about prewriting, see Chapter 2, pp. 18–21.

Process Analysis Process analysis is a type of exposition. (Definition, division and classification, comparison and contrast, illustration, and cause and effect analysis are the others.) Process analysis answers the question *how?* and explains how something works or gives step-by-step directions for doing something. See Chapter 7 for a detailed discussion of process analysis. See also *Exposition*.

Publication The publication stage of the writing process is when the writer shares his or her writing with the intended audience. Publication can take the form of a typed or an oral presentation, a photocopy, or a commercially printed rendition. What's important is that the writer's words are read in what amounts to their final form.

Purpose Purpose is what the writer wants to accomplish in a particular piece of writing. Purposeful writing seeks to *relate* (narration), to *describe* (description), to *explain* (process analysis, definition, division and classification, comparison and contrast, and cause and effect analysis), or to *convince* (argument).

Revision During the revision stage of the writing process, the writer determines what in the draft needs to be developed or clarified so that the essay says what the writer intends it to say. Often the writer needs to revise several times before the essay is "right." Comments from peer evaluators can be invaluable in helping writers determine what sorts of changes need to be made. Such changes can include adding material, deleting material, changing the order of presentation, and substituting new material for old.

Rhetorical Question A rhetorical question is a question that is asked but requires no answer from the reader. "When will nuclear proliferation end?" is such a question. Writers use rhetorical questions to introduce topics they plan to discuss or to emphasize important points.

Rough Draft See *Draft*.

Sequence Sequence refers to the order in which a writer presents information. Writers commonly select chronological order, spatial order, order of importance, or order of complexity to arrange their points. See also *Organization*.

Simile See *Figures of Speech*.

Slang   Slang is the unconventional, very informal language of particular sub-groups of a culture. Slang, such as *bummed, coke, split, hurt, dis, blow off,* and *cool,* is acceptable in formal writing only if it is used purposefully.

Slanting   The use of certain words or information that results in a biased viewpoint.

Specific/General   *General words* name groups or classes of objects, qualities, or actions. *Specific words,* in contrast, name individual objects, qualities, or actions within a class or group. To some extent, the terms *general* and *specific* are relative. For example, *dessert* is a class of things. *Pie,* however, is more specific than *dessert* but more general than *pecan pie* or *chocolate cream pie.*

Good writing judiciously balances the general with the specific. Writing with too many general words is likely to be dull and lifeless. General words do not create vivid responses in the reader's mind as concrete, specific words can. However, writing that relies exclusively on specific words may lack focus and direction — the control that more general statements provide.

Strategy   A strategy is a means by which a writer achieves his or her purpose. Strategy includes the many rhetorical decisions that the writer makes about organization, paragraph structure, syntax, and diction. In terms of the whole essay, strategy refers to the principal rhetorical mode that the writer uses. If, for example, a writer wishes to show how to make chocolate chip cookies, the most effective strategy would be process analysis. If it is the writer's purpose to show why sales of American cars have declined in recent years, the most effective strategy would be cause and effect analysis.

Style   Style is the individual manner in which a writer expresses ideas. Style is created by the author's particular selection of words, construction of sentences, and arrangement of ideas.

Subject   The subject of an essay is its content, what the essay is about. Depending on the author's purpose and the constraints of space, a subject may range from one that is broadly conceived to one that is narrowly defined.

Subjective   See *Objective/Subjective.*

Supporting Evidence   See *Evidence.*

Syllogism   A syllogism is an argument that utilizes deductive reasoning and consists of a major premise, a minor premise, and a conclusion. For example:

All trees that lose leaves are deciduous. (*Major premise*)

Maple trees lose their leaves. (*Minor premise*)

Therefore, maple trees are deciduous. (*Conclusion*)

See also *Deduction.*

Symbol   A symbol is a person, place, or thing that represents something beyond itself. For example, the eagle is a symbol of the United States, and the bear is a symbol of Russia.

Syntax   Syntax refers to the way in which words are arranged to form phrases, clauses, and sentences as well as to the grammatical relationship among the words themselves.

Technical Language   Technical language, or jargon, is the special vocabulary of a trade or profession. Writers who use technical language do so with an awareness of their audience. If the audience is a group of peers, technical language may be used freely. If the audience is a more general one, technical language should be used sparingly and carefully so as not to sacrifice clarity. See also *Diction.*

Thesis   A thesis is a statement of the main idea of an essay. Also known as the *controlling idea,* a thesis may sometimes be implied rather than stated directly.

Title   A title is a word or phrase set off at the beginning of an essay to identify the subject, to capture the main idea of the essay, or to attract the reader's attention.

A title may be explicit or suggestive. A subtitle, when used, extends or restricts the meaning of the main title.

Tone   Tone is the manner in which a writer relates to an audience — the "tone of voice" used to address readers. Tone may be described as friendly, serious, distant, angry, cheerful, bitter, cynical, enthusiastic, morbid, resentful, warm, playful, and so forth. A particular tone results from a writer's diction, sentence structure, purpose, and attitude toward the subject. See also *Attitude*.

Topic Sentence   The topic sentence states the central idea of a paragraph and thus limits and controls the subject of the paragraph. Although the topic sentence most often appears at the beginning of the paragraph, it may appear at any other point, particularly if the writer is trying to create a special effect. Also see *Paragraph*.

Transitions   Transitions are words or phrases that link sentences, paragraphs, and larger units of a composition to achieve coherence. These devices include parallelism, pronoun references, conjunctions, and the repetition of key ideas, as well as the many conventional transitional expressions, such as *moreover, on the other hand, in addition, in contrast*, and *therefore*. Also see *Coherence*.

Unity   Unity is achieved in an essay when all the words, sentences, and paragraphs contribute to its thesis. The elements of a unified essay do not distract the reader. Instead, they all harmoniously support a single idea or purpose.

Verb   Verbs can be classified as either strong verbs (*scream, pierce, gush, ravage*, and *amble*) or weak verbs (*be, has, get*, and *do*). Writers prefer to use strong verbs to make their writing more specific, more descriptive, and more action filled.

Voice   Verbs can be classified as being in either the active or the passive voice. In the active voice, the doer of the action is the grammatical subject. In the passive voice, the receiver of the action is the subject:

Active: Glenda questioned all of the children.

Passive: All of the children were questioned by Glenda.

Writing Process   The writing process consists of five major stages: prewriting, writing drafts, revision, editing, and publication. The process is not inflexible, but there is no mistaking the fact that most writers follow some version of it most of the time. Although orderly in its basic components and sequence of activities, the writing process is nonetheless continuous, creative, and unique to each individual writer. See Chapter 2 for a detailed discussion of the writing process. See also *Draft, Editing, Prewriting, Publication, Revision*.

Acknowledgments

Carl M. Cannon. "The Real Computer Virus." From *American Journalism Review*, April 2001. Copyright © 2001 American Journalism Review. Reprinted with permission of the publisher.

Rachel Carson. "The Obligation to Endure." Chapter 2 of *Silent Spring* by Rachel Carson. Copyright © 1962 by Rachel Carson. Renewed 1990 by Roger Christie. Reprinted by permission of Houghton Mifflin Company. All rights reserved.

Bruce Catton. "Grant and Lee: A Study in Contrasts." Originally published in *The American Story*, edited by Earl Schneck Miers (1956). Copyright © Capitol Historical Society, 1956. Reprinted with permission. All rights reserved.

Katrina Clark. "My Father Was an Anonymous Sperm Donor." From the *Washington Post*, December 17, 2006, B1. Copyright © 2006. Reprinted by permission of the author.

Elizabeth Corcoran. "Don't Marry A Lazy Man." From *Forbes.com*, August 23, 2006. Copyright © 2007 Forbes.com. Reprinted by permission of Forbes.com LLC™. All rights reserved.

Annie Dillard. From *An American Childhood* by Annie Dillard. Copyright © 1987 by Annie Dillard. Reprinted by permission of HarperCollins Publishers, Inc.

Dave Ehrenfeld. "A Techno-Pox Upon the Land." Originally entitled "Agricultural Biotechnology Presents Health Risks." From the October 1997 issue of *Harper's Magazine*. Copyright © 1997 by Harper's Magazine. Reprinted by special permission. All rights reserved.

Lars Eighner. "On Dumpster Diving." From *Travels With Lizbeth* by Lars Eighner. Copyright © 1993 by Lars Eighner. Reprinted by permission of St. Martin's Press, LLC.

Linda Flower. "Writing for an Audience." From *Problem Solving Strategies for Writing*, Fourth Edition, by Linda Flower. Copyright © 1993. Reprinted by permission of Heinie, a division of Thomson Learning: www.thomsonrights. com. Fax: 800 730-2215.

Thomas L. Friedman. "My Favorite Teacher." From *The New York Times*, January 9, 2001, Op-ed. Copyright © 2001 by The New York Times Company. Reprinted by permission.

Nikki Giovanni. "Campus Racism 101." From *Racism 101* by Nikki Giovanni. Copyright © 1994 by Nikki Giovanni. Reprinted by permission of HarperCollins Publishers.

Natalie Goldberg. "Be Specific" from *Writing Down The Bones: Freeing the Writer Within* by Natalie Goldberg. Copyright © 1986 by Natalie Goldberg. Reprinted by permission of Shambhala Publications, Inc., Boston, MA. www.shambhala.com.

G. Anthony Gorry. "Steal This MP3 File: What is Theft?" First published in *Chronicle of Higher Education*, Vol. 49, Issue 37, May 23, 2003, p. B20. Copyright © 2003. Reprinted by permission of G. Anthony Gorry, Friedkin Professor of the Management and Professor of Computer Science, Rice University.

S. I. Hayakawa. "How Dictionaries Are Made." From *Language in Thought and Action*, Fourth Edition, by S. I. Hayakawa and Alan R. Hayakawa.

Mothers' Gardens: Womanist Prose. Copyright © 1974 by Alice Walker. Reprinted by permission of Harcourt, Inc. "Women" From *Revolutionary Petunias & Other Poems* by Alice Walker. Copyright © 1970 by Alice Walker. Reprinted by permission of Harcourt, Inc.

Rosalind Wiseman. "The Queen Bee" excerpt from *Queen Bees & Wannabes* by Rosalind Wiseman. Copyright © 2002 by Rosalind Wiseman. Used by permission of Crown Publishers, a division of Random House, Inc.

Mary Winstead. "Up In Smoke." First published in *Minnesota Magazine,* July/August 2006. Copyright © 2006 Mary Winstead. Reprinted by permission of Mary Winstead.

Barry Winston. "Stranger Than True." Copyright © 1986 by *Harper's Magazine.* All rights reserved. Reproduced from the December issue by special permission.

William Zinsser. "Simplicity." Copyright © 1976, 1980, 1985, 1988, 1990, 1994, 1998, 2001, 2006 by William K. Zinsser. Reprinted by permission of the author.

PHOTO CREDITS

7, Nancy Ostertag/Getty Images; **40**, Richard Howard/Time Life Pictures/ Getty Images; **44**, Mark Richards; **49**, Courtesy of Linda Flower; **53**, Courtesy of William Zinsser; **57**, University of New Hampshire Photo Services; **76**, AP/Wide World Photos; **81**, Richard Howard/Time & Life Pictures/ Getty Images; **87**, Winreaux Studios; **93**, Courtesy of David Bardeen; **94**, Bob Daemmrich/The Image Works; **99**, Courtesy of Mary Winstead; **118**, Courtesy of Cherokee Paul McDonald; **123**, Jack Dykinga; **129**, Cheron Bayna; **135**, Courtesy of Robert Ramirez; **137**, Tim Sloan/AFP/Getty Images; **141**, © Syracuse Newspapers/Frank Ordonez/The Image Works; **162**, Ritch Davidson; **166**, Michael L. Abramson/Time Life Pictures/Getty Images; **171**, farwellphotography. com; **181**, AP/Wide World Photos; **193**, AP/Wide World Photos; **199**, Tom & Dee Ann McCarthy/Corbis; **220**, Alfred Eisenstaedt/ Pix Inc./Time Life Pictures/Getty Images; **240**, Courtesy of Japanese American National Museum; **244**, Kathleen McPartland, Inside Chico State, California State University, Chico; **249**, Courtesy of Nikki Giovanni; **252**, © Flip Schulke/Corbis; **272**, © Corbis; **276**, Courtesy of Suzanne Britt; **280**, Kaku Kurita/Time Life Pictures/Getty Images; **285**, Hank Walker/Time Life Pictures/Getty Images; **286**, Time Life Pictures/ Mansell/Getty Images; **288**, AP Photos/Wide World; **293**, farwellphotography. com; **315**, Courtesy of Rosalind Wiseman; **318**, Stefanie Felix/Susie Fitzhugh Photography; **330**, Courtesy of Carolina A. Miranda; **334**, Milton Viorst; **341**, Photo by Robert J. Laramie; **353**, © Flip Schulke/Corbis; **382**, Courtesy of Jonathan Rauch; **388**, Courtesy of G. Anthony Gorry; **394**, AP/Wide World Photos; **395**, © A. Inden/zefa/Corbis; **398**, *USA Today.* September 30, 2004. Reprinted with Permission. Photo By Tim Dillon, *USA Today;* **421**, James Lattanzio; **426**, AP/Wide World Photos; **432**, Peter Kramer/Getty Images for TFF; **433**, Staci Schwartz for *The Village Voice;* **437**, Liz Lynch; **446**, Courtesy of Kennedy P. Maize; **474**, © Bettmann/Corbis; **480**, Courtesy of Richard Lederer; **486**,

© Flip Schulke/Corbis; **492**, Courtesy of Michael Parenti; **494**, © Kevin Fleming/Corbis; **500**, Katrina Clark; **519**, Photo by Barry Myers; **522**, Courtesy of Robert D. King; **536**, Courtesy of David Ehrenfeld; **542**, Courtesy of Jane E. Brody; **562**, Courtesy of Lars Eighner; **564**, Christopher S. Johnson/Stock, Boston; **567**, Erich Hartmann/Magnum Photos; **575**, Jeff Smith/FOTOSMITH; **588**, AP/Wide World Photos; **597**, Time & Life Pictures/Getty Images.

Index